CICERO
XVIII

LCL 141

CICERO

TUSCULAN DISPUTATIONS

WITH AN ENGLISH TRANSLATION BY

J. E. KING

HARVARD UNIVERSITY PRESS

CAMBRIDGE, MASSACHUSETTS

LONDON, ENGLAND

First published 1927
Revised 1945

LOEB CLASSICAL LIBRARY® is a registered trademark
of the President and Fellows of Harvard College

ISBN 978-0-674-99156-9

Printed on acid-free paper and bound by
The Maple-Vail Book Manufacturing Group

CONTENTS

PREFACE TO SECOND EDITION

This book was partly revised by the translator, and the revision was completed by the Editors after his death.

A second appendix has been added giving a list of passages quoted by Cicero in this work from early Latin writers which have been translated in *Remains of Old Latin*, by E. H. Warmington, published in the Loeb Classical Library (four volumes).

July, 1943

LIST OF CICERO'S WORKS
SHOWING ARRANGEMENT
IN THIS EDITION

LIST OF CICERO'S WORKS

LIST OF CICERO'S WORKS

LETTERS. 8 VOLUMES

INTRODUCTION

THE Tusculan Disputations were written in the
year 45 B.C. after Cicero had completed the *De
Finibus* and before he began the *De Natura Deorum.*
When Caesar paid a visit to Cicero in the month
of December of that year there was no word of
politics, the talk was confined to literature and
may very well have touched upon the Tusculans.
Almost all Cicero's philosophical works belong to
this and the following year. "I write," as he tells
Atticus, "from morning till night."[1] First he wrote
the *Consolatio,*[2] then the *Hortensius,*[3] then the
Academica,[4] then the *De Finibus,*[5] and about July
he began the Tusculan Disputations which take
their name from his villa at Tusculum. They are
in the form of dialogues, not of the dramatic type
with which we are familar in Plato, but of a later
kind where there is much less of question and
answer and much more of continuous exposition.
To explain the speed with which Cicero's philosophical writings were produced we have to remember that they do not claim to be original
work. In answer to the question how he managed
to write them so quickly he says himself in a letter
to Atticus: ἀπόγραφα *sunt: minore labore funt;
verba tantum adfero, quibus abundo.*[6] He took, that

---

[1] *Ad Att.* xii. 20.   [2] I. § 65.   [3] II. § 4.
[4] II. § 4.   [5] V. § 32.   [6] *Ad Att.* xii. 52. 3.

is to say, the work of some Greek authority: he did not just translate but borrowed as much as he thought fit according to his own judgment and choice.[1] For the setting of the composition with its elaborate introduction, as well as for the episodes and illustrations taken from Roman history and literature he was himself responsible. The style in which he wrote was his own and he had to find Latin equivalents for the Greek philosophical terminology. Often, especially in the second book of the Tusculans, he brings in quotations from the Latin and Greek poets, which do not always fit in very aptly, but which serve to show his knowledge of his native literature as well as his skill in translation, of which he was evidently proud. Plutarch indeed tells us that at this time Cicero's ready turn for poetry afforded him amusement, and he was capable of composing 500 verses in a night.

The chief passages translated by Cicero in this work from Greek authors have been given in an Appendix, and readers can judge for themselves how far he is successful in giving the meaning of the original and how far in his metrical versions he has any claim to be considered a poet.

His letters to friends, as well as the introductions to the different books, explain his motives in writing. The study of philosophy was, he found, his only comfort in distress. He had suffered cruelly in his family life. He had quarrelled with and divorced his wife Terentia, his second marriage was a failure, and in Feb. 45 B.C. his beloved daughter Tullia had died. The public life in which he still longed to play his part was no longer open to a man of

[1] Cf. *De Off*. I. § 6.

his convictions. The days were evil. There was nothing, he felt, for him to do in the Senate or the courts of law. Since the glories of his consulship in 63 B.C. his political life had been one long disappointment. He had refused to join, as he might have done, the first triumvirate, and was punished by being left to the mercies of his bitter enemy Clodius and banished. After his return from exile he was forced to observe a muzzled tranquillity to which he could not be reconciled. When the civil war came, after much hesitation he decided to join Pompey, and about a year after the battle of Pharsalia he made his peace with Caesar. His personal relations with Caesar had constantly been friendly. In 54 B.C. he wrote to his brother Quintus,[1] " I have taken Caesar to my bosom and will never let him slip," and Caesar had always been untiring in his efforts to win Cicero to his side. But Cicero's loyalty to the Republic prevented him from attaching himself to Caesar. There came, it is true, a moment in 46 B.C., on the occasion of the pardon of Marcus Marcellus at the wish of the Senate, when Cicero conceived the hope that Caesar meant to be the leader in a free State, and in his delight he pronounced a splendid eulogy of the Dictator's career. But the hope died away, as Caesar made it more and more plain that his rule was to be despotic.

Apart from the motives which kept him out of public life, Cicero was anxious to redeem Roman literature from the reproach of having neglected philosophy. He wished to do his countrymen a service and hoped that, as the glory of free oratory

[1] *Ad Q. F.* II. 11. 1.

passed away from Senate and law-courts, a new study would take its place. He uses far-fetched arguments to show that philosophy had already left its mark in early Italian and Roman history.[1] He will not admit the superiority of the Greek language for the purposes of philosophy,[2] and will not hear of any incapacity in Roman intellect to engage in philosophical inquiries.[3]

According to tradition, philosophy was first introduced to Rome when the Athenians sent their famous embassy of three philosophers in 155 B.C.,[4] and Cato the Censor, dreading the effect upon the old Roman discipline, procured their dismissal. His attitude resembled that of Frederick William of Prussia, when the theologians of Halle accused the philosopher Wolf of heterodoxy. The king was much perplexed to know what it all meant, but when one of his generals told him that Wolf's ideas about oaths and duty might mean that a grenadier could desert without sin, he ordered Wolf to quit the country within forty-eight hours. Later on he read Wolf's works, just as Cato in his old age learnt Greek, and saw that he had been mistaken. As the position of Rome became established, as wealth and luxury increased and the old religious beliefs decayed, the leading spirits felt the need of some influence strong enough to stem the tide of demoralization. Philosophers of the different Greek sects migrated to Rome and took up their quarters in the houses of influential nobles, as Panaetius did with Scipio Aemilianus. Gradually philosophy became recognized as a part of liberal education.

[1] IV. § 2.　　　　　[2] II. § 35.
[3] IV. § 5.　　　　　[4] IV. § 5.

INTRODUCTION

Like Neoptolemus,[1] the Romans thought that a little philosophy was a good thing, though it would not be like a Roman to give up law and war and administration and devote the whole of life to its study. Their general attitude was that of Tacitus, who says of Agricola, that in his youth he devoted himself too eagerly to the study of philosophy and would have gone "further than was befitting to a Roman and a Senator," had not the wisdom of his mother restrained him.[2]

Cicero set himself to make Greek philosophy accessible in a Roman form. There were, it is true, Roman writers on the subject. He tells us of Amafinius[3] and his imitators who had popularized the knowledge of Epicureanism. Their popularity he admits. Their style of writing he condemns, but of Lucretius, the one writer of genius on their side, he makes no mention. Apart from his wish to put Greek philosophy in a Roman form he was an enemy of Epicureanism. He thought it led to the luxury, indifference, and idleness[4] which he deplored in many of the nobles of the day, like Lucullus, and which paved the way for the coming of the Empire. Besides schooling his own soul in his troubles he hoped to rouse and fortify a more manly spirit in his contemporaries.

Cicero was well equipped for his purpose. He tells us of the youthful enthusiasm[5] with which he had embraced the study of philosophy. Before he was twenty his first teacher had been Phaedrus the Epicurean, and he had heard the lectures of Diodotus[6] the Stoic, after whom he surrendered

[1] II. § 1.   [2] Tacit., *Agric.* 4.   [3] IV. § 6.
[4] V. § 78.   [5] V. § 5.   [6] V. § 113.

himself to the influence of Philo[1] of the Academy. Two whole years, 79 to 77 B.C., were spent, as part of his oratorical training, with Greek philosophers and rhetoricians, and one of those from whom he learnt most was Antiochus[2] of Ascalon. At Rhodes he formed a friendship with the Stoic Posidonius.[3] Even after 77 B.C., when his active career began, he kept up his knowledge by reading and conversation, and when after his consulship his leisure increased he returned to the life of a student. In 51 B.C. he revisited Athens and stayed with Aristus[4] the brother of Antiochus, and met Cratippus the Peripatetic at Mytilene. He was thus prepared by thought and study as well as by personal acquaintance with the leaders of different schools for the task which he set himself at the age of sixty.

At the beginning of Bk. V. Cicero sketches the history of philosophy, in a passage derived possibly from a work of Posidonius. Philosophy began with the ancients and the study of the phenomena of Nature. The early Ionic philosophers tried to discover the primitive ground or principle of all things. To Thales it was water, to Anaximenes it was air: Pythagoras was the first to give philosophy its name and to the Pythagoreans number was the essence of all things. Of other early philosophers Cicero mentions Zeno[5] the Eleatic, claimed as the originator of dialectic; Empedocles[6] the Sicilian who first taught that there were four indestructible elements; Heraclitus[7] who named the world an ever-living fire;

[1] II. § 26.   [2] III. § 59.   [3] II. § 61.   [4] V. § 21.
[5] II. § 52.   [6] I. § 19.   [7] V. § 105.

INTRODUCTION

Democritus [1] of Abdera, the author of the atomic theory and, last of the earlier philosophers, Anaxagoras,[2] who held that mind was the ultimate principle of things.

Socrates begins the next stage in the history of philosophy, for he called it down from the heavens to the earth and brought it into the life of men in their cities and homes. After his death three schools claimed to be Socratic, the Cynics, founded by Antisthenes,[3] whose ideal of virtue consisted only in freedom from desires and was caricatured by the disregard of knowledge and contempt of propriety shown by Diogenes [4] of Sinope; the Cyrenaics, founded by Aristippus [5] of Cyrene, who pronounced the pleasure of the moment to be the supreme good; the Megaric school, of which Euclid of Megara was the chief, who held that the only end was reason and knowledge. These three schools were one-sided developments of parts of the teaching of Socrates. His true successors were Plato and Aristotle. Plato, whom of all philosophers Cicero most venerated, was the founder of the Old Academy, and Aristotle, with whose works Cicero was less well acquainted, founded the Peripatetic school. Their schools survived them, but neither the Academy nor the Peripatetics maintained the reputation and influence of their founders.

After Aristotle there was a changed world, and the spirit and aims of philosophy changed with it. The earlier philosophers were citizens of the old Greek city-state with its ideals of liberty and independence. The conquests of Alexander the Great

[1] I. § 22. [2] I. § 104. [3] V. § 26.
[4] I. § 104. [5] II. § 15.

spread Greek civilization and culture over a far wider area than before and brought them into contact with Oriental influences; new centres of population like Alexandria arose. But under the Macedonians and later under the Romans the old political freedom came to an end. Men's thoughts were turned inward and they sought to obtain within themselves that peace and happiness which they could not find in the external world. It became the aim of philosophy to establish a moral standard rather than a theory of knowledge. It was this that made philosophy popular, and philosophers became preachers who taught the art of right living to those who desired a teaching which could satisfy their needs.

Of the post-Aristotelian schools Stoicism was founded by Zeno, a native of Cyprus who began by being a Cynic. He was followed by Cleanthes[1] and Chrysippus.[2] Of the later Stoics, who modified the doctrines of their school to meet the needs of Romans, Panaetius[3] and Posidonius[4] are mentioned in these books. Only fragments remain of the works of these Stoic philosophers, and for further knowledge of their teaching we depend upon Cicero and other writers.

About the same time as the Stoa there arose the school founded by Epicurus. Besides these two schools, and the schools of the Academy and the Peripatetics, surviving from the earlier period, there were the Sceptics, of whom Cicero mentions Pyrrho,[5] and allied to these the New Academy, the school to which Cicero himself belonged, founded by

[1] II. § 60. [2] I. § 108. [3] I. § 42.
[4] II. § 61. [5] II. § 15.

INTRODUCTION

Arcesilas who was followed by Carneades,[1] a vigorous opponent of the Stoics, whilst Philo[2] aimed at bringing the Stoa and the Academy nearer together, and Antiochus of Ascalon[3] his pupil tried to find a middle course between Zeno, Aristotle and Plato.

In Cicero's time, and after, students of philosophy were to be found mainly in the Stoic or Epicurean camp, but only a brief sketch of their doctrines can be given here. No sect adhered so closely to the teaching of its founder as the Epicureans, but in the course of its long history the teaching of the Stoics was much altered, to meet the needs of the practical Roman mind and parry the assaults of Carneades, though it retained the spirit of its founders. It is noteworthy that of the earlier Stoics not one was a native of Greece proper. Zeno was the "Phoenician," Cleanthes and Chrysippus came from Asia Minor. They introduced a Semitic spirit into Greek philosophy, "an intense but narrow earnestness, averse on the whole to science and art but tending to enthusiasm and even fanaticism for abstract ideas of religion and morality."[4] To the Stoics philosophy was the training-school of virtue, the science of the principles on which a virtuous life is to be formed. Of the three parts of ancient philosophy the function of *Dialectic* was to determine what is the standard of truth, and of *Physics* to ascertain the nature of the universe and its laws, which in *Ethics* are applied to the practical life of men. The Stoics accepted the Logic of Aristotle, but developed its forms with painful minuteness.[5] According to their

[1] III. § 54.   [2] II. § 26.   [3] III. § 59.
[4] Grant, *Essay on The Ancient Stoics.*   [5] II. § 42.

xix

theory of knowledge all perceptions come from the senses, perception gives rise to memory and repeated acts of memory to experience; from experience are formed conceptions, and from the formation of conceptions comes knowledge. True perceptions are distinguished by the strength with which they force themselves upon our notice and compel the assent of judgment. When the Stoic, spoken of by Aulus Gellius (xix. 1), turned pale in a storm at sea he explained that a sudden shock anticipates reason, but when it is found that there is nothing really to be feared the assent of judgment to the alarm is refused.

In their Physics the Stoics held that nothing exists but body, for this only can act and be acted upon. The ultimate ground of things is at once spirit and matter—ether conceived as fiery breath which is transmuted into the four elements from which all things are formed. All things are permeated by the divine ether and this makes the universe one. Between God and the primitive substance there is no difference. In this original state God and the world are one. The world is a living thing of which God is the rational soul, the inner necessity which subjects all to unalterable law. All in the world comes out of the divine whole and returns into it again in a never-ending series of cycles. Much of their Physics the Stoics derived from Aristotle,[1] but it was from Heraclitus, the old Ionian philosopher, that they took their principle of the unity of all being and the conception of God as the fiery, heat-giving power now called spiritual breath, now creative fire, now the

---

[1] I. § 40.

ether; the soul, mind or reason of the world and also law, nature, destiny and providence.

The soul of man, like the soul of the universe, of which it is part, is a fiery breath;[1] it is fed from the blood and grows with the growth of the body. The soul has no distinct parts but there are currents permeating the body and connecting the ruling principle of reason in the heart with the extremities. The soul is not immortal[2] and can only survive until the general conflagration at the end of the cycle.

The Ethics of the Stoics were based upon their Physics. The primary impulse of every being is toward self-preservation. The supreme good or end of man's endeavour is to adapt himself to the universal law, to nature as they conceived it, summed up in the rule, "live in agreement with nature," as a rational part of the rational whole. Virtue is the sole end of man as a rational being, his sole happiness, his sole good;[3] only to act in conformity with nature can make him happy. Pleasure is not a good: it is involved in virtue but as a consequence, not as an end to be aimed at. External goods like health and wealth are indifferent. Some, as conforming to nature, are preferable to others,[4] but they are not positive goods. Virtue is good in itself apart from consequences, an indivisible whole which we possess entirely or not at all.[5] He only is good who is perfectly good. Anyone who is irrational or wrong in any way is vicious. There is no middle term between vice and virtue any more than between truth and falsehood. Further, all good actions are

[1] I. § 19.   [2] I. § 78.   [3] II. § 29.
[4] V. § 47.   [5] II. § 32.

equally right, all bad actions equally wrong. Virtue consists in absolute judgment, absolute control of the soul over pain, absolute mastery of desire and lust, absolute justice. Emotion is not merely to be regulated but suppressed,[1] for, as the soul is entirely rational, emotion is due to erroneous judgment and is therefore under man's control.[2] The Stoic teaching assumed a concrete form in the "wise man" who alone is free and happy, never led into error or hurried into emotion, endowed with true wealth and beauty, in no way inferior to Zeus himself.

Many questions were raised which led the later Stoics to abate the rigidity of their teaching. If no actual instance of the "wise man" could be named, did that mean that all mankind were fools? Were there no degrees amongst the good and the bad? If self-preservation was man's primary impulse, how could health, for instance, be a matter of indifference? If goods did not differ in degree, how was rational choice possible? If all things were absolutely determined by unalterable law, how was freedom of choice possible? How could irrational impulses enter a reasonable soul? How could there be evil in a world that was divine?

Cicero rejected the fatalism and pantheism of the Stoics. He was repelled by their pedantic formalism,[3] he disliked their uncouthness of manner and the contempt of ordinary feeling, which they derived from the Cynics, he rejected their paradoxes that all bad men are equally bad and all vices of equal magnitude. But more and more, as he grew older, he was drawn to the Stoics. There was a grandeur in their utterances about morality which appealed to

---

[1] IV. § 57.   [2] IV. § 83.   [3] II. §§ 29, 30.

him. They carried their doctrine of duties into details, they represented man as independent of external circumstances, they made the morally good alone at all times expedient. In fact he confesses to an uneasy feeling that they may be the only true philosophers.[1]

Epicurus rejected the older Dialectic and appealed to the common sense of the plain man. Logic called Canonic [2] was the test-science of truth. In Physics, the study of which set men free from superstitious fears, he adopted the atomic theory of Democritus.[3] The atoms stream from the infinite void with power to swerve from the perpendicular, and from their chance collisions, indefinitely multiplied, our world was evolved. The soul is mortal and material but its matter is incomparably finer than that of other things. All knowledge comes from the senses. Bodies constantly give off films or husks which can be lodged in the mind and give rise to notions. Reason depends upon sense and cannot correct the impressions of sense nor can one sense correct another. For instance the sun is no bigger than it appears to be [4]—about a foot across, and this shows that Epicurus paid no regard to exact sciences like mathematics and astronomy.

In ethics pleasure is the only standard of conduct.[5] As the Stoics said " it is pleasant because it is good," the Epicureans said " it is good because it is pleasant." Virtue can have no value in itself, but only so far as it offers us something. By pleasure is understood, not the excitement of the moment, but permanent, tranquil satisfaction. Many a pleasure must be

---

[1] IV. § 53.
[2] τὸ κανονικόν reckoned an appendage to Physics.
[3] I. 22.   [4] Lucret. V. 564.   [5] III. § 41.

rejected as bringing only pain, many a pain accepted as bringing only a greater pleasure. The wise man seeks his supreme good for the whole of life, not for the moment as the Cyrenaics said. Natural desires are easily satisfied:[1] artificial desires like ambition, which are stimulated by the opinion of others, bring no pleasure at all. Virtue should be pursued not as an end in itself but as a means to happiness. As happiness consists in imperturbable tranquillity of spirit, in the feeling of inner worth, of superiority to the blows of fate, it was possible for Epicurus to maintain that pleasure and happiness were inseparable from virtue and that the wise man could be happy even in torment.[2]

In Cicero's day, as has been said, the Stoic and Epicurean schools had most adherents at Rome. The Stoics had the greater influence and the more earnest adherents. Stoicism was more akin to the national spirit. The old Roman worthies, it has been said, were unconscious Stoics, and Cato of Utica, who rather than submit to Caesar had refused to live, became to later ages the pattern of unbending Roman virtue. The Stoic view of religion, which rationalized the myths[3] and interpreted the divinities of polytheism as manifestations of one Supreme Being, justified Roman statesmen in the maintenance of popular beliefs and cults of which they felt the practical necessity. The gods of Epicurus, on the other hand, were useless for State purposes, for they took no part in the government of the world, since that would destroy their happiness. The Roman lawyers, too, were allies of Stoicism. The *Ius Gentium*, which was first developed to meet the

[1] V. § 93.   [2] II. § 17.   [3] I. § 28.

INTRODUCTION

needs of intercourse with foreigners, was held to be the lost code of Nature, the part of the law which natural reason appoints for all mankind, worked into Roman jurisprudence by the praetor's edicts.

The Peripatetics were few. The works of their founder Aristotle were neglected and it was not till the days of the medieval schoolmen that the greatness of Aristotle was better understood. In fact the theories of knowledge constructed by both Plato and Aristotle had little vitality after their death, and even the Academy forgot Plato's doctrine of ideas in days when all the schools agreed in deriving knowledge from the senses. Cicero himself claimed to belong to the New Academy,[1] connected with the names of Arcesilas and Carneades. Regarding, like the Sceptics, absolute certainty as out of reach, they developed the doctrine of probability,[2] but the impossibility of knowledge did not exclude the possibility of conviction.[3] Their tenets were best adapted to the purposes of oratory ; and eloquence, Cicero says, is the child of the Academy.[4] By nature and training Cicero was attracted to them. He disliked arrogant claims : as a lawyer he was accustomed to weigh evidence, and he thought that in every subject all the arguments for and against should be considered and a balance of probability struck. He claims to sip the best of every school[5] and free himself and others from the mists of error. So indifferent was he to the charge of inconsistency

---

[1] II. § 9, IV. § 47. 　　　[2] I. § 17, V. § 30.
[3] Cf. the argument that "probabilities which did not reach to logical certainty might create a mental certitude" (Newman, *Apologia*).
[4] Cf. II. § 9. 　　　[5] V. § 82.

that in V. § 38 he maintains a view at variance with the whole of the fourth book of the *De Finibus* which he had just written. When, however, it comes to questions of morality, Cicero uses the freedom of opinion, which he claimed, to dissociate himself entirely from Carneades and his negative attitude. From being a supporter of Carneades and later of Antiochus he passes to the Stoic view in the Tusculans and *De Officiis.* He begs his former friends not to make confusion, to cease from giving an uncertain sound [1] and to admit that the happiness of the wise man can never be impaired.

The Tusculan Disputations like the *De Officiis* are addressed to the general reader for purposes of edification. The first book deals with the fear of death, the second with endurance of pain, the third with the alleviation of distress, the fourth with the remaining disorders of the soul, the fifth with the sufficiency of virtue for a happy life. They are intended to lift all men, especially young men of generous instincts, to a higher level, to strengthen their souls and inspire them to better ways of life. Cicero adapts his language to the setting in which he has placed the Disputations, a discussion at a gathering of friends rather than a treatise meant for a philosopher in his study. In maintaining the form of a dialogue, though mainly in the mouth of one speaker, he frequently does not adhere to strict grammatical rule. A sentence begins with one construction, breaks off with a parenthesis, and is then resumed with a different construction, or else the original sentence is left in the air and a new sentence takes its place.[2] This is not to be explained by hasty

[1] V. § 75.   [2] I. § 30, II. §§ 3, 17, III. § 16, V. §§ 54, 63.

writing or negligence but is deliberately done to preserve the conversational character of the composition.

Moreover his train of reasoning is sometimes hard to follow.[1] The transitional particles occasionally seem to refer to some thought or passage other than that which immediately precedes. In fact he appears at times to be employing a conversational logic as well as conversational grammar, and to skate with something of a flourish over thin places in the ice.

We do not know who are supposed to have been present at the Tusculan villa. We do not know who the interlocutors M. and A. were. M. may stand for *Marcus* or *Magister*: A. may stand for *Adolescens* or *Auditor* or Cicero's friend Atticus, but this last is not likely as he was over sixty.[2] In letters of the year 46 B.C. Cicero alludes to the presence of friends of Caesar at his Tusculan villa. Plutarch tells us that at this period Cicero bestowed his leisure upon young men of the best families who were desirous of instruction in philosophy. In July he had with him at Tusculum his scape-grace son-in-law Dolabella and Hirtius, one of Caesar's chief lieutenants. *Hirtium ego et Dolabellam dicendi discipulos habeo, cenandi magistros*, he says in a letter[3] of the time. He gave them lessons in rhetoric and in return they instructed him in the art of dining, and they only left him to make his peace with Caesar. Now in the Tusculans the earlier part of the day is stated to have been spent in declamation, showing that rhetoric came first; later the company descend to the *ambulatio*[4] or place of exercise and there before dinner the philosophical discussions were

---

[1] *e.g.* I. § 30, IV. § 29.   [2] A., in II. § 28, is *adolescens*.
[3] *Ad Fam.* IX. 16. 7.   [4] II. § 9.

held. It may be that, after their rhetorical exercises,[1] Hirtius and Dolabella and any others present were willing to gain some knowledge of philosophy, for which their busy lives had left them little time, but with which educated Romans were now expected to have some acquaintance. The five books, it is true, are dedicated to the austere Brutus, but in the first instance they may have been intended to meet the needs of men like Pansa, Hirtius and Dolabella, who, however willing to have their knowledge extended, might have been repelled by too technical a treatment of the subject. Cicero's aim then would be not to go deeper than his audience were prepared to follow him, and not to exhaust their interest either by the form or matter of what was meant for their benefit. He was a preacher, but a preacher in polite or even corrupt society, dealing with men who respected his pre-eminence as an orator but who had little inclination for philosophical truth. His style throughout adapts itself to the matter. Sometimes he banters Zeno or Epicurus, at other times he uses the language of earnest appeal; in the narrative passages he is flowing and vivid; in explaining philosophical doctrines he aims at being precise without being obscure and passes rapidly over the necessary definitions and distinctions. Then when he dwells upon the order of the universe, its wonder and beauty, or upon the grandeur of the moral law, the level of his language rises and his subject carries him away in a swelling stream of majestic eloquence.

As has been already said, Cicero usually had the work of some Greek authority before him, the substance of which he followed or adapted as he chose.

[1] II. § 9.

INTRODUCTION

The books of the *De Officiis*, for instance, were based upon a work of Panaetius. It is more difficult to decide what writer Cicero followed for the Tusculans and to what school that writer belonged. In the first book he cites the opinions of different philosophers upon the nature of the soul, he translates passages from Plato, names Chrysippus as his authority for funeral observances, and in another place appears to be using a work of Crantor's.[1] These passages may have been the result of his own reading or have been found in the authority he was using. If this authority was Stoic Cicero has certainly not accepted Stoic conclusions. He prefers with Plato to believe in the pre-existence and immortality of the soul, and rejects the Stoic doctrine of a limited existence after death. In the spirit of the New Academy he leaves the nature and place of the soul undetermined.[2] The nearest approach to certainty is the soul's conviction of its own existence.[3]

In the second book, which deals with the endurance of pain, he rejects the views of the Cyrenaics and Epicureans as well as those of the Stoics, and his remarks about the Stoic method of reasoning and about Zeno could not come from a Stoic source.[4] His position is that of the New Academy. He finds fault with the Stoics, not for denying that pain is an evil, but for raising a question which for purposes of practical morality is indifferent.[5] He accepts the division of the soul into rational and irrational parts,[6] contrary to the teaching of the Stoics, but declares that this is done in the interests of practical morality,

[1] I. § 92 ff.   [2] I. §§ 60, 67.   [3] I. § 53.
[4] II. § 29.   [5] II. § 42.   [6] II. § 47.

and he refuses to make any closer determination of the two parts.

In the third book Cicero's standpoint is that of the New Academy. He has a strong leaning towards the Stoics, but though he accepts their definition of distress [1] he does not deny an irrational part to the soul as they did, and the choice between the Stoic and Peripatetic view of evil is left open.[2] The Stoic teaching is praised as manliest and bravest: [3] it may not be possible to carry it out, but it is best for man to set the moral demand high, even if it is beyond him.

In dealing with the other disorders of the soul in the fourth book Cicero uses the Stoic dialectic but prefers a wider treatment of the subject. He adopts their definitions but clings to the psychology of Plato. He upholds Chrysippus against Carneades and attacks the Peripatetics who advocated the regulation of the passions instead of their extirpation. As in the third book, he gives the preference to the dogmatic views not because of their theoretical truth, but because of their practical utility.

In the fifth book, again, Cicero is more interested in practice than in theory. He wishes to show that virtue is sufficient for happiness. Portions of the book are so much coloured now by Stoic, now by Peripatetic, now by Epicurean teaching, that he has been supposed by some critics to have used three different and conflicting authorities. The explanation is that it is his aim to prove that the sufficiency of virtue for happiness is a truth consistent with the ethical theory and teaching of all the different schools.

---

[1] III. § 75, *i.e.* that of the older Stoics, for Posidonius differed from Chrysippus on this point.
[2] III. § 77 ff.   [3] III. § 22.

INTRODUCTION

If the work which Cicero followed in writing the Tusculans was a Stoic work by Chrysippus, Panaetius or more probably Posidonius, then it is clear that though he has accepted much from the Stoics, yet he has felt himself at liberty, as a follower of the New Academy, to deal freely with his material, to accept or reject as he chooses and to combine it with the teaching of other schools. If on the other hand Cicero had before him the work of a writer belonging to the New Academy, it does not seem likely that Antiochus was his authority, for in the fifth book [1] he expressly contests his views. Philo is more likely, who was actually reproached with his strong leaning to Stoicism in spite of his being a follower of Carneades.

As Cicero wrote in haste and depended upon others, it may be asked what permanent value attaches to his philosophical writings. To Mommsen in his history of Rome Cicero is only a " phrase-maker," a " journalist," but Mommsen's Prussian contempt for Cicero the politician, who had a conscience and was loyal to the Republic in a time of revolution, has been extended to Cicero the author.

Montaigne in one of his Essays [2] is gentler but still severe : " To confess the truth boldly, Cicero's manner of writing seems to me tiresome. His prefaces, definitions, divisions and etymologies take up the chief part of his work . . . the greater part of the time I find only wind, for he has not yet come to the arguments which serve his purpose. . . . I only wish to become wiser, not more learned and eloquent. . . . I understand quite well what death

[1] V. § 22.   [2] II. 17.

is and what pleasure, which there is no amusement
in anatomizing. I look for good, strong reasons to
instruct me in making the effort to get to the point.
. . . I want discourses which go straight to the
strongest part of doubt : his languidly beat about the
bush." Montaigne would perhaps have agreed with
Macaulay where he says, " Words and more words and
nothing but words had been all the fruit of all the
toil of all the most renowned sages of antiquity." [1]

On the other side we have St. Augustine. In
the *Confessions*,[2] speaking of his 19th year, he writes
in reference, it is true, to the lost *Hortensius* and
not to the Tusculans : " In the ordinary course of
study I fell upon a certain book of Cicero whose
speech almost all admire, not so his heart. This
book of his contains an exhortation to philosophy
and is called *Hortensius*. But this book altered my
affections and turned my prayers to thyself, O Lord ;
and made me have other purposes and desires.
Every vain hope at once became worthless to me ;
and I longed with an incredibly burning desire for
an immortality of wisdom, and began now to arise
that I might return to thee. . . . Not to sharpen
my tongue did I employ that book ; nor did it
infuse into me its style but its matter."

Again, Erasmus writing to a friend, and in this
instance about the Tusculans, says : " When I was
a boy I was fonder of Seneca than of Cicero, and
till I was twenty years old could not bear to spend
any time reading him. . . . Whether my judgment
be improved by age I know not ; but am certain
that Cicero never pleased me so much, when I was
fond of those juvenile studies, as he does now, when

---

[1] *Essay on Bacon.*   [2] III. 4.

INTRODUCTION

I am grown old; not only for the divine felicity of his style but the sanctity of his heart and morals: in short he inspired my soul and made me feel myself a better man."

A writer who makes such an appeal to men like St. Augustine and Erasmus cannot be dismissed as merely a phrase-maker. Cicero was not an original thinker and greater names have taken the place his once occupied in philosophy. His importance rests for one thing on the fact that he was not simply a student but a man of affairs as well. He was the leader of the Roman bar; during his consulship and at the end of his life, as the opponent of Antony, he directed the policy of the Roman State: in Cilicia he showed himself an able administrator. When men of his gifts and his experience are also genuinely interested in great subjects like philosophy, the conclusions to which they have come upon the meaning of life exercise an influence and have a permanent value quite apart from the technical qualifications they may possess. Historically Cicero is of the greatest importance, for he gives us most that we know of a number of Greek philosophers whose thought inspired the civilized world of their day, and his influence was felt by the Latin fathers of the Church, at the Revival of learning and in the eighteenth century, at all the chief turning-points of Western thought, not to speak of the many generations of the young whose first steps he has guided in the paths of moral philosophy, and what in his writings may seem commonplace to us is commonplace because it has been "absorbed into the fabric of civilized society."[1] In fact, as Strachan-

[1] Mackail, *Latin Literature.*

INTRODUCTION

Davidson said in Cicero's *Life*: [1] "If we were required to decide what ancient writings have most directly influenced the modern world, the award must probably go in favour of Plutarch's *Lives* and of the philosophical writings of Cicero."

BOOKS

Zeller's *Stoics, Epicureans and Sceptics*, trans. Reichel.

Zielinski, *Cicero im Wandel der Jahrhunderte*, 1912.

Grant's Essay on "The Ancient Stoics," *Ethics of Aristotle*, vol I.

Introduction, Reid's *Academica*.

Roman Philosophy, R. D. Hicks in *Companion to Latin Studies* and the article on philosophy in *Companion to Greek Studies*, Cambridge Press.

Among editions of the Tusculans are those of Davies first printed in 1709, Orelli's Oxford edition of 1834, a translation of Tischer and Sorof by the Rev. T. K. Arnold, and the edition of T. W. Dougan and R. M. Henry, Cambridge, 1905 and 1934; also the volume by G. Fohlen and J. Humbert in the *Budé* series. Orelli's Oxford edition contains the emendations of Bentley as well as the lectures of F. A. Wolf and other commentaries upon the Tusculans.

We have now (1971) H. Drexler's edition, Milan 1964. For this translation Klotz, and Baiter and Kayser chiefly have been used for the text, and Kühner (Hanover, 1874) for the meaning.

[1] Heroes of the Nations Series.

ARGUMENTS

Book II.—On Enduring Pain.

the morally right is the chief good, 44, 45. **Control yourself, control your lower nature, 46–48.** Examples of Zeno of Elea, Anaxarchus, Callanus, Marius, 52, 53. Resolution must be braced, 53, 54. Think of the disgrace of crying out, 55–57. How noble to endure calmly, 58; heroes in battle, 59; Dionysius the apostate, 60; Posidonius, 61; hardship for the sake of glory, 62, 63; the verdict of conscience, 64. Endurance of pain, coming from reason, must be uniform and unvarying, 65.

Conclusion. Pain, if an evil, is a slight one. Virtue makes it insignificant and death is a ready refuge, 66, 67.

Book III. — On the Alleviation of Distress.

Praise of philosophy as the medicine of the soul, 1–7.

Proposition. "The wise man is susceptible of distress." But distress is disorder of soul, therefore unsoundness of mind. Latin and Greek terms compared, 7–11.

There is weakness in our nature which philosophy must remove, 12, 13. The Stoic arguments: fortitude and distress are incompatible, 14, 15; distress is disorder of soul from which the wise man is free, 15; the wise man is σώφρων, *frugi,* 16–18; anger is distress, 19; pity and envy are distress; from all these the wise man is free, 20, 21.

Wider treatment, the Peripatetic doctrine of the "mean," and the terms πάθος and *aegritudo,* 20–23. The cause of distress and all disorders is opinion and judgment. There are four disorders, 24, 25: delight, desire, distress, fear; distress is worst,

26, 27. The element of unexpectedness, 28–31. The Epicurean view that relief of distress is found in diverting attention, 32, 33 : its refutation, 34–51. The Cyrenaic view that distress comes from the unexpected, 52–54. Time brings alleviation but reflection is the true remedy, 55–59. Fortify experience by reason. Refutation of Carneades who denies that reflection on man's lot brings relief, 59, 60.

The cause of distress lies in opinion and judgment, 61. Men think it right to feel distress, 62–65. It can be got rid of, 66; it is useless; those who suffer most bear it more easily, 67. Wise men are not distressed at their short-comings, 68, 69. Distress must not be yielded to as natural, 70–74. The Stoic definition, 75.

The duty of comforters in removing or lessening distress, 76; the different methods illustrated, 77–80.

Conclusion. Distress is not natural but voluntary and due to mistaken opinion, 81–84.

Book IV.—On the Remaining Disorders of the Soul.

Praise of Roman progress and history of philosophy at Rome, 1–7.

Proposition. " The wise man does not seem to be free from all disorders of soul." But he is free from distress, why not from others ? 8.

9–33. Begin with Stoic definitions. Disorder (πάθος) comes from erroneous judgment, alien to right reason, against nature, a disturbance of the soul. Opposed to it is equability (εὐπάθεια). Disorder is longing or aversion. Its objects are present or

future. There are four disorders: Delight, Lust, Distress, Fear, 9–15. The subdivisions of distress and fear, 16; their definitions, 17–19; delight and lust, 20, 21. Intemperance the source of all, 22.

Comparison of diseases of soul and body. To diseases and sicknesses of the soul which are desires are opposed aversions like misogyny, 23–27. Some men prone to one, some to others, 27, 28. Disease, sickness, and defects in the soul, 29, 30. Analogy of body and soul in good things, 31. Disease and disorder of soul come from contempt of reason. Defects are easiest to remove, 32.

34–57. The wise not susceptible of disorders. From virtue comes right reason, from vice disorder, 34–38. The Peripatetic view that disorders are natural and useful and that in all things the " mean " is best, 39–46. Oppose to this the Stoic definition, 47. Take separate disorders ; anger, 48 ; is it necessary to fortitude ? 49–53 ; to private life ? 54 ; to the orator ? 55. Lust, rivalry, envy, compassion, 55, 56. All disorders must be rooted out, 57.

58–84. Remedies for disorders. Either show that the object which occasions the disorder is not the good or evil it seems, or that all disorders in themselves are neither natural nor necessary, 58–61. How to deal with separate disorders, 62, 63. Distress, fear, delight, lust, 64–67. Love, 68–76. Anger, 77–79. As disorders come from error, equability comes from knowledge. The soul is curable as the soul of Socrates was, 80, 81.

Conclusion. All disorders and the worst of them, distress, come from errors of judgment and are voluntary. Philosophy roots out error, 82–84.

ARGUMENTS

ARGUMENTS

Epicurus, Peripatetics, Old Academy and Stoics, 73–79. Cicero supports the Stoics, 80–82.

What of different views about the highest good? 83, 84. Views stated, 84–87; particularly that of Epicurus, 88, 89. Illustrations, 90–92. Epicurus on kinds of desire, natural and necessary, 93; pleasures, 94–96; food, 97–101; wealth, 102; honours, 103–105; exile, 106–109; bodily infirmities, 110–117.

Conclusion. Epicurus thinks the wise men always happy, much more then must the philosophers who go back to Plato think so, 119, 120.

TUSCULAN DISPUTATIONS

M. TULLI CICERONIS TUSCULANARUM
DISPUTATIONUM

LIBER I

I. Cum defensionum laboribus senatoriisque mune-
ribus aut omnino aut magna ex parte essem aliquando
liberatus, rettuli me, Brute, te hortante maxime ad
ea studia, quae retenta animo, remissa temporibus,
longo intervallo intermissa revocavi, et, cum omnium
artium, quae ad rectam vivendi viam pertinerent,
ratio et disciplina studio sapientiae, quae philosophia
dicitur, contineretur, hoc mihi Latinis litteris illus-
trandum putavi, non quia philosophia Graecis et
litteris et doctoribus percipi non posset, sed meum
semper iudicium fuit omnia nostros aut invenisse
per se sapientius quam Graecos aut accepta ab illis
fecisse meliora, quae quidem digna statuissent in
2 quibus elaborarent. Nam mores et instituta vitae
resque domesticas ac familiares nos profecto et
melius tuemur et lautius, rem vero publicam nostri

---

[1] He prefers to speak of defence rather than accusation.
Indeed he could regard his attacks on Verres and Catiline as
made in defence of the republic.

[2] Cicero wished to encourage his countrymen. As he says
in his *Brutus*: *multum tribueram Latinis, vel ut hortarer alios,
vel quod amarem meos.* The Romans were at their worst in
the exact sciences and abstract studies. What they needed

M. TULLIUS CICERO'S TUSCULAN
DISPUTATIONS

BOOK I

I. On at last securing a complete or at any rate
a considerable release from the toils of advocacy [1]
and from my senatorial duties, I have once more—
chiefly, Brutus, on your encouragement—returned to
those studies, which, though stored in memory, had
been put aside through circumstances, and are now
revived after a long interval of neglect. My view
was that, inasmuch as the system and method of
instruction in all the arts which have a bearing upon
the right conduct of life is bound up with the study
of wisdom which goes by the name of philosophy,
it was incumbent on me to throw light upon that
study by a work in the Latin tongue; not that philosophy could not be learnt from Greek writers and
teachers, but it has always been my conviction that
our countrymen have shown more wisdom everywhere than the Greeks, either in making discoveries
for themselves, or else in improving upon what they
had received from Greece—in such subjects at least
as they had judged worthy of the devotion of their
efforts.[2] For morality, rules of life, family and
household economy are surely maintained by us in a
better and more dignified way; and beyond question

they borrowed from the Greeks, and the same applies to
medicine and geography, but not to engineering, law or war.

maiores certe melioribus temperaverunt et institutis
et legibus. Quid loquar de re militari? in qua cum
virtute nostri multum valuerunt tum plus etiam
disciplina. Iam illa, quae natura, non litteris
adsecuti sunt, neque cum Graecia neque ulla cum
gente sunt conferenda. Quae enim tanta gravitas,
quae tanta constantia, magnitudo animi, probitas,
fides, quae tam excellens in omni genere virtus in
ullis fuit, ut sit cum maioribus nostris comparanda?
3 Doctrina Graecia nos et omni litterarum genere
superabat, in quo erat facile vincere non repugnantes.
Nam cum apud Graecos antiquissimum e doctis
genus sit poëtarum, si quidem Homerus fuit
et Hesiodus ante Romam conditam, Archilochus
regnante Romulo, serius poëticam nos accepimus.
Annis fere cccccx post Romam conditam Livius
fabulam dedit C. Claudio Caeci filio M. Tuditano
consulibus, anno ante natum Ennium, qui fuit maior
natu quam Plautus et Naevius.

II. Sero igitur a nostris poëtae vel cogniti vel
recepti. Quamquam est in Originibus solitos esse
in epulis canere convivas ad tibicinem de clarorum
hominum virtutibus, honorem tamen huic generi
non fuisse declarat oratio Catonis, in qua obiecit
ut probrum M. Nobiliori, quod is in provinciam
poëtas duxisset. Duxerat autem consul ille in
Aetoliam, ut scimus, Ennium. Quo minus igitur

---

[1] Greek lyric poet, 720–676 B.C.

[2] 240 B.C. Livius Andronicus, the earliest Roman poet.

[3] A historical work, of which fragments survive, written
by M. Porcius Cato, the Censor, d. 149 B.C. Cf. iv. § 3.

[4] Q. Ennius, the Roman poet, born 239 B.C. He was a
Greek by birth, a friend of Scipio Africanus the elder, and
buried in the tomb of the Scipios, § 13. He obtained Roman
citizenship from the son of Fulvius Nobilior the consul.

our ancestors have adopted better regulations and laws than others in directing the policy of government. What shall I say of the art of war? In this sphere our countrymen have proved their superiority by valour as well as in an even greater degree by discipline. When we come to natural gifts apart from book-learning they are above comparison with the Greeks or any other people. Where has such earnestness, where such firmness, greatness of soul, honesty, loyalty, where has such surpassing merit in every field been found in any of mankind to justify comparison with our ancestors? In learning Greece surpassed us and in all branches of literature, and victory was easy where there was no contest. For while with the Greeks the poets are the oldest literary class, seeing that Homer and Hesiod lived before the foundation of Rome and Archilochus [1] lived in the reign of Romulus, poetry came to us at a later date. About five hundred and ten years after the foundation of Rome Livius [2] produced a play in the consulship of C. Claudius, son of Caecus, and M. Tuditanus in the year before the birth of Ennius, who was older than Plautus and Naevius.

II. At a late date then were poets either known or welcomed by our countrymen. Though it is stated in the *Origines* [3] that guests were in the habit of singing at banquets in honour of the virtues of famous men to the playing of a piper, yet a speech of Cato's shows that this kind of talent was not held in respect, for in it he censured M. Nobilior for having, as he declares, taken poets in his suite to his province. It is, as we know, matter of fact that Nobilior when consul had taken Ennius [4] to Aetolia. The lighter then the esteem in which poetry was

5

honoris erat poëtis, eo minora studia fuerunt, nec
tamen, si qui magnis ingeniis in eo genere exstiterunt, non satis Graecorum gloriae responderunt.
4 An censemus, si Fabio nobilissimo homini laudi
datum esset quod pingeret, non multos etiam apud
nos futuros Polyclitos et Parrhasios fuisse? Honos
alit artes omnesque incenduntur ad studia gloria
iacentque ea semper, quae apud quosque impro-
bantur. Summam eruditionem Graeci sitam censebant in nervorum vocumque cantibus: igitur et
Epaminondas princeps meo iudicio Graeciae fidibus
praeclare cecinisse dicitur Themistoclesque aliquot
ante annis, cum in epulis recusaret lyram, est habitus
indoctior. Ergo in Graecia musici floruerunt disce-
bantque id omnes nec qui nesciebat satis excultus
5 doctrina putabatur. In summo apud illos honore
geometria fuit, itaque nihil mathematicis illustrius:
at nos metiendi ratiocinandique utilitate huius artis
terminavimus modum.

III. At contra oratorem celeriter complexi sumus,
nec eum primo eruditum, aptum tamen ad dicendum,
post autem eruditum. Nam Galbam, Africanum,
Laelium doctos fuisse traditum est, studiosum autem
eum, qui iis aetate anteibat, Catonem; post vero
Lepidum, Carbonem, Gracchos; inde ita magnos

---

[1] Fabius Pictor, 302 B.C., on the walls of the temple of Salus.
He belonged to an ancient aristocratic house, and his grandson was the earliest Roman historian.

[2] Polyclitus was a famous Greek sculptor and Parrhasius
a painter.

[3] M. Porcius Cato, known as the Censor, lived from 234–
149 B.C., and Servius Galba, Scipio Africanus Minor, C.
Laelius Sapiens were younger contemporaries. M. Aemilius
Lepidus, Papirius Carbo, Tiberius and Caius Sempronius
Gracchus formed the next group of orators.

held, the less was the devotion paid to it, and yet
such writers as have by virtue of great natural
endowments proved themselves poets, have not
failed to be a worthy match for the glory of the
Greeks. Or do we suppose that if Fabius Pictor,
a man of noble family, had managed to win fame for
his painting,[1] we too should not have had many a
Polyclitus[2] and Parrhasius? Public esteem is the
nurse of the arts, and all men are fired to application by fame, whilst those pursuits which meet with
general disapproval, always lie neglected. The
Greeks held that the proof of the highest education
was found in instrumental and vocal music : thus it
is that Epaminondas, to my mind the leading man
in Greek history, was, we are told, an accomplished
singer to the accompaniment of the harp, whilst
Themistocles, to go back many years previously, was
held to show a lack of culture in refusing to play
the lyre at banquets. Musicians accordingly flourished in Greece ; everyone would learn music, and
the man who was unacquainted with the art was not
regarded as completely educated. With the Greeks
geometry was regarded with the utmost respect, and
consequently none were held in greater honour than
mathematicians, but we Romans have restricted this
art to the practical purposes of measuring and
reckoning.

III. But on the other hand we speedily welcomed
the orator—not at first the cultivated but the ready
speaker—and at a later date the cultivated orator.
For Galba, Africanus and Laelius were, as tradition
has told us, well-read, while Cato who preceded
them was a diligent student ; next came Lepidus,
Carbo and the Gracchi ;[3] after them up to our day

7

nostram ad aetatem, ut non multum aut nihil omnino Graecis cederetur. Philosophia iacuit usque ad hanc aetatem nec ullum habuit lumen litterarum Latinarum quae illustranda et excitanda nobis est, ut, si occupati profuimus aliquid civibus nostris, 6 prosimus etiam, si possumus, otiosi. In quo eo magis nobis est elaborandum, quod multi iam esse libri Latini dicuntur scripti inconsiderate ab optimis illis quidem viris, sed non satis eruditis. Fieri autem potest ut recte quis sentiat et id, quod sentit, polite eloqui non possit; sed mandare quemquam litteris cogitationes suas, qui eas nec disponere nec illustrare possit nec delectatione aliqua adlicere lectorem, hominis est intemperanter abutentis et otio et litteris. Itaque suos libros ipsi legunt cum suis nec quisquam attingit praeter eos, qui eandem licentiam scribendi sibi permitti volunt. Qua re si aliquid oratoriae laudis nostra attulimus industria, multo studiosius philosophiae fontes aperiemus, e quibus etiam illa manabant.

7   IV. Sed ut Aristoteles, vir summo ingenio, scientia, copia, cum motus esset Isocratis rhetoris gloria, dicere docere etiam coepit adolescentes et pru-

---

[1] Cf. iv. § 6.

[2] Aristotle, born at Stagira in Macedonia 384 B.C., became a pupil of Plato 365 B.C., tutor to Alexander the Great 342 B.C., and returned to Athens in 335 B.C. and taught at the Lyceum. From the walks (περίπατοι) round the Lyceum his followers were called Peripatetics.

[3] Isocrates, "that old man eloquent," who committed suicide in 338 B.C. after the battle of Chaeronea. With

orators of such power that little or no ground at all
was yielded in favour of the Greeks. Philosophy
has lain neglected to this day, and Latin literature
has thrown no light upon it: it must be illuminated
and exalted by us, so that, if in the active business
of life I have been of service to my countrymen, I
may also, if I can, be of service to them in my
leisure. And I must exert myself all the more
actively because there are now, it is said, a number
of books in Latin[1] written without due care by
writers who with all their merits are yet insufficiently
equipped. Now it is possible for an author to hold
right views and yet be unable to express them in a
polished style; but to commit one's reflections to
writing, without being able to arrange or express
them clearly or attract the reader by some sort of
charm, indicates a man who makes an unpardonable
misuse of leisure and his pen. The result is that
such writers read their own books themselves along
with their own circle, and none of them reaches any
wider public than that which wishes to have the
same privilege of scribbling extended to itself. For
this reason, if by my assiduity I have won for our
countrymen some measure of oratorical renown, I
shall with far greater enthusiasm lay bare the springs
of philosophy, which were also the source from which
those earlier efforts of mine took their rise.

IV. But just as Aristotle,[2] a man of supreme genius,
knowledge and fertility of speech, under the stimulus
of the fame of the rhetorician Isocrates,[3] began like
him to teach the young to speak and combine

reference to his rivalry with Isocrates Aristotle made, it
was said, constant use of the line, αἰσχρὸν σιωπᾶν, Ἰσοκράτην
δ᾽ ἐᾶν λέγειν. Cf. de Orat. III. 35. 141.

dentiam cum eloquentia iungere, sic nobis placet
nec pristinum dicendi studium deponere et in hac
maiore et uberiore arte versari. Hanc enim perfectam philosophiam semper iudicavi, quae de maximis quaestionibus copiose posset ornateque dicere,
in quam exercitationem ita nos studiose dedimus, ut
iam etiam scholas Graecorum more habere audere-
mus: ut nuper tuum post discessum in Tusculano,
cum essent complures mecum familiares, temptavi
quid in eo genere possem. Ut enim antea declami-
tabam causas, quod nemo me diutius fecit, sic haec
mihi nunc senilis est declamatio. Ponere iubebam
de quo quis audire vellet: ad id aut sedens aut
8 ambulans disputabam. Itaque dierum quinque
scholas, ut Graeci appellant, in totidem libros con-
tuli. Fiebat autem ita, ut, cum is, qui audire vellet,
dixisset quid sibi videretur, tum ego contra dicerem.
Haec est enim, ut scis, vetus et Socratica ratio
contra alterius opinionem disserendi. Nam ita
facillime quid veri simillimum esset inveniri posse
Socrates arbitrabatur. Sed quo commodius disputationes nostrae explicentur, sic eas exponam, quasi
agatur res, non quasi narretur. Ergo ita nascetur
exordium.

9   V. A. Malum mihi videtur esse mors. M. Iisne,

---

¹ *Declamitare*, to practise constantly the delivery of speeches
beforehand. *Declamatio* was the name given to the speech
which a pupil in a school of rhetoric had to deliver by way of
practice upon a given theme. Cicero represents himself as
having gone to school again in his old age. Cf. II. § 26.
² It is uncertain whom the initials A. and M. stand for.
A. may stand for *Adolescens* or *Auditor*. It is not likely to

wisdom with eloquence, similarly it is my design not
to lay aside my early devotion to the art of expression,
but to employ it in this grander and more fruitful
art : for it has ever been my conviction that philosophy in its finished form enjoys the power of treating the greatest problems with adequate fulness and
in an attractive style. To this endeavour I devoted
myself with such energy that I actually reached the
point of venturing to give dissertations in the manner
of the Greeks : for instance, recently after your
departure, as there were a number of close friends
staying with me, I attempted in my house at Tusculum to see what I could do in this sort of exercise :
for just as in my youth I used to be constantly
declaiming speeches for the courts—and no one
ever did so longer—so this is now a declamation [1] of
my old age. I called upon my friends to put forward
any subject which any of them wished to hear
discussed, and this I debated either as I sat or
walked about. The result is that I have put together
into five books the dissertations, as the Greeks term
them, of as many days. The procedure was that,
after the would-be listener had expressed his view,
I opposed it. This, as you know, is the old Socratic
method of arguing against your adversary's position ;
for Socrates thought that in this way the probable
truth was most readily discovered ; but in order that
the course of our discussions may be more conveniently followed I shall put them before you in
the form of a debate and not in narrative form. This
then will be the manner of its opening :

V. A.[2] To my thinking death is an evil. M. To the

stand for Cicero's friend Atticus, then sixty-five. M. may
stand for Marcus, Cicero's own name, or for *Magister*.

qui mortui sunt, an iis, quibus moriendum est?
A. Utrisque. M. Est miserum igitur, quoniam
malum. A. Certe. M. Ergo et ii, quibus evenit
iam ut morerentur, et ii, quibus eventurum est,
miseri. A. Mihi ita videtur. M. Nemo ergo non
miser. A. Prorsus nemo. M. Et quidem, si tibi
constare vis, omnes, quicumque nati sunt eruntve,
non solum miseri, sed etiam semper miseri. Nam
si solos eos diceres miseros, quibus moriendum esset,
neminem tu quidem eorum, qui viverent, exciperes—
moriendum est enim omnibus—, esset tamen miseriae
finis in morte; quoniam autem etiam mortui miseri
sunt, in miseriam nascimur sempiternam. Necesse
est enim miseros esse eos, qui centum milibus annorum ante occiderunt, vel potius omnes, quicumque
10 nati sunt. A. Ita prorsus existimo. M. Dic quaeso:
num te illa terrent, triceps apud inferos Cerberus,
Cocyti fremitus, travectio Acherontis, "mento summam aquam attingens enectus siti Tantalus?" tum
illud, quod

Sisyphus versat
Saxum sudans nitendo neque proficit hilum?

fortasse etiam inexorabiles iudices, Minos et Rhadamanthus? apud quos nec te L. Crassus defendet nec
M. Antonius nec, quoniam apud Graecos iudices res
agetur, poteris adhibere Demosthenem: tibi ipsi pro
te erit maxima corona causa dicenda. Haec fortasse
metuis et idcirco mortem censes esse sempiternum
malum.

---

[1] Cf. § 98, and for the terrors of the lower world, Lucret.
III. 978 ff., Virg. *Aen.* VI. 548 ff.
[2] The chief orators of the generation preceding Cicero.
[3] Cf. V. § 103.

dead or to those who have to die? A. To both. M. As it is an evil it is therefore wretchedness. A. Certainly. M. Then those whose lot it has already been to die and those whose lot it is to be are wretched. A. I think so. M. There is no one then who is not wretched. A. Absolutely no one. M. And in fact, if you wish to be consistent, everyone who has been born or will be born is not only wretched but always wretched as well. For if your meaning were that only those who had to die were wretched, you would make an exception of no living person—for all have to die—still there would have been an end of wretchedness in death; seeing however that the dead too are wretched we are born to eternal wretchedness. For it must follow that those who died a hundred thousand years ago are wretched, or rather everyone who has been born. A. That is precisely my opinion. M. Tell me, pray! You are not terrified, are you, by the stories of three-headed Cerberus in the lower world, the roar of Cocytus, the passage of Acheron, and " chin the water touching, Tantalus worn out with thirst " ? [1] Again, are you frightened at the tale that Sisyphus

Rolleth the stone as he sweateth in toil yet never advanceth?

Or it may be also at the pitiless judges Minos and Rhadamanthus? At whose bar L. Crassus will not defend you nor M. Antonius,[2] nor—since the case will be tried before Greek judges—will you be able to engage Demosthenes: [3] you will have to plead your cause in person before a vast audience. From such prospects it may be you shrink and therefore consider death an unending evil.

MARCUS TULLIUS CICERO

VI. A. Adeone me delirare censes, ut ista esse credam? **M.** An tu haec non credis? **A.** Minime vero. **M.** Male hercule narras. **A.** Cur? quaeso. **M.** Quia disertus esse possem, si contra ista dicerem. 11 **A.** Quis enim non in eius modi causa? aut quid negotii est haec poëtarum et pictorum portenta convincere? **M.** Atqui pleni libri sunt contra ista ipsa disserentium philosophorum. **A.** Inepte sane. Quis enim est tam excors quem ista moveant? **M.** Si ergo apud inferos miseri non sunt, ne sunt quidem apud inferos ulli. **A.** Ita prorsus existimo. **M.** Ubi sunt ergo ii, quos miseros dicis, aut quem locum incolunt? Si enim sunt, nusquam esse non possunt. **A.** Ego vero nusquam esse illos puto. **M.** Igitur ne esse quidem? **A.** Prorsus isto modo, et tamen 12 miseros ob id ipsum quidem, quia nulli sint. **M.** Iam mallem Cerberum metueres, quam ista tam inconsiderate diceres. **A.** Qui tandem? **M.** Quem esse negas, eundem esse dicis. Ubi est acumen tuum? cum enim miserum esse dicis, tum eum, qui non sit, dicis esse. **A.** Non sum ita hebes, ut istud dicam. **M.** Quid dicis igitur? **A.** Miserum esse verbi causa M. Crassum, qui illas fortunas morte dimiserit, miserum Cn. Pompeium, qui tanta gloria sit orbatus, omnes denique miseros, qui hac luce careant. **M.** Revolveris eodem. Sint enim oportet,

---

[1] A. should have said that the copula "*is*" is simply a connecting particle and implies no notion of existence, as is clear in such a proposition as " He is a nonentity."

[2] M. Licinius Crassus the Triumvir, killed at Carrhae fighting with the Parthians in 53 B.C.

[3] Killed in Egypt after his defeat at Pharsalus in 48 B.C., cf. § 86.

VI. A. Do you suppose me so crazy as to believe such tales? M. You don't believe them true? A. Certainly not. M. My word! that's a sad story. A. Why so? M. Because I could have been so eloquent in speaking against such tales. A. Who could not on such a theme? Or what trouble is there in proving the falsity of these hobgoblins of poets and painters? M. And yet there are portly volumes in which philosophers argue against these self-same fables. A. They must have little to do; for who is so stupid as to be influenced by such things? M. If then the wretched are not in the lower world, there cannot be any beings in the lower world at all. A. I am precisely of that opinion. M. Where then are those whom you describe as wretched, or what is their place of habitation? For if they exist they must be somewhere. A. Well! I suppose they are not anywhere. M. Therefore you suppose they have no existence either. A. Exactly as you say; still I suppose them to be wretched for the simple reason that they do not exist at all. M. I must say now I should have preferred you to quail at Cerberus rather than find you making such rash statements. A. How so, pray? M. You are affirming the existence of the being whose existence you deny. Where have your wits gone? Once say a being who does not exist *is* miserable and you affirm his existence.[1] A. I am not so dull as to say such a thing. M. What do you say then? A. I say that M. Crassus[2] for example, because he lost a noble fortune by death, is wretched, that Cn. Pompeius[3] is wretched because he was robbed of a splendid reputation, in a word that all are wretched who quit the light of day. M. You come back to the same

15

si miseri sunt : tu autem modo negabas eos esse, qui
mortui essent. Si igitur non sunt, nihil possunt
esse : ita ne miseri quidem sunt. A. Non dico fortasse etiam quod sentio. Nam istuc ipsum, non esse,
13 cum fueris, miserrimum puto. M. Quid ? miserius
quam omnino numquam fuisse ? Ita qui nondum
nati sunt miseri iam sunt, quia non sunt, et nos, si
post mortem miseri futuri sumus, miseri fuimus ante
quam nati. Ego autem non commemini, ante quam
sum natus, me miserum : tu si meliore memoria es,
velim scire ecquid de te recordere. VII. A. Ita
iocaris, quasi ego dicam eos miseros, qui nati non
sint, et non eos, qui mortui sint. M. Esse ergo eos
dicis. A. Immo, quia non sint, cum fuerint, eo
miseros esse. M. Pugnantia te loqui non vides ?
Quid enim tam pugnat quam non modo miserum,
sed omnino quidquam esse qui non sit ? An tu
egressus porta Capena, cum Calatini, Scipionum,
Serviliorum, Metellorum sepulcra vides, miseros
putas illos ? A. Quoniam me verbo premis, posthac
non ita dicam *miseros esse,* sed tantum *miseros,* ob id
ipsum, quia non sint. M. Non dicis igitur *Miser est
M. Crassus,* sed tantum *Miser M. Crassus.* A. Ita
14 plane. M. Quasi non necesse sit, quidquid isto

---

[1] Family tombs on the Appian Way, which entered the city
by the *Porta Capena.*

16

position, for they must exist if they *are* wretched:
but just now you said that the dead did not exist.
Now if they do not exist they cannot be anything.
Therefore they cannot be wretched either. A. I do
not perhaps yet express my meaning. I think that
the mere fact of not existing, when one has existed,
is utter wretchedness. M. What? more wretched
than never to have existed at all? It follows that
those who are not yet born are wretched now,
because they do not exist, and that we, if we are to
be wretched after death, have been wretched before
we were born. My recollections previous to my
birth do not report me wretched: if you have a
better memory I should like to know what your
recollections of your state are. VII. A. You are
poking fun at me as if my position, instead of being
that those who are dead are wretched, were that
those who are unborn are wretched. M. You say
then they exist. A. Not so. I say they are wretched
because they do not exist, after having existed. M.
Don't you see that your statements are self-contradictory? What can be more of a contradiction than
to say that a being, who does not exist, not merely
is wretched but *is* anything at all? When you come
out of the Porta Capena and see the tombs of Calatinus, the Scipios, the Servilii, the Metelli,[1] do you
think them wretched? A. You are pushing me
hard with a verbal argument, and so I shall hence-
forward not say as before that they *are* wretched,
but merely say " wretched," for the simple reason
that they do not exist. M. You do not say then
" M. Crassus is wretched," but simply " wretched M.
Crassus." A. Quite so. M. As if anything stated
in a proposition of such a kind must not necessarily

modo pronunties, id aut esse aut non esse. An tu dialecticis ne imbutus quidem es? In primis enim hoc traditur: omne pronuntiatum—sic enim mihi in praesentia occurrit ut appellarem ἀξίωμα: utar post alio, si invenero melius,—id ergo est pronuntiatum, quod est verum aut falsum. Cum igitur dicis *Miser M. Crassus,* aut hoc dicis *Miser est M. Crassus,* ut possit iudicari verum id falsumne sit, aut nihil dicis omnino. A. Age iam concedo non esse miseros, qui mortui sint, quoniam extorsisti ut faterer, qui omnino non essent, eos ne miseros quidem esse posse. Quid? qui vivimus, cum moriundum sit, nonne miseri sumus? Quae enim potest in vita esse iucunditas, cum dies et noctes cogitandum sit iam iamque esse moriendum?

15 VIII. M. Ecquid ergo intelligis quantum mali de humana condicione deieceris? A. Quonam modo? M. Quia, si mori etiam mortuis miserum esset, infinitum quoddam et sempiternum malum haberemus in vita: nunc video calcem, ad quam cum sit decursum, nihil sit praeterea extimescendum. Sed tu mihi videris Epicharmi, acuti nec insulsi hominis, ut Siculi, sententiam sequi. A. Quam? Non enim novi. M. Dicam, si potero, Latine. Scis enim me Graece loqui in Latino sermone non plus solere quam in Graeco Latine. A. Et recte quidem. Sed quae tandem est Epicharmi ista sententia?

---

[1] For logical purposes every proposition must be formally resolved into its logical elements of subject, copula and predicate, *e.g. Fire burns* into *Fire is burning.*

[2] With Phormis the originator of the plot in comedy. Born 540 B.C.

either be or not be. Have you not taken so much as a first step in logic? This is an elementary lesson. Every proposition—this is the word that at the moment it has occurred to me to use for the term ἀξίωμα: I shall employ another word later if I can find a better—a proposition then is a statement which is true or false: therefore when you say " wretched Marcus Crassus," either you say " Marcus Crassus is wretched," so that it can be settled whether the statement is true or false, or you say nothing at all.[1] A. Well! I grant now that the dead are not wretched, seeing that you forced me to admit that those who did not exist at all could not be wretched either. But what of this? Are not we the living wretched, seeing that we have to die? What satisfaction can there be in living, when day and night we have to reflect that at this or that moment we must die?

VIII. M. Now do you realise at all from what a load of misery you have lightened the lot of mankind? A. How do you mean? M. In this way: if death had been wretchedness even for the dead, we should have been subject in life to an unlimited and eternal condition of evil: as it is I see a goal, and when we have reached it there is nothing left to be so much afraid of. But you seem to me to agree with the aphorism of Epicharmus,[2] who was, as one expects in a Sicilian, a man of keen insight and not without taste. A. What aphorism? I am not acquainted with it. M. I shall give it if I can in Latin: you know I am no more in the habit of using Greek in speaking Latin than of using Latin in speaking Greek. A. Quite right. But what, pray, is this aphorism of Epicharmus?

MARCUS TULLIUS CICERO

M. *Emori nolo, sed me esse mortuum nihili aestimo.*[1]

A. Iam agnosco Graecum. Sed quoniam coëgisti ut concederem, qui mortui essent, eos miseros non esse, perfice, si potes, ut ne moriendum quidem esse 16 miserum putem. **M.** Iam istuc quidem nihil negotii est, maiora molior. **A.** Quo modo hoc nihil negotii est? aut quae sunt tandem ista maiora? **M.** Quia, quoniam post mortem mali nihil est, ne mors quidem est malum, cui proximum tempus est post mortem, in quo mali nihil esse concedis: ita ne moriendum quidem esse malum est: id est enim, perveniendum esse ad id, quod non esse malum confitemur. **A.** Uberius ista, quaeso. Haec enim spinosiora prius ut confitear me cogunt quam ut adsentiar. Sed quae sunt ea, quae dicis te maiora moliri? **M.** Ut doceam, si possim, non modo malum non esse, sed bonum etiam esse mortem. **A.** Non postulo id quidem, aveo tamen audire. Ut enim non efficias quod vis, tamen mors ut malum non sit efficies. Sed nihil te interpellabo: continentem orationem audire malo. 17 **M.** Quid? si te rogavero aliquid, nonne respondebis? **A.** Superbum id quidem est, sed, nisi quid necesse erit, malo non roges. **IX. M.** Geram tibi morem et ea, quae vis, ut potero, explicabo, nec tamen quasi Pythius Apollo, certa ut sint et fixa quae dixero, sed ut homunculus unus e multis, probabilia coniectura sequens.[3] Ultra enim quo progrediar quam ut veri

---

[1] H. Sauppe conjectures the Greek to have been: ἀποθανεῖν οὐχ ἀνδάνει μοι· τεθνάναι δ' οὐ διαφέρει.

[2] Like an oracle, ὡς ἐκ τρίποδος.

[3] Cicero follows the teaching of the New Academy represented by Carneades who said that though certitude is impossible, various degrees of probability are within our reach.

M. Dying I shun: of being dead I nothing reck.[1]

A. Now I recognise the Greek. But since you compelled me to admit that the dead were not wretched, go on if you can to make me think that to have to die is not wretchedness either. M. Surely that is no serious undertaking, I have greater aims in view. A. How no serious matter? Or what do you mean by the greater aims you speak of? M. Because, inasmuch as after death there is no evil, death, which is at once succeeded by time in which by your admission there is no evil, is not an evil either: it follows that to have to die is not an evil either, for it means having to reach a condition which we admit is not an evil. A. Explain more fully, I beg; for your last remarks are somewhat intricate and compel me to agree before I am convinced. But what do you mean by the greater aims you have in view? M. To show you if I can that death is not merely no evil but positively a good. A. I do not ask so much as that, all the same I am eager to hear it: for though you may not succeed in your wish, still you will succeed in showing that death is not an evil. But I shall not interrupt you: I wish to hear a continuous speech. M. What? If I put a question to you, will you make no reply? A. That would be discourteous: but I prefer you to refrain from questions except where necessary. IX. M. I shall humour you and explain what you wish as best I can, not however as if I were the Pythian Apollo making statements to be regarded as certain and unalterable,[2] but following out a train of probabilities[3] as one poor mortal out of many. For further than likelihood

similia videam non habeo. Certa dicent ii, qui et percipi ea posse dicunt et se sapientes esse profitentur. A. Tu, ut videtur: nos ad audiendum parat_i sumus.

18 M. Mors igitur ipsa, quae videtur notissima res esse, quid sit primum est videndum. Sunt enim qui discessum animi a corpore putent esse mortem : sunt qui nullum censeant fieri discessum, sed una animum et corpus occidere animumque in corpore exstingui. Qui discedere animum censent, alii statim dissipari, alii diu permanere, alii semper. Quid sit porro ipse animus aut ubi aut unde, magna dissensio est. Aliis cor ipsum animus videtur, ex quo *excordes, vecordes concordes*que dicuntur et Nasica ille prudens bis consul *Corculum* et

> *Egregie cordatus homo, catus Aelius Sextus.*

19 Empedocles animum esse censet cordi suffusum sanguinem. Aliis pars quaedam cerebri visa est animi principatum tenere. Aliis nec cor ipsum placet nec cerebri quandam partem esse animum, sed alii in corde, alii in cerebro dixerunt animi esse sedem et locum; animum autem alii animam, ut

---

1 Publius Cornelius Scipio Nasica Corculum, cons. 162 B.C., celebrated for his knowledge of pontifical and civil law.
2 Sextus Aelius Paetus Catus was consul 198 B.C.; cf. App. II.
3 Empedocles, of Agrigentum in Sicily, about 490 B.C.

as I see it I cannot get. Certainty will be for those who say such things can be known and who claim wisdom for themselves. A. Take the course you think best: for our part we are ready to hear.

M. We must first then consider what death, which seems to be a thing well known to everyone, is in itself. Some consider death the separation of the soul from the body; some think there is no such separation, but that soul and body perish together and the soul is annihilated with the body. Of those who think that there is a separation of the soul some hold that it is at once dispersed in space, others that it survives a long time, others that it survives for ever. Further, as to what the soul itself is in itself, or where its place in us, or what its origin, there is much disagreement. Some think the soul is the actual heart, and so we get the words "without heart," "wanting heart" and "of one heart," meaning "senseless," "feeble-minded" and "of one mind"; and the wise statesman Nasica,[1] twice consul, got the name of "Goodheart" or "Sagacious," and so too

the man of matchless heart, shrewd Aelius Sextus.[2]

Empedocles[3] holds that the soul is blood permeating the heart: others thought that a particular part of the brain had claim to the primacy of soul; others do not regard the actual heart or a particular portion of the brain as being the soul, but some of them have said that the heart is the local habitation of the soul, whilst others place it in the brain; others however identify soul and breath as we Romans practically do—the name explains this, for we speak

fere nostri—declarat nomen ; nam et *agere animam*
et *efflare* dicimus et *animosos* et *bene animatos* et *ex
animi sententia ;* ipse autem animus ab anima dictus
est—Zenoni Stoico animus ignis videtur.

X. Sed haec quidem, quae dixi, cor, cerebrum,
animam, ignem vulgo : reliqua fere singuli, ut
multo[1] ante veteres, proxime autem Aristoxenus,
musicus idemque philosophus, ipsius corporis inten-
tionem quandam, velut in cantu et fidibus quae
harmonia dicitur, sic ex corporis totius natura et
figura varios motus cieri tamquam in cantu sonos.
20 Hic ab artificio suo non recessit et tamen dixit
aliquid, quod ipsum quale esset erat multo ante et
dictum et explanatum a Platone. Xenocrates animi
figuram et quasi corpus negavit esse ullum,[2] numerum dixit esse, cuius vis, ut iam ante Pythagorae
visum erat, in natura maxima esset. Eius doctor
Plato triplicem finxit animum, cuius principatum, id
est rationem in capite sicut in arce posuit, et duas
partes ei parere voluit, iram et cupiditatem, quas suis

---

[1] *multi* MSS. : *multo* Bentley.
[2] *verum* is the reading of the best MSS. Bentley proposed
merum.

---

[1] *i.e.* the opinion that "soul" and "breath" are the same
seems to be supported by Latin phrases in which *animus* and
anima are used with the same meaning.

[2] Zeno the founder of the Stoic philosophy, a native of
Cyprus who settled at Athens, and lived, it is said, till
250 B.C.

[3] *Veteres* are philosophers before Socrates.

[4] Aristoxenus of Tarentum, who first studied philosophy
with the Pythagoreans and then became a pupil of Aristotle.

[5] Phaedo 89, ψυχὴν δὲ ἁρμονίαν τινὰ ἐκ τῶν κατὰ τὸ σῶμα
ἐντεταμένων ξυγκεῖσθαι.

[6] Xenocrates of Chalcedon, pupil of Plato (cf. § 24) and
head of the Academy 339-315 B.C.

of "giving up the ghost" and "expiring" and of "spirited people" and "people of good spirit" and "to the best of one's belief"[1]; moreover the actual word for "soul" has come from the word for "breath" in Latin;—Zeno[2] the Stoic holds the soul to be fire.

X. Now the views I have mentioned, that the soul is heart, brain, life or fire are those ordinarily held: the remaining views are as a rule peculiar to individual thinkers, just as philosophers of old[3] held individual views long ago, but nearest in date to our time there was Aristoxenus,[4] musician as well as philosopher, who held the soul to be a special tuning-up of the natural body analogous to that which is called harmony in vocal and instrumental music; answering to the nature and conformation of the whole body, vibrations of different kinds are produced just as sounds are in vocal music: this thinker has not gone outside the limits of his own art, but all the same he has made a contribution of value, the proper meaning of which had long before been plainly stated by Plato.[5] Xenocrates[6] denied that the soul had form or any substance, but said that it was number, and the power of number, as had been held by Pythagoras[7] long before, was the highest in nature. His teacher Plato imagined the soul to be of three-fold nature;[8] the sovereign part, that is reason, he placed in the head as the citadel, and the other two parts, anger and desire, he wished to be

[7] For Pythagoras cf. V. §§ 8, 9, 10. He declared the soul to be ἀριθμὸν ἑαυτὸν κινοῦντα.

[8] νοῦς (ratio), θυμός (ira), ἐπιθυμία (cupiditas). Their seat in man is given in the Timaeus, 69. Principatus is for the Greek term τὸ ἡγεμονικόν, cf. § 80.

locis iram in pectore, cupiditatem subter praecordia
21 locavit. Dicaearchus autem in eo sermone, quem
Corinthi habitum tribus libris exponit, doctorum
hominum disputantium primo libro multos loquentes
facit: duobus Pherecraten quendam Phthiotam
senem, quem ait a Deucalione ortum, disserentem
inducit, nihil esse omnino animum et hoc esse
nomen totum inane frustraque animalia et animantes
appellari, neque in homine inesse animum vel
animam nec in bestia, vimque omnem eam, qua vel
agamus quid vel sentiamus, in omnibus corporibus
vivis aequabiliter esse fusam nec separabilem a corpore esse, quippe quae nulla sit nec sit quidquam
nisi corpus unum et simplex, ita figuratum, ut tem-
22 peratione naturae vigeat et sentiat. Aristoteles
longe omnibus—Platonem semper excipio—praestans et ingenio et diligentia, cum quattuor nota
illa genera principiorum esset complexus, e quibus
omnia orerentur, quintam quandam naturam censet
esse, e qua sit mens; cogitare enim et providere et
discere et docere et invenire aliquid et meminisse,[1]
et tam multa alia, amare odisse, cupere timere, angi
laetari; haec et similia eorum in horum quattuor
generum inesse nullo putat: quintum genus adhibet

---

[1] *et tam multa alia meminisse* in MSS. : emended by Heine.

[1] Dicaearchus, pupil of Aristotle and fellow-pupil of
Aristoxenus.
[2] The four elements, τὰ ἁπλᾶ τῶν σωμάτων, are earth, fire,
air and water. The fifth element αἰθήρ is the substance of
the heavenly bodies. Aristotle does not seem to have in-

subservient, and these he fixed in their places, anger
in the breast and desire below the diaphragm. On
the other hand Dicaearchus [1] in the discussion, of
which the scene is laid in Corinth and of which he
gives an account in three books, introduces a number
of the learned men who took part in the discussion
as speakers in the first book; in the other two he
represents Pherecrates, an old native of Phthiotis,
descendant he says of Deucalion, as arguing that
the soul is wholly non-existent and the name quite
meaningless, and that the terms "animalia" and
"animantes" denoting "creatures and plants possessed of soul" are applied without reason; neither
in man nor in beast is there a spiritual or physical
principle answering to soul, and all the capacity we
have of action or sensation is uniformly diffused in all
living bodies and cannot be separated from the body,
seeing that it has no separate existence and that
there is nothing apart from one single body fashioned
in such a way that its activity and power of sensation
are due to the natural combination of the parts.
Aristotle, who far excels everyone—always with the
exception of Plato—in genius and industry, after
grasping the conception of the well-known four classes
of elements [2] which he held to be the origin of
all things, considers that there is a special fifth
nature from which comes mind; for mind reflects and
foresees and learns and teaches and makes discoveries
and remembers and a multitude of other things:
mind loves, hates, desires, fears, feels pain and joy;
these and similar activities are to be found, he thinks,
in none of the four first classes: he employs a fifth

vented these classes himself. The soul Aristotle says is
immaterial (ἀσώματος).

vacans nomine et sic ipsum animum ἐνδελέχειαν
appellat novo nomine quasi quandam continuatam
motionem et perennem.

XI. Nisi quae me forte fugiunt, haec sunt fere de
animo sententiae. Democritum enim, magnum illum
quidem virum, sed levibus et rotundis corpusculis
efficientem animum concursu quodam fortuito, omittamus. Nihil est enim apud istos quod non atomorum
23 turba conficiat. Harum sententiarum quae vera sit
deus aliqui viderit : quae veri simillima magna
quaestio est. Utrum igitur inter has sententias
diiudicare malumus an ad propositum redire ? A.
Cuperem equidem utrumque, si posset, sed est difficile confundere. Qua re si, ut ista non disserantur,
liberari mortis metu possumus, id agamus : sin id
non potest nisi hac quaestione animorum explicata,
nunc, si videtur, hoc, illud alias. M. Quod malle te
intelligo, id puto esse commodius. Efficiet enim
ratio, ut, quaecumque vera sit earum sententiarum,
quas exposui, mors aut malum non sit aut sit bonum
24 potius. Nam si cor aut sanguis aut cerebrum est
animus, certe, quoniam est corpus, interibit cum
reliquo corpore ; si anima est, fortasse dissipabitur ;
si ignis, exstinguetur ; si est Aristoxeni harmonia,

---

[1] It looks as if Cicero had confused two different words,
ἐνδελέχεια and ἐντελέχεια. In Aristotle the word used is
ἐντελέχεια, *actus*, *perfectio*, the perfect state of a thing:
ἐνδελέχεια on the other hand is *continuatio*, as when the constant dropping of water hollows out stone. This is movement, and Aristotle denies any movement to the soul. It
seems then that if Cicero wrote ἐντελέχεια he has given it a
wrong meaning: if he wrote ἐνδελέχεια he has not used
Aristotle's word. That the difficulty about the two words
is a very old one is shown by Lucian's Δίκη Φωναέντων 10,
where δέλτα accuses ταῦ of filching ἐνδελέχεια illegally and
getting it turned into ἐντελέχεια.

class without a name and accordingly applies to the actual soul a new term, $\dot{\epsilon}\nu\delta\epsilon\lambda\dot{\epsilon}\chi\epsilon\iota\alpha$,[1] descriptive of a sort of uninterrupted and perpetual movement.

XI. These, unless I happen to have missed any, are pretty nearly the views held about the soul. There is, it is true, Democritus,[2] a man of undoubted power, but, as he makes the soul consist of minute smooth round bodies brought together in some sort of accidental collision, let us pass him over; for there is nothing which thinkers of his school cannot construct out of a swarm of atoms. Which of these views is the true one it is for a divine being to determine: which is most probable is a difficult question. Are we in favour of deciding between these views or of going back to the subject first put forward?[3] A. My wish would be for both courses if it could be managed, but it is a difficult matter to combine the two. Therefore if, without discussing these further questions, we can get free from the fear of death, let this be our aim; but if that is impossible, unless this problem of the nature of the soul is first unravelled, let us take that problem first and the other question later. M. I think the course I understand you to prefer is the more convenient; for rational investigation will show that, whichever of the views I have stated is the true one, death is either not an evil or, better, a positive good. For if the soul is the heart or blood or brain, then assuredly, since it is material, it will perish with the rest of the body; if it is breath it will perhaps be dispersed in space; if fire it will be quenched; if it is the harmony of Aristoxenus

[2] Democritus of Abdera, about 460 B.C., the founder of the atomic theory.
[3] § 9.

dissolvetur. Quid de Dicaearcho dicam, qui nihil omnino animum dicat esse? His sententiis omnibus nihil post mortem pertinere ad quemquam potest; pariter enim cum vita sensus amittitur; non sentientis autem nihil est ullam in partem quod intersit. Reliquorum sententiae spem adferunt, si te hoc forte delectat, posse animos, cum e corporibus excesserint, in caelum quasi in domicilium suum pervenire. A. Me vero delectat, idque primum ita esse velim, deinde, etiam si non sit, mihi persuaderi tamen velim. M. Quid tibi ergo opera nostra opus est? Num eloquentia Platonem superare possumus? Evolve diligenter eius eum librum, qui est de animo, amplius quod desideres nihil erit. A. Feci mehercule et quidem saepius; sed nescio quo modo, dum lego, adsentior; cum posui librum et mecum ipse de immortalitate animorum coepi cogitare, adsensio illa
25 omnis elabitur. M. Quid hoc? dasne aut manere animos post mortem aut morte ipsa interire? A. Do vero. M. Quid, si maneant? A. Beatos esse concedo. M. Sin intereant? A. Non esse miseros, quoniam ne sint quidem: nam istuc coacti a te paullo ante concessimus. M. Quo modo igitur aut cur mortem malum tibi videri dicis? quae aut beatos nos efficiet animis manentibus aut non miseros sensu carentes?

---

[1] Cicero refers to Plato's *Phaedo*.

[2] As *adsensio* is the Latin for the Stoic συγκατάθεσις, there may be a reference to the philosophical meaning of the term, the assent given by the mind to a perception.

it will vanish away. Why speak of Dicaearchus, a thinker who says the soul is nothing at all? According to all these views nothing can appertain to anyone after death, for along with life is lost the power of sensation; moreover there is nothing to make any sort of difference to a being without sensation. The views of the rest of the teachers offer the hope, if this happen to rejoice you, that souls, on their separation from the body, find their way to heaven as to their dwelling-place. A. It does rejoice me, and best of all I should like this to be the truth, and next I should like, even should it not prove true, to be persuaded of it all the same. M. What need have you then of our help? We cannot, can we, surpass Plato in eloquence? Turn over with attention the pages of his book upon the soul.[1] You will be conscious of no further need. A. I have done so, be sure, and done so many times; but somehow I am sorry to find that I agree while reading, yet when I have laid the book aside and begin to reflect in my own mind upon the immortality of souls, all my previous sense of agreement[2] slips away. M. What do you mean by this? do you grant that souls either survive after death, or else perish by the mere fact of death? A. I do grant it. M. Well then—suppose they survive? A. I admit that they are happy. M. But suppose they perish? A. I admit that they are not wretched, since by hypothesis they have no existence: for this admission we made a little while back under the force of your argument. M. In what sense then or for what reason do you say that you consider death an evil, when it will either render us happy if our souls survive, or free from wretchedness if we are without sensation?

31

26 XII. A. Expone igitur, nisi molestum est, primum, si potes, animos remanere post mortem; tum, si minus id obtinebis—est enim arduum,—docebis carere omni malo mortem. Ego enim istuc ipsum vereor ne malum sit, non dico carere sensu, sed carendum esse. M. Auctoribus quidem ad istam sententiam, quam vis obtineri, uti optimis possumus, quod in omnibus causis et debet et solet valere pluri-mum, et primum quidem omni antiquitate, quae quo propius aberat ab ortu et divina progenie, hoc melius

27 ea fortasse, quae erant vera, cernebat. Itaque unum illud erat insitum priscis illis, quos *cascos* appellat Ennius, esse in morte sensum neque excessu vitae sic deleri hominem, ut funditus interiret: idque cum multis aliis rebus tum e pontificio iure et e caerimo-niis sepulcrorum intelligi licet, quas maximis ingeniis praediti nec tanta cura coluissent nec violatas tam inexpiabili religione sanxissent, nisi haereret in eorum mentibus mortem non interitum esse omnia tollentem atque delentem, sed quandam quasi migrationem commutationemque vitae, quae in claris viris et feminis dux in caelum soleret esse, in ceteris

28 humi retineretur et permaneret tamen. Ex hoc et

---

[1] *Cascus*, a word for "old," said by Varro to be of Sabine origin.   Ennius' line, is *Quam prisci casci populi tenuere Latini*, cf. App. II.

[2] The general Roman belief was that, if the body were properly buried, the ghost or shade passed beneath the earth to join the whole body of Manes in the underworld and would only return at certain fixed times: if the body were not properly burnt and buried, the ghost would "walk" and was dangerous, cf. *Mids. Night's Dream*, Act 3, Sc. 2. The

XII. A. Show clearly, then, if it is not troublesome, in the first place, if you can, that souls survive
after death, and next, if you fail to establish this—
for it is a difficult matter—you are to prove that
death is free from any evil. For the point I am
afraid of is precisely this, namely that it be found
an evil, I do not say to be without sensation, but to
have to face the prospect of being without it. M. As
for authorities for that view which you wish to see
established, we can employ the highest, a point
which in all cases ought to have great weight and
usually does so: and, to begin with, we can quote
all antiquity which, it may be, had a clearer vision
of the truth in proportion to its nearness to its origin
and divine ancestry. Accordingly we find in those
men of old whom Ennius styled the "ancients"[1]
the fixed belief that there is sensation in the state
of death, and that in quitting life man is not annihilated so as to perish utterly; this may be gathered,
among many other instances, from pontifical law and
the rites of burial, for these rites would not have
been so scrupulously observed by men of commanding
ability and their profanation forbidden under penalty
of guilt admitting of no atonement, if there had not
been a fixed conviction in their minds that death
was not annihilation obliterating and destroying all
things, but a kind of shifting and changing of life
which often served as a guide to heaven for illustrious
men and women, while for all others the ghostly life
was kept underground, yet all the same survived.[2]

Roman festivals connected with the cult of the dead were
Parentalia (February) and *Lemuria* (May). The souls of the
righteous and illustrious dead passed at once to heaven, as
Cicero argues at greater length in the dream of Scipio (*De
Republica*, Bk. VI.), cf. § 106.

nostrorum opinione " Romulus in caelo cum dis agit
aevom," ut famae adsentiens dixit Ennius, et apud
Graecos indeque perlapsus ad nos et usque ad
Oceanum Hercules tantus et tam praesens habetur
deus : hinc Liber Semela natus eademque famae
celebritate Tyndaridae fratres, qui non modo adiu-
tores in proeliis victoriae populi Romani, sed etiam
nuntii fuisse perhibentur. Quid? Ino Cadmi filia
nonne Λευκοθέα nominata a Graecis Matuta habetur a
nostris ? Quid? totum prope caelum, ne plures
persequar, nonne humano genere completum est?

29   XIII. Si vero scrutari vetera et ex iis ea, quae
scriptores Graeciae prodiderunt, eruere coner, ipsi
illi maiorum gentium di qui habentur hinc profecti
in caelum reperientur. Quaere quorum demonstren-
tur sepulcra in Graecia, reminiscere, quoniam es
initiatus, quae tradantur mysteriis, tum denique
quam hoc late pateat intelliges. Sed qui nondum
ea, quae multis post annis tractari coepta sunt,[1]
physica didicissent tantum sibi persuaserant, quantum
natura admonente cognoverant, rationes et causas
rerum non tenebant, visis quibusdam saepe move-

---

[1]   *coepissent*, MSS. : *coepta sunt*, Keil.

[1] Cf. App. II.
[2] Before starting for Italy Hannibal made his vows to
Hercules (Melcarth) at Gades, Livy xxi. 21.
[3] Liber, the name of an ancient Italian deity of agri-
culture, applied by Roman poets to the Greek Bacchus or
Dionysus the God of Wine, the son of Zeus and Semele of
Thebes.
[4] The Dioscuri, Castor and Pollux. Their worship was
introduced to Rome after the battle at Lake Regillus, the
news of which they brought to Rome.
[5] Matuta, an old Italian goddess of the dawn and identified
with the Greek Ino who threw herself into the sea and was
changed into the marine goddess Leucothea.

Hence, in the belief of our countrymen, " in heaven Romulus lives ever with the gods," as Ennius [1] wrote in obedience to tradition, and with the Greeks there is the belief, which passed from them to us and on as far as Ocean, that Hercules [2] is a great and helpful god. From this belief it comes that Liber son of Semele is held a god,[3] and that the same tale is told of the brethren, sons of Tyndareus,[4] who have not only helped the Romans to victory in battle, but have, so runs the rede, been messengers of victory as well. What? Is not Ino, daughter of Cadmus, named by the Greeks Λευκοθέα, reverenced as Matuta [5] by our countrymen? Again, is not almost the whole of heaven, to avoid the search for further instances, filled with gods of mortal origin?

XIII. In fact, if I were to investigate old records and rummage out of them the instances given by Greek writers, the actual beings who are regarded as the gods of first enrolment [6] have started, we shall find, on their heavenly pilgrimage by this road. Inquire whose tombs are pointed out in Greece; recall, as you have been initiated, the lore imparted to you in the mysteries: then indeed you will realize how far this belief extends. The fact is that men, as they had not yet become acquainted with natural philosophy which first began to be studied many years later, had only such convictions as they had gained from the suggestions of nature; they had no grasp of a reasoned system of causation and were influenced by the frequent sight of apparitions, mostly

[6] The 100 senators chosen by Romulus were called *maiorum gentium*. This term applied to the gods means the *Dii Consentes* of Ennius (cf. App. II.), *i.e.*
Iuno, Vesta, Minerva, Ceres, Diana, Venus, Mars, Mercurius, Iovis, Neptunus, Volcanus, Apollo.

bantur iisque maxime nocturnis, ut viderentur ei, qui vita excesserant, vivere.

30 Ut porro firmissimum hoc adferri videtur, cur deos esse credamus, quod nulla gens tam fera, nemo omnium tam est immanis, cuius mentem non imbuerit deorum opinio—multi de dis prava sentiunt, id enim vitioso more effici solet, omnes tamen esse vim et naturam divinam arbitrantur, nec vero id collocutio hominum aut consensus[1] effecit, non institutis opinio est confirmata, non legibus, omni autem in re consensio omnium gentium lex naturae putanda est —quis est igitur qui suorum mortem primum non eo lugeat, quod eos orbatos vitae commodis arbitretur? Tolle hanc opinionem, luctum sustuleris. Nemo enim maeret suo incommodo: dolent fortasse et anguntur: sed illa lugubris lamentatio fletusque maerens ex eo est, quod eum, quem dileximus, vitae commodis privatum arbitramur idque sentire. Atque haec ita sentimus natura duce, nulla ratione nullaque doctrina.

31 XIV. Maximum vero argumentum est naturam ipsam de immortalitate animorum tacitam iudicare, quod omnibus curae sunt et maximae quidem, quae

---

[1] *consensus* is not used in the sense it has in § 35. *Consessus* has been suggested, or *consensus* may be a gloss to explain *collocutio*. It is certainly awkward, coming as it does so close to *consensio*.

---

[1] Cf. § 36.

[2] Convention, συνθήκη, as opposed to nature, φύσις.

[3] This passage is hard to follow. Cicero seems to be arguing that *as* general consent is a proof of the existence of the gods, *so* it is of the immortality of the soul, cf. § 35. We should therefore have expected "*As* the surest basis for our belief in gods is the unanimity of mankind, so the surest basis for belief in immortality is the unanimity with which

seen in the hours of night, to think that those who had departed from life still lived.

Furthermore, as this seems to be advanced as the surest basis for our belief in the existence of gods, that there is no race so uncivilized, no one in the world, we are told, so barbarous that his mind has no inkling of a belief in gods :—true it is that many men have wrong notions about the gods, for this is usually the result of a corrupt nature ; nevertheless all men think that a divine power and divine nature exist,[1] and that is not the result of human conference or convention,[2] it is not belief established by regulation or by statute, but in every inquiry the unanimity of the races of the world must be regarded as a law of nature. Is there then any being so constituted that he does not in the first instance mourn for his dear ones because they have been deprived, as he thinks, of the comforts of life ?[3] Do away with this belief and you will at once do away with mourning. It is not for his own discomfort that anyone grieves ; men feel, it may be, sorrow and anguish ; but our customary melancholy wailing and weeping for grief come from the thought that the being we have loved is robbed of the comforts of life and is sensible of their loss ; and this feeling of ours is due, not to any process of reasoning or instruction, but to the promptings of nature.

XIV. But the principal proof is that nature herself gives an unspoken judgment on the immortality of souls, because all men are anxious and indeed deeply anxious about what will happen

everyone mourns his dead, because they have been deprived of the comforts of this life and are, it is thought, sensible of their loss."

post mortem futura sint. *Serit arbores, quae alteri saeclo prosint*, ut ait Statius[1] in Synephebis, quid spectans nisi etiam postera saecula ad se pertinere? Ergo arbores seret diligens agricola, quarum aspiciet bacam ipse numquam; vir magnus leges, instituta, rem publicam non seret? Quid procreatio liberorum, quid propagatio nominis, quid adoptationes filiorum, quid testamentorum diligentia, quid ipsa sepulcrorum monumenta, elogia significant nisi nos futura 32 etiam cogitare? Quid illud? num dubitas quin specimen naturae capi deceat ex optima quaque natura? Quae est melior igitur in hominum genere natura quam eorum, qui se natos ad homines iuvandos, tutandos, conservandos arbitrantur? Abiit ad deos Hercules; numquam abisset, nisi, cum inter homines esset, eam sibi viam munivisset. Vetera iam ista et religione omnium consecrata.

XV. Quid in hac re publica tot tantosque viros ob rem publicam interfectos cogitasse arbitramur? iisdemne ut finibus nomen suum quibus vita terminaretur? Nemo umquam sine magna spe immortalitatis 33 se pro patria offerret ad mortem. Licuit esse otioso Themistocli, licuit Epaminondae, licuit, ne et vetera et externa quaeram, mihi, sed nescio quo modo

---

[1] The MSS. give no subject for *ait*. *Statius*, the name of the poet, inserted by Beroaldus. Caecilius Statius, Roman comic poet, died 168 B.C. cf. App. II.

after death. "Trees does he sow to be of service to the coming age," as *Statius* says in the *Synephebi*, and what notion is in his mind except that even succeeding ages are his concern? Shall then a farmer industriously sow trees, no berry of which his eyes will ever see, and a great man not sow the seed of laws, regulations and public policy? The begetting of children, the prolongation of a name, the adoption of sons, the careful preparation of wills, the very burial monuments, the epitaphs—what meaning have they except that we are thinking of the future as well as the present? And what of this point? Can you doubt that properly our ideal of human nature should be formed from the finest natures we meet with? What better type of nature therefore can we find among human beings than the men who regard themselves as born into the world to help and guard and preserve their fellow-men? Hercules passed away to join the gods : he would never have so passed, unless in the course of his mortal life he had built for himself the road he travelled. Such instances are by now time-worn and hallowed by the religious feeling of the world.

XV. Again, in this commonwealth of ours, with what thought in their minds do we suppose such an army of illustrious men have lost their lives for the commonwealth? Was it that their name should be restricted to the narrow limits of their life? No one would ever have exposed himself to death for his country without good hope of immortality. Themistocles might have led a quiet life, Epaminondas might have done so, and not to quote old-time instances from foreign history, I might have done so; but somehow it comes about that there is

inhaeret in mentibus quasi saeclorum quoddam augurium futurorum, idque in maximis ingeniis altissimisque animis et exsistit maxime et apparet facillime. Quo quidem dempto quis tam esset amens qui 34 semper in laboribus et periculis viveret? Loquor de principibus: quid poëtae? nonne post mortem nobilitari volunt? Unde ergo illud?

> *Aspicite, o cives, senis Enni imaginis formam:*
> *Hic vestrum panxit maxuma facta patrum.*

Mercedem gloriae flagitat ab iis, quorum patres adfecerat gloria, idemque:

> *Nemo me lacrumis decoret nec funera fletu*
> *Faxit. Cur? volito vivus per ora virum.*

Sed quid poëtas? opifices post mortem nobilitari volunt. Quid enim Phidias sui similem speciem inclusit in clipeo Minervae, cum inscribere non liceret? Quid nostri philosophi? nonne in iis libris ipsis, quos scribunt de contemnenda gloria, sua 35 nomina inscribunt? Quod si omnium consensus naturae vox est omnesque, qui ubique sunt, consentiunt esse aliquid quod ad eos pertineat, qui vita cesserint, nobis quoque idem existimandum est et si, quorum aut ingenio aut virtute animus excellit, eos

in men's minds a sort of deeply rooted presentiment of future ages, and this feeling is strongest and most evident in men of the greatest genius and the loftiest spirit. Take this feeling away and who would be such a madman as to pass his life continually in toil and peril? So far, I am speaking of statesmen, but what of poets? Have they no wish to become famous after death? What then is the meaning of the passage? :—

> Behold, my fellow-countrymen, old Ennius' sculptured face!
> He told the glorious story of your fathers' mighty race. [1]

He demands the recompense of fame from those whose fathers he had rendered famous, and the same poet writes:

> Let no one honour me with tears or on my ashes weep.
> For why? from lips to lips of men I pass and living keep. [1]

But why stop at the poets? Artists wish to become famous after death. Or why did Phidias insert his likeness on the shield of Minerva, though not allowed to inscribe his name on it? What of our philosophers? Do they not inscribe their names upon the actual books they write about contempt of fame? But if universal agreement is the voice of nature, and all men throughout the world agree that there is something appertaining to those who have passed away from life, we too are bound to hold the same opinion; and if we think that spirits of outstanding ability or moral worth have the clearest insight into the mean-

---

[1] Cf. App. II.

arbitramur, quia natura optima sint, cernere naturae vim maxime, veri simile est, cum optimus quisque maxime posteritati serviat, esse aliquid, cuius is post mortem sensum sit habiturus.

36 XVI. Sed ut deos esse natura opinamur, quales sint ratione cognoscimus, sic permanere animos arbitramur consensu nationum omnium, qua in sede maneant qualesque sint ratione discendum est. Cuius ignoratio finxit inferos easque formidines, quas tu contemnere non sine causa videbare. In terram enim cadentibus corporibus iisque humo tectis, e quo dictum est humari, sub terra censebant reliquam vitam agi mortuorum ; quam eorum opinionem magni 37 errores consecuti sunt, quos auxerunt poëtae. Frequens enim consessus theatri, in quo sunt mulierculae et pueri, movetur audiens tam grande carmen :

Adsum atque advenio Acherunte vix via alta atque
 ardua
Per speluncas saxis structas asperis, pendentibus,
Maxumis, ubi rigida constat crassa caligo inferum,

tantumque valuit error, qui mihi quidem iam sublatus videtur, ut, corpora cremata cum scirent, tamen ea fieri apud inferos fingerent, quae sine

---

[1] *Humare*, to bury, is derived from *humus*, soil.
[2] Lines from some tragedy unknown, spoken perhaps by the ghost of a Trojan prince, as in Eur. *Hecuba* 1, ἥκω νεκρῶν κευθμῶνα, cf. App. II.

ing of nature, because they are blest with the highest nature, then, inasmuch as all the best characters do most service for posterity, the probability is that there is something of which they will have sensation after death.

XVI. But just as it is by natural instinct that we believe in the existence of gods, and by the exercise of reason that we learn to know their nature, so it is that resting upon the agreement of all races of mankind we think that souls have an abiding life, and it is by reason we must learn their place of abode and their nature. It is ignorance of this that has invented the world below and the terrors which not without reason you appeared to despise. Bodies fall into the ground and are covered with earth, and this is the origin of our word for burial,[1] and so men held that the subsequent life of the dead was passed underground ; this belief resulted in serious deceptions which poets exaggerated. The crowded concourse in the theatre with its contingent of silly women and children is stirred at the sound of the swelling strain :

> Here out of Acheron straight I come by steep and
>   toilsome road,
> Through caves of rugged rocks piled high that
>   threaten from above,
> Stupendous, where Hell's darkness makes a thick,
>   substantial gloom.[2]

And such was the extent of deception, now to my thinking dissipated, that though they knew that the bodies of the dead were consumed with fire, yet they imagined that events took place in the lower world

43

corporibus nec fieri possunt nec intelligi; animos enim per se ipsos viventes non poterant mente complecti, formam aliquam figuramque quaerebant. Inde Homeri tota νέκυια, inde ea, quae meus amicus Appius νεκυομαντεῖα faciebat, inde in vicinia nostra Averni lacus,

> Unde animae excitantur obscura umbra aperto *ex ostio*
> Altae Acheruntis, falso[1] sanguine, mortuorum ima-
> gines.

Has tamen imagines loqui volunt, quod fieri nec sine lingua nec sine palato nec sine faucium, laterum, pulmonum vi et figura potest; nihil enim animo 38 videre poterant, ad oculos omnia referebant. Magni autem est ingenii sevocare mentem a sensibus et cogitationem ab consuetudine abducere. Itaque credo equidem etiam alios tot saeculis; sed, quod litteris exstet, Pherecydes Syrius primus dixit animos esse hominum sempiternos, antiquus sane; fuit enim meo regnante gentili. Hanc opinionem discipulus eius, Pythagoras, maxime confirmavit: qui cum Superbo regnante in Italiam venisset, tenuit Magnam

---

[1] *salso* is another reading and Bentley proposed *fuso*.

---

[1] Cf. *Odyssey* xi, where Ulysses calls up the ghosts of the dead.

[2] Places where the spirits of the dead can be called up to give answers, or else the ceremonies used for calling up the spirits to be consulted. Appius (Appius Claudius Pulcher, consul 54 B.C. and, like Cicero, an augur), it seems, either frequented the places or performed the necessary rites. Cf. § 115.

[3] At Cumae in Campania.

[4] *Falso sanguine*, the shades of the dead really required human blood to revivify them, but in place of it the blood of animals is substituted on a principle of make-believe familiar in folk-lore, cf. App. II.

which cannot take place and are not intelligible
without bodies; the reason was that they were
unable to grasp the conception of souls living an
independent life and tried to find for them some
sort of appearance and shape. This is the origin of
Homer's entire νέκυια,[1] this is the origin of the
νεκυομαντεῖα [2] which my friend Appius practised and
of Lake Avernus in our neighbourhood,[3]

> Whence souls are raised in murky shade out of the
>   yawning mouth
> Of Acheron deep by man's blood feigned,[4] the
>   phantoms of the dead.

Yet none the less they wish the phantoms to speak
and this cannot take place without tongue and
palate, or without a formed throat and chest and
lungs in active working. It was because they could
frame no mental vision; everything was brought to
the test of eyesight: and indeed it requires a
powerful intellect to abstract the mind from the
senses and separate thought from the force of habit.
There must in my belief have been other thinkers in
the long succession of the centuries, but so far as literature tells us, Pherecydes of Syros [5] was the first who
pronounced the souls of men to be eternal, and he
was decidedly venerable, for he lived when my
clansman [6] was upon the throne. This belief his
disciple Pythagoras strongly supported, who, after
coming to Italy in the reign of Superbus, became

[5] Pherecydes of Syros lived in the sixth century B.C., and
is said to have been teacher of Pythagoras.
[6] Servius Tullius, whom Cicero jestingly takes as the
founder of his *gens*, the *gens Tullia*.

illam Graeciam cum honore disciplinae, tum etiam
auctoritate, multaque saecula postea sic viguit Pythagoreorum nomen, ut nulli alii docti viderentur.

XVII. Sed redeo ad antiquos. Rationem illi sententiae suae non fere reddebant, nisi quid erat
39 numeris aut descriptionibus explicandum. Platonem
ferunt, ut Pythagoreos cognosceret, in Italiam venisse et didicisse Pythagorea omnia, primumque de
animorum aeternitate non solum sensisse idem quod
Pythagoram, sed rationem etiam attulisse. Quam,
nisi quid dicis, praetermittamus et hanc totam spem
immortalitatis relinquamus. A. An tu, cum me in
summam exspectationem adduxeris, deseris ? Errare
mehercule malo cum Platone, quem tu quanti facias
scio et quem ex tuo ore admiror, quam cum istis
40 vera sentire. M. Macte virtute ! ego enim ipse cum
eodem isto non invitus erraverim. Num igitur du-
bitamus sicut pleraque—quamquam hoc quidem
minime ; persuadent enim mathematici—terram in
medio mundo sitam ad universi caeli complexum
quasi puncti instar obtinere, quod κέντρον illi vocant ?
eam porro naturam esse quattuor omnia gignentium
corporum, ut, quasi partita habeant inter se ac

---

[1] When the disciples of Pythagoras were asked the reasons
for any statement they had made in the course of a philosophical discussion, they used to reply : *ipse dixit*, αὐτὸς ἔφα,
"the Master said so." Cf. V. §§ 8–10.

[2] As followers of Carneades who only look for probability,
not certainty. Cf. § 17.

[3] Plato, *Phaedo*, 108 E, Aristotle, *De Caelo* 2.14. Mathematics included astrology, geometry, arithmetic and music.

paramount in the region known as Magna Graecia
both by reason of the honour paid to his system of
training and by his personal influence as well, and
many centuries after, the name of Pythagorean still
stood so high that none outside the sect were thought
learned.

XVII. But I return to the old Pythagoreans.
They did not generally give a reasoned proof of
their opinion[1] apart from the interpretation to be
imparted by numbers and geometrical figures. The
story goes that Plato came to Italy to study the
Pythagoreans and learnt all the Pythagorean
doctrine, and not merely agreed with Pythagoras
about the eternity of souls but was the first to
furnish reasoned proof as well: but unless you
demur let us ignore this proof and abandon the
whole problem of the hope of immortality. A. After
having raised me to the highest pitch of expectancy
do you propose, pray, to leave me in the lurch? I
prefer, before heaven, to go astray with Plato, your
reverence for whom I know, and admiration for
whom I learn from your lips, rather than hold true
views with his opponents. M. Well done! I should
not myself be unwilling to go astray with that same
thinker. Surely then we have no doubts, have we,
as we have on a great number of subjects[2]—yet this
at any rate we cannot possibly doubt, for the mathematicians are convincing—I mean, that the earth is
placed in the centre of the universe[3] and in comparison with the compass of the sky occupies space
in extent like a point, called by mathematicians
κέντρον? Furthermore we do not doubt that the
nature of the four elements from which all things
are begotten is such that, as though their laws of

47

divisa momenta, terrena et humida suopte nutu et
suo pondere ad pares angulos in terram et in mare
ferantur, reliquae duae partes, una ignea, altera ani-
malis, ut illae superiores in medium locum mundi
gravitate ferantur et pondere, sic hae rursum rectis
lineis in caelestem locum subvolent, sive ipsa natura
superiora appetente sive quod a gravioribus leviora
natura repellantur.   Quae cum constent, perspicuum
debet esse animos, cum e corpore excesserint, sive
illi sint animales, id est, spirabiles, sive ignei, sublime
41 ferri.   Si vero aut numerus quidam est animus, quod
subtiliter magis quam dilucide dicitur, aut quinta
illa non nominata magis quam non intellecta natura,
multo etiam integriora ac puriora sunt, ut a terra
longissime se efferant.   Horum igitur aliquid animus,[1] ne tam vegeta mens aut in corde cerebrove
aut in Empedocleo sanguine demersa iaceat.

XVIII. Dicaearchum vero cum Aristoxeno aequali
et condiscipulo suo, doctos sane homines, omittamus,
quorum alter ne condoluisse quidem umquam videtur, qui animum se habere non sentiat, alter ita
delectatur suis cantibus, ut eos etiam ad haec trans-
ferre conetur.   Harmoniam autem ex intervallis
sonorum nosse possumus, quorum varia compositio
etiam harmonias efficit plures, membrorum vero situs

---

[1] Many editors supply *est*.

---

[1] These are Stoic views derived from Aristotle.
[2] Cf. § 22.

motion were mutually apportioned and divided, the earthy and the moist are carried perpendicularly into land and sea by their own tendency and weight, while the two remaining parts, one fiery, the other airy, precisely as the two first-mentioned are carried into the centre of the universe by heaviness and weight, so the last two on the contrary fly vertically upward into the heavenly region, whether this be due to an upward tendency inherent in their nature, or because bodies naturally lighter are driven away from heavier bodies.[1] And since these facts are established it ought to be clear that souls, on quitting the body, whether they are airy, that is to say, of the nature of breath, or fiery, are carried aloft. If, however, the soul is a number, a suggestion more subtle than clear, or is Aristotle's fifth nature, unnamed rather than not understood,[2] then there are substances of a purity so much more uncontaminated that they transport themselves as far as possible away from earth. The soul then is some one or other of these things, so that the mind, with all its activity, has not to lie buried in the heart or brain, or in the blood of Empedocles' theory.

XVIII. But as for Dicaearchus, along with his contemporary and fellow-pupil Aristoxenus, in spite of their undoubted learning, let us ignore them. The one appears never to have felt so much as a pang at not noticing that he had a soul; the other is so pleased with his own tunes that he attempts to bring them into philosophy as well. But we can recognize the melody arising out of the distances in pitch between sounds, and the different combination of these sounds again produces further melodies; I fail to see, however, how the position of the limbs

49

et figura corporis vacans animo quam possit harmoniam efficere non video. Sed hic quidem, quamvis eruditus sit, sicut est, haec magistro concedat Aristoteli, canere ipse doceat. Bene enim illo Graecorum proverbio praecipitur:

Quam quisque norit artem, in hac se exerceat.

42 Illam vero funditus eiiciamus individuorum corporum levium et rotundorum concursionem fortuitam, quam tamen Democritus concalefactam et spirabilem, id est, animalem, esse volt. Is autem animus, qui si est horum quattuor generum, ex quibus omnia constare dicuntur, ex inflammata anima constat, ut potissimum videri video Panaetio, superiora capessat necesse est; nihil enim habent haec duo genera proni et supera semper petunt. Ita, sive dissipantur, procul a terris id evenit, sive permanent et conservant habitum suum, hoc etiam magis necesse est ferantur ad caelum et ab iis perrumpatur et dividatur crassus hic et concretus aër, qui est terrae proximus; calidior est enim vel potius ardentior animus, quam est hic aër, quem modo dixi crassum atque concretum; quod ex eo sciri potest, quia corpora nostra terreno principiorum genere confecta, ardore animi concalescunt.

---

[1] ἔρδοι τις ἣν ἕκαστος εἰδείη τέχνην, Ar., *Wasps* 1431.

[2] Democritus said the soul was a kind of fire and hot: the atoms of fire and soul were round, and these atoms were a seed-magazine, πανσπερμία, for all nature. Arist. *De Anima*, I. 2.

[3] According to the Stoics the soul was πνεῦμα ἔνθερμον. Following the old Ionian philosopher Heraclitus they held that all the aspects of the universe are in one way or another manifestations of πῦρ τεχνικόν, creative fire, which is God.

[4] Panaetius of Rhodes, a Stoic philosopher and friend of Scipio Africanus Minor, § 79.

and the attitude of the body, where there is no soul, is to produce melody. But let this musician, in spite of his being, as indeed he was, very learned, leave philosophy in the hands of his master Aristotle, and for himself continue his singing lessons: for it is a good rule laid down in the well-known Greek saying:

> The art which each man knows, in this let him employ himself.[1]

Let us further utterly reject the notion of a soul made of indivisible smooth round bodies brought into accidental concurrence, in spite of the fact that Democritus[2] holds it to be heated and airy, that is of the nature of breath. On the other hand, if the soul, as we regard it, belongs to the four classes of elements of which all things are said to consist, it consists of kindled air,[3] as I see is the view which most commends itself to Panaetius,[4] and such a soul necessarily strives to reach higher regions; for the two lighter classes have no downward tendency and always seek the heights. Consequently if souls are dispersed in space, this takes place at a distance from the earth; if they survive and preserve their quality, all the more reason for their being carried to heaven and breaking their way through and parting asunder our dense and compact air which is nearest to earth; for the soul is hotter or, preferably, more glowing than our air which I just now described as dense and compact; and this may be known from the fact that our bodies, which are fashioned from the earthy class of elements,[5] are heated by the glow of the soul.

[5] Flesh and bones from earth, moisture and sweat from water, breath from air, warmth from fire.

43   XIX. Accedit ut eo facilius animus evadat ex hoc
aëre, quem saepe iam appello, eumque perrumpat,
quod nihil est animo velocius: nulla est celeritas,
quae possit cum animi celeritate contendere. Qui
si permanet incorruptus suique similis, necesse est
ita feratur, ut penetret et dividat omne caelum hoc,
in quo nubes, imbres ventique coguntur, quod et
humidum et caliginosum est propter exhalationes
terrae. Quam regionem cum superavit animus natu-
ramque sui similem contigit et agnovit, iunctis ex
anima tenui et ex ardore solis temperato ignibus
insistit et finem altius se efferendi facit. Cum enim
sui similem et levitatem et calorem adeptus est,
tamquam paribus examinatus ponderibus nullam in
partem movetur, eaque ei demum naturalis est sedes,
cum ad sui simile penetravit, in quo nulla re egens
aletur et sustentabitur iisdem rebus, quibus astra
44 sustentantur et aluntur. Cumque corporis facibus
inflammari soleamus ad omnes fere cupiditates eoque
magis incendi, quod iis aemulemur, qui ea habeant,
quae nos habere cupiamus, profecto beati erimus,
cum corporibus relictis et cupiditatum et aemula-
tionum erimus expertes; quodque nunc facimus,
cum laxati curis sumus, ut spectare aliquid velimus
et visere, id multo tum faciemus liberius totosque
nos in contemplandis rebus perspiciendisque pone-
mus, propterea quod et natura inest in mentibus

---

[1] In the *De Natura Deorum*, ii. 46. 118, Cicero says that
the stars are of fiery nature, and fed on the vapours which
are drawn by the sun from the warmed fields and waters of
the earth.

XIX. Add that the soul comes to make its escape
all the more readily from our air, which I have
frequently so named, and breaks its way through,
because there is nothing swifter than the soul :
there is no sort of speed which can match the speed
of the soul. If it survives unadulterated and unchanged in substance, it is of necessity carried away
so rapidly as to pierce and part asunder all this
atmosphere of ours, in which clouds, storms and
winds collect because of the moisture and mist produced by evaporation from the earth. When the
soul has passed this tract and reaches to and recognizes a substance resembling its own, it stops amongst
the fires which are formed of rarefied air and the
modified glow of the sun and ceases to make higher
ascent. For when it has reached conditions of light-
ness and heat resembling its own, it becomes quite
motionless, as though in a state of equilibrium with
its surroundings, and then, and not before, finds its
natural home, when it has pierced to conditions
resembling its own, and there, with all its needs
satisfied, it will be nourished and maintained on the
same food which maintains and nourishes the stars.[1]
And as it is the fires of the flesh in our bodies
which commonly enkindle us to almost all desires,
and the flame is heightened by envy of all who
possess what we desire to possess, assuredly we shall
be happy when we have left our bodies behind and
are free from all desirings and envyings ; and as
happens now, when the burden of care is relaxed,
we feel the wish for an object of our observation and
attention, this will happen much more freely then,
and we shall devote our whole being to study and
examination, because nature has planted in our

nostris insatiabilis quaedam cupiditas veri videndi et
orae ipsae locorum illorum, quo pervenerimus, quo
faciliorem nobis cognitionem rerum caelestium, eo
45 maiorem cognoscendi cupiditatem dabunt. Haec
enim pulcritudo etiam in terris "patritam illam et
avitam," ut ait Theophrastus, philosophiam cognitionis cupiditate incensam excitavit. Praecipue vero
fruentur ea qui tum etiam, cum has terras incolentes
circumfusi erant caligine, tamen acie mentis dispicere
cupiebant.

XX. Etenim si nunc aliquid adsequi se putant,
qui ostium Ponti viderunt et eas angustias, per quas
penetravit ea, quae est nominata

> *Argo, quia Argivi in ea dilecti viri*
> *vecti petebant pellem inauratam arietis,*

aut ii, qui Oceani freta illa viderunt,

> *Europam Libyamque rapax ubi dividit unda,*

quod tandem spectaculum fore putamus, cum totam
terram contueri licebit eiusque cum situm, formam,
circumscriptionem, tum et habitabiles regiones et
rursum omni cultu propter vim frigoris aut caloris
46 vacantes? Nos enim ne nunc quidem oculis cernimus ea, quae videmus : neque est enim ullus sensus
in corpore, sed ut non physici solum docent, verum

---

[1] πατρῷος καὶ παππῷος. For Theophrastus, cf. III. § 21.
[2] Cf. App. II. : see also Eurip. *Med.* 5,

> ἀνδρῶν ἀριστέων οἳ τὸ πάγχρυσον δέρος
> Πελίᾳ μετῆλθον.

minds an insatiable longing to see truth; and the more the vision of the borders only of the heavenly country, to which we have come, renders easy the knowledge of heavenly conditions, the more will our longing for knowledge be increased. For the beauty of that vision even here on earth called into being that philosophy "of sires and grandsires,"[1] as Theophrastus terms it, which was first kindled by longing for knowledge. But theirs will be the chief enjoyment who, even in the days they sojourned on earth amid the encircling gloom, longed all the same to pierce it by the keenness of mental vision.

XX. For if now men think it an achievement when they have seen Pontus and the famous narrows through which the vessel passed named

Argo, for her picked Argive heroes once
Sailed out to win the ram's bright golden fleece,[2]

or those who saw the famous straits[3] of Ocean,

Where from the Libyan shore the hungry wave
    sundereth Europe,

what, pray, do we think the panorama will be like when we shall be free to embrace the whole earth in our survey, its situation, shape, and circumference, as well as both the districts that are habitable and those again that are left wholly uncultivated because of the violence of cold or heat? We do not even now distinguish with our eyes the things we see; for there is no perception in the body, but, as is taught not only by natural philosophers but also

The Argonauts sailed under the leadership of Jason to the Euxine to get the golden fleece.   [3] Of Gibraltar.

etiam medici, qui ista aperta et patefacta viderunt,
viae quasi quaedam sunt ad oculos, ad aures, ad
nares a sede animi perforatae. Itaque saepe aut
cogitatione aut aliqua vi morbi impediti apertis atque
integris et oculis et auribus nec videmus nec audi-
mus, ut facile intelligi possit animum et videre et
audire, non eas partes, quae quasi fenestrae sint
animi, quibus tamen sentire nihil queat mens, nisi
id agat et adsit. Quid? quod eadem mente res
dissimillimas comprehendimus, ut colorem, saporem,
calorem, odorem, sonum? quae numquam quinque
nuntiis animus cognosceret, nisi ad eum omnia
referrentur et is omnium iudex solus esset. Atque
ea profecto tum multo puriora et dilucidiora cernen-
tur, cum quo natura fert liber animus pervenerit.

47 Nam nunc quidem, quamquam foramina illa, quae
patent ad animum a corpore, callidissimo artificio
natura fabricata est, tamen terrenis concretisque
corporibus sunt intersaepta quodam modo: cum
autem nihil erit praeter animum, nulla res obiecta
impediet quo minus percipiat quale quidque est.

XXI. Quamvis copiose haec diceremus, si res
postularet, quam multa, quam varia, quanta specta-
cula animus in locis caelestibus esset habiturus.

48 Quae quidem cogitans soleo saepe mirari non
nullorum insolentiam philosophorum, qui naturae

---

[1] The arteries, found empty by the ancients on dissection
and supposed to be air-tubes.

[2] Plutarch quotes a line from the comic poet Epicharmus
(cf. § 15):

νοῦς ὁρῇ καὶ νοῦς ἀκούει, τἆλλα κωφὰ καὶ τυφλά.

by the experts of medicine, who have seen the proofs openly disclosed, there are, as it were, passages[1] bored from the seat of the soul to eye and ear and nose. Often, therefore, we are hindered by absorption in thought or by some attack of sickness, and though eyes and ears are open and uninjured, we neither see nor hear, so that it can be readily understood that it is the soul[2] which both sees and hears, and not those parts of us which serve as windows to the soul, and yet the mind can perceive nothing through them, unless it is active and attentive. What of the fact that by using the same mind we have perception of things so utterly unlike as colour, taste, heat, smell, sound? These the soul would never have ascertained by its five messengers, unless it had been sole court of appeal and only judge of everything. Moreover, surely objects of far greater purity and transparency will be discovered when the day comes on which the mind is free and has reached its natural home. For in our present state, although the apertures which, as has been said, are open from the body to the soul, have been fashioned by nature with cunning workmanship, yet they are in a manner fenced in with a compound of earthy particles: when, however, there shall be soul and nothing else, no physical barrier will hinder its perception of the true nature of everything.

XXI. Did the occasion demand, one might speak at any length on the number, variety and magnitude of the wondrous sights the soul will have before it in heavenly places. Indeed on reflecting over them I often find myself wondering at the extravagance of some philosophers who marvel at natural science,

cognitionem admirantur eiusque inventori et principi
gratias exsultantes agunt eumque venerantur ut
deum; liberatos enim se per eum dicunt gravissimis
dominis, terrore sempiterno et diurno ac nocturno
metu.   Quo terrore? quo metu? quae est anus tam
delira quae timeat ista, quae vos videlicet, si physica
non didicissetis, timeretis, "*Acherunsia templa alta
Orci, pallida Leti, obnubila tenebris loca?*"   Non
pudet philosophum in eo gloriari, quod haec non
timeat et quod falsa esse cognoverit?   E quo intelligi potest quam acuti natura sint, qui haec
49 sine doctrina credituri fuerint.[1]   Praeclarum autem
nescio quid adepti sunt, quod didicerunt se, cum
tempus mortis venisset, totos esse perituros.   Quod
ut ita sit—nihil enim pugno—, quid habet ista res
aut laetabile aut gloriosum?   Nec tamen mihi sane
quidquam occurrit cur non Pythagorae sit et Platonis
vera sententia.   Ut enim rationem Plato nullam
adferret—vide quid homini tribuam—, ipsa auctoritate me frangeret: tot autem rationes attulit, ut
velle ceteris, sibi certe persuasisse videatur.

> [1] Or *quoniam . . . fuerunt* have good authority.

---

[1] Lucretius, V. 8, says of Epicurus :
  Dicendum est, deus ille fuit, deus, inclyte Memmi,
  Qui princeps vitae rationem invenit eam quae
  Nunc appellatur sapientia, quique per artem
  Fluctibus e tantis vitam tantisque tenebris
  In tam tranquillo et tam clara luce locavit.

[2] Lucr. I. 120 :
  Etsi praeterea tamen esse Acherusia templa
  Ennius aeternis exponit versibus edens
  Quo neque permaneant animae neque corpora nostra
  Sed quaedam simulacra modis pallentia miris.

and in the excess of their joy render thanks to its discoverer and founder and do reverence to him as a god [1] : they say that through him they have been set free from tyrannous masters, from unending terror and daily and nightly fear. What terror? What fear? Where is the crone so silly as to be afraid of the bugbears of which you gentlemen would, it is obvious, have been afraid, if you had not studied natural philosophy? [2] " The lofty Acherunsian temples of Orcus,[3] wan haunts of Death, regions clouded over with darkness." Should not a philosopher blush to boast of not being afraid of such things and of having discovered their falsity? And from this we can realize the natural intelligence of those folk who would, without instruction, have believed them true. Yes, but it is a notable achievement to have learnt that, when once the hour of death had come, they would wholly perish ! And granted that it be so—I am not contesting it— what ground is there in this for joy or boasting? And yet no reason really suggests itself to my mind why the belief of Pythagoras and Plato [4] should not be true. For though Plato produced no reasoned proof—note the tribute I pay the man—he would crush me by the mere weight of his authority : he has, on the contrary, produced such a number of proofs that it seems he wished to convince others, and beyond doubt he seems to have convinced himself.

[3] *Acheron* and *Orcus* are names for the place of the dead. *Templum* is used properly of a space in the sky marked out for observation by augurs, and is then applied to any place held sacred. The line is from Ennius' *Andromacha*, cf. App. II.
[4] Cf. § 39.

50   XXII. Sed plurimi contra nituntur animosque
quasi capite damnatos morte mulctant, neque aliud
est quidquam cur incredibilis iis animorum videatur
aeternitas nisi quod nequeunt qualis animus sit
vacans corpore intelligere et cogitatione compre-
hendere.   Quasi vero intelligant qualis sit in ipso
corpore, quae conformatio, quae magnitudo, qui
locus. At,[1] si iam possent in homine vivo cerni
omnia, quae nunc tecta sunt, casurusne in conspec-
tum videatur animus an tanta sit eius tenuitas, ut
51 fugiat aciem? Haec reputent isti, qui negant animum sine corpore se intelligere posse: videbunt
quem in ipso corpore intelligant.   Mihi quidem
naturam animi intuenti multo difficilior occurrit
cogitatio multoque obscurior, qualis animus in corpore sit tamquam alienae domui, quam qualis, cum
exierit et in liberum caelum quasi domum suam
venerit.   Nisi enim, quod numquam vidimus, id
quale sit intelligere non possumus, certe et deum
ipsum et divinum animum corpore liberatum cogitatione complecti possumus.   Dicaearchus quidem et
Aristoxenus, quia difficilis erat animi quid aut qualis
esset intelligentia, nullum omnino animum esse
52 dixerunt.   Est illud quidem vel maximum animo
ipso animum videre et nimirum hanc habet vim
praeceptum Apollinis, quo monet ut se quisque
noscat.   Non enim, credo, id praecipit, ut membra

_____

[1] The MSS. have *ut*: *at* Pearce, others *vel*.

_____

[1] Cf. § 41.

XXII. But quite a number of thinkers contend against this belief and by a sort of capital sentence punish souls with death, and yet they have no reason for thinking the immortality of souls incredible except that they are unable to understand or grasp the conception of the nature of soul without body. As if indeed they understood its nature, its shape, its size, its position whilst actually in the body. But supposing for the moment that all that is now concealed were discernible in the living man, would it seem likely that the soul could come within the scope of vision, or rather be of such fine substance as to escape the eye? Let the thinkers who say they cannot understand soul without body reflect upon these considerations, and they will see how far they understand soul while it is actually in the body. For my part, when I study the nature of the soul, the conception of it in the body, as it were in a home that is not its own, presents itself as one much more difficult, much more doubtful than the conception of the nature of the soul when it has quitted the body and come into the free heaven, as it were to its home. For unless we are unable to realize the nature of what we have never seen, beyond doubt we can form a conception of God Himself and the divine soul set free from the body. It is true that Dicaearchus and Aristoxenus [1] said that the soul had no existence at all because of the difficulty of understanding what the soul was or what its nature was. It is a point of the utmost importance to realize that the soul sees by means of the soul alone, and surely this is the meaning of Apollo's maxim advising that each one should know himself. For I do not suppose the meaning of the

61

nostra aut staturam figuramve noscamus; neque nos corpora sumus, nec ego tibi haec dicens corpori tuo dico. Cum igitur : *Nosce te*, dicit, hoc dicit : *Nosce animum tuum*. Nam corpus quidem quasi vas est aut aliquod animi receptaculum : ab animo tuo quidquid agitur, id agitur a te. Hunc igitur nosse nisi divinum esset, non esset hoc acrioris cuiusdam animi praeceptum tributum deo.[1]

53 Sed si qualis sit animus ipse animus nesciet, dic, quaeso, ne esse quidem se sciet, ne moveri quidem se ? Ex quo illa ratio nata est Platonis, quae a Socrate est in Phaedro explicata, a me autem posita est in sexto libro de re publica. XXIII. "Quod semper movetur, aeternum est : quod autem motum adfert alicui quodque ipsum agitatur aliunde, quando finem habet motus, vivendi finem habeat necesse est. Solum igitur, quod se ipsum movet, quia numquam deseritur a se, numquam ne moveri quidem desinit : quin etiam ceteris, quae moventur, hic 54 fons, hoc principium est movendi. Principii autem nulla est origo : nam e principio oriuntur omnia, ipsum autem nulla ex re alia nasci potest : nec enim esset id principium, quod gigneretur aliunde. Quod si numquam oritur, ne occidit quidem umquam : nam principium exstinctum nec ipsum ab alio renascetur nec ex se aliud creabit, si quidem necesse est a principio oriri omnia. Ita fit ut motus principium

---

[1] The MSS. have *a deo sit hoc se ipsum posse cognoscere.* Wesenberg's reading based on *Leg.* 1. 22. 58 has been adopted.

---

[1] The words γνῶθι σεαυτόν, inscribed in the vestibule of the temple of Apollo at Delphi. Pausanias X. 24. 1.
[2] This maxim was generally attributed to one of the seven wise men of Greece, Thales or Chilo or Solon.

maxim is that we should know our limbs, our height or shape ; our selves are not bodies, and in speaking as I do to you, I am not speaking to your body. When then Apollo says, " Know thyself," [1] he says, " Know thy soul." For the body is as it were a vessel or a sort of shelter for the soul : every act of your soul is an act of yours. Unless then it had been godlike to know the soul, this maxim, which marks a soul of superior penetration,[2] would not have been attributed to the god.

But if the soul itself prove to be without knowledge of the nature of soul, tell me, pray, will it not have knowledge even of its existence? or even of its movement? This thought gave rise to Plato's well-known argument, developed by Socrates in the *Phaedrus* [3] and placed by me in the sixth book of my work *On the State*. XXIII. "That which is always in motion is eternal; but that which causes movement to something else and is itself set in motion from elsewhere, when it ceases to move must also cease to live. Only that then which is self-moving, because it never abandons itself, never ceases to move either; nay, this is also the source, this is the beginning of movement to all else which moves. On the other hand a beginning has no birth, for all things have origin in a beginning, but the beginning itself can be born from nothing else, for the thing that should be begotten from anything else would not be a beginning. Now if it never has origin, it never perishes either; for a beginning once destroyed will not be itself reborn from anything else, nor will it create anything else from itself, seeing that all things must have origin in a beginning. It results

[3] Plato, *Phaedrus* 245.

63

ex eo sit, quod ipsum a se movetur; id autem nec
nasci potest nec mori, vel concidat omne caelum
omnisque natura consistat necesse est nec vim ullam
nanciscatur, qua a primo impulsa moveatur. Cum
pateat igitur aeternum id esse, quod se ipsum
moveat, quis est qui hanc naturam animis esse tributam neget? Inanimum est enim omne, quod
pulsu agitatur externo; quod autem est animal, id
motu cietur interiore et suo. Nam haec est propria
natura animi atque vis, quae si est una ex omnibus,
quae se ipsa moveat, neque nata certe est et aeterna
est."

55   Licet concurrant omnes plebeii philosophi—sic
enim ii, qui a Platone et Socrate et ab ea familia
dissident, appellandi videntur—, non modo nihil
umquam tam eleganter explicabunt, sed ne hoc
quidem ipsum quam subtiliter conclusum sit intelli-
gent. Sentit igitur animus se moveri: quod cum
sentit, illud una sentit se vi sua, non aliena moveri,
nec accidere posse ut ipse umquam a se deseratur.
Ex quo efficitur aeternitas, nisi quid habes ad haec.
A. Ego vero facile sum passus ne in mentem quidem
mihi aliquid contra venire : ita isti faveo sententiae.

56   XXIV. M. Quid? illa tandem num leviora censes,
quae declarant inesse in animis hominum divina
quaedam? quae si cernerem quem ad modum nasci

64

that the beginning of motion comes from that which is self-moved; moreover it cannot be born or die, else the whole heavens must collapse and all creation come to a standstill and find no power under the impulse of which movement could begin from the outset. Since it is clear, then, that that which is self-moving is eternal, who is there to say that this property has not been bestowed on souls? For everything which is set in motion by impulse from the outside is soulless; what on the other hand has soul is stirred by movement from within and its own. For this is the peculiar essence and character of the soul which, if it is out of all things the one which is self-moving, has assuredly not been born and is eternal."

All the common crowd of philosophers—for such a title seems appropriate to those who disagree with Plato and Socrates and their school—though they lay their heads together, will not only never unravel any problem so neatly, but will not even appreciate the accuracy of this particular conclusion. The soul then is conscious that it is in motion, and when so conscious it is at the same time conscious of this, that it is self-moved by its own power and not an outside power, and that it cannot ever be abandoned by itself; and this is proof of eternity—unless you have anything to advance. A. I have found it easy to let no argument to the contrary so much as enter my head; I therefore support the view you have given.

XXIV. M. Again, can you think, pray, those views of less importance which pronounce that there are divine elements in human souls? Could I discern how such elements could come into being I

possent, etiam quem ad modum interirent viderem.
Nam sanguinem, bilem, pituitam, ossa, nervos, venas,
omnem denique membrorum et totius corporis figuram videor posse dicere unde concreta et quo modo
facta sint : animum ipsum, si nihil esset in eo nisi
id, ut per eum viveremus, tam natura putarem
hominis vitam sustentari quam vitis, quam arboris :
haec enim etiam dicimus vivere.   Item si nihil
haberet animus hominis, nisi ut appeteret aut
fugeret, id quoque esset ei commune cum bestiis.

57   Habet primum memoriam et eam infinitam rerum
innumerabilium : quam quidem Plato recordationem
esse vult superioris vitae.   Nam in illo libro, qui
inscribitur Μένων, pusionem quendam Socrates in-
terrogat quaedam geometrica de dimensione quad-
rati : ad ea sic ille respondet, ut puer, et tamen ita
faciles interrogationes sunt, ut gradatim respondens
eodem perveniat quo si geometrica didicisset ; ex
quo effici vult Socrates ut discere nihil aliud sit nisi
recordari.   Quem locum multo etiam accuratius
explicat in eo sermone, quem habuit eo ipso die,
quo excessit e vita ; docet enim quemvis, qui omnium rerum rudis esse videatur, bene interroganti
respondentem declarare se non tum illa discere, sed
reminiscendo recognoscere, nec vero fieri ullo modo

---

[1] The four humours, blood, black bile, yellow bile, phlegm.
Cf. IV. § 23.

[2] ἀνάμνησις, the recollection of things seen in a previous
state of existence.   Plato, *Phaed.* 73 A.

should also see how they came to an end. For it seems to me that I can tell from what the blood, bile, phlegm,[1] bones, sinews, veins, in fact all the framework of the limbs and the whole body have been compounded and how they were fashioned: as for the soul itself, if it had no characteristic except that through it we have life, I should think that the life of men was supported by natural process much as the life of a vine or a tree is, for such things we say have life. Also, if man's soul had no characteristic except that of seeking out or avoiding things, that also it would share with the beasts.

In the first place, soul has memory, a memory too without limit of things without number; and this Plato wishes to make the recollection[2] of a previous life. For in the book entitled *Meno* Socrates asks a little lad certain geometrical questions about the measurement of the square. To these questions the boy makes answer as a boy would, yet though the questions are easy,[3] by giving his answers step by step he gets to the same conclusion as he would if he had learnt geometry: this Socrates regards as proof that learning is nothing but recollecting. This subject he develops too with much greater care in the conversation which he held on the very day he departed this life; for he there teaches that anyone, though to all appearance totally ignorant, shows in answer to skilful questioning that he is not at the time learning a lesson but taking knowledge of things afresh by remembrance; indeed in no other way was it possible for us to possess from

[3] The point is that the boy is led step by step to the conclusion which he already has in his mind without having learnt geometry.

posse ut a pueris tot rerum atque tantarum insitas
et quasi consignatas in animis notiones, quas ἐννοίας
vocant, haberemus, nisi animus, ante quam in corpus
58 intravisset, in rerum cognitione viguisset. Cumque
nihil esset, ut omnibus locis a Platone disseritur—
nihil enim putat esse quod oriatur et intereat, idque
solum esse, quod semper tale sit, quale est ; [1] ἰδέαν
appellat ille, nos speciem—, non potuit animus haec
in corpore inclusus agnoscere, cognita attulit : ex
quo tam multarum rerum cognitionis admiratio
tollitur. Neque ea plane videt animus, cum repente
in tam insolitum tamque perturbatum domicilium
immigravit, sed, cum se collegit atque recreavit,
tum agnoscit illa reminiscendo : ita nihil est aliud
discere nisi recordari.

59 Ego autem maiore etiam quodam modo memoriam
admiror. Quid est enim illud, quo meminimus, aut
quam habet vim aut unde natam ? Non quaero
quanta memoria Simonides fuisse dicatur, quanta

---

[1] *est* is not written in the MSS.

---

[1] A metaphor taken by Zeno from the impressions made
by a seal-ring in wax.

[2] Called ἔννοιαι by the Stoics. Plato held that general
notions, ἰδέαι, were brought into this life from a previous
life by man at his birth ; the Stoics, that general notions,
κοιναὶ ἔννοιαι, were formed out of experience got from the
perceptions of external objects by the bodily senses.

[3] Cicero is summing up the teaching of the *Phaedo*.
Absolute justice, beauty, goodness, etc., are "ἰδέαι," and
knowledge of them cannot be obtained through the senses.
These "ideas" are unchanging, are always what they are
and do not admit of variation. We acquired knowledge of
them before we were born. Objects perceived by the senses
are always changing and hardly ever the same. The soul is
akin to the invisible and unchanging : the body to the visible

childhood such a number of important ideas, innate and as it were impressed[1] on our souls and called ἔννοιαι,[2] unless the soul, before it had entered the body, had been active in acquiring knowledge. And since there is no true existence in any sensible object, as Plato everywhere argues—for he thinks that nothing that has a beginning and an ending exists, and only that exists which is always constant to its nature; this he calls ἰδέα and we "idea"— the soul in the prison-house of the body could not have apprehended ideas; it brought the knowledge with it: consequently our feeling of wonder at the extent of our knowledge is removed. Yet the soul, when suddenly shifted into such an unaccustomed and disordered dwelling-place, does not clearly see ideas, but when it has composed and recovered itself it apprehends them by remembrance. Thus, according to Plato, learning is nothing but recollecting.[3]

But for my part I wonder at memory[4] in a still greater degree. For what is it that enables us to remember, or what character has it, or what is its origin? I am not inquiring into the powers of memory which, it is said, Simonides possessed, or

and changing. The body drags the soul into the region of the visible and changing, and the soul wanders and is confused. We make the nearest approach to knowledge when we have the least possible connection or fellowship with the body. If the soul had had no life apart from its association with the body, it could not have acquired knowledge of the true realities, the "ideas."

[4] Cicero here leaves the Platonic doctrine of the recollection by the soul of knowledge acquired before it entered the body, and considers the powers of memory by which we retain the knowledge of things we learn in this life, and which he seems to think more wonderful than Plato's ἀνάμνησις.

Theodectes, quanta is, qui a Pyrrho legatus ad
senatum est missus, Cineas, quanta nuper Charmadas,
quanta, qui modo fuit, Scepsius Metrodorus, quanta
noster Hortensius : de communi hominum memoria
loquor et eorum maxime, qui in aliquo maiore studio
et arte versantur, quorum quanta mens sit difficile
est existimare : ita multa meminerunt.

60   XXV. Quorsus igitur haec spectat oratio ? Quae
sit illa vis et unde sit, intelligendum puto. Non est
certe nec cordis nec sanguinis nec cerebri nec
atomorum : animae sit ignisne nescio, nec me pudet,
ut istos, fateri nescire quod nesciam : illud, si ulla
alia de re obscura adfirmare possem, sive anima sive
ignis sit animus, eum iurarem esse divinum. Quid
enim ? obsecro te, terrane tibi hoc nebuloso et
caliginoso caelo aut sata aut concreta videtur tanta
vis memoriae ? Si quid sit hoc non vides, at quale
sit vides : si ne id quidem, at quantum sit profecto

61 vides. Quid igitur ? utrum capacitatem aliquam in
animo putamus esse, quo tamquam in aliquod vas ea,
quae meminimus, infundantur ? Absurdum id quidem. Qui enim fundus aut quae talis animi figura
intelligi potest aut quae tanta omnino capacitas ?
An imprimi quasi ceram animum putamus et esse
memoriam signatarum rerum in mente vestigia ?

---

[1] All instances of men with great powers of memory, the
best known of them being Simonides the lyric poet, Cineas
the philosopher and Hortensius, Cicero's rival at the Roman
bar.

[2] St. Augustine speaks of the "caverns of memory,"
according to Beroaldus.

Theodectes, or the powers of Cineas, whom Pyrrhus sent as ambassador to the Senate, or the powers in recent days of Charmadas, or of Metrodorus of Scepsis, who was lately alive, or the powers of our own Hortensius.[1] I am speaking of the average memory of man, and chiefly of those who are engaged in some higher branch of study and art, whose mental capacity it is hard to estimate, so much do they remember.

XXV. What then is the object of what I am saying? I think it must be clear by now what the power so displayed is and whence it comes. Certainly it is not a quality of heart or blood or brain or atoms. Whether it is of breath or fire I know not, and I am not ashamed, as those others were, of admitting my ignorance where I am ignorant: this I do say, if I could make any other assertions on a subject of such difficulty, I should be ready to swear that, whether soul is breath or fire, it is divine. For consider, I pray, can you really think that it is from earth, where our atmosphere is so watery and foggy, that the prodigious power of memory has originated or been formed? If you do not see the right answer to the question, yet you see the problem it involves: if you do not see even that much, yet surely you see its importance. What then? Do we think that there is in the soul a sort of roominess into which the things we remember can be poured as if into a kind of vessel? That would be ridiculous; what can we understand as the bottom or shape of such a soul, or what room at all can it have that is adequate?[2] Or do we think that like wax the soul has marks impressed upon it and that memory consists of the traces of things registered

Quae possunt verborum, quae rerum ipsarum esse vestigia, quae porro tam immensa magnitudo quae illa tam multa possit effingere?

Quid? illa vis quae tandem est, quae investigat occulta, quae inventio atque cogitatio dicitur? Ex hacne tibi terrena mortalique natura et caduca 62 concreta ea videtur, aut qui primus, quod summae sapientiae Pythagorae visum est, omnibus rebus imposuit nomina, aut qui dissipatos homines congregavit et ad societatem vitae convocavit, aut qui sonos vocis, qui infiniti videbantur, paucis litterarum notis terminavit, aut qui errantium stellarum cursus, praegressiones, institiones notavit? Omnes magni, etiam superiores, qui fruges, qui vestitum, qui tecta, qui cultum vitae, qui praesidia contra feras invenerunt, a quibus mansuefacti et exculti a necessariis artificiis ad elegantiora defluximus. Nam et auribus oblectatio magna parta est inventa et temperata varietate et natura sonorum et astra suspeximus cum ea, quae sunt infixa certis locis, tum illa non re, sed vocabulo errantia: quorum conversiones omnesque motus qui vidit, is docuit similem animum suum eius esse, qui ea fabricatus esset in caelo.

---

[1] As for instance in the apparent movements of the planet Mars.

[2] In the *De Natura Deorum*, II. 2. 51, Cicero says that the five planets, Saturn, Jupiter, Mars, Venus and Mercury,

in the mind? What can be the traces of words, of actual objects, what further could be the enormous space adequate to the representation of such a mass of material?

Again, what, I ask, is the power which investigates hidden secrets, which is known as discovery and contrivance? Do you think it was formed out of this earthy, mortal and perishable substance? Or was the man so formed who first assigned a name to everything, an achievement which Pythagoras thought one of supreme wisdom; or the man who first united the scattered human units into a body and summoned them to the fellowship of social life; or the man who by a few written characters defined the meaning of the endless variety, as it seemed, of the sounds of the voice; or the man who marked down the paths of the wandering stars, their passings in front of one another, their stoppings?[1] All these were great men; earlier still the men who discovered the fruits of the earth, raiment, dwellings, an ordered way of life, protection against wild creatures—men under whose civilizing and refining guidance we have gradually passed on from the indispensable handicrafts to the finer arts. For through them our ears have gained keen delight from the discovery of the due combinations of musical sounds of diverse quality, and we have looked up at the stars, both those that are fixed in certain spots and those that by name are wandering,[2] though not really so, and he who has seen their revolutions and all their movements has taught that his soul resembles His whose word had fashioned them in the heavens. For when

are wrongly called "wandering stars," for nothing wanders which in all eternity preserves a constant and settled course.

63 Nam cum Archimedes lunae, solis, quinque errantium motus in sphaeram illigavit, effecit idem quod
ille qui in Timaeo mundum aedificavit Platonis deus,
ut tarditate et celeritate dissimillimos motus una
regeret conversio. Quod si in hoc mundo fieri sine
deo non potest, ne in sphaera quidem eosdem motus
Archimedes sine divino ingenio potuisset imitari.

64   XXVI. Mihi vero ne haec quidem notiora et illu-
striora carere vi divina videntur, ut ego aut poëtam
grave plenumque carmen sine caelesti aliquo mentis
instinctu putem fundere aut eloquentiam sine maiore
quadam vi fluere abundantem sonantibus verbis
uberibusque sententiis : philosophia vero, omnium
mater artium, quid est aliud nisi, ut Plato, donum,
ut ego, inventum deorum ? Haec nos primum ad
illorum cultum, deinde ad ius hominum, quod situm
est in generis humani societate, tum ad modestiam
magnitudinemque animi erudivit, eademque ab
animo tamquam ab oculis caliginem dispulit, ut
omnia supera infera, prima ultima media videremus.

65   Prorsus haec divina mihi videtur vis, quae tot res
efficiat et tantas. Quid est enim memoria rerum et
verborum ? quid porro inventio ? Profecto id, quo

---

¹ The globe of Archimedes was an orrery or clockwork
model by which the movements of the sun and moon and
five planets were reproduced when it was set in motion.
On the capture of Syracuse in the Second Punic War M.
Marcellus carried it away. It is described by Cicero in
De Republica I. 14.

² In the *Timaeus* 38, Plato says, "God made the sun and
moon and five other stars, which are called the planets, in
order to distinguish and preserve the numbers of time, and
when he had made them he assigned to them their orbits."

Archimedes fastened on a globe[1] the movements of moon, sun and five wandering stars, he, just like Plato's God who built the world in the *Timaeus*,[2] made one revolution of the sphere control several movements utterly unlike in slowness and speed. Now if in this world of ours phenomena cannot take place without the act of God, neither could Archimedes have reproduced the same movements upon a globe without divine genius.

XXVI. To my mind even better known and more famous fields of labour do not seem removed from divine influence, or suffer me to think that the poet pours out his solemn, swelling strain without some heavenly inspiration, or that eloquence flows in a copious stream of echoing words and fruitful thoughts without some higher influence: as to philosophy, the mother of all arts, what else is it except, as Plato held, the gift,[3] or, as I hold, the discovery of the gods? It instructed us first in the worship of gods, then in the justice of mankind at large which is rooted in the social union of the race of men, and next taught us the lessons of temperance and greatness of soul, and thus dispersed the darkness from the eyes as it were of the mind, so that we saw all things above, below, things first and last and in between.

A power able to bring about such a number of important results is to my mind wholly divine. For what is the memory of facts and words? What further is discovery?[4] Assuredly nothing can be

---

[3] Plato, *Timaeus* 47, τῷ θνητῷ γένει δωρηθὲν ἐκ θεῶν. How much more, says Cicero, if not simply given but created !
[4] "Inventio" is taken in a general sense in § 61. It was also a division of Dialectic and a technical rhetorical term.

ne in deo quidem quidquam maius intelligi potest.
Non enim ambrosia deos aut nectare aut Iuventate
pocula ministrante laetari arbitror, nec Homerum
audio, qui Ganymeden ab dis raptum ait propter
formam, ut Iovi bibere ministraret: non iusta causa
cur Laomedonti tanta fieret iniuria. Fingebat haec
Homerus et humana ad deos transferebat: divina
mallem ad nos. Quae autem divina? Vigere,
sapere, invenire, meminisse. Ergo animus, ut ego
dico, divinus est, ut Euripides dicere audet, deus:
et quidem, si deus aut anima aut ignis est, idem
est animus hominis; nam ut illa natura caelestis et
terra vacat et humore, sic utriusque harum rerum
humanus animus est expers. Sin autem est quinta
quaedam natura ab Aristotele inducta primum, haec
et deorum est et animorum.

66   Hanc nos sententiam secuti his ipsis verbis in
Consolatione hoc expressimus: XXVII. " Animorum
nulla in terris origo inveniri potest; nihil enim est
in animis mixtum atque concretum aut quod ex terra
natum atque fictum esse videatur, nihil ne aut
humidum quidem aut flabile aut igneum. His enim
in naturis nihil inest quod vim memoriae, mentis,
cogitationis habeat, quod et praeterita teneat et
futura provideat et complecti possit praesentia: quae
sola divina sunt nec invenietur umquam unde ad

---

[1] Homer *Il.* 20, 233, says that Tros had three sons, Ilus,
Assaracus, and Ganymede, and that Laomedon was the son
of Ilus. Cicero seems to regard Laomedon as Ganymede's
father. To appease the gods because he had broken his word,
Laomedon had to sacrifice a daughter. When he broke his
word to Heracles also, the latter killed all Laomedon's sons
except Priam.

[2] Euripides frag. 1007, ὁ νοῦς γὰρ ἡμῶν ἐστὶν ἐν ἑκάστῳ θεός.

[3] Cf. § 22.

comprehended even in God of greater value than this. I do not think the gods delight in ambrosia or nectar or Hebe filling the cups, and I do not listen to Homer who says that Ganymede was carried off by the gods for his beauty to serve as cup-bearer to Zeus: there was no just reason why such cruel wrong should be inflicted on Laomedon.[1] Homer imagined these things and attributed human feelings to the gods: I had rather he had attributed divine feelings to us. But what do we understand by divine attributes? Activity, wisdom, discovery, memory. Therefore the soul is, as I say, divine, as Euripides dares to say, God:[2] and in fact, if God is either air or fire, so also is the soul of man; for just as the heavenly nature is free from earth and moisture, so the human soul is without trace of either element. But if there is a kind of fifth nature, first introduced by Aristotle,[3] this is the nature of both gods and souls.

This view we have supported and given the sense of in these precise words in the *Consolatio* :[4] XXVII. "No beginning of souls can be discovered on earth; for there is no trace of blending or combination in souls or any particle that could seem born or fashioned from earth, nothing even that partakes either of moist or airy or fiery. For in these elements there is nothing to possess the power of memory, thought, reflection, nothing capable of retaining the past, or foreseeing the future and grasping the present, and these capacities are nothing but divine; and never will there be found any

---

[4] Cicero wrote his *Consolatio*, a work now lost, to console his grief at the death of his daughter Tullia in 45 B.C.

hominem venire possint nisi a deo. Singularis est
igitur quaedam natura atque vis animi, seiuncta ab
his usitatis notisque naturis. Ita quidquid est illud,
quod sentit, quod sapit, quod vivit, quod viget,
caeleste et divinum ob eamque rem aeternum sit
necesse est. Nec vero deus ipse, qui intelligitur a
nobis, alio modo intelligi potest nisi mens soluta
quaedam et libera, segregata ab omni concretione
mortali, omnia sentiens et movens ipsaque praedita
67 motu sempiterno." Hoc e genere atque eadem e
natura est humana mens.

Ubi igitur aut qualis est ista mens?—Ubi
tua aut qualis? potesne dicere? an, si omnia
ad intelligendum non habeo, quae habere vellem,
ne iis quidem, quae habeo, mihi per te uti
licebit?—Non valet tantum animus, ut se ipse[1]
videat: at ut oculus, sic animus se non videns alia
cernit. Non videt autem, quod minimum est,
formam suam—quamquam fortasse id quoque, sed
relinquamus—: vim certe, sagacitatem, memoriam,
motus[2] celeritatem videt. Haec magna, haec divina,
haec sempiterna sunt. Qua facie quidem sit aut ubi
habitet ne quaerendum quidem est.
68 XXVIII. Ut cum videmus speciem primum
candoremque caeli, dein conversionis celeritatem
tantam, quantam cogitare non possumus, tum vicis-
situdines dierum ac noctium commutationesque
temporum quadrupertitas ad maturitatem frugum et

---

[1] *se ipsum ipse* in MSS. : *se ipse*, Davies.
[2] *motum* in MSS. : *motus*, Bentley.

---

[1] Revolving round the earth, which was fixed, in twenty-
four hours.

source from which they can come to men except from God. There is then a peculiar essential character belonging to the soul, distinct from these common and well-known elements. Accordingly, whatever it is that is conscious, that is wise, that lives, that is active must be heavenly and divine and for that reason eternal. And indeed God Himself, who is comprehended by us, can be comprehended in no other way save as a mind unfettered and free, severed from all perishable matter, conscious of all and moving all and self-endowed with perpetual motion." Of such sort and of the same nature is the human mind.

Where then and what is such a mind?—Where and what is yours? Can you say? Or if I do not possess all the faculties for comprehension I could have wished, will you not give me leave to use even those which I have?—The soul has not the power of itself to see itself, but, like the eye, the soul, though it does not see itself, yet discerns other things. But it does not see, what is a matter of very little moment, its own shape,—and yet possibly it may do that too, but still no matter—assuredly it sees its power, wisdom, memory, rapidity of movement. These things are of real moment, these are divine, these are everlasting. About its outward aspect or place of habitation we need not even enquire.

XXVIII. Just as when we see first the beauty and the brightness of the sky, then the amazing speed,[1] which our thought cannot grasp, of its revolution, next the succession of day and night and the changes of the seasons divided into four to suit the ripening of the fruits of the earth and the constitu-

ad temperationem corporum aptas eorumque omnium
moderatorem et ducem solem, lunamque accre-
tione et deminutione luminis quasi fastorum notan-
tem et significantem dies, tum in eodem orbe
in duodecim partes distributo quinque stellas ferri,
eosdem cursus constantissime servantes, disparibus
inter se motibus, nocturnamque caeli formam undique sideribus ornatam, tum globum terrae eminentem
e mari, fixum in medio mundi universi loco, duabus
oris distantibus habitabilem et cultum, quarum
altera, quam nos incolimus,

> *Sub axe posita ad stellas septem, unde horrifer*
> *Aquilonis stridor gelidas molitur nives,*

altera australis, ignota nobis, quam vocant Graeci
69 ἀντίχθων, ceteras partes incultas, quod aut frigore
rigeant aut urantur calore : hic autem, ubi habitamus,
non intermittit suo tempore

> *Caelum nitescere, arbores frondescere,*
> *Vites laetificae pampinis pubescere,*
> *Rami bacarum ubertate incurvescere,*
> *Segetes largiri fruges, florere omnia,*
> *Fontes scatere, herbis prata convestirier,*

tum multitudinem pecudum partim ad vescendum,
partim ad cultus agrorum, partim ad vehendum,
partim ad corpora vestienda, hominemque ipsum

---

[1] This is the *signifer orbis* called by the Greeks ζωδιακός.

Sunt aries, taurus, gemini, cancer, leo, virgo,
Libraque, scorpius, arcitenens, caper, amphora, pisces.

[2] Aristotle, Plato and the Stoics held the earth to be
spherical. What Cicero means here is not clear. Sea and
land are included in the spherical outline and the geographer
Strabo, II. 5, says that in so large a mass the parts that rise
above the rest do not affect the general outline.

tion of living bodies, and the sun their ruler and guide, and the moon marking as it were and indicating the days in the calendar by the waxing and waning of her light; then the five planets carried along in the same vault with its twelve divisions,[1] unchangingly keeping the same courses, in spite of the mutual difference of their movements, and the aspect of the heavens at night decked everywhere with stars, then the ball of the earth rising from the sea,[2] set firmly in the centre of the universe, habitable and cultivated in two separate zones of which the one in which we dwell is:

> Beneath the pole set toward the seven stars [3] from whence
> The dreadful North wind whistling drives the frozen snow,

the other, the Southern, unknown to us, called by the Greeks ἀντίχθων [4]: all other parts are uncultivated, because we gather they are either frozen with cold or parched with heat: here, however, where we live, there cease not in due season:

> Skies to be shining and trees in leaf blossoming,
> Tendrils of joy-giving vines to be burgeoning,
> Foison of berries the boughs to be burdening,
> Fields to be rich with crops, flowers out everywhere,
> Fountains to bubble and grasses the meads cover:

then the vast number of domestic animals used in part for food, in part for tillage, in part for draught, in part for clothing, and man himself formed as

---

[3] The Bear, *i.e.* Septentriones, seven ploughing oxen.
[4] *i.e.* counter-earth, called ἀντίποδες in *Acad.* II. 39. 123—a southern land-mass, nothing to do with our "Antipodes."

quasi contemplatorem caeli ac terrarum[1] cultorem
atque hominis utilitati agros omnes et maria parentia
70 —: haec igitur et alia innumerabilia cum cernimus,
possumusne dubitare quin iis praesit aliquis vel
effector, si haec nata sunt, ut Platoni videtur, vel, si
semper fuerunt, ut Aristoteli placet, moderator tanti
operis et muneris? Sic mentem hominis, quamvis
eam non videas, ut deum non vides, tamen, ut deum
agnoscis ex operibus eius, sic ex memoria rerum et
inventione et celeritate motus omnique pulcritu-
dine virtutis vim divinam mentis agnoscito.

XXIX. In quo igitur loco est? Credo equidem
in capite, et cur credam adferre possum. Sed alias
ubi sit animus, certe quidem in te est. Quae est ei
natura? Propria puto et sua. Sed fac igneam, fac
spirabilem: nihil ad id, de quo agimus. Illud
modo video, ut deum noris, etsi eius ignores et
locum et faciem, sic animum tibi tuum notum esse
71 oportere, etiam si ignores et locum et formam. In
animi autem cognitione dubitare non possumus, nisi
plane in physicis plumbei sumus, quin nihil sit animis
admixtum, nihil concretum, nihil copulatum, nihil
coagmentatum, nihil duplex: quod cum ita sit, certe

---

[1] *terrarum* is Bentley's emendation of the *deorum* of the
MSS., which is not appropriate when Cicero is giving proofs
of the existence of God. Still in *Nat. Deorum* II. § 140 he
says that man standing erect contemplates the sky and
learns to know the gods, and he may, arguing loosely, say
the same here, cf. Ovid, *Met.* 1.85:

Os homini sublime dedit ; caelumque tueri
Iussit et erectos ad sidera tollere vultus.

---

[1] Plato, *Phaedo* 78 C, says that the compound or composite
may be supposed to be naturally capable, as of being compounded, so also of being dissolved ; but that which is un-

it were to observe the heavens and cultivate the soil, and lastly all fields and seas made subject to the service of man—when then we behold all these things and countless others, can we doubt that some being is over them, or some author, if these things have had beginning, as Plato holds, or, if they have always existed, as Aristotle thinks, some governor of so stupendous a work of construction? So with the mind of man, though thou seest it not, as thou seest not God, nevertheless as thou recognizest God from His works, so from memory, power of discovery, rapidity of movement and all the beauty of virtue, thou shalt recognize the divine power of mind.

XXIX. Where then is its place? I for my part believe, in the head, and I can furnish reasons for my belief. But the place of the soul I shall explain another time. Beyond doubt it is in you. What is its substance? Special to it I think and individual. But suppose it fiery, suppose it airy: that has nothing to do with our purpose. Note now that just as you may know God, though you are ignorant both of His place of dwelling and aspect, so your soul should be known to you, even if you are ignorant of its place and shape. In studying the soul moreover we cannot doubt, unless we are regular blockheads in natural philosophy, that in souls there is no mingling of ingredients, no compounding or combining or cementing, nothing of two-fold nature;[1] and, this being so, it is assuredly

compounded (*i.e.* the soul), and that only, must be, if anything is, indissoluble, and the uncompounded may be assumed to be the same and unchanging, whereas the compound is always changing and never the same. With this, however, compare §§ 20, 80. Clearly the soul could be contaminated, § 72.

nec secerni nec dividi nec discerpi nec distrahi
potest, ne interire quidem igitur; est enim interitus
quasi discessus et secretio ac diremptus earum par-
tium, quae ante interitum coniunctione[1] aliqua
tenebantur. His et talibus rationibus adductus
Socrates nec patronum quaesivit ad iudicium capitis
nec iudicibus supplex fuit adhibuitque liberam con-
tumaciam a magnitudine animi ductam, non a super-
bia, et supremo vitae die de hoc ipso multa disseruit
et paucis ante diebus, cum facile posset educi e
custodia, noluit et tum paene in manu iam morti-
ferum illud tenens poculum locutus ita est, ut
non ad mortem trudi, verum in caelum videretur
escendere.

72   XXX. Ita enim censebat itaque disseruit, duas
esse vias duplicesque cursus animorum e corpore
excedentium: nam qui se humanis vitiis contamina-
vissent et se totos libidinibus dedissent, quibus
caecati vel domesticis vitiis atque flagitiis se inquina-
vissent vel re publica violanda fraudes inexpiabiles
concepissent, iis devium quoddam iter esse, seclusum
a concilio deorum; qui autem se integros castosque
servavissent quibusque fuisset minima cum corporibus
contagio seseque ab iis semper sevocavissent essent-
que in corporibus humanis vitam imitati deorum, iis
ad illos, a quibus essent profecti, reditum facilem
73   patere.   Itaque commemorat, ut cygni, qui non sine
causa Apollini dicati sint sed quod ab eo divinationem

---

[1] Madvig's alteration of *iunctione*.

---

[1] Socrates was tried and condemned in 399 B.C. In the
Phaedo Plato describes him as spending his last hours, before
drinking the hemlock, in discussing the immortality of the
soul.

impossible for the soul to be severed or divided, or
plucked asunder, or torn apart; impossible, therefore,
for it to perish either; for perishing is like the
separation and severance and divorcing of the parts
which before destruction were maintained in some
sort of union. Influenced by these and similar
reasons Socrates sought out no advocate, when on
trial for his life,[1] and was not humble to his judges,
but showed a noble obstinacy derived from greatness
of soul, not from pride, and on the last day of his
life he discussed at length this very subject; and a
few days before, though he could easily have been
removed from prison, he refused, and then, with the
fatal cup almost actually in his hands, he spoke in
language which made him seem not as one thrust
out to die, but as one ascending to the heavens.

XXX. The tenor of his thought and the arguments
he used were that there are two paths, a twofold
course for souls on departure from the body: for
those, he said, who had polluted themselves with the
sins that men commit, and delivered themselves over
wholly to their lusts, and under their blinding influence had either defiled themselves by private sins
and iniquities or had by public outrages been guilty
of offences that could not be atoned, had before them
a road apart, remote from the company of the gods;
they, on the other hand, who had kept themselves
pure and chaste, who had suffered least contact with
the body and always separated themselves from it
and in the bodies of men had followed the life of
the gods, had an easy way of return before them to
those from whom they had set out. And so he
relates that just as the swans—who have been conse-
crated to Apollo, not undesignedly, but because from

85

habere videantur, qua providentes quid in morte
boni sit cum cantu et voluptate moriantur, sic omnibus bonis et doctis esse faciendum. Nec vero de hoc
quisquam dubitare posset, nisi idem nobis accideret
diligenter de animo cogitantibus, quod iis saepe usu
venit, qui cum[1] acriter oculis deficientem solem
intuerentur, ut aspectum omnino amitterent, sic
mentis acies se ipsa intuens non numquam hebescit,
ob eamque causam contemplandi diligentiam amit-
timus. Itaque dubitans, circumspectans, haesitans,
multa adversa reverens tamquam in rate in mari
immenso nostra vehitur oratio.[2]

74 Sed haec et vetera et a Graecis. Cato autem sic
abiit e vita, ut causam moriendi nactum se esse
gauderet: vetat enim dominans ille in nobis deus
iniussu hinc nos suo demigrare: cum vero causam
iustam deus ipse dederit, ut tunc Socrati, nunc
Catoni, saepe multis, ne ille, medius fidius, vir
sapiens laetus ex his tenebris in lucem illam ex-
cesserit, nec tamen illa vincla carceris ruperit—leges
enim vetant—, sed tamquam a magistratu aut ab
aliqua potestate legitima, sic a deo evocatus atque
emissus exierit. *Tota* enim *philosophorum vita*, ut ait
idem, *commentatio mortis est.*

[1] Some editors bracket *cum* to get rid of the difficulty of
the *cum*-clause followed by an *ut*-clause. Another suggestion is to alter *ut* to *vel*.
[2] Many editors alter *oratio* to *ratio*, but in IV. § 33 we have
enavigavit oratio. The word λόγος, in the passage of Plato
which Cicero had in mind, can mean *ratio* or *oratio* and therefore is not decisive. *Oratio* implies *ratio* as in § 112.

[1] This Cicero takes from Plato's *Phaedo* 84 E.
[2] Cf. Plato's *Phaedo* 85 D. δεῖ . . . τὸν γοῦν βέλτιστον τῶν
ἀνθρωπίνων λόγων λαβόντα . . . ἐπὶ τούτου ὀχούμενον, ὥσπερ
ἐπὶ σχεδίας κινδυνεύοντα διαπλεῦσαι τὸν βίον. In Plato the
λόγος is the raft upon which man is embarked.

Apollo they seem to have the gift of prophecy, and thus have a foretaste of the blessing death brings— die with a song of rapture,[1] so must all good and learned men do likewise. And in fact no one could entertain a doubt of this, unless in thinking attentively about the soul we suffer the same experience as often comes from gazing intently at the setting sun, that is of losing entirely the sense of sight; in the same way the mind's vision, in gazing upon itself sometimes waxes dim, and for that reason we relax the steadiness of contemplation. And so doubting, watching, wavering, fearing many an adverse chance, our argument is driven as if on a skiff in a boundless sea.[2]

This, however, is ancient history and Greek history too: but Cato[3] departed from life with a feeling of joy in having found a reason for death; for the God who is master within us forbids our departure without his permission; but when God Himself has given a valid reason as He did in the past to Socrates, and in our day to Cato, and often to many others, then of a surety your true wise man will joyfully pass forthwith from the darkness here into the light beyond. All the same he will not break the bonds of his prison-house—the laws forbid it—but as if in obedience to a magistrate or some lawful authority, he will pass out at the summons and release of God.[4] For the whole life of the philosopher, as the same wise man says, is a preparation for death.[5]

[3] M. Porcius Cato, who killed himself after the Battle of Thapsus, 46 B.C., rather than submit to punishment or pardon from the victorious Caesar.

[4] He will not quit his prison until the power that put him there gives him leave to depart.

[5] Plato, *Phaedo* 67 D. τὸ μελέτημα αὐτὸ τοῦτό ἐστι τῶν φιλοσόφων, λύσις καὶ χωρισμὸς ψυχῆς ἀπὸ σώματος.

75 XXXI. Nam quid aliud agimus, cum a voluptate,
id est, a corpore, cum a re familiari, quae est ministra
et famula corporis, cum a republica, cum a negotio
omni sevocamus animum : quid, inquam, tum agimus
nisi animum ad se ipsum advocamus, secum esse
cogimus maximeque a corpore abducimus? Secernere
autem a corpore animum ecquid aliud est quam mori
discere? Qua re hoc commentemur, mihi crede,
disiungamusque nos a corporibus, id est, consuescamus
mori. Hoc, et dum erimus in terris, erit illi caelesti
vitae simile, et cum illuc ex his vinclis emissi fere-
mur, minus tardabitur cursus animorum. Nam qui
in compedibus corporis semper fuerunt, etiam cum
soluti sunt, tardius ingrediuntur, ut ii, qui ferro
vincti multos annos fuerunt. Quo cum venerimus,
tum denique vivemus ; nam haec quidem vita mors
76 est, quam lamentari possem, si liberet. A. Satis tu
quidem in Consolatione es lamentatus, quam cum
lego, nihil malo quam has res relinquere : his vero
modo auditis, multo magis. M. Veniet tempus et
quidem celeriter, sive retractabis sive properabis :
volat enim aetas. Tantum autem abest ab eo, ut
malum mors sit, quod tibi dudum videbatur, ut
verear ne homini nihil sit non malum aliud, certe
sit [1] nihil bonum aliud potius, si quidem vel di
ipsi vel cum dis futuri sumus. A. Quid refert?

---

[1] *certe sed* in MSS. : *sit* Wesenberg.

---

[1] Cf. § 65.   [2] Cf. § 23.

XXXI. For what else do we do when we sequester the soul from pleasure, for that means from the body; from private property, the handmaid and servant of the body; from public interests; from any kind of business: what, I say, do we then do except summon the soul to its own presence, force it to companionship with itself and withdraw it completely from the body? But is severance of the soul from the body anything else than learning how to die? Let us, therefore, believe me, make this preparation and dissociation of ourselves from our bodies, that is, let us habituate ourselves to die. This will, both for the time of our sojourn on earth, resemble heavenly life, and when we shall be released from our chains here, the progress of our soul will be less retarded. For they who have always been caught in the shackles of the body, even when they are set free, advance more slowly, like men who have been many years bound with chains. And when we have come yonder, then and not before shall we live; for this life is indeed death, and I could sorrow over it if so I would. A. You have sorrowed over life sufficiently in your *Consolatio*,[1] and when I read it I wish for nothing better than to quit this world, and on hearing what you have just said I wish it much more. M. The hour will come and that quickly, whether you shrink back or are in a hurry, for life-time is fleeting. So wide of the truth, however, is the view that death is an evil, as you thought not long ago, that I incline to think that for a human being there is nothing else that is not an evil;[2] assuredly there is no other good that is to be preferred to it, if indeed we are to be either ourselves gods, or be in company with the gods. A. What does it

89

M. Adsunt enim, qui haec non probent; ego autem
numquam ita te in hoc sermone dimittam, ulla uti
77 ratione mors tibi videri malum possit. A. Qui
potest, cum ista cognoverim? M. Qui possit rogas?
Catervae veniunt contra dicentium, nec solum Epi-
cureorum, quos equidem non despicio, sed nescio
quo modo doctissimus quisque contemnit, acerrime
autem deliciae meae Dicaearchus contra hanc immortalitatem disseruit. Is enim tris libros scripsit,
qui *Lesbiaci* vocantur, quod Mytilenis sermo habetur,
in quibus vult efficere animos esse mortales. Stoici
autem usuram nobis largiuntur tamquam cornicibus:
diu mansuros aiunt animos, semper negant.

XXXII. Num non vis igitur audire cur, etiam si
ita sit, mors tamen non sit in malis? A. Ut vide-
78 tur, sed me nemo de immortalitate depellet. M.
Laudo id quidem, etsi nihil nimis oportet confidere;
movemur enim saepe aliquo acute concluso, labamus
mutamusque sententiam clarioribus etiam in rebus;
in his est enim aliqua obscuritas. Id igitur si
acciderit, simus armati. A. Sane quidem, sed ne
accidat providebo. M. Num quid igitur est causae
quin amicos nostros Stoicos dimittamus? eos dico,
qui aiunt manere animos, cum e corpore excesserint,
sed non semper. A. Istos vero, qui, quod tota in

---

[1] What difference is there between "not an evil" and "a
good"?

[2] Cf. I. § 22.

[3] Cf. Hor. *Odes* III. 17. 13, *annosa cornix.*

matter?[1]   M. O it does, for there are those here
who are not satisfied with our conclusions; however,
in this discussion of ours I shall never let you go
with the possibility of your thinking on any ground
that death is an evil.   A.   How can it be, seeing I
have recognized the truth of what you say?   M. How
can it, do you ask?   Crowds of opponents are coming,
not merely Epicureans—whom for my part I do not
despise, though somehow or other to my regret all
the best philosophers are contemptuous of them—
but my favourite Dicaearchus[2] has argued most
incisively against the immortality of the soul.   For
he has written three books, with the title of *Lesbian*,
because the discussion, in which he aims at proving
the mortality of souls, took place at Mytilene.   The
Stoics, on the other hand, grant us, as though to
make us crows,[3] a generous lease of life: they say
chat souls will survive a long time, not for ever.

XXXII. You do not disdain, do you, to hear why,
even if this view be true, death is still not reckoned
among evils?   A. As you like, but no one will drive
me to give up immortality.   M. That I approve, and
yet we ought not to be over-confident in anything:
for we are often influenced by some cleverly drawn
conclusion, we waver and change our opinion even
in questions that are comparatively clear: much
more in this question, for it has an element of
obscurity.   Let us therefore be armed in case we
find ourselves in such a plight.   A. Quite so, but I
shall take care we do not.   M. Is there any reason
then to stop us from sending our friends the Stoics
about their business?   I mean those who say that
souls survive on their departure from the body, but
not for ever?   A. O send *them* surely, seeing that

hac causa difficillimum est, suscipiant, posse animum
manere corpore vacantem, illud autem, quod non
modo facile ad credendum est, sed eo concesso, quod
volunt, consequens, id circumcidant,[1] ut, cum diu
permanserit, ne intereat.   M. Bene reprehendis, et
79 se isto modo res habet.   Credamus igitur Panaetio a
Platone suo dissentienti ?   Quem enim omnibus locis
divinum, quem sapientissimum, quem sanctissimum,
quem Homerum philosophorum appellat, huius hanc
unam sententiam de immortalitate animorum non
probat.   Vult enim, quod nemo negat, quidquid
natum sit interire, nasci autem animos, quod declaret
eorum similitudo, qui procreentur, quae etiam in
ingeniis, non solum in corporibus appareat.   Alteram
autem adfert rationem, nihil esse quod doleat quin
id aegrum esse quoque possit: quod autem in morbum cadat, id etiam interiturum: dolere autem
animos, ergo etiam interire.

80   XXXIII. Haec refelli possunt.   Sunt enim ignor-
antis, cum de aeternitate animorum dicatur, de mente
dici, quae omni turbido motu semper vacet, non de
partibus iis, in quibus aegritudines, irae libidinesque
versentur, quas is, contra quem haec dicuntur, se-
motas a mente et disclusas putat.   Iam similitudo

----

[1] Most MSS. have *idcirco :* other suggestions are *id non
concedant* and *id vero non dant : circumcidant,* Madvig.

----

[1] Cf. § 42.
[2] Cf. § 20. Plato, *Rep.* iv. 439, distinguishes in the soul
the rational (λογιστικόν) and the irrational (ἄλογον), which
last he subdivides into the appetitive (ἐπιθυμητικόν) and the
passionate (θυμικόν). The Stoics rejected the assumption of
irrational faculties. They held that the soul was a unity :
man feels and wills and knows with the whole soul. Cicero
sides with Plato; but cf. § 56, where he agrees with Plato's

they maintain that the soul can survive without
a body, the point of greatest difficulty in the whole
problem, but chop away what is not only easy of
belief, but, if their view is granted, a logical consequence, namely that the soul does not perish when
it has survived a long time.   M. Your criticism is
just, and that is how the case stands.   Are we then
to believe Panaetius[1] when he disagrees with his
revered Plato? for whilst he calls him at every
mention of his name inspired, the wisest, the most
saintly of men, the Homer of philosophers, he yet
fails to approve of this one opinion of his about the
immortality of souls.   For he holds what nobody
denies, that whatever has been born perishes; but
he asserts that souls are born, as is shown by the
resemblance of children to their parents, which is
manifest in dispositions and not only in bodily
features.   He alleges next as his second proof that
there is nothing sensible of pain without being also
susceptible of sickness; all, however, that is subject
to disease, will also perish; now souls are sensible of
pain, therefore they also perish.

XXXIII. These arguments can be refuted.   For
they show his ignorance of the fact that, when a
statement is made about the eternity of souls, it
is made about the mind which is always free from
disorderly impulse, and not about those parts of us
which are subject to the attacks of distress, anger
and lust, and these Plato, against whom his arguments are directed, regards as remote and isolated
from the mind.[2]   Then as to resemblance, this is

view in the *Phaedo* 78, that the soul is *simplex*, uncompounded,
ἀξύνθετος. Here he introduces another term, *mens*, without
defining its relation to soul (*animus*).

magis apparet in bestiis, quarum animi sunt rationis
expertes; hominum autem similitudo in corporum
figura magis exstat et ipsi animi magni refert quali
in corpore locati sint; multa enim e corpore exsistunt
quae acuant mentem, multa quae obtundant. Aristoteles quidem ait omnes ingeniosos melancholicos
esse, ut ego me tardiorem esse non moleste feram.
Enumerat multos, idque quasi constet, rationem cur
ita fiat adfert. Quod si tanta vis est ad habitum
mentis in iis, quae gignuntur in corpore—ea sunt autem, quaecumque sunt, quae similitudinem faciunt—,
nihil necessitatis adfert, cur nascantur animi, simili-
81 tudo. Omitto dissimilitudines.[1] Vellem adesse
posset Panaetius—vixit cum Africano— : quaererem
ex eo, cuius suorum similis fuisset Africani fratris
nepos, facie vel patris, vita omnium perditorum ita
similis, ut esset facile deterrimus; cuius etiam similis P. Crassi, et sapientis et eloquentis et primi
hominis, nepos multorumque aliorum clarorum virorum, quos nihil attinet nominare, nepotes et filii.
Sed quid agimus? oblitine sumus hoc nunc nobis
esse propositum, cum satis de aeternitate dixissemus,
ne si interirent quidem animi, quidquam mali esse
in morte? A. Ego vero memineram, sed te de

---

[1] Bentley's correction of *similitudines*.

---

[1] Arist. *Probl.* XXX. 1. περιττοί εἰσι πάντες οἱ μελαγχο-
λικοί, all atrabilious men are remarkable.

[2] Quintus Fabius Maximus Allobrogicus, a man of pro-
fligate character, was son of Q. Fabius Maximus Aemilianus
Allobrogicus, Consul 121 B.C., and grandson of Q. Fabius
Maximus Aemilianus, the brother of Scipio Africanus Minor.

more obvious in animals whose souls have no trace
of reason; besides in man resemblance is found
more in the conformation of the body, and it makes
a great difference what sort of body it is in which
souls are actually placed; for there are many
conditions of the body tending to sharpen the mind
and many to deaden it. Indeed Aristotle says that
men of talent are atrabilious and so makes me less
distressed at being rather slow-witted.[1] He gives a
long list of instances and, as if the point were
settled, adds a reason for the phenomenon. Now if
natural conditions begotten in the body exert such
an influence upon the disposition of the mind—
whatever they are, it is such conditions that cause
the resemblance—resemblance implies no necessary
reason for the birth of souls. I pass over cases
where there are no features of resemblance. I
could have wished that Panaetius could have been
here—he lived in intimacy with Africanus—: I
should have asked him which member of the family
Africanus' great-nephew[2] had resembled, who was
the image of his father in face, but in manner of
life resembled all debauchees, with this distinction,
that he was easily the most degraded; I should
have asked too whom the grandson of P. Crassus,
a wise, eloquent and leading man, resembled, and
the grandsons and sons of many other celebrities
whom there is no object in naming. But what are
we about? have we forgotten that at present the
subject of consideration, after we had spoken sufficiently about eternity, was that not even if souls
perished was there any evil in death?[3] A. I had not
forgotten, but I readily submitted to your wandering

[3] §§ 23, 77.

aeternitate dicentem aberrare a proposito facile patiebar.

82 XXXIV. M. Video te alte spectare et velle in caelum migrare. Spero fore ut contingat id nobis. Sed fac, ut isti volunt, animos non remanere post mortem: video nos, si ita sit, privari spe beatioris vitae. Mali vero quid adfert ista sententia? Fac enim sic animum interire, ut corpus: num igitur aliquis dolor aut omnino post mortem sensus in corpore est? Nemo id quidem dicit, etsi Democritum insimulat Epicurus, Democritii negant. Ne in animo quidem igitur sensus remanet: ipse enim nusquam est. Ubi igitur malum est, quoniam nihil tertium est? an quod[1] ipse animi discessus a corpore non fit sine dolore? Ut credam ita esse, quam est id exiguum! Sed falsum esse arbitror et fit plerumque sine sensu, non numquam etiam cum voluptate, totumque hoc leve est, qualecumque est: fit enim 83 ad punctum temporis. Illud angit vel potius excruciat, discessus ab omnibus iis, quae sunt bona in vita Vide ne a malis dici verius possit. Quid ego nunc lugeam vitam hominum? Vere et iure possum. Sed quid necesse est, cum id agam, ne post mortem miseros nos putemus fore, etiam vitam efficere deplorando miseriorem? Fecimus hoc in eo libro, in quo nosmet ipsos quantum potuimus consolati sumus. A malis igitur mors abducit, non a bonis, verum si

---

[1] *quoniam* in the MSS.

[1] His *Consolatio*, § 65.

from the subject when you were speaking about eternity.

XXXIV. M. I see that you have lofty aims and that you wish to be a pilgrim heavenward. I hope that this will be our lot. But suppose, as these thinkers hold, that souls do not survive after death: I see that in that case we are deprived of the hope of a happier life. But what evil does such a view imply? For suppose that the soul perishes like the body: is there then any definite sense of pain or sensation at all in the body after death? There is no one who says so, though Epicurus accuses Democritus of this, but the followers of Democritus deny it. And so there is no sensation in the soul either, for the soul is nowhere. Where, then, is the evil, since there is no third thing? Is it because the actual departure of soul from body does not take place without sense of pain? Though I should believe this to be so, how petty a matter it is! But I think it false, and the fact is that often the departure takes place without sensation, sometimes even with a feeling of pleasure; and the whole thing is trivial, whatever the truth, for departure takes place in a moment of time. What does cause anguish, or rather torture, is the departure from all those things that are good in life. Take care it may not more truly be said, from all its evils! Why should I *now* bewail the life of man? I could do so with truth and justice. But what need is there, when my object is to avoid the thought that we shall be wretched after death, of rendering life still more wretched by lamentation? We have done this in the book in which we did our utmost to console ourselves.[1] Death then withdraws us from evil, not

quaerimus. Et quidem hoc a Cyrenaico Hegesia sic
copiose disputatur, ut is a rege Ptolemaeo prohibitus
esse dicatur illa in scholis dicere, quod multi iis
84 auditis mortem sibi ipsi consciscerent. Callimachi
quidem epigramma in Ambraciotam Cleombrotum
est, quem ait, cum ei nihil accidisset adversi, e muro
se in mare abiecisse lecto Platonis libro. Eius
autem, quem dixi, Hegesiae liber est, Ἀποκαρτερῶν,
in quo a vita quidam per inediam discedens revocatur
ab amicis, quibus respondens vitae humanae enumerat incommoda. Possem idem facere, etsi minus
quam ille, qui omnino vivere expedire nemini putat.
Mitto alios : etiamne nobis expedit ? qui et domesticis et forensibus solaciis ornamentisque privati certe,
si ante occidissemus, mors nos a malis, non a bonis
abstraxisset.
85 XXXV. Sit igitur aliquis qui nihil mali habeat,
nullum a fortuna vulnus acceperit : Metellus ille
honoratis quattuor filiis, at quinquaginta Priamus, e
quibus septemdecim iusta uxore natis : in utroque
eandem habuit fortuna potestatem, sed usa in altero
est ; Metellum enim multi filii filiae, nepotes neptes
in rogum imposuerunt, Priamum tanta progenie
orbatum cum in aram confugisset, hostilis manus

---

[1] Ptolemy Philadelphus of Egypt, reigned 283–246 B.C.

[2] Callimachus, grammarian, poet, and librarian at Alexandria in the reign of Philadelphus.

[3] *i.e.* killing himself by abstinence from food.

[4] *Domesticus* refers to the death of his daughter Tullia,
forensibus to his inactivity under the absolute rule of
Caesar.

[5] Caecilius Metellus Macedonicus, d. 115 B.C.   He had
been consul, censor, augur, and had had the honour of a
Triumph.

from good, if truth is our object. Indeed this thought is discussed by Hegesias the Cyrenaic with such wealth of illustration that the story goes that he was stopped from lecturing on the subject by King Ptolemy,[1] because a number of his listeners afterwards committed suicide. There is an epigram of Callimachus [2] upon Cleombrotus of Ambracia who, he says, without having met with any misfortune, flung himself from the city wall into the sea after reading Plato's book. Now in the book of Hegesias whom I have mentioned, Ἀποκαρτερῶν,[3] there appears a man who was passing away from life by starvation and is called back by his friends, and in answer to their remonstrances, details the discomforts of human life. I could do the same, but I should not go so far as he does in thinking it no advantage at all for anyone to live. Other cases I wave aside : is it an advantage still to me ? I have been robbed of the consolations of family life [4] and the distinctions of a public career, and assuredly, if we had died before this happened, death would have snatched us from evil, not from good.

XXXV. Grant then the existence of someone distinguished by suffering no evil, receiving no blow from the hand of fortune. The famous Metellus [5] had four sons who became dignitaries of state, but Priam had fifty, and seventeen of them born in lawful wedlock : in both these instances fortune had the same power of control, but exercised it in one ; for a company of sons, daughters, grandsons and granddaughters placed Metellus upon the funeral pyre, Priam was bereft of his numerous family and slain by the hand of his enemy after he had fled

interemit. Hic si vivis filiis incolumi **regno occidis-**
set,

> . . . *astante ope barbarica*
> *Tectis caelatis, laqueatis,*

utrum tandem a bonis an a malis discessisset? Tum
profecto videretur a bonis. At certe ei melius even-
isset nec tam flebiliter illa canerentur:

> *Haec omnia vidi inflammari,*
> *Priamo vi vitam evitari,*
> *Iovis aram sanguine turpari.*

Quasi vero ista vi quidquam tum potuerit ei melius accidere. Quod si ante occidisset, talem eventum omnino
amisisset, hoc autem tempore sensum amisit malorum.
86 Pompeio, nostro familiari, cum graviter aegrotaret
Neapoli, melius est factum. Coronati Neapolitani
fuerunt, nimirum etiam Puteolani, vulgo ex oppidis
publice gratulabantur. Ineptum sane negotium et
Graeculum, sed tamen fortunatum. Utrum igitur,
si tum esset exstinctus, a bonis rebus an a malis
discessisset? Certe a miseris. Non enim cum
socero bellum gessisset, non imparatus arma sump-
sisset, non domum reliquisset, non ex Italia fugisset,
non exercitu amisso nudus in servorum ferrum et

---

¹ Priam, King of Troy, at the end of ten years' siege by
the Achaeans, was killed by Neoptolemus, the son of
Achilles, at the altar of Zeus, in the sack of the city.

² Cf. App. II.

³ Julius Caesar, whose daughter, Julia, Pompey married in
59 B.C. She died five years later in 54 B.C., and her death
made the estrangement of Pompey and Caesar easier.

for refuge to the altar.[1] Had he died with his
sons alive, his throne secure :

> His barbarous opulence at hand
> And fretted ceilings richly carved,[2]

would he have departed from good or from evil?
At that date assuredly he would have seemed to
depart from good. Certainly it would have been a
better fate, and strains so melancholy would not
have been sung :

> By the flames I saw all things devoured,
> Priam's life by violence shortened,
> Jove's altar by bloodshed polluted.[2]

As if in such a scene of violence anything better
could have happened for him in that hour ! But if
he had died previously he would have wholly escaped so sad an ending : but by dying at the
moment he did he escaped the sense of the evils
about him. Our dear friend, Pompey, on the occasion of his serious illness at Naples, got better.
The Neapolitans set garlands on their heads; so, be
sure, did the inhabitants of Puteoli; public con-
gratulations kept pouring in from the towns : silly
behaviour no doubt and in Greekish taste, but all
the same it may count as a proof of good fortune.
Had his life come to an end then, would he have
left a scene of good or a scene of evil? Certainly
he would have escaped wretchedness. He would
not have gone to war with his father-in-law,[3] he
would not have taken up arms when unprepared, he
would not have left home, he would not have fled
from Italy, would not have lost his army and fallen
unprotected into the hands of armed slaves ; his poor

manus incidisset, non liberi defleti, non fortunae
omnes a victoribus possiderentur.[1] Qui si mortem
tum obisset, in amplissimis fortunis occidisset, is
propagatione vitae quot, quantas, quam incredibiles
hausit calamitates! XXXVI. Haec morte effugiun-
tur, etiam si non evenerunt, tamen, quia possunt
evenire; sed homines ea sibi accidere posse non
cogitant: Metelli sperat sibi quisque fortunam,
proinde quasi aut plures fortunati sint quam infelices
aut certi quidquam sit in rebus humanis aut sperare
sit prudentius quam timere.

87   Sed hoc ipsum concedatur, bonis rebus homines
morte privari: ergo etiam carere mortuos vitae
commodis idque esse miserum? Certe ita dicant
necesse est.[2] An potest is, qui non est, re ulla
carere? Triste enim est nomen ipsum carendi,
quia subiicitur haec vis: habuit, non habet, desiderat,
requirit, indiget. Haec, opinor, incommoda sunt
carentis: caret oculis, odiosa caecitas: liberis, orbitas.
Valet hoc in vivis, mortuorum autem non modo vitae
commodis, sed ne vita quidem ipsa quisquam caret.
De mortuis loquor, qui nulli sunt: nos, qui sumus,
num aut cornibus caremus aut pinnis? ecquis id
dixerit? Certe nemo. Quid ita? Quia, cum id
non habeas, quod tibi nec usu nec natura sit aptum,

---

[1] *incidisset* seems to be the natural end of the sentence
and the thought. From *non liberi* to *possiderentur* may be a
gloss. To alter *defleti* to *deleti* does not help, as Pompey's
sons survived him and fought against Caesar, and one of
them, Sextus, lived till 35 B.C.

[2] There is no subject for *dicant*, and the sentence is
suspected of being a gloss.

children, his wealth, would not have passed into the
power of his conquerors. Had he died at Naples, he
would have fallen at the zenith of his prosperity,
whilst by the prolongation of life what repeated,
bitter draughts of inconceivable disaster he came to
drain! XXXVI. Such things are evaded by death,
because although they have not taken place, yet
they may take place; but men do not think it possible
they can happen to themselves: each one hopes for
himself the good fortune of Metellus, just as if more
men were lucky than unlucky, or there were certainty in men's affairs or hope were wiser than
apprehension.

But let us go so far as to make the admission that
mankind are deprived of blessings by death: must
we therefore also grant that the dead feel the need
of the comforts of life, and that this is a condition of
wretchedness? Assuredly that is what they must
say. Is it possible for the man who does not exist to
" feel the need " of anything? The mere term
" feeling the need of " has a melancholy sound,
because the meaning that underlies it is, he had, he
has not; he misses, looks for, wants. These, I think,
are the discomforts of one who " feels the need of ";
he " feels the need of " eyes, blindness is hateful; of
children, barrenness is hateful. This holds good among
the living, but as regards the dead, no one " feels the
need," I do not say of the comforts of life, but even
of life itself. I say this of the dead who do not exist;
but do we who exist " feel the need " in this sense of
horns or feathers? Can anyone make such a statement? Undoubtedly none. Why so? Because, as
you are without that for which you are suited neither
by acquired skill nor by nature, you cannot " feel the

88 non careas, etiam si sentias te non habere. Hoc
premendum etiam atque etiam est argumentum
confirmato illo, de quo, si mortales animi sunt,
dubitare non possumus, quin tantus interitus in
morte sit, ut ne minima quidem suspicio sensus
relinquatur : hoc igitur probe stabilito et fixo illud
excutiendum est, ut sciatur quid sit carere, ne
relinquatur aliquid erroris in verbo. Carere igitur
hoc significat, egere eo, quod habere velis; inest
enim velle in carendo, nisi cum sic tamquam in febri
dicitur alia quadam notione verbi. Dicitur enim alio
modo etiam carere, cum aliquid non habeas et non
habere te sentias, etiam si id facile patiare. Carere
in malo [1] non dicitur : nec enim esset dolendum :
dicitur illud, bono carere, quod est malum. Sed ne
vivus quidem bono caret, si eo non indiget. Sed in
vivo intelligi tamen potest regno te carere—dici
autem hoc in te satis subtiliter non potest, posset in
Tarquinio, cum regno esset expulsus—at in mortuo

---

[1] The readings of the MSS. are *carere morte, carere in morte,
carere in malo*. The last reading has least support but gives
the best sense.

---

[1] Cicero says that there is a sense of wish in the word
carere, "to feel the need of," "to be without something you
wish to have," for *carere* is used of being without pleasant
and useful things. (1) In the phrase, however, *carere febri*
the words mean "to be free from fever," where one has not
got fever and knows one has not got fever and is quite content
that it should be so. (2) We cannot say *carere* in connection
with evil, for to "feel the need of evil" would mean that
evil was not a thing to grieve about but the reverse. (3)
We can say *carere bono*, for to "feel the need of" good is of
itself an evil. (4) Only the living feel and only the living
"feel the need of" anything : the dead do not feel and
therefore cannot "feel the need of" anything.

need of " it, even if you should be conscious that you
do not possess it. This argument must be repeatedly
insisted upon when we have firmly established the
point, about which, we can have
no doubt, namely, that souls are mortal, if destruction in death is so
complete that not even the faintest vestige of sensation is left behind : when that, then, is properly
settled for once and all, we must thoroughly sift, so
as to be sure of it, the meaning of " feeling the need
of," that there may be no possibility of mistake in
using the phrase. This then is the meaning of
" feeling the need of,"[1] to be in want of anything
you wish to possess ; for there is a notion of wish in
" feeling the need of,"—except when the word *carere*
is used in another sense, as for instance of a fever,
meaning " to be without fever." For it is using the
word in quite a different sense to use it where one
has not got something and is conscious of not having
it, even if one can readily put up with being without
it. To " feel the need of " is not used in connection
with evil ; for then evil would not be a thing to
grieve about : the expression " to feel the need of "
a good is used, and that amounts to an evil. But not
even a living man " feels the need of " a good, if he
does not want it. In the case of a living man it is,
however, intelligible to say that you " feel the need
of " a throne—that, however, cannot be said quite
accurately in your case, though it could have been in
the case of Tarquin after he had been dethroned [2]— :

[2]   My ancestors did from the streets of Rome
    The Tarquin drive, when he was called a King,

says Brutus in *Julius Caesar*, Act II. Sc. 1, and Cicero is continually dropping his hints to Brutus about Caesar in these
books, sometimes as here with little reference to the argument.

ne intelligi quidem; carere enim sentientis est,
nec sensus in mortuo: ne carere quidem igitur in
mortuo est.

89   XXXVII. Quamquam quid opus est in hoc philosophari, cum rem non magno opere philosophia
egere videamus? Quotiens non modo ductores
nostri, sed universi etiam exercitus ad non dubiam
mortem concurrerunt! Quae quidem si timeretur,
non L. Brutus arcens eum reditu tyrannum, quem
ipse expulerat, in proelio concidisset, non cum Latinis
decertans pater Decius, cum Etruscis filius, cum
Pyrrho nepos se hostium telis obiecissent, non uno
bello pro patria cadentes Scipiones Hispania vidisset,
Paullum et Geminum Cannae, Venusia Marcellum,
Litana Albinum, Lucani Gracchum. Num quis
horum miser hodie? Ne tum quidem post spiritum
extremum; nec enim potest esse miser quisquam
90 sensu perempto. At id ipsum odiosum est, sine
sensu esse. Odiosum, si id esset carere. Cum vero
perspicuum sit nihil posse in eo esse, qui ipse non sit,
quid potest esse in eo odiosum, qui nec careat
nec sentiat? Quamquam hoc quidem nimis saepe,
sed eo, quod in hoc inest omnis animi contractio ex metu mortis. Qui enim satis viderit, id
quod est luce clarius, animo et corpore consumpto

---

[1] Tarquinius Superbus, expelled from Rome 510 B.C.

[2] Decius Mus (1) against the Latins, 340 B.C.; (2) against
the Samnites, 295 B.C.; (3) against Pyrrhus, 279 B.C., but this
last is not historical.

[3] Publius and Cnaeus Scipio, defeated by Hasdrubal in
Spain, 211 B.C. *Scipiadas, belli fulmen, Carthaginis horror*,
Lucr. 3.1035.

[4] 216 B.C.   [5] 208 B.C.   [6] 215 B.C.   [7] 213 B.C.

still in the case of a dead man it is not even intelligible, for " to feel the need of " is appropriate to a sentient being, and in a dead man there is no sensation : in a dead man therefore there is no possibility either of " feeling the need of."

XXXVII. And yet what need to philosophize where we see that the question does not to any great extent require philosophy ? How often have our leaders, and not only they but whole armies, rushed on certain death ! If death indeed had been their fear, L. Brutus would not have fallen in battle, preventing the return of the tyrant [1] whom he had himself driven out ; the elder Decius in desperate conflict with the Latins, his son in conflict with the Etruscans, his grandson fighting Pyrrhus [2] would not have flung themselves upon the weapons of the enemy ; Spain would not have seen the Scipios [3] falling for their country in the selfsame war ; Cannae would not have seen the fall of Paullus and Geminus,[4] Venusia of Marcellus,[5] Litana of Albinus [6] and Lucania of Gracchus.[7] Can any one of these at the present day be wretched ? Not even on the day they fell, after their last breath, for no one can be wretched when sensation has entirely gone. But, it may be objected, the mere absence of sensation is hateful. Hateful, yes, if it meant " feeling the need of " ; since, however, it is quite plain that there is nothing left in the man who has no existing self, what can there be hateful where the man has neither feeling of need nor power of sensation ? Too often it is true this notion exists, but it is due to the fact that in it lurks all the shrinking of the soul from the fear of death. For it is clearer than daylight that, when soul and body have been made away with, the

totoque animante deleto et facto interitu universo
illud animal, quod fuerit, factum esse nihil, is plane
perspiciet inter Hippocentaurum, qui numquam
fuerit, et regem Agamemnonem nihil interesse, nec
pluris nunc facere M. Camillum hoc civile bellum,
quam ego vivo illo fecerim Romam captam. Cur
igitur et Camillus doleret, si haec post trecentos et
quinquaginta fere annos eventura putaret, et ego
doleam, si ad decem milia annorum gentem aliquam
urbe nostra potituram putem? Quia tanta caritas
patriae est, ut eam non sensu nostro, sed salute
ipsius metiamur.

91   XXXVIII. Itaque non deterret sapientem mors
quae propter incertos casus cotidie imminet, propter
brevitatem vitae numquam potest longe abesse, quo
minus in omne tempus rei publicae suisque consulat,
ut posteritatem ipsam, cuius sensum habiturus non
sit, ad se putet pertinere. Qua re licet etiam
mortalem esse animum iudicantem aeterna moliri,
non gloriae cupiditate, quam sensurus non sit, sed
virtutis, quam necessario gloria, etiam si tu id non
agas, consequatur.

Natura vero si[1] se sic habet, ut, quo modo
initium nobis rerum omnium ortus noster adferat,
sic exitum mors: ut nihil pertinuit ad nos ante
ortum, sic nihil post mortem pertinebit. In quo

---

[1] *si* is not in the MSS., but is generally inserted by
editors.

---

[1] Cf. Lucr. v. 878.

whole living being destroyed, and complete annihilation has ensued, the creature which has existed has
become nothing; and the man who has once grasped
this will realize quite plainly that there is no
difference between a Hippocentaur[1] who has never
existed and King Agamemnon, and that M. Camillus
makes no more account of the present civil war than
I should make now of the capture of Rome in his
lifetime. Why then should Camillus have felt pain,
had he thought that some 350 years after his lifetime
the present troubles would come, and why should
i feel pain if I should think that some nation would
get possession of our city at a date 10,000 years
hence? Because so great is love of country that we
measure it not by what we feel but by the salvation
of our country itself.

XXXVIII. Consequently death, which because of
the changes and chances of life is daily close at
hand, and because of the shortness of life can never
be far away, does not frighten the wise man from
considering the interests of the State and of his
family for all time; and it follows that he regards
posterity, of which he is bound to have no consciousness, as being really his concern. And so the
man who concludes that the soul is mortal may yet
attempt deeds that will not die, not from a thirst
for fame, of which he will have no enjoyment, but
from a thirst for virtue, which of necessity secures
fame, even if it be not its object.

If it is nature's law that, as our birth brings the
beginning of all things, so death brings us the end
of all: then, as we brought nothing into the world
at birth, so we take nothing out of the world at
death. What evil can there be in this, seeing that

quid potest esse mali, cum mors nec ad vivos pertineat nec ad mortuos? Alteri nulli sunt, alteros
92 non attinget. Quam qui leviorem faciunt, somni simillimam volunt esse, quasi vero quisquam ita nonaginta annos velit vivere, ut cum sexaginta confecerit, reliquos dormiat: ne sui quidem id velint, non modo ipse. Endymion vero, si fabulas audire volumus, ut nescio quando in Latmo obdormivit, qui est mons Cariae, nondum, opinor, est experrectus. Num igitur eum curare censes, cum Luna laboret, a qua consopitus putatur, ut eum dormientem oscularetur? Quid curet autem, qui ne sentit quidem? Habes somnum imaginem mortis eamque cotidie induis, et dubitas quin sensus in morte nullus sit, cum in eius simulacro videas esse nullum sensum?

93 XXXIX. Pellantur ergo istae ineptiae paene aniles, ante tempus mori miserum esse. Quod tandem tempus? Naturaene? At ea quidem dedit usuram vitae tamquam pecuniae nulla praestituta die. Quid est igitur quod querare, si repetit, cum vult? Ea enim condicione acceperas. Idem, si puer parvus occidit, aequo animo ferendum putant: si vero in cunis, ne querendum quidem. Atqui ab hoc acerbius exegit natura quod dederat. "Nondum

---

[1] Death cannot be where life is; where life is there is no death.

[2] Homer speaks of sleep as death's brother, κασίγνητος Θανάτοιο, *Il.* xiv. 231.

[3] *Laborare* is a word used for an eclipse of the moon, cf. *Una laboranti poterit succurrere lunae,* Juv. 6. 443. Endymion was a shepherd, and from his story came the proverb, *Endymionis somnum dormire,* to express a long sleep. Cicero is again perhaps thinking of the *Phaedo,* where Socrates says, "If there were no alternation between sleeping and

death does not appertain either to the living or to
the dead? The dead do not exist, the living it will
not touch.[1] Those who minimize it are for making
it closely resemble sleep:[2] just as if anyone would
wish to live for ninety years on condition of sleeping
the remainder after he had completed sixty. Even
his family would not wish it, apart from the man's
own wishes. Endymion, if we are inclined to listen
to fairy-tales, once upon a time fell asleep on Latmus,
a mountain in Caria, and has not yet awoke I fancy.
You do not think then that he is anxious over the
worries[3] of the moon, by whom it is thought he was
lulled to sleep, that she might kiss him in his slumber.
Nay, why should he be anxious who has not so much
as the power of sensation? You have sleep, death's
counterfeit, and this you daily put on like a garment,
and you doubt the fact of there being no sensation
in death, though you see that in its counterfeit there
is no sensation?

XXXIX. Let such follies then as thinking that
it is wretched to die before our time be pushed
aside as old wives' fables, which they pretty nearly
are. What "time," pray? Nature's? Why, she
it is who has granted the use of life like a loan,
without fixing any day for repayment. What is
there then for you to complain of, if she calls it
in when she will? Those were the terms on which
you had accepted the loan. The same grumblers
think that if a small child dies, the loss must be
borne calmly; if an infant in the cradle, there must
not even be a lament. And yet in this latter case
nature has called in her gift with greater cruelty.

waking, the story of the sleeping Endymion would in the
end have no meaning."

gustaverat," inquiunt, " vitae suavitatem : hic autem
iam sperabat magna, quibus frui coeperat." At id
quidem in ceteris rebus melius putatur, aliquam
partem quam nullam attingere : cur in vita secus ?
Quamquam non male ait Callimachus *multo saepius
lacrimasse Priamum quam Troilum*. Eorum autem,
94 qui exacta aetate moriuntur, fortuna laudatur. Cur ?
nam, reor, nullis, si vita longior daretur, posset esse
iucundior. Nihil enim est profecto homini prudentia
dulcius, quam, ut cetera auferat, adfert certe senectus. Quae vero aetas longa est aut quid omnino
homini longum ? Nonne

> *Modo pueros, modo adolescentes in cursu a tergo
> insequens*
> *Nec opinantes assecuta est*

senectus ? Sed quia ultra nihil habemus, hoc longum dicimus. Omnia ista, perinde ut cuique data
sunt pro rata parte, aut longa aut brevia dicuntur.
Apud Hypanim fluvium, qui ab Europae parte in
Pontum influit, Aristoteles ait bestiolas quasdam
nasci, quae unum diem vivant. Ex his igitur hora
octava quae mortua est, provecta aetate mortua est ;
quae vero occidente sole, decrepita, eo magis, si
etiam solstitiali die. Confer nostram longissimam
aetatem cum aeternitate : in eadem propemodum
brevitate qua illae bestiolae reperiemur.

95 XL. Contemnamus igitur omnes ineptias—quod

---

[1] Troilus, a son of Priam, killed by Achilles in the Trojan
War. For Callimachus, cf. § 84. [2] The Būg.

"The infant had not yet tasted the sweetness of life," they say: "but the other was already forming high hopes, which he was beginning to enjoy." But in all other matters this is counted better—to get a part rather than nothing: why otherwise in life? And yet it is no bad saying of Callimachus that "Priam had shed tears far more often than Troilus." [1] On the other hand, the lot of those who die at the close of their prime is applauded. Why should it be? I imagine to no men could a longer life, if it were granted them, prove more agreeable. For there is, assuredly, nothing dearer to a man than wisdom, and though age takes away all else, it undoubtedly brings us that. What lifetime in fact is long, or what is there long at all for a human being? Has not old age

> Now the children, now the young men, following
>   closely in the race,
> Overtaken unsuspecting?

But, because we have nothing beyond, we speak of its length. All such things are spoken of as long or short according to the proportion in which they are in each case allotted. By the river Hypanis,[2] which flows into the Pontus from a part of Europe, Aristotle says that a kind of small animal is born, which lives for a single day. One of these creatures then that died in the eighth hour has died at an advanced age; that which died at sunset is decrepit, and all the more if it happen on Midsummer Day. Contrast our longest lifetime with eternity: we shall be found almost in the same category of short-lived beings as those tiny creatures.

XL. Let us then despise all follies—what milder

enim lenius huic levitati nomen imponam?—to.
tamque vim bene vivendi in animi robore ac magnitudine et in omnium rerum humanarum contemptione
ac despicientia et in omni virtute ponamus; nam
nunc quidem cogitationibus mollissimis effeminamur,
ut, si ante mors adventet, quam Chaldaeorum pro-
missa consecuti sumus, spoliati magnis quibusdam
96 bonis, illusi destitutique videamur. Quod si ex-
spectando et desiderando pendemus animi, cruciamur,
angimur, pro di immortales! quam illud iter iucun-
dum esse debet, quo confecto nulla reliqua cura,
nulla sollicitudo futura sit! Quam me delectat
Theramenes, quam elato animo est! Etsi enim
flemus, cum legimus, tamen non miserabiliter vir
clarus emoritur: qui cum coniectus in carcerem
triginta iussu tyrannorum venenum ut sitiens ob-
duxisset, reliquum sic e poculo eiecit, ut id resonaret,
quo sonitu reddito adridens: *Propino*, inquit, *hoc
pulcro Critiae*, qui in eum fuerat taeterrimus; Graeci
enim in conviviis solent nominare cui poculum tradi-
turi sint. Lusit vir egregius extremo spiritu, cum
iam praecordiis conceptam mortem contineret, vere-
que ei, cui venenum praebiberat, mortem eam est
97 auguratus, quae brevi consecuta est. Quis hanc
maximi animi aequitatem in ipsa morte laudaret, si

---

[1] "Chaldaean," once the name of a nation, became the
name for soothsayers, cf. *gipsy* from *Egyptian*.

[2] The game κότταβος was much in use at ancient Athenian
banquets. Its object was to throw a small quantity of wine
at a mark and make a sound in doing so. The mark was
either a saucer floating in a big bowl of water or else a
saucer attached to the rod of a special apparatus. Theramenes
combined this with a toast. He was an Athenian statesman
of moderate views and hence nicknamed κόθορνος (buskin,
fitting either foot), "trimmer," and was put to death by the
thirty tyrants, of whom Critias was the leader, in 404 B.C.

name could I apply to such triviality?—and set the
whole meaning of right living in strength and greatness of soul, in disdain and scorn for all human vicissitudes and in the practice of all virtue; for as it is
these modern times we are made unmanly by the
most mawkish imaginations, and the result is that,
should death come upon us before we have realized
the promises of soothsayers,[1] we look upon ourselves
as defrauded of sundry blessings of importance and
as mocked and cheated men. But if our minds are
kept in the suspense and torture and anguish of
expectation and longing, ye immortal gods! how
delightful should the journey prove which at its
close leaves us no further care, no anxiety for the
future! How charmed I am with Theramenes!
How lofty a spirit is his! For though we shed
tears as we read, nevertheless a notable man dies
a death that is not pitiable: he was flung into
prison by order of the thirty tyrants, and when he
had swallowed the poison like a thirsty man he
tossed the remainder out of the cup[2] to make a
splash, and with a laugh at the sound it made, "I
drink this," said he, "to the health of fair Critias,"
the man who had treated him abominably; I may
explain that at their banquets the Greeks make a
practice of naming the guest to whom they are
going to pass the cup. This noble spirit jested
with his last breath, though he already had within
him the death his vitals had absorbed, and in reality
he prophesied for the man he had toasted in the
poison the death which shortly overtook him.[3] Who
would applaud this calmness of a great spirit in the

[3] In the battle between the thirty tyrants and the exiles
under Thrasybulus at Piraeus in 403 B.C., a year afterwards.

mortem malum iudicaret? Vadit in eundem carcerem atque in eundem paucis post annis scyphum
Socrates, eodem scelere iudicum quo tyrannorum
Theramenes. Quae est igitur eius oratio, qua facit
eum Plato usum apud iudices iam morte mulc-
tatum?

XLI. "Magna me" inquit "spes tenet, iudices,
bene mihi evenire, quod mittar ad mortem; necesse
est enim sit alterum de duobus, ut aut sensus
omnino omnes mors auferat aut in alium quendam
locum ex his locis morte migretur. Quam ob rem
sive sensus exstinguitur morsque ei somno similis
est, qui non numquam etiam sine visis somniorum
placatissimam quietem adfert, di boni, quid lucri
est emori! aut quam multi dies reperiri possunt,
qui tali nocti anteponantur, cui si[1] similis futura
est perpetuitas omnis consequentis temporis, quis
98 me beatior? Sin vera sunt quae dicuntur, migrationem esse mortem in eas oras, quas qui e vita
excesserunt incolunt, id multo iam beatius est.
Tene, cum ab iis, qui se iudicum numero haberi
volunt, evaseris, ad eos venire, qui vere iudices
appellentur, Minoem, Rhadamanthum, Aeacum,
Triptolemum, convenireque eos, qui iuste et cum
fide vixerint: haec peregrinatio mediocris vobis
videri potest? Ut vero colloqui cum Orpheo,
Musaeo, Homero, Hesiodo liceat, quanti tandem
aestimatis? Equidem saepe emori, si fieri posset,
vellem, ut ea, quae dico, mihi liceret invenire.

---

[1] si supplied by Bentley.

---

[1] Plato, *Apol.* 40 C.   [2] Cf. § 10.

hour of death, did he judge death to be an evil?
A few years later, Socrates passed to the same prison
and the same bowl as Theramenes, condemned by
a sentence of judges as criminal as that of the
tyrants on Theramenes. What then is the speech
which Plato represents Socrates as having given
before his judges when the death sentence had
been pronounced?[1]

XLI. "I entertain, gentlemen of the jury, high
hopes," said he, "that it is for my good that I am sent
to death; for there must follow one of two consequences, either that death takes away all sensation
altogether, or that by death a passage is secured
from these regions to another place. Accordingly, if
sensation is obliterated and death resembles the
sleep which sometimes brings the calmest rest,
untroubled even by the appearances of dreams, good
gods, what gain it is to die! or how many days can
be found preferable to such a night, and if the
coming endless succession of ensuing time resembles
this sleep, who can be happier than I? But if there
is truth in the tale that death is a passage to those
shores which are inhabited by the departed dead,
that is surely happier still. To think that, when
thou hast escaped from those who wish to be reckoned
judges, thou art coming to those who can really be
called judges, Minos, Rhadamanthus, Aeacus and
Triptolemus,[2] and meetest the men who have lived
righteous and faithful lives: does this seem to you
an ordinary pilgrimage? What value, pray, do you
set upon the privilege of actually conversing with
Orpheus, Musaeus, Homer and Hesiod? For my
part I could feel in my heart the wish to die many
times, that I might have the privilege of finding what

117

Quanta delectatione autem adficerer, cum Palamedem, cum Aiacem, cum alios iudicio iniquo circumventos convenirem! Temptarem etiam summi regis, qui maximas copias duxit ad Troiam, et Ulixi Sisyphique prudentiam, nec ob eam rem, cum haec exquirerem, sicut hic faciebam, capite damnarer. Ne vos quidem, iudices ii, qui me absolvistis, mortem

99 timueritis. Nec enim cuiquam bono mali quidquam evenire potest nec vivo nec mortuo, nec umquam eius res a dis immortalibus negligentur, nec mihi ipsi hoc accidit fortuito. Nec vero ego iis, a quibus accusatus aut a quibus condemnatus sum, habeo quod suscenseam, nisi quod mihi nocere se crediderunt." Et haec quidem hoc modo; nihil autem melius extremo: "Sed tempus est" inquit "iam hinc abire me, ut moriar, vos, ut vitam agatis. Utrum autem sit melius di immortales sciunt: hominem quidem scire arbitror neminem."

XLII. Ne ego haud paullo hunc animum malim quam eorum omnium fortunas, qui de hoc iudicaverunt: etsi, quod praeter deos negat scire quemquam, id scit ipse, utrum sit melius—nam dixit ante—; sed suum illud, nihil ut adfirmet, tenet ad

100 extremum. Nos autem teneamus, ut nihil censeamus esse malum, quod sit a natura datum omnibus, intelligamusque, si mors malum sit, esse sempiternum malum. Nam vitae miserae mors finis esse videtur; mors si est misera, finis esse nullus potest.

---

[1] Heroes of the Trojan War: Palamedes put to death on a false charge of treachery; Ajax defeated in the contest for the arms of Achilles. For Sisyphus below, cf. § 10.

I am speaking of. What delight now should I feel at meeting Palamedes, at meeting Ajax [1] and at meeting others overthrown by an unjust sentence! I might test the wisdom of the supreme king who led the mighty host to Troy, and the wisdom of Ulysses and Sisyphus, without risk of a capital sentence for putting my questions to them as I used to do here. Do not you either, the judges who have voted for my acquittal, have fear of death. For no evil can befall any good man either in life or in death, nor will his troubles ever be disregarded by the immortal gods, nor has my own lot come by accident. In truth I have no ground for anger with my accusers or those who have condemned me, except that they have believed that they are doing me an injury." So much he said in this fashion; yet nothing is better than the close: "but the time has now come," he says, "for departure, I to die, you to go on with your lives. Which of the two, however, is better the immortal gods know; no human being, I think, does know."

XLII. Verily I should prefer above measure to have such a soul to the possessions of all those who passed sentence upon him: and yet he does himself know what is known, he says, to no one except the gods, which of the two is better—for he has said previously that he knew—; but he holds firmly to the last his principle of asserting nothing. Let us on our side hold fast the principle of accounting nothing evil which has been bestowed by nature upon all mankind, and of realizing that if death be an evil it is an everlasting evil. For death seems to be the end of a wretched life; if death is wretched, there can be no end to its wretchedness.

MARCUS TULLIUS CICERO

Sed quid ego Socratem aut Theramenem, praestantes viros virtutis et sapientiae gloria, commemoro ? cum Lacedaemonius quidam, cuius ne nomen quidem proditum est, mortem tanto opere contempserit, ut, cum ad eam duceretur damnatus ab ephoris et esset vultu hilari atque laeto, dixissetque ei quidam inimicus : *Contemnisne leges Lycurgi ?* responderit : *Ego vero illi maximam gratiam habeo, qui me ea poena mulctaverit, quam sine mutuatione et sine versura possem dissolvere.* O virum Sparta dignum ! ut mihi quidem, qui tam magno animo fuerit, innocens damnatus 101 esse videatur. Tales innumerabiles nostra civitas tulit. Sed quid duces et principes nominem, cum legiones scribat Cato saepe alacres in eum locum profectas, unde redituras se non arbitrarentur ? Pari animo Lacedaemonii in Thermopylis occiderunt, in quos Simonides :

> *Dic, hospes, Spartae nos te hic vidisse iacentes,*
> *Dum sanctis patriae legibus obsequimur.*[1]

E quibus unus, cum Perses hostis in colloquio dixisset glorians : *Solem prae iaculorum multitudine et sagittarum non videbitis, In umbra igitur*, inquit, 102 *pugnabimus.* Viros commemoro : qualis tandem Lacaena ? quae cum filium in proelium misisset et

---

[1] The MSS. have here : "Quid ille dux Leonidas dicit ? *Prandete animo forti, Lacedaemonii : hodie apud inferos fortasse cenabimus.*—Fuit haec gens fortis, dum Lycurgi leges vigebant !" but the passage is generally condemned as a spurious insertion.

---

[1] He passes now to less famous examples.
[2] The Greek of this famous epigram of Simonides is :

> ὦ ξεῖν', ἀγγέλλειν Λακεδαιμονίοις ὅτι τῇδε
> κείμεθα τοῖς κείνων ῥήμασι πειθόμενοι.

But why do I quote the examples of Socrates and Theramenes, men pre-eminently famous for virtue and wisdom?[1] There was a Lacedaemonian (and not so much as his name has been reported) who had such utter scorn of death that when, after being sentenced by the ephors, he was led out to execution with a cheerful and joyous look, and an enemy said to him, " Do you scorn the laws of Lycurgus? " he replied : " I am deeply grateful to him for inflicting upon me a penalty which I could pay without borrowing from friend or usurer." A man of whom Sparta could be proud ! So much so, that to my thinking a man of such high spirit was undeservedly condemned. Such examples our State has produced in countless numbers. But why should I name leaders and chiefs, seeing that Cato records that the legions often marched cheerfully to a position from which they did not think they would come back again? Of like spirit were the Lacedaemonians who fell at Thermopylae, on whom Simonides wrote :

> Stranger, the Spartans tell that here in the grave
>   you beheld us
>   Keeping the laws of our land by an obedience
>   due.[2]

One of them, when a Persian foeman in conversation had said in boast, " You will not see the sun for the number of our javelins and arrows," " Then," said he, " we shall fight in the shade."[3] I am quoting examples of men : of what temper, pray, was the Spartan woman ? When she had sent her son to

[3] Herodotus, 7. 266, states that the conversation was held not with a Persian but with a Greek.

interfectum audisset: *Idcirco*, inquit, *genueram, ut esset qui pro patria mortem non dubitaret occumbere.*

XLIII. Esto, fortes et duri Spartiatae, magnam habet vim rei publicae disciplina. Quid? Cyrenaeum Theodorum, philosophum non ignobilem, nonne miramur? cui cum Lysimachus rex crucem minaretur: *Istis, quaeso*, inquit, *ista horribilia minitare purpuratis tuis: Theodori quidem nihil interest humine an sublime putescat.* Cuius hoc dicto admoneor, ut aliquid etiam de humatione et sepultura dicendum existimem; rem non difficilem, iis praesertim cognitis, quae de nihil sentiendo paullo ante dicta sunt; de qua Socrates quidem quid senserit apparet in eo libro, in quo moritur, de quo iam tam multa 103 diximus. Cum enim de immortalitate animorum disputavisset et iam moriendi tempus urgueret, rogatus a Critone quem ad modum sepeliri vellet: *Multam vero*, inquit, *operam, amici, frustra consumpsi; Critoni enim nostro non persuasi me hinc avolaturum neque mei quidquam relicturum. Verum tamen, Crito, si me adsequi potueris aut sicubi nanctus eris, ut tibi videbitur, sepelito. Sed, mihi crede, nemo me vestrum, cum hinc excessero, consequetur.* Praeclare id quidem, qui et amico permiserit et se ostenderit de hoc toto 104 genere nihil laborare. Durior Diogenes et is quidem idem sentiens, sed ut Cynicus asperius, proiici se

---

[1] "Cyrenaeus" may mean "of the Cyrenaic school of philosophy"; for in another treatise Cicero says, *Theodorus Cyrenaicus.*

[2] Plat. *Phaed.* 115.

battle and heard the news of his death, "To that end," said she, "had I borne him, to be a man who should not hesitate to meet death for his country."

XLIII. Be it so, you brave and hardy Spartans; the training of the State has a mighty power. Yes, but do we not admire Theodorus of Cyrene,[1] no mean philosopher? When King Lysimachus threatened him with crucifixion: "Make, I beg," said he, "your abominable threats to those courtiers of yours in the scarlet liveries: it makes no difference to Theodorus whether he rots on the ground or in the air." And this saying suggests the thought that I ought to say a word about interment and burial—no difficult matter, particularly after we have mastered what was said a little while back about absence of sensation; and as a matter of fact Socrates' view on the subject is given clearly in the book which relates his death, of which we have already said so much.[2] For after he had discussed the immortality of souls and the hour of death was close at hand, when asked by Crito how he wished to be buried, "My friends," said he, "I have indeed spent a deal of labour to no purpose, for I have not convinced our friend Crito that I shall fly hence and leave nothing of me behind. But all the same, Crito, if you can catch me or light upon me, you shall bury me as you think fit. But, believe me, none of you will come up with me when I have gone hence." That was indeed nobly said, for he gave his friend a free hand and yet showed that no thought of this sort troubled him at all. Diogenes was rougher; his feeling it is true was the same, but like a Cynic he spoke more harshly and required that he should be flung out unburied. Upon which

MARCUS TULLIUS CICERO

iussit inhumatum. Tum amici : *Volucribusne et feris?*
Minime vero, inquit, *sed bacillum propter me quo abigam*
ponitote. Qui poteris? illi, *non enim sentis. Quid*
igitur mihi ferarum laniatus oberit nihil sentienti?
Praeclare Anaxagoras, qui cum Lampsaci moreretur,
quaerentibus amicis velletne Clazomenas in patriam,
si quid ei accidisset, auferri : *Nihil necesse est,* inquit,
undique enim ad inferos tantumdem viae est. Totaque
de ratione humationis unum tenendum est, ad
corpus illam pertinere, sive occiderit animus sive
vigeat; in corpore autem perspicuum est vel
exstincto animo vel elapso nullum residere sensum.

105   XLIV. Sed plena errorum sunt omnia. Trahit
Hectorem ad currum religatum Achilles : lacerari
eum et sentire, credo, putat. Ergo hic ulciscitur, ut
quidem sibi videtur ; at illa sicut acerbissimam rem
maeret :

> *Vidi videre quod sum passa aegerrime,*
> *Hectorem curru quadriiugo raptarier.*

Quem Hectorem aut quam diu ille erit Hector?
Melius Accius et aliquando sapiens Achilles :

> *Immo enimvero corpus Priamo reddidi, Hectorem*
> *abstuli.*

Non igitur Hectorem traxisti, sed corpus, quod

---

[1] Anaxagoras, an Ionian philosopher, 500–428 B.C., who lived
for thirty years at Athens and was the friend of Pericles.
[2] Cf. App. II.
[3] Accius, Roman tragic poet, born in 170 B.C.

his friends said: "To the birds and wild beasts?" "Certainly not," said he, "but you must put a stick near me to drive them away with." "How can you, for you will be without consciousness?" they replied. "What harm, then, can the mangling of wild beasts do me if I am without consciousness?" It was a noble saying of Anaxagoras[1] on his death-bed at Lampsacus, in answer to his friends' inquiry whether he wished in the event of need to be taken away to Clazomenae, his native land: "There is no necessity," said he, "for from any place the road to the lower world is just as far." Accordingly one principle must be adhered to in dealing with the whole purpose of burial, that it has to do with the body, whether the soul has perished or is still vigorous: in the body, however, it is plain that, when the soul has either been annihilated or made its escape, there is no remnant of sensation.

XLIV. But this whole subject is full of deceptions. Achilles fastens Hector to his chariot and drags him: he thinks, I imagine, that Hector is being torn to bits and has sensation. Therefore, he wreaks his vengeance, or thinks he does; but the poor woman mourns this as a cruel outrage:

I saw what I have suffered bitterly to see,
Hector behind the four-horse chariot dragged along.[2]

Hector indeed! How long will he be Hector? Far better Accius[3] and Achilles at last become wise:

Nay, sure to Priam have I the corpse restored,
Hector's life have I taken.

You have not dragged Hector then, but the body

106 fuerat Hectoris. Ecce alius exoritur e terra, qui matrem dormire non sinat:

> *Mater, te appello, tu quae curam somno suspensam levas,*
> *Neque te mei miseret, surge et sepeli natum tuum.*

—Haec cum pressis et flebilibus modis, qui totis theatris maestitiam inferant, concinuntur, difficile est non eos, qui inhumati sint, miseros iudicare—

prius quam ferae

Volucresque . . . .

—metuit ne laceratis membris minus bene utatur, ne combustis non extimescit—

> *Neu reliquias, quaeso, meas sieris denudatis ossibus*
> *Per terram sanie delibutas foede divexarier.*

107 —Non intelligo quid metuat, cum tam bonos septenarios fundat ad tibiam.—Tenendum est igitur nihil curandum esse post mortem, cum multi inimicos etiam mortuos poeniuntur. Exsecratur luculentis sane versibus apud Ennium Thyestes, primum ut naufragio pereat Atreus: durum hoc sane; talis enim interitus non est sine gravi sensu: illa inania:

---

[1] Deiphilus, son of Iliona, daughter of Priam, and of Polymnestor, King of Thrace, who killed him by mistake instead of Polydorus, son of Priam. Pacuvius adopted this story for his tragedy *Iliona*. Cf. App. II.

[2] Cf. § 27 and note.

[3] Eight-foot really, *octonarii*. Perhaps *VIII narios* became *VII narios*, *septenarios*, in the MSS.

[4] Cf. App. II.

which had been Hector's.   See! another spirit[1]
rises from the earth, to prevent his mother from
sleeping:

> Mother, 'tis you I call, you that your care with
>   sleep's relief suspend,
> Nor pity of me have you: rise, and to your son
>   give burial.

Such words when chanted in measured and plaintive
numbers, suited to inspire whole audiences with
sadness, make it difficult to avoid the thought that
all who are unburied[2] are wretched—

> before wild beasts
> And birds . . .

He fears she will be neglectful of his mangled
limbs; he has no terror that she will so treat what
has been burnt with fire—

> And suffer not my poor remains, I pray, with
>   bones all stripped and bare,
> Along the ground with gore besmeared in pieces
>   to be foully torn.

I do not understand what he is afraid of, seeing
that he pours out such a stream of fine seven-foot
verses.[3] We must therefore hold fast the principle
that there is no need, when you see numbers of men
punishing even dead enemies, to be anxious about
anything after death.   In Ennius[4] Thyestes utters
curses in quite magnificent verses, praying first
that Atreus may die by shipwreck: a cruel prayer
this no doubt; for such an end involves grievous
consciousness of death: the following means
nothing:

Ipse summis saxis fixus asperis, evisceratus,
Latere pendens, saxa spargens tabo, sanie et sanguine
atro.

Non ipsa saxa magis sensu omni vacabunt quam ille
" latere pendens," cui se hic cruciatum censet optare.
Quae [1] essent dura, si sentiret ; nulla sunt sine sensu !
Illud vero perquam inane :

Neque sepulcrum quo recipiat habeat portum corporis,
Ubi remissa humana vita corpus requiescat malis.

Vides quanto haec in errore versentur : portum esse
corporis et requiescere in sepulcro putat mortuum,
magna culpa Pelopis, qui non erudierit filium nec
docuerit quatenus esset quidque curandum.

108   XLV. Sed quid singulorum opiniones animadver-
tam, nationum varios errores perspicere cum liceat?
Condiunt Aegyptii mortuos et eos servant domi,
Persae etiam cera circumlitos condunt, ut quam
maxime permaneant diuturna corpora ; Magorum
mos est non humare corpora suorum, nisi a feris sint
ante laniata ; in Hyrcania plebs publicos alit canes,
optimates domesticos : nobile autem genus canum
illud scimus esse, sed pro sua quisque facultate parat

----

[1] *quae* for the *quam* of the MSS., and *sunt* supplied after
nulla, Ernestius and Tregder.

Right on the top of rugged rocks transfixed and
    burst asunder,
Hung by the flank, the rocks with filth, gore
    and black blood he spatters.

The very rocks will not be more destitute of sensation than he "hung by the flank"; for whom
Thyestes imagines he is desiring torments. They
would have been cruel, had the victim the power of
sensation; without sensation they are non-existent.
The following is perfectly meaningless:

Let him have no tomb to hide in like a haven for
    the body
Where, resigned when human life is, respite he
    may find from evils.

You see how deep the deception in which they live:
he thinks the grave is the body's haven and that
the dead man finds peace in the grave, to the great
discredit of Pelops for not having instructed his son
and taught him what were the limits of anxiety in
each particular situation.

XLV. But why should I notice the beliefs of
individuals, since we may observe the varied deceptions under which races of mankind labour? The
Egyptians embalm their dead and keep them in the
house; the Persians even smear them with wax before
burial, that the bodies may last for as long a time as
possible; it is the custom of the Magi not to bury
the bodies of their dead unless they have been
first mangled by wild beasts; in Hyrcania the
populace support dogs for the benefit of the community, while the nobles keep them for family use:
it is as we know a famous breed of dogs, but in
spite of the cost, each householder procures animals

a quibus lanietur, eamque optimam illi esse censent
sepulturam. Permulta alia colligit Chrysippus, ut
est in omni historia curiosus, sed ita taetra sunt
quaedam, ut ea fugiat et reformidet oratio. Totus
igitur hic locus est contemnendus in nobis, non
negligendus in nostris, ita tamen, ut mortuorum
109 corpora nihil sentire vivi sentiamus. Quantum
autem consuetudini famaeque dandum sit, id curent
vivi, sed ita, ut intelligant nihil ad mortuos pertinere.

Sed profecto mors tum aequissimo animo oppetitur,
cum suis se laudibus vita occidens consolari potest.
Nemo parum diu vixit, qui virtutis perfectae perfecto
functus est munere. Multa mihi ipsi ad mortem
tempestiva fuerunt, quam [1] utinam potuissem obire !
Nihil enim iam acquirebatur, cumulata erant officia
vitae, cum fortuna bella restabant. Qua re si ipsa
ratio minus perficiet ut mortem negligere possimus,
at vita acta perficiat ut satis superque vixisse videamur. Quamquam enim sensus aberit, tamen suis
et propriis bonis laudis et gloriae, quamvis non sentiant, mortui non carent. Etsi enim nihil habet in
se gloria cur expetatur, tamen virtutem tamquam
110 umbra sequitur. XLVI. Verum multitudinis iudi-

---

[1] *quam* for the *quae* of the MSS., Davies.

---

[1] Chrysippus, born in 280 B.C., became head of the Stoic
School and was regarded as its second founder.

in proportion to his means, to mangle him, and that they consider the best mode of burial. Chrysippus [1] collects a large number of other instances as suits his inquisitive way in making any investigation, but there are details so disgusting that language avoids them with abhorrence. This whole subject then must be treated with contempt as regards ourselves, but not ignored in the case of those connected with us—with this proviso, however, that we, the living, are conscious that the bodies of the dead have no consciousness. Let the living, however, attend to funeral observance to the extent to which they must make a compromise with custom and public opinion, but with the understanding that they realize that in no way does it concern the dead.

But assuredly death is encountered with most equanimity when the failing life can find solace in the reputation it has won. No one has lived too short a life who has discharged the perfect work of perfect virtue. In my life there have been many occasions when death would have been timely, and would I could have found it! for there was no longer anything to be won; life's duties had been discharged in full; the war with fortune alone remained. If therefore my arguments fail to convince us that we can ignore death, yet let a life completed make us think that we have lived sufficiently and more. For though consciousness will have gone, nevertheless the dead, unconscious though they be, are not without their own peculiar blessings of fame and glory. There is, it may be, nothing in glory that we should desire it, but none the less it follows virtue like a shadow. XLVI. The true judgment of popular opinion about good

cium de bonis si quando est, magis laudandum est quam illi ob eam rem beati. Non possum autem dicere, quoquo modo hoc accipietur, Lycurgum, Solonem legum et publicae disciplinae carere gloria: Themistoclem, Epaminondam bellicae virtutis. Ante enim Salamina ipsam Neptunus obruet quam Salaminii tropaei memoriam, priusque Boeotia Leuctra tollentur quam pugnae Leuctricae gloria. Multo autem tardius fama deseret Curium, Fabricium, Calatinum, duo Scipiones, duo Africanos, Maximum, Marcellum, Paullum, Catonem, Laelium, innumerabiles alios; quorum similitudinem aliquam qui adripuerit, non eam fama populari, sed vera bonorum laude metiens fidenti animo, si ita res feret, gradietur ad mortem, in qua aut summum bonum aut nullum malum esse cognovimus. Secundis vero suis rebus volet etiam mori; non enim tam cumulus bonorum

111 iucundus esse potest quam molesta decessio. Hanc sententiam significare videtur Laconis illa vox, qui, cum Rhodius Diagoras, Olympionices nobilis, uno die duo suos filios victores Olympiae vidisset, accessit ad senem et gratulatus; *Morere, Diagora;* inquit: *non enim in caelum ascensurus es.* Magna haec et nimium fortasse Graeci putant vel tum potius putabant, isque, qui hoc Diagorae dixit, permagnum existimans tris Olympionicas una e domo prodire cunctari

---

[1] For *carere* cf. § 88.

[2] This is illustrated by a passage from Pindar's *Pyth.* x. 22, which says, "Happy and glorious in the eyes of the wise is the man who by prowess of hand or foot has prevailed and won victory by daring and strength, and has seen his son duly win Pythian crowns. The brazen heaven he cannot ever scale" (ὁ χάλκεος οὐρανὸς οὔ ποτ' ἀμβατὸς αὐτῷ). He has reached the height of human felicity and cannot hope for more.

men, if ever it is given, is a thing to be commended rather than a cause of happiness to them. Still I cannot bring myself to say (however my statement shall be received) that Lycurgus and Solon are without[1] the fame of legislators and political organizers, or Themistocles and Epaminondas without the fame of military leaders. For Neptune will overwhelm the island of Salamis sooner than the memory of the trophy of the victory at Salamis, and Boeotian Leuctra will be obliterated sooner than the fame of the battle of Leuctra. Far more slowly will the glory fade of Curius, Fabricius, Calatinus, the two Scipios, the two Africani, Maximus, Marcellus, Paullus, Cato, Laelius and countless others; he who has once managed to gain some shadow of resemblance to these men, measuring it not by popular repute, but by the genuine approval of good men, will with confident spirit, if so it is to be, advance to meet death, in which we have found that the highest good or at any rate no evil lies. Indeed he will even be ready to die in the midst of prosperity; for no accumulation of successes can afford so much delight as their diminution will cause annoyance. This seems to be the meaning of the well-known utterance of the Lacedaemonian who, when Diagoras of Rhodes, a famous Olympian victor, had seen his two sons victorious on one day at Olympia, approached the old man and, congratulating him, said, " Die, Diagoras, for you are not destined to ascend to heaven."[2] Such achievements the Greeks think glorious—too much so perhaps—or rather thought so in that day, and he, who spoke in this way to Diagoras, considered it very glorious for three Olympian victors to come from one home, and

illum diutius in vita fortunae obiectum ınutile putabat ipsi.

Ego autem tibi quidem, quod satis esset, paucis verbis, ut mihi videbar, responderam ; concesseras enim nullo in malo mortuos esse, sed ob eam causam contendi, ut plura dicerem, quod in desiderio et luctu haec est consolatio maxima. Nostrum enim et nostra causa susceptum dolorem modice ferre debemus, ne nosmet ipsos amare videamur : illa suspicio intolerabili dolore cruciat, si opinamur eos, quibus orbati sumus, esse cum aliquo sensu in iis malis quibus vulgo opinantur. Hanc excutere opinionem mihimet volui radicitus, eoque sui fortasse

112 longior. XLVII. A. Tu longior ? Non mihi quidem. Prior enim pars orationis tuae faciebat ut mori cuperem, posterior ut modo non nollem, modo non laborarem : omni autem oratione illud certe perfectum est, ut mortem non ducerem in malis. M. Num igitur etiam rhetorum epilogum desideramus ? an hanc iam artem plane relinquimus ? A. Tu vero istam ne reliqueris, quam semper ornasti, et quidem iure ; illa enim te, verum si loqui volumus, ornaverat. Sed quinam est iste epilogus ? aveo enim audire quidquid est.

113   M. Deorum immortalium iudicia solent in scholis

---

[1] § 14.

judged it inexpedient for the father to linger longer in life exposed to the buffets of fortune.

Now I had already given you in a few words an answer, which was, as it seemed to me, at any rate sufficient, for you had admitted[1] that the dead were in no evil plight, but the reason why I have striven to speak at greater length is that in this admission of yours we find our chief solace in seasons of longing and sorrow. For our own grief, and grief felt on our account, we ought to bear in a spirit of moderation, that we may not seem to be lovers of self; it is a notion of unendurable torment if we believe that those, of whom we have been bereft, have some feeling of consciousness amid the evils in which ordinary belief imagines them involved. It has been my wish to root up this belief from my mind and cast it out, and for that reason it may be I have been too lengthy. XLVII. A. You, too lengthy? Not to my thinking. During the first part of what you said the effect was to make me long for death, whilst the effect of the latter part was sometimes to make me feel not unwilling, sometimes feel untroubled; the net result of all you said, however, is that I do not reckon death among evils. M. Do we then require in addition the epilogue usual with rhetoricians? Or has the time come for completely turning our backs on rhetoric? A. Nay, do not you turn your back on the art on which you have always brought honour, and with good reason; for to tell the truth it had first brought honour to you. But what is this epilogue? I wish to hear it whatever it be.

M. In dissertations it is the practice to quote the judgments of the immortal gods on death, and not

proferre de morte, nec vero ea fingere ipsi, sed Herodoto auctore aliisque pluribus. Primum Argivae sacerdotis Cleobis et Biton filii praedicantur. Nota fabula est: cum enim illam ad solemne et statum sacrificium curru vehi ius esset, satis longe ab oppido ad fanum, morarenturque iumenta, tunc iuvenes ii, quos modo nominavi, veste posita, corpora oleo perunxerunt, ad iugum accesserunt. Ita sacerdos advecta in fanum, cum currus esset ductus a filiis, precata a dea dicitur, ut id iis praemium daret pro pietate, quod maximum homini dari posset a deo ; post epulatos cum matre adolescentes somno se 114 dedisse, mane inventos esse mortuos. Simili precatione Trophonius et Agamedes usi dicuntur : qui cum Apollini Delphis templum exaedificavissent, venerantes deum petiverunt mercedem non parvam quidem operis et laboris sui, nihil certi, sed quod esset optimum homini. Quibus Apollo se id daturum ostendit post eius diei diem tertium, qui ut illuxit, mortui sunt reperti. Iudicavisse deum dicunt et eum quidem deum, cui reliqui di concessissent ut praeter ceteros divinaret.

XLVIII. Adfertur etiam de Sileno fabella quaedam, qui cum a Mida captus esset, hoc ei muneris pro sua missione dedisse scribitur : docuisse regem

---

[1] Hdt. 1. 31.
[2] A demigod, nurse and attendant of Dionysus.

the inventions of individual fancy, but with the authority of Herodotus and many other authors. The foremost place is given to the story of Cleobis and Biton, the sons of the priestess of Argos.[1] It is a well-known tale : religious observance required that on a fixed annual date of sacrifice she should be drawn to the spot in a chariot, and it was some distance from the town to the shrine ; the animals conveying her were lagging, whereupon the youths, whom I named just now, stripped and anointed their bodies with oil and took their place at the yoke. In this way the priestess was conveyed to the shrine and, according to the tale, as the car had been drawn by her sons, she prayed the goddess to grant them for their filial love the greatest boon that could be bestowed on man by God ; after they had feasted with their mother the young men fell asleep and in the morning were found dead. It is said Trophonius and Agamedes offered a similar prayer, for after completing the building of the temple to Apollo at Delphi they worshipped the god and asked in return for their toil and the work they had accomplished a recompense, no light one it is true, nothing definite, but what was best for man. Apollo made known to them that he would grant their prayer the third ensuing day, and when it dawned they were found dead. The god, they say, gave definite judgment, and he was the god to whom the rest of the gods had granted the gift of prophecy beyond all others.

XLVIII. There is further a story told of Silenus,[2] who had been taken captive by Midas and to gain his release had granted him, according to the record, the following boon : he instructed the king that it

non nasci homini longe optimum esse, proximum
115 autem quam primum mori. Qua est sententia in
Cresphonte usus Euripides:

> *Nam nos decebat coetus celebrantes domum*
> *Lugere, ubi esset aliquis in lucem editus,*
> *Humanae vitae varia reputantes mala:*
> *At, qui labores morte finisset graves,*
> *Hunc omni amicos laude et laetitia exsequi.*

Simile quiddam est in Consolatione Crantoris: ait
enim Terinaeum quendam Elysium, cum graviter
filii mortem maereret, venisse in psychomantium
quaerentem quae fuisset tantae calamitatis causa:
huic in tabellis tris huius modi versiculos datos:

> *Ignaris homines in vita mentibus errant:*
> *Euthynous potitur fatorum numine leto.*
> *Sic fuit utilius finiri ipsique tibique.*

116 His et talibus auctoribus usi confirmant causam
rebus a dis immortalibus iudicatam. Alcidamas
quidem, rhetor antiquus in primis nobilis, scripsit
etiam laudationem mortis, quae constat ex enumera-
tione humanorum malorum; cui rationes eae, quae
exquisitius a philosophis colliguntur, defuerunt,
ubertas orationis non defuit. Clarae vero mortes
pro patria oppetitae non solum gloriosae rhetoribus,
sed etiam beatae videri solent. Repetunt ab Erech-

---

[1] Cf. § 37.

was far the best thing for man not to be born at all, but the next best was to die as soon as possible. Euripides has made use of this maxim in the *Cresphontes* :

> For we should mourn in sorrowing throngs the
> house
> Where a man child is born to light of day,
> When reckoning o'er the ills of human life :
> But who by death has ended grievous toils,
> Him let his friends bear forth with praise and joy.

A similar thought is found in the *Consolation* of Crantor. For he says that a certain Elysius of Terina, in deep grief over the death of a son, came to the place where spirits are called up,[1] and on his asking what had been the reason for his sad misfortune, three lines to the following effect were given to him on writing-tablets :

> In life men wander with unknowing minds :
> By death Euthynoüs wins the award of fate.
> So better end comes for himself and thee.

By quoting these and similar authorities rhetoricians maintain that in this trial the immortal gods have given their verdict by facts. Alcidamas, for instance, an ancient rhetorician of the first distinction, actually wrote an encomium on death which consists of a list of the evils to which mankind are exposed ; he has failed to give those deeper arguments which the philosophers bring together, but he has not failed in wealth of eloquence. But noble deaths, sought voluntarily, for the sake of country, are not only commonly reckoned glorious by rhetoricians but also happy. They go back to Erechtheus, whose daugh-

139

theo, cuius etiam filiae cupide mortem expetiverunt pro vita civium : Codrum,[1] qui se in medios immisit hostes veste famulari, ne posset agnosci, si esset ornatu regio, quod oraculum erat datum, si rex interfectus esset, victrices Athenas fore ; Menoeceus non praetermittitur, qui item oraculo edito largitus est patriae suum sanguinem ; Iphigenia Aulide duci se immolandam iubet, "ut hostium eliciatur suo."

Veniunt inde ad propiora. XLIX. Harmodius in ore est et Aristogiton ; Lacedaemonius Leonidas, Thebanus Epaminondas vigent. Nostros non norunt, quos enumerare magnum est : ita sunt multi, quibus 117 videmus optabiles mortes fuisse cum gloria. Quae cum ita sint, magna tamen eloquentia est utendum atque ita velut superiore e loco contionandum, ut homines mortem vel optare incipiant vel certe timere desistant. Nam si supremus ille dies non exstinctionem, sed commutationem adfert loci, quid optabilius? sin autem perimit ac delet omnino, quid melius quam in mediis vitae laboribus obdormiscere et ita coniventem somno consopiri sempiterno? Quod si fiat, melior Ennii quam Solonis oratio. Hic enim noster :

> Nemo me lacrumis decoret, inquit, nec funera fletu
> Faxit !

[1] Some word like commemorant seems needed after Codrum.

---

[1] Menoeceus, son of Creon, King of Thebes, in obedience to the seer Tiresias who promised victory if he sacrificed his life. Erechtheus and Codrus were legendary kings of Athens.

[2] § 34, cf. App. II

ters sought even with eagerness for death to save the lives of their fellow-citizens; they give the tale of Codrus who flung himself into the midst of the enemy in the costume of a slave to avoid the recognition, which would have ensued had he worn the dress of a king, because of an oracle which said that if the king should fall, Athens would be victorious; the example of Menoeceus [1] is not passed over, who, on a similar announcement of an oracle, freely shed his blood for his country; Iphigenia required that she should be led to sacrifice at Aulis "that by her blood blood should be drawn from foemen's veins."

From those days they advance to nearer days. XLIX. Harmodius and Aristogiton are often on the lips of rhetoricians: the Spartan Leonidas, Epaminondas of Thebes, are much in evidence. Our Roman examples they do not know of, and it would be an undertaking to give the long roll of names: so numerous are those who made, as we see, the choice of death with honour. This being the case, we must employ the resources of eloquence and deliver as from a pulpit the message to mankind, either to begin to wish for death, or at any rate cease to fear it. For if the final day brings, not annihilation but a change of place, what more can be wished for? But if on the other hand that day brings total destruction and obliteration, what can be better than to fall asleep in the midst of the toils of life and so, closing one's eyes, be lulled in everlasting slumber? Were that so, the language of Ennius is better than Solon's. For our poet says:

Let no one honour me with tears or on my ashes weep,[2]

At vero ille sapiens :

Mors mea ne careat lacrimis : linquamus amicis
Maerorem, ut celebrent funera cum gemitu.

118 Nos vero, si quid tale acciderit, ut a deo denuntia-
tum videatur ut exeamus e vita, laeti et agentes
gratias pareamus emittique nos e custodia et levari
vinclis arbitremur, ut aut in aeternam et plane
nostram domum remigremus aut omni sensu molesti-
aque careamus : sin autem nihil denuntiabitur, eo
tamen simus animo, ut horribilem illum diem aliis,
nobis faustum putemus nihilque in malis ducamus
quod sit vel a dis immortalibus vel a natura parente
omnium constitutum.   Non enim temere nec fortuito
sati et creati sumus, sed profecto fuit quaedam vis
quae generi consuleret humano nec id gigneret aut
aleret quod cum exanclavisset omnes labores, tum
incideret in mortis malum sempiternum : portum
119 potius paratum nobis et perfugium putemus.   Quo
utinam velis passis pervehi liceat!   Sin reflantibus
ventis reiiciemur, tamen eodem paullo tardius refera-
mur necesse est.   Quod autem omnibus necesse est,
idne miserum esse uni potest ?

Habes epilogum, ne quid praetermissum aut re-
lictum putes. A. Ego vero, et quidem fecit etiam
iste me epilogus firmiorem. M. Optime, inquam.

but here is what your wise Solon says :

> Let not my death lack tears, and let us leave
> Sorrow to friends, that burying us they grieve !

For our part, if it so fall out that it seems a sentence delivered by God, that we depart from life, let us obey joyfully and thankfully and consider that we are being set free from prison and loosed from our chains, in order that we may pass on our way to the eternal home which is clearly ours, or else be free of all sensation and trouble ; but if on the other hand no sentence is delivered, let us all the same make up our minds to regard that day as auspicious for us, though to others it seems terrible, and to count nothing as an evil which is due to the appointment of the immortal gods or of nature, the mother of all things. For not to blind hazard or accident is our birth and our creation due, but assuredly there is a power to watch over mankind, and not one that would beget and maintain a race which, after exhausting the full burden of sorrows, should then fall into the everlasting evil of death : let us regard it rather as a haven and a place of refuge prepared for us. Would that we might be wafted there under full sail ! but if contrary winds shall throw us back, all the same we must be brought again to the same point a little later. But can that which is necessary for all be wretched for one alone ?

There you have the epilogue, so that you may not think that there has been anything neglected or left undone. A. Indeed I have it and I may tell you that your epilogue has really strengthened me. M. Excellent, say I ; but for the present let us make

Sed nunc quidem valetudini tribuamus aliquid, cras autem et quot dies erimus in Tusculano, agamus haec et ea potissimum, quae levationem habeant aegritudinum, formidinum, cupiditatum, qui omni e philosophia est fructus uberrimus.

some concession to the claims of health; to-morrow, however, and all the days we shall be staying here at Tusculum let us busy ourselves with such questions and particularly with all that tends to alleviate distresses, terrors, lusts, for here is the richest fruit of the whole field of philosophy.

M. TULLI CICERONIS TUSCULANARUM
DISPUTATIONUM

LIBER II

1 I. Neoptolemus quidem apud Ennium philosophari sibi ait necesse esse, sed paucis; nam omnino
haud placere : ego autem, Brute, necesse mihi quidem
esse arbitror philosophari; nam quid possum, praesertim nihil agens, agere melius? sed non paucis, ut
ille. Difficile est enim in philosophia pauca esse ei
nota, cui non sint aut pleraque aut omnia : nam nec
pauca nisi e multis eligi possunt nec qui pauca per-
ceperit non idem reliqua eodem studio persequetur.
2 Sed tamen in vita occupata atque, ut Neoptolemi
tum erat, militari pauca ipsa multum saepe prosunt
et ferunt fructus, si non tantos, quanti ex universa
philosophia percipi possunt, tamen eos, quibus aliqua
ex parte interdum aut cupiditate aut aegritudine aut
metu liberemur; velut ex ea disputatione, quae mihi
nuper habita est in Tusculano, magna videbatur
mortis effecta contemptio, quae non minimum valet

---

[1] In a tragedy by Ennius, cf. App. II.: for Neoptolemus
cf. I. § 85.

[2] In Plato's *Gorgias*, 484 C, Callicles says, φιλοσοφία γάρ τοί
ἐστι χαρίεν, ἄν τις αὐτοῦ μετρίως ἅψηται ἐν τῇ ἡλικίᾳ· ἐὰν δὲ
περαιτέρω τοῦ δέοντος ἐνδιατρίψῃ, διαφθορὰ τῶν ἀνθρώπων. Cf.
also Tacitus, *Agric.* IV, where he says that Agricola

M. TULLIUS CICERO'S TUSCULAN
DISPUTATIONS

BOOK II

I. Neoptolemus in Ennius [1] says that he must play the philosopher, but only a little way, for of doing so entirely he did not approve:[2] I on the other hand, Brutus, think that for my part I " must " play the philosopher; for what can I busy myself with better, above all at a time when I have nothing to busy myself with? But not " a little way " as Neoptolemus said, for it is difficult to have a little knowledge in philosophy without having either a great deal or all that there is: for neither can a little be selected except from much nor, when a man has learnt a little, will he not also go on with the same eagerness to master what remains. All the same in a busy life and the life of a soldier, as Neoptolemus then was, only a little is often of great benefit and bears fruit—if not the heavy crop which can be gathered from the whole field of philosophy, yet fruit that can at times free us in a measure from lust or distress or fear; as for instance the discussion I lately held at my house at Tusculum seemed to result in a noble scorn of death, and this is of no

prima in juventa studium philosophiae acrius, ultra quam concessum Romano ac senatori, hausisse, ni prudentia matris incensum ac flagrantem animum coercuisset.

ad animum metu liberandum: nam qui id, quod
vitari non potest, metuit, is vivere animo quieto
nullo modo potest; sed qui, non modo quia necesse
est mori, verum etiam quia nihil habet mors quod
sit horrendum, mortem non timet, magnum is sibi
3 praesidium ad beatam vitam comparavit. Quamquam non sumus ignari multos studiose contra esse
dicturos, quod vitare nullo modo potuimus, nisi nihil
omnino scriberemus. Etenim si orationes, quas nos
multitudinis iudicio probari volebamus—popularis
est enim illa facultas et effectus eloquentiae est
audientium approbatio—, sed si reperiebantur non
nulli qui nihil laudarent nisi quod se imitari posse
confiderent, quemque sperandi sibi, eundem bene
dicendi finem proponerent, et, cum obruerentur
copia sententiarum atque verborum, ieiunitatem et
famem se malle quam ubertatem et copiam dicerent,
unde erat exortum genus Atticorum iis ipsis, qui id
sequi se profitebantur, ignotum, qui iam conticuerunt
paene ab ipso foro irrisi: quid futurum putamus,
cum adiutore populo, quo utebamur antea, nunc
4 minime nos uti posse videamus? Est enim philosophia paucis contenta iudicibus, multitudinem con-
sulto ipsa fugiens eique ipsi et suspecta et invisa, ut

---

[1] In the *Brutus* Cicero says that the consummate orator
must make the people think he is one.

[2] The ancients recognized three styles of oratory, Asiatic,
Attic and Rhodian. The Asiatic was rich and redundant;
the Attic simple and concise; the Rhodian held a middle
position between the two others. The Roman imitators of
the Attic style, according to Cicero, in avoiding ornament
and redundancy succeeded only in being dry and poverty-
stricken.

[3] Cicero says that the speeches he delivered in former days

slight value in setting the soul free from fear, for the man who is afraid of the inevitable can by no manner of means live with a soul at peace; but the man who is without fear of death, not simply because it is unavoidable but also because it has no terrors for him, has secured a valuable aid towards rendering life happy. And yet I am well assured that many will argue eagerly against my view, but this it was by no means in my power to avoid except by writing nothing at all. For as regards the speeches in which I sought for the approval of the multitude (for oratory is a popular art and the true aim of eloquence is to win the approval of the hearers [1])—still if a certain number of critics were found to refuse praise to anything unless they thought they could successfully imitate it, and to regard the limits of their own individual powers as the highest flight of eloquence; and, when they found themselves overwhelmed with a flood of thoughts and words, to claim that they preferred their own poverty-stricken barrenness to rich luxuriance (this being the origin of the "Attic style," [2] about which the very gentlemen who professed to copy it knew nothing and have now become dumb and almost jeered out of the courts)—what prospect for us do we think there is when it is clear we have at present no opportunity at all of relying upon the populace on whose support we previously relied? [3] For philosophy is content with few judges, and of set purpose on her side avoids the multitude and is in her turn an object of suspicion and dislike to them, with the result that if anyone should be disposed to

were criticised by would-be Atticists for being turgid, but they were popular. What is to happen to him in his new venture, when he can no longer count on popular support?

vel si quis universam velit vituperare, secundo id
populo facere possit, vel si in eam, quam nos maxime
sequimur, conetur invadere, magna habere possit
auxilia a reliquorum philosophorum disciplinis. II.
Nos autem universae philosophiae vituperatoribus re-
spondimus in Hortensio, pro Academia autem quae
dicenda essent satis accurate in Academicis quattuor
libris explicata arbitramur; sed tamen tantum abest
ut scribi contra nos nolimus, ut id etiam maxime
optemus; in ipsa enim Graecia philosophia tanto in
honore numquam fuisset, nisi doctissimorum conten-
tionibus dissensionibusque viguisset.

5   Quam ob rem hortor omnes, qui facere id possunt,
ut huius quoque generis laudem iam languenti
Graeciae eripiant et transferant in hanc urbem,
sicut reliquas omnes, quae quidem erant expetendae,
studio atque industria sua maiores nostri transtulerunt. Atque oratorum quidem laus ita ducta ab
humili venit ad summum, ut iam, quod natura fert
in omnibus fere rebus, senescat brevique tempore
ad nihilum ventura videatur:[1] philosophia nascatur
Latinis quidem litteris ex his temporibus eamque
nos adiuvemus, nosque ipsos redargui refellique
patiamur. Quod ii ferunt animo iniquo, qui certis
quibusdam destinatisque sententiis quasi addicti et
consecrati sunt eaque necessitate constricti, ut, etiam
quae non probare soleant, ea cogantur constantiae
causa defendere: nos, qui sequimur probabilia nec

---

[1] Most editors have a comma at *videatur* and make *nascatur*
depend upon *ut*, which gives a very awkward sequence of
thought, though a possible one.

---

[1] Like insolvent debtors passing into the power of their
creditors.

[2] Cf. I. § 17.

revile all philosophy he could count on popular support, or if he should try to attack the school of which we are in the main adherents, he would have powerful assistance from the other schools of philosophy. II. In the *Hortensius*, however, we have replied to the revilers of philosophy as a whole, whilst in the four books of the *Academics* we have set out, as we think with sufficient precision, all that could be urged on behalf of the Academy : all the same we are so far from deprecating criticism that we should even welcome it heartily, for even in its best days Greek philosophy would never have been held in such high honour, if the rivalries and disagreements of its chief exponents had not maintained its activity.

For this reason I encourage all, who have the capacity, to wrest from the now failing grasp of Greece the renown won from this field of study and transfer it to this city, just as our ancestors by their indefatigable zeal transferred here all the other really desirable avenues to renown. And in oratory indeed our fame, from humble beginnings, has reached its zenith, with the result that now, as is the law of nature in almost everything, it is beginning its decline and seems destined in a short while to come to nothing : in consequence of these evil days let it be now the birthday of philosophy in Latin literature and let us lend it our support and submit to contradiction and refutation. That indeed is endured impatiently by those who are in a way bound over [1] and dedicated to certain definite fixed opinions and compulsorily tied hand and foot to the obligation of even supporting for the sake of consistency views which they do not usually approve : we, however, whose guide is probability [2] and who are unable to

ultra quam ad id, quod veri simile occurrit, progredi possumus, et refellere sine pertinacia et refelli sine iracundia parati sumus.

6 Quod si haec studia traducta erunt ad nostros, ne bibliothecis quidem Graecis egebimus, in quibus multitudo infinita librorum propter eorum est multitudinem, qui scripserunt; eadem enim dicuntur a multis, ex quo libris omnia referserunt: quod accidet etiam nostris, si ad haec studia plures confluxerint. Sed eos, si possumus, excitemus, qui liberaliter eruditi adhibita etiam disserendi elegantia ratione et via

7 philosophantur. III. Est enim quoddam genus eorum, qui se philosophos appellari volunt, quorum dicuntur esse Latini sane multi libri, quos non contemno equidem, quippe quos numquam legerim; sed quia profitentur ipsi illi, qui eos scribunt, se neque distincte neque distribute neque eleganter neque ornate scribere, lectionem sine ulla delectatione negligo. Quid enim dicant et quid sentiant ii, qui sunt ab ea disciplina, nemo ne mediocriter quidem doctus ignorat. Quam ob rem, quoniam quem ad modum dicant ipsi non laborant, cur legendi sint nisi ipsi inter se, qui idem sentiunt, non intelligo.

8 Nam, ut Platonem reliquosque Socraticos et deinceps eos, qui ab his profecti sunt, legunt omnes, etiam qui illa aut non approbant aut non studiosissime consectantur, Epicurum autem et Metrodorum non fere praeter suos quisquam in manus sumit, sic hos

---

[1] Cf. I. § 6. He refers to Amafinius and other writers who popularized Epicureanism.

[2] Metrodorus was a pupil of Epicurus and called by Cicero in *De Finibus* "*paene alter Epicurus.*" He is not the same as the Metrodorus of Scepsis in I. § 59.

advance further than the point at which the likelihood of truth has presented itself, are prepared both to refute without obstinacy and be refuted without anger.

But once these studies are transferred to ourselves, we shall have no need even of Greek libraries, in which there is an endless number of books due to the crowd of writers; for the same things are said by many since the day they crammed the world with books: and things will be the same here too if a larger stream of writers sets toward these studies. But let us, if we can, stimulate those who, possessing a liberal education and the power of arguing with precision, can deal orderly and methodically with philosophical questions. III. For there is a class of men, who wish to be called philosophers and are said to be responsible for quite a number of books in Latin,[1] which I do not for my part despise, for I have never read them; but as on their own testimony the writers claim to be indifferent to definition, arrangement, precision and style I forbear to read what affords no pleasure. What followers of this school say and what they think is not unknown to anyone of even moderate learning. Inasmuch therefore as by their own showing they do not trouble how they express themselves, I do not see why they should be read except in the circle of those who hold the same views and read their books to one another. For everyone, even those who do not accept their teaching or are not enthusiastic disciples, reads Plato and the rest of the Socratic school and after them their followers, whilst scarcely anyone beyond their own adherents takes up the works of Epicurus and Metrodorus;[2] similarly these Latin writers are only read

Latinos ii soli legunt, qui illa recte dici putant.
Nobis autem videtur, quidquid litteris mandetur, id
commendari omnium eruditorum lectioni decere;
nec, si id ipsi minus consequi possumus, idcirco
9 minus id ita faciendum esse sentimus. Itaque mihi
semper Peripateticorum Academiaeque consuetudo
de omnibus rebus in contrarias partes disserendi non
ob eam causam solum placuit, quod aliter non posset
quid in quaque re veri simile esset inveniri, sed etiam
quod esset ea maxima dicendi exercitatio; qua princeps usus est Aristoteles, deinde eum qui secuti sunt.
Nostra autem memoria Philo, quem nos frequenter
audivimus, instituit alio tempore rhetorum praecepta
tradere, alio philosophorum: ad quam nos consuetudinem a familiaribus nostris adducti, in Tusculano,
quod datum est temporis nobis, in eo consumpsimus.
Itaque cum ante meridiem dictioni operam dedis-
semus, sicut pridie feceramus, post meridiem in
Academiam descendimus, in qua disputationem habi-
tam non quasi narrantes exponimus, sed eisdem fere
verbis, ut actum disputatumque est.

10 IV. Est igitur ambulantibus ad hunc modum
sermo ille nobis institutus et a tali quodam ductus
exordio: A. Dici non potest quam sim hesterna
disputatione tua delectatus vel potius adiutus; etsi

---

[1] Philo of Larissa, who brought the teaching of the Academic school nearer to that of the Stoics. He came to Rome in 88 B.C., when Cicero made his acquaintance and listened to him eagerly.

[2] Cicero had two gymnasia at his Tusculan villa, an upper one called *Lyceum* and a lower one called *Academia*. Caesar's day on his visit to Cicero, described in *Ad Att.* XIII. 52, was:

by those who approve their tenets. Our opinion on the other hand is that everything committed to writing should approve itself to the taste of all educated readers, and if we ourselves are unable quite to succeed in this, we do not for that reason think we should abate our efforts to do so. Accordingly these considerations always led me to prefer the rule of the Peripatetics and the Academy of discussing both sides of every question, not only for the reason that in no other way did I think it possible for the probable truth to be discovered in each particular problem, but also because I found it gave the best practice in oratory. Aristotle first employed this method and later those who followed him. Philo,[1] however, as we remember, for we often heard him lecture, made a practice of teaching the rules of the rhetoricians at one time, and those of the philosophers at another. I was induced by our friends to follow this practice, and in my house at Tusculum I thus employed the time at our disposal. Accordingly, after spending the morning in rhetorical exercises, we went in the afternoon, as on the day before, down to the Academy,[2] and there a discussion took place which I do not present in narrative form, but as nearly as I can in the exact words of our actual discussion.

IV. As then we walked about the gymnasium our debate was started, originating in a beginning of pretty much the following character. A. It is impossible for me to express the delight or rather the feeling of comfort I derived from yesterday's dis-

business till midday, then a walk on the shore (but exercise might be taken in the villa), then the bath, then dinner about half-past one, and after that conversation.

enim mihi sum conscius numquam me nimis vitae
cupidum fuisse, tamen interdum obiiciebatur animo
metus quidam et dolor cogitanti fore aliquando finem
huius lucis et amissionem omnium vitae commodorum.
Hoc genere molestiae sic, mihi crede, sum liberatus,
11 ut nihil minus curandum putem. M. Minime mirum
id quidem ; nam efficit hoc philosophia : medetur
animis, inanes sollicitudines detrahit, cupiditatibus
liberat, pellit timores. Sed haec eius vis non idem
potest apud omnes : tum valet multum, cum est ido-
neam complexa naturam. "Fortes" enim non modo
"fortuna adiuvat," ut est in vetere proverbio, sed
multo magis ratio, quae quibusdam quasi praeceptis
confirmat vim fortitudinis. Te natura excelsum
quendam videlicet et altum et humana despicientem
genuit; itaque facile in animo forti contra mortem
habita insedit oratio. Sed haec eadem num censes
apud eos ipsos valere nisi admodum paucos, a quibus
inventa, disputata, conscripta sunt ? Quotus enim
quisque philosophorum invenitur qui sit ita moratus,
ita animo ac vita constitutus, ut ratio postulat ? qui
disciplinam suam non ostentationem scientiae, sed
legem vitae putet ? qui obtemperet ipse sibi et
12 decretis suis pareat ? Videre licet alios tanta levitate
et iactatione, ut iis fuerit non didicisse melius, alios

cussion, for though I am not aware of having ever been over-anxious to live, nevertheless a shadow of fear and pain occasionally crossed my mind at the thought that one day there would be an end of this light of day and a loss of all the comforts of life. From this kind of distress, believe me, I have been relieved so completely that I think that nothing should be less a source of anxiety. M. There is nothing astonishing in that, for it shows the effect of philosophy: it is a physician of souls, takes away the load of empty troubles, sets us free from desires and banishes fears. But its influence cannot be the same for all: its effect is great when it has secured a hold upon a character suited to it. For it is not only true that "fortune helps the brave," as the old proverb says, but philosophic thought does so in a far higher degree, and by its lessons strengthens as it were the quality of bravery. Nature clearly gave you at your birth a certain elevated and lofty spirit that looks down on things earthly, and so a speech delivered against death readily found a resting place in a brave soul. But can you think that these same arguments have real influence, apart from quite a few exceptions, with the very men by whom these arguments were discovered, reasoned out and committed to writing? How few philosophers are found to be so constituted and to have principles and a rule of life so firmly settled as reason requires! how few there are to think that the tenets of their school are not a display of knowledge but a law of life! to control themselves of their own will and obey their own dogmas! Some of them we may see guilty of such frivolity and vanity that it would have been far better for them never to have been students; others

pecuniae cupidos, gloriae non nullos, multos libidinum servos, ut cum eorum vita mirabiliter pugnet
oratio; quod quidem mihi videtur esse turpissimum.
Ut enim si grammaticum se professus quispiam
barbare loquatur aut si absurde canat is, qui se
haberi velit musicum, hoc turpior sit, quod in eo
ipso peccet, cuius profiteatur scientiam, sic philosophus in vitae ratione peccans hoc turpior est, quod
in officio, cuius magister esse vult, labitur artemque
vitae professus delinquit in vita. V. A. Nonne
verendum est igitur, si est ita, ut dicis, ne philosophiam falsa gloria exornes? Quod est enim maius
argumentum nihil eam prodesse quam quosdam
13 perfectos philosophos turpiter vivere? M. Nullum
vero id quidem argumentum est: nam ut agri non
omnes frugiferi sunt, qui coluntur, falsumque illud
Accii:

> Probae etsi in segetem sunt deteriorem datae
> Fruges, tamen ipsae suapte natura enitent,

sic animi non omnes culti fructum ferunt. Atque,
ut in eodem simili verser, ut ager quamvis fertilis
sine cultura fructuosus esse non potest, sic sine
doctrina animus. Ita est utraque res sine altera
debilis. Cultura autem animi philosophia est: haec
extrahit vitia radicitus et praeparat animos ad satus
accipiendos eaque mandat iis et, ut ita dicam, serit,

---

[1] Cf. Juvenal, *Sat.* II. 3, who speaks of hypocritical Stoics,
Qui Curios simulant et Bacchanalia vivunt.

[2] I. § 105, cf. App. II.

we see greedy of gain, not a few of fame, many slaves to lust, so that there is a strange contradiction between their public utterances and their life;[1] and this seems to me a black disgrace. For just as it is if a teacher claiming to be a grammarian were guilty of solecisms, or one who should wish to be regarded as a musician were to sing out of tune; the disgrace would be enhanced by the fact of his failure in the very subject of which he professed the knowledge; similarly the philosopher who fails to observe his rule of life is the more deeply disgraced, because he stumbles in the duty of which he aims at being the teacher and fails in the conduct of life though professing to give the rule of life. V. A. If it is as you say, have we not reason to fear that you are tricking out philosophy in borrowed plumes? What stronger proof of its uselessness can there be than to find instances of completely trained philosophers who lead disgraceful lives? M. That is really no proof, for not all cultivated fields are productive, and the dictum of Accius[2] is false:

Though placed in poorer soil good seed can yet
Of its own nature bear a shining crop,

and in the same way not all educated minds bear fruit. Moreover, to continue the same comparison, just as a field, however good the ground, cannot be productive without cultivation, so the soul cannot be productive without teaching. So true it is that the one without the other is ineffective. Now the cultivation of the soul is philosophy; this pulls out vices by the roots and makes souls fit for the reception of seed, and commits to the soul and, as we may say, sows in it seed of a kind to bear the richest fruit

quae adulta fructus uberrimos ferant. Agamus igitur,
ut coepimus. Dic, si vis, de quo disputari velis.

14 A. Dolorem existimo maximum malorum omnium.
M. Etiamne maius quam dedecus? A. Non audeo
id quidem dicere et me pudet tam cito de sententia
esse deiectum. M. Magis esset pudendum, si in
sententia permaneres. Quid enim minus est dignum
quam tibi peius quidquam videri dedecore, flagitio,
turpitudine, quae ut effugias, quis est non modo non
recusandus, sed non ultro appetendus, subeundus,
excipiendus dolor? A. Ita prorsus existimo. Qua
re ne sit sane summum malum dolor, malum certe
est. M. Videsne igitur quantum breviter admonitus
15 de doloris terrore deieceris? A. Video plane, sed
plus desidero. M. Experiar equidem, sed magna
res est, animoque mihi opus est non repugnante.
A. Habebis id quidem. Ut enim heri feci, sic nunc
rationem quo ea me cumque ducet sequar.

VI. M. Primum igitur de imbecillitate multorum
et de variis disciplinis philosophorum loquar, quorum
princeps et auctoritate et antiquitate, Socraticus
Aristippus, non dubitavit summum malum dolorem
dicere; deinde ad hanc enervatam muliebremque
sententiam satis docilem se Epicurus praebuit; hunc
post Rhodius Hieronymus vacare dolore summum
bonum dixit: tantum in dolore duxit mali. Ceteri
praeter Zenonem, Aristonem, Pyrrhonem idem fere

---

[1] Aristippus, pupil of Socrates and founder of the Cyrenaic
school, to whom the pleasure of the moment was the highest
good.

[2] Hieronymus belonged to the Peripatetic school and lived
about 300 B.C.

[3] For Zeno cf. I. § 19. Aristo was a pupil of Zeno; Pyrrho
was a painter and accompanied Alexander the Great in his
expeditions. He was founder of the Sceptical School.

when fully grown. Let us go on then as we have begun; tell me if you will, what subject you wish to have discussed.

A. I consider pain the greatest of all evils. M. Greater even than disgrace? A. I do not venture to go so far as that and I am ashamed of having been dislodged so speedily from my position. M. You should have been still more ashamed had you clung to it. For what is more unworthy than for you to regard anything as worse than disgrace, crime and baseness? And to escape these, what pain should be, I do not say rejected, but should not rather be voluntarily invited, endured and welcomed? A. I am entirely of that opinion. So then, granted that pain be not indeed the chief evil, an evil it assuredly is. M. Do you see how much of the dread of pain you have got rid of, thanks to my brief reminder? A. I see clearly, but I want fuller explanation. M. Well, I shall try; but it is a serious undertaking and I shall need a soul that does not put up any resistance. A. That you can count upon, for as I did yesterday so to-day I shall follow the argument whithersoever it leads me.

VI. M. In the first place then I shall deal with the feebleness of many philosophers belonging to different schools of thought. First among them both in influence and date is Aristippus the Socratic,[1] who had no hesitation in pronouncing pain to be the chief evil; next Epicurus lent himself quite obediently to the support of this backboneless, effeminate view; after him Hieronymus[2] of Rhodes said that the highest good was to be free of pain: so much evil he thought lay in pain. The rest, with the exception of Zeno,[3] Aristo and Pyrrho, held

quod modo tu : malum illud quidem, sed alia peiora.
16 Ergo id, quod natura ipsa et quaedam generosa virtus
statim respuit, ne scilicet dolorem summum malum
diceres oppositoque dedecore sententia depellerere,
in eo magistra vitae philosophia tot saecula permanet.
Quod huic officium, quae laus, quod decus erit tanti
quod adipisci cum dolore corporis velit, qui dolorem
summum malum sibi esse persuaserit? Quam porro
quis ignominiam, quam turpitudinem non pertulerit,
ut effugiat dolorem, si id summum malum esse de-
creverit? Quis autem non miser non modo tunc,
cum premetur summis doloribus, si in iis est summum malum, sed etiam cum sciet id sibi posse
evenire? et quis est cui non possit? Ita fit ut
17 omnino nemo esse possit beatus. Metrodorus quidem perfecte eum beatum putat, cui corpus bene
constitutum sit et exploratum ita semper fore : quis
autem est iste cui id exploratum possit esse?

VII. Epicurus vero ea dicit, ut mihi quidem risus
captare videatur. Adfirmat enim quodam loco, si
uratur sapiens, si crucietur, exspectas fortasse dum
dicat, "patietur, perferet, non succumbet" : magna
mehercule laus et eo ipso, per quem iuravi, Hercule
digna, sed Epicuro, homini aspero et duro, non est

---

[1] Cicero has already excepted Zeno, Aristo and Pyrrho, so
that he cannot mean all philosophers here, but only that all
along some philosophers held that pain was the chief evil.
[2] Cf. § 8.

pretty nearly the view you stated just now, namely that pain was admittedly an evil but that there were other worse evils. We see then that, though natural instinct and a sense of native worth at once revolted against your saying that pain is the highest evil, and forced you, when faced with disgrace, to abandon your opinion, yet philosophy, the teacher of life, has maintained that view for all these centuries.[1] What duty, what reputation, what glory will be of such value that the man who has once convinced himself that pain is the highest evil will be willing to seek to secure them at the cost of bodily pain? And further what shame, what degradation will a man not submit to in order to avoid pain, if he has once decided it to be the highest evil? Who moreover will not feel wretched, not merely at the moment that he is overtaken by attacks of extreme pain, if they involve the highest evil, but also when he is conscious that there is the prospect of pain? And who is there beyond its reach? The result is that absolutely no one can be happy. Metrodorus[2] no doubt thinks that man completely happy who has a good constitution and an assurance that he will always enjoy it: but who is there who can have such assurance?

VII. As for Epicurus, however, he speaks in a way that makes him seem to my mind to be provoking laughter. For in one passage he asserts that if the wise man be burnt, if he be tortured—you are waiting perhaps for him to say, "he will submit, will endure, will not yield": high praise by Hercules and worthy of the great god Hercules whose name I invoked; but this is not enough for Epicurus, that hard stern spirit; if the wise man finds himself

hoc satis: in Phalaridis tauro si erit, dicet: " Quam
suave est, quam hoc non curo!" Suave etiam ? an
parum est, si non amarum ? At id quidem illi ipsi,
qui dolorem malum esse negant, non solent dicere,
cuiquam suave esse cruciari: asperum, difficile, odiosum, contra naturam dicunt, nec tamen malum: hic,
qui solum hoc malum dicit et malorum omnium
extremum, sapientem censet id suave dicturum.

18 Ego a te non postulo, ut dolorem eisdem verbis
adficias, quibus Epicurus,[1] homo, ut scis, voluptarius.
Ille dixerit sane idem in Phalaridis tauro, quod, si
esset in lectulo: ego tantam vim non tribuo sapientiae contra dolorem. Si fortis [2] in perferendo, officio
satis est; ut laetetur etiam, non postulo; tristis
enim res est sine dubio, aspera, amara, inimica
naturae, ad patiendum tolerandumque difficilis.

19 Aspice Philoctetam, cui concedendum est gementi;
ipsum enim Herculem viderat in Oeta magnitudine
dolorum eiulantem. Nihil igitur hunc virum sagittae,
quas ab Hercule acceperat, tum consolantur, cum

> *E viperino morsu venae viscerum*
> *Veneno imbutae taetros cruciatus cient.*

Itaque exclamat auxilium expetens, mori cupiens:

[1] The MSS. have *voluptatem* after *Epicurus*, which is struck
out on Bentley's authority.
[2] For *si forte* of MSS.

---

[1] Phalaris was a Sicilian tyrant of the sixth century B.C.
who burnt his victims in a brazen bull. What Epicurus said
was that the wise man was happy even on the rack, κἂν
στρεβλωθῇ.
[2] The Stoics.
[3] Philoctetes, son of Poeas, alone consented to light the
funeral pyre for Hercules, and received his bow and arrows
as a reward. In the Trojan expedition Philoctetes was

inside Phalaris' bull,[1] he will say: "How sweet;
how indifferent I am to this!" Actually sweet?
Or is "not bitter" a bit inadequate? And yet those
very philosophers[2] who deny that pain is an evil
do not generally go so far as to say that it is sweet
to be tortured; they say that it is unpleasing, difficult, hateful, contrary to nature, and yet that it is
not an evil: Epicurus, who says that pain is the only
evil and the worst of all evils, thinks that the wise
man will pronounce it sweet. For my part I do not
require you to describe pain in the same words as
Epicurus, that devotee, as you know, of pleasure.
Let him, if he likes, say the same inside the bull of
Phalaris as he would have said, had he been in his
own bed: I do not attribute to wisdom such wonderful power against pain. It is enough for duty if the
wise man is brave in endurance; I do not require
him to rejoice; for pain is a melancholy condition
beyond doubt, unpleasing, distasteful, repugnant to
nature, difficult to submit to and bear. Look at
Philoctetes whose moans we must pardon, for he
had seen the mighty Hercules on Oeta shrieking
aloud in the extremity of his pains.[3] No comfort,
therefore, did the arrows he had received from
Hercules give this hero when

From vipers' bite the veins of all his flesh,
Tainted with venom, cruel tortures stir.

And thus he cries out in the longing for aid and
desire of death:

wounded in the foot by one of Hercules' poisoned arrows.
His outcries forced the Greeks to leave him on the island of
Lemnos.

MARCUS TULLIUS CICERO

Heu ! quas salsis fluctibus mandet
Me ex sublimo vertice saxi ?
Iam iam absumor : conficit animam
 Vis volneris, ulceris aestus.

Difficile dictu videtur eum non in malo esse et
magno quidem, qui ita clamare cogatur.
20 VIII. Sed videamus Herculem ipsum, qui tum dolore frangebatur, cum immortalitatem ipsa morte
quaerebat : quas hic voces apud Sophoclem in
Trachiniis edit ! cui cum Deianira sanguine Centauri
tinctam tunicam induisset inhaesissetque ea visceribus, ait ille :

O multa dictu gravia, perpessu aspera,
Quae corpore exanclata atque animo pertuli !
Nec mihi Iunonis terror implacabilis
Nec tantum invexit tristis Eurystheus mali,
Quantum una vaecors Oenei partu edita.
Haec me irretivit veste furiali inscium,
Quae lateri inhaerens morsu lacerat viscera
Urguensque graviter pulmonum hauait spiritus :
Iam decolorem sanguinem omnem exsorbuit.
Sic corpus clade horribili absumptum extabuit :
Ipse illigatus peste interemor textili.
Hos non hostilis dextra, non Terra edita
Moles Gigantum, non biformato impetu
Centaurus ictus corpori inflixit meo,

---

[1] These and the preceding verses are from the *Philocteta*
of Accius, cf. App. II.
[2] Cicero's rendering of Soph. *Trach.* 1046 foll. ; see
Appendix. Hercules had killed Nessus the Centaur for
insulting his wife Deianira, shooting him with one of the
arrows poisoned in the blood of the Hydra. The Centaur

Ah! who to the salt sea-waves can consign
Me from the summit of the cliff on high?
Now, now pierces the pain and the killing
    Might of the wound and the ulcer's fire.[1]

It seems hard to say that he is not involved in evil,
and that serious evil, when compelled to cry out in
this way.

VIII. But let us look at Hercules himself who
broke down under stress of pain at the moment
when death itself was opening the gate of immortality. What cries he utters in the *Trachiniae* of
Sophocles! When Deianira had got the shirt,
steeped in the Centaur's blood, put upon him and it
had stuck to his flesh, he says:[2]

O cruel to tell of, harsh to be endured,
Body and soul have drained the cup of woe!
Not Juno's dreadful wrath implacable,
Not dark Eurystheus[3] brought such evil on me
As Oeneus' frantic daughter, she alone.
She netted me unwitting in this robe
Of hell that clinging rends and gnaws my flesh,
And suffocating drains my panting lungs:
Now has it sucked out all my blood discoloured.
My strength, by dread disaster spent, is gone;
And caught in web of ruin am I slain.
Not hand of foeman nor Earth's massive brood
Of Giants,[4] not onset of twin-natured form
Of Centaur struck these blows upon my body,

persuaded Deianira to collect his poisoned blood for a love
charm. Subsequently when jealous of Iole she steeped a
shirt in the blood and sent it to Hercules.

[3] Who imposed the twelve labours on Hercules.

[4] In the battle of gods and giants on the Phlegraean plain.

Non Graia vis, non barbara ulla immanitas,
Non saeva terris gens relegata ultimis,
Quas peragrans undique omnem ecferitatem expuli :
Sed feminae vir, feminea interemor manu.
IX. *O nate, vere hoc nomen usurpa patri,*
Neve [1] *occidentem matris superet caritas.*
Huc adripe ad me manibus abstractam piis.
Iam cernam mene an illam potiorem putes.
21 *Perge, aude, nate, illacrima patris pestibus,*
Miserere ! Gentes nostras flebunt miserias.
Heu ! virginalem me ore ploratum edere,
Quem vidit nemo ulli ingemescentem malo !
Ecfeminata virtus adflicta occidit.
Accede, nate, adsiste, miserandum aspice
Eviscerati corpus laceratum patris !
Videte, cuncti, tuque, caelestum sator,
Iace, obsecro, in me vim coruscam fulminis,
Nunc, nunc dolorum anxiferi torquent vertices,
Nunc serpit ardor. O ante victrices manus,
22 *O pectora, o terga, o lacertorum tori !*
Vestrone pressu quondam Nemeaeus leo
Frendens efflavit graviter extremum halitum ?
Haec dextra Lernam, taetra mactata excetra,
Pacavit, haec bicorporem adflixit manum,
Erymanthiam haec vastificam abiecit beluam,
Haec e Tartarea tenebrica abstractum plaga
Tricipitem eduxit Hydra generatum Canem :
Haec interemit tortu multiplicabili
Draconem auriferam obtutu adservantem arborem :
Multa alia victrix nostra lustravit manus,
Nec quisquam e nostris spolia cepit laudibus.

Possumusne nos contemnere dolorem, cum ipsum
Herculem tam intoleranter dolere videamus?

[1] For *ne me* of the MSS., Wolf.

Not might of Greeks, no barbarous savagery,
Not cruel race banished to earth's last bounds
Through which I wandered cleansing all the land,
But me, a man, a woman's hand hath slain.
IX. O son [1]—that name be true to for thy sire,
Nor o'er my death let mother-love prevail.
Wrest forth with filial hand and drag her here.
Now shall I see if her or me you choose.
Come, dare my son! weep for thy father's pangs!
Have pity! nations will these miseries weep.
Ah! think of my lips uttering girls' laments,
Whom none saw groaning over any ill!
Crushed is my manhood, fallen effeminate.
Approach, son, stand nigh, see how pitiful
Thy father's body mangled here and torn!
Look all, and thou begetter of heaven's gods
Hurl at me, I pray, the gleaming thunderbolt!
Now racks the torturing crisis of my pains,
Now creeps the fire.   O once victorious hands,
O breast, O back, O muscles of my arms,
Beneath your grip did once the Nemean lion
Gnashing his teeth gasp painfully his last?
Did this hand pacify Lerna when was slain
The loathly snake, this crush the band two-shaped,
From Erymanthus fling the wasting beast,
This drag from Tartarus' black tract of gloom
The dog three-headed that the Hydra bore,
This slay the dragon with its myriad coils
Whose watching kept the tree that carried gold?
Much else this conquering hand of ours hath faced,
And none hath booty made of our renown.

Can we scorn pain, seeing that we find the mighty
Hercules bear it so impatiently?

---

[1] Hyllus, son of Hercules and Deianira.

MARCUS TULLIUS CICERO

23 X. Veniat Aeschylus, non poëta solum, sed etiam
Pythagoreus; sic enim accepimus. Quo modo fert
apud eum Prometheus dolorem, quem excipit ob
furtum Lemnium!

> *Unde ignis cluet mortalibus clam*
> *Divisus : eum doctus Prometheus*
> *Clepsisse dolo poenasque Iovi*
>   *Fato expendisse supremo.*

Has igitur poenas pendens, adfixus ad Caucasum,
dicit haec :

> *Titanum suboles, socia nostri sanguinis,*
> *Generata Caelo, aspicite religatum asperis*
> *Vinctumque saxis, navem ut horrisono freto*
> *Noctem paventes timidi adnectunt navitae.*
> *Saturnius me sic infixit Iuppiter,*
> *Iovisque numen Mulciberi ascivit manus.*
> *Hos ille cuneos fabrica crudeli inserens,*
> *Perrupit artus : qua miser sollertia*
> *Transverberatus castrum hoc Furiarum incolo.*
24 *Iam tertio me quoque funesto die*
> *Tristi advolatu aduncis lacerans unguibus*
> *Iovis satelles pastu dilaniat fero.*
> *Tum iecore opimo farta et satiata alfatim,*
> *Clangorem fundit vastum et sublime avolans*
> *Pinnata cauda nostrum adulat sanguinem.*
> *Cum vero adesum inflatu renovatum est iecur,*
> *Tum rursus taetros avida se ad pastus refert.*
> *Sic hanc custodem maesti cruciatus alo,*
> *Quae me perenni vivum foedat miseria.*

---

[1] The Προμηθεὺς Λυόμενος, a lost play. Prometheus, one
of the Titans, stole fire from Vulcan's island of Lemnos and
gave it to men. For this he was chained to Caucasus and
torn by the eagle. The Titans were the Chorus in this play.

X. Let Aeschylus come forward, not merely a poet but a Pythagorean as well, for so we are told he was; how does Prometheus in Aeschylus' play [1] bear the pain which he suffers for the theft of Lemnos!

> Whence it is said that in secret to mortals
> Fire was allotted; it cunning Prometheus
> Stole by his craft and the punishment rendered
>   By fate overruling to Jove.

Paying this punishment therefore when nailed to the Caucasus he speaks as follows:

> Offspring of Titans, linked in blood to ours,
> Children of Heaven, see bound to rugged cliffs
> A prisoner, like a ship on roaring seas
> Which timid sailors anchor, fearing night.
> Jupiter, Saturn's son, thus nailed me here,
> Jove's power claimed the hands of Mulciber; [2]
> These wedges he by cruel art pinned in
> And burst my limbs, and by his skill, poor wretch,
> Pierced through, I make this Furies' fort my
>   home.
> More, each third fatal day Jove's minister,
> In gloomy flight swoops here with talons bent,
> And tears me piecemeal for a savage feast.
> Then crammed with liver fat and gorged in full
> Pours forth an echoing scream and soaring up
> With feathered tail he strokes away my blood.
> When liver gnawn is swollen and grown afresh,
> Greedy he then comes back to hideous meal.
> Thus nourish I this guard of my sad torture
> Which mars my living frame with endless woe.

[2] A surname of Vulcan.

Namque, ut videtis, vinclis constrictus Iovis,
Arcere nequeo diram volucrem a pectore.
25 *Sic me ipse viduus pestes excipio anxias,*
Amore mortis terminum anquirens mali.
Sed longe a leto numine aspellor Iovis.
Atque haec vetusta saeclis glomerata horridis
Luctifica clades nostro infixa est corpori,
E quo liquatae solis ardore excidunt
Guttae, quae saxa adsidue instillant Caucasi.

XI. Vix igitur posse videmur ita adfectum non
miserum dicere et, si hunc miserum, certe dolorem
malum.

26 A. Tu quidem adhuc meam causam agis. Sed
hoc mox videro. Interea, unde isti versus? Non
enim agnosco. M. Dicam hercle; etenim recte
requiris. Videsne abundare me otio? A. Quid
tum? M. Fuisti saepe, credo, cum Athenis esses,
in scholis philosophorum. A. Vero ac libenter
quidem. M. Animadvertebas igitur, etsi tum nemo
erat admodum copiosus, verum tamen versus ab his
admisceri orationi. A. Ac multos quidem a Dionysio
Stoico. M. Probe dicis. Sed is quasi dictata, nullo
delectu, nulla elegantia. Philo et proprium numerum
et lecta poëmata et loco adiungebat. Itaque post-
quam adamavi hanc quasi senilem declamationem,
studiose equidem utor nostris poëtis, sed, sicubi illi

---

[1] Cf. I. § 7.

For, as ye see, bound in the chains of Jove
I cannot keep that fell bird from my breast.
Reft of myself I wait the torturing hour
Looking for end of ill in hoping death.
But far from death Jove's power repulses me.
For age-long centuries massed in stern array
This dolorous doom is fastened on my body
From which distilled by heat of sun there rain
Drops which aye wet the rocks of Caucasus.

XI. We seem then scarcely able to say that one
so afflicted was not wretched, and if we pronounce
him wretched assuredly we admit that pain is an
evil.

A. You are in fact so far pleading my case: but
this I shall soon find out; meanwhile where do the
lines you quoted come from? For I do not recognize
them.   M. I shall tell you fast enough, for it is
right of you to ask.   You see, do you not, that I
have plenty of leisure?   A. Well, what follows?
M. You have, I imagine, as you stayed at Athens,
often attended philosophic lectures?   A. Certainly,
and I did so readily.   M. You noted then that
although at that date no one was very eloquent, yet
pieces of poetry were interwoven in their discourses.
A. Yes, Dionysius the Stoic frequently did so.   M.
You are right.   But he recited poetry as if he were
dictating a lesson, without choice or appropriateness:
our Philo used to give the verse its proper rhythm,
and the passages he introduced were well-chosen
and apposite.   And so since I have fallen in love
with this sort of school-exercise [1] of my old age, I
follow the example given and make diligent use of
our poets; but whenever they fail me I have often

defecerunt, verti etiam [1] multa de Graecis, ne quo ornamento in hoc genere disputationis careret
27 Latina oratio. Sed videsne poëtae quid mali adferant? Lamentantes inducunt fortissimos viros, molliunt animos nostros, ita sunt deinde dulces, ut non legantur modo, sed etiam ediscantur. Sic ad malam domesticam disciplinam vitamque umbratilem et delicatam cum accesserunt etiam poëtae, nervos omnes virtutis elidunt. Recte igitur a Platone eiiciuntur ex ea civitate, quam finxit ille cum optimos mores et optimum rei publicae statum exquireret. At vero nos, docti scilicet a Graecia, haec a pueritia et legimus et discimus, hanc eruditionem liberalem et doctrinam putamus.

28 XII. Sed quid poëtis irascimur? Virtutis magistri, philosophi, inventi sunt qui summum malum dolorem dicerent. At tu, adolescens, cum id tibi paullo ante dixisses videri, rogatus a me etiamne maius quam dedecus, verbo de sententia destitisti. Roga hoc idem Epicurum : maius dicet esse malum mediocrem dolorem quam maximum dedecus; in ipso enim dedecore mali nihil esse, nisi sequantur dolores. Quis igitur Epicurum sequitur dolor, cum hoc ipsum dicit, summum malum esse dolorem? quo dedecus maius a philosopho nullum exspecto. Qua re satis mihi dedisti, cum respondisti maius tibi

---

[1] For *verti enim* of the MSS.

---

[1] Plato, *Rep.* II. 398 A.
[2] *I.e.*, directly I had spoken, § 14.
[3] For Epicurus said disgrace was no evil unless it was followed by pain; yet if pain ever attends disgrace he ought to have suffered pain for saying what he did.

translated from the Greek poets as well, that Latin eloquence might not lack any embellishment in this kind of discussion. But do you note the harm which poets do? They represent brave men wailing, they enervate our souls, and besides this they do it with such charm that they are not merely read, but learnt by heart. Thus when the influence of the poets is combined with bad family discipline and a life passed in the shade of effeminate seclusion, the strength of manliness is completely sapped. Plato[1] was right then in turning them out of his imaginary State, when he was trying to find the highest morality and the best conditions for the community. We, however, taught no doubt by Greek example, both read and learn by heart from boyhood the words of the poets and regard such instruction and teaching as a free man's heritage.

XII. But why are we angry with the poets? Philosophers, the teachers of virtue, have been found ready to say that pain was the highest evil. But you, young man, after saying a little while ago that you shared this view, when asked by me whether you thought that it was a greater evil even than disgrace, at a word[2] abandoned your opinion. Put the same question to Epicurus: he will say that a moderate degree of pain is worse evil than the deepest disgrace, for no evil is involved in disgrace alone, unless it should be attended by painful circumstances. What pain then does Epicurus feel when he actually affirms that pain is the greatest evil?[3] And yet I cannot look to find any worse disgrace than such a sentiment in the mouth of a philosopher. You therefore gave me all I wanted when you replied that you regarded disgrace as a

videri malum dedecus quam dolorem. Hoc ipsum
enim si tenebis, intelliges quam sit obsistendum
dolori; nec tam quaerendum est dolor malumne sit
quam firmandus animus ad dolorem ferendum.

29 Concludunt ratiunculas Stoici cur non sit malum,
quasi de verbo, non de re laboretur.—Quid me
decipis, Zeno? Nam cum id, quod mihi horribile
videtur, tu omnino malum negas esse, capior et scire
cupio quo modo id, quod ego miserrimum existimem,
ne malum quidem sit.—" Nihil est," inquit, " malum,
nisi quod turpe atque vitiosum est."—Ad ineptias
redis. Illud enim, quod me angebat, non eximis.
Scio dolorem non esse nequitiam; desine id me
docere : hoc doce, doleam necne doleam nihil interesse.—" Numquam quidquam," inquit, "ad beate
quidem vivendum, quod est in una virtute positum,
sed est tamen reiiciendum." Cur? "Asperum est,
contra naturam, difficile perpessu, triste, durum."

30 XIII. Haec est copia verborum, quod omnes uno
verbo malum appellamus, id tot modis posse dicere.
Definis tu mihi, non tollis dolorem, cum dicis asperum,
contra naturam, vix quod ferri tolerarique possit, nec
mentiris, sed re succumbere non oportebat, verbis
gloriantem. Nihil bonum nisi quod honestum, nihil
malum nisi quod turpe : optare hoc quidem est, non

---

[1] Such as—what is evil hurts, what hurts makes worse, pain
does not make worse, therefore pain is not an evil—which
may secure verbal assent but does not convince. Cf. § 42.

[2] I. 19.

[3] It counts amongst *relectanea*, ἀποπροηγμένα, things to be
rejected, but not "evils."

greater evil than pain. For if you hold fast simply to this truth you will realize the resistance which must be offered to pain, and we must not endeavour so much to ask whether pain be an evil as to strengthen the soul for the endurance of pain. The Stoics construct foolish syllogisms[1] to prove pain no evil, just as if the difficulty in question were a verbal one and not one of matter of fact. Why deceive me, Zeno?[2] When you say that what is dreadful in my eyes is not an evil at all, I am attracted and long to know how it can be true that the condition I regard as utter wretchedness is not even evil. "There is nothing evil," says he, "except what is base and wicked." Now you are talking foolishly, for you do not take away the cause of my torment: I know that pain is not villainy; stop teaching me that; tell me that it makes no difference whether I am in pain or not in pain. "It never makes any difference," says he, "to the fact of leading a happy life, which is based on virtue alone; but, all the same, pain is to be shunned."[3] Why? "It is unpleasing, against nature, hard to endure, melancholy, cruel."

XIII. Here is a flood of words, all to get a number of different expressions for what we call in a single word "evil." You are giving me a definition of pain, you are not removing it, when you say that it is unpleasing, against nature, a thing that can scarcely be borne or endured, and you do not lie. But you should not have really yielded the point under a cloak of vaunting words. "Nothing good but what is honourable, nothing evil but what is base:" this is mere aspiration, not proof. The

177

docere. Illud et melius et verius, omnia, quae natura aspernetur, in malis esse: quae asciscat, in bonis. Hoc posito et verborum concertatione sublata tantum tamen excellet illud, quod recte amplexantur isti, quod honestum, quod rectum, quod decorum appellamus, quod idem interdum virtutis nomine amplectimur, ut omnia praeterea, quae bona corporis et fortunae putantur, perexigua et minuta videantur, nec malum ullum ne si in unum quidem locum collata omnia sint, cum turpitudinis malo comparandum.[1] Qua re si, ut initio concessisti, turpitudo peius est quam dolor, nihil est plane dolor; nam dum tibi turpe nec dignum viro videbitur gemere, eiulare, lamentari, frangi, debilitari dolore, dum honestas, dum dignitas, dum decus aderit, tuque in ea intuens te continebis, cedet profecto virtuti dolor et animi inductione languescet; aut enim nulla virtus est aut contemnendus omnis dolor. Prudentiamne vis esse, sine qua ne intelligi quidem ulla virtus potest? Quid ergo? ea patieturne te quidquam facere nihil proficientem et frustra[2] laborantem, an temperantia sinet te immoderate facere quidquam, an coli iustitia poterit ab homine propter vim doloris enuntiante commissa, prodente conscios, multa officia relinquente? Quid? fortitudini comi-

31

32

---

[1] For *comparanda* of MSS. which would go back to *omnia*: Halm.

[2] *frustra* is not in the MSS.: its insertion is due to Bentley.

---

[1] As Plato, Aristotle and their followers say.

[2] Whether pain is *malum* or *reiectaneum*.

[3] § 14.

[4] Cicero invokes the four cardinal virtues, *prudentia* or

better and truer statement is that all such things as nature rejects are counted evils, all such things as nature accepts count as goods.[1] Once determine this and do away with the verbal controversy,[2] and it will be found that what the Stoics are right in clinging to, what we call honourable, right, becoming, and sometimes comprehend under the name of virtue—this will still stand out in such pre-eminence that, in comparison, all things which are held to be goods of body and fortune will seem insignificant and paltry, whilst it will also be found that no evil, even if all evils were heaped together, is to be compared with the evil of disgrace. Therefore if, as you admitted at the outset, disgrace is worse than pain,[3] pain is clearly of no account; for whilst you shall hold it base and unworthy of a man to groan, shriek aloud, wail, break down and be unnerved; so long as honour, so long as nobility, so long as worth remain, and so long as you control yourself by keeping your eyes upon them, assuredly pain will lead to virtue and grow fainter by a deliberate effort of will; for either no virtue exists or all pain is to be despised. Do you believe in the existence of prudence, without which we cannot so much as realize the meaning of any virtue? What then? Will prudence[4] suffer you to do anything without thereby gaining any advantage and so only wasting effort uselessly; or can it be that temperance will allow you to act without self-restraint; can justice be practised by a man who discloses secrets, betrays accomplices, and turns his back on a multitude of obligations because of the violence of pain? How, I ask, will you answer the

practical wisdom (φρόνησις), *temperantia* (σωφροσύνη), *fortitudo* (ἀνδρεία), *iustitia* (δικαιοσύνη), cf. III. § 16.

tibusque eius, magnitudini animi, gravitati, patientiae, rerum humanarum despicientiae quo modo respondebis? Adflictusne et iacens et lamentabili voce deplorans audieris: "O virum fortem"? Te vero ita adfectum ne virum quidem quisquam dixerit. Amittenda igitur fortitudo est aut sepeliendus dolor.

XIV. Ecquid nescis igitur, si quid de Corinthiis tuis amiseris, posse habere te reliquam supellectilem salvam, virtutem autem si unam amiseris, etsi amitti non potest virtus, sed si unam confessus fueris te non habere, nullam esse te habiturum? 33 Num igitur fortem virum, num magno animo, num patientem, num gravem, num humana contemnentem potes dicere aut Philoctetam illum—? a te enim malo discedere; sed ille certe non fortis, qui iacet

> *in tecto humido,*
> *Quod eiulatu, questu, gemitu, fremitibus*
> *Resonando mutum flebiles voces refert.*

Non ego dolorem dolorem esse nego,—cur enim fortitudo desideraretur?—sed eum opprimi dico patientia, si modo est aliqua patientia: si nulla est, quid exornamus philosophiam aut quid eius nomine gloriosi sumus? Pungit dolor, vel fodiat sane: si

---

[1] Precious vases of metal. The Emperor Augustus was a collector and called *Corinthiarius*; cf. IV. § 32.

[2] As to whether virtue could be lost or not the Stoics differed. Cleanthes said it was ἀναπόβλητον, Chrysippus ἀποβλητόν.

[3] The Stoic teaching was that all the virtues were inseparable and the man who had one, had all: τὰς ἀρετὰς λέγουσιν οἱ Στωικοὶ ἀντακολουθεῖν ἀλλήλοις καὶ τὸν μίαν ἔχοντα πάσας ἔχειν (Diog. Laert. VII. 125). The wise man did all things in accordance with all the virtues.

claims of courage and its attendant train, greatness of soul, dignity, endurance and contempt of the vicissitudes of life? When you lie crushed and prostrate, bemoaning your fate in pitiful accents, will you hear the words "O how brave a man!" said over you? If you are reduced to such straits no one will so much as say you are a man. Courage must therefore go by the board or else a grave be found for pain.

XIV. Are you then unaware that, if you lose one of your Corinthian vases,[1] you can possess the rest of your goods in safety, but that if you lose a single virtue (and yet virtue cannot be lost)[2]—still if you once admit there is a virtue you do not possess,[3] do you not know that you will possess none at all? Can you then possibly regard as a brave man, as a man of high spirit, enduring, dignified, as a man who despised fortune, either the Philoctetes of the poem—?[4] for I prefer not to take you as my instance; but that was certainly not a brave character, who lies

> in dwelling dank,
> Where from dumb walls re-echo piteous sounds
> Of lamentation, plaints and groans and cries.[5]

I do not deny the reality of pain—why else should courage be wanted?—but I say that it is overcome by patience if only there is a measure of patience: if there is none, why do we glorify philosophy and why vaunt ourselves in its name? Pain stings—or if you like let it strike deep; if you are defenceless,

---

[4] Instead of saying, "Philoctetes or you," Cicero breaks off politely.   [5] cf. App. II.

nudus es, da iugulum : sin tectus Volcaniis armis, id
est, fortitudine, resiste. Haec enim te, nisi ita
34 facies, custos dignitatis relinquet et deseret. Cretum
quidem leges, quas sive Iuppiter sive Minos sanxit
de Iovis quidem sententia, ut poëtae ferunt, itemque
Lycurgi, laboribus erudiunt iuventutem, venando
currendo, esuriendo sitiendo, algendo aestuando.
Spartae vero pueri ad aram sic verberibus accipi-
untur,

Ut multus e visceribus sanguis exeat,

non numquam etiam, ut, cum ibi essem, audiebam,
ad necem ; quorum non modo nemo exclamavit umquam, sed ne ingemuit quidem. Quid ergo ? hoc
pueri possunt, viri non poterunt ? et mos valet, ratio
non valebit ?

35   XV. Interest aliquid inter laborem et dolorem.
Sunt finitima omnino, sed tamen differunt aliquid.
Labor est functio quaedam vel animi vel corporis
gravioris operis et muneris, dolor autem motus
asper in corpore, alienus a sensibus. Haec duo
Graeculi illi, quorum copiosior est lingua quam
nostra, uno nomine appellant ; itaque industrios
homines illi studiosos vel potius amantes doloris

---

[1] Cicero refers to the arms of Achilles made for him by
the god Hephaestus (Vulcan) at the request of his mother
Thetis, *Il.* 18. 478. Cf. also Virg. *Aen.* 8. 33, where Venus
appeals to Vulcan for arms for her son Aeneas.

[2] Because Minos, King of Crete, was Διὸς μεγάλου ὀαριστής
(*Od.* 19. 179), and the laws were communicated to him by
Jupiter (Zeus).

[3] Annually at the altar of Artemis Orthia. The contest
was called διαμαστίγωσις.

[4] Greek has two distinct terms, πόνος, *labor*, and ἄλγος,
dolor. A Greek might have pointed out to Cicero that *laborare* sometimes has a meaning like that of *dolere*, cf. § 61,

offer your throat; if you are cased in the armour of Vulcan,[1] that is fortitude, resist; for if you do not resist, this guardian of your honour will leave you desolate. The laws of Crete for instance—whether ratified by Jupiter or by Minos [2] according to Jupiter's decision as the poets relate—and also the laws of Lycurgus educate youth by hardships, hunting and running, hunger and thirst, exposure to heat and cold; moreover at the altar [3] Spartan boys are submitted to such a shower of stripes

> That from the flesh the blood comes forth in streams,

sometimes even, as I heard on the occasion of a visit, resulting in death; not one of them ever uttered a cry nor even so much as a groan. What then? Can boys do this and shall men prove unable? Has custom the power and shall reason not have the power?

XV. There is some difference between toil and pain; they are certainly closely related, but there is a difference: toil is a mental or physical execution of work or duty of more than usual severity; pain on the other hand is disagreeable movement in the body, repugnant to the feelings. To these two things our Greek friends, whose language is richer than ours, apply a single term,[4] and accordingly they call diligent men devotees of, or rather lovers of, pain;[5] we

---

quod vehementer eius artus laborarent. For similar remarks about Greek and Latin cf. III. § 7.

[5] φιλόπονος has the meaning of *industrius* or *laboriosus*. In contrast to Cicero Lucretius complains of *patrii sermonis egestas:* so do Seneca and Quintilian. The Greek Tiro, Cicero's amanuensis, freedman and friend, must have been rather aghast at these remarks of his.

appellant, nos commodius laboriosos. Aliud est enim
laborare, aliud dolere. O verborum inops interdum,
quibus abundare te semper putas, Graecia ! Aliud,
inquam, est dolere, aliud laborare. Cum varices
secabantur C. Mario, dolebat; cum aestu magno
ducebat agmen, laborabat. Est inter haec quaedam
tamen similitudo : consuetudo enim laborum per-
36 pessionem dolorum efficit faciliorem. Itaque illi,
qui Graeciae formam rerum publicarum dederunt,
corpora iuvenum firmari labore voluerunt; quod
Spartiatae etiam in feminas transtulerunt, quae
ceteris in urbibus mollissimo cultu "parietum umbris
occuluntur." Illi autem voluerunt nihil horum
simile esse

> *apud Lacaenas virgines,*
> *Quibus magis palaestra, Eurota, sol, pulvis, labor*
> *Militiae studio est quam fertilitas* [1] *barbara.*

Ergo his laboriosis exercitationibus et dolor inter-
currit non numquam : impelluntur, feriuntur, abiici-
untur, cadunt, et ipse labor quasi callum quoddam
obducit dolori.
37   XVI. Militia vero—nostram dico, non Spartiata-

---

[1] *fertilitas* probably refers to a number of children like the
50 children of foreigners, such as Priam, Danaus, Aegyptus.
Rhea the wife of Cronos "*indoluit fertilitate sua,*" Ovid,
Fast. iv. 202. Others understand it to mean opulence,

more aptly call them toilers, for toiling is one thing,
feeling pain another. O Greece, you are sometimes
deficient in the words of which you think you have
such a plentiful supply! toiling I say is one thing,
feeling pain another. When C. Marius had his vari-
cose veins cut out he felt pain;[1] when he led his
column under a blazing sun he was toiling. All the
same there is a sort of resemblance between the two
things, for the habit of toil renders the endurance of
pain easier. Accordingly those who gave to Greece
the specific form of her governments were in favour
of having young men's bodies strengthened by toil;
the citizens of Sparta applied the same rule to women,
who in all other cities lead a luxurious mode of life
and are "sequestered behind the shadow of walls."
The Spartans, however, wished for nothing of that
sort

in Spartan maids
Whose cares are wrestling, sun, Eurotas, dust and
        toil
Of drill[2] far more than barbarous fecundity.

It follows that pain sometimes intervenes in these
toilsome exercises : the victims are driven on, struck,
flung aside or fall, and toil of itself brings a certain
callousness to pain.

XVI. Military service in fact—I mean our own
and not that of the Spartans who march to a measure

---

[1] Cf. § 53. Marius was born of obscure parentage at
Arpinum, Cicero's native place.
[2] Spartan girls were exercised in running, wrestling, and
throwing the discus and javelin.

---

luxury, πλησμονὴ τῶν βαρβάρων. Emendations, e.g *futilitas*,
teneritas, have been proposed.

rum, quorum procedit agmen [1] ad tibiam nec adhibetur ulla sine anapaestis pedibus hortatio—, nostri
exercitus primum unde nomen habeant vides, deinde
qui labor quantus agminis, ferre plus dimidiati mensis
cibaria, ferre si quid ad usum velint, ferre vallum;
nam scutum, gladium, galeam in onere nostri milites
non plus numerant quam humeros, lacertos, manus;
arma enim membra militis esse dicunt; quae
quidem ita geruntur apte, ut, si usus ferat, abiectis
oneribus, expeditis armis ut membris pugnare possint. Quid? exercitatio legionum, quid? ille cursus,
concursus, clamor quanti laboris est! Ex hoc ille
animus in proeliis paratus ad vulnera. Adduc pari
animo inexercitatum militem, mulier videbitur.
38 Cur tantum interest inter novum et veterem exercitum quantum experti sumus? Aetas tironum
plerumque melior, sed ferre laborem, contemnere
vulnus consuetudo docet. Quin etiam videmus ex
acie efferri saepe saucios et quidem rudem illum et
inexercitatum quamvis levi ictu ploratus turpissimos
edere: at vero ille exercitatus et vetus ob eamque

---

[1] The MSS. have *quorum procedit ad modum ad tibiam.*
Iter may have fallen out after the *it* of *procedit* or *agmen* may
be concealed in *ad modum.*

---

[1] The Spartans marched slowly to the sound of the flute,
ἵνα ὁμαλῶς μετὰ ῥυθμοῦ βαίνοντες προσέλθοιεν, Thuc. V. 70.
Cf. Milton, *Par. Lost*, I. 550:

> Anon they move
> In perfect Phalanx to the Dorian mood
> Of Flutes and soft Recorders; such as rais'd
> To highth of noblest temper Hero's old.

accompanied by the flute,[1] and no word of encouragement is given except with the beat of anapaests [2]—as for our "army" (*exercitus*) you can see first what it gets its name from ;[3] then the toil, the great toil of the march ; the load of more than half a month's provisions, the load of any requisite needed, the load of the stake for intrenchment ; for shield, sword, helmet are reckoned a burden by our soldiers as little as their shoulders, arms and hands ; for weapons they say are the soldiers' limbs, and these they carry handy so that, should need arise, they fling aside their burdens and have their weapons as free for use as their limbs. Look at the training of the legions, the double, the attack, the battle-cry,[4] what an amount of toil it means ! Hence comes the courage in battle that makes them ready to face wounds. Bring up a force of untrained soldiers of equal courage : they will seem like women. Why is there such a difference between raw and veteran soldiers as we have lately had experience of ?[5] Recruits have usually the advantage in age, but it is habit which teaches men to endure toil and despise wounds. Nay, we see too wounded men frequently carried out of the line of battle, and the raw untrained soldier on the one hand uttering disgraceful lamentations however trifling his wound, whilst on the other hand the trained veteran, made more brave by the advantage of training, only wants the

---

[2] The marching metre ◡◡ – – | as in Tyrtaeus,

ἄγετ' ὦ Σπάρτας ἔνοπλοι κοῦροι, ποτὶ τὰν Ἄρεως κίνασιν.

[3] "Exercitando," according to Varro.

[4] Called *baritus* and given when the lines engaged.

[5] Cicero is thinking of Caesar's veterans and Pompey's untrained troops in 48 B.C.

rem fortior, medicum modo requirens a quo
obligetur :

> *O Patricoles, inquit, ad vos adveniens, auxilium et*
> *vestras manus*
> *Peto, prius quam oppeto malam pestem mandatam*
> *hostili manu,*
> *(Neque sanguis ullo potis est pacto profluens consistere,)*
> *Si qui sapientia magis vestra mors devitari potest.*
> *Namque Aesculapi liberorum saucii opplent porticus ;*
> *Non potest accedi.   P. Certe Eurypylus hic quidem*
> *est.   Hominem exercitum !* [1]

39 XVII. Ubi tantum luctus continuatur, vide quam
non flebiliter respondeat, rationem etiam adferat
cur aequo animo sibi ferendum sit :

> *E. Qui alteri exitum parat,*
> *Eum scire oportet sibi paratam pestem ut participet*
> *parem.*

Abducet Patricoles, credo, ut collocet in cubili, ut
vulnus obliget.   Si quidem homo esset, sed nihil
vidi minus.[2]   Quaerit enim quid actum sit :

> *P. Eloquere, eloquere, res Argivum proelio ut se*
> *sustinet.*

---

[1] Some editors take *Hominem exercitum* (or *exercitatum*) as
the beginning of Cicero's comment and governed by *vide*.
[2] *Vidimus* in most MSS.

---

[1] The lines are taken, it seems, from a tragedy of Ennius
entitled, perhaps, *Achilles*, cf. App. II.
[2] Podalirius and Machaon the Greek surgeons, *Il.* 2. 732 :
for the interview of Eurypylus and Patroclus cf. *Il.* 11. 804.
Eurypylus does not go to the surgeons but to Patroclus to
have his wound treated.

surgeon to put the bandage on him and says like
Eurypylus:[1]

> E. To you for aid I come, Patroclus, and your helping
>   hands I beg
> Before a cruel death encountering by foeman's
>   hand bestowed,
> (And by no shift is't possible the stream of flowing
>   blood to staunch,)
> To see if some way by your wisdom death can better
>   be escaped,
> For wounded crowd the entrance ways of the
>   sons[2] of Aesculapius,
> There is no access. P. This surely is Eurypylus.
>   Poor sufferer!

XVII. Where lament succeeds lament so fast,[3] yet
note how he is not plaintive in his reply, and even
gives a reason why suffering must be borne calmly.

>   E. Who for his enemy death contrives
> Should know like end's for him contrived, that he
>   may equal ruin share.

Patroclus will take him away, I suppose, to set him
on the bed, to bind up the wound.[4] Yes, if he had
the feelings of a human being. But nothing less
so. He asks what has taken place:

> P. Speak, speak, the cause of the Argives, how
>   is it now maintained?

---

[3] The "lament" refers either to the woes of Eurypylus
already given, or to a speech in the play not quoted by
Cicero because it was well known.

[4] As he does in Homer, but not in the sterner Latin poet,
for Patroclus wants to have news of the battle.

MARCUS TULLIUS CICERO

E. *Non potest ecfari tantum dictis, quantum factis*
   suppetit.
P. Laberis.[1]

Quiesce igitur et vulnus alliga.[2]   Etiam si Eurypylus
posset, non posset Aesopus.

E. *Ubi fortuna Hectoris nostram acrem aciem inclina-*
   tam . . .

et cetera explicat in dolore.   Sic est enim intemperans militaris in forti viro gloria.   Ergo haec
veteranus miles facere poterit, doctus vir sapiensque
non poterit?   Ille vero melius ac non paullo
40 quidem.   Sed adhuc de consuetudine exercitationis
loquor, nondum de ratione et sapientia.   Aniculae
saepe inediam biduum aut triduum ferunt: subduc
cibum unum diem athletae, Iovem Olympium, eum
ipsum, cui se exercebit, implorabit, ferre non posse se
clamabit.   Consuetudinis magna vis est.   Pernoctant
venatores in nive in montibus; uri se patiuntur Indi;[3]
pugiles caestibus contusi ne ingemescunt quidem.
41 Sed quid hos, quibus Olympiorum victoria consulatus
ille antiquus videtur?   gladiatores, aut perditi homines aut barbari, quas plagas perferunt!   quo modo

---

   [1] *Laberis* is Bentley's emendation for the *laboris* of the
MSS.
   [2] *Quiesce* to *alliga* are sometimes printed as part of the
verse.   They seem better taken as Cicero's comment in the
character of a spectator at the play, cf. *vidi minus* above.
   [3] For the *inde* of the MSS., Davies.

---

   [1] A famous Roman actor and friend of Cicero.   Though he
could act the part of Eurypylus upon the stage, he could not
have borne the pain of a real wound in battle like the trained
soldier Eurypylus.

E. The words that I can give fall short o' the
mighty deeds that there are done.

P. See, you faint!

Be quiet then and tie up the wound! Even if
Eurypylus could, Aesopus[1] could not.

E. Where Hector's fortune our keen line of battle
driven in . . .

and then he goes on to unfold the rest of the story
in his pain: so uncontrollable in a brave man is the
soldier's love of glory. Shall then the veteran
soldier be able to act like this, and the trained
philosopher be unable? He will assuredly be better
able, and in no stinted measure. But so far I am
dealing with the habit which comes from training,
and not as yet with reasoned philosophy. Old
women often endure going without food for two or
three days: take away an athlete's food for a single
day; he will entreat Olympian Jove, the great god
in whose honour he is in training; he will cry out
that he cannot endure it. The force of habit is
great. Hunters pass the night in the snow on the
mountains: Indians suffer themselves to be burnt;
boxers battered by the gauntlets[2] do not so much
as utter a groan. But why mention those who
regard an Olympic victory as equal to the consulship of olden days?[3] Look at gladiators, who are
either ruined men or barbarians, what blows they

---

[2] The gauntlets were of ox-hide stiffened with lead and
iron, cf. Virg. *Aen.* 5. 425.

[3] Cicero means that in the old days the consulship was
prized as the reward of merit: the dictator Caesar gave it
to his friends and even appointed one of them consul for a
single day.

illi, qui bene instituti sunt, accipere plagam malunt
quam turpiter vitare! quam saepe apparet nihil eos
malle quam vel domino satis facere vel populo!
mittunt etiam vulneribus confecti ad dominos qui
quaerant quid velint: si satis iis factum sit, se velle
decumbere. Quis mediocris gladiator ingemuit,
quis vultum mutavit umquam? quis non modo stetit,
verum etiam decubuit turpiter? quis cum decubuis-
set, ferrum recipere iussus collum contraxit? Tantum exercitatio, meditatio, consuetudo valet. Ergo
hoc poterit

Samnis, spurcus homo, vita illa dignus locoque:

vir natus ad gloriam ullam partem animi tam mollem
habebit quam non meditatione et ratione corro-
boret? Crudele gladiatorum spectaculum et in-
humanum non nullis videri solet, et haud scio an ita
sit, ut nunc fit: cum vero sontes ferro depugnabant,
auribus fortasse multae, oculis quidem nulla poterat
esse fortior contra dolorem et mortem disciplina.

42   XVIII. De exercitatione et consuetudine et com-
mentatione dixi. Age, sis, nunc de ratione videamus,

---

[1] Cf. Byron, *Child Harold's Pilgrimage*, Canto IV. cxl.

> I see before me the gladiator lie:
> He leans upon his hand—his manly brow
> Consents to death, but conquers agony.

[2] Cicero was killed in the proscription of 43 B.C. When
the executioners overtook him he thrust his neck as far
forward as he could out of the litter and bade them do their
work.

[3] A verse of the satirist Lucilius. *Samnis* was a gladiator
armed in the fashion of the old Samnites and often a native
of Samnium, cf. App. II.

[4] In Boswell's *Journal* Dr. Johnson says, " I am sorry that

endure! See, how men, who have been well trained, prefer to receive a blow rather than basely avoid it! How frequently it is made evident that there is nothing they put higher than giving satisfaction to their owner or to the people! Even when weakened with wounds they send word to their owners to ascertain their pleasure: if they have given satisfaction to them they are content to fall. What gladiator of ordinary merit has ever uttered a groan or changed countenance? Who of them has disgraced himself, I will not say upon his feet, but who has disgraced himself in his fall?[1] Who after falling has drawn in his neck when ordered to suffer the fatal stroke?[2] Such is the force of training, practice and habit. Shall then

> The Samnite,[3] filthy fellow, worthy of his life and place,

be capable of this, and shall a man born to fame have any portion of his soul so weak that he cannot strengthen it by systematic preparation? A gladiatorial show is apt to seem cruel and brutal to some eyes, and I incline to think that it is so, as now conducted. But in the days when it was criminals who crossed swords in the death struggle, there could be no better schooling against pain and death at any rate for the eye,[4] though for the ear perhaps there might be many.

XVIII. I have dealt with training, habit and preparation. Come if you will and let us consider the question from the philosophic side, unless you

prize-fighting is gone out. . . . Prize-fighting made people accustomed not to be alarmed at seeing their own blood or feeling a little pain from a wound."

nisi quid vis ad haec. A. Egone ut te interpellem?
Ne hoc quidem vellem : ita me ad credendum tua
ducit oratio. M. Sitne igitur malum dolere necne
Stoici viderint, qui contortulis quibusdam et minutis
conclusiunculis nec ad sensus permanantibus effici
volunt non esse malum dolorem. Ego illud, quidquid
sit, tantum esse quantum videatur non puto, falsaque
eius visione et specie moveri homines dico vehementius doloremque omnem esse tolerabilem. Unde
igitur ordiar ? an eadem breviter attingam, quae
modo dixi, quo facilius oratio progredi possit longius?

43 Inter omnes igitur hoc constat nec doctos homines
solum, sed etiam indoctos, virorum esse fortium et
magnanimorum et patientium et humana vincentium
toleranter dolorem pati ; nec vero quisquam fuit qui
eum, qui ita pateretur, non laudandum putaret. Quod
ergo et postulatur a fortibus et laudatur, cum fit, id
aut extimescere veniens aut non ferre praesens
nonne turpe est? Atquin vide ne, cum omnes
rectae animi adfectiones virtutes appellentur, non
sit hoc proprium nomen omnium, sed ab ea, quae
una ceteris excellebat, omnes nominatae, sint.
Appellata est enim ex viro virtus ; viri autem propria
maxime est fortitudo, cuius munera duo sunt maxima
mortis dolorisque contemptio. Utendum est igitur

---

[1] Cf. § 29.

wish to comment on what has been said.   A. Are
you asking me to interrupt you ?   I could not even
entertain the wish to do so : so conducive to belief
do I find your words.   M. Whether then the sense
of pain is an evil or no, let the Stoics settle in their
attempt to prove that pain is not an evil by a string
of involved and pettifogging syllogisms, which fail
to make any impression on the mind.[1]   For my part,
whatever pain is, I do not think it deserves its
apparent importance, and I say that men are unduly
influenced by a spurious image of it in our fancy,
and that all pain is endurable.   At what point then
shall I begin ?   What do you say to my touching
briefly on the same points I have already mentioned,
in order that by doing so I may more easily make
still further progress in my argument ?   It is univer-
sally agreed then, not merely by the learned but
by the unlearned as well, that it is characteristic
of men who are brave, high-spirited, enduring, and
superior to human vicissitudes to suffer pain with
patience ; nor was there anyone, we said, who did
not think that the man who suffered in this spirit
was deserving of praise.   When then this endurance
is both required of brave men and praised when
found, is it not base either to shrink from the
coming of pain or fail to bear its visitation ?   And
yet, perhaps, though all right-minded states are
called virtue, the term is not appropriate to all
virtues, but all have got the name from the single
virtue which was found to outshine the rest, for it
is from the word for " man " that the word virtue is
derived ; but man's peculiar virtue is fortitude, of
which there are two main functions, namely scorn
of death and scorn of pain.   These then we must

his, si virtutis compotes vel potius si viri volumus
esse, quoniam a viris virtus nomen est mutuata.
Quaeres fortasse, quo modo, et recte.   Talem enim
medicinam philosophia profitetur.

44   XIX. Venit Epicurus, homo minime malus vel
potius vir optimus : tantum monet, quantum intelligit : " Neglige " inquit " dolorem."   Quis hoc dicit ?
Idem qui dolorem summum malum.   Vix satis constanter.   Audiamus.   " Si summus dolor est " inquit,
" brevem necesse est esse."

Itera dum eadem istaec mihi !

Non enim satis intelligo quid summum dicas esse,
quid breve.   "Summum, quo nihil sit superius :
breve, quo nihil brevius.   Contemno magnitudinem
doloris, a qua me brevitas temporis vindicabit ante
paene quam venerit."   Sed si est tantus dolor quantus Philoctetae ?   " Bene plane magnus mihi quidem
videtur, sed tamen non summus : nihil enim dolet
nisi pes : possunt oculi : potest caput, latera, pul-
mones, possunt omnia : longe   igitur   abest   a
summo dolore."   " Ergo," inquit " dolor diuturnus
45 habet laetitiae plus quam molestiae."   Hunc ego
non possum tantum hominem nihil sapere dicere,
sed nos ab eo derideri puto.   Ego summum dolorem—summum autem dico, etiam si decem atomis
est maior alius—, non continuo esse dico brevem
multosque possum bonos viros nominare, qui com-

---

[1] From the *Iliona* of Pacuvius, cf. I. § 106.
[2] Diog. Laert. X. 140. αἱ πολυχρόνιοι τῶν ἀρρωστιῶν
πλεόναζον ἔχουσι τὸ ἡδόμενον ἐν τῇ σαρκὶ ἥπερ τὸ ἀλγοῦν.
Epicurus also said that we think many pains superior to
pleasures whenever a greater pleasure comes after we have
endured pains for a long time.

exercise if we wish to prove possessors of virtue, or rather, since the word for " virtue " is borrowed from the word for " man," if we wish to be men. You will perhaps ask how, and rightly so, for such an art of healing philosophy claims to possess.

XIX. Epicurus steps forward,—in no sense an ill-meaning person, or rather a gentleman of the best intentions, he gives advice to the extent of his ability. " Ignore pain," he says. Who says this? The same thinker who pronounces pain the highest evil. This is not quite consistent. Let us listen. " If pain is at its highest," says he, " it must be short."

> " Repeat that once again to me!" [1]

For I do not quite understand what you mean by "at its highest" and what you mean by "short." " By at the highest I mean that which has nothing higher; by short I mean that which has nothing shorter. I scorn a degree of pain from which a brief space of time will deliver me almost before it has come." But what if the pain be as severe as that of Philoctetes? " I admit it seems to me pretty severe, but all the same it is not at the highest ; for his pain is only in the foot ; there can be pain in the eyes, pain in the head, sides, lungs, pain everywhere. He is therefore far from suffering pain at the highest. Therefore," says he, " continuous pain admits of more of gladness than of vexation." [2] Now I cannot say that a man of his eminence is without any sense, but I think he is mocking us. I say that the highest pain—and I say "highest" even if there is another ten atoms worse—is not necessarily short, and I can name a number of worthy men who, according to their

plures annos doloribus podagrae crucientur maximis.
Sed homo catus numquam terminat nec magnitudinis
nec diuturnitatis modum, ut sciam quid summum
dicat in dolore, quid breve in tempore. Omittamus
hunc igitur nihil prorsus dicentem cogamusque confiteri non esse ab eo doloris remedia quaerenda, qui
dolorem malorum omnium maximum dixerit, quamvis idem forticulum se in torminibus et in stranguria
sua praebeat. Aliunde igitur est quaerenda medicina
et maxime quidem, si quid maxime consentaneum
sit quaerimus, ab iis, quibus quod honestum sit,
summum bonum, quod turpe, summum videtur
malum. His tu praesentibus gemere et iactare
te non audebis profecto. Loquetur enim eorum
voce virtus ipsa tecum :

46   XX. Tune, cum pueros Lacedaemone, adolescentes Olympiae, barbaros in arena videris excipientes
gravissimas plagas et ferentes silentio, si te forte
dolor aliquis pervellerit, exclamabis ut mulier, non
constanter et sedate feres ?—Ferri non potest :
natura non patitur.—Audio. Pueri ferunt gloria
ducti, ferunt pudore alii, multi metu, et tamen
veremur ut hoc, quod a tam multis et quod tot locis
perferatur, natura patiatur ? Illa vero non modo
patitur, verum etiam postulat ; nihil enim habet
praestantius, nihil quod magis expetat quam honestatem, quam laudem, quam dignitatem, quam decus.
Hisce ego pluribus nominibus unam rem declarari

---

[1] Cicero is referring to a letter written to a friend by
Epicurus on his death-bed, saying that he was happy in
spite of stranguria and dysentery ; against this he set the
delight his soul felt in the memory of past discussions with
his friend.   Diog. Laert. X. 22, and Cic. *De Fin.* II. 30. 96.
[2] The Stoics.

own account, have suffered tortures of pain from
gout for several years. But the cunning rogue
never fixes the limit either of the degree or the
continuance, so as to let me know what he means
by " highest " in pain or " short " in time. Let us
then pass him over as saying absolutely nothing and
compel him to admit that means of relief from pain
are not to be sought from one who has pronounced
pain to be the greatest of all evils, however resolutely the same person may show a touch of bravery
in an attack of colic or a difficulty in passing water.[1]
We must then seek for a remedy from another
quarter and principally, in fact, if we are looking for
what best fits the case, from those in whose eyes the
honourable is the highest good and the base the
highest evil.[2] In their presence you will assuredly
not dare to groan and toss about in pain, for virtue
will itself remonstrate with you by their voice.

XX. Will you, though you have seen boys in
Lacedaemon, young men at Olympia, barbarians in
the arena submitting to the heaviest blows and
enduring them in silence—will you, if some pain
happen to give you a twitch, cry out like a woman
and not endure resolutely and calmly? " It is unbearable; nature cannot put up with it." Very
well. Boys endure from love of fame, others endure
for shame's sake, many from fear, and yet are we
afraid that nature cannot put up with what so many
have endured in such a number of different places?
Nature in fact not only puts up with but even
demands it; for she offers nothing more excellent,
nothing more desirable than honour, than renown,
than distinction, than glory. By all this number of
terms there is only one thing that I want to express,

volo, sed utor, ut quam maxime significem, pluribus.
Volo autem dicere illud homini longe optimum esse,
quod ipsum sit optandum per se, a virtute profectum
vel in ipsa virtute situm, sua sponte laudabile, quod
quidem citius dixerim solum quam [1] summum bonum.
Atque ut haec de honesto, sic de turpi contraria:
nihil tam taetrum, nihil tam aspernandum, nihil
homine indignius.

47 Quod si tibi persuasum est—principio enim dixisti
plus in dedecore mali tibi videri quam in dolore—,
reliquum est ut tute tibi imperes. Quamquam hoc
nescio quo modo dicitur, quasi duo simus, ut alter
imperet, alter pareat; non inscite tamen dicitur.
XXI. Est enim animus in partes tributus duas,
quarum altera rationis est particeps, altera expers.
Cum igitur praecipitur, ut nobismet ipsis impere-
mus, hoc praecipitur, ut ratio coerceat temeritatem.
Est in animis omnium fere natura molle quiddam,
demissum, humile, enervatum quodam modo et
languidum. Si nihil esset aliud, nihil esset homine
deformius; sed praesto est domina omnium et
regina ratio, quae conixa per se et progressa longius
fit perfecta virtus. Haec ut imperet illi parti animi,
48 quae obedire debet, id videndum est viro. Quonam
modo? inquies. Vel ut dominus servo vel ut impe-

---

[1] Most MSS. have *non summum* with the sense "rather
than deny it to be the highest good."

---

[1] Cf. I. 80.

but I employ a number, in order to make my meaning as clear as possible. What I want to say in fact is that far the best for man is that which is desirable in and for itself, has its source in virtue or rather is based on virtue, is of itself praiseworthy, and in fact I should prefer to describe it as the only rather than the highest good. Moreover, just as we use language like this in speaking of what is honourable, so we use the opposite in speaking of what is base: there is nothing so revolting, nothing so despicable, nothing more unworthy of a human being.

And if you are so far convinced—for you said at the outset that you thought there was more evil in disgrace than in pain—it remains for you to be master of yourself. And yet in some way or other we so express ourselves, just as if we had two selves, one to be master and one to obey: still the phrase shows insight. XXI. For the soul is divided into two parts,[1] one of which is gifted with reason, while the other is destitute of it. When then we are directed to be masters of ourselves, the meaning of the direction is that reason should be a curb upon recklessness. As a rule, all men's minds contain naturally an element of weakness, despondency, servility, a kind of nervelessness and flaccidity. Had human nature nothing else, no creature would be more hideous than man; but reason, the mistress and queen of the world, stands close at hand and striving by her own strength and pressing onward she becomes completed virtue. It is man's duty to enable reason to have rule over that part of the soul which ought to obey. How is it to be done? you will say. Even as the master

rator militi vel ut parens filio. Si turpissime se illa
pars animi geret, quam dixi esse mollem, si se lamen-
tis muliebriter lacrimisque dedet, vinciatur et con-
stringatur amicorum propinquorumque custodiis ;
saepe enim videmus fractos pudore, qui ratione nulla
vincerentur. Ergo hos quidem ut famulos vinclis
prope ac custodia, qui autem erunt firmiores nec
tamen robustissimi, hos admonitu oportebit ut bonos
milites revocatos dignitatem tueri. Non nimis in
Niptris ille sapientissimus Graeciae saucius lamentatur vel modice potius :

> *Pedetemptim*, inquit, *et sedato nisu,*
> *Ne succussu adripiat maior*
> *Dolor.*

49 Pacuvius hoc melius quam Sophocles—apud illum
enim perquam flebiliter Ulixes lamentatur in vulnere :
tamen huic leniter gementi illi ipsi, qui ferunt
saucium, personae gravitatem intuentes non dubitant
dicere :

> *Tu quoque, Ulixes, quamquam graviter*
> *Cernimus ictum, nimis paene animo es*
> *Molli, qui consuetus in armis*
> *Aevom agere . . . . . .*

Intelligit poëta prudens ferendi doloris consuetudi-
50 nem esse non contemnendam magistram. Atque
ille non immoderate magno in dolore :

---

[1] Pacuvius translated or imitated a play of Sophocles
(Νίπτρα ἢ Ὀδυσσεὺς ἀκανθοπλήξ) in which the plot turns upon
the death of Ulysses from the bone of the sting-ray shot by
his son Telegonus, cf. App. II.

over the slave, or the general over the soldier, or
the parent over the son. If the part of the soul,
which I have described as yielding, conducts itself
disgracefully, if it give way in womanish fashion to
lamentation and weeping, let it be fettered and
tightly bound by the guardianship of friends and
relations; for often we find men crushed by a sense
of shame who would never be overcome by any
reason. Such persons therefore we shall have almost
to keep in chains and guard closely like slaves, whilst
those who shall be found more steadfast, though
not of the highest strength, we shall have to warn
to be mindful of honour, like good soldiers recalled
to duty. The wisest hero of Greece when wounded
does not wail extravagantly, in the *Niptra*; rather
should we say he shows due restraint in saying:

> March step by step evenly straining
> Lest from a jolt there seize me a keener
> Pain.

Pacuvius[1] in this surpasses Sophocles — for in
Sophocles the wounded Ulysses wails very pitifully:
all the same the bearers of the wounded man,
having an eye to the dignity of his character,
actually do not hesitate to say to him when he
softly groans:

> You too Ulysses albeit grievously
> Stricken we see, yet a well-nigh effeminate
> Spirit you show for a soldier to warfare
> Life-long accustomed.

The wise poet sees that the custom of bearing pain
is a teacher not to be despised. And then Ulysses
not at all extravagantly in his great pain says:

> *Retinete, tenete : opprimit ulcus :*
> *Nudate, heu, miserum me : excrucior.*

Incipit labi ; deinde ilico desinit :

> *Operite, abscedite, iamiam,*
> *Mittite ; nam attrectatu et quassu*
> *Saevum amplificatis dolorem.*

Videsne ut obmutuerit non sedatus corporis, sed castigatus animi dolor ? Itaque in extremis Niptris alios quoque obiurgat idque moriens :

> *Conqueri fortunam advorsam, non lamentari decet ;*
> *Id viri est officium : fletus muliebri ingenio additus.*

Huius animi pars illa mollior rationi sic paruit, ut severo imperatori miles pudens.

51 XXII. In quo vero erit perfecta sapientia—quem adhuc nos quidem vidimus neminem, sed philosophorum sententiis qualis hic futurus sit, si modo aliquando fuerit, exponitur—, is igitur sive ea ratio, quae erit in eo perfecta atque absoluta, sic illi parti imperabit inferiori, ut iustus parens probis filiis ; nutu quod volet conficiet, nullo labore, nulla molestia ; eriget ipse se, suscitabit, instruet, armabit, ut tamquam hosti sic obsistat dolori. Quae sunt ista arma ?

---

[1] The title Niptra (washing) seems to point to some scene in the play based on *Odyssey* 19. 349, where Euryclea washes the feet of Odysseus. Cf. V. § 45.

Hold back! nay hold! overpowering is the sore,
Lay it bare; misery! I am in torture.

He begins to lose hold of himself; then at once he
pulls up:

Cover up, cover up, and away forthwith;
Make ye despatch; by your handling and shaking
Ye increase the cruel pain of the wounded.

Do you see how it is not the pain of the body which
has been quieted and reduced to silence, but the
pain of the soul which has been chastened by rebuke
and reduced to silence? And so at the end of the
Niptra[1] he rebukes others as well, and that in his
last moments:

It befits you to complain of adverse fortune, not
bemoan;
This man's duty is: on women's nature weeping
was bestowed.

The weaker part of his soul was submissive to reason
in the same way that the disciplined soldier obeys
the strict commander.

XXII. But the man in whom there shall be
perfect wisdom—we have never, it is true, seen a
living example hitherto, but his character, if only
one day he can be found, is described in the words
of philosophers—, such a wise man then, or rather
such a reason as will be found in him in complete
and perfect measure, will govern the lower part of
his nature in the same way as a righteous parent
governs sons of good character; he will secure the
carrying out of his wishes by a hint, without trouble
and without vexation; he will rouse and bestir
himself, make ready and arm himself to face pain
like an enemy. What are the weapons he will

Contentio, confirmatio sermoque intimus, cum ipse
secum : "Cave turpe quidquam, languidum, non
52 virile." Obversentur species honestae viro: Zeno
proponatur Eleates, qui perpessus est omnia potius
quam conscios delendae tyrannidis indicaret; de
Anaxarcho Democritio cogitetur, qui cum Cypri in
manus Timocreontis regis incidisset, nullum genus
supplicii deprecatus est neque recusavit. Callanus
Indus, indoctus ac barbarus, in radicibus Caucasi
natus, sua voluntate vivus combustus est, nos, si pes
condoluit, si dens—sed fac totum dolere corpus—
ferre non possumus; opinio est enim quaedam
effeminata ac levis nec in dolore magis quam eadem
in voluptate, qua cum liquescimus fluimusque
mollitia, apis aculeum sine clamore ferre non pos-
53 sumus. At vero C. Marius, rusticanus vir, sed plane
vir, cum secaretur, ut supra dixi, principio vetuit se
adligari, nec quisquam ante Marium solutus dicitur
esse sectus. Cur ergo postea alii ? Valuit auctori-
tas. Videsne igitur opinionis esse, non naturae
malum ? Et tamen fuisse acrem morsum doloris
idem Marius ostendit; crus enim alterum non
praebuit. Ita et tulit dolorem ut vir et ut homo
maiorem ferre sine causa necessaria noluit. Totum
igitur in eo est, ut tibi imperes.

---

[1] Not the founder of the Stoic philosophy, but a native of
Magna Graecia, about 460 B.C.

[2] Anaxarchus, a native of Thrace, was a companion of
Alexander the Great, and after his death was killed by the
King of Cyprus, Timocreon or Nicocreon.

[3] Alexander the Great made friends with Callanus after
the fall of Babylon. Callanus was a gymnosophist, as the
Greeks called the Hindu ascetic philosophers, cf. V. § 77,
and was said to have predicted Alexander's death.

[4] The Hindu Kush.   [5] § 35 and V. § 56.

need?   He will brace and strengthen and commune with himself by saying, " Beware of anything base, slack, unmanly."   Let the ideals which a true man honours be kept constantly before his eyes : let him call up the image of Zeno of Elea[1] who endured every torment rather than be brought to divulge his accomplices in the plot to overthrow tyranny ; let him reflect on the story of Anaxarchus[2] the follower of Democritus, who fell into the power of King Timocreon in Cyprus, and without appealing for mercy recoiled from no form of torture. Callanus the Indian,[3] an untutored savage, born at the foot of the Caucasus,[4] of his own free-will was burnt alive. We, on the contrary, cannot bear a pain in the foot, or a toothache (but suppose the whole body is in pain) ; the reason is that there is a kind of womanish and frivolous way of thinking exhibited in pleasure as much as in pain, which makes our self-control melt and stream away through weakness, and so we cannot endure a bee-sting without crying out.   But as a matter of fact C. Marius, a countryman by extraction yet undoubtedly a man, when under the surgeon's knife, as I related earlier,[4] refused from the outset to be bound, and there is no record of anyone before Marius having been operated on without being tied up.   Why then did others afterwards do like him?   It was the force of example. Do you see then that evil is a creature of the imagination, not a reality of nature?   And yet the same Marius showed that the sting of the pain was severe, for he did not offer his other leg ; thus being a man he bore pain, being human he refused to bear greater pain without actual necessity.   The whole point then is to be master of yourself.

Ostendi autem quod esset imperandi genus, atque
haec cogitatio, quid patientia, quid fortitudine, quid
magnitudine animi dignissimum sit, non solum
animum comprimit, sed ipsum etiam dolorem nescio
54 quo pacto mitiorem facit. XXIII. Ut enim fit in
proelio, ut ignavus miles ac timidus, simul ac viderit
hostem, abiecto scuto fugiat quantum possit ob
eamque causam pereat non numquam etiam integro
corpore, cum ei, qui steterit, nihil tale evenerit,
sic qui doloris speciem ferre non possunt abiiciunt se
atque ita adflicti et exanimati iacent; qui autem
restiterunt discedunt saepissime superiores; sunt
enim quaedam animi similitudines cum corpore. Ut
onera contentis corporibus facilius feruntur, remissis
opprimunt, simillime animus intentione sua depellit
pressum omnem ponderum, remissione autem sic
55 urguetur, ut se nequeat extollere. Et, si verum
quaerimus, in omnibus officiis persequendis animi
est adhibenda contentio; ea est sola officii tamquam
custodia. Sed hoc quidem in dolore maxime est
providendum, ne quid abiecte, ne quid timide, ne
quid ignave, ne quid serviliter muliebriterve faciamus, in primisque refutetur ac reiiciatur Philocteteus
ille clamor. Ingemescere non numquam viro concessum est idque raro, eiulatus ne mulieri quidem.
Et hic nimirum est lessus,[1] quem duodecim tabulae

---

[1] The MSS. have *fletus*, but *lessus* is the word used in
the XII Tables as quoted by Cicero, *Leg.* II. 23. 59, *Mulieres
genas ne radunto, neve lessum funeris ergo habento.*

---

[1] Cf. Hor. *Od.* 3. 2. 14, *Mors et fugacem persequitur virum.*
[2] It is difficult to make any difference in English between
contentio and *intentio*. The root meaning of both words is
"stretching." *Contentio* suits the joint effort of sailors

But I have now made clear the character of self-mastery, and such consideration of the conduct most worthy of endurance, courage and greatness of soul not only brings the soul under submission, but actually serves somehow to mitigate pain as well. XXIII. For, just as it happens in battle that the cowardly and faint-hearted soldier throws away his shield as soon as he has caught sight of the enemy and flies as fast as he can, and for that reason loses his life [1] sometimes without even a wound on his body, whereas nothing of the kind has happened meanwhile to the soldier who has stood his ground : similarly those who cannot bear the sight of pain throw themselves away and lie stricken and slain, whilst those on the other hand who have faced the attack very often quit the field victorious. For the soul has certain analogies to the body : weights are more easily carried by straining every nerve of the body : relax the strain and the weights are too heavy ; quite similarly the soul by its intense [2] effort throws off all the pressure of burdens, but by relaxation of effort is so weighed down that it cannot recover itself. And if we would have the truth, the soul must strain every nerve in the performance of all duties ; in this alone does duty find its safeguard. But the principal precaution to be observed in the matter of pain is to do nothing in a despondent, cowardly, slothful, servile or womanish spirit, and before all to resist and spurn those Philoctetean outcries. Sometimes, though seldom, it is allowable for a man to groan aloud ; to shriek, not even for a woman ; and this no doubt is the form of wailing of

hauling a cable, *intentio* a musician tightening the strings of his instrument.

56 in funeribus adhiberi vetuerunt. Nec vero umquam
ne ingemescit quidem vir fortis ac sapiens, nisi forte
ut se intendat ad firmitatem, ut in stadio cursores
exclamant quam maxime possunt; faciunt idem,
cum exercentur, athletae; pugiles vero, etiam
cum feriunt adversarium, in iactandis caestibus
ingemescunt, non quod doleant animove succumbant,
sed quia profundenda voce omne corpus intenditur
venitque plaga vehementior.

XXIV. Quid? qui volunt exclamare maius, num
satis habent latera, fauces, linguam intendere, e
quibus eiici vocem et fundi videmus? Toto corpore
atque omnibus ungulis, ut dicitur, contentioni vocis
57 adserviunt. Genu mehercule M. Antonium vidi, cum
contente pro se ipse lege Varia diceret, terram
tangere. Ut enim balistae lapidum et reliqua tormenta telorum eo graviores emissiones habent, quo
sunt contenta atque adducta vehementius, sic vox,
sic cursus, sic plaga hoc gravior, quo est missa
contentius. Cuius contentionis cum tanta vis sit,
si gemitus in dolore ad confirmandum animum
valebit, utemur; sin erit ille gemitus elamentabilis,
si imbecillus, si abiectus, si flebilis, ei qui se dederit,
vix eum virum dixerim. Qui quidem gemitus si
levationis aliquid adferret, tamen videremus quid
esset fortis et animosi viri : cum vero nihil imminuat

---

[1] Lit. "with all the hoofs." The phrase is said to come
from the action of horses drawing a load up a steep place
when they strike the ground with the front edge of the
hoof. Our "tooth and nail" is like the Greek ὀδοῦσι καὶ ὄνυξι.

[2] Cf. I. § 10.

[3] The principle of these engines was to have two horizontal
arms fixed in tightly twisted ropes : the arms were connected
by a cord which was released by a trigger. A windlass was
needed to set the machine.

which the Twelve Tables forbade the use at funerals. Nor in fact does the brave, wise man so much as ever groan aloud, unless perhaps to make an intense effort for steadfastness, in the way that runners shout on the race-course as loudly as they can. Athletes do the same in training; boxers in fact, at the moment of striking their opponent, groan in the act of swinging their gauntlets, not that they feel pain or are losing heart, but because by the burst of sound the whole body is made more tense and the blow comes with greater force.

XXIV. Again, when men want to shout louder it is not enough, is it, to intensify the effort of sides and throat and tongue from which we see the voice jerked out with such a burst? No! With the whole force of the body, with tooth and nail,[1] as the saying is, they second the straining of the voice. Great heavens, I have seen M. Antonius,[2] when straining every nerve in defence of himself under the Varian law, touch the ground with his knee. For just as engines for hurling stones and the other machines for throwing missiles give a more powerful discharge in proportion to the tightness of the strain upon the cords,[3] so it is with the voice, so it is with running, and the boxer's blow is heavier in proportion to the strain exerted. And as the effect of strain is so powerful, we shall indulge in a groan at an access of pain, if it can avail to strengthen the soul; but if the groan is melancholy, weak, despondent, piteous I can scarcely give the name of man to him who has succumbed. Should a groan indeed bring some degree of relief, we should nevertheless find it consistent with the character of a brave and spirited man: seeing, however, that it

doloris, cur frustra turpes esse volumus? Quid est
58 enim fletu muliebri viro turpius? Atque hoc praeceptum, quod de dolore datur, patet latius: omnibus
enim rebus, non solum dolori, simili contentione
animi resistendum est. Ira exardescit, libido con-
citatur: in eandem arcem confugiendum est, eadem
sunt arma sumenda; sed quoniam de dolore loquimur, illa omittamus. Ad ferendum igitur dolorem
placide atque sedate plurimum proficit toto pectore,
ut dicitur, cogitare quam id honestum sit. Sumus
enim natura, ut ante dixi—dicendum est enim
saepius—, studiosissimi appetentissimique honestatis,
cuius si quasi lumen aliquod aspeximus, nihil est
quod, ut eo potiamur, non parati simus et ferre
et perpeti. Ex hoc cursu atque impetu animorum
ad veram laudem atque honestatem illa pericula
adeuntur in proeliis; non sentiunt viri fortes in acie
vulnera, vel sentiunt, sed mori malunt quam tantum
59 modo de dignitatis gradu demoveri. Fulgentes
gladios hostium videbant Decii, cum in aciem
eorum irruebant: his levabat omnem vulnerum
metum nobilitas mortis et gloria. Num tum in-
gemuisse Epaminondam putas, cum una cum
sanguine vitam effluere sentiret? Imperantem
enim patriam Lacedaemoniis relinquebat, quam acceperat servientem. Haec sunt solacia, haec
fomenta summorum dolorum.
60   XXV. Dices, quid in pace, quid domi, quid in

---

[1] But Ovid says, *Expletur lacrimis egeriturque dolor.* *Trist.*
IV. 3. 38.
[2] For *honestum, honestas,* see page 494.
[3] Cf. I. 89.
[4] At the battle of Mantinea, 362 B.C. Cf. I. § 4.

abates nothing of the pain,[1] why do we wish to disgrace ourselves to no purpose? What is more disgraceful for a man than womanish weeping? Moreover this rule which is laid down for pain has a wider scope, for we must resist everything and not merely pain with a similar straining of every nerve of the soul. Anger blazes up, lust is roused: we must hasten for refuge to the same citadel, we must take up the same weapons;—but as pain is our subject, let us leave other illustrations on one side. To enable us to bear pain quietly and calmly it is a very great gain to reflect with all our heart and mind, as the saying is, how honourable[2] it is to do so. Nature has made us, as I have said before—it must often be repeated—enthusiastic seekers after honour, and once we have caught, as it were, some glimpse of its radiance, there is nothing we are not prepared to bear and go through in order to secure it. It is from this rush, this impulse of our souls towards true renown and reputation that the dangers of battle are encountered; brave men do not feel wounds in the line of battle, or feel them, but prefer death rather than move a step from the post that honour has appointed. The Decii[3] saw the gleaming swords of the enemy when they charged their line of battle; the fame and glory of death lessened for them all fear of wounds. You cannot think that Epaminondas uttered a groan at the moment he felt life ebbing with the gush of blood?[4] for the country he had found enslaved he left mistress of the Lacedaemonians. These are the consolations, these the alleviations, of extreme pain.

XXV. But what, you will say, have we in time of

lectulo? Ad philosophos me revocas, qui in aciem non saepe prodeunt, e quibus homo sane levis Heracleotes Dionysius, cum a Zenone fortis esse didicisset, a dolore dedoctus est. Nam cum ex renibus laboraret, ipso in eiulatu clamitabat falsa esse illa, quae antea de dolore ipse sensisset. Quem cum Cleanthes condiscipulus rogaret quaenam ratio eum de sententia deduxisset, respondit: "Quia si,[1] cum tantum operae philosophiae dedissem, dolorem tamen ferre non possem, satis esset argumenti malum esse dolorem. Plurimos autem annos in philosophia consumpsi nec ferre possum : malum est igitur dolor." Tum Cleanthem, cum pede terram percussisset, versum ex Epigonis ferunt dixisse :

Audisne haec, Amphiaraë sub terram abdite?

Zenonem significabat, a quo illum degenerare dolebat. At non noster Posidonius, quem et ipse saepe vidi et id dicam, quod solebat narrare Pompeius, se, cum Rhodum venisset decedens ex

---

[1] The MSS. have *qui cum* or *quia cum* and *opere* or *opera*. The reading adopted is that of Madvig. The argument is in syllogistic form.

---

[1] Socrates fought at Delium, 424 B.C., and saved the life of Alcibiades at Potidaea, 432 B.C. Plat. *Symp.* 221.

[2] A native of Magna Graecia, who for his desertion of Zeno was named μεταθέμενος, turncoat.

[3] Cleanthes was Zeno's successor as head of the Stoic school.

[4] A syllogism after the Stoic manner, but a bad one, for the major premiss is not distributed, being particular : *if I*, not universal : *if all men had given*.

[5] A tragedy of Aeschylus translated by Accius : Amphiaraus the Argive seer went with Adrastus on the expedition

peace, at home, in our easy chairs ?   You call me back
to the philosophers who do not often[1] step into
the battle-line, and one of whom, Dionysius of
Heraclea,[2] a person certainly of little resolution,
after learning from Zeno to be brave was taught
by pain to forget his lesson.   For upon an attack
of kidney trouble, even amid his shrieks, he kept
on crying out that the opinions he had himself
previously held about pain were false.   And on
being asked by Cleanthes,[3] his fellow-pupil, what
was the reason that had seduced him from his
former opinion, he replied : " Because if, after I
had given such devoted attention to philosophy, I
yet proved unable to bear pain, that would be
sufficient proof that pain was an evil.   Now I have
spent many years in studying philosophy and am
unable to bear pain : pain is therefore an evil." [4]
Then Cleanthes stamped with his foot upon the
ground and, according to the story, recited a line
from the *Epigoni* : [5]

Do you hear this, Amphiaraus, in your home
    beneath the earth ?

meaning Zeno and grieving that Dionysius was false
to his teaching.   It was not so with our Posidonius,[6]
whom I have often seen with my own eyes, and I
shall repeat the story Pompey liked to tell, that
after reaching Rhodes on giving up Syria [7] he felt

against Thebes and was swallowed up by the earth.
Cleanthes applies the line to his master Zeno who was
numbered amongst the dead.

[6] A native of Syria, a Stoic philosopher and teacher and
friend of Cicero.

[7] Pompey returned to Italy from his command in the East
in 62 B.C.

Syria, audire voluisse Posidonium, sed cum audisset
eum graviter esse aegrum, quod vehementer eius
artus laborarent, voluisse tamen nobilissimum philosophum visere : quem ut vidisset et salutavisset
honorificisque verbis prosecutus esset molesteque se
dixisset ferre, quod eum non posset audire, at ille :
"Tu vero," inquit, "potes ; nec committam ut dolor
corporis efficiat ut frustra tantus vir ad me venerit."
Itaque narrabat eum graviter et copiose de hoc ipso,
nihil esse bonum nisi quod esset honestum, cubantem
disputavisse, cumque quasi faces ei doloris ad-
moverentur, saepe dixisse : "Nihil agis, dolor!
quamvis sis molestus, numquam te esse confitebor
malum."

62 XXVI. Omninoque omnes clari et nobilitati labores contendendo fiunt etiam tolerabiles. Videmusne
apud quos eorum ludorum, qui gymnici nominantur,
magnus honos sit, nullum ab iis, qui in id certamen
descendant, devitari dolorem ? apud quos autem
venandi et equitandi laus viget, qui hanc petessunt,
nullum fugiunt dolorem. Quid de nostris ambitioni-
bus, quid de cupiditate honorum loquar ? quae
flamma est per quam non cucurrerunt ii, qui haec
olim punctis singulis colligebant ? Itaque semper
Africanus Socraticum Xenophontem in manibus
habebat : cuius in primis laudabat illud, quod diceret eosdem labores non aeque graves esse
imperatori et militi, quod ipse honos laborem

---

[1] *faces*, torches, used metaphorically here for accesses of
pain : in I. § 44 for temptations of the flesh.
[2] Before the ballot was introduced in 139 B.C. votes were
given by word of mouth and the reply noted down by a

a wish to hear Posidonius; but on learning that he was seriously ill with an attack of gout in the joints, he wished at all events to go to see so famous a philosopher: when he had seen him and offered his respects, he paid him distinguished compliments and said that he regretted that he was not able to hear him, but Posidonius said, " You can hear me, nor will I suffer bodily pain to be a reason for allowing a man of your eminence to visit me for nothing." And accordingly Pompey related that from his sick bed the philosopher had earnestly and fully discussed this very proposition, "that there is nothing good except what is honourable," and as often as a paroxysm[1] of pain attacked him, continually repeated: " It is no use, pain! for all the distress you cause I shall never admit that you are an evil."

XXVI. And in all cases all toils that bring glory and distinction are by the effort they demand rendered endurable.   Do we not see, with those who hold in high esteem the sports called gymnastic, that no pain is shunned by the competitors who enter for them?   Moreover men with whom a name for hunting and horsemanship is valued shrink from no pain in their constant quest of this reputation.   Why should I speak of our candidature at elections, our desire for offices of State?   Would fire and water stop the men who once used to gather in such prizes vote by vote?[2]   And so, Africanus, who continually had Xenophon, the follower of Socrates, in his hand, used particularly to praise him for saying that the same toils in war were not equally severe for general and soldier, because his position alone made the toil

prick on a tablet opposite the name of the candidate preferred.

63 leviorem faceret imperatorium. Sed tamen hoc
evenit ut in vulgus insipientium opinio valeat
honestatis, cum ipsam videre non possint ; itaque
fama et multitudinis iudicio moventur, cum id
honestum putent, quod a plerisque laudetur. Te
autem, si in oculis sis multitudinis, tamen eius
iudicio stare nolim nec quod illa putet idem putare
pulcherrimum : tuo tibi iudicio est utendum ; tibi
si recta probanti placebis, tum non modo tete viceris,
quod paullo ante praecipiebam, sed omnes et omnia.

64 Hoc igitur tibi propone : amplitudinem animi et
quasi quandam exaggerationem quam altissimam
animi, quae maxime eminet contemnendis et de-
spiciendis doloribus, unam esse omnium rem pul-
cherrimam eoque pulchriorem, si vacet populo neque
plausum captans se tamen ipsa delectet. Quin etiam
mihi quidem laudabiliora videntur omnia, quae sine
venditatione et sine populo teste fiunt, non quo
fugiendus sit—omnia enim bene facta in luce se
collocari volunt—, sed tamen nullum theatrum
virtuti conscientia maius est.

65 XXVII. Atque in primis meditemur illud, ut haec
patientia dolorum, quam saepe iam animi intentione
dixi esse firmandam, in omni genere se aequabilem
praebeat. Saepe enim multi, qui aut propter

---

[1] Xen., *Cyr.* 1. 6. 25. ἐπικουφίζει τι ἡ τιμὴ τοὺς πόνους τῷ
ἄρχοντι. The general shares the private soldier's toils, their
bodies are similar, but the general's toil is lightened by his
position.

of the general lighter.[1] But all the same it does come about that an imperfect notion of honour has its influence with the unphilosophical vulgar, since they cannot see its true nature; and so they are swayed by reputation and the verdict of the mob in thinking that honourable which the majority would approve. In your case, however, should you become a figure in the eyes of the mob, I should nevertheless not like you to be dependent on their judgment, nor wish you to accept their view of what is fairest: you must use your own judgment; if you are content with yourself in approving the right, then you will not only win a victory over self, a rule I laid down a little while back, but over the world of men and things. Make this your aim: consider that largeness of soul and, if I may say so, a certain exaltation of soul to the highest possible pitch, which best shows itself in scorn and contempt for pain, is the one fairest thing in the world and all the fairer, should it be independent of popular approval and without trying to win applause nevertheless find joy in itself. Nay more, to my mind all things seem more praiseworthy which are done without glorification and without publicity, not that this is to be avoided—for all things done well tend to be set in the light of day—but all the same there is no audience for virtue of higher authority than the approval of conscience.

XXVII. Moreover let us first of all reflect upon this point, that the endurance of pain, which, as I have often said, must be strengthened by an intense effort of the soul, should show itself at the same level in every field. For on many occasions numbers of men have bravely received and bravely borne

victoriae cupiditatem aut propter gloriae aut etiam,
ut ius suum et libertatem tenerent, vulnera ex-
ceperunt fortiter et tulerunt, idem omissa contentione dolorem morbi ferre non possunt. Neque
enim illum, quem facile tulerant, ratione aut
sapientia tulerant, sed studio potius et gloria.
Itaque barbari quidam et immanes ferro decertare
acerrime possunt, aegrotare viriliter non queunt;
Graeci autem homines non satis animosi, prudentes,
ut est captus hominum, satis, hostem aspicere non
possunt, eidem morbos toleranter atque humane
ferunt. At Cimbri et Celtiberi in proeliis exsultant,
lamentantur in morbo: nihil enim potest esse
aequabile quod non a certa ratione proficiscatur.

66 Sed cum videas eos, qui aut studio aut opinione
ducantur, in eo persequendo atque adipiscendo
dolore non frangi, debeas existimare aut non esse
malum dolorem aut, etiam si, quidquid asperum
alienumque natura sit, id appellari placeat malum,
tantulum tamen esse, ut a virtute ita obruatur, ut
nusquam appareat. Quae meditare, quaeso, dies et
noctes; latius enim manabit haec ratio et aliquanto
maiorem locum quam de uno dolore occupabit; nam
si omnia fugiendae turpitudinis adipiscendaeque
honestatis causa faciemus, non modo stimulos doloris, sed etiam fulmina fortunae contemnamus

---

[1] Aristotle, *Pol.* 4. 7. 3, says that the Greek race was both
ἔνθυμον καὶ διανοητικόν, not like the northern races who were
courageous but unintellectual, or the Asiatics who were
intellectual but spiritless.

[2] The Cimbri were German, the Celtiberi Spanish.

wounds, either from thirst for victory or fame, or
even to maintain their own right or freedom, and
yet the same men, when the strain of effort is
relaxed, are unable to bear the pain of disease ; the
reason is that the pain they had readily endured,
they had endured, not from principle or the teaching
of philosophy, but from motives rather of ambition
and fame. We find accordingly some uncivilized
barbarians able to fight desperately to the end with
the sword but unable to behave like men in sickness.
The Greeks on the other hand, who are not so very
courageous but have a sufficiency of sense answering
to their mental powers, cannot look an enemy in
the face ; [1] and yet these same men show endurance
and spirit, as human beings should, in bearing sickness, while the Cimbri and Celtiberians [2] revel in
battle and wail in sickness. For nothing can keep
the same level unless it starts with fixed principle.
But since one finds that men acting from ambition or
upon unverified opinion do not break down under
pain in the pursuit and attainment of their object,
it should be a duty to think either that pain is not
an evil, or even if it should be decided to give the
name of evil to all that is unpleasant and unnatural,
nevertheless, that this is of such trifling importance
that it is eclipsed by virtue so completely as to be
nowhere visible. Reflect on these considerations, I
pray, by day and night, for this principle will spread
more widely in its application and cover a field a
good deal larger than the consideration of pain
alone ; for if we are to do everything with the object
of avoiding baseness and securing honour, we shall
have the right of despising not merely the stings
of pain but the bolts of fortune as well, especially

licebit, praesertim cum paratum sit illud ex hesterna
67 disputatione perfugium. Ut enim si cui naviganti,
quem praedones si[1] insequantur, deus qui dixerit :
" Eiice te e navi : praesto est qui excipiat, vel
delphinus, ut Arionem Methymnaeum, vel equi
Pelopis illi Neptunii, qui ʻper undas currus suspen-
sos rapuisse' dicuntur, excipient te et quo velis
perferent," omnem omittat timorem, sic urguentibus
asperis et odiosis doloribus, si tanti sint, ut ferendi
non sint, quo sit confugiendum vides. Haec fere
hoc tempore putavi esse dicenda. Sed tu fortasse
in sententia permanes. A. Minime vero, meque
biduo duarum rerum, quas maxime timebam, spero
liberatum metu. M. Cras ergo ad clepsydram : sic
enim diximus, et tibi hoc video non posse deberi.
A. Ita prorsus. Et illud quidem ante meridiem,
hoc eodem tempore. M. Sic faciemus tuisque
optimis studiis obsequemur.

---

[1] The second *si* is not in the MSS., but is usually supplied
before or after *praedones.*

---

[1] The story of Arion is given in Hdt. 1. 23. The sailors
of the ship on which he was returning from Italy to Lesbos
threw him into the sea, and a dolphin bore him safely to land.
[2] Pelops sought the help of Neptune in his contest with

as such a mansion of refuge has been prepared for us as a result of yesterday's discussion. For if a god should say to some navigator confronted with a chase by pirates: "Cast yourself from the ship; there is either a dolphin ready to pick you up like Arion of Methymna,[1] or else the famous horses of Neptune, which aided Pelops[2] and are said 'to have hurried the car afloat over the waves,' will pick you up and carry you whither you will," he would cast off all fear; similarly when unpleasing and hateful pains assail you, if they should be too keen to be borne, you see the refuge to which you must fly. This is pretty nearly what I thought should be said in the time available. But it may be you adhere to your opinion. A. By no means so, and it is my hope that I have in two days been set free from the fear of two things of which I was desperately afraid. M. To-morrow then we will practise declamation by the water-clock, for so we have arranged and I see that this cannot be refused you. A. Exactly so : the practice in the morning and the discussion at the same time as to-day. M. It shall be so, and we shall comply with your excellent inclinations.

Oenomaus for the hand of Hippodamia his daughter, and the god gave him a golden chariot and fleet horses.

M. TULLI CICERONIS TUSCULANARUM DISPUTATIONUM

LIBER III

1 I. Quidnam esse, Brute, causae putem cur, cum constemus ex animo et corpore, corporis curandi tuendique causa quaesita sit ars atque eius utilitas deorum immortalium inventioni consecrata, animi autem medicina nec tam desiderata sit, ante quam inventa, nec tam culta, postea quam cognita est, nec tam multis grata et probata, pluribus etiam suspecta et invisa? An quod corporis gravitatem et dolorem animo iudicamus, animi morbum corpore non sentimus? Ita fit ut animus de se ipse tum iudicet, 2 cum id ipsum, quo iudicatur, aegrotet. Quod si tales nos natura genuisset, ut eam ipsam intueri et perspicere eademque optima duce cursum vitae conficere possemus, haud erat sane quod quisquam rationem ac doctrinam requireret. Nunc parvulos nobis dedit igniculos, quos celeriter malis moribus

---

[1] Apollo and his son Aesculapius. Cf. II. § 38.
[2] Zeno the Stoic said that the τέλος φύσεως was τὸ ὁμολογουμένως τῇ φύσει ζῆν, ὅπερ ἐστὶ κατ᾿ ἀρετὴν ζῆν.

M. TULLIUS CICERO'S TUSCULAN DISPUTATIONS

BOOK III

I. Seeing, Brutus, that we are made up of soul and body, what am I to think is the reason why for the care and maintenance of the body there has been devised an art which from its usefulness has had its discovery attributed to immortal gods,[1] and is regarded as sacred, whilst on the other hand the need of an art of healing for the soul has not been felt so deeply before its discovery, nor has it been studied so closely after becoming known, nor welcomed with the approval of so many, and has even been regarded by a greater number with suspicion and hatred? Is it because with the soul we judge of bodily lassitude and pain, whilst with the body we cannot realize the sickness of the soul? The result is that the soul passes judgment upon its own condition at a moment when the actual instrument of judgment is sick. Now if at our birth nature had granted us the ability to discern her, as she truly is, with insight and knowledge,[2] and under her excellent guidance to complete the course of life, there would certainly have been no occasion for anyone to need methodical instruction: as it is, she has given us some faint glimmering of insight which, under the corrupting influence of bad habits

opinionibusque depravati sic restinguimus, ut nusquam naturae lumen appareat. Sunt enim ingeniis nostris semina innata virtutum, quae si adolescere liceret, ipsa nos ad beatam vitam natura perduceret: nunc autem, simul atque editi in lucem et suscepti sumus, in omni continuo pravitate et in summa opinionum perversitate versamur, ut paene cum lacte nutricis errorem suxisse videamur. Cum vero parentibus redditi, dein magistris traditi sumus, tum ita variis imbuimur erroribus, ut vanitati veritas et 3 opinioni confirmatae natura ipsa cedat. II. Accedunt etiam poëtae, qui cum magnam speciem doctrinae sapientiaeque prae se tulerunt, audiuntur, leguntur, ediscuntur et inhaerescunt penitus in mentibus; cum vero eodem quasi maximus quidam magister populus accessit atque omnis undique ad vitia consentiens multitudo, tum plane inficimur opinionum pravitate a naturaque desciscimus, ut nobis optime naturae vim vidisse[1] videantur, qui nihil melius homini, nihil magis expetendum, nihil praestantius honoribus, imperiis, populari gloria iudicaverunt; ad quam fertur optimus quisque, veramque illam honestatem expetens, quam unam natura maxime anquirit, in summa inanitate versatur consectaturque nullam eminentem effigiem virtutis, sed adumbratam imaginem gloriae. Est enim gloria

---

[1] *naturam invidisse*, MSS. : *naturae vim vidisse*, Madvig.

---

[1] If the father was prepared to "acknowledge" a newborn child, he lifted it from the ground and thus showed that he was willing to rear it as his own.

[2] *I.e.* erroneous ideas, opinions and prejudices due to upbringing and society.

[3] Cf. II. § 27.

and beliefs, we speedily quench so completely that no flicker of nature's light remains. The seeds of virtue are inborn in our dispositions and, if they were allowed to ripen, nature's own hand would lead us on to happiness of life; as things are, how-ever, as soon as we come into the light of day and have been acknowledged,[1] we at once find ourselves in a world of iniquity amid a medley of wrong beliefs, so that it seems as if we drank in deception with our nurse's milk; but when we leave the nursery to be with parents and later on have been handed over to the care of masters, then we become infected with deceptions so varied that truth gives place to unreality and the voice of nature itself to fixed prepossessions.[2] II. Add too the poets [3] who hold out a fair prospect of wise teaching and are therefore heard, read, learnt, and penetrate deeply into our minds; but when to all this is added public opinion as a sort of finishing master, with all the mob combining in a general tendency to error,—then obviously we are tainted with vicious beliefs, and our revolt from nature is so complete that we come to think that the clearest insight into the meaning of nature has been gained by the men who have made up their minds that there is no higher ambition for a human being, nothing more desirable, nothing more excellent than civil office, military command and popular glory; it is to this that all the noblest are attracted, and in their quest for the true honour which alone is the object of nature's eager search, they find themselves where all is vanity, and strain to win no lofty image of virtue, but a shadowy phantom of glory.[4] For true glory

[4] Cicero seems to have Julius Caesar in his mind.

solida quaedam res et expressa, non adumbrata : ea est
consentiens laus bonorum, incorrupta vox bene iudi-
cantium de excellenti virtute, ea virtuti resonat
tamquam imago : quae quia recte factorum plerumque
4 comes est, non est bonis viris repudianda ; illa autem,
quae se eius imitatricem esse vult, temeraria atque
inconsiderata et plerumque peccatorum vitiorumque
laudatrix, fama popularis, simulatione honestatis formam eius pulcritudinemque corrumpit : qua caecati [1]
homines, cum quaedam etiam praeclara cuperent
eaque nescirent nec ubi nec qualia essent, funditus
alii everterunt suas civitates, alii ipsi occiderunt.
Atque hi quidem optima petentes non tam voluntate
quam cursus errore falluntur. Quid ? qui pecuniae
cupiditate, qui voluptatum libidine feruntur, quorum-
que ita perturbantur animi, ut non multum absint ab
insania, quod insipientibus contingit omnibus, iis
nullane est adhibenda curatio ? Utrum, quod minus
noceant animi aegrotationes quam corporis, an quod
corpora curari possint, animorum medicina nulla sit ?
5   III. At et morbi perniciosiores pluresque sunt
animi quam corporis. Hoc [2] enim ipso odiosi sunt,
quod ad animum pertinent eumque sollicitant, *animus-
que aeger,* ut ait Ennius, *semper errat, neque poti* [3]

---

[1] *caecitate*, MSS. : *caecati*, Schlenger.
[2] *Hi enim ipsi*, MSS. : *hoc . . . ipso*, Bake.
[3] *Pati*, MSS. : *poti (potiri)*, Ribbeck.

---

[1] *eminens statua* is the statue upright and standing out
prominently ; *expressa* when the marble has been worked so
that the likeness of the person it is meant for is discernible :
adumbrata is the sketchy delineation of the statue that is
to be.

[2] He seems to be thinking of Caesar and Pompey.

[3] Such as avarice, ambition. Cicero omits to deal with

is a thing of real substance and clearly wrought, no shadowy phantom :[1] it is the agreed approval of good men, the unbiassed verdict of judges deciding honestly the question of pre-eminent merit ; it gives back to virtue the echo of her voice ; and as it generally attends upon duties rightly performed it is not to be disdained by good men. The other kind of glory, however, which claims to be a copy of the true, is headstrong and thoughtless, and generally lends its support to faults and errors ; it is public reputation, and by a counterfeit mars the fair beauty of true honour. By this illusion human beings, in spite of some noble ambitions, are blinded and, as they do not know where to look or what to find, some of them bring about the utter ruin of their country and others their own downfall.[2] Now such men at any rate are misled in their quest of the best, not so much of set purpose as by a mistake in direction. What of others ? Where men are carried away by desire of gain, lust of pleasure, and where mens' souls are so disordered that they are not far off unsoundness of mind (the natural consequence for all who are without wisdom), is there no treatment which should be applied to them ? Is it that the ailments of the soul are less injurious than physical ailments, or is it that physical ailments admit of treatment while there is no means of curing souls ? III. But diseases of the soul[3] are both more dangerous and more numerous than those of the body. For the very fact that their attacks are directed at the soul makes them hateful, "and a sick soul," as Ennius says, "is always astray and cannot either attain or

their being more numerous, and this is excusable in the conversational style he adopts.

neque perpeti potest : cupere numquam desinit. Quibus
duobus morbis, ut omittam alios, aegritudine et
cupiditate, qui tandem possunt in corpore esse
graviores ? Qui vero probari potest, ut sibi mederi
animus non possit, cum ipsam medicinam corporis
animus invenerit cumque ad corporum sanationem
multum ipsa corpora et natura valeat nec omnes, qui
curari se passi sint, continuo etiam convalescant,
animi autem, qui se sanari voluerint praeceptisque
sapientium paruerint, sine ulla dubitatione sanentur ?
6 Est profecto animi medicina, philosophia, cuius
auxilium non ut in corporis morbis petendum est
foris, omnibusque opibus atque [1] viribus, ut nosmet
ipsi nobis mederi possimus, elaborandum est : quamquam de universa philosophia, quanto opere et expetenda esset et colenda, satis, ut arbitror, dictum
est in Hortensio. De maximis autem rebus nihil
fere intermisimus postea nec disputare nec scribere ;
his autem libris exposita sunt ea, quae a nobis cum
familiaribus nostris in Tusculano erant disputata.
Sed quoniam duobus superioribus de morte et de dolore dictum est, tertius dies disputationis hoc tertium
7 volumen efficiet. Ut enim in Academiam nostram
descendimus inclinato iam in postmeridianum tempus
die, poposci eorum aliquem, qui aderant, causam
disserendi. Tum res acta sic est.

IV. A. Videtur mihi cadere in sapientem aegritudo.

---

[1] *atque* supplied by Bentley.

---

[1] As we read now in newspapers, "The operation was
carried out successfully, but the patient subsequently succumbed from weakness."
[2] Bk. II. § 4.   [3] II. § 9.

endure: never does it cease to desire;" and to say nothing of others, what bodily diseases can be more serious, pray, than these two diseases of distress and desire? And then how can we accept the notion that the soul cannot heal itself, seeing that the soul has discovered the actual art of healing the body, and seeing that men's constitutions of themselves, as well as nature, contribute a good deal to the cure of the body, and not all of those who have submitted to treatment succeed at once in making recovery as well,[1] whereas we see, on the contrary, that souls which have been ready to be cured and have obeyed the instructions of wise men, are undoubtedly cured? Assuredly there is an art of healing the soul—I mean philosophy, whose aid must be sought not, as in bodily diseases, outside ourselves, and we must use our utmost endeavour, with all our resources and strength, to have the power to be ourselves our own physicians. However, as regards philosophy in general I think I have in the *Hortensius*[2] adequately expressed the paramount reasons which make its study desirable. Moreover, since that time, I have almost without cessation discussed and written on the most momentous subjects; in these books, however, the discussions held by us with our friends in my house at Tusculum have been set out in full. But as on the two previous days we dealt with death and pain, the third day's discussions will make up this third book. For when we came down to our Academy,[3] after the day had drawn towards afternoon, I called upon one of those present to propose a subject for debate. This was the subsequent course of our proceedings.

IV. A. The wise man it seems to me is susceptible

MARCUS TULLIUS CICERO

M. Num reliquae quoque perturbationes animi, formidines, libidines, iracundiae? Haec enim fere sunt eius modi, quae Graeci πάθη appellant; ego poteram morbos et id verbum esset e verbo, sed in consuetudinem nostram non caderet: nam misereri, invidere, gestire, laetari, haec omnia morbos Graeci appellant, motus animi rationi non obtemperantes; nos autem hos eosdem motus concitati animi recte, ut opinor, perturbationes dixerimus, morbos autem non satis 8 usitate, nisi quid aliud tibi videtur. A. Mihi vero isto modo. M. Haecine igitur cadere in sapientem putas? A. Prorsus existimo. M. Ne ista gloriosa sapientia non magno aestimanda est, si quidem non multum differt ab insania. A. Quid? tibi omnisne animi commotio videtur insania? M. Non mihi quidem soli, sed, id quod admirari saepe soleo, maioribus quoque nostris hoc ita visum intelligo multis saeculis ante Socratem, a quo haec omnis quae est de vita et de moribus philosophia manavit. A. Quonam tandem modo? M. Quia nomen insaniae significat mentis aegrotationem et morbum [id est,

---

¹ *Aegritudo* translates the Greek λύπη, cf. § 83 for its forms. *Tristitia*, "sorrow," is St. Augustine's word, cf. § 77.

² νόσος (cf. IV. § 23 νόσημα) is the equivalent of *morbus* and πάθος of *perturbatio*. For a similar error due to Cicero's zeal in defence of Latin cf. II. § 35. As a matter of fact Greek is better able to express the abstract notions of philosophy than Latin, cf. I. § 22. The Stoics distinguished four classes of πάθη (irrational emotions) given in Virg. *Aen*. 6. 733. *Hinc metuunt cupiuntque dolent gaudentque.* The Stoic order was ἐπιθυμία, φόβος, λύπη, ἡδονή.

³ These would be πάθη coming under the head of λύπη, *aegritudo*, and not allowable in the wise man who was ἀπαθής and did not feel desire, grief, anger or joy. The Peripatetics

of distress.[1]   M. Surely not of the other disorders of
the soul too, terrors, lusts, fits of anger? These
belong, speaking generally, to the class of emotions
which the Greeks term πάθη: I might have called
them "diseases," and this would be a word-for-word
rendering :[2] but it would not fit in with Latin usage.
For pity, envy, exultation, joy,[3] all these the Greeks
term diseases, movements that is of the soul which
are not obedient to reason;[4] we on the other
hand should, I think, rightly say that these same
movements of an agitated soul are "disorders," but
not "diseases" in the ordinary way of speaking,
unless you are of another opinion.   A. I think as you
do.   M. Do you think that these emotions come
upon the wise man?   A. Unquestionably so, I think.
M. 'Pon my word, that vaunted wisdom of yours is
not to be rated at a high value, as it is much the same
as unsoundness of mind.[5]   A. What do you mean?
Do you regard every agitation of the soul as
unsoundness of mind?   M. It is not my opinion
only, but our ancestors too—a fact which often stirs
my admiration—held the same opinion, I understand,
many centuries before Socrates, the fountain-head of
all modern philosophy that deals with life and
conduct.[6]   A. How do you make that out, pray?
M. Because the term "unsoundness" means sickness
and disease of the mind [that is a condition of

and Academy thought that these emotions were natural in
origin but needed restraint.

[4] ἄλογος καὶ παρὰ φύσιν ψυχῆς κίνησις.

[5] It was a Stoic paradox that all fools are mad, πάντες οἱ
μωροὶ μαίνονται.

[6] Of the three parts (*dialectica, physica, ethica*) into which
philosophy was divided, *ethica* is referred to Socrates,
cf. V. § 68.

insanitatem et aegrotum animum, quam appellarunt
9 insaniam.   Omnes autem perturbationes animi morbos philosophi appellant negantque stultum quemquam his morbis vacare; qui autem in morbo sunt,
sani non sunt, et omnium insipientium animi in
morbo sunt: omnes insipientes igitur insaniunt].[1]
Sanitatem enim animorum positam in tranquillitate
quadam constantiaque censebant: his rebus mentem
vacuam appellarunt insaniam, propterea quod in
perturbato animo sicut in corpore sanitas esse non
posset.

10   V. Nec minus illud acute, quod animi adfectionem
lumine mentis carentem nominaverunt amentiam
eandemque dementiam; ex quo intelligendum est
eos, qui haec rebus nomina posuerunt, sensisse hoc
idem, quod a Socrate acceptum diligenter Stoici
retinuerunt, omnes insipientes esse non sanos.   Qui
est enim animus in aliquo morbo—morbos autem hos
perturbatos motus, ut modo dixi, philosophi appellant
—non magis est sanus quam id corpus, quod in morbo
est.   Ita fit ut sapientia sanitas sit animi, insipientia
autem quasi insanitas quaedam, quae est insania
eademque dementia; multoque melius haec notata
sunt verbis Latinis quam Graecis, quod aliis quoque
multis locis reperietur. Sed id alias; nunc quod instat.

---

[1] This passage is bracketed as a later insertion.   From *id*
to *insaniam* is mere repetition: from *omnes* to *insaniunt* is
Stoic reasoning and out of place where Cicero is speaking of
the ancient Romans.

---

[1] Our ancestors.
[2] *Amens* is the man whose mind has gone: *demens* the man
whose mind has wandered from the right way.
[3] In II. § 35 he criticizes Greek terms in comparison with
Latin.   Here his point seems to be that the Latin terms
emphasize better than Greek the loss of healthiness and

unhealthiness and sickness of soul which they have termed "unsoundness." Now philosophers apply the term disease to all disorders of the soul and they say that no foolish person is free from such diseases; sufferers from disease, however, are not sound, and the souls of all unwise persons are diseased : therefore all unwise persons are of "unsound" mind]. For they[1] considered that the sound health of souls consisted in a state of equable calm : they applied the term "unsoundness" to the mind that was not in this state, because they thought that in a disordered soul, as in a disordered body, soundness of health was impossible.

V. And there was no less insight in their giving to a condition of the soul, marked by an absence of the illuminating influence of the mind, the name of "mindlessness" as well as "aberration of mind" :[2] and from this we must understand that those who gave these names to such conditions held the view which the Stoics took from Socrates and steadily adhered to, that all unwise persons are in an "unsound" state. For the soul which is suffering from some disease—now philosophers as I have said apply the term disease to these disordered movements—is no more in a sound condition than the body which is diseased. It follows that wisdom is a sound condition of the soul, unwisdom on the other hand a sort of unhealthiness which is unsoundness and also aberration of mind ; and these attributes are much better connoted by the Latin terms than by the Greek, as will be found also in many other instances.[3] But of that elsewhere ; now for the business in hand.

---

intellect that a disordered mind implies. He forgets ἄφρων and παράνοια. Tiro, his Greek secretary, could have told him.

MARCUS TULLIUS CICERO

11 Totum igitur id, quod quaerimus, quid et quale sit
verbi vis ipsa declarat. Eos enim sanos quoniam
intelligi necesse est, quorum mens motu quasi morbo
perturbata nullo sit: qui contra adfecti sint, hos
insanos appellari necesse est. Itaque nihil melius
quam quod est in consuetudine sermonis Latini, cum
exisse ex potestate dicimus eos, qui effrenati feruntur
aut libidine aut iracundia: quamquam ipsa iracundia
libidinis est pars. Sic enim definitur iracundia,
ulciscendi libido. Qui igitur exisse ex potestate
dicuntur, idcirco dicuntur, quia non sunt in potestate
mentis, cui regnum totius animi a natura tributum
est. Graeci autem μανίαν unde appellent non facile
dixerim: eam tamen ipsam distinguimus nos melius
quam illi; hanc enim insaniam, quae iuncta stultitia
patet latius, a furore disiungimus. Graeci volunt
illi quidem, sed parum valent verbo: quem nos
furorem, μελαγχολίαν illi vocant. Quasi vero atra
bili solum mens ac non saepe vel iracundia graviore
vel timore vel dolore moveatur, quo genere Atha-
mantem, Alcmaeonem, Aiacem, Orestem furere
dicimus. Qui ita sit adfectus, eum dominum esse

---

¹ *sanus.*

² Lit. "have passed out of (their own) control." Gk.
ἐξίστασθαι ἑαυτοῦ.

³ For lust is a general term for all desire, and wrath is a
particular desire or lust of getting satisfaction for an injury.
For *ira* and *iracundia* cf. IV. § 27.

⁴ The root of μανία comes in the related words, μένος,
μέμονα, μαίνομαι, *memini, mens, mind.*

⁵ The verb μελαγχολᾶν is used by Aristophanes of craziness,
cf. *Birds* 14. Black bile was one of the four humours and a
mixture of cold and hot. It made men querulous or gay or
crazy or sleepy. Modern psychology would speak of "bio-
chemical processes," cf. I. § 80.

⁶ Instances of madness in Greek mythology and poetry.

The nature then and meaning of the whole question at issue is shown by the exact force of the term.[1] For seeing that it must be understood that those, whose mind has not been thrown into disorder by any movement of the nature of a disease, are in a "sound" condition, the term "unsound" must be applied to those who on the contrary are suffering from disorder. Consequently there is nothing better than the usage of the Latin language, where we say that those who are unbridled in the indulgence of either lust or wrath are beside themselves [2] (though in fact wrath itself comes under the head of lust, for the definition of wrath is lust of vengeance).[3] Those then who are described as beside themselves are so described because they are not under the control of mind to which the empire of the whole soul has been assigned by nature. Now I cannot readily give the origin of the Greek term μανία : [4] the meaning it actually implies is marked with better discrimination by us than by the Greeks, for we make a distinction between "unsoundness" of mind, which from its association with folly has a wider connotation, and "frenzy." The Greeks wish to make the distinction but fall short of success in the term they employ : what we call frenzy they call μελαγχολία,[5] just as if the truth were that the mind is influenced by black bile only and not in many instances by the stronger power of wrath or fear or pain, in the sense in which we speak of the frenzy of Athamas, Alcmaeon, Ajax and Orestes.[6] Whosoever is so afflicted is not allowed by the Twelve Tables [7] to

[7] The code of laws drawn up by the *Decemviri legibus scribendis* appointed 451 B.C.

Tab. V. 7. *Si furiosus escit, adgnatum gentiliumque in eo pecuniaque eius potestas esto*, cf. App. II.

rerum suarum vetant duodecim tabulae; itaque non
est scriptum, si insanus, sed SI FURIOSUS ESCIT. Stultitiam enim censuerunt constantia, id est, sanitate,
vacantem posse tamen tueri mediocritatem officiorum
et vitae communem cultum atque usitatum; furorem
autem esse rati sunt mentis ad omnia caecitatem.
Quod cum maius esse videatur quam insania, tamen
eius modi est, ut furor in sapientem cadere possit,
non possit insania. Sed haec alia quaestio est: nos
ad propositum revertamur.

12 VI. Cadere, opinor, in sapientem aegritudinem
tibi dixisti videri. A. Et vero ita existimo. M. Humanum id quidem, quod ita existimas. Non enim
silice nati sumus, sed est natura[1] in animis tenerum
quiddam atque molle, quod aegritudine quasi tem-
pestate quatiatur. Nec absurde Crantor ille, qui
in nostra Academia vel in primis fuit nobilis:
"Minime" inquit "adsentior iis, qui istam nescio
quam indolentiam magno opere laudant, quae nec
potest ulla esse nec debet. Ne aegrotus sim: si
sim, qui fuerat[2] sensus adsit, sive secetur quid sive
avellatur a corpore. Nam istuc nihil dolere non

---

[1] *naturabile*, MSS. : *natura*, Lambinus: *natura fere*,
Bentley.
[2] *nec aegrotassem si inquit, fuerat*, most MSS. : Halm's
correction adopted.

---

[1] The wise man, according to the Stoics, could not become
insane, for insanity is the same as folly, and the wise man
could not be foolish. He was still a wise man when he was
asleep, and similarly he maintained his title even if attacked
with frenzy.
[2] *Odyssey*, 19. 163, οὐ γὰρ ἀπὸ δρυός ἐσσι παλαιφάτου οὐδ᾽
ἀπὸ πέτρης : *Aen.* 4, 366, *duris genuit te cautibus horrens
Caucasus.*

remain in control of his property; and consequently
we find the text runs, not "if of unsound mind," but
"if he be frenzied." For they thought that folly,
though without steadiness, that is to say, soundness
of mind, was nevertheless capable of charging itself
with the performance of ordinary duties and the
regular routine of the conduct of life: frenzy, however, they regarded as a blindness of the mind in all
relations. And though this seems to be worse than
unsoundness of mind, nevertheless there is this to
be noted, that frenzy can come upon the wise man,
unsoundness of mind cannot.[1] But this is a different
problem: let us return to our subject.

VI. You said, I think, that in your view the wise
man is susceptible of distress. A. That is assuredly
my opinion. M. It is natural at any rate for you to
have this opinion; for we are not sprung from rock,[2]
but our souls have a strain of tenderness and sensi-
tiveness of a kind to be shaken by distress as by a
storm. And it is not ridiculous of the famous
Crantor,[3] who held the foremost place of distinction
in our Academy, to say, "I do not in the least agree
with those who are so loud in their praise of that
sort of insensibility[4] which neither can nor ought to
exist. Let me escape illness: should I be ill, let
me have the capacity for feeling I previously
possessed, whether it be knife or forceps that are to
be applied to my body. For this state of apathy is

---

[3] A native of Cilicia, pupil of Xenocrates and author of a
work περὶ πένθους (*de consolatione*) which Cicero imitated,
cf. I. § 115.

[4] ἀναλγησία, the Stoic ideal. As their critics pointed out,
Stoics might root out the wheat of good emotions with the
tares of evil and reduce themselves to a torpid state of
feeling.

sine magna mercede contingit, immanitatis in animo,
13 stuporis in corpore." Sed videamus ne haec oratio
sit hominum adsentantium nostrae imbecillitati et
indulgentium mollitudini, nos autem audeamus non
solum ramos amputare miseriarum, sed omnes radi-
cum fibras evellere. Tamen aliquid relinquetur
fortasse: ita sunt altae stirpes stultitiae: sed relinquetur id solum, quod erit necessarium. Illud
quidem sic habeto, nisi sanatus animus sit, quod
sine philosophia fieri non potest, finem miseriarum
nullum fore. Quam ob rem, quoniam coepimus,
tradamus nos ei curandos: sanabimur, si vole-
mus. Et progrediar quidem longius; non enim de
aegritudine solum, quamquam id quidem primum,
sed de omni animi, ut ego posui, perturbatione—
morbo, ut Graeci volunt—explicabo. Et primo, si
placet, Stoicorum more agamus, qui breviter astrin-
gere solent argumenta; deinde nostro instituto
vagabimur.

14   VII. Qui fortis est, idem est fidens, quoniam confidens mala consuetudine loquendi in vitio ponitur,
ductum verbum a confidendo, quod laudis est; qui
autem est fidens, is profecto non extimescit; dis-
crepat enim a timendo confidere. Atqui in quem
cadit aegritudo, in eundem timor; quarum enim
rerum praesentia sumus in aegritudine, easdem

---

¹ Cicero's summary of the Stoic arguments, with digres-
sions, continues to the end of § 21, and he imitates their
brief concise style.

² The parasite in the *Phormio* of Terence is *homo confidens*,
i.e. has assurance.

not attained except at the cost of brutishness in the
soul and callousness in the body." But let us have
a care lest this be the language of those who flatter
the infirmity of our nature and regard its weakness
with complacency; for ourselves let us have the
courage, not merely to lop the branches of wretchedness, but tear out all the fibres of its roots. Yet
even then there will, perhaps, be some left; the
roots of folly go so deep; yet only that much
will be left which must be left. Be persuaded
at any rate of this, that there will be no end
to wretchedness unless the soul is cured, and
without philosophy this is impossible. Therefore
let us put ourselves in the hands of philosophy
for treatment, since we have made a beginning: we
shall be cured if we will. And indeed I shall go a
step further, for I shall deal not merely with the
subject of distress, though that will come first, but,
as I have stated, with the whole subject of disturbance—"disease" as the Greeks prefer—of the soul.
And to begin with, if you agree, let us follow the
example of the Stoics whose practice it is to give
briefly a compendious statement of their proofs;
after that we shall roam at large in our accustomed
way.

VII.[1] The brave man is also self-reliant; for "confident" is by a mistaken usage of speech used in a
bad sense, though the word is derived from *confidere*,
"to have trust," which implies praise.[2] The self-
reliant man, however, is assuredly not excessively
fearful; for there is a difference between confidence
and timidity. And yet the man who is accessible to
distress is also accessible to fear. For where things
cause us distress by their presence, we are also

impendentes et venientes timemus. Ita fit ut
fortitudini aegritudo repugnet. Veri simile est igitur,
in quem cadit aegritudo, cadere in eundem timorem
et infractionem quidem animi et demissionem; quae
in quem cadunt, in eundem cadit ut serviat, ut
victum, si quando, se esse fateatur; quae qui recipit,
recipiat idem necesse est timiditatem et ignaviam.
Non cadunt autem haec in virum fortem: igitur
ne aegritudo quidem. At nemo sapiens nisi fortis:
15 non cadet ergo in sapientem aegritudo. Praeterea
necesse est, qui fortis sit, eundem esse magni
animi; qui magni animi sit, invictum; qui invictus
sit, eum res humanas despicere atque infra se
positas arbitrari; despicere autem nemo potest eas
res, propter quas aegritudine adfici potest; ex quo
efficitur fortem virum aegritudine numquam adfici;
omnes autem sapientes fortes: non cadit igitur in
sapientem aegritudo. Et quem ad modum oculus
conturbatus non est probe adfectus ad suum munus
fungendum, et reliquae partes totumve corpus statu
cum est motum, deest officio suo et muneri, sic
conturbatus animus non est aptus ad exsequendum
munus suum. Munus autem animi est ratione
bene uti et sapientis animus ita semper adfectus est,
ut ratione optime utatur; numquam igitur est
perturbatus; at aegritudo perturbatio est animi:
semper igitur ea sapiens vacabit.
16   VIII. Veri etiam simile illud est, qui sit tem-

---

[1] The argument loses itself in a long digression on terminology written in the *conversational* irregular style, which
Cicero often adopts in his dialogues, and is only resumed in
§ 18 with the words *Qui sit frugi igitur*.

afraid of the menace of their approach. So it comes
that distress is incompatible with fortitude. It is
therefore probable that the man who is susceptible
of distress is also susceptible of fear, and indeed
of dejection and depression of soul. Where
men are susceptible of these emotions there also
comes a feeling of subjection, a readiness to
admit themselves beaten should occasion arise. He
who makes this admission has to admit fear and
cowardice as well. But of such feelings the brave
man is not susceptible : therefore he is not susceptible
of distress either. But no one is wise if he is not
brave. Therefore the wise man will not be susceptible of distress. Moreover the brave man must
also be high-souled, and the high-souled must be
unconquered ; and the unconquered must look down
on human vicissitudes and consider them beneath
him. But no one can look down upon the things
which can make him suffer distress. And from this
it follows that the brave man never suffers distress.
But all wise men are brave. Therefore the wise
man is not susceptible of distress. And just as the
eye, if out of order, is not in a right condition for
discharging its function, and the other members, or
the body as a whole, if it is not in its normal condition, fails to perform its function and work : similarly the soul, if disquieted, is not fitted to carry out
its work. But the work of the soul is the right use
of reason, and the soul of the wise man is always
in a condition to make the best use of reason.
Therefore it is never in a disordered state. But
distress is a disorder of the soul. Therefore the wise
man will always be free from it.

VIII. It is also probable that the temperate man [1]

perans,—quem Graeci σώφρονα appellant eamque
virtutem σωφροσύνην vocant, quam soleo equidem tum
temperantiam, tum moderationem appellare, non
numquam etiam modestiam, sed haud scio an recte
ea virtus frugalitas appellari possit, quod angustius
apud Graecos valet, qui frugi homines χρησίμους
appellant, id est, tantum modo utiles; at illud est
latius; omnis enim abstinentia, omnis innocentia—
quae apud Graecos usitatum nomen nullum habet,
sed habere potest ἀβλάβειαν: nam est innocentia
adfectio talis animi, quae noceat nemini—reliquas
etiam virtutes frugalitas continet; quae nisi tanta
esset et si iis angustiis, quibus plerique putant,
teneretur, numquam esset L. Pisonis cognomen
17 tanto opere laudatum. Sed quia nec qui propter
metum praesidium reliquit, quod est ignaviae, nec
qui propter avaritiam clam depositum non reddidit,
quod est iniustitiae, nec qui propter temeritatem
male rem gessit, quod est stultitiae, *frugi* appellari
solet, eo tris virtutes, fortitudinem, iustitiam, prudentiam, frugalitas complexa est—: etsi hoc quidem

---

[1] *Frugi, frugalitas* are words which describe the virtue of
the older Romans. Applied to a field *frugi* means that it is
productive; when transferred to human beings it means an
upright, energetic, prudent, self-controlled man who keeps
the right measure in all that he does, cf. IV. § 36. *Frugi*
was employed as a surname; it could also be applied

—the Greeks call him σώφρων, and they apply the
term σωφροσύνη to the virtue which I usually call,
sometimes temperance, sometimes self-control, and
occasionally also discretion; but, it may be, the
virtue could rightly be called "frugality,"[1] the term
corresponding to which has a narrower meaning
with the Greeks, who call "frugal" men χρήσιμοι,
that is to say simply useful; but our term has a
wider meaning, for it connotes all abstinence and
inoffensiveness (and this with the Greeks has no
customary term, but it is possible to use ἀβλάβεια,
harmlessness; for inoffensiveness is a disposition of
the soul to injure no one)—well, "frugality" embraces all the other virtues as well; had its meaning
not been so comprehensive and had it been confined
to the narrow limits of ordinary acceptation,[2] it would
never have become the much eulogized surname of
L. Piso.[3] But because neither the man who through
fear has deserted his post, which is a proof of
cowardice, nor the man who through avarice has
failed to restore a trust privately committed to him,
which is a proof of unrighteousness, nor the man
who through rashness has mismanaged a business
transaction, which is a proof of folly, are usually
called "frugal," "frugality" has come to include
the three virtues of fortitude, justice and prudence :
(though this is a feature common to the virtues ; for

to good slaves. The meaning of *frugalitas* in the main is
that of σωφροσύνη, for that virtue bids us use right reason in
all that we undertake, and implies temperance, self-control,
moderation, steadfastness and continence.

[2] *i.e.* "economical," as in Horace, *Sat.* 1. 3. 49, *Parcius hic
vivit, frugi dicatur.*

[3] Lucius Calpurnius Piso, who gained the cognomen of
Frugi, was Consul 133 B.C.

commune est virtutum: omnes enim inter se nexae et iugatae sunt—: reliqua igitur est, quarta virtus ut sit, ipsa frugalitas. Eius enim videtur esse proprium motus animi appetentis regere et sedare semperque adversantem libidini moderatam in omni re servare constantiam: cui contrarium vitium
18 nequitia dicitur. *Frugalitas*, ut opinor, a *fruge*, qua nihil melius e terra, *nequitia* ab eo—etsi erit hoc fortasse durius, sed temptemus; lusisse putemur, si nihil sit—, ab eo, quod *nequidquam* est in tali homine, ex quo idem *nihili* dicitur. Qui sit frugi igitur vel, si mavis, moderatus et temperans, eum necesse est esse constantem; qui autem constans, quietum; qui quietus, perturbatione omni vacuum, ergo etiam aegritudine; et sunt illa sapientis: aberit igitur a sapiente aegritudo.

IX. Itaque non inscite Heracleotes Dionysius ad ea disputat, quae apud Homerum Achilles queritur hoc, ut opinor, modo:

Corque meum penitus turgescit tristibus iris,
Cum decore atque omni me orbatum laude recordor.

19 Num manus adfecta recte est, cum in tumore est, aut num aliud quodpiam membrum tumidum ac

---

¹ The virtues overlap. In Plato, *Gorgias* 507, Socrates argues that ὁ σώφρων τὰ προσήκοντα πράττοι ἂν καὶ περὶ θεοὺς καὶ περὶ ἀνθρώπους. If the temperate man performs his duties to men, he will also be just, and if he avoids and pursues the things he ought to, he will also be courageous. The "frugal" man, Cicero says, shows fortitude, justice and prudence. "Frugality" embraces these three and also has its own peculiar quality, therefore, says Cicero, "frugality" is left for the fourth virtue, temperance. But it cannot be said that his "therefore" is clear.

they are all mutually linked and bound together).[1] Therefore I count " frugality " by itself as left to be the fourth virtue. For it seems to be its special function to guide and compose the eager impulses of the soul and, by a constant opposition to lust, to preserve on every occasion a tempered firmness : and the vice which is its opposite is " worthlessness." " Frugality," as I think, is derived from " fruit " and nothing better comes from the earth : " worthlessness " is derived (the derivation, it may be, will be somewhat harsh ; but all the same let us make the attempt ; let it be taken as a jest if it should come to nothing) from that which is *nequidquam*, " for nothing," in a man of that kind ; hence he is also said to be " good for nothing." The man therefore who is " frugal " or, should you prefer it, self-restrained and temperate must be firm ; the firm man must be calm ; the calm man must be free from all disturbance, therefore free from distress as well. All these are characteristic of the wise man. Therefore distress will keep far away from the wise man.

IX. And so in dealing with the passage in Homer where Achilles laments to this effect, I think :

Big is the heart in my breast with a gloomy swelling of anger,
When I remember that I have been robbed of my honour and glory,[2]

Dionysius of Heraclea[3] argues not unskilfully— Can the hand be in a right condition when suffering from a swelling ? or can any other limb fail to be

<hr>

[2] *Il.* 9. 646.   [3] Cf. II. § 60.

turgidum non vitiose se habet? Sic igitur inflatus
et tumens animus in vitio est. Sapientis autem
animus semper vacat vitio, numquam turgescit, numquam tumet; at irati animus eius modi est: numquam igitur sapiens irascitur. Nam si irascitur,
etiam concupiscit; proprium est enim irati cupere,
a quo laesus videatur, ei quam maximum dolorem
inurere ; qui autem id concupierit, eum necesse est,
si id consecutus sit, magno opere laetari : ex quo fit
ut alieno malo gaudeat; quod quoniam non cadit in
sapientem, ne ut irascatur quidem cadit. Sin autem
caderet in sapientem aegritudo, caderet etiam
iracundia: qua quoniam vacat, aegritudine etiam
20 vacabit. Etenim si sapiens in aegritudinem incidere
posset, posset etiam in misericordiam, posset in invidentiam : non dixi in invidiam, quae tum est, cum
invidetur ; ab invidendo autem invidentia recte dici
potest, ut effugiamus ambiguum nomen invidiae,
quod verbum ductum est a nimis intuendo fortunam
alterius, ut est in Melanippo :

> *Quisnam florem liberum invidit meum ?*

Male Latine videtur, sed praeclare Accius : ut enim
videre, sic *invidere florem* rectius quam *flori*. Nos

---

[1] Cf. § 11.

[2] For compassion and envy come under the head of the
πάθος *aegritudo*, λύπη. In the *Pro Ligario*, however, speaking
in praise of Caesar, Cicero says, *Nulla de tuis virtutibus
plurimis nec gratior nec admirabilior misericordia est.*

[3] *Invidia* has two senses, *altera invidum, altera invidiosum
facit,* "the one makes an envious man, the other a man who
rouses envy," Quint. VI. 2. 21. *Invidere* in the *Melanippus*
has the meaning of βασκαίνειν, *fascinare,* "to cast an evil
eye on."

[4] Cf. App. II.

defective when in a swollen and inflamed state?
Similarly then the soul, when puffed up and swollen,
is in a defective state. But the soul of the wise
man is always free from defect and never in an
inflamed, never in a swollen state; but this is the
condition of the angry soul : therefore the wise
man is never angry. For if he is angry he is also
covetous. The covetousness peculiar to the angry
man is the desire to stamp the brand of uttermost
pain upon the person by whom he considers himself
injured.[1] Moreover the man who has coveted this
end must necessarily be greatly rejoiced if he has
secured it. Hence it comes about that he rejoices
in another's misfortune. As the wise man is incapable of this, he is also incapable of feeling anger
either. But should the wise man be susceptible of
distress, he would also be susceptible of anger, and
as he is free from anger he will also be free from
distress. For if the wise man could be capable of
feeling distress he could be also of feeling compassion,[2] he could feel envy. (I have not said
invidia for envy, as it is used where a person is the
object of envy; the word *invidentia*, however, derived from *invidere*, can be rightly used to avoid the
ambiguity of *invidia*[3] which comes from eyeing the
prosperity of a rival too narrowly, as in the
Melanippus : [4]

> Who has looked askance upon the promise of my
> children ?

Bad Latin, it seems; but admirably said by Accius;
for just as *videre*, " to look at," takes the accusative,
so *invidere florem*, " to look askance upon the
promise," is truer than the use of *flori* the dative.

consuetudine prohibemur; poëta ius suum tenuit et
21 dixit audacius.   X. Cadit igitur in eundem et
misereri et invidere; nam qui dolet rebus alicuius
adversis, idem alicuius etiam secundis dolet, ut
Theophrastus interitum deplorans Callisthenis sodalis
sui rebus Alexandri prosperis angitur, itaque dicit
Callisthenem incidisse in hominem summa potentia
summaque fortuna, sed ignarum quem ad modum
rebus secundis uti conveniret.   Atqui quem ad
modum misericordia aegritudo est ex alterius rebus
adversis, sic invidentia aegritudo est ex alterius rebus
secundis; in quem igitur cadit misereri, in eundem
etiam invidere; non cadit autem invidere in sapientem: ergo ne misereri quidem.   Quod si aegre ferre
sapiens soleret, misereri etiam soleret: abest ergo a
sapiente aegritudo.

22   Haec sic dicuntur a Stoicis concludunturque con-
tortius; sed latius aliquanto dicenda sunt et diffusius,
sententiis tamen utendum eorum potissimum, qui
maxime forti et, ut ita dicam, virili utuntur ratione
atque sententia: nam Peripatetici, familiares nostri,
quibus nihil est uberius, nihil eruditius, nihil gravius,

---

[1] The passage in brackets is an explanation of Cicero's,
parenthetical to the comment of Dionysius of Heraclea on
the passage of Homer.

[2] Callisthenes was fellow-pupil with Alexander the Great
of Aristotle.   He was put to death by Alexander in Asia on

The usage of language bars *us* from doing this; the poet has claimed his right and spoken with greater freedom.)[1] X. The same person therefore is susceptible of pity and envy. For the man who is pained by another's misfortunes is also pained by another's prosperity. For instance, Theophrastus in lamenting the death of his friend Callisthenes[2] is vexed at the prosperity of Alexander; and so he says that Callisthenes fell in with a man of supreme power and unparalleled good fortune, but one who did not know how to turn prosperity to good account. And yet, as compassion is distress due to a neighbour's misfortunes, so envy is distress due to a neighbour's prosperity. Therefore the man who comes to feel compassion comes also to feel envy. The wise man, however, does not come to feel envy; therefore he does not come to feel compassion either. But if the wise man were accustomed to feel distress he would also be accustomed to feel compassion. Therefore distress keeps away from the wise man.

This is how the Stoics state the case, reasoning in a way that is unduly intricate. But the subject needs expansion and stating with considerably greater amplification. None the less we must above all make use of the opinions of thinkers who in the method they use and the opinion they adopt show a highly courageous and so to speak manly spirit. For the Peripatetics, friends of ours as they are and unequalled in resourcefulness, in learning and in earnestness, do not quite succeed in convincing me

a charge of conspiracy. Theophrastus of Lesbos, cf. V. § 24, a pupil of Plato and Aristotle, wrote a book in memory of his friend.

mediocritates vel perturbationum vel morborum animi mihi non sane probant. Omne enim malum, etiam mediocre, malum [1] est; nos autem id agimus, ut id in sapiente nullum sit omnino. Nam ut corpus, etiam si mediocriter aegrum est, sanum non est, sic in animo ista mediocritas caret sanitate.

Itaque praeclare nostri, ut alia multa, molestiam, sollicitudinem, angorem propter similitudinem corporum aegrorum aegritudinem nominaverunt.

23 Hoc propemodum verbo Graeci omnem animi perturbationem appellant; vocant enim πάθος, id est, morbum, quicumque est motus in animo turbidus: nos melius; aegris enim corporibus simillima animi est aegritudo; at non similis aegrotationis est libido, non immoderata laetitia, quae est voluptas animi elata et gestiens. Ipse etiam metus non est morbi admodum similis, quamquam aegritudini est finitimus, sed proprie ut aegrotatio in corpore, sic aegritudo in animo nomen habet non seiunctum a dolore. Doloris huius igitur origo nobis explicanda est, id est causa efficiens aegritudinem in animo tamquam aegrotationem in corpore; nam ut medici causa morbi inventa curationem esse inventam putant, sic

---

[1] *magnum*, MSS.: *malum*, Bouhier.

---

[1] Gk. μεσότητες. The Peripatetics taught Aristotle's doctrine of the "mean," a balance between two extremes. Virtue is the mean between two extremes, as for instance courage is the "mean" between rashness and cowardice, cf. § 74. The "mean" expresses the Greek notion of the beauty of virtue in its harmony and proportion rather than the absolute difference between right and wrong. But Aristotle said that in its essence virtue was an extreme utterly remote from vice. The difference between virtue and vice was not merely quantitative as Cicero seems to think the Peripatetics supposed.

of their "mean"[1] or moderate states either of disturbances or of diseases of the soul. For every evil, even a moderate one, is an evil; but our object is that there should be no evil at all in the wise man. For as the body, even if moderately ailing, is not healthy;[2] so in the soul the so-called mean or moderate state is without health.

And so our countrymen, as in many other instances, showed a fine instinct in giving the name of "distress" to vexation, anxiety, and anguish, because of their resemblance to the condition of bodies out of health. By almost the same term the Greeks describe all disturbance of the soul; for they use πάθος,[3] that is to say, "disease," for any troubled movement whatever in the soul. We do better; for distress of soul closely resembles the condition of bodies out of health; but lust does not resemble sickness, intemperate joy does not, which is an excited and exuberant pleasure of the soul. Actual fear too is not very like disease, though closely akin to distress. But it is appropriate that, like sickness in the body, so distress in the soul has a name which in meaning is not distinct from the meaning of pain. We must therefore trace out the origin of this pain which is the efficient cause of distress in the soul, as if we were diagnosing sickness in the body. For physicians consider that, when they have discovered the cause of disease, they have also discovered the method of treating it, and similarly we, when we

---

[2] The Peripatetics did not admit the "mean" in a bad state. There can be violent sickness or trifling ailment, but no "mean" between them that is good, Arist. *Eth.* II. 6. 17.

[3] Cf. § 7.

nos causa aegritudinis reperta medendi facultatem reperiemus.

24   XI. Est igitur causa omnis in opinione nec vero aegritudinis solum, sed etiam reliquarum omnium perturbationum,—quae sunt genere quattuor, partibus plures. Nam cum omnis perturbatio sit animi motus vel rationis expers vel rationem aspernans vel rationi non obediens, isque motus aut boni aut mali opinione citetur bifariam, quattuor perturbationes aequaliter distributae sunt: nam duae sunt ex opinione boni, quarum altera, voluptas gestiens, id est, praeter modum elata laetitia, opinione praesentis magni alicuius boni, altera, quae est[1] immoderata appetitio opinati magni boni rationi non obtemper-
25 ans, vel cupiditas recte vel libido dici potest. Ergo haec duo genera, voluptas gestiens et libido, bonorum opinione turbantur, ut duo reliqua, metus et aegritudo, malorum. Nam et metus opinio magni mali impendentis et aegritudo est opinio magni mali praesentis et quidem recens opinio talis mali, ut in eo rectum videatur esse angi; id autem est, ut is, qui doleat, oportere opinetur se dolere. His autem perturbationibus, quas in vitam hominum stultitia quasi quasdam furias immittit atque incitat, omnibus viribus atque opibus repugnandum est, si volumus hoc, quod datum est vitae, tranquille placideque traducere. Sed cetera alias: nunc aegritudinem, si possumus, depellamus. Id enim sit propositum, quando quidem eam tu videri tibi in sapientem

---

[1] The order of words is confused in the MSS. and has been corrected by Davies.

---

[1] He deals with the other disturbances in Book IV.

have discovered the cause of distress, shall find the
possibility of curing it.

XI. It is then wholly in an idea that we find the
cause not merely indeed of distress but of all other disturbances as well, and these can be classified as four
with numerous subdivisions. For as all disturbance
is a movement of the soul either destitute of reason,
or contemptuous of reason, or disobedient to reason,
and as such a movement is provoked in two ways,
either by an idea of good or idea of evil, we have
four disturbances equally divided. For there are
two proceeding from an idea of good, one of which
is exuberant pleasure, that is to say, joy excited
beyond measure by the idea of some great present
good ; the second is the intemperate longing for a
supposed great good, and this longing is disobedient
to reason, and may be rightly termed desire or lust.
Therefore these two classes, exuberant pleasure and
lust springing from the idea of good, disturb the
soul just as the two remaining, fear and distress,
cause disturbances by the idea of evil. For fear is
the idea of a serious threatening evil and distress
is the idea of a serious present evil and indeed an
idea freshly conceived of an evil of such sort that it
seems a due reason for anguish ; now that means
that the man who feels the pain believes that he
ought to feel pain. We must, however, with all our
might and main resist these disturbances which folly
looses and launches like a kind of evil spirit upon
the life of mankind, if we wish to pass our allotted
span in peace and quiet. But let us deal with the
rest another time ;[1] for the present let us get rid
of distress if we can. In fact let that be our object,
since you have said that you think the wise man

cadere dixisti, quod ego nullo modo existimo ; taetra
enim res est, misera, detestabilis, omni contentione,
26 velis, ut ita dicam, remisque fugienda. XII. Qualis
enim tibi ille videtur

> *Tantalo prognatus, Pelope natus, qui quondam a*
> *socro*
> *Oenomao rege Hippodameam raptis nanctust nuptiis ?*

Iovis iste quidem pronepos. Tamne ergo abiectus
tamque fractus ?

> *Nolite,* inquit, *hospites ad me adire ! Ilico istic,*
> *Ne contagio mea bonis umbrave obsit,*
> *Meo* [1] *tanta vis sceleris in corpore haeret.*

Tu te, Thyesta, damnabis orbabisque luce propter
vim sceleris alieni ? Quid ? illum filium Solis nonne
patris ipsius luce indignum putas ?

> *Refugere oculi : corpus macie extabuit :*
> *Lacrimae peredere humore exsanguis genas :*
> *Situm inter* [2] *oris barba pedore horrida atque*
> *Intonsa infuscat pectus illuvie scabrum.*

Haec mala, o stultissime Aeeta, ipse tibi addidisti :
non inerant in iis, quae tibi casus invexerat, et
quidem inveterato malo, cum tumor animi resed-
isset—est autem aegritudo, ut docebo, in opinione

---

[1] Inserted by Bentley.
[2] *Situ nitoris* MSS. : corrected by Lachmann.

---

[1] He gives the Stoic doctrine : the Peripatetics said, " We
shall grieve, but with restraint ; we shall desire, but with
moderation ; we shall be angry, but not implacably."
[2] Thyestes, cf. I. § 107, was son of Pelops, grandson of
Tantalus, great-grandson of Jupiter, and yet breaks down
ignobly. Pelops won Hippodamea by victory in a chariot
race, II. § 67, cf. App. II.

susceptible of distress, an opinion I by no means share. For distress is loathsome, wretched, execrable, to be avoided so to speak with full spread of sail and reach of oars.[1] What think you of that hero of tragedy,

> Tantalus' descendant, son of Pelops,[2] who from her
>   royal sire
> Oenomaus won Hippodamea by forced nuptials
>   once?

Yes, he was Jupiter's great-grandson! Is he then to be so despondent, so broken down?

> Forbear you my friends to approach me; at once
>   fly,
> Lest on good men my shadow infection be working,
> So strong in my body crime's power is lurking.

Will you, Thyestes, pass sentence on yourself and deprive yourself of the sight of men because of the power of another man's crime?—Or again, do you not think that the famed child of the Sun was unworthy of his own father's light?

> My eyes are dim, my frame with wasting thinned,
> The dew of tears my bloodless cheeks has
>   marred;
> On face uncared for, stiff with filth my beard
> Blackens unshorn a breast that's rough with
>   grime.

Such ills O foolish Aeetes you have heaped upon yourself; they were not in the list of those which misfortune brought upon you, and in fact you made them into a rooted evil, when the fever once settled in the soul—distress, however, as I shall

mali recenti [1]—; sed maeres videlicet regni desiderio, non filiae; illam enim oderas et iure fortasse: regno non aequo animo carebas. Est autem impudens luctus maerore se conficientis, quod imperare non

27 liceat liberis. Dionysius quidem tyrannus Syracusis expulsus Corinthi pueros docebat: usque eo imperio carere non poterat. Tarquinio vero quid impudentius, qui bellum gereret cum iis, qui eius non tulerant superbiam? Is cum restitui in regnum nec Veientium nec Latinorum armis potuisset, Cumas contulisse se dicitur inque ea urbe senio et aegritudine esse confectus. XIII. Hoc tu igitur censes sapienti accidere posse, ut aegritudine opprimatur, id est, miseria? Nam cum omnis perturbatio miseria est, tum carnificina est aegritudo. Habet ardorem libido, levitatem laetitia gestiens, humilitatem metus, sed aegritudo maiora quaedam, tabem, cruciatum, adflictationem, foeditatem; lacerat, exest animum planeque conficit. Hanc nisi exuimus sic, ut abiiciamus, miseria carere non possumus.

28 Atque hoc quidem perspicuum est, tum aegritudinem exsistere, cum quid ita visum sit, ut magnum quoddam malum adesse et urguere videatur. Epicuro autem placet opinionem mali aegritudinem esse

---

[1] *recentis* MSS.: *recenti* Bake.

---

[1] Cicero seems to be following the *Medus* of Pacuvius, where Aeetes is deprived of his throne by his brother Perses because of the loss of the golden fleece which Medea helped Jason to win, cf. App. II.

[2] Dionysius the younger, who succeeded his father 367 B.C. Cicero has Julius Caesar in his mind as well as Aeetes and Tarquin.

show, lies in the freshly conceived idea of evil; but your grief, we must suppose, is due to the loss of your throne and not of your daughter.[1] For her you hated and maybe with good reason; you could not patiently do without a throne. Still there is shamelessness in the sorrow of a man wasting himself with grief because he is not allowed to rule over free men. There is the instance of the tyrant Dionysius,[2] who after his expulsion from Syracuse became a schoolmaster at Corinth; so complete was his inability to do without the right to rule. What indeed could be more shameless than Tarquin in making war on the men who had refused to endure his pride? When he found that his restoration to the throne by the help of the arms of Veientines or Latins was impossible, he withdrew, we are told, to Cumae, and in that city was brought to the grave by old age and distress of mind. XIII. Do you suppose then that there is any possibility of the wise man being overwhelmed with distress, that is to say, with wretchedness? Indeed, while all disturbance is wretchedness, "distress" means being actually put upon the rack. Lust involves passion, exuberant joy frivolity, fear degradation; but distress involves worse things, it means decay, torture, agony, hideousness; it rends and corrodes the soul and brings it to absolute ruin. Unless we strip it off[3] and manage to fling it away we cannot be free from wretchedness.

Moreover this at any rate is clear, that distress arises from the impression of some great evil which seems to be closely besetting us. Now Epicurus holds that the distress which the idea of evil pro-

natura, ut quicumque intueatur in aliquod maius
malum, si id sibi accidisse opinetur, sit continuo in
aegritudine. Cyrenaici non omni malo aegritudinem
effici censent, sed insperato et necopinato malo.
Est id quidem non mediocre ad aegritudinem augen-
dam; videntur enim omnia repentina graviora. Ex
hoc et illa iure laudantur:

> Ego cum genui, tum morituros scivi et ei rei sustuli.
> Praeterea ad Troiam cum misi ob defendendam
>   Graeciam,
> Scibam me in mortiferum bellum, non in epulas
>   mittere.

29   XIV. Haec igitur praemeditatio futurorum malorum lenit eorum adventum, quae venientia longe
ante videris. Itaque apud Euripidem a Theseo dicta
laudantur; licet enim, ut saepe facimus, in Latinum
illa convertere:

> Nam qui haec audita a docto meminissem viro,
> Futuras mecum commentabar miserias:
> Aut mortem acerbam aut exsili maestam fugam,
> Aut semper aliquam molem meditabar mali,
> Ut, si qua invecta diritas casu foret,
> Ne me imparatum cura laceraret repens.

30   Quod autem Theseus a docto se audisse dicit, id de
se ipso loquitur Euripides; fuerat enim auditor

---

[1] Natural and necessary, Gk. φυσικῶς. The Stoics held
distress to be contrary to nature and voluntary.
[2] By the Cyrenaics, cf. II. § 15, as showing that evils
anticipated are not so distressing as unexpected evils. The
lines are from Ennius' *Telamo*, where Telamon is speaking of
his sons Ajax and Teucer, whom he had sent to war, cf. App. II.

duces is a natural[1] effect, in the sense that anyone who contemplates some considerable evil at once feels distress, should he imagine that it has befallen him. The Cyrenaics consider that distress is not caused by every evil but by an unlooked for and unexpected evil. That, it is true, has no ordinary effect in heightening distress, for all sudden visitations seem more serious than others. Hence it is that these lines are rightly praised:[2]

I begat them and begetting knew that them for
    death I reared.
Also when to Troy I sent them Greece to fight
    for and defend,
Well I knew to deadly warfare not for feasting
    sent I them.

XIV. This anticipation therefore of the future mitigates the approach of evils whose coming one has long foreseen. And so the words Euripides has put into the mouth of Theseus[3] are praised, for it is allowable, according to our frequent practice, to turn them into Latin:

For since this lesson from wise lips I learnt,
Within my heart I pondered ills to come:
Untimely death or exile's sullen flight,
Or other weight of woe I mused on aye,
That if dread chance should bring calamity,
No sudden care should rend me unprepared.

By the lesson which Theseus says he learnt from a wise man, Euripides means a lesson which he had learnt himself. For he had been a pupil of Anaxa-

---

[3] From a lost tragedy. The Greek lines are quoted in Plutarch's *Moralia*, 112 D, see page 563.

Anaxagorae, quem ferunt nuntiata morte filii dixisse: " Sciebam me genuisse mortalem." Quae vox declarat iis esse haec acerba, quibus non fuerint cogitata. Ergo id quidem non dubium, quin omnia, quae mala putentur, sint improvisa graviora. Itaque quamquam non haec una res efficit maximam aegritudinem, tamen, quoniam multum potest provisio animi et praeparatio ad minuendum dolorem, sint semper omnia homini humana meditata. Et nimirum haec est illa praestans et divina sapientia et perceptas penitus et pertractatas res humanas habere, nihil admirari cum acciderit, nihil, ante quam evenerit, non evenire posse arbitrari.

> Quam ob rem omnes, cum secundae res sunt maxume, tum maxume
> Meditari secum oportet quo pacto advorsam aerumnam ferant:
> Pericla, damna, peregre rediens semper secum cogitet,
> Aut fili peccatum aut uxoris mortem aut morbum filiae:
> Communia esse haec, ne quid horum umquam accidat animo novum:
> Quidquid praeter spem eveniat, omne id deputare esse in lucro.

31 XV. Ergo hoc Terentius a philosophia sumptum cum tam commode dixerit, nos, e quorum fontibus id haustum est, non et dicemus hoc melius et con-

---

[1] Cf. I. § 104.
[2] The evening before the Ides of March Caesar supped with Lepidus and there arose a question, "What kind of death was the best?" and Caesar, answering before them all, cried out, "A sudden one."
[3] *Phormio*, 2. 1. 11.

goras,[1] who, according to the story, said when he heard of his son's death, "I knew that I had begotten a mortal." This saying shows that such events are cruel for those who have not reflected upon them. Therefore it does not admit of doubt that everything which is thought evil is more grievous if it comes unexpectedly.[2] And so, though this is not the one cause of the greatest distress, yet as foresight and anticipation have considerable effect in lessening pain, a human being should ponder all the vicissitudes that fall to man's lot. And do not doubt that here is found the ideal of that wisdom which excels and is divine, namely in the thorough study and comprehension of human vicissitudes, in being astonished at nothing when it happens, and in thinking, before the event is come, that there is nothing which may not come to pass.

Wherefore everyone, when fortune smiles her
    brightest, closely then
Ponder should within his heart how hardship's
    onset he may bear:
Let him think on perils, losses, from abroad as he
    returns,
Son's misdeed or wife's departing or disease of
    daughter loved;
Think these things man's common lot are, lest
    one strike the mind as strange:
Luck that passes expectation should be reckoned
    all as gain.

XV. Now when Terence[3] has given such apt expression to a lesson gained from philosophy, shall we, from whose springs the draught was drawn, fail to express it in better terms and feel it more stead-

stantius sentiemus? Hic est enim ille vultus semper idem, quem dicitur Xanthippe praedicare solita
in viro suo fuisse Socrate, eodem semper se vidisse
exeuntem illum domo et revertentem. Nec vero ea
frons erat, quae M. Crassi illius veteris, quem semel
ait in omni vita risisse Lucilius, sed tranquilla et
serena; sic enim accepimus : iure autem erat semper
idem vultus, cum mentis, a qua is fingitur, nulla
fieret mutatio.

Qua re accipio equidem a Cyrenaicis haec arma
contra casus et eventus, quibus eorum advenientes
impetus diuturna praemeditatione frangantur, simul-
que iudico malum illud opinionis esse, non naturae ;
32 si enim in re esset, cur fierent provisa leviora ? Sed
est iisdem de rebus quod dici possit subtilius, si
prius Epicuri sententiam viderimus, qui censet
necesse esse omnes in aegritudine esse, qui se in
malis esse arbitrentur, sive illa ante provisa et
exspectata sint sive inveteraverint. Nam neque
vetustate minui mala nec fieri praemeditata leviora,
stultamque etiam esse meditationem futuri mali aut
fortasse ne futuri quidem ; satis esse odiosum malum
omne, cum venisset : qui autem semper cogitavisset
accidere posse aliquid adversi, ei fieri illud sempiternum malum; si vero ne futurum quidem sit,

---

¹ M. Crassus known as Agelastus, ἀγέλαστος, praetor 105
B.C. and grandfather of the triumvir.

fastly? For here we have that look of the wise man—that look ever the same which, according to the story, Xanthippe used to claim her husband Socrates wore, for she said she saw him going out and returning home with his countenance always unchanged. And his was in no way the severe brow of our old M. Crassus [1] who, according to Lucilius, laughed but once in the whole course of his life, but a calm and sunny look; for so history tells us: and with good right was his look ever the same, since the mind from which the countenance receives its mould underwent no change.

And therefore, for my part, in confronting the changes and chances of life I accept indeed from the Cyrenaics such weapons as they provide to enable me, with the help of long previous consideration, to break the coming of life's assaults, and at the same time I judge the evil we speak of to lie in belief and not in nature; for if it were downright reality, why should it be rendered lighter by anticipation? But a more accurate statement upon this same subject is possible, if we first consider the opinion of Epicurus, who supposes that all men must necessarily feel distress, if they think themselves encompassed by evils, whether previously foreseen and anticipated, or long established. For according to him evils are not lessened by duration nor lightened by previous consideration, and besides, he thinks it folly to dwell upon an evil which has still to come or maybe will not come at all; all evil, he says, is hateful enough when it has come; but the man, who is always thinking a mishap may come, is making that evil perpetual: but if it is not destined to come at all, he is needlessly the victim of a

265

frustra suscipi miseriam voluntariam : ita semper
33 angi aut accipiendo aut cogitando malo.   Levationem
autem aegritudinis in duabus rebus ponit, avoca-
tione a cogitanda molestia et revocatione ad con-
templandas voluptates.   Parere enim censet animum
rationi posse et quo illa ducat sequi.   Vetat igitur
ratio intueri molestias, abstrahit ab acerbis cogitationibus, hebetem facit[1] aciem ad miserias contem-
plandas : a quibus cum cecinit receptui, impellit
rursum et incitat ad conspiciendas totaque mente
contrectandas varias voluptates, quibus ille et
praeteritarum memoria et spe consequentium sapientis vitam refertam putat.   Haec nostro more nos
diximus, Epicurii dicunt suo ; sed quae dicant
videamus, quo modo, negligamus.

34   XVI. Principio male reprehendunt praemedita-
tionem rerum futurarum.   Nihil est enim quod tam
obtundat elevetque aegritudinem quam perpetua in
omni vita cogitatio nihil esse, quod non accidere
possit, quam meditatio condicionis humanae, quam
vitae lex commentatioque parendi, quae non hoc
adfert, ut semper maereamus, sed ut numquam.
Neque enim qui rerum naturam, qui vitae varieta-
tem, qui imbecillitatem generis humani cogitat,
maeret, cum haec cogitat, sed tum vel maxime
sapientiae fungitur munere.   Utrumque enim consequitur, ut et considerandis rebus humanis proprio

----

[1] *facit*, inserted by Wesenberg.

----

[1] *Revocatio* is a military metaphor, e.g. *receptui signum aut
revocationem a bello audire non possumus*, cf. II. § 48.   The
word is used of calling anyone back from a course he has
begun to an earlier right course.

[2] Which was uncultivated, for Epicurus said, Παιδείαν
πᾶσαν, μακάριε, φεῦγε.

wretchedness he has brought upon himself: thus he is always tortured either by undergoing or by reflecting on the evil. Alleviation of distress, however, Epicurus finds in two directions, namely in calling the soul away from reflection upon vexation and in a " recall " [1] to the consideration of pleasures. For he thinks the soul able to obey reason and follow its guidance. Reason therefore (in his view) forbids attention to vexations, withdraws the soul from morose reflections, blunts its keenness in dwelling upon wretchedness and, sounding a retreat from such thoughts, eagerly urges it on again to descry a variety of pleasures and engage in them with all the powers of the mind; and according to this philosopher the wise man's life is packed with the recollection of past and the prospect of future pleasures. This view we have stated in our usual style, the Epicureans state it in theirs. But let us look at their meaning; their style [2] let us ignore.

XVI. In the first place they are wrong in censuring the consideration of evils beforehand. For there is nothing so well fitted to deaden and alleviate distress as the continual life-long reflection that there is no event which may not happen; nothing so serviceable as the consideration of our state as human beings, as the study of the law of our being and the practice of obedience to it; and the effect of this is not to make us always sad but to prevent us from being so at all. For the man who reflects upon nature, upon the diversity of life and the weakness of humanity, is not saddened by reflecting upon these things, but in doing so he fulfils most completely the function of wisdom. For he gains doubly, in that by considering the vicissitudes of

267

philosophiae fruatur officio et adversis casibus tri-
plici consolatione sanetur : primum quod posse
accidere diu cogitavit, quae cogitatio una maxime
molestias omnes extenuat et diluit; deinde quod
humana humane ferenda intelligit; postremo quod
videt malum nullum esse nisi culpam, culpam autem
nullam esse, cum id, quod ab homine non potuerit
praestari, evenerit.

35 Nam revocatio illa, quam adfert, cum a contuendis
nos malis avocat, nulla est : non est enim in nostra
potestate fodicantibus iis rebus, quas malas esse
opinemur, dissimulatio vel oblivio : lacerant, vexant,
stimulos admovent, ignes adhibent, respirare non
sinunt. Et tu oblivisci iubes, quod contra naturam
est, qui quod a natura datum est auxilium extorqueas
inveterati doloris ? Est enim tarda illa quidem
medicina, sed tamen magna, quam adfert longinqui-
tas et dies. Iubes me bona cogitare, oblivisci
malorum. Diceres aliquid et magno quidem philosopho dignum, si ea bona esse sentires, quae essent
homine dignissima.

36 XVII. Pythagoras mihi si diceret aut Socrates
aut Plato : " Quid iaces aut quid maeres aut cur
succumbis cedisque fortunae ? quae pervellere te
forsitan potuerit et pungere, non potuit certe vires

---

[1] Cf. II. § 61.

human life he has the enjoyment of the peculiar duty of philosophy, and in adversity he finds a threefold relief to aid his restoration ; first because he has long since reflected on the possibility of mishap, and this is far the best method of lessening and weakening all vexation ; secondly because he understands that the lot of man must be endured in the spirit of a man ; lastly because he sees that there is no evil but guilt, but that there is no guilt when the issue is one against which a man can give no guarantee.

As for that " recall " which Epicurus advises, when he calls us away from the contemplation of evil, I do not add it, for it is null and void. For under the sting of circumstances which we regard as evil, concealment or forgetfulness is not within our control : circumstances tear us in pieces, worry and goad us ; their touch is fiery ;[1] they do not allow us to breathe. And do you, Epicurus, bid me "forget," though to forget is contrary to nature, while you wrest from my grasp the aid which nature has supplied for the relief of long-standing pain ? For there is a remedy, slow-working it is true but effectual, brought about by the long lapse of time. You bid me reflect on good, forget evil. There would be something in what you say and something worthy of a great philosopher, were you sensible that those things are good which are most worthy of a human being.

XVII. Should Pythagoras, Socrates or Plato say to me : " Why are you prostrated, or why do you mourn, or why do you tamely yield to fortune ? She may possibly have pinched and pricked you, she cannot assuredly have undermined your strength.

frangere. Magna vis est in virtutibus : eas excita,
si forte dormiunt. Iam tibi aderit princeps fortitudo,
quae te animo tanto esse coget, ut omnia, quae
possint homini evenire, contemnas et pro nihilo
putes ; aderit temperantia, quae est eadem moderatio,
a me quidem paullo ante appellata frugalitas, quae te
turpiter et nequiter facere nihil patietur. Quid est
autem nequius aut turpius effeminato viro ? Ne
iustitia quidem sinet te ista facere, cui minimum
esse videtur in hac causa loci, quae tamen ita dicet
dupliciter esse te iniustum, cum et alienum appetas,
qui mortalis natus condicionem postules immortalium et graviter feras te quod utendum acceperis
37 reddidisse. Prudentiae vero quid respondebis do-
centi virtutem sese esse contentam quo modo ad
bene vivendum, sic etiam ad beate ? Quae si
extrinsecus religata pendeat et non et oriatur a se
et rursus ad se revertatur et omnia sua complexa
nihil quaerat aliunde, non intelligo cur aut verbis
tam vehementer ornanda aut re tanto opere expetenda videatur." Ad haec bona me si revocas,
Epicure, pareo, sequor, utor te ipso duce, obliviscor
etiam malorum, ut iubes, eoque facilius, quod ea
ne in malis quidem ponenda censeo. Sed traducis
cogitationes meas ad voluptates. Quas ? Corporis,
credo, aut quae propter corpus vel recordatione vel
spe cogitentur. Num quid est aliud ? Rectene

---

¹ § 16.
² The subject of Book V. It is the function of prudence
to distinguish between bad and good.
³ 'Αρχὴ καὶ ῥίζα παντὸς ἀγαθοῦ ἡ τῆς γαστρὸς ἡδονή. τιμη-
τέον τὸ καλὸν καὶ τὰς ἀρετὰς καὶ τὰ τοιουτότροπα, ἐὰν ἡδονὴν
παρασκευάζῃ are the words of Epicurus, Athen. VII. 279 F.

There is a mighty power in the virtues ; rouse them,
if maybe they slumber. At once you will have the
foremost of all, I mean Fortitude, who will compel
you to assume a spirit that will make you despise and
count as nothing all that can fall to the lot of men.
Next will come Temperance, who is also self-control,
and called by me a little while ago 'frugality,'[1]
and will not suffer you to do anything disgraceful
and vile. But what is more vile or disgraceful than a
womanish man ? Justice even will not suffer you to
act in such a way ; there seems but little need for
her in this case, but yet her plea will be that you
are doubly unjust, since in demanding, in spite of your
mortal origin, the attribute of the immortal gods,
and in repining at the repayment of the gift you
have received as a loan, you are longing for what
is not your own. What answer moreover will you
make to Prudence when she tells you that, for her,
virtue is self-sufficient for leading a good life as well
as a happy one?[2] And should Prudence be tied and
bound to dependence on external things, and not
owe her beginning to herself and return again to
herself, so that in full self-dependence she seeks
nothing from elsewhere, I do not understand why
she should be held deserving of such passionate
worship in words or such an eager quest in act."
If you "recall" me to goods like this, Epicurus, I
obey, I follow, I take you as my only guide, I "forget"
evils too, as you bid, and the more readily because
I think they are not so much as to be reckoned as
evils. But you are turning my thoughts towards
pleasures. What pleasures?[3] Bodily, I fancy, or
such pleasures as for the body's sake find their place
in memory or expectation. There is nothing else, is

interpretor sententiam tuam? Solent enim isti
38 negare nos intelligere quid dicat Epicurus. Hoc
dicit et hoc ille acriculus me audiente Athenis
senex Zeno, istorum acutissimus, contendere et
magna voce dicere solebat, eum esse beatum, qui
praesentibus voluptatibus frueretur confideretque se
fruiturum aut in omni aut in magna parte vitae
dolore non interveniente aut, si interveniret, si
summus foret, futurum brevem, sin productior, plus
habiturum iucundi quam mali : haec cogitantem
fore beatum, praesertim si et ante perceptis bonis
contentus esset et nec mortem nec deos extimesceret.
Habes formam Epicuri vitae beatae verbis Zenonis
expressam, nihil ut possit negari.

39   XVIII. Quid ergo? huiusne vitae propositio et
cogitatio aut Thyestem levare poterit aut Aeetam,
de quo paullo ante dixi, aut Telamonem pulsum
patria exsulantem atque egentem? in quo haec
admiratio fiebat :

> *Hicine est ille Telamon, modo quem gloria ad caelum*
>   *extulit,*
> *Quem aspectabant, cuius ob os Graii ora obvertebant*
>   *sua ?*

40 Quod si cui, ut ait idem, *simul animus cum re concidit,*
a gravibus illis antiquis philosophis petenda medicina
est, non ab his voluptariis. Quam enim isti bonorum
copiam dicunt? Fac sane esse summum bonum non

---

¹ Zeno the Epicurean, a contemporary of Cicero, and
named the *coryphaeus* of Epicurus. He called Socrates
scurra Atticus and spoke of Chrysippus invariably as
Chrysippa, in scorn of his title of "father," cf. Hor. *Sat.*
1. 3. 127 : *Non nosti, quid pater, inquit, Chrysippus dicat.*
² Cf. II. § 44.

there? Do I give a true interpretation of your view? No, say his disciples, who aver that I do not understand what Epicurus says. He does say this, and so that little spitfire Zeno,[1] who had the keenest intellect of them all, used in his old age to insist at the top of his voice in my hearing at Athens—that *he* was happy who had the enjoyment of present pleasure and the assurance that he would have enjoyment either throughout life or for a great part of life without the intervention of pain, or, should pain come, that it would be short-lived if extreme, but if prolonged it would imply more that was pleasant than evil;[2] reflection on this would make him happy, particularly if he had had the satisfaction of good things previously enjoyed and were without undue fear of death or gods. You have Epicurus' notion of a happy life, as formulated in the words of Zeno, so that there is no possibility of denial.

XVIII. What then? Will the idea and thought of such a life avail to relieve either Thyestes or Aeetes of whom I spoke a little while back, or Telamon banished from his country to be an exile, and a needy one as well, at sight of whom men asked in astonishment:

> See we here the famous Telamon whom to heaven
>   glory raised,
> Whom men gazed on and Greek faces towards his
>   face were ever turned?

But if anyone find, as the same poet says, that "spirit at once with fortune fell," he must look for a remedy from those earnest philosophers of old, not from these devotees of pleasure. For what do these triflers mean by abundance of good? Suppose, if

dolere : quamquam id non vocatur voluptas, sed non
necesse est nunc omnia : idne est, quo traducti
luctum levemus? Sit sane summum malum dolere :
in eo igitur qui non est, si malo careat, continuone
41 fruitur summo bono? Quid tergiversamur, Epicure,
nec fatemur eam nos dicere voluptatem, quam tu
idem, cum os perfricuisti, soles dicere? Sunt haec
tua verba necne? In eo quidem libro, qui continet
omnem disciplinam tuam,—fungar enim iam inter-
pretis munere, ne quis me putet fingere—dicis haec :
"Nec equidem habeo quod intelligam bonum illud,
detrahens eas voluptates, quae sapore percipiuntur,
detrahens eas, quae auditu et cantibus, detrahens
eas etiam, quae ex formis percipiuntur oculis, suaves
motiones, sive quae aliae voluptates in toto homine
gignuntur quolibet sensu. Nec vero ita dici potest,
mentis laetitiam solam esse in bonis ; laetantem
enim mentem ita novi, spe eorum omnium, quae
supra dixi, fore ut natura iis potiens dolore careat."
42 Atque haec quidem his verbis, quivis ut intelligat
quam voluptatem norit Epicurus. Deinde paullo
infra : "Saepe quaesivi" inquit "ex iis, qui appella-
bantur sapientes, quid haberent quod in bonis re-
linquerent, si illa detraxissent, nisi si vellent voces

---

[1] For it is an intermediate state of neither joy nor pain.
[2] e.g. the dancing of the daughter of Herodias, Matth.
xiv. 6. Epicurus' own words were, οὐ γὰρ ἔγωγε δύναμαι
νοῆσαι τἀγαθὸν ἀφαιρῶν μὲν τὰς διὰ χυλῶν ἡδονάς, ἀφαιρῶν δὲ
τὰς δι' ἀφροδισίων, ἀφαιρῶν δὲ τὰς δι' ἀκροαμάτων, ἀφαιρῶν δὲ
τὰς διὰ μορφῆς κατ' ὄψιν ἡδείας κινήσεις, Athen. VII. 280.

you like, that the highest good is absence of pain;
although that is not termed pleasure[1]—but there
is no need to go into everything now—is it to
this we have been led on to find relief for sorrow?
Grant, if you like, that pain is the highest evil;
does the man who is not in pain at once enjoy the
highest good if he be free from evil? Why do we
shirk the question, Epicurus, and why do we not
confess that we mean by pleasure what you habitually say it is, when you have thrown off all sense of
shame? Are these your words or not? For instance, in that book which embraces all your teaching (for I shall now play the part of translator, that
no one may think I am inventing) you say this:
"For my part I find no meaning which I can attach
to what is termed good, if I take away from it the
pleasures obtained by taste, if I take away the
pleasures which come from listening to music, if I
take away too the charm derived by the eyes from
the sight of figures in movement,[2] or other pleasures
produced by any of the senses in the whole man.
Nor indeed is it possible to make such a statement
as this—that it is joy of the mind which is alone to
be reckoned as a good; for I understand by a mind
in a state of joy, that it is so, when it has the hope
of all the pleasures I have named—that is to say the
hope that nature will be free to enjoy them without
any blending of pain." And this much he says in
the words I have quoted, so that anyone you please
may realize what Epicurus understands by pleasure.
Then a little lower: " I have often," he says, " asked
men who were called wise what content could be
left in a good, if they took away the advantages
named, unless it were to be supposed that it was

inanes fundere; nihil ab iis potui cognoscere: qui
si virtutes ebullire volent et sapientias, nihil aliud
dicent nisi eam viam, qua efficiantur eae voluptates,
quas supra dixi." Quae sequuntur in eadem sententia sunt, totusque liber, qui est de summo bono,
43 refertus et verbis et sententiis talibus. Ad hancine
igitur vitam Telamonem illum revocabis, ut leves
aegritudinem, et si quem tuorum adflictum maerore
videris, huic acipenserem potius quam aliquem
Socraticum libellum dabis? hydrauli hortabere ut
audiat voces potius quam Platonis? expones quae
spectet florida et varia? fasciculum ad nares ad-
movebis? incendes odores? sertis redimiri iubebis
et rosa? Si vero aliquid etiam . . ., tum plane
luctum omnem absterseris.

44   XIX. Haec Epicuro confitenda sunt aut ea, quae
modo expressa ad verbum dixi, tollenda de libro vel
totus liber potius abiiciundus; est enim confertus
voluptatibus. Quaerendum igitur quem ad modum
aegritudine privemus eum, qui ita dicat:

> . . . . *Pol mihi fortuna magis nunc defit quam*
> *genus.*
> *Namque regnum suppetebat mı, ut scias quanto e loco,*
> *Quantis opibus, quibus de rebus lapsa fortuna ac-*
> *cidat.*

---

[1] They talk grandiloquently about virtue, but all they mean
is that virtue is useful for securing pleasure; cf. *De Fin.*
V. § 80: *Dixerit hoc idem Epicurus, semper beatum esse
sapientem; quod quidem solet ebullire nonnunquam*, and
Madvig's note.

[2] Περὶ τέλους.

[3] *Apud antiquos piscium nobilissimus*, Plin. IX. 17. 27.

[4] The grosser Epicurean pleasures Cicero forbears to
mention.

their wish to utter sentences destitute of meaning;
I have been able to learn nothing from these men;
if they choose to go on babbling about ' virtues ' or
' wisdoms,' [1] they will mean nothing but the way in
which the pleasures I have named are brought
about." What follows is to the same effect, and the
whole book,[2] which deals with the highest good, is
packed with words and sentiments of similar
character. Is this then the life to which you will
" recall " the hero Telamon for the relief of his
distress? and, if you find any of your relatives
broken down by grief, will you give him a sturgeon [3]
rather than a Socratic treatise, will you urge him
to listen to the music of a water organ rather than
that of Plato, will you set out variegated blooms
for him to look at, will you hold a nosegay to his
nostrils, burn spices and bid him wreathe his head
with garlands and roses? If indeed something else [4]
—then clearly you will have wiped away all tears
from his eyes.

XIX. These admissions Epicurus must make or
else remove from his book all that I have rendered
word for word, or preferably the whole book should
be flung away, for it is brimful of pleasures. We
must inquire then how a man is to be rid of his
distress who speaks thus

Truly Fortune at the moment fails me more than
    noble birth,
For the throne once mine can show men from
    what haughty pride of place,
Pride of power, wealth of riches, fortune, fallen is
    my lot.[5]

[5] Cf. App. II.

MARCUS TULLIUS CICERO

Quid? huic calix mulsi impingendus est, ut plorare
desinat aut aliquid eius modi? Ecce tibi ex altera
parte ab eodem poëta:

>   *Ex opibus summis opis egens, Hector, tuae.*

Huic subvenire debemus; quaerit enim auxilium:

>   *Quid petam praesidi aut exsequar, quove nunc*
>   *Auxilio exsili aut fuga freta sim?*
>   *Arce et urbe orba sum. Quo accidam? quo applicem?*
>   *Cui nec arae patriae domi stant, fractae et disiectae*
>   *iacent,*
>   *Fana flamma deflagrata, tosti alti stant parietes,*
>   *Deformati atque abiete crispa. . . .*

Scitis quae sequantur et illa in primis:

>   *O pater, o patria, o Priami domus,*
>   *Saeptum altisono cardine templum,*
>   *Vidi ego te, astante ope barbarica,*
>   *Tectis caelatis, laqueatis,*
>   *Auro, ebore instructam regifice.*

45 O poëtam egregium! quamquam ab his cantoribus
Euphorionis contemnitur. Sentit omnia repentina
et necopinata esse graviora. Exaggeratis igitur
regiis opibus, quae videbantur sempiternae fore,
quid adiungit?

>   *Haec omnia vidi inflammari,*
>   *Priamo vi vitam evitari,*
>   *Iovis aram sanguine turpari.*

---

[1] These verses are from Ennius' *Andromacha*, cf. App. II.
[2] Euphorion of Chalcis of the third century B.C. In
Cicero's time he had admirers who preferred him to the old
Roman poet Ennius. Euphorion belonged to the artificial
Alexandrian School.

What? must we thrust upon the poor man a goblet of mead to make him stop lamenting? or something of that kind? Here on the other side you have from the same poet:

Once high in power, now, Hector, thine aid lost.[1]

We ought to help her, for she is asking for help:

Where to seek or to find sure defence? How rely
Can I on hope of aid, way of flight or retreat?
Fortress and city gone! Whom can I supplicate?
Altars of my country stand not, broken, wrenched apart they lie,
Temples by the flames devoured, lofty walls stand burnt with fire,
All disfigured, and the pine beams wrinkled up. . . .

You know what follows; and above all the lines:

Father, O country, O palace of Priam,
Temple made sure by the echoing hinge,
In barbarous opulence I saw you
With ceilings fretted, and panelled roof
Royally wrought with ivory and gold.

O wonderful poet! Whatever our modern imitators of Euphorion[2] may say in depreciation. He is sensible that the sudden and unexpected is more grievous to bear. What therefore does he add after this heightened picture of the royal wealth which was, it seemed, to endure for ever?

All this did I see by the flames consumed,
And Priam's life by violence shortened,
Jove's high altar by bloodshed polluted.[3]

[3] Cf. I. § 85.

46 Praeclarum carmen! Est enim et rebus et verbis
et modis lugubre. Eripiamus huic aegritudinem.
Quo modo! Collocemus in culcita plumea, psaltriam
adducamus, hedychri incendamus scutellam, dulci-
culae potionis aliquid videamus et cibi : haec tandem bona sunt, quibus aegritudines gravissimae
detrahantur ; tu enim paullo ante ne intelligere
quidem te alia ulla dicebas. Revocari igitur oportere a maerore ad cogitationem bonorum conveniret
mihi cum Epicuro, si quid esset bonum conveniret.

XX. Dicet aliquis : Quid ergo ? tu Epicurum
existimas ista voluisse aut libidinosas eius fuisse
sententias? Ego vero minime ; video enim ab eo
dici multa severe, multa praeclare. Itaque, ut
saepe dixi, de acumine agitur eius, non de moribus :
quamvis spernat voluptates eas, quas modo laudavit,
ego tamen meminero quod videatur ei summum
bonum. Non enim verbo solum posuit voluptatem,
sed explanavit quid diceret. "Saporem" inquit
"et corporum complexum et ludos atque cantus et
formas eas, quibus oculi iucunde moveantur." Num
fingo, num mentior ? Cupio refelli ; quid enim
laboro nisi ut veritas in omni quaestione explicetur ?
47 At idem ait non crescere voluptatem dolore detracto
summamque esse voluptatem nihil dolere. Paucis
verbis tria magna peccata. Unum, quod secum ipse

---

[1] *e.g.* οὐκ ἔστιν ἡδέως ζῆν ἄνευ τοῦ φρονίμως καὶ καλῶς καὶ
δικαίως. Diog. Laert. X. 140.

A magnificent strain; it breathes melancholy in the story, the diction and the rhythm. Let us tear away her distress. How? Let us pop her into a feather-bed, bring in a harpist, burn a platter of sweet balsam, look out a drop of soothing syrup and something to eat. Here we have at last the good things which enable us to get rid of the most grievous distresses. For *you* explained a little while ago that you did not even understand any others. I should therefore agree with Epicurus about the duty of a "recall" from mourning to reflection upon what was good, if we were agreed upon the meaning of good.

XX. Someone will say: What then? Do you think Epicurus meant that sort of thing, or that his views were licentious? I certainly do not. For I see that many of his utterances breathe an austere and many a noble spirit.[1] Consequently, as I have often said, the question at issue is his intelligence, not his morality. However much he may scorn the pleasures he has just approved, yet I shall remember what it was that he thinks the highest good. For he has not only used the term pleasure, but stated clearly what he meant by it. "Taste," he says, "and embraces and spectacles and music and the shapes of objects fitted to give a pleasant impression to the eyes." I am not inventing, I am not misrepresenting, am I? I long to be refuted. For why am I exerting myself except to get the truth in every problem unravelled? But wait! Epicurus also says that pleasure does not increase when pain has been removed, and that the highest pleasure is the absence of pain. Three big mistakes in a few words. One

pugnat; modo enim ne suspicari quidem se quidquam bonum, nisi sensus quasi titillarentur voluptate : nunc autem summam voluptatem esse dolore carere. Potestne magis secum ipse pugnare? Alterum peccatum, quod, cum in natura tria sint, unum gaudere, alterum dolere, tertium nec gaudere nec dolere, hic primum et tertium putat idem esse nec distinguit a non dolendo voluptatem. Tertium peccatum commune cum quibusdam, quod, cum virtus maxime expetatur eiusque adipiscendae causa philosophia quaesita sit, ille a virtute summum
48 bonum separavit. "At laudat saepe virtutem." Et quidem C. Gracchus, cum largitiones maximas fecisset et effudisset aerarium, verbis tamen defendebat aerarium. Quid verba audiam, cum facta videam? L. Piso ille Frugi semper contra legem frumentariam dixerat : is lege lata consularis ad frumentum accipiundum venerat. Animum advertit Gracchus in contione Pisonem stantem; quaerit audiente populo Romano qui sibi constet, cum ea lege frumentum petat, quam dissuaserit. "Nolim" inquit "mea bona, Gracche, tibi viritim dividere libeat, sed si facias, partem petam." Parumne declaravit vir gravis et sapiens lege Sempronia

---

[1] Cyrenaics and others.
[2] The *Lex Frumentaria* of 123 B.C. by which cheap corn was distributed to citizens was proposed by C. Sempronius Gracchus and hence called, as lower down, *Lex Sempronia*. The anecdote about Piso (for whom cf. § 16) is introduced to mark its evil consequences.

because he contradicts himself. For just now he said that he had not even an inkling of any good, unless the senses were in some sort tickled with pleasure; now, on the contrary, he says that the highest pleasure is freedom from pain. Is it possible to be more self-contradictory? The second mistake is that, as there are three natural states, one of joy, the second of pain, the third of neither joy nor pain, he here thinks the first and third identical and makes no distinction between pleasure and absence of pain. The third mistake he shares with certain philosophers,[1] that, though virtue is the object of our eager seeking and philosophy has been devised for the sake of securing it, Epicurus has severed the highest good from virtue. "Yes, but he often praises virtue." He does, and so too C. Gracchus, after he had granted extravagant doles and poured out the funds of the treasury like water, none the less, in his words, posed as the protector of the treasury. Why am I to listen to words, seeing that I have the deeds before my eyes? The famous Piso, named Frugi, had spoken consistently against the Corn-law.[2] When the law was passed, in spite of his consular rank, he was there to receive the corn. Gracchus noticed Piso standing in the throng; he asked him in the hearing of the Roman people what consistency there was in coming for the corn under the terms of the law which he had opposed. "I shouldn't like it, Gracchus, to come into your head to divide up my property among all the citizens; but should you do so I should come for my share." Did not the words of this serious and sagacious statesman show with sufficient clearness that the public inheritance was squandered by the Sempronian

patrimonium publicum dissipari? Lege orationes
49 Gracchi : patronum aerarii esse dices. Negat Epicurus iucunde posse vivi nisi cum virtute vivatur,
negat ullam in sapientem vim esse fortunae, tenuem
victum antefert copioso, negat ullum esse tempus
quo sapiens non beatus sit : omnia philosopho digna,
sed cum voluptate pugnantia. "Non istam dicit
voluptatem." Dicat quamlibet : nempe eam dicit,
in qua virtutis nulla pars insit. Age, si voluptatem
non intelligimus, ne dolorem quidem? Nego igitur
eius esse, qui dolore summum malum metiatur, men-
tionem facere virtutis.

50 XXI. Et queruntur quidem [1] Epicurei, viri optimi
—nam nullum genus est minus malitiosum—, me
studiose dicere contra Epicurum. Ita, credo, de
honore aut de dignitate contendimus. Mihi summum in animo bonum videtur, illi autem in corpore :
mihi in virtute, illi in voluptate. Et illi pugnant et
quidem vicinorum fidem implorant ; multi autem
sunt qui statim convolent. Ego sum is, qui dicam
me non laborare, actum habiturum quod egerint.
51 Quid enim? de bello Punico agitur? de quo ipso
cum aliud M. Catoni, aliud L. Lentulo videretur,
nulla inter eos concertatio umquam fuit. Hi nimis

---

[1] Some editors adopt the reading *quidam*. Cicero means
Roman Epicureans.

---

[1] A political contest and not a philosophical one in which
heat and bitterness are unworthy.

[2] At the call of the Epicureans all those who want an
excuse for a life of pleasure flock in to help.

[3] A proverbial expression to intimate that they may have
their own way, that the matter is not worth his troubling
about ; see Tyrrell on Cic. *ad Fam.* 16. 23. 1.

law? Read Gracchus' *speeches* and you will say
he was protector of the treasury. Epicurus says
a pleasurable life is impossible unless accompanied
by virtue; he says that fortune has no power over
the wise man; he prefers a plain to a rich diet;
he says there is no season when the wise man is
not happy: all thoughts worthy of a philosopher
but at variance with pleasure. "He does not mean
your idea of pleasure." Let him mean any pleasure
he pleases; surely he means pleasure of the kind
that has no share in virtue. Come, if we do not
understand pleasure, do we understand pain either?
Therefore I say that it is not open to the man who
measures the highest evil by the standard of pain
to introduce the name of virtue.

XXI. And yet the Epicureans, excellent creatures
that they are (for never was a set of beings less
artful), complain that I argue against Epicurus like
a partisan. Ah! then, I suppose the contest between
us is one for office or position.[1] To my thinking the
highest good is in the soul, to Epicurus it is in the body;
for me it is in virtue, for him in pleasure. It is the
Epicureans who fight, yes, and appeal to the loyalty
of their neighbours; and there are plenty of them
ready to flock in on the instant:[2] it is I who am the
one to say that I am not troubling, that I shall look
upon what they have settled as settled.[3] For what
is at stake? is it a question of war with Carthage?
When M. Cato and L. Lentulus took different sides
upon this very question,[4] there was never any heated
controversy between them. The Epicureans show

[4] Cato's view was expressed in the famous *delenda est
Carthago*; Lentulus opposed this, but though it was a question
of imperial politics, the controversy was not embittered.

iracunde agunt, praesertim cum ab iis non sane
animosa defendatur sententia, pro qua non in senatu,
non in contione, non apud exercitum neque ad
censores dicere audeant. Sed cum istis alias, et
eo quidem animo, nullum ut certamen instituam,
verum dicentibus facile cedam : tantum admonebo ;
si maxime verum sit ad corpus omnia referre
sapientem sive, ut honestius dicam, nihil facere nisi
quod expediat sive omnia referre ad utilitatem suam,
quoniam haec plausibilia non sunt, ut in sinu gau-
deant, gloriose loqui desinant.

52 XXII. Cyrenaicorum restat sententia, qui tum
aegritudinem censent exsistere, si necopinato quid
evenerit. Est id quidem magnum, ut supra dixi :
etiam Chrysippo ita videri scio, quod provisum ante
non sit, id ferire vehementius : sed non sunt in hoc
omnia. Quamquam hostium repens adventus magis
aliquanto conturbat quam exspectatus et maris subita
tempestas quam ante provisa terret navigantes
vehementius, et eius modi sunt pleraque. Sed cum
diligenter necopinatorum naturam consideres, nihil
aliud reperias nisi omnia videri subita maiora, et
quidem ob duas causas, primum quod quanta sint
quae accidunt considerandi spatium non datur,
deinde, cum videtur praecaveri potuisse, si provisum
esset, quasi culpa contractum malum aegritudinem

---

[1] §§ 28, 30.

an excess of irritation, particularly as the view that they support is not one that inspires a generous enthusiasm, and they would not venture to advocate it in the Senate, at a public meeting, in front of an army or before the Censors. But let us deal with these gentry another time and in any case with the intention, not of entering the lists, but of yielding readily to words of truth. I shall merely drop this hint : if it is perfectly true that the wise man judges everything by the standard of the body, or to speak more fittingly, does nothing except what is profitable, or judges everything by the standard of his own advantage, then, as such truths are not likely to win applause, let them keep their joy in their own breasts, let them cease to speak so boastfully.

XXII. There remains the Cyrenaic view ; they hold that distress arises where an event has happened unexpectedly. This is indeed an important point, as I have said before ;[1] I know that it is the view of Chrysippus too that what has not been previously foreseen brings a more violent shock : but surprise is not everything. Yet it is true that a sudden advance of the enemy causes a good deal more consternation than an advance which is expected, and a sudden storm at sea causes more intense alarm than one that is anticipated, and there are many instances of the kind. But on a careful consideration of the nature of the unexpected you would find nothing else, except that all sudden occurrences are magnified, and that for two reasons : first because no scope is given for weighing the magnitude of the occurrences ; secondly because, where it seems that previous precautions could have been taken if sufficient foresight had been shown, the evil incurred,

53 acriorem facit. Quod ita esse dies declarat, quae
procedens ita mitigat, ut iisdem malis manentibus
non modo leniatur aegritudo, sed in plerisque tollatur. Karthaginienses multi Romae servierunt,
Macedones rege Perse capto; vidi etiam in Pelo-
ponneso, cum essem adolescens, quosdam Corinthios.
Hi poterant omnes eadem illa de Andromacha
deplorare,

Haec omnia vidi. . . .

Sed iam decantaverant fortasse. Eo enim erant
vultu, oratione, omni reliquo motu et statu, ut eos
Argivos aut Sicyonios diceres, magisque me move-
rant Corinthi subito aspectae parietinae quam ipsos
Corinthios, quorum animis diuturna cogitatio callum
54 vetustatis obduxerat. Legimus librum Clitomachi,
quem ille eversa Karthagine misit consolandi causa
ad captivos cives suos : in eo est disputatio scripta
Carneadis, quam se ait in commentarium rettulisse.
Cum ita positum esset, videri fore in aegritudine
sapientem patria capta, quae Carneades contra
dixerit scripta sunt. Tanta igitur calamitatis praesentis adhibetur a philosopho medicina, quanta in [1]
inveterata ne desideratur quidem, nec si aliquot
annis post idem ille liber captivis missus esset, vul-

---

[1] Most MSS. omit *in.*

---

[1] During his exile, 58 B.C., however, Cicero wrote to
Atticus, *dies non modo non levat luctum hunc sed etiam auget.*
[2] After Pydna, 168 B.C.
[3] Cf. § 45.
[4] Corinth was ruined by the siege and capture of 146 B.C.
[5] A Carthaginian and successor of Carneades, who belonged to the New Academy, b. 215 B.C. Carneades was
an opponent of Zeno.

as implying blame, makes the distress keener. That
this is so is shown by lapse of time, the passage of
which has such an alleviating effect, that, in spite
of the continuance of the same evils, not only is
the sense of distress rendered less poignant, but it
is in a number of instances removed.[1] Many Car-
thaginians were slaves at Rome, many Macedonians
after the capture of King Perses.[2] I have seen too
in the Peloponnese in my youthful days some natives
of Corinth who were slaves.   All of them could have
made the same lament as that in the *Andromacha* :

" All this did I see . . .," [3]

but by the time I saw them they had ceased, it may
be, to chant dirges.   Their features, speech, all the
rest of their movements and postures would have
led one to say they were freemen of Argos or
Sicyon ; and at Corinth the sudden sight of the
ruins [4] had more effect upon me than upon the
actual inhabitants, for long contemplation had had
the hardening effect of length of time upon their
souls.   I have read the book which Clitomachus [5]
sent by way of comfort to his captive fellow-citizens
after the destruction of Carthage ; it contains in its
pages a lecture of Carneades which Clitomachus says
he had entered in his notebook : the question that
had been proposed for discussion was that the wise
man, it seemed, would feel distress at the fall of his
country, and the arguments used by Carneades in
opposing this proposition are given at length.   The
remedy therefore effectively applied to a recent
disaster by the philosopher is one which no one
even feels the want of in a disaster of long standing ;
and if that same book had been sent to the captives

289

neribus mederetur, sed cicatricibus; sensim enim et
pedetemptim progrediens extenuatur dolor, non quo
ipsa res immutari soleat aut possit, sed id, quod
ratio debuerat, usus docet minora esse ea, quae sint
visa maiora.

55 XXIII. Quid ergo opus est, dicet aliquis, ratione
aut omnino consolatione illa, qua solemus uti, cum
levare dolorem maerentium volumus? Hoc enim
fere tum habemus in promptu, nihil oportere inopinatum videri. At[1] qui tolerabilius feret incom-
modum qui cognoverit necesse esse homini tale
aliquid accidere? Haec enim oratio de ipsa summa
mali nihil detrahit, tantum modo adfert nihil eve-
nisse, quod non opinandum fuisset. Neque tamen
genus id orationis in consolando non valet, sed id
haud sciam an plurimum. Ergo ista necopinata non
habent tantam vim, ut aegritudo ex iis omnis oriatur;
feriunt enim fortasse gravius, non id efficiunt ut ea,
quae accidant, maiora videantur; maiora videntur,[2]
56 quia recentia sunt, non quia repentina. Duplex est
igitur ratio veri reperiendi, non in iis solum, quae
mala, sed in iis etiam, quae bona videntur; nam aut
ipsius rei natura qualis et quanta sit quaerimus, ut
de paupertate non numquam, cuius onus disputando
levamus, docentes quam parva et quam pauca sint

---

[1] *Aut* is another reading.
[2] The words *maiora videntur* are omitted in many MSS.,
and in some they come after *recentia sunt.* The order adopted
is Moser's.

some years after, it would not have been a remedy
for wounds but only for scars. For step by step,
by slow degrees, pain is lessened as it goes on, not
that the actual conditions are ordinarily changed or
can be so, but experience teaches the lesson which
reason should have taught before, that the things
once magnified are smaller than they seemed.

XXIII. What need is there, then, someone will say,
of argument, or what need at all of the comfort we
usually give when we wish to alleviate the grief
of mourners? For we have on the tip of our tongues
as a rule the words " nothing should seem unexpected." But how will the burden of loss be more
endurable for the man who has recognized that
something of the kind must happen to a human
being? For this way of speaking takes nothing
from the actual sum of evil; all it does is to suggest that nothing has taken place which should
not have been expected. And yet such a mode of
speaking is not without effect in imparting comfort ;
I should rather be inclined to think it had very great
effect. Therefore such things as are unexpected
do not have enough influence to account for all
distress that arises; for the shock they cause is
perhaps heavier, but they do not make the occurrences seem more serious; they seem more serious
because their impression is still fresh, not because
of their suddenness. The method therefore of discovering the truth is twofold, not merely in the
case of things that seem evil, but also of things
that seem good. For we either inquire into the
character of the actual occurrence and its magnitude,
as for instance in dealing occasionally with poverty,
the burden of which we lighten in argument by

quae natura desideret, aut a disputandi subtilitate
orationem ad exempla traducimus. Hic Socrates
commemoratur, hic Diogenes, hic Caecilianum illud :

Saepe est etiam sub palliolo sordido sapientia.

Cum enim paupertatis una eademque sit vis, quidnam dici potest quam ob rem C. Fabricio tolerabilis
57 ea fuerit, alii negent se ferre posse ? Huic igitur
alteri generi similis est ea ratio consolandi, quae
docet humana esse quae acciderint; non enim
solum id continet ea disputatio, ut cognitionem
adferat generis humani, sed significat tolerabilia esse
quae et tulerint et ferant ceteri.

XXIV. De paupertate agitur : multi patientes
pauperes commemorantur ; de contemnendo honore :
multi inhonorati proferuntur et quidem propter id
ipsum beatiores, eorumque, qui privatum otium
negotiis publicis antetulerunt, nominatim vita laudatur, nec siletur illud potentissimi regis anapaestum,
qui laudat senem et fortunatum esse dicit, quod
inglorius sit atque ignobilis ad supremum diem
58 perventurus. Similiter commemorandis exemplis
orbitates quoque liberum praedicantur eorumque,
qui gravius ferunt, luctus aliorum exemplis leniun-

---

[1] Caecilius Statius, Roman writer of comedies, d. 168 B.C.,
cf. App. II.
[2] Like Cincinnatus, a model of ancient Roman virtue. He
rejected the bribes of Pyrrhus in 280 B.C.
[3] Cf. II. § 37. The king is Agamemnon.

pointing out how small and few natural needs are;
or leaving aside niceties of argument we give instances: now Socrates is quoted, now Diogenes, now
Caecilius'[1] well-known line:

> Even underneath the tattered mantle oft doth
> wisdom hide.

For, as the stress of poverty is one and the same,
what reason can be given why C. Fabricius[2] found
it endurable whilst others say it is unbearable?
Similar to this second method of comforting is that
which teaches that all that has happened is natural
to human life. For such a line of argument not
only includes a recognition of the facts of man's
condition, but indicates that what the rest of men
have borne and are bearing is endurable.

XXIV. In dealing with poverty many instances of
patient endurance are quoted: in dealing with scorn
of office many are given of men who have not
obtained office and have been happier for that very
reason, and praise is bestowed expressly upon the
life of men who have preferred the retirement of
private life to a public career, and the well-known
anapaests[3] of that most mighty king are not passed
over, in which he praises the old man and calls him
blessed for being destined to reach his latest day
unhonoured and unknown.[4] Similarly, too, attention is called to those who have lost their children,
by giving instances, and so the sorrow of those
whose grief is excessive is softened by the examples

---

[4] Eurip., *Iph. in Aul.* 15:

ζηλῶ σε, γέρον,
ζηλῶ δ' ἀνδρῶν, ὃς ἀκίνδυνον
βίον ἐξεπέρασ' ἀγνὼς ἀκλεής.

tur: sic perpessio ceterorum facit ut ea, quae
acciderint, multo minora quam quanta sint existi-
mata videantur. Ita fit sensim cogitantibus ut
quantum sit ementita opinio appareat. Atque hoc
idem et Telamon ille declarat:

Ego cum genui . . .

et Theseus:

Futuras mecum commentabar miserias . . .

et Anaxagoras: *Sciebam me genuisse mortalem.* Hi
enim omnes diu cogitantes de rebus humanis in-
telligebant eas nequaquam pro opinione vulgi esse
extimescendas. Et mihi quidem videtur idem fere
accidere iis, qui ante meditantur, quod iis, quibus
medetur dies, nisi quod ratio quaedam sanat illos,
hos ipsa natura, intellecto eo, quod rem continet,
illud malum, quod opinatum sit esse maximum,
nequaquam esse tantum, ut vitam beatam possit
59 evertere. Hoc igitur efficitur, ut ex illo necopinato
plaga maior sit, non, ut illi putant, ut, cum duobus
pares casus evenerint, is modo aegritudine adficiatur,
cui ille necopinato casus evenerit. Itaque dicuntur
non nulli, in maerore, cum de hac communi hominum
condicione audivissent, ea lege esse nos natos, ut nemo
in perpetuum esse posset expers mali, gravius etiam

---

¹ § 28.   ² § 29.   ³ § 30.
⁴ Unexpected misfortune is not the only cause of distress,
and so we find men grieving at the inevitable conditions of
human life. When Solon was mourning the death of his
son, someone said to him, "That will do no good;" and

of others who have suffered : in this way the endurance of the others makes mishaps seem of far less magnitude than the estimate first formed of them. So it is that by reflection men gradually realize the extreme falsity of their belief. Moreover, the famous Telamon points the same moral in :

I when I begat,[1]

and Theseus :

Within my heart I pondered ills to come,[2]

and Anaxagoras : " I knew that I had begotten a mortal." [3] For all these, by dint of long reflection upon the lot of mankind, understood that it must by no means be regarded with the excessive fear which fits in with popular belief. And to my mind the effect upon wise men of previous consideration is pretty much the same as the effect of lapse of time upon others ; only it is a process of reasoning which restores the former, while nature left to herself restores the latter, when once the root of the matter is grasped, namely that the evil which was greatest in anticipation is by no means great enough to ruin a happy life. All, therefore, we need conclude is that the shock from the unexpected is more severe, not, as the Cyrenaics think, that, where two men have met with equal misfortune, only the one on whom the misfortune has come unexpectedly is a victim to distress. And so [4] some, it is said, when sadness comes, have felt a still deeper pang on being told of this common lot of mankind, namely that it is the law of our entry into this world that no one

Solon replied, " It is for that very reason I weep, because I can do no good."

tulisse. XXV. Quocirca Carneades, ut video nostrum
scribere Antiochum, reprehendere Chrysippum
solebat laudantem Euripideum carmen illud:

> *Mortalis nemo est quem non attingat dolor*
> *Morbusque; multis sunt humandi liberi,*
> *Rursum creandi, morsque est finita omnibus,*
> *Quae generi humano angorem nequiquam adferunt.*
> *Reddenda terrae est terra, tum vita omnibus*
> *Metenda, ut fruges. Sic iubet Necessitas.*

60 Negabat genus hoc orationis quidquam omnino
ad levandam aegritudinem pertinere; id enim ipsum dolendum esse dicebat, quod in tam crude-
lem necessitatem incidissemus; nam illam quidem
orationem ex commemoratione alienorum malorum
ad malevolos consolandos esse accommodatam. Mihi
vero longe videtur secus; nam et necessitas ferendae
condicionis humanae quasi cum deo pugnare prohibet admonetque esse hominem, quae cogitatio
magno opere luctum levat, et enumeratio exemplorum, non ut animum malevolorum oblectet,
adfertur, sed ut ille, qui maeret, ferendum sibi id
censeat, quod videat multos moderate et tranquille
61 tulisse. Omnibus enim modis fulciendi sunt, qui
ruunt nec cohaerere possunt propter magnitudinem
aegritudinis; ex quo ipsam aegritudinem λύπην
Chrysippus, quasi solutionem totius hominis appella-
tam putat: quae tota poterit evelli, explicata, ut

---

[1] Antiochus, a native of Syria, pupil of Philo and friend of
Cicero. He attempted to harmonize the Stoic and Peripatetic systems with the Academy, cf. V. § 21.

[2] From the *Hypsipyla*, a lost play. *Necessitas* of the last
line is the Greek ἀνάγκη, what must happen independently
of the will of gods or men by the necessity of a fixed order
of nature.

can permanently escape evil. XXV. It was for this reason that Carneades, as I see our friend Antiochus[1] states, habitually censured Chrysippus for his approval of the well-known passage in Euripides:

No mortal is there but pain finds him out
And sickness; many must their children bury,
And sow fresh issue; death is end for all;
In vain do these things vex the race of men,
Earth must go back to earth: then life by all
Like crops is reaped. So bids Necessity.[2]

He said that this way of speaking had no bearing at all on the alleviation of distress; for he argued that the actual call to grief came from the fact that we were subject to a necessity so cruel. For Euripides' way of speaking was suited to bring comfort to ill-disposed people from the recital of the evils of others. My view, however, is far different. For the thought that the lot of man must be endured prevents us from contending as it were against God and also warns us that we are human: and this reflection is a great relief to sorrow, and the detailed instances cited are not given to delight the mind of the ill-natured, but to lead the mourner to think that he must bear the burdens which he sees many men have borne in a spirit of quiet restraint. For we must, as it were, shore up in every way those who are toppling over and unable to stand because of the extent of their distress. Hence, Chrysippus thinks that distress gets its own name λύπη[3] as being a dissolution of the whole man, and it can be entirely rooted out when we have

---

[3] Deriving λύπη from λύω (διάλυσις) as Plato does in the *Cratylus*, 419 C.

principio dixi, causa aegritudinis; est enim nulla
alia nisi opinio et iudicium magni praesentis atque
urguentis mali. Itaque et dolor corporis, cuius est
morsus acerrimus, perfertur spe proposita boni et
acta aetas honeste ac splendide tantam adfert
consolationem, ut eos, qui ita vixerint, aut non
attingat aegritudo aut perleviter pungat animi
dolor.

XXVI. Sed ad hanc opinionem magni mali cum
illa etiam opinio accessit, oportere, rectum esse, ad
officium pertinere ferre illud aegre, quod acciderit,
tum denique efficitur illa gravis aegritudinis per-
62 turbatio. Ex hac opinione sunt illa varia et de-
testabilia genera lugendi : pedores, muliebres
lacerationes genarum, pectoris, feminum, capitis
percussiones. Hinc ille Agamemno Homericus et
idem Accianus

Scindens dolore identidem intonsam comam,

in quo facetum illud Bionis, perinde stultissimum
regem in luctu capillum sibi evellere quasi calvitio
63 maeror levaretur. Sed haec omnia faciunt opinantes
ita fieri oportere. Itaque et Aeschines in Demosthenem invehitur, quod is septimo die post filiae
mortem hostias immolavisset. At quam rhetorice,
quam copiose, quas sententias colligit, quae verba
contorquet! ut licere quidvis rhetori intelligas.
Quae nemo probaret, nisi insitum illud in animis
haberemus, omnes bonos interitu suorum quam

---

[1] *e.g.* at the death of relatives or friends.
[2] *Il.* 10. 15 and a play of Accius.
[3] Bion of Borysthenes, a Cyrenaic philosopher of the third
century B.C., and celebrated for his sayings.
[4] In the speech *contra Ctesiph.* § 77.

disentangled its cause, as I said at the outset. For it is nothing else than the idea and conviction of an instant and pressing great evil. Consequently physical pain, the smart of which is exceedingly keen, is endured when we can see before us the promise of good, and a life spent honourably and brilliantly affords a solace so complete that either no touch of distress approaches those who have lived such a life, or else the prick of pain in the soul is only superficial.

XXVI. But when, in addition to the idea of serious evil, we entertain also the idea that it is an obligation, that it is right, that it is a matter of duty to be distressed at what has happened,[1] then, and not before, the disturbing effect of deep distress ensues. In consequence of this idea come the different odious forms of mourning, neglect of person, women's rending of the cheeks, beatings of the breast and thighs and head. Hence the famous Agamemnon of Homer and Accius too,[2]

Oft tearing in his grief his unshorn hair,

which inspired the witticism of Bion[3] that the fool of a monarch plucked out his hair in his grief, for all the world as though baldness were a relief to sadness. But all this is due to the belief that it is a duty. Accordingly Aeschines[4] attacks Demosthenes for having offered up victims at a sacrifice of thanksgiving a week after his daughter's death. "But what rhetorical skill, what wealth of language, what a collection of maxims, what a hail of phrases!" so that you see the rhetorician may say anything. All this no one could approve except for the rooted idea that it is a duty for all good men to

gravissime maerere oportere. Ex hoc evenit ut in
animi doloribus alii solitudines captent, ut ait
Homerus de Bellerophonte :

> *Qui miser in campis maerens errabat Aleïs,*
> *Ipse suum cor edens, hominum vestigia vitans,*

et Nioba fingitur lapidea propter aeternum, credo,
in luctu silentium ; Hecubam autem putant propter
animi acerbitatem quandam et rabiem fingi in
canem esse conversam.   Sunt autem alii, quos in
luctu cum ipsa solitudine loqui saepe delectat, ut
illa apud Ennium nutrix :

> *Cupido cepit miseram nunc me proloqui*
> *Caelo atque terrae Medeaï miserias.*

64   XXVII. Haec omnia recta, vera, debita putantes
faciunt in dolore, maximeque declarat hoc quasi
officii iudicio fieri, quod, si qui forte, cum se in luctu
esse vellent, aliquid fecerunt humanius aut si
hilarius locuti sunt, revocant se rursus ad maestitiam
peccatique se insimulant, quod dolere intermiserint :
pueros vero matres et magistri castigare etiam
solent, nec verbis solum, sed etiam verberibus, si
quid in domestico luctu hilarius ab iis factum est

---

[1] *Il.* 6. 201.   After Tullia's death Cicero tells Atticus,
Itaque solitudinem sequor.   See *ad. Att.* XII. 23.
[2] Niobe was changed to stone after her children had been
slain by Apollo and Artemis, *Il.* 24. 617.
[3] *Sed torva canino latravit rictu,* Juv. X. 271.
[4] Cf. App. II. and Eurip. *Med.* 56.

show the deepest possible sorrow at the death of
relations. Hence it comes that, in times when the
soul is grieved, others seek out solitude, as Homer
says of Bellerophon:[1]

> In the Aleïan plain he desolate wandered in
> sorrow,
> Eating his heart out alone, and the footsteps of
> men he avoided.

And Niobe[2] is imagined in stone to represent, I
suppose, everlasting silence in sorrow, while they
think that Hecuba on the other hand, by reason of
a sort of fierceness and fury of soul, was imagined
to have been changed into a bitch.[3] There are,
moreover, other mourners who often find delight in
holding converse with solitude itself, like the well-
known nurse in Ennius:

> Longing has come upon me now, poor wretch,
> To heav'n and earth to tell Medea's woes.[4]

XXVII. All these things they do in the hour of
grief, in the idea that such things are right and
proper and obligatory, and the chief proof that they
are done from a sort of conviction of duty is shown
by the fact that, if any of those who think they
should be sorrowful chance to act more humanly
or speak more cheerfully, they resume a gloomy
demeanour and accuse themselves of misconduct
because of this interruption to their grief: indeed
mothers and teachers are even accustomed to punish
children, if in the midst of family sorrow they show
any undue cheerfulness in act or speech, and not
merely with words but even with the whip they

aut dictum, plorare cogunt. Quid? ipsa remissio luctus cum est consecuta intellectumque est nihil profici maerendo, nonne res declarat fuisse totum 65 illud voluntarium? Quid ille Terentianus ipse se poeniens, id est, ἑαυτὸν τιμωρούμενος?

Decrevi tantisper me minus iniuriae,
Chreme, meo gnato facere, dum fiam miser.

Hic decernit ut miser sit. Num quis igitur quidquam decernit invitus?

Malo quidem me quovis dignum deputem.

Malo se dignum deputat, nisi miser sit? Vides ergo opinionis esse, non naturae malum. Quid, quos res ipsa lugere prohibet? ut apud Homerum cotidianae neces interitusque multorum sedationem maerendi adferunt, apud quem ita dicitur:

Namque nimis multos atque omni luce cadentes
Cernimus ut nemo possit maerore vacare.
Quo magis est aequum tumulis mandare peremptos
Firmo animo et luctum lacrimis finire diurnis.

66 Ergo in potestate est abiicere dolorem, cum velis, tempori servientem. An est ullum tempus—quoniam quidem res in nostra potestate est—cui non ponendae curae et [1] aegritudinis causa serviamus?

---

[1] *et* is omitted in most MSS.

---

[1] Lines 147-8.
[2] *Il.* 19. 226.

force them to shed tears. What is the meaning of this? When actual cessation of sorrow has ensued and it is thus realized that nothing is gained by mourning, do not the facts of the case show that it is entirely a matter of will? What does the self-tormenting character—in Greek ἑαυτὸν τιμωρούμενος—say in Terence?

> Chremes, at heart I am convinced I do
> My boy less wrong so long as I'm unhappy.[1]

He resolves to be miserable. Can you think anyone takes a resolution against his will?

> Worthy of any ill should I esteem myself.

He esteems himself "worthy of ill" if he be not "miserable?" You see therefore that evil comes from belief, not from nature. What of those whom the circumstances of the case prevent from mourning? For instance in Homer the daily loss of numbers of lives produces an assuagement of mourning; and so we find the lines:

> Too many every day falling in death we see
>   always,
> So that no respite there is for any from sorrow
>   of mourning;
> Therefore the more is it right to bury the dead
>   in the barrows,
> Keeping a pitiless heart, and but one day give to
>   our weeping.[2]

Therefore it is in one's power to throw grief aside when one will, in obedience to the call of the hour. Or seeing that in any case the first step rests with us, is there any hour whose call we cannot obey with the object of laying anxiety and distress aside? It

Constabat eos, qui concidentem vulneribus Cn. Pompeium vidissent, cum in illo ipso acerbissimo miserrimoque spectaculo sibi timerent, quod se classe hostium circumfusos viderent, nihil aliud tum egisse nisi ut remiges hortarentur et ut salutem adipiscerentur fuga : postea quam Tyrum venissent, tum adflictari lamentarique coepisse. Timor igitur ab his aegritudinem potuit repellere, ratio ab sapienti viro[1] non poterit ?

XXVIII. Quid est autem quod plus valeat ad ponendum dolorem, quam cum est intellectum nihil profici et frustra esse susceptum? Si igitur deponi potest, etiam non suscipi potest ; voluntate igitur et 67 iudicio suscipi aegritudinem confitendum est. Idque indicatur eorum patientia, qui cum multa sint saepe perpessi, facilius ferunt quidquid accidit obduruisseque iam sese contra fortunam arbitrantur, ut ille apud Euripidem :

Si mihi nunc tristis primum illuxisset dies,
Nec tam aerumnoso navigavissem salo,
Esset dolendi causa, ut iniecto eculei
Freno repente tactu exagitantur novo ;
Sed iam subactus miseriis obtorpui.

Defetigatio igitur miseriarum aegritudines cum faciat leniores, intelligi necesse est non rem ipsam causam atque fontem esse maeroris.

---

[1] *ac sapientia vera* MSS.: corrected by Bentley.

---

[1] In Egypt, 48 B.C.
[2] Eurip. Frag. 818 quoted by Galen from the *Phrixus.*

was common talk that those who saw Cn. Pompeius [1] sinking under his wounds, in the alarm they felt for their own safety on witnessing that cruel and pitiful scene, because they saw themselves surrounded by the enemies' fleet, did nothing else at the time except urge on the rowers and secure their safety by flight; only on reaching Tyre did they begin to indulge in grief and lamentation. Therefore fear had the power to drive away their distress, and shall not reason have power to drive it away from the wise man?

XXVIII. What, however, has more effect in putting grief aside than the realization of the fact that it gains us no advantage and that indulgence in it is useless? If then it can be set aside, it is also possible to refrain from indulging in it. It must therefore be admitted that distress is an indulgence due to an act of will and to conviction. And that is signified by the endurance of those who submit more readily to any mishap after they have frequently been through many experiences and who think they have at last succeeded in hardening themselves against fortune, like the character in Euripides:

Were this sad day the first that dawned for me,
Such sea of troubles had I not long sailed,
Good cause had been to toss like new-yoked colt
But lately brought to bear the touch of bit;
But quelled and numb with miseries am I now. [2]

Since, then, the exhaustion brought by miseries renders distresses milder, it must be understood that it is not the misfortune itself that is the cause and origin of mourning.

68 Philosophi summi neque dum tamen sapientiam consecuti nonne intelligunt in summo se malo esse? Sunt enim insipientes, neque insipientia ullum maius malum est; neque tamen lugent. Quid ita? quia huic generi malorum non. adfingitur illa opinio, rectum esse et aequum et ad officium pertinere aegre ferre quod sapiens non sis, quod idem adfingimus huic aegritudini, in qua luctus inest, quae 69 omnium maxima est. Itaque Aristoteles veteres philosophos accusans, qui existimavissent philosophiam suis ingeniis esse perfectam, ait eos aut stultissimos aut gloriosissimos fuisse, sed se videre, quod paucis annis magna accessio facta esset, brevi tempore philosophiam plane absolutam fore. Theophrastus autem moriens accusasse naturam dicitur, quod cervis et cornicibus vitam diuturnam, quorum id nihil interesset, hominibus, quorum maxime interfuisset, tam exiguam vitam dedisset : quorum si aetas potuisset esse longinquior, futurum fuisse ut omnibus perfectis artibus omni doctrina hominum vita erudiretur. Querebatur igitur se tum, cum illa videre coepisset, exstingui. Quid? ex ceteris philosophis nonne optimus et gravissimus quisque confitetur multa se ignorare et multa sibi etiam atque

---

[1] According to the Stoics those who had not completely attained wisdom were utterly wretched and there was no difference between their life and that of the worst of mankind. For this and other paradoxes Cicero laughs at them, *Pro Murena* 61.

[2] The best philosophers realize the imperfection of their knowledge and the folly of the world, but they are not therefore overcome by distress. And so Aristotle was consoled for imperfection by thinking of the future progress of philosophy, and Theophrastus by the thought that longer life would have brought perfection.

Do not philosophers of the highest eminence, who all the same have not yet attained the state of "wisdom," understand that they are in a plight of utter evil?[1] For they are unwise, and there is no greater evil than unwisdom; yet they do not lament. Why is this? Because to this kind of evil there is no adapting the belief that it is right and regular and a matter of duty to feel distressed at not being wise,[2] whereas we do adapt this belief to the kind of distress that involves mourning, and such distress is the greatest of all. And so Aristotle in upbraiding the philosophers of old for thinking, according to him, that thanks to their genius philosophy had reached perfection, says that they had been guilty of extreme folly or boastfulness; all the same he adds that he saw that, as a consequence of the great advance made in a few years, philosophy would be absolutely complete. Theophrastus,[3] on the other hand, on his death-bed is said to have reproached nature for having bestowed a long life on stags and crows,[4] creatures to whom such a gift made no difference, whereas mankind to whom it made the greatest difference had so short a time of life bestowed on them: could their life have been prolonged, the result would have been that all systems would have been brought to perfection and human life enriched with the acquisition of all learning. He complained therefore that he was passing away when he had a glimpse of the promised land. Again, is it not true that all the best and most influential of the other philosophers admit that there is much they do not know, and much they must

---

[3] Peripatetic philosopher, pupil of Plato and Aristotle, cf. § 21 and I. § 45.   [4] Cf. I. § 77.

70 etiam esse discenda? Neque tamen, cum se in
media stultitia, qua nihil est peius, haerere intelligant, aegritudine premuntur; nulla enim admiscetur
opinio officiosi doloris. Quid, qui non putant lu-
gendum viris? qualis fuit Q. Maximus efferens filium
consularem, qualis L. Paullus duobus paucis diebus
amissis filiis, qualis M. Cato praetore designato
mortuo filio, quales reliqui, quos in Consolatione
71 collegimus. Quid hos aliud placavit nisi quod
luctum et maerorem esse non putabant viri? Ergo
id, quod alii rectum opinantes aegritudini se solent
dedere, id hi turpe putantes aegritudinem reppule-
runt: ex quo intelligitur non in natura, sed in
opinione esse aegritudinem.

XXIX. Contra dicuntur haec: Quis tam demens,
ut sua voluntate maereat? Natura adfert dolorem,
cui quidem Crantor, inquiunt, vester cedendum
putat. Premit enim atque instat nec resisti potest.
Itaque Oïleus ille apud Sophoclem, qui Telamonem
antea de Aiacis morte consolatus esset, is, cum
audivisset de suo, fractus est; de cuius commutata
mente sic dicitur:

Nec vero tanta praeditus sapientia
Quisquam est qui aliorum aerumnam dictis adlevans
Non idem, cum fortuna mutata impetum
Convertat, clade subita frangatur sua,
Ut illa ad alios dicta et praecepta excidant.

---

[1] Q. Fabius Maximus Cunctator the Dictator of 218 B.C.,
Lucius Aemilius Paullus conqueror of Macedonia and M.
Porcius Cato the Censor.
[2] Cf. I. § 115. The Academy and the Peripatetics held
that distress was natural and insensibility harsh and savage.
The Peripatetics said that men should neither be insensible,
ἀπαθεῖς, nor over-sensitive, δυσπαθεῖς.

learn over and over again? And yet though they
realize that they are stuck fast in a slough of folly,
and nothing is worse than this, they are not overcome with distress. For their thoughts are not
coloured by the idea of a grief that duty requires.
What of those who do not think that men should
show their grief? Men like Q. Maximus carrying
to the grave a son of consular rank, like L. Paullus
who lost two sons within a few days, like M. Cato [1]
on the death of a son who was praetor elect, like
the other examples I have brought together in my
Consolation. What else was it made them tranquil
except the thought that sorrow and mourning were
unbefitting in a man? Therefore, where others are
accustomed to surrender themselves to distress in
the belief that it is right, these men spurned distress
in the thought that it was degrading. From this it
is understood that distress is not natural but a
matter of belief.

XXIX. In opposition to this view it is urged:
Who is so mad as to mourn of his own free choice?
It is nature that causes grief, and your Crantor,[2]
they say, thinks that we must give way to it. For
its attack is pressed home and cannot be resisted.
And so the hero Oïleus in Sophocles,[3] though he
had previously consoled Telamon for the death of
Ajax, yet broke down when he heard of his own
son's death. His change of mind is thus described:

And there is none of wisdom so possessed,
Who with mild words has soothed another's woes,
But does not, when a turn of fortune comes,
Fall broken by his own calamity;
So words, for others wise, his own need fail.

[3] From Αἴας Λοκρός, a lost tragedy.

Haec cum disputant, hoc student efficere, naturae obsisti nullo posse: ii tamen fatentur graviores aegritudines suscipi quam natura cogat. Quae est igitur amentia? ut nos quoque idem ab illis requiramus.

72 Sed plures sunt causae suscipiendi doloris. Primum illa opinio mali, quo viso atque persuaso aegritudo insequitur necessario; deinde etiam gratum mortuis se facere, si graviter eos lugeant, arbitrantur. Accedit superstitio muliebris quaedam; existimant enim dis immortalibus se facilius satis facturos, si eorum plaga perculsi adflictos se et stratos esse fateantur. Sed haec inter se quam repugnent plerique non vident. Laudant enim eos, qui aequo animo moriantur; qui alterius mortem aequo animo ferant, eos putant vituperandos: quasi fieri ullo modo possit, quod in amatorio sermone dici solet, ut quisquam 73 plus alterum diligat quam se. Praeclarum illud est et, si quaeris, rectum quoque et verum, ut eos, qui nobis carissimi esse debeant, aeque ac nosmet ipsos amemus; ut[1] vero plus, fieri nullo pacto potest. Ne optandum quidem est in amicitia, ut me ille plus quam se, ego illum plus quam me; perturbatio vitae, si ita sit, atque officiorum omnium consequatur. XXX. Sed de hoc alias: nunc illud satis est, non attribuere ad amissionem amicorum miseriam nostram,

[1] The *at* which many MSS. have would require an interrogative sentence.

[1] The opponents who say, "Who is so mad as to mourn of his own choice?" But they admit that in feeling distress men go further than nature requires. "Well, are they not then as 'mad' as those who mourn voluntarily?" answers Cicero.

When they[1] argue in this way their object is to prove that there is no possible means of withstanding nature: yet they admit that men are victims of distress more grievous than nature enforces. What then is the "madness" they speak of?—to put to them the same question as they put to us.

But there are more reasons than one for falling a victim to grief. First there is the belief already spoken of that a thing is evil, and at the sight of it and the conviction of its presence distress inevitably follows. Secondly men also think that by the intensity of their grief they are gratifying the dead. Add to these a certain womanish superstition; for they think they will more easily satisfy the immortal gods, if they admit that they are crushed and prostrated by an overwhelming blow. But the majority do not see how inconsistent these ideas are. For they praise those who, they think, meet death calmly; any who bear another's death with calmness they consider deserving of censure. As if it were in any sense possible, as is often said in lovers' talk, that anyone should love another more than himself. It is an excellent thing, and if you look into it, a right and just thing too to love those, who should be our dearest, as well as we do ourselves; but to love them more than ourselves is in no way possible. It is not to be desired in friendship either that my friend should love me more than himself, or I love him more than myself; if it could be so, it would result in an upset of life and all its obligations. XXX. But this question can be dealt with at another time: for the present it is enough to refrain from making ourselves wretched as well as losing our friends, for fear our love go further than

ne illos plus quam ipsi velint, si sentiant, plus certe quam nosmet ipsos diligamus.

Nam quod aiunt plerosque consolationibus nihil levari adiunguntque consolatores ipsos confiteri se miseros, cum ad eos impetum suum fortuna[1] converterit, utrumque dissolvitur; sunt enim ista non naturae vitia, sed culpae; stultitiam autem accusare quamvis copiose licet. Nam et qui non levantur ipsi se[2] ad miseriam invitant et qui suos casus aliter ferunt atque ut auctores aliis ipsi fuerunt, non sunt vitiosiores quam fere plerique, qui avari avaros, gloriae cupidos gloriosi reprehendunt; est enim proprium stultitiae aliorum vitia cernere, oblivisci 74 suorum. Sed nimirum hoc maximum est experimentum, cum constet aegritudinem vetustate tolli, hanc vim non esse in die positam, sed in cogitatione diuturna. Nam si eadem res est et idem est homo, qui potest quidquam de dolore mutari, si neque de eo, propter quod dolet, quidquam est mutatum neque de eo, qui dolet? Cogitatio igitur diuturna nihil esse in re mali dolori medetur, non ipsa diuturnitas.

XXXI. Hic mihi adferunt mediocritates, quae si naturales sunt, quid opus est consolatione? Natura enim ipsa terminabit modum; sin opinabiles, opinio

---

[1] *fortuna* is generally omitted in the MSS., but it is needed.

[2] *se* omitted in MSS.: supplied by Davies.

---

[1] Cf. § 71.

[2] The folly of being wretched from our own fault.

[3] That distress is due to ourselves and not to nature.

[4] Cf. § 22: μεδιοπάθειαι, for there is a "mean" in πάθη as well as in πράξεις, Arist., *Eth.* II. 6. Right feeling as well as right action lay in a "mean" between two extremes of excess and defect.

they themselves would wish if they were conscious, certainly further than our love for ourselves.

As to their objection[1] that most men get no relief from words of comfort, and the additional one, that the comforters themselves admit that they are wretched when fortune has shifted her attack to them, each statement admits of refutation. For the fault here is not nature's, the blame rests with us; and the folly[2] of it you may attack as much as you like. For both those who get no relief are wretched by their own invitation, and those, who bear their own misfortunes in a spirit different from that which they have themselves advocated in the case of others, are not worse than, as a rule, many avaricious men who censure the avaricious, or ambitious men who censure the ambitious; for it is a peculiarity of folly to discern the faults of others and be forgetful of its own. But beyond question, since it is agreed that distress is removed by long continuance, the chief proof[3] is the fact that it is not the mere lapse of time that produces this effect, but continued reflection. For if the circumstances are the same and the person is the same, how can there be any change in the grief felt, if there is no change either in the reason for the grief or in the person who feels it? Continued reflection therefore that there is no evil in the circumstances has a healing effect upon pain, not the continuance of time alone.

XXXI. At this point they confront me with their "mean"[4] states. If these are based upon nature, what need is there of giving comfort? For nature will herself fix the limit; but if they are based on belief, then let the belief be completely set aside.

tota tollatur.   Satis dictum esse arbitror aegritudinem
esse opinionem mali praesentis, in qua opinione illud
insit, ut aegritudinem suscipere oporteat.

75   Additur ad hanc definitionem a Zenone recte, ut
illa opinio praesentis mali sit recens; hoc autem
verbum sic interpretantur, ut non tantum illud
recens esse velint, quod paullo ante acciderit, sed,
quam diu in illo opinato malo vis quaedam insit, ut[1]
vigeat et habeat quandam viriditatem, tam diu
appelletur recens.   Ut Artemisia illa, Mausoli Cariae
regis uxor, quae nobile illud Halicarnassi fecit
sepulcrum, quam diu vixit, vixit in luctu, eodemque
etiam confecta contabuit.   Huic erat illa opinio
cotidie recens, quae tum denique non appellatur
recens, cum vetustate exaruit.

Haec igitur officia sunt consolantium, tollere
aegritudinem funditus aut sedare aut detrahere
quam plurimum aut supprimere nec pati manare
76 longius aut ad alia traducere.   Sunt qui unum
officium consolantis putent docere[2] malum illud
omnino non esse, ut Cleanthi placet.   Sunt qui non
magnum malum, ut Peripatetici.   Sunt qui abducant
a malis ad bona, ut Epicurus.   Sunt qui satis putent
ostendere nihil inopinati accidisse, ut Cyrenaici.[3]
Chrysippus autem caput esse censet in consolando

---

[1] *et* MSS. : *ut* Bentley.
[2] Lambinus supplied *docere* which is not in MSS.
[3] *nihil mali* MSS. : *ut Cyrenaici* Davies.   The context
requires this, cf. § 28.

---

[1] The πάθη, *perturbationes*, emotions, were according to the
Stoics voluntary, and judgments (κρίσεις) resting on an idea
or belief (δόξα).   Time could weaken their effect, but if they
retained their vigour, they counted as "fresh" or newly
conceived.

It has, I think, been sufficiently insisted on that distress is the idea of a present evil with this implication in it, that it is a duty to feel distress.

An addition to this definition is rightly made by Zeno, namely that this idea of a present evil is a "fresh"[1] one. This word, however, his followers interpret to mean that not only, according to their view, is that "fresh" which has taken place a short time previously, but that so long as the imagined evil preserves a certain power of being vigorous and retaining so to speak its greenness,[2] it is termed "fresh." For instance the famous Artemisia, wife of Mausolus, King of Caria, who built the celebrated burial monument at Halicarnassus, lived in sorrow all her days and wasted away under its enfeebling influence. The idea of her sorrow was "fresh" for her every day, and this idea only ceases to be termed "fresh" when it has withered away by length of time.

These therefore are the duties of comforters: to do away with distress root and branch, or allay it, or diminish it as far as possible, or stop its progress and not allow it to extend further, or to divert it elsewhere. There are some who think it the sole duty of a comforter to insist that the evil has no existence at all, as is the view of Cleanthes;[3] some, like the Peripatetics, favour the lesson that the evil is not serious. Some again favour the withdrawal of attention from evil to good, as Epicurus does; some, like the Cyrenaics, think it enough to show that nothing unexpected has taken place. Chrysippus on the other hand considers that the main thing in giving

[2] Cf. the phrase "to keep the bones green," or Falstaff s "green wound," 2 *Hen. IV.* II. I.   [3] II. § 60.

detrahere illam opinionem maerenti, si se officio
fungi putet iusto atque debito. Sunt etiam qui haec
omnia genera consolandi colligant—alius enim alio
modo movetur—ut fere nos in Consolatione omnia
in consolationem unam coniecimus; erat enim in
tumore animus et omnis in eo temptabatur curatio.

Sed sumendum tempus est non minus in animorum morbis quam in corporum, ut Prometheus ille
Aeschyli, cui cum dictum esset:

Atqui, Prometheu, te hoc tenere existimo,
Mederi posse orationem iracundiae,

respondit:

Si quidem qui tempestivam medicinam admovens
Non adgravescens vulnus illidat manu.

77 XXXII. Erit igitur in consolationibus prima medicina docere aut nullum malum esse aut admodum
parvum; altera et de communi condicione vitae et
proprie, si quid sit de ipsius, qui maereat, disputan-
dum, tertia summam esse stultitiam frustra confici
maerore, cum intelligas nihil posse profici. Nam
Cleanthes quidem sapientem consolatur, qui consolatione non eget; nihil enim esse malum quod
turpe non sit, si lugenti persuaseris, non tu illi

---

¹ Aesch., *Prom. Vinct.* 377:

Ωκ. οὐκουν, Προμηθεῦ, τοῦτο γιγνώσκεις, ὅτι
ὀργῆς ζεούσης εἰσὶν ἰατροὶ λόγοι;
Πρ. ἐάν τις ἐν καιρῷ γε μαλθάσσῃ κέαρ
καὶ μὴ σφριγῶντα θυμὸν ἰσχναίνῃ βίᾳ.

² Cicero is picking up § 76. Cleanthes comforts by showing that the occasion of distress is not real, for baseness is
the only evil. But for the "wise man" who is not base
this is superfluous. It does not take away sorrow from the

comfort is to remove from the mind of the mourner the belief already described, in case he should think he is discharging a regular duty which is obligatory. There are some too in favour of concentrating all these ways of administering comfort (for one man is influenced in one way, one in another) pretty nearly as in my *Consolation* I threw them all into one attempt at consolation; for my soul was in a feverish state and I attempted every means of curing its condition.

But it is necessary in dealing with diseases of the soul, just as much as in dealing with bodily diseases, to choose the proper time, as was shown by the famous Prometheus, who after the words

> And yet, Prometheus, this I think you know,
> That speech physician is to wrathful heart,

replied:

> Yes, if a man applies a timely cure,
> And crushes not the wound with heavy hand.[1]

XXXII. The first remedial step therefore in giving comfort will be to show that either there is no evil or very little; the second will be to discuss the common lot of life and any special feature that needs discussion in the lot of the individual mourner; the third will be to show that it is utter folly to be uselessly overcome by sorrow when one realizes that there is no possible advantage. For Cleanthes[2] comforts the "wise man" who does not want comfort. For if you succeed in convincing the mourner that nothing is evil provided it is not disgraceful, you will succeed in removing

sorrowing, but only shows them that sorrow is folly, and that at the wrong time.

luctum, sed stultitiam detraxeris; alienum autem
tempus docendi. Et tamen non satis mihi videtur
vidisse hoc Cleanthes, suscipi aliquando aegritudinem posse ex eo ipso, quod esse summum malum
Cleanthes ipse fatebatur. Quid enim dicemus, cum
Socrates Alcibiadi persuasisset, ut accepimus, eum
nihil hominis esse nec quidquam inter Alcibiadem
summo loco natum et quemvis baiulum interesse,
cum se Alcibiades adflictaret lacrimansque Socrati
supplex esset, ut sibi virtutem traderet turpitudi-
nemque depelleret, quid dicemus, Cleanthe? num
in illa re, quae aegritudine Alcibiadem adficiebat,
78 mali nihil fuisse? Quid? illa Lyconis qualia sunt?
qui aegritudinem extenuans parvis ait eam rebus
moveri, fortunae et corporis incommodis, non animi
malis. Quid ergo? illud, quod Alcibiades dolebat,
non ex animi malis vitiisque constabat? Ad Epicuri
consolationem satis est ante dictum.

79   XXXIII. Ne illa quidem firmissima consolatio est,
quamquam et usitata est et saepe prodest: "Non
tibi hoc soli." Prodest haec quidem, ut dixi, sed
nec semper nec omnibus; sunt enim qui respuant,
sed refert quo modo adhibeatur. Ut enim tulerit
quisque eorum, qui sapienter tulerunt, non quo
quisque incommodo adfectus sit praedicandum est.

---

[1] This story is not in Plato. It is given in Augustine *C.D.*
XIV. 8. Socrates showed Alcibiades that he was wretched
because of his folly. Alcibiades was distressed because he
was not what he ought to have been, *i.e.* was base, which
Cleanthes says is the worst of all evils. Cleanthes can only
say that the "wise man" is free from evil and cannot feel
distress or sorrow : Lyco says that distress is occasioned by
trifles. What can either of them do for Alcibiades? Is his
distress real or not? Is it or is it not due to "evil"? To
St. Augustine it is sorrow (*tristitia*), akin to the "godly
sorrow" of 2 Cor. 7. 10, cf. § 7.

his folly, not his sorrow; the season for the lesson is, however, unfavourable. And yet it seems to me Cleanthes has not quite seen that the feeling of distress can sometimes arise from the very thing which he himself admits to be the worst evil of all. For what shall we say—seeing that Socrates, as we are told, convinced Alcibiades that he was in no true sense a man and that there was no difference, for all his high position, between him and any poor porter, whereupon Alcibiades was much distressed and implored Socrates with tears to teach him virtue and drive baseness away,—what shall we say, Cleanthes?[1] Surely not that there was no evil in the cause which made Alcibiades feel distress? Another point: what is the meaning of Lyco's words?[2] By way of minimizing distress he says that it is occasioned by trifling circumstances, discomforts of fortune and of body, not by evils of the soul. I ask you then—the grief which Alcibiades felt, did it not come from evils and flaws in the soul? As for the comfort Epicurus suggests, enough has been previously said.

XXXIII. Not even the comforting effect of the phrase, "You are not the only one," in spite of its constant use and frequent benefit, is perfectly reliable. It is beneficial, as I have said, but not always and not in all cases. For there are some who scorn it, but it does make a difference how the remedy is applied. For we have to point out how each of those who bore his sufferings wisely, managed to bear them, and not point out the inconvenience under which he laboured. The comfort

[2] A native of Phrygia and head of the Peripatetic school.

Chrysippi ad veritatem firmissima est, ad tempus
aegritudinis difficilis. Magnum opus est probare
maerenti illum suo iudicio et, quod se ita putet
oportere facere, maerere. Nimirum igitur, ut in
causis non semper utimur eodem statu—sic enim
appellamus controversiarum genera—, sed ad tempus, ad controversiae naturam, ad personam accom-
modamus, sic in aegritudine lenienda quam quisque
curationem recipere possit videndum est.

80 Sed nescio quo pacto ab eo, quod erat a te propositum, aberravit oratio. Tu enim de sapiente
quaesieras, cui aut malum videri nullum potest quod
vacet turpitudine aut ita parvum malum, ut id
obruatur sapientia vixque appareat, qui nihil opinione
adfingat adsumatque ad aegritudinem, nec id putet
esse rectum, se quam maxime excruciari luctuque
confici, quo pravius nihil esse possit. Edocuit tamen
ratio, ut mihi quidem videtur, cum hoc ipsum proprie non quaereretur hoc tempore, num quid[1] esset
malum, nisi quod idem dici turpe posset, tamen ut
videremus, quidquid esset in aegritudine mali, id
non naturale esse, sed voluntario iudicio et opinionis
81 errore contractum. Tractatum est autem a nobis id

---

[1] *nunc quod* most MSS. : *num quid* Wesenberg.

[1] § 76.
[2] *Status* or *constitutio* is the term used for the line adopted
by counsel conducting a case. It might be *coniecturalis*,
question of fact, *iuridicialis*, question of justification, *defini-
tiva*, question of name to be applied. *Status*, στάσις, is what

suggested by Chrysippus,[1] regarded in the abstract, is the most reliable, but difficult for a time of distress. It is a hard matter to prove to a mourner that he is mourning of his own choice and because he thinks he ought to do so. No need to wonder then that in the conduct of cases in court we do not always take up the same position[2] (this is the term we apply to lines of argument in disputes), but we adapt the line we take to the occasion, to the character of the dispute, to the personality of the litigant; we act similarly in the alleviation of distress, for we have to consider what method of treatment is admissible in each particular case.

But our argument in some manner has wandered away from the subject you put forward for discussion. Your statement referred to the wise man who cannot think that there is any evil where there is no disgrace, or else thinks the evil so insignificant that it is overwhelmed by wisdom and is scarcely visible; for the wise man does not call in any imaginary belief to buttress distress, or think it right to let himself be cruelly tortured and weakened by sorrow, as he thinks nothing can be more degraded. Nevertheless the course of our argument has shown, it appears to me, that though the actual question, whether anything was evil unless it could also be described as disgraceful, was not specifically put at the time—nevertheless, I say, we have come to see that, whatever evil there is in distress, it is not due to nature, but brought to a head by a judgment of the will and by mistaken belief. Moreover we have dealt with the one most poignant form of

armies manœuvre for before battle, or wrestlers before taking hold.

genus aegritudinis, quod unum est omnium maximum, ut eo sublato reliquorum remedia ne magno
opere quaerenda arbitraremur.

XXXIV. Sunt enim certa quae de paupertate,
certa quae de vita inhonorata et ingloria dici soleant:
separatim certae scholae sunt de exsilio, de interitu
patriae, de servitute, de debilitate, de caecitate, de
omni casu, in quo nomen poni solet calamitatis.
Haec Graeci in singulas scholas et in singulos libros
dispertiunt; opus enim quaerunt: quamquam plenae
82 disputationes delectationis sunt.   Et tamen ut
medici toto corpore curando minimae etiam parti, si
condoluit, medentur, sic philosophia, cum universam
aegritudinem sustulit, sustulit etiam,[1] si quis error
alicunde exstitit, si paupertas momordit, si ignominia
pupugit, si quid tenebrarum offudit exsilium aut
eorum, quae modo dixi, si quid exstitit; etsi singularum rerum sunt propriae consolationes, de quibus
audies tu quidem, cum voles.   Sed ad eundem
fontem revertendum est, aegritudinem omnem procul
abesse a sapiente, quod inanis sit, quod frustra
suscipiatur, quod non natura exoriatur, sed iudicio,
sed opinione, sed quadam invitatione ad dolendum,
83 cum id decreverimus ita fieri oportere.   Hoc detracto, quod totum est voluntarium, aegritudo erit
sublata illa maerens, morsus tamen et contractiun-

---

[1] *tamen* MSS. : *sustulit etiam* Keil.

---

[1] Though these discussions may seem unnecessary.
[2] In Book IV.

distress, in order that, by getting it out of the way, we might consider that there need be no troublesome search for a means of healing the other forms of distress.

XXXIV. For there are definite words of comfort habitually used in dealing with poverty, definite words in dealing with a life spent without obtaining office and fame; there are distinctly definite forms of discourse dealing with exile, ruin of country, slavery, infirmity, blindness, every accident upon which the term disaster can be fixed. These subjects the Greeks divide up under separate heads of discourse, and deal with in separate books; for they are on the look-out for subjects to work at; all the same the discussions are full of charm. And yet,[1] just as physicians in attending to the body as a whole also treat the smallest part, if there has been previous suffering, so philosophy, when it did away with distress as a whole, did away with any mistaken idea due to any special cause, be it the sting of poverty, the prick of disgrace, the dark shadow of exile, or any of the possibilities I have just given; and yet there are modes of comforting peculiar to the several circumstances, about which in fact you shall hear when you are ready.[2] But in each case we must go back to the one fountain-head, that all distress is far remote from the wise man, because it is meaningless, because it is indulged in to no purpose, because it does not originate in nature but in an act of judgment, of belief, in a kind of call to grief when we have made up our minds that it is a duty to feel it. By the removal of what is wholly an act of will, the distress of mourning which we have spoken of will at once be done away with;

culae quaedam animi relinquentur. Hanc dicant
sane naturalem, dum aegritudinis nomen absit grave,
taetrum, funestum, quod cum sapientia esse atque,
ut ita dicam, habitare nullo modo possit. At quae
stirpes sunt aegritudinis, quam multae, quam amarae !
quae ipso trunco everso omnes eligendae sunt et, si
necesse erit, singulis disputationibus. Superest
enim nobis hoc, cuicuimodi est, otium. Sed ratio
una omnium est aegritudinum, plura nomina ; nam
et invidere aegritudinis est et aemulari et obtrectare
et misereri et angi, lugere, maerere, aerumna adfici,
lamentari, sollicitari, dolere, in molestia esse, ad-
84 flictari, desperare. Haec omnia definiunt Stoici,
eaque verba, quae dixi, singularum rerum sunt, non,
ut videntur, easdem res significant, sed aliquid
differunt, quod alio loco fortasse tractabimus. Haec
sunt illae fibrae stirpium, quas initio dixi, persequen-
dae et omnes eligendae, ne unquam ulla possit
exsistere. Magnum opus et difficile, quis negat ?
quid autem praeclarum non idem arduum ? sed
tamen id se effecturam philosophia profitetur, nos
modo curationem eius recipiamus. Verum haec
quidem[1] hactenus : cetera, quotienscumque voletis,
et hoc loco et aliis parata vobis erunt.

---

[1] *quidem haec* MSS. : *haec quidem* Wesenberg.

---

[1] See p. 343.
[2] The main disturbance, distress, of which all others are offshoots.
[3] Because he had now withdrawn from public life, cf. I. § 1.
[4] Cf. § 7.
[5] Cf. χαλεπὰ τὰ καλά, the proverb attributed to Solon.

all the same the sting and certain minor symptoms of shrinking[1] of soul will be left. Let them say that this is quite natural, provided the term distress with its harsh, ugly, melancholy associations is not used, for it is a term that cannot go along with wisdom and cannot, so to speak, in any way share its habitation. But how far-reaching the roots of distress, how numerous, how bitter! All of them, when the trunk itself[2] is overturned, must be picked out, and, if need be, by a discussion for each separate one. For I have this single boon left to me, whatever its worth, of leisure.[3] There is one principle in all forms of distress; their names are many. For envy[4] is a form of distress, and rivalry and jealousy and compassion and trouble, lament, mourning, attacks of suffering, wailing, agitation, grief, vexation, torment and despondency. All these the Stoics define, and the terms I have given are used for each manifestation of distress; they do not, as it appears, mean the same, but there is a difference which we shall, it may be, deal with in another place. These, however, are the filaments of the roots of which I spoke at the outset, and are to be followed up and picked out, so that none of them can ever be found again. A great undertaking and a hard one, who denies it? But what noble undertaking is not also hard?[5] Yet, all the same, philosophy claims that she will succeed: only let us consent to her treatment. But so much at any rate so far. All else, as often as you will, whether in this spot or in others, will be in readiness for you.

M. TULLI CICERONIS TUSCULANARUM
DISPUTATIONUM

LIBER IV

1   I. Cum multis locis nostrorum hominum ingenia
virtutesque, Brute, soleo mirari, tum maxime in his
studiis, quae sero admodum expetita in hanc civitatem e Graecia transtulerunt: nam cum a primo
urbis ortu regiis institutis, partim etiam legibus,
auspicia, caerimoniae, comitia, provocationes, patrum
consilium, equitum peditumque discriptio, tota res
militaris divinitus esset constituta, tum progressio
admirabilis incredibilisque cursus ad omnem ex-
cellentiam factus est dominatu regio re publica
liberata. Nec vero hic locus est ut de moribus
institutisque maiorum et disciplina ac temperatione
civitatis loquamur: aliis haec locis satis accurate a
nobis dicta sunt maximeque in iis sex libris, quos de
2 Republica scripsimus. Hoc autem loco consideranti
mihi studia doctrinae multa sane occurrunt, cur ea
quoque arcessita aliunde neque solum expetita, sed

M. TULLIUS CICERO'S TUSCULAN DISPUTATIONS

BOOK IV

I. WHILE on many grounds, Brutus, I regard with a constant wonder the genius and virtues of our countrymen, I do so above all in those studies which at quite a late period became the object of their aspiration and were transferred to this State from Greece: for though from the first beginnings of the city, the auspices, the religious rites, the assemblies of the people, the appeals, the Council of the Fathers, the distribution of horse and foot, and the whole military system had been established in an admirable way by the usages—to some extent too by the laws—prevalent under the Kings, later on, when once the commonwealth was set free from the tyranny of monarchy, a wonderful advance was made towards general excellence at a rate that surpasses belief. But this is by no means the place for me to speak of the customs and regulations of our ancestors and the direction and organization of the State; these things I have described with sufficient care in other places and in particular in the six books I have written upon the Commonwealth. Now, however, that I am engaged in considering learned studies quite a number of reasons present themselves why these too, derived as they have been from an outside source, appear not only to

etiam conservata et culta videantur. Erat enim illis
paene in conspectu praestanti sapientiae nobilitate[1]
Pythagoras, qui fuit in Italia temporibus iisdem,
quibus L. Brutus patriam liberavit, praeclarus auctor
nobilitatis tuae. Pythagorae autem doctrina cum
longe lateque flueret, permanavisse mihi videtur in
hanc civitatem, idque cum coniectura probabile est
tum quibusdam etiam vestigiis indicatur. Quis
enim est qui putet, cum floreret in Italia Graecia
potentissimis et maximis urbibus, ea quae magna
dicta est, in iisque primum ipsius Pythagorae, deinde
postea Pythagoreorum tantum nomen esset, nostrorum hominum ad eorum doctissimas voces aures
3 clausas fuisse ? Quin etiam arbitror propter Pythagoreorum admirationem Numam quoque regem
Pythagoreum a posterioribus existimatum : nam
cum Pythagorae disciplinam et instituta cognos-
cerent regisque eius aequitatem et sapientiam a
maioribus suis accepissent, aetates autem et tem-
pora ignorarent propter vetustatem, eum, qui
sapientia excelleret, Pythagorae auditorem crediderunt fuisse.

II. Et de coniectura quidem hactenus; vestigia
autem Pythagoreorum quamquam multa colligi
possunt, paucis tamen utemur, quoniam non id
agitur hoc tempore : nam cum carminibus soliti illi
esse dicantur et praecepta quaedam occultius
tradere et mentes suas a cogitationum intentione

---

[1] *sapientia et nobilitate* MSS. : *sapientiae nobilitate* Madvig.

[1] Numa Pompilius, 715–673 B.C. Pythagoras, 580–500 B.C.
[2] " For " refers to " many traces."
[3] ἔλεγόν τε καὶ οἱ ἄλλοι Πυθαγόρειοι μὴ εἶναι πρὸς πάντας
πάντα ῥητά. Diog. Laert. VIII. 15. The disciples were
divided into ἐσωτερικοί and ἐξωτερικοί.

have been made objects of aspiration but cultivated with constant attention as well. This is not strange, for almost within sight of our ancestors Pythagoras, who was pre-eminent for the fame of his wisdom, lived in Italy at the same time that L. Brutus, the founder of your famous house, set his country free. Now, as the teaching of Pythagoras spread far and wide, it penetrated, as I think, into our State, and this, besides being likely as a conjecture, has also definite pieces of evidence in its favour. For as there were at that time great and powerful Greek cities in Italy, the district in which they flourished being called Magna Graecia, and as the name of Pythagoras himself and after him of the Pythagoreans had such remarkable influence in those cities, who can imagine that the ears of our countrymen were closed to the echo of their wisdom? Nay, I think too that admiration for the Pythagoreans was also the reason why King Numa was considered a Pythagorean by posterity. For as men were acquainted with the training and the regulations of Pythagoras and had heard from their ancestors of the impartiality and wisdom of the king, while in consequence of the long lapse of years they were ignorant of the chronology of the past,[1] they believed that Numa because of his surpassing wisdom had been a scholar of Pythagoras.

II. And so much indeed by way of conjecture. But though many traces of the Pythagoreans can be brought together, I shall nevertheless make sparing use of them, as this is not my present object. For,[2] as it was their habit, according to what we are told, to convey certain instruction more guardedly[3] in the form of verse, and to withdraw their thoughts

cantu fidibusque ad tranquillitatem traducere,
gravissimus auctor in Originibus dixit Cato morem
apud maiores hunc epularum fuisse, ut deinceps qui
accubarent canerent ad tibiam clarorum virorum
laudes atque virtutes : ex quo perspicuum est et
cantus tum fuisse descriptos [1] vocum sonis et car-
4 mina. Quamquam id quidem etiam xii. tabulae
declarant, condi iam tum solitum esse carmen, quod
ne liceret fieri ad alterius iniuriam, lege sanxerunt.
Nec vero illud non eruditorum temporum argumentum est, quod et deorum pulvinaribus et epulis
magistratuum fides praecinunt, quod proprium eius
fuit, de qua loquor, disciplinae.   Mihi quidem etiam
Appii Caeci carmen, quod valde Panaetius laudat
epistola quadam, quae est ad Q. Tuberonem, Pythagoreum videtur.   Multa etiam sunt in nostris institutis ducta ab illis, quae praetereo, ne ea, quae
repperisse [2] ipsi putamur, aliunde didicisse vide-
5 amur.   Sed, ut ad propositum redeat oratio, quam
brevi tempore quot et quanti poëtae, qui autem
oratores exstiterunt ! facile ut appareat nostros
omnia consequi potuisse, simul ut velle coepissent.

---

[1] *rescriptos* MSS. : *descriptos* Gronovius.
[2] *perperisse* MSS. : *repperisse* Davies.

---

[1] Cf. I. § 3.
[2] Tabula VIII. *Qui malum carmen incantassit*, cf. App. II.
[3] *Pulvinaria* were couches, and upon occasion the senate
ordered that statues of deities should be laid upon these
couches in pairs and banquets served to them, and this
solemnity was called *Lectisternium*.
[4] Consisting probably of moral maxims, one of which is
said to have been *Fabrum esse suae quemque fortunae.* Appius
Claudius Caecus as Censor in 312 B.C. built the *Via Appia.*

from intense meditation by the use of song and the
music of the harp to calm their minds, Cato, a writer
of great authority, has stated in his *Origines*[1]
that at banquets it was the custom of our ancestors
for the guests at table to sing one after the other
to the accompaniment of the flute in praise of the
merits of illustrious men. And from this it is clear
that, in addition to poems, songs set to music were
already at that date written down to guide the
voice of the singer. And yet as much as this is
formally shown also by the Twelve Tables, namely,
that by that time the composition of songs was
regularly practised : because it is expressly enacted
that this may not be done to a neighbour's detri-
ment.[2] And it is by no means a proof of an uninstructed age that stringed instruments play a
prelude at the festivals[3] of the gods and the feasts
of the magistrates : and this was a special feature
of the Pythagorean training of which I am speaking.
For my part too I think that the poem[4] of Appius
Caecus, which is highly praised by Panaetius in a
certain letter addressed to Q. Tubero, was Pythagorean. In our ancient usages too there is much
that has been taken over from the Pythagoreans,
which I pass by, that it may not appear that we
have learned from other sources the things we are
thought to have discovered for ourselves. But to
come back to the main argument, how short is the
period of time in which there have appeared such
a number of great poets and such famous orators
besides ! So that it can be readily seen that our
countrymen had the power to achieve success in
all directions, as soon as they conceived the wish
to do so.

III. Sed de ceteris studiis alio loco et dicemus, si usus fuerit, et saepe diximus. Sapientiae studium vetus id quidem in nostris, sed tamen ante Laelii aetatem et Scipionis non reperio quos appellare possim nominatim ; quibus adolescentibus Stoicum Diogenem et Academicum Carneadem video ad senatum ab Atheniensibus missos esse legatos, qui cum rei publicae nullam umquam partem attigissent essetque eorum alter Cyrenaeus, alter Babylonius, numquam profecto scholis essent excitati neque ad illud munus electi, nisi in quibusdam principibus temporibus illis fuissent studia doctrinae. Qui cum cetera litteris mandarent, alii ius civile, alii orationes suas, alii monumenta maiorum, hanc amplissimam omnium artium, bene vivendi disciplinam, vita magis 6 quam litteris persecuti sunt. Itaque illius verae elegantisque philosophiae, quae ducta a Socrate in Peripateticis adhuc permansit et idem alio modo dicentibus Stoicis, cum Academici eorum contro- versias disceptarent, nulla fere sunt aut pauca admodum Latina monumenta sive propter magni- tudinem rerum occupationemque hominum sive etiam, quod imperitis ea probari posse non arbitra- bantur : cum interim illis silentibus C. Amafinius exstitit dicens, cuius libris editis commota multitudo

---

155 B.C. Diogenes the Stoic, Carneades of the Academy and Critolaus the Peripatetic were the Athenian ambassadors, in the absence of statesmen properly so called.

[2] In the fourth book of the *De Finibus* Cicero criticizes Zeno the founder of the Stoics for stating doctrines, which he accepted from his predecessors, in different language out of a desire for novelty.

[3] cf. I. § 6.

III. But of the other studies we shall both speak elsewhere, should need arise, and have often done so. The study of wisdom, at any rate to the extent I have shown, was of long standing among our countrymen, but nevertheless I do not find any I can expressly call philosophers before the days of Laelius and Scipio. In their young days I see that Diogenes the Stoic and Carneades of the Academy were sent as ambassadors[1] to the senate by the Athenians, and as these men had never taken any part in public life and one of them was a native of Cyrene and the other of Babylon, they would assuredly never have been called out of their lecture rooms or chosen for this office, unless the study of philosophy had been familiar to some of the leading Romans of that day. But though they committed other subjects to writing, some the rules of civil law, some their speeches, some the memorials of their ancestors, yet this the most fruitful of all arts, which teaches the way of right living, they promoted more by their lives than by their writings. Consequently of that true and refined philosophy which starting with Socrates has found its home till now among the Peripatetics (with the Stoics[2] too saying the same thing in different language, whereas the Academic school discussed the points of controversy between the two) there are almost no Latin memorials or very few, whether the want is due to the absorption of the race in great practical undertakings, or whether again to the thought that such studies could not be commended to ignorant readers. To fill the gap their silence left came the voice of C. Amafinius,[3] and by the publication of his works the crowd had its interest stirred, and flocked

contulit se ad eam potissimum disciplinam, sive
quod erat cognitu perfacilis, sive quod invitabantur
illecebris blandae voluptatis, sive etiam, quia nihil
erat prolatum melius, illud, quod erat, tenebant.
7 Post Amafinium autem multi eiusdem aemuli
rationis multa cum scripsissent, Italiam totam occu-
paverunt, quodque maximum argumentum est non
dici illa subtiliter, quod et tam facile ediscantur et
ab indoctis probentur, id illi firmamentum esse
disciplinae putant.

IV. Sed defendat quod quisque sentit; sunt enim
iudicia libera: nos institutum tenebimus nulliusque[1]
unius disciplinae legibus astricti, quibus in philosophia necessario pareamus, quid sit in quaque re
maxime probabile semper requiremus; quod cum
saepe alias tum nuper in Tusculano studiose egimus.
Itaque expositis tridui disputationibus quartus dies
hoc libro concluditur; ut enim in inferiorem ambu-
lationem descendimus, quod feceramus idem superioribus diebus, acta res est sic.

8 M. Dicat, si quis vult, qua de re disputari velit.
A. Non mihi videtur omni animi perturbatione posse
sapiens vacare. M. Aegritudine quidem hesterna
disputatione videbatur, nisi forte temporis causa
nobis adsentiebare. A. Minime vero; nam mihi
egregie probata est oratio tua. M. Non igitur
existimas cadere in sapientem aegritudinem. A.
Prorsus non arbitror. M. Atqui, si ista perturbare

---

[1] *nullisque* MSS. : *nulliusque* Bentley.

---

[1] cf. II. § 9.

to the teaching he advocated in preference to any other, whether because it was so easy to grasp, or because of the seductive allurements of pleasure, or possibly also because, in the absence of any better teaching, they clung to what there was. After Amafinius again there came a number of imitators of the same system and by their writings took all Italy by storm : and whereas the chief proof that their arguments are stated without precision lies in the fact that their doctrine is so easily grasped and so much to the taste of the unlearned, *they* imagine this to be its main support.

IV. But let everyone defend his views, for judgment is free : I shall cling to my rule and without being tied to the laws of any single school of thought which I feel bound to obey, shall always search for the most probable solution in every problem ; and as has been my frequent practice on other occasions, so I was careful to act lately in my house at Tusculum. Accordingly, now that the discussions of three days have been set out in full, the fourth day is comprised in this book. For when we went down to the lower place of exercise,[1] as we had done on the previous days, the proceedings were as follows.

M. Let anyone, who will, state the subject he wishes discussed. A. It does not appear to me that the wise man can be free from all disorder of soul. M. It appeared from yesterday's discussion that he was at any rate free from distress, unless it may be you agreed with me for the sake of expediency. A. Certainly not, for your line of argument commended itself to me in an extraordinary way. M. You do not think then that the wise man is liable to distress ? A. Not at all, in my opinion. M. And yet if such a

335

animum sapientis non potest, nulla poterit. Quid
enim? metusne conturbet? At earum rerum est
absentium metus, quarum praesentium est aegritudo. Sublata igitur aegritudine sublatus est metus.
Restant duae perturbationes, laetitia gestiens et
libido: quae si non cadent in sapientem, semper
9 mens erit tranquilla sapientis. A. Sic prorsus intelligo. M. Utrum igitur mavis? statimne nos vela
facere an quasi e portu egredientes paullulum remi-
gare? A. Quidnam est istuc? Non enim intelligo.
V. M. Quia Chrysippus et Stoici, cum de animi perturbationibus disputant, magnam partem in his
partiendis et definiendis occupati sunt, illa eorum
perexigua oratio est, qua medeantur animis nec eos
turbulentos esse patiantur; Peripatetici autem ad
placandos animos multa adferunt, spinas partiendi
et definiendi praetermittunt: quaerebam igitur
utrum panderem vela orationis statim an eam ante
paullulum dialecticorum remis propellerem. A.
Isto modo vero; erit enim hoc totum, quod quaero,
10 ex utroque perfectius. M. Est id quidem rectius,
sed post requires, si quid fuerit obscurius. A.
Faciam equidem: tu tamen, ut soles, dices ista ipsa
obscura planius quam dicuntur a Graecis. M.
Enitar equidem, sed intento opus est animo, ne

---

[1] cf. I. § 108.

feeling cannot bring disorder into the soul of the wise man, none can do so. For tell me this. Can fear disturb him? The answer is that fear is felt of things not present, the presence of which causes distress. Take away distress then and fear is taken away. There remain two disorders, exuberant delight and lust, and if it is found that the wise man is not liable to them, the mind of the wise man will always be at peace. A. I am quite of this opinion. M. Which course do you prefer then? Shall we at once spread our sails, or like sailors working out of harbour use the oars for a bit? A. What does that mean? I do not understand. V. M. Because Chrysippus [1] and the Stoics in discussing disorders of the soul have devoted considerable space to subdividing and defining them, that part of their treatment of the subject where they claim to cure the soul and hinder it from being disquieted is quite small; the Peripatetics on the contrary adduce a number of arguments for tranquillizing the soul and leave on one side the thorny points of subdivision and definition: my question therefore meant, should I spread the sails of eloquence at once or push on first for a little with the oars of dialectic? A. This last way, to be sure. For all sides of the question I raise will be more completely dealt with by the use of both methods. M. That, it is true, is the more correct way; but if there is any obscurity you must ask questions afterwards. A. For my part I shall be ready; on your side all the same you must state these selfsame obscurities in a clearer fashion than is employed by the Greeks. M. For my part I shall do my best; but strict attention is needed, for fear the whole fabric fall to pieces if some one point

omnia dilabantur, si unum aliquid effugerit. Quoniam, quae Graeci πάθη vocant, nobis perturbationes appellari magis placet quam morbos, in his explicandis veterem illam equidem Pythagorae primum, dein Platonis discriptionem sequar, qui animum in duas partes dividunt, alteram rationis participem faciunt, alteram expertem. In participe rationis ponunt tranquillitatem, id est, placidam quietamque constantiam, in illa altera motus turbidos cum irae 11 tum cupiditatis contrarios inimicosque rationi. Sit igitur hic fons ; utamur tamen in his perturbationibus describendis Stoicorum definitionibus et partitionibus, qui mihi videntur in hac quaestione versari acutissime.

VI. Est igitur Zenonis haec definitio, ut perturbatio sit, quod πάθος ille dicit, aversa a recta ratione contra naturam animi commotio. Quidam brevius perturbationem esse appetitum vehementiorem, sed vehementiorem eum volunt esse, qui longius discesserit a naturae constantia. Partes autem perturbationum volunt ex duobus opinatis bonis nasci et ex duobus opinatis malis, ita esse quattuor : ex bonis *libidinem* et *laetitiam*, ut sit laetitia praesentium bonorum, libido futurorum, ex malis *metum* et *aegritudinem* nasci censent, metum futuris, aegritudinem praesentibus ; quae enim venientia metuun-12 tur, eadem adficiunt aegritudine instantia. *Laetitia* autem et *libido* in bonorum opinione versantur, cum

---

[1] cf. III. § 7.

[2] Pythagoras taught that νοῦς and θυμός were in all animals, φρένες in man alone, and that τὸ φρόνιμον, reason, was immortal. Diog. Laert. VIII. 30. For Plato cf. I. § 20, II. § 47.

[3] ἢ ἄλογος καὶ παρὰ φύσιν ψυχῆς κίνησις ἢ ὁρμὴ πλεονάζουσα. Diog. Laert. VII. 110.

escapes notice. Inasmuch as we prefer to apply the term "disorders"[1] rather than "diseases" to what the Greeks call πάθη, I shall for my part, in tracing them out, follow the time-honoured distinction made first by Pythagoras[2] and after him by Plato, who divide the soul into two parts : to the one they assign a share in reason, to the other none; that which has a share of reason they make the seat of peacefulness, that is, a consistent state of quiet and tranquillity; the other part they make the seat of stormy emotions both of anger and desire which are contrary and hostile to reason. Let this then be the starting-point; let us nevertheless in depicting these disorders employ the definitions and sub-divisions of the Stoics who, it appears to me, show remarkable penetration in dealing with this problem.

VI. This then is Zeno's definition of disorder, which he terms πάθος, that it is an agitation of the soul alien from right reason and contrary to nature.[3] Certain philosophers more briefly define disorder as a too violent longing, but by too violent they mean the longing which is removed too far from the equability of nature. They hold furthermore that there are divisions of disorder originating in two kinds of expected good and two of expected evil, with the result that there are four in all : *lust* and *delight*, in the sense of delight in present good and lust of future good, originate in what is good ; *fear* and *distress*, they consider, originate in what is evil, fear in future and distress in present evil. For events whose coming is feared also cause distress by their presence. *Delight* and *lust* on the other hand rest upon belief of prospective good, since lust

libido ad id, quod videtur bonum, illecta et inflammata rapiatur, laetitia ut adepta iam aliquid concupitum efferatur et gestiat : natura enim omnes ea,
quae bona videntur, sequuntur fugiuntque contraria ;
quam ob rem simul obiecta species est cuiuspiam
quod bonum videatur, ad id adipiscendum impellit
ipsa natura. Id cum constanter prudenterque fit,
eius modi appetitionem Stoici βούλησιν appellant,
nos appellemus *voluntatem*. Eam illi putant in solo
esse sapiente, quam sic definiunt : voluntas est, quae
quid cum ratione desiderat. Quae autem a ratione
aversa incitata est vehementius, ea libido est vel
cupiditas effrenata, quae in omnibus stultis invenitur.

13 Itemque cum ita movemur, ut in bono simus aliquo,
dupliciter id contingit : nam cum ratione animus
movetur placide atque constanter, tum illud *gaudium*
dicitur ; cum autem inaniter et effuse animus exsultat, tum illa *laetitia gestiens* vel *nimia* dici potest,
quam ita definiunt, sine ratione animi elationem.
Quoniamque, ut bona natura appetimus, sic a malis
natura declinamus, quae declinatio cum [1] ratione
fiet, *cautio* appelletur eaque intelligatur in solo esse
sapiente ; quae autem sine ratione et cum exanimatione humili atque fracta, nominetur metus : est
14 igitur *metus* a ratione aversa cautio. Praesentis

---

[1] Bentley's correction for *si cum* of MSS.

---

[1] τῇ δὲ ἐπιθυμίᾳ ἐναντίαν φασὶν εἶναι τὴν βούλησιν, οὖσαν
εὔλογον. Diog. Laert. VII. 116.
[2] τὴν χαρὰν ἐναντίαν φασὶν εἶναι τῇ ἡδονῇ. Diog. Laert. VII.
114.

kindled by temptation is hurried away to the apparent good, and delight shows itself in exuberant transport at having at length secured some coveted object : for by a law of nature all men pursue apparent good and shun its opposite ; for which reason, as soon as the semblance of any apparent good presents itself, nature of itself prompts them to secure it. Where this takes place in an equable and wise way the Stoics employ the term βούλησις for this sort of longing,[1] we should employ the term *wish*. That, they think, is found in the wise man alone and they define it in this way : wish is a rational longing for anything. Where, however, wish is alien from reason and is too violently aroused, it is lust or unbridled desire, which is found in all fools. And also, where we are satisfied that we are in possession of some good, this comes about in two ways : for when the soul has this satisfaction rationally and in a tranquil and equable way, then the term *joy*[2] is employed ; when on the other hand the soul is in a transport of meaningless extravagance, then the satisfaction can be termed *exuberant* or *excessive delight* and this they define as irrational excitement of the soul. And since we naturally desire good in the same manner as we naturally turn away from evil, and such a turning away, when rational, would be called *precaution*,[3] and is consequently found in the wise man only ; but when dissociated from reason and associated with mean and abject pusillanimity, it would be named fear ; therefore *fear* is precaution alien from reason. The wise man, however, is not

[3] τὴν εὐλάβειαν ἐναντίαν φασὶν εἶναι τῷ φόβῳ. Diog. Laert. VII. 116.

autem mali sapientis adfectio nulla est; stultorum[1] aegritudo est, eaque[2] adficiuntur in malis opinatis animosque demittunt et contrahunt rationi non obtemperantes. Itaque haec prima definitio est, ut aegritudo sit animi adversante ratione contractio. Sic quattuor *perturbationes* sunt, tres *constantiae*, quoniam aegritudini nulla constantia opponitur.

VII. Sed omnes perturbationes iudicio censent fieri et opinione; itaque eas definiunt pressius, ut intelligatur non modo quam vitiosae, sed etiam quam in nostra sint potestate. Est ergo *aegritudo* opinio recens mali praesentis, in quo demitti contrahique animo rectum esse videatur; *laetitia* opinio recens boni praesentis, in quo efferri rectum esse videatur; *metus* opinio impendentis mali, quod intolerabile esse videatur, *libido* opinio venturi boni, quod sit ex usu iam praesens esse atque adesse. 15 Sed quae iudicia quasque opiniones perturbationum esse dixi, non in eis perturbationes solum positas esse dicunt, verum illa etiam, quae efficiuntur perturbationibus, ut aegritudo quasi morsum aliquem doloris efficiat, metus recessum quendam animi et fugam, laetitia profusam hilaritatem, libido effrenatam appetentiam. *Opinationem* autem, quam in omnes definitiones superiores inclusimus, volunt esse imbecillam adsensionem.

---

[1] *stultorum* for the *stulta* or *stulti autem* of MSS.
[2] *ea qua* MSS.: *eaque* Bake.

---

[1] *contractio*, cf. § 66 and I. § 90, answers to Greek συστολή. Joy is expansion, grief contraction. In II. § 41 *contrahere collum* is used of shrinking from a sword-stroke.
[2] εὐπάθειαι in Greek.

subject to the influence of present evil; fools are subject to distress and feel its influence in the face of expected evil, and their souls are downcast and shrunken together in disobedience to reason. And consequently the first definition of distress is that it is a shrinking together [1] of the soul in conflict with reason. Thus there are four *disorders*, three *equable states*,[2] since there is no equable state in opposition to distress.

VII. But all disorders are, they think, due to judgment and belief. Consequently they define them more precisely, that it may be realized not only how wrong they are but to what extent they are under our control. *Distress* then is a newly formed belief of present evil, the subject of which thinks it right to feel depression and shrinking of soul; *delight* is a newly formed belief of present good, and the subject of it thinks it right to feel enraptured; *fear* is a belief of threatening evil which seems to the subject of it insupportable; *lust* is a belief of prospective good and the subject of this thinks it advantageous to possess it at once upon the spot. But they do not think that only the disorders depend upon the judgments and beliefs from which disorders, as I have said, come, but that on them also depend the results of the disorders; and so it is that distress results in some sting as it were of pain, fear in a kind of withdrawal and flight of the soul, delight in extravagant gaiety, lust in unbridled longing. Moreover the *act of belief* which we have included in all previous definitions they hold to be a weak acquiescence.[3]

[3] The Stoic word for *adsensio*, assent of judgment, was συγκατάθεσις, cf. Introd. p. xvi.

16 Sed singulis perturbationibus partes eiusdem generis plures subiiciuntur, ut *aegritudini* invidentia—utendum est enim docendi causa verbo minus usitato, quoniam invidia non in eo, qui invidet, solum dicitur, sed etiam in eo, cui invidetur—aemulatio, obtrectatio, misericordia, angor, luctus, maeror, aerumna, dolor, lamentatio, sollicitudo, molestia, adflictatio, desperatio et si quae sunt de genere eodem. Sub *metum* autem subiecta sunt pigritia, pudor, terror, timor, pavor, exanimatio, conturbatio, formido; *voluptati* malevolentia laetans malo alieno, delectatio, iactatio et similia; *libidini* ira, excandescentia, odium, inimicitia, discordia, indigentia, desiderium et cetera eius modi.

17 VIII. Haec autem definiunt hoc modo: *invidentiam* esse dicunt aegritudinem susceptam propter alterius res secundas, quae nihil noceant invidenti; nam si qui doleat eius rebus secundis, a quo ipse laedatur, non recte dicatur invidere, ut si Hectori Agamemno; qui autem, cui alterius commoda nihil noceant, tamen eum doleat his frui, is invideat profecto. *Aemulatio* autem dupliciter illa quidem

---

The Greek terms for most of the different disorders named by Cicero are given in Diog. Laert. VII. 111.

[1] φθόνος.	[2] ζῆλος.	[3] ζηλοτυπία.	[4] ἔλεος.
[5] ἄχθος.	[6] ὀδύνη.	[7] ἀνία.	[8] ἐνόχλησις.
[9] ὄκνος.	[10] αἰσχύνη.	[11] ἔκπληξις.	[12] δεῖμα.
[13] ἀγωνία.	[14] θόρυβος.	[15] ἐπιχαιρεκακία.	
[16] κήλησις.	[17] ὀργή.	[18] θυμός.	[19] μῆνις.
[20] μῖσος.	[21] σπάνις.	[22] ἵμερος.	

But numerous subdivisions of the same class are brought under the head of the separate disorders, as for instance under the head of *distress* come *invidentia*,[1] " envy " (for we must employ the less usual word for the sake of clearness, since *invidia* is used not only of the person who feels envy but also of the person of whom envy is felt), rivalry,[2] jealousy,[3] compassion,[4] anxiety,[5] mourning, sadness, troubling,[6] grief, lamenting, depression, vexation,[7] pining,[8] despondency and anything of the same kind. Under the head of *fear* moreover are brought sluggishness,[9] shame,[10] fright,[11] timidity,[12] consternation, pusillanimity,[13] bewilderment,[14] faintheartedness ; under *pleasure* malice [15] (taking delight in another's evil), rapture,[16] ostentation and the like ; under *lust* anger,[17] rage,[18] hatred,[19] enmity,[20] wrath, greed,[21] longing, [22] and the rest of this kind.

VIII. These moreover they define in this way : *envy* they say is distress incurred by reason of a neighbour's prosperity, though it does no harm to the envious person ; for if anyone were to be grieved by the prosperity of one by whom he conceives himself injured, he would not rightly be described as envious, as for instance if Agamemnon were said to envy Hector ; anyone however who, without being at all injured by his neighbour's advantages, is yet grieved at his enjoyment of them would assuredly be envious. But *rivalry* [23] is for its part used in a twofold way, so that it has both a

---

[23] The Greek word ζῆλος, emulation, rivalry, has more often a good sense. In *Galatians* V. 20 it comes with ἔχθραι, ἔρις, θυμοί in St. Paul's list of the works of the flesh. Tarsus, his native city, was a centre of Stoic philosophy, and Antipater one of the Stoic leaders came from Tarsus, cf. V. § 107.

dicitur, ut et in laude et in vitio nomen hoc sit;
nam et imitatio virtutis aemulatio dicitur—sed ea
nihil hoc loco utimur; est enim laudis—et est
aemulatio aegritudo, si eo, quod concupierit, alius
18 potiatur, ipse careat. *Obtrectatio* autem est, ea
quam intelligi ζηλοτυπίαν volo, aegritudo ex eo, quod
alter quoque potiatur eo, quod ipse concupiverit.
Misericordia est aegritudo ex miseria alterius iniuria
laborantis; nemo enim parricidae aut proditoris
supplicio misericordia commovetur; *angor* aegritudo
premens, *luctus* aegritudo ex eius, qui carus fuerit,
interitu acerbo, *maeror* aegritudo flebilis, *aerumna*
aegritudo laboriosa, *dolor* aegritudo crucians, *lamentatio* aegritudo cum eiulatu, *sollicitudo* aegritudo cum
cogitatione, *molestia* aegritudo permanens, *adflictatio*
aegritudo cum vexatione corporis, *desperatio* aegri-
19 tudo sine ulla rerum exspectatione meliorum. Quae
autem subiecta sunt sub *metum*, ea sic definiunt:
pigritiam metum consequentis laboris [*pudorem*
metum sanguinem diffundentem][1] . . . *terrorem* metum concutientem, ex quo fit ut pudorem rubor,
terrorem pallor et tremor et dentium crepitus consequatur, *timorem* metum mali appropinquantis,
pavorem metum mentem loco moventem; ex quo
illud Ennii:

> *Tum pavor sapientiam omnem mi exanimato expectorat;*

[1] Supplied from *quaeri potest quamobrem pudor sanguinem
diffundat,* Aulus Gell. xix. 6, and *pudorem rubor consequatur*
below. The MSS. mark a lacuna.

---

[1] λύπη βαρύνουσα.

[2] A definition of *pudor* should come after that of *pigritia*
and has fallen out or been forgotten. The Stoics said that

good and a bad sense. For one thing, rivalry is used of the imitation of virtue (but this sense we make no use of here, for it is praiseworthy); and rivalry is distress, should another be in possession of the object desired and one has to go without it oneself. *Jealousy* on the other hand is what I understand to be the meaning of ζηλοτυπία, distress arising from the fact that the thing one has coveted oneself is in the possession of the other man as well as one's own. *Compassion* is distress arising from the wretchedness of a neighbour in undeserved suffering, for no one is moved by compassion for the punishment of a murderer or a traitor. *Anxiety* [1] is oppressive distress; *mourning* is distress arising from the untimely death of a beloved object; *sadness* is tearful distress; *trouble* is burdensome distress; deep *grief* is torturing distress; *lamenting* is distress accompanied by wailing; *depression* is distress accompanied by brooding; *vexation* is lasting distress; *pining* is distress accompanied by bodily suffering; *despondency* is distress without any prospect of amelioration. The divisions under the head of fear are defined in this way: *sluggishness* as fear of ensuing toil [*shame* [2] as fear causing diffusion of blood]; *fright* as paralyzing fear which causes paleness, trembling and chattering of teeth, just as blushing is caused by shame; *timidity* as the fear of approaching evil; *consternation* as fear upsetting the mental balance: and hence the line of Ennius: [3]

Consternation drives all wisdom from my nerveless bosom forth;

αἰσχύνην εἶναι φόβον ἀδοξίας for which the Latin would be *pudorem metum infamiae.*   [3] Cf. App. II.

exanimationem metum subsequentem et quasi comi·
tem pavoris, *conturbationem* metum excutientem
cogitata, *formidinem* metum permanentem.

20 IX. Voluptatis autem partes hoc modo describunt,
ut *malevolentia* sit voluptas ex malo alterius sine
emolumento suo, *delectatio* voluptas suavitate auditus
animum deleniens, et qualis est haec aurium, tales
sunt et oculorum et tactionum et odorationum et
saporum, quae sunt omnes unius generis, ad per-
fundendum animum tamquam illiquefactae voluptates. *Iactatio* est voluptas gestiens et se efferens
21 insolentius. Quae autem libidini subiecta sunt, ea
sic definiunt, ut *ira* sit libido poeniendi eius, qui
videatur laesisse iniuria, *excandescentia* autem sit ira
nascens et modo exsistens, quae θύμωσις Graece
dicitur, *odium* ira inveterata, *inimicitia* ira ulciscendi
tempus observans, *discordia* ira acerbior, intimo
animo[1] et corde concepta, *indigentia* libido inexple-
bilis, *desiderium* libido eius, qui nondum adsit,
videndi. Distinguunt illud etiam, ut libido sit
earum rerum, quae dicuntur de quodam aut quibusdam, quae κατηγορήματα dialectici appellant, ut
habere divitias, capere honores: indigentia rerum
22 ipsarum est, ut honorum, ut pecuniae. Omnium
autem perturbationum fontem esse dicunt *intemperantiam,* quae est a tota mente et a recta ratione
defectio sic aversa a praescriptione rationis, ut nullo
modo appetitiones animi nec regi nec contineri

---

[1] *odio* MSS. : *animo* Lambinus.

---

[1] The Stoics were fond of subtle distinctions. *Desiderium,*
πόθος, can be used of longing for the thing itself, *e.g. desiderium
urbis.* To make the sentence clear *desiderium* has to be
supplied with *libido sit,* and *libido* with *indigentia est.*

pusillanimity as fear following on the heels of fright like an attendant; *confusion* as fear paralyzing thought; *faintheartedness* as lasting fear.

IX. Further, the divisions of pleasure are described in this way, that *malice* is pleasure derived from a neighbour's evil which brings no advantage to oneself; that *rapture* is pleasure soothing the soul by charm of the sense of hearing, and similar to this pleasure of the ear are those of sight and touch and smell and taste which are all of one class resembling liquefied pleasures, if I may say so, to steep the soul in. *Ostentation* is pleasure shown in outward demeanour and puffing oneself out extravagantly. The divisions again under the head of lust are defined in such a way that *anger* is the lust of punishing the man who is thought to have inflicted an undeserved injury; *rage* on the other hand is anger springing up and suddenly showing itself, termed in Greek θύμωσις: *hate* is inveterate anger; *enmity* is anger watching an opportunity for revenge; *wrath* is anger of greater bitterness conceived in the innermost heart and soul; *greed* is insatiable lust; *longing* is the lust of beholding someone who is not present. They distinguish another sense of longing and make it also mean lust of the predicates affirmed of a person or persons (the terms used by the logicians being κατηγορήματα), as for instance a man longs *to have* riches, *to obtain* distinctions; while greed is lust of the actual things, as for instance of distinctions, of money.[1] Further, they say that the fountain-head of all disorders is *intemperance*, which is a revolt from all guidance of the mind and right reason, so completely alien from the control of reason that the cravings of the soul cannot be

queant. Quem ad modum igitur temperantia sedat
appetitiones et efficit ut eae rectae rationi pareant
conservatque considerata iudicia mentis, sic huic
inimica intemperantia omnem animi statum inflam-
mat, conturbat, incitat; itaque et aegritudines et
metus et reliquae perturbationes omnes gignuntur
ex ea.

23 X. Quem ad modum cum sanguis corruptus est
aut pituita redundat aut bilis, in corpore morbi
aegrotationesque nascuntur, sic pravarum opinionum
conturbatio et ipsarum inter se repugnantia sanitate
spoliat animum morbisque perturbat. Ex perturbationibus autem primum morbi conficiuntur, quae
vocant illi νοσήματα, eaque, quae sunt eis morbis
contraria, quae habent ad res certas vitiosam offen-
sionem atque fastidium, deinde aegrotationes, quae
appellantur a Stoicis ἀρρωστήματα, hisque item
oppositae contrariae offensiones. Hoc loco nimium
operae consumitur a Stoicis, maxime a Chrysippo,
dum morbis corporum comparatur morborum
animi similitudo: qua oratione praetermissa minime
necessaria ea, quae rem continent, pertractemus.

24 Intelligatur igitur perturbationem iactantibus se
opinionibus inconstanter et turbide in motu esse
semper; cum autem hic fervor concitatioque animi
inveteraverit et tamquam in venis medullisque
insederit, tum exsistit et morbus et aegrotatio et

---

[1] For the four humours, cf. I. § 56.

[2] Diseases and sicknesses of soul, like love of glory, come
from the disorders of lust and delight: they have "opposites" in aversions and disgusts which spring from the disorder of fear, as for instance hatred of mankind, for love is
the opposite of hate. In logical opposition black is the

guided or curbed. Therefore just as temperance allays the cravings and causes them to obey right reason, and maintains the well-considered judgments of the mind, so intemperance its enemy kindles, confounds and agitates the whole condition of the soul, with the result that from it come distress and fear and all other disorders.

X. Just as when the blood is in a bad state or there is an overflow of phlegm or bile,[1] bodily disease and sickness begin, so the disturbing effect of corrupt beliefs warring against one another robs the soul of health and introduces the disorder of disease. Moreover from disorders are produced, in the first place, diseases (for which the term is νοσήματα), and besides these the affections which are the opposites of such diseases and which are accompanied by unwholesome aversion and loathing for certain things; secondly there are produced sicknesses, termed by the Stoics ἀρρωστήματα, and these too have corresponding aversions which are their "opposites."[2] At this point far too much attention is devoted by the Stoics, principally by Chrysippus, to drawing an analogy between diseases of the soul and diseases of the body. Let us neglect such passages as quite unnecessary and busy ourselves only with the pith of their argument. Let it be understood then that, as the waves of belief toss in capricious confusion, disorder is in perpetual motion ; when however this feverish excitement of the soul is become chronic and settled as it were in the veins and marrow of our bones—then there come

"contrary" of white and love of hate. Both diseases and sicknesses have severally corresponding aversions which are "contrary" to them and are their "opposites."

offensiones eae, quae sunt eis morbis aegrotationi-
busque contrariae.

XI. Haec, quae dico, cogitatione inter se differunt,
re quidem copulata sunt, eaque oriuntur ex libidine
et ex laetitia : nam cum est concupita pecunia nec
adhibita continuo ratio quasi quaedam Socratica
medicina, quae sanaret eam cupiditatem, permanat
in venas et inhaeret in visceribus illud malum
exsistitque morbus et aegrotatio, quae evelli inveti-
rata non possunt, eique morbo nomen est *avaritia ;*
25 similiterque ceteri morbi, ut *gloriae cupiditas,* ut
mulierositas, ut ita appellem eam, quae Graece
φιλογυνία dicitur, ceterique similiter morbi aegrotationesque nascuntur.   Quae autem sunt his contraria, ea nasci putantur a metu, ut *odium mulierum,*
quale in Μισογύνῳ Atilii [1] est, ut *in hominum universum
genus,* quod accepimus de Timone, qui μισάνθρωπος
appellatur, ut *inhospitalitas* est : quae omnes aegrotationes animi ex quodam metu nascuntur earum
26 rerum, quas fugiunt et oderunt.   Definiunt autem
animi *aegrotationem* opinationem vehementem de re
non expetenda, tamquam valde expetenda sit, inhaerentem et penitus insitam.   Quod autem nascitur
ex offensione ita definiunt, opinionem vehementem
de re non fugienda inhaerentem et penitus insitam
tamquam fugienda : haec autem opinatio est iudi-
catio se scire quod nesciat.   *Aegrotationi* autem talia
quaedam subiecta sunt : *avaritia, ambitio, mulierositas,*

---

[1] As Atilius is little known, and his play only a guess,
Bentley proposed to read *odium in mulieres quale* μισογύνου
Hippolyti, cf. § 27.   Μισογύνη has been suggested for μισογύνῳ
to correspond with the title of Menander's play.

---

[1] Atilius, comic poet about 200 B.C., who perhaps translated
Menander's play Μισογύνης.

both disease and sickness and those aversions which are the " opposites " of disease and sickness.

XI. Whilst there is theoretically a difference between the ailments I am dealing with, in practice at any rate they are combined and their origin is found in lust and delight. For when money is coveted and reason is not at once applied as a kind of Socratic remedy to cure the desire, the evil circulates in the veins and fastens on the vital organs, and disease and sickness ensue, things which cannot be plucked out when they are long established; and for such a disease the name is *avarice*. And similarly the other diseases like *thirst for fame*, like *love of women*, to give this term to what the Greeks call φιλογυνία, and all other diseases and sicknesses originate in similar fashion. It is thought moreover that fear is the origin of their opposites like *hatred of women*, as for instance in the Μισόγυνος of Atilius,[1] like the *hatred of all mankind* felt we are told by Timon[2] who is termed μισάνθρωπος, and like *inhospitality* : and all these sicknesses of the soul originate in a certain fear of the things they avoid and hate. Furthermore they define *sickness* of soul as an intense belief, persistent and deeply rooted, which regards a thing that is not desirable as though it were eminently desirable. The product of aversion moreover is defined as an intense belief, persistent and deeply rooted, which regards a thing that need not be shunned as though it ought to be shunned : further this sort of belief is an act of judging that one has knowledge where one has none. There are moreover certain subdivisions of *sickness* of the following kind : *avarice, ambition, love of*

---

[2] Timon belonged to the age of Socrates.

pervicacia, ligurritio, vinolentia, cuppedia et si qua
similia. Est autem avaritia opinatio vehemens de
pecunia, quasi valde expetenda sit, inhaerens et
penitus insita, similisque est eiusdem generis de-
27 finitio reliquarum. *Offensionum* autem definitiones
sunt eius modi, ut *inhospitalitas* sit opinio vehemens
valde fugiendum esse hospitem eaque inhaerens et
penitus insita, similiterque definitur et *mulierum
odium,* ut Hippolyti, et, ut Timonis, *generis humani.*

XII. Atque ut ad valetudinis similitudinem veniamus eaque collatione utamur aliquando, sed parcius
quam solent Stoici, ut sunt alii ad alios morbos pro-
cliviores, itaque dicimus gravedinosos quosdam,
quosdam torminosos, non quia iam sint, sed quia
saepe, sic alii ad metum, alii ad aliam perturbationem: ex quo in aliis *anxietas,* unde anxii, in aliis
iracundia dicitur, quae ab *ira* differt, estque aliud
iracundum esse, aliud iratum, ut differt *anxietas* ab
angore; neque enim omnes anxii qui anguntur aliquando nec qui anxii semper anguntur, ut inter
ebrietatem et ebriositatem interest aliudque est
amatorem esse, aliud amantem. Atque haec aliorum
ad alios morbos proclivitas late patet; nam pertinet
28 ad omnes perturbationes. In multis etiam vitiis

*women, stubbornness, love of good living, intoxica-
tion, daintiness* and anything similar. Avarice again
is an intense belief, persistent and deeply rooted,
which regards money as being eminently desirable,
and the definition of the other members of the same
class is similar. The definitions of *aversions* moreover are of the type that *inhospitality* is an intense
belief, persistent and deeply rooted, that a visitor is
to be carefully avoided; a similar definition too is
given of *hatred of women* like that of Hippolytus,
and *hatred of mankind* like that of Timon.

XII. Now to come to the analogy of health and
to make use at last of this comparison (but more
sparingly than is the way of the Stoics), as some
men are more prone to some diseases and other men
to others, and so we say of certain people that they
are liable to catch cold, certain others to attacks of
colic, not because they are suffering at the moment
but because they frequently do so; in the same way
some men are prone to fear, others to another
disorder, in consequence of which in some cases we
speak of an *anxious temper* and hence of anxious
people, in other cases of *irascibility* which is different
from *anger*, and it is one thing to be irascible, another
thing to be angry, just as an *anxious temper* is
different from *feeling anxiety*; for not all men who
are at times anxious are of an anxious temper, nor
are those who have an anxious temper always
feeling anxious, just as for instance there is a
difference between intoxication and habitual drunkenness, and it is one thing to be a gallant and another thing to be in love. Moreover this proneness
of some men to one disease and others to another is
of wide application; for it applies to all disorders.

apparet, sed nomen res non habet. Ergo et invidi et malevoli [et lividi][1] et timidi et misericordes, quia proclives ad eas perturbationes, non quia semper feruntur. Haec igitur proclivitas ad suum quodque genus a similitudine corporis aegrotatio dicatur, dum ea intelligatur ad aegrotandum proclivitas. Sed haec in bonis rebus, quod alii ad alia bona sunt aptiores, *facilitas* nominetur, in malis *proclivitas*, ut significet lapsionem, in neutris habeat superius nomen.

XIII. Quo modo autem in corpore est morbus, est aegrotatio, est vitium, sic in animo. *Morbum* appellant totius corporis corruptionem, *aegrotationem*
29 morbum cum imbecillitate, *vitium*, cum partes corporis inter se dissident, ex quo pravitas membrorum, distortio, deformitas. Itaque illa duo, morbus et aegrotatio, ex totius valetudinis corporis conquassatione et perturbatione gignuntur; vitium autem integra valetudine ipsum ex se cernitur. Sed in animo tantum modo cogitatione possumus morbum ab aegrotatione seiungere; *vitiositas* autem est habitus aut adfectio in tota vita inconstans et a se ipsa dissentiens. Ita fit ut in altera corruptione opinionum morbus efficiatur et aegrotatio, in altera inconstantia et repugnantia; non enim omne vitium pares habet dissensiones,[2] ut eorum, qui non longe

[1] *et lividi* bracketed as unnecessary by Wesenberg.
[2] *partes habet dissentientis* MSS. : *pares h. dissensiones* Bentley.

---

[1] For the difference between *vitia* and *perturbationes* cf. the beginning of § 30.
[2] *i.e.* moral defectiveness, in § 34 "viciousness," as the same rendering does not suit all contexts.

It is apparent also in a number of defects[1]; but for this there is no name. Men therefore are called both envious and malicious (and jealous) and fearful and compassionate because of a proneness to such disorders, not because they are always being hurried into them. This proneness then of each individual to his own peculiar disorder would on the analogy of the body be called sickness, provided it be understood as proneness to sickness. But in the case of what is good, because some men are better adapted to one sort of good and others to another, let it be named *inclination ;* in the case of what is evil let it be named *proneness* so as to suggest slipping ; in the case of what is neither good nor bad let it have the earlier name.

XIII. Now as the body is liable to disease, to sickness, to defect, so is the soul. *Disease* is the term applied to a break-down of the whole body, *sickness* to disease attended by weakness, *defect* when the parts of the body are not symmetrical with one another and there ensue crookedness of the limbs, distortion, ugliness. And so the first two, disease and sickness, are a result of shock and disorder to the bodily health as a whole; defect, however, is discernible of itself, though the general health is unimpaired. But in the soul we can only separate disease from sickness theoretically. *Defectiveness,*[2] however, is a habit or a disposition which is throughout life inconsistent and out of harmony with itself. So it comes that in the one perversion of beliefs the result is disease and sickness, in the other the result is inconsistency and discord. For not every defect involves equal want of harmony, as for instance the disposition of those who are not far off

357

a sapientia absunt, adfectio est illa quidem dis
crepans sibi ipsa, dum est insipiens, sed non
distorta nec prava. Morbi autem et aegrotationes partes sunt vitiositatis, sed perturbationes
30 sintne eiusdem partes quaestio est : vitia enim
adfectiones sunt manentes, perturbationes autem
moventes, ut non possint adfectionum manentium
partes esse. Atque ut in malis attingit animi
naturam corporis similitudo, sic in bonis ; sunt enim
in corpore praecipua, pulcritudo, vires, valetudo,
firmitas, velocitas, sunt item in animo. Ut enim
corporis temperatio, cum ea congruunt inter se, e
quibus constamus, sanitas, sic animi dicitur, cum
eius iudicia opinionesque concordant, eaque animi
est virtus, quam alii ipsam temperantiam dicunt
esse, alii obtemperantem temperantiae praeceptis et
eam subsequentem nec habentem ullam speciem
suam, sed, sive hoc sive illud sit, in solo esse
sapiente. Est autem quaedam animi sanitas, quae
in insipientem etiam cadat, cum curatione[1] medi-
31 corum conturbatio mentis aufertur. Et ut corporis
est quaedam apta figura membrorum cum coloris

---

[1] *curatione et perturbatione* MSS. : *curatione* Victorius.

---

[1] The meaning of this passage is difficult to follow. Cicero
seems to be distinguishing between two states of moral defect,
the one a "habit," the other a "disposition." Both are due
to perversion of belief, but vicious "habit" means depravity,
vicious "disposition" means only inconsistency, sometimes
more, sometimes less. A "disposition" by long indulgence
can become a "habit." When Dr. Johnson was urged by
Hannah More to take a little wine, "I can't take a little,
child," he answered ; "therefore I never touch it," for he did
not intend the "disposition" to become a "habit." On the
other hand Johnson declared himself "a hardened and shame-

wisdom is indeed out of harmony with itself, as long as it is unwise, but it is not distorted or perverse.[1] Disease, however, and sickness are subdivisions of defectiveness, but it is a question whether disorders are subdivisions of the same class. For defects are permanent dispositions, but disorders are shifting, so that they cannot be subdivisions of permanent dispositions. Moreover as in evil the analogy of the body extends to the nature of the soul, so it does in good. For the chief blessings of the body are beauty, strength, health, vigour, agility ; so are they of the soul. For as in the body the adjustment of the various parts, of which we are made up, in their fitting relation to one another is health, so health of the soul means a condition when its judgments and beliefs are in harmony, and such health of soul is virtue, which some say is temperance alone,[2] others a condition obedient to the dictates of temperance and following close upon it and without specific difference, but whether it be the one or the other, it exists, they say, in the wise man only. There is furthermore a certain kind of health of the soul which the unwise too can enjoy, when agitation of mind is removed by medical treatment. And as in the body a certain symmetrical shape of the limbs combined

less tea-drinker," for "disposition" had been allowed to become "habit." Horace recognizes the distinction between the man who has the "habit" of vice and who rejoices in iniquity, and the man who has the "disposition" to vice but is at war with himself, *Sat.* II. 7. 6 :

> Pars hominum vitiis gaudet constanter et urget
> Propositum ; pars multa natat, modo recta capessens,
> Interdum pravis obnoxia.

cf. also Seneca *Epist. Moral.* 75.

  [2] cf. § 22.

quadam suavitate eaque dicitur pulcritudo, sic in
animo opinionum iudiciorumque aequabilitas et
constantia cum firmitate quadam et stabilitate virtutem subsequens aut virtutis vim ipsam continens
pulcritudo vocatur. Itemque viribus corporis et
nervis et efficacitati similes similibus quoque verbis
animi vires nominantur. Velocitas autem corporis
celeritas appellatur, quae eadem ingenii etiam laus
habetur propter animi multarum rerum brevi tempore percursionem. XIV. Illud animorum corpo-
rumque dissimile, quod animi valentes morbo
temptari non possunt, ut[1] corpora possunt, sed
corporum offensiones sine culpa accidere possunt,
animorum non item, quorum omnes morbi et perturbationes ex aspernatione rationis eveniunt, itaque
in hominibus solum exsistunt ; nam bestiae simile
quiddam faciunt, sed in perturbationes non incidunt.
32 Inter acutos autem et inter hebetes interest, quod
ingeniosi, ut aes Corinthium in aeruginem, sic illi
in morbum et incidunt tardius et recreantur ocius,
hebetes non item. Nec vero in omnem morbum
ac perturbationem animus ingeniosi cadit ; non enim
in ulla[2] efferata et immania : quaedam autem humanitatis quoque habent primam speciem, ut miseri-

---

[1] *ut* supplied by Bentley.
[2] *multa* MSS. : *in ulla* Bentley.

---

[1] cf. *Merchant of Venice*, Act IV. Sc. 1, where Shylock says,
    As there is no firm reason to be render'd,
    Why he cannot abide a gaping pig ;
    Why he, a harmless necessary cat ;
    Why he, a wauling bag-pipe.
Such idiosyncrasies are physical aversions without blame,
but the lines which follow show an aversion of the soul in
contempt of reason:

with a certain charm of colouring is described as
beauty; so in the soul the name of beauty is given to
an equipoise and consistency of beliefs and judgments, combined with a certain steadiness and
stability, following upon virtue or comprising the
true essence of virtue. And so strength of soul
resembling the strength and sinews and effectiveness
of the body is also described by similar terms.
Agility of body again is termed quickness, and the
same term is held to imply praise when applied to
the intellect as well, because of the soul's rapid
survey of a number of things in a short space of
time. XIV. There is this dissimilarity between soul
and body, that the strong soul cannot be attacked by
disease as bodies can, but physical aversions can
occur without blame,[1] while it is not so with aversions
of the soul in which all diseases and disorders are
the result of contempt of reason. Consequently they
are only found in human beings; for while animals
act in a way that is comparable, yet they are not
attacked by disorders of the soul. There is, however,
this difference between quick-witted and dull-witted
men, that gifted men resemble Corinthian bronze
which is slow to be attacked by rust, and similarly
they are both slower to be attacked by disease and
quicker in recovery, while with the dull-witted it is
not so. Nor is the soul of the gifted man by any means
liable to every disease and disorder, for it is not so
to anything savage and monstrous; and some of its
disorders such as compassion, distress, fear, bear at

> So can I give no reason, nor I will not,
> More than a lodg'd hate and a certain loathing
> I bear Antonio, that I follow thus
> A losing suit against him.

cordia, aegritudo, metus. Aegrotationes autem
morbique animorum difficilius evelli posse putantur
quam summa illa vitia, quae virtutibus sunt contraria;
morbis enim manentibus vitia sublata esse possunt,
quia hi[1] non tam celeriter sanantur quam illa tollun-
33 tur. Habes ea, quae de perturbationibus enucleate
disputant Stoici, quae logica appellant, quia dis-
seruntur subtilius : ex quibus quoniam tamquam ex
scrupulosis cotibus enavigavit oratio, reliquae disputationis cursum teneamus, modo satis illa dilucide
dixerimus pro rerum obscuritate. A. Prorsus satis,
sed si quae diligentius erunt cognoscenda, quaere-
mus alias : nunc vela, quae modo dicebas, exspecta-
mus et cursum.

34 XV. M. Quando, ut aliis locis de virtute et diximus et saepe dicendum erit—pleraeque enim quaes-
tiones, quae ad vitam moresque pertinent, a virtutis
fonte ducuntur,—quando igitur virtus est adfectio
animi constans conveniensque, laudabiles efficiens
eos, in quibus est, et ipsa per se, sua sponte separata
etiam utilitate laudabilis, ex ea proficiscuntur
honestae voluntates, sententiae, actiones omnisque
recta ratio, quamquam ipsa virtus brevissime recta
ratio dici potest. Huius igitur virtutis contraria est
vitiositas—sic enim malo quam malitiam appellare

---

[1] *hi* supplied by Lambinus.

---

[1] cf. § 9. Cicero has worked his way out to sea by using
the oars of dialectic and is now clear of all the thorny distinctions and definitions of the Stoics, which he here com-

first the semblance even of humanity. Moreover it is thought that sicknesses and diseases of the soul are extirpated with greater difficulty than those extreme defects which are the opposites of the virtues. For whilst diseases persist, defects may be got rid of, because diseases are not cured so quickly as defects can be got rid of. You now have the pith of the Stoic discussions about disorders, which they term "logical conclusions," because they are argued out with special precision. And now that our argument has worked its way, as it were, clear of these rocks with all their catchy points,[1] let us pursue the course of the discussion that remains, provided only I have given an account which is adequately clear, considering the difficulty of the subject. A. Perfectly clear; but if any points call for more searching inquiry, we shall put questions at another time; for the present we are waiting for the sails you just now mentioned and a clear run.

XV. M. Since, as I have both said on other occasions and shall frequently have to say again (for there are a number of problems connected with life and morality which have virtue as their fountain-head)— since therefore virtue is an equable and harmonious disposition of the soul making those praiseworthy in whom it is found, and is of its own nature and by itself praiseworthy, apart from any question of expediency, there spring from it good inclinations, opinions, actions and all that makes right reason; though indeed virtue itself can best be summed up as right reason. The opposite then of such virtue is viciousness (for I prefer this term to "malice"

pares to rocks with jagged ends which catch the vessel. Now that he is happily clear he can spread his sails.

eam, quam Graeci κακίαν appellant; nam malitia
certi cuiusdam vitii nomen est, vitiositas omnium,—
ex qua concitantur [1] perturbationes, quae sunt, ut
paullo ante diximus, turbidi animorum concitatique
motus, aversi a ratione et inimicissimi mentis vitae-
que tranquillae. Important enim aegritudines
anxias atque acerbas animosque adfligunt et debili-
tant metu; iidem inflammant appetitione nimia,
quam tum cupiditatem, tum libidinem dicimus, impotentiam quandam animi a temperantia et modera-
35 tione plurimum dissidentem. Quae si quando
adepta erit id, quod ei fuerit concupitum, tum effere-
tur alacritate, " ut nihil ei constet " quod agat, ut
ille, qui " voluptatem animi nimiam summum esse
errorem " arbitratur. Eorum igitur malorum in una
virtute posita sanatio est.

XVI. Quid autem est non miserius solum, sed
foedius etiam et deformius quam aegritudine quis
adflictus, debilitatus, iacens? Cui miseriae proximus
est is, qui appropinquans aliquod malum metuit
exanimatusque pendet animi. Quam vim mali
significantes poëtae impendere apud inferos saxum
Tantalo faciunt

Ob scelera animique impotentiam et superbiloquentiam.

---

[1] *cogitantur* MSS. : *concitantur* Manutius : *oriuntur* Bentley.

---

[1] κακία means " badness " as opposed to ἀρετή, ' excellence."
In the plural κακίαι would mean "defects" and answer to
vitia, cf. III. § 7 (note).
[2] Quoted from Trabea a Roman comic writer about 200 B.C.
Part comes in *De Finibus* II. 4. 13 and part in a letter of

which the Greeks term κακία,[1] for "malice" is the
name of a particular definite vice, viciousness is
applicable to all); and by it comes the agitation of
disorders which are, as we said a little while back,
troubled and agitated movements of the soul alien
from reason and bitterly hostile to peace of mind and
peaceful life. For they introduce worrying and
cruel distresses and depress the soul and enfeeble it
with fear; they also kindle passionate longing which
at one time we name desire, at another lust, a sort of
ungovernableness of soul widely at variance with
temperance and self-control. And if ever the soul
has secured the object of its desire it will be transported with eagerness, "so that there is no rule"
in what it does, as says the poet who thinks that
"excessive pleasure of the soul is utter folly."[2] Of
such evils therefore the cure is found in virtue alone.

XVI. What again is not only more wretched but
more degraded and hideous than a man depressed,
enfeebled and prostrate with distress? And to this
state of wretchedness that man comes nearest who
is in fear of the approach of some evil, and whose
soul is paralyzed with suspense. And it is as a
symbol of this power of evil that the poets imagine
the rock hanging over Tantalus in the world below,[3]

> Punishing his sin and want of self-control and
> boastful tongue.

Cicero's *Ad. Fam.* II. 9. 2 out of which Bentley constructed
the lines
> *Tanta laetitia auctus sum, ut nihil constet,*

and
> *Ego voluptatem animi nimiam summum esse errorem*
> *arbitror.*

[3] cf. I. § 3.

Ea communis poena stultitiae est; omnibus enim, quorum mens abhorret a ratione, semper aliqui talis

36 terror impendet. Atque ut hae tabificae mentis perturbationes sunt, aegritudinem dico et metum, sic hilariores illae, cupiditas avide semper aliquid expetens et inanis alacritas, id est laetitia gestiens, non multum differunt ab amentia. Ex quo intelligitur qualis ille sit, quem tum moderatum, alias modestum, tum temperantem, alias constantem continentemque dicimus; non numquam haec eadem vocabula ad frugalitatis nomen tamquam ad caput referre volumus. Quod nisi eo nomine virtutes continerentur, numquam ita pervulgatum illud esset, ut iam proverbii locum obtineret *hominem frugi omnia recte facere.* Quod idem cum Stoici de sapiente dicunt, nimis admirabiliter nimisque magnifice dicere videntur.

37 XVII. Ergo hic, quisquis est, qui moderatione et constantia quietus animo est sibique ipse placatus, ut nec tabescat molestiis nec frangatur timore nec sitienter quid expetens ardeat desiderio nec alacritate futili gestiens deliquescat, is est sapiens, quem quaerimus, is est beatus, cui nihil humanarum rerum aut intolerabile ad demittendum animum aut nimis laetabile ad efferendum videri potest. Quid enim videatur ei magnum in rebus humanis, cui aeternitas omnis totiusque mundi nota sit magnitudo? Nam quid aut in studiis humanis aut in tam exigua brevi-

---

[1] cf. III. § 16.

Such is the general penalty of folly; for in all cases
where the mind recoils from reason there is always
some such kind of overhanging dread. Moreover
just like these carking disorders of the mind, I mean
distress and fear, so those gayer emotions—desire
that is always greedily coveting something, and
empty eagerness, that is, exuberant delight—are not
far different from aberration of mind. And hence is
realized the character of the man whom I describe
now as restrained, at other times as sober, now as
temperate, at other times as equable and moderate;
sometimes I am inclined to refer these same
appellations to the term frugality[1] as their prime
source. For unless the virtues had been comprehended in this term it would never have come
so widely into common use that by now it passes for
a proverb that "the frugal man does everything
aright," exactly what the Stoics say of the "wise
man," but when *they* do so, their language is held to
be too high-flown and grandiloquent.

XVII. Therefore the man, whoever he is, whose
soul is tranquillized by restraint and consistency and
who is at peace with himself, so that he neither pines
away in distress, nor is broken down by fear, nor
consumed with a thirst of longing in pursuit of some
ambition, nor maudlin in the exuberance of meaningless eagerness—he is the wise man of whom we are in
quest, he is the happy man who can think no human
occurrence insupportable to the point of dispiriting
him, or unduly delightful to the point of rousing him
to ecstasy. For what can seem of moment in human
occurrences to a man who keeps all eternity before
his eyes and knows the vastness of the universe?
Nay, what either in human ambitions or in the short

tate vitae magnum sapienti videri potest, qui semper animo sic excubat, ut ei nihil improvisum accidere possit, nihil inopinatum, nihil omnino novum?

38 Atque idem ita acrem in omnes partes aciem intendit, ut semper videat sedem sibi ac locum sine molestia atque angore vivendi, ut, quemcumque casum fortuna invexerit, hunc apte et quiete ferat: quod qui faciet non aegritudine solum vacabit, sed etiam perturbationibus reliquis omnibus. His autem vacuus animus perfecte atque absolute beatos efficit, idemque concitatus et abstractus ab integra certaque ratione non constantiam solum amittit, verum etiam sanitatem.

Quocirca mollis et enervata putanda est Peripateticorum ratio et oratio, qui perturbari animos necesse dicunt esse, sed adhibent modum quendam, quem

39 ultra progredi non oporteat. Modum tu adhibes vitio? an vitium nullum est non parere rationi? an ratio parum praecipit nec bonum illud esse, quod aut cupias ardenter aut adeptus efferas te insolenter, nec porro malum, quo aut oppressus iaceas aut, ne opprimare, mente vix constes? eaque omnia aut nimis tristia aut nimis laeta errore fieri? Qui si error stultis extenuetur die, ut, cum res eadem maneat, aliter ferant inveterata, aliter recentia,

span of our brief life can seem of moment to the wise man whose soul is ever on the watch to prevent the occurrence of anything unforeseen, anything unexpected, anything whatever that is strange? Further he also directs so searching a glance in all directions with the constant aim of finding an assured retreat for a life free from vexation and worry, that, whatever reverse fortune may inflict, he shoulders his burden tranquilly : and he who shall do this will not only be free from distress but from all other disorders as well. But when the soul is freed from such ailments, it renders men completely and entirely happy, while the man who is agitated and alienated from sure and perfect reason, also loses not only equability but health of mind as well.

And therefore the views and utterances of the Peripatetics must be regarded as weak and effeminate, when they say that souls are necessarily subject to disorders, but fix a certain limit beyond which disorders should not pass. Do you I ask prescribe a limit for vice ? Or is there no vice in refusing to obey reason ? or is reason so backward in teaching, either that the thing one either passionately desires or feels extravagant transports at securing is not good? or further, that the burden, beneath the pressure of which one either lies prostrate or the pressure of which one scarcely has the resolution to resist, is not evil? and that all instances either of excessive sadness or excessive delight are due to deception ? And if this deception should in the case of fools have its impression weakened by lapse of time (with the result that, though the same process of deception continually goes on, they bear what is of long standing in one way, what is of

40 sapientes ne attingat quidem omnino. Etenim quis
erit tandem modus iste? Quaeramus enim modum
aegritudinis, in qua operae plurimum ponitur.
Aegre tulisse P. Rupilium fratris repulsam consulatus scriptum apud Fannium est; sed tamen trans-
isse videtur modum, quippe qui ob eam causam a
vita recesserit: moderatius igitur ferre debuit.
Quid? si, cum id ferret modice, mors liberorum
accessisset? Nata esset aegritudo nova; sit[1] ea
modica: magna tamen facta esset accessio. Quid?
si deinde dolores graves corporis, si bonorum amissio, si caecitas, si exsilium? si pro singulis malis
aegritudines accederent, summa ea fieret, quae non
sustineretur.

41 XVIII. Qui modum igitur vitio quaerit similiter
facit, ut si posse putet eum, qui se e Leucata prae-
cipitaverit, sustinere se, cum velit. Ut enim id non
potest, sic animus perturbatus et incitatus nec co-
hibere se potest nec quo loco vult insistere; omninoque, quae crescentia perniciosa sunt, eadem sunt
42 vitiosa nascentia. Aegritudo autem ceteraeque perturbationes amplificatae certe pestiferae sunt: igitur
etiam susceptae continuo in magna pestis parte
versantur. Etenim ipsae se impellunt, ubi semel
a ratione discessum est, ipsaque sibi imbecillitas
indulget in altumque provehitur imprudens nec

[1] *sed* MSS. : *sit* Bentley.

---

[1] Cicero resumes the question of the Peripatetic "limit."
[2] C. Fannius was son-in-law of Laelius and wrote history
or annals. He was a contemporary of Tiberius Gracchus.
P. Rupilius Lupus was consul 132 B.C.
[3] At the south end of the island of Leucas there was a
promontory with a temple of Apollo at whose annual festival
a criminal was flung from the promontory into the sea.

recent occurrence in another), yet wise men would not be so much as touched by it at all. For [1] what, I ask, will the suggested "limit" be? Let us inquire for instance into the limit of distress to which they devote most attention. It has been recorded in Fannius [2] that P. Rupilius was distressed at his brother's failure to be elected to the consulship. But all the same he seems to have passed the limit, since he died of chagrin. He ought therefore to have shown more restraint. Well, suppose that, though he showed moderation under this blow, there had come in addition the loss of children? a new distress would have arisen: grant it a moderate one: still an addition of consequence would have been made. Well, suppose that subsequently severe bodily pains, suppose loss of property, suppose blindness, suppose exile had followed. If there were an addition of distress to match each separate evil, there would be a sum total impossible to bear.

XVIII. He therefore who looks for a "limit" to vice is doing much the same as if he were to think that a man who has flung himself headlong from Leucas [3] can stop his fall when he will. For just as that is impossible, so it is impossible for a disordered and excited soul to control itself or stop where it wishes; and, speaking generally, things which are ruinous in their development are vicious also in their origin. Moreover distress and all other forms of disorder, when intensified, are assuredly deadly; therefore, also, when experienced, their tendency is from the outset to a great extent deadly. For they are forced on by their nature, when once the severance from reason has begun, and weakness is by its nature self-indulgent and is carried out to sea with-

reperit locum consistendi. Quam ob rem nihil
interest utrum moderatas perturbationes approbent
an moderatam iniustitiam, moderatam ignaviam,
moderatam intemperantiam; qui enim vitiis modum
apponit, is partem suscipit vitiorum; quod cum
ipsum per se odiosum est, tum eo molestius, quia
sunt in lubrico incitatique semel proclivi labuntur
sustinerique nullo modo possunt.

43   XIX. Quid? quod iidem Peripatetici perturbationes istas, quas nos exstirpandas putamus, non
modo naturales esse dicunt, sed etiam utiliter a
natura datas; quorum est talis oratio. Primum
multis verbis iracundiam laudant: cotem fortitudinis
esse dicunt, multoque et in hostem et in improbum
civem vehementiores iratorum impetus esse, leves
autem ratiunculas eorum, qui ita cogitarent: "proelium rectum est hoc fieri, convenit dimicare pro
legibus, pro libertate, pro patria;" haec nullam
habere[1] vim nisi ira excanduerit[2] fortitudo. Nec
vero de bellatoribus solum disputant; imperia
severiora nulla esse putant sine aliqua acerbitate
iracundiae; oratorem denique non modo accusantem,
sed ne defendentem quidem probant sine aculeis
iracundiae, quae etiam si non adsit, tamen verbis
atque motu simulandam arbitrantur, ut auditoris
iram oratoris incendat actio. Virum denique videri
negant, qui irasci nesciat, eamque, quam lenitatem

---

[1] *habent* MSS. : *habere* Bentley.
[2] *excanduit* MSS. : *excanduerit* Bake.

---

[1] "Sudden anger stands in our nature for self-defence. . . .
There are plainly cases . . . in which there is no time for
consideration, and yet to be passive is certain destruction."
Bishop Butler, *Upon Resentment.*

out knowing it and finds no means of stopping. And therefore it makes no difference whether the Peripatetics are in favour of limited disorders or limited injustice, limited sloth, limited intemperance; for he who sets a limit to vices, admits a part of them; and this is both in and for itself hateful, and all the more grievous because the ground is slippery, and once started they slide swiftly downhill and cannot by any means be stopped.

XIX. Again, what of the contention of the same Peripatetics that these selfsame disorders which we think need extirpating are not only natural but also bestowed on us by nature for a useful end? This is the language they use. In the first place they praise irascibility [1] at great length; they name it the whetstone of bravery and say that the assaults of angry men upon an enemy or disloyal citizen show greater vehemence; but that there is no substance in the petty logic of those who coldly argue like this: " It is *right* to fight this battle; it is *proper* to contend for laws, for liberty, for country; " that these words have no meaning unless bravery breaks out in a blaze of anger. And they do not argue about warriors only; no stern commands in time of need are given, they think, without something of the keen edge of irascibility. Finally they do not approve of an orator unless he uses the prickles of irascibility, not merely in bringing an accusation but even in conducting a defence, and though the anger be not genuine, yet it should, they think, be feigned in language and gesture, that the delivery of the orator may kindle the anger of the hearer. In fine they say that they do not regard anyone, who does not know how to be angry,

nos dicimus, vitioso lentitudinis nomine appellant.
44 Nec vero solum hanc libidinem laudant—est enim
ira, ut modo definivi, ulciscendi libido,—sed ipsum
illud genus vel libidinis vel cupiditatis ad summam
utilitatem esse dicunt a natura datum ; nihil enim
quemquam nisi quod libeat praeclare facere posse.
Noctu ambulabat in publico Themistocles, quod
somnum capere non posset, quaerentibusque re-
spondebat Miltiadis tropaeis se e somno suscitari.
Cui non sunt auditae Demosthenis vigiliae? qui
dolere se aiebat, si quando opificum antelucana
victus esset industria. Philosophiae denique ipsius
principes numquam in suis studiis tantos progressus
sine flagranti cupiditate facere potuissent. Ultimas
terras lustrasse Pythagoram, Democritum, Platonem
accepimus ; ubi enim quidquid esset quod disci
posset, eo veniendum iudicaverunt. Num putamus
haec fieri sine summo cupiditatis ardore potuisse ?
45 XX. Ipsam aegritudinem, quam nos ut taetram et
immanem beluam fugiendam diximus, non sine
magna utilitate a natura dicunt constitutam, ut
homines castigationibus, reprehensionibus, igno-
miniis adfici se in delicto dolerent. Impunitas enim
peccatorum data videtur eis, qui ignominiam et
infamiam ferunt sine dolore : morderi est melius

---

[1] "One may venture to affirm that there is scarce a man in
the world, but would have it (*i.e.* deliberate anger or resentment) upon some occasions." Butler, *Upon Resentment.*

[2] In Aristotle, *Eth.* II. 7. 10, the excess of anger is
ὀργιλότης, *iracundia*, the defect is ἀοργησία, *lentitudo*, and the
mean is πραότης, *lenitas.*

[3] cf. § 21.

[4] Cicero has to use *libido* even of feigned anger, for *libido*
is the genus of which anger, love, etc., are species, § 14. He
couples it with *cupiditas.* If *cupiditas* stood alone he could

as a man,[1] and to what we call mildness,[2] they apply the term indifference with a bad meaning. And indeed they do not only praise lust of this sort (for anger is as I defined it lately the lust of vengeance),[3] but they say that this selfsame kind of emotion, call it lust[4] or desire, has been bestowed by nature for purposes of the highest utility; for no one is able to do anything really well except he has a lust for it. Themistocles walked by night in a public place because he was, he said, unable to sleep, and in answer to questions replied that he was kept awake by the trophies of Miltiades. Who has not heard of the sleeplessness of Demosthenes? who said that he was grieved if ever he had been beaten by the diligence of workmen rising before the break of day. Lastly the leaders of philosophy itself would never have been able to make such prodigious advance in their studies without a fiery longing. We have been told that Pythagoras, Democritus, Plato journeyed to the ends of the earth; for they judged it their duty to go where there was something to be learnt, whatever it might be. We cannot think, can we, that this would have been possible without deep and passionate longing?

XX. As for distress itself, which we have said is to be shunned as an abominable and savage monster, they say it has been provided by nature not without considerable advantage, in order that mankind if guilty of trespass should feel pain at incurring correction, censure and disgrace. For escape from the penalty of trespasses seems granted to those who endure disgrace and shame without pain; it is better

have said below *nisi quod cupiat*, but to pick up *libido* he says *nisi quod libeat*.

conscientia. Ex quo est illud e vita ductum ab Afranio ; nam cum dissolutus filius :

Heu me miserum !

tum severus pater :

> *Dum modo doleat aliquid, doleat quidlubet.*

46 Reliquas quoque partes aegritudinis utiles esse dicunt, misericordiam ad opem ferendam et calamitates hominum indignorum sublevandas ; ipsum illud aemulari, obtrectare non esse inutile, cum aut se non idem videat consecutum quod alium aut alium idem quod se ; metum vero si qui sustulisset, omnem vitae diligentiam sublatam fore, quae summa esset in eis, qui leges, qui magistratus, qui paupertatem, qui ignominiam, qui mortem, qui dolorem timerent. Haec tamen ita disputant, ut resecanda esse fateantur, evelli penitus dicant nec posse nec opus esse, et in omnibus fere rebus mediocritatem esse optimam existimant. Quae cum exponunt, nihilne tibi videntur an aliquid dicere ? A. Mihi vero dicere aliquid ; itaque exspecto quid ad ista.

47 XXI. M. Reperiam fortasse, sed illud ante. Videsne quanta fuerit apud Academicos verecundia ? Plane enim dicunt quod ad rem pertineat. Peripateticis respondetur a Stoicis. Digladientur illi per me licet, cui nihil est necesse nisi ubi sit illud,

---

[1] Cicero wishes to show that the followers of the Academy, of whom he was one, do not endeavour to support a preconceived opinion or to engage in the war of sects, but to find out the view which is nearest to the truth.

to suffer the stings of conscience. Hence the passage in Afranius is true to life; for when the prodigal son says:

"Ah misery!"

the stern father replies:

"So pain comes, let that pain be what it will."

They say too that the remaining subdivisions of distress are useful, compassion, for instance, to make us give assistance and relieve the misfortunes of men who do not deserve them; even feelings of rivalry, of jealousy are not without their use, they say, when he who feels them sees either that he has not made the same gain as another, or another has gained the same as himself; if indeed anyone succeeded in getting rid of fear, the careful conduct of life which is found at its highest in those who fear the laws, fear the magistrates, fear poverty, fear disgrace, fear death, fear pain, would be got rid of entirely. Yet in arguing in this way they admit the need of the pruning knife, but say that complete extirpation is neither possible nor necessary, and consider that in almost all circumstances the "mean" is best. And when they state their case thus, do you think that it amounts to anything or nothing? *A.* To me, certainly, it seems to amount to something, and consequently I am waiting to see what you will say in answer.

XXI. *M.* I shall find a way perhaps; but this much first. Do you see the admirable reserve [1] shown by the followers of the Academy? For they say simply what they think to the purpose. The answer to the Peripatetics is given by the Stoics. Let these parties cross swords in a life and death struggle, for all I care, who ask for nothing except

quod veri simillimum videatur, anquirere. Quid est
igitur quod occurrat in hac quaestione quo [1] possit
attingi aliquid veri simile? quo longius mens humana progredi non potest. Definitio perturbationis,
qua recte Zenonem usum puto; ita enim definit,
ut *perturbatio sit aversa a ratione contra naturam
animi commotio*, vel brevius, ut *perturbatio sit
appetitus vehementior*, vehementior autem intelligatur
48 is, qui procul absit a naturae constantia. Quid ad
has definitiones possint dicere? Atque haec pleraque sunt prudenter acuteque disserentium: illa
quidem ex rhetorum pompa, *ardores animorum
cotesque virtutum*. An vero vir fortis nisi stomachari
coepit non potest fortis esse? Gladiatorium id
quidem; quamquam in eis ipsis videmus saepe
constantiam:

> *Colloquuntur, congrediuntur, quaerunt aliquid, pos-
> tulant,*

ut magis placati quam irati esse videantur. Sed
in illo genere sit sane Pacideianus aliquis hoc
animo, ut narrat Lucilius:

> *Occidam illum equidem et vincam, si id quaeritis,
> inquit.*
> *Verum illud credo fore: in os prius accipiam ipse,*

> [1] *e qua* most MSS.: *quo* Bouhier.

---

[1] cf. § 11.
[2] *Pompa* is properly a procession, which would carry with
it banners and other ornaments.
[3] The source of this quotation is unknown.
[4] C. Lucilius, the satirist, was a Roman knight and served
in the Numantine war, 133 B.C. He died *c*. 102 B.C. Pacidei-

to look carefully for the solution which seems most probable. What is there then to be found in this problem, by the help of which we may make the port of probability? Further than this the mind of man cannot advance. There is the definition of disorder which I think Zeno rightly employed; for his definition[1] is that "disorder is an agitation of the soul alien from reason, contrary to nature," or more briefly that "disorder is a longing of undue violence," unduly violent however being understood to mean a longing which is far removed from the equability of nature. What, I ask, can the Peripatetics advance against these definitions? Besides, the words of the Stoics are in the main those of men arguing with wisdom and insight: the others deal in rhetorical fireworks,[2] "kindlings of souls and whetstones of virtues." Or is it the fact that a brave man cannot be brave unless he begins to lose his temper? True for gladiators—yes; and yet in these selfsame men we often see an equable spirit:

> Converse hold they, meet together, questions ask
> and make requests,[3]

so that they seem to be cool rather than angry. But suppose, if you like, there be in this class of men some Pacideianus of the spirit described by Lucilius:[4]

> Kill him for my part I shall and shall conquer, he
> says, if you ask this.
> This is the programme I think: in the face I shall
> first be to get one,

anus was a famous gladiator, and is mentioned by Horace, *Sat.* II. 7. 96. Cf. App. II.

MARCUS TULLIUS CICERO

Quam gladium in stomacho spurci[1] ac pulmonibus
   sisto.
Odi hominem, iratus pugno, nec longius quidquam
Nobis quam dextrae gladium dum accommodet alter :
Usque adeo studio atque odio illius ecferor ira.

49   XXII. At sine hac gladiatoria iracundia videmus
progredientem apud Homerum Aiacem multa cum
hilaritate, cum depugnaturus est cum Hectore ;
cuius ut arma sumpsit, ingressio laetitiam attulit
sociis, terrorem autem hostibus, ut ipsum Hectorem,
quem ad modum est apud Homerum, toto pectore
trementem provocasse ad pugnam poeniteret.   Atque hi collocuti inter se, prius quam manum con-
sererent, leniter et quiete nihil ne in ipsa quidem
pugna iracunde rabioseve fecerunt.   Ego ne Tor-
quatum quidem illum, qui hoc cognomen invenit,
iratum existimo Gallo torquem detraxisse nec Marcellum apud Clastidium ideo fortem fuisse, quia
50 fuerit iratus.   De Africano quidem, quia notior est
nobis propter recentem memoriam, vel iurare possum non illum iracundia tum inflammatum fuisse,
cum in acie M. Allienum Pelignum scuto protexerit
gladiumque hosti in pectus infixerit.   De L. Bruto

---

[1] *sura*, most MSS., but a wound in the calf does not fit
the passage: *spurci*, a Lucilian word, Scyffert.   Bentley
suggests *Furiae* as the name of the rival gladiator.

---

[1] *Il.* VII. 211.
[2] Homer says the Trojans trembled, not Hector.
[3] T. Manlius Torquatus, 361 B.C., slew a gigantic Gaul in
single combat and took the collar (*torquis*) from his neck.
[4] M. Claudius Marcellus, a hero of the second Punic war,
killed Viridomarus king of the Gauls in battle at Clastidium,

Ere in his swinish guts or his lungs my sword
  come to a standstill.
Hate for the fellow I feel, fight in anger, and wait
  we no longer
Than for us each to fit tight our swords to the
  grip of the right hand :
Such is the passion of hate that I feel in my
  transport of anger.

XXII. But in Homer [1] we find Ajax with no sign
of this irascibility of the gladiator going out with
great cheerfulness to fight his deadly duel with
Hector; and his entry, upon taking up his arms,
brought delight to friends and dread to foes, so
much so that Hector himself, according to Homer's
account,[2] with his heart all aquake repented of
having given the challenge to battle. Moreover
they conversed together with a calm courtesy before
they set themselves to close combat, and even in the
actual fighting showed no irascibility or frenzy. I
do not think either that the famous soldier who won
the surname of Torquatus [3] was angry when he
dragged the torque off the Gaul, or that Marcellus [4]
at Clastidium was brave for the reason that he was
angry. Of Africanus [5] indeed, of whom we have
better knowledge, because his memory is fresh in
our minds, I can even take my oath that he was not
in a blaze of irascibility when on the field of battle
he covered M. Allienus Pelignus with his shield and
planted his sword in the breast of his enemy. I

222 b.c., and was the third Roman to dedicate the *spolia
opima* to Jupiter Feretrius.
  [5] P. Cornelius Scipio Africanus Minor, conqueror of
Carthage, 146 b.c., and Numantia, 133 b.c.

fortasse dubitarim an propter infinitum odium tyranni
effrenatius in Arruntem invaserit; video enim utrumque comminus ictu cecidisse contrario.   Quid igitur
huc adhibetis iram? an fortitudo nisi insanire coepit
impetus suos non habet?   Quid?   Herculem, quem
in caelum ista ipsa, quam vos iracundiam esse
vultis, sustulit fortitudo, iratumne censes conflixisse
cum Erymanthio apro aut leone Nemeaeo?   an
etiam Theseus Marathonii tauri cornua compre-
hendit iratus?   Vide ne fortitudo minime sit rabiosa
sitque iracundia tota levitatis; neque enim est ulla
fortitudo, quae rationis est expers.

51   XXIII. Contemnendae res humanae sunt, negli-
genda mors est, patibiles et dolores et labores
putandi: haec cum constituta sunt iudicio atque
sententia tum est robusta illa et stabilis fortitudo,
nisi forte, quae vehementer, acriter, animose fiunt,
iracunde fieri suspicamur.   Mihi ne Scipio quidem
ille pontifex maximus, qui hoc Stoicorum verum
esse declaravit, numquam privatum esse sapientem,
iratus videtur fuisse Ti. Graccho tum, cum consulem languentem reliquit atque ipse privatus, ut
si consul esset, qui rem publicam salvam esse vel-
52 lent, se sequi iussit.   Nescio ecquid ipsi nos fortiter
in re publica fecerimus: si quid fecimus, certe irati
non fecimus.   An est quidquam similius insaniae

---

[1] Every now and again there are hints of what was
expected of Marcus Brutus in regard to Caesar, cf. § 2.
[2] P. Cornelius Scipio Serapio, consul 138 B.C., was responsible for the death of Tiberius Gracchus, 133 B.C.

could not be so sure of L. Brutus; it may be that unbounded hatred of the tyrant[1] made him dash more impetuously upon Arruns; for I see that each of them fell by a wound from the hand of the other. Why then do you bring in anger here? Is it that bravery has no impulses of its own unless it begins to lose its wits? Again, do you think that Hercules, who was raised to heaven by that selfsame bravery you would have to be irascibility, was angry when he struggled with the boar of Erymanthus or the lion of Nemea? or Theseus too when he gripped the horns of the bull of Marathon? Have a care lest bravery contain no jot of frenzy, and irascibility be wholly trumpery; for there is no bravery that is devoid of reason.

XXIII. The chances of mortal life are to be despised, death is to be disregarded, pains and toils are to be considered endurable. When such principles have been established by judgment and thought, then appears the strong and steady bravery we are looking for, unless, it may be, our notion is that acts done in an impetuous, fiery and high-spirited way are done in a mood of irascibility. To my mind even that Scipio,[2] the chief pontiff, who verified the truth of the Stoic maxim that the wise man is never out of office, does not seem to have been angry with Tiberius Gracchus when he left the spiritless consul and, though himself holding no official position, called, as though he were consul, upon all who desired the safety of the commonwealth to follow him. I cannot say whether I myself have acted bravely in public life: if ever I have so acted, assuredly I have not acted in anger. Or is there anything more like unsoundness of mind than anger?

quam ira? quam bene Ennius *initium* dixit *insaniae.*
Color, vox, oculi, spiritus, impotentia dictorum ac
factorum quam partem habent sanitatis? Quid
Achille Homerico foedius, quid Agamemnone in
iurgio? Nam Aiacem quidem ira ad furorem
mortemque perduxit. Non igitur desiderat fortitudo advocatam iracundiam. Satis est instructa,
parata, armata per sese. Nam isto modo quidem
licet dicere utilem vinolentiam ad fortitudinem,
utilem etiam dementiam, quod et insani et ebrii
multa faciunt saepe vehementius. Semper Aiax
fortis, fortissimus tamen in furore; nam

—*Facinus fecit maximum, cum Danais inclinantibus*
Summam rem perfecit manu, restituit proelium in-
saniens.

53 XXIV. Dicamus igitur utilem insaniam? Tracta
definitiones fortitudinis: intelliges eam stomacho
non egere. Fortitudo est igitur adfectio animi legi
summae in perpetiendis rebus obtemperans, vel
conservatio stabilis iudicii in eis rebus, quae for-
midolosae videntur, subeundis et repellendis, vel
scientia rerum formidolosarum contrariarumque aut
omnino negligendarum, conservans earum rerum
stabile iudicium, vel brevius, ut Chrysippus—nam

---

[1] *Il.* I. 122, because Agamemnon took Briseis away from
Achilles.
[2] cf. *Od.* XI. 542, 563. In the contest for the arms of
Achilles Ulysses was preferred to Ajax, and hence came the
anger and madness of Ajax.

With what truth Ennius called it "the beginning of unsoundness of mind!" What share have change of colour, voice, eyes, breathing, ungovernableness of speech and act in soundness of mind? What more degraded than Homer's Achilles, than his Agamemnon in their brawl?[1] Ajax[2] I need not quote, for him at any rate anger led on to madness and death. Bravery then does not need the backing of irascibility. It is of itself sufficiently equipped, prepared and armed. Sufficiently I say, for there is, no doubt, a sense in which we may call drunkenness of use to bravery, aberration of mind too of use, because the madman and the drunkard often do many things with uncommon impetuosity. Ajax is always brave but bravest in frenzy; for

> Glorious was the deed he wrought when Danaan ranks were falling back;
> The common safety he secured: in fury he the fray renewed.[3]

XXIV. Are we therefore to say that unsoundness of mind is useful? Examine the definitions of bravery; you will realize that it stands in no need of loss of temper. Bravery then is a disposition of the soul obedient to the highest law in enduring vicissitudes; or the maintenance of a steady judgment in meeting and repulsing vicissitudes which seem dreadful; or the knowledge of vicissitudes which are dreadful and the opposite of dreadful or wholly to be ignored, maintaining a steady judgment of such vicissitudes, or more briefly as Chrysippus

---

[3] Perhaps from a tragedy of Pacuvius. The story of Ajax's repulse of the Trojans from the ships is given in *Iliad* XV. 742, ἦ καὶ μαιμώων ἔφεπ' ἔγχεϊ ὀξυόεντι.

superiores definitiones erant Sphaeri, hominis in
primis bene definientis, ut putant Stoici; sunt enim
omnino omnes fere similes, sed declarant communes
notiones, alia magis alia—, quo modo igitur Chrysippus? Fortitudo est, inquit, scientia rerum per-
ferendarum vel adfectio animi in patiendo ac perferendo summae legi parens sine timore. Quamvis
licet insectemur istos, ut Carneades solebat, metuo
ne soli philosophi sint; quae enim istarum defini-
tionum non aperit notionem nostram, quam habemus
omnes de fortitudine tectam atque involutam? qua
aperta quis est qui aut bellatori aut imperatori aut
oratori quaerat aliquid neque eos existimet sine
54 rabie quidquam fortiter facere posse? Quid? Stoici,
qui omnes insipientes insanos esse dicunt, nonne
ista colligunt? Remove perturbationes maximeque
iracundiam; iam videbuntur monstra dicere. Nunc
autem ita disserunt, sic se dicere, omnes stultos
insanire, ut male olere omne coenum. At non
semper. Commove: senties. Sic iracundus non
semper iratus est; lacesse: iam videbis furentem.
Quid? ista bellatrix iracundia, cum domum rediit,
qualis est cum uxore, cum liberis, cum familia? an
tum quoque est utilis? Est igitur aliquid quod
perturbata mens melius possit facere quam constans? An quisquam potest sine perturbatione

---

[1] Sphaerus, a Stoic philosopher of Thracian birth and
pupil of Zeno.

[2] Attack the Stoics as Carneades attacked Chrysippus.

[3] The Stoic conclusion covers all cases of disorder of the
soul. Disorders are diseases and the unwise who suffer from
them are mad. Argue that irascibility or any other disorder is justifiable and has its uses, and the Stoics are made
to talk nonsense.

[4] cf. § 28.

says (for the foregoing definitions are due to
Sphaerus,[1] a man pre-eminent in framing definitions
according to the Stoics: no matter, for in any case
their definitions have a common family resemblance,
but they explain more or less the ideas generally
held)—how then does Chrysippus speak? Bravery
is, he says, the knowledge of enduring vicissitudes
or a disposition of soul in suffering and enduring,
obedient to the supreme law of our being without
fear. However we may attack [2] such men, as was
the way of Carneades, I have a misgiving they are
the only true philosophers; for which of the definitions I have given does not reveal the meaning of
the idea we all have of bravery, hidden though it be
behind a veil? And when revealed, who is there to
ask for any further support for warrior or general or
orator and to think them incapable of any brave
deed without frenzy? Again, do not the Stoics,
who say that everyone who is not wise is mad, bring
together in their conclusion the instances we have
given? Take out disorders and above all irascibility; the result is they will seem to be talking
rubbish.[3] But, as it is, their line of argument is
to assert that all fools are mad in the same way
that all mud stinks. Surely not always.[4] Stir it
and you will see! Similarly the irascible man is
not always angry; rouse him! now you will see him
in a rage. Again, this combative irascibility of
yours,[5] when it has got back home, what is it like
with wife, with children, with household? Or do
you think it useful there as well as in battle? Is
there a thing that the disordered mind can do
better than the equable mind? Or is anyone at all

[5] Which the Peripatetics praise.

mentis irasci? Bene igitur nostri, cum omnia
essent in *moribus* vitia, quod nullum erat iracundia
foedius, iracundos solos *morosos* nominaverunt.

55 XXV. Oratorem vero irasci minime decet, simu-
lare non dedecet. An tibi irasci tum videmur, cum
quid in causis acrius et vehementius dicimus? quid?
cum iam rebus transactis et praeteritis orationes
scribimus, num irati scribimus?

> *Ecquis hoc animadvertit? vincite!*

Num aut egisse umquam iratum Aesopum aut scrip-
sisse existimas iratum Accium? Aguntur ista praeclare et ab oratore quidem melius, si modo est
orator, quam ab ullo histrione, sed aguntur leniter
et mente tranquilla. Libidinem vero laudare cuius
est libidinis? Themistoclem mihi et Demosthenem
profertis: additis Pythagoram, Democritum, Platonem. Quid? vos studia libidinem vocatis? quae
vel optimarum rerum, ut ea sunt, quae profertis,
sedata tamen et tranquilla esse debent. Iam aegritudinem laudare unam rem maxime detestabilem
quorum est tandem philosophorum? At commode
dixit Afranius:

> *Dum modo doleat aliquid, doleat quidlubet.*

Dixit enim de adolescente perdito ac dissoluto; nos

---

[1] Part of a verse from the *Atreus* of Accius, cf. App. II.

[2] "If Garrick really believed himself to be that monster,
Richard the Third, he deserved to be hanged every time he
performed it." Boswell's *Johnson*.

[3] As instances of *libido* cf. § 44.

[4] The Peripatetics are represented as quoting Afranius to
show that grief is useful.

able to be angry without disorder of mind? Therefore, as all vices are "moral defects," our countrymen have done well to give the name of "morose"
to irascible men alone, because no vice is more
degraded than irascibility.

XXV. But of all men an orator should not be
irascible; to feign to be so is not unbecoming. Or
do you think I am irascible at the time I plead in
court in a more fiery and forcible strain than usual?
Again, after the trial is over and done with and I
write my speeches out, surely you do not think that
I am angry as I write?

"Does no one punish this? Bring fetters!"[1]

Surely one does not think Aesopus was ever angry
when he played this part[2] or Accius angry when he
wrote it? Such parts are finely played and better
indeed by the orator, if only he is an orator, than by
any actor; but they are played without bitterness
and with a mind at peace. Then as to lust—what a
wanton thing it is to praise that! You put forward
the instances[3] of Themistocles and Demosthenes,
you throw in Pythagoras, Democritus, Plato. What
do you mean? Do you call devotion lust? devotion
which though shown, as in the instances you put
forward, in quite the highest aims ought nevertheless
to be composed and peaceful. And more, what
philosophers can praise distress, the one most
hateful ailment of all? But, you will say,[4] Afranius
aptly said:

So long as pain comes, let that pain be what it
    will.

Yes, for he spoke of a ruined and profligate youth;

389

autem de constanti viro ac sapienti quaerimus. Et
quidem ipsam illam iram centurio habeat aut signifer vel ceteri, de quibus dici non necesse est, ne
rhetorum aperiamus mysteria. Utile est enim uti
motu animi, qui uti ratione non potest: nos autem,
ut testificor saepe, de sapiente quaerimus.

56 XXVI. At etiam aemulari utile est, obtrectare,
misereri. Cur misereare potius quam feras opem,
si id facere possis? an sine misericordia liberales
esse non possumus? Non enim suscipere ipsi aegritudines propter alios debemus, sed alios, si possumus, levare aegritudine. Obtrectare vero alteri aut
illa vitiosa aemulatione, quae rivalitati similis est,
aemulari quid habet utilitatis, cum sit aemulantis
angi alieno bono, quod ipse non habeat, obtrectantis
autem angi alieno bono, quod id etiam alius habeat?
Quis id approbare possit, aegritudinem suscipere
pro experientia, si quid habere velis? nam solum
57 habere velle summa dementia est. Mediocritates
autem malorum quis laudare recte possit? Quis
enim potest, in quo libido cupiditasve sit, non
libidinosus et cupidus esse? in quo ira, non iracundus? in quo angor, non anxius? in quo timor,
non timidus? Libidinosum igitur et iracundum et

---

[1] Cicero refers to orators, of whom he was one. Rhetoricians taught that speech must be adapted to the different
dispositions of different men, but philosophy was concerned
with the "wise man" alone.
[2] cf. III. § 22.

but our question is concerned with the consistent and wise man. And by all means let the centurion have the selfsame anger which the Peripatetics praise or the standard-bearer or the others named,[1] of whom there is no need to speak, for fear I disclose the secrets of rhetoricians. For it is expedient for the man who cannot resort to reason, to resort to an emotion of the soul: we on the other hand are asking, as I frequently testify, about the wise man.

XXVI. It is urged too that it is useful to feel rivalry, to feel envy, to feel pity. Why pity rather than give assistance if one can? Or are we unable to be open-handed without pity? We are able, for we ought not to share distresses ourselves for the sake of others, but we ought to relieve others of their distress if we can. But what use is there in envying a neighbour, or in " emulation " in the bad sense (the word which resembles "rivalry "), seeing that the mark of rivalry is to be worried by one's neighbour's good if one is conscious of not possessing it oneself, while the mark of the envious man is to be worried by a neighbour's good because he is conscious that another possesses it as well as he? Who could approve of allowing oneself to be distressed instead of making an effort to get a thing one wants to possess? for to want to possess and do nothing is downright aberration of mind. Again, who can rightly approve of " mean " states [2] in their application to evil? For who can fail to be lustful or covetous if he harbours lust or covetousness within? to be irascible if he harbours anger? to be anxious if he harbours anxiety? to be fearful if he harbours fear? Do we therefore suppose that the

anxium et timidum censemus esse sapientem? de
cuius excellentia multa quidem dici quamvis fuse
lateque possunt, sed brevissime illo modo, sapientiam esse rerum divinarum et humanarum scientiam
cognitionemque, quae cuiusque rei causa sit; ex
quo efficitur, ut divina imitetur, humana omnia
inferiora virtute ducat. In hanc tu igitur tamquam
in mare, quod est ventis subiectum, perturbationem
cadere tibi dixisti videri? Quid est quod tantam
gravitatem constantiamque perturbet? an improvisum aliquid aut repentinum? Quid potest accidere
tale ei, cui nihil quod homini evenire possit [non
praemeditatum sit]?[1] Nam quod aiunt nimia resecari
oportere, naturalia relinqui, quid tandem potest esse
naturale, quod idem nimium esse possit? Sunt
enim omnia ista ex errorum orta radicibus, quae
evellenda et extrahenda penitus, non circumcidenda
nec amputanda sunt.

58 XXVII. Sed quoniam suspicor te non tam de
sapiente quam de te ipso quaerere—illum enim
putas omni perturbatione esse liberum, te vis—,
videamus quanta sint quae a philosophia remedia
morbis animorum adhibeantur. Est enim quaedam
medicina certe, nec tam fuit hominum generi in-
fensa atque inimica natura, ut corporibus tot res
salutares, animis nullam invenerit, de quibus hoc
etiam est merita melius, quod corporum adiumenta

---

[1] The bracketed words are not in most MSS. Bentley
would read *an improvisum aut repentinum quid accidere
potest ei; cui nihil tale, quod homini evenire possit?*

---

[1] "For" refers to the Peripatetic contention that the
"mean" in all things was best and natural and that all
excess was unnatural and should be pruned away, cf. § 47.

wise man is lustful and irascible and anxious and fearful ? Of his superiority there is indeed much that can be said as fully and widely as you will, but quite briefly it may be said that wisdom is the knowledge of things divine and human and acquaintance with the cause of each of them, with the result that wisdom copies what is divine, whilst it regards all human concerns as lower than virtue. Do you then say that in your opinion wisdom falls into the disorder we have described, as it were into a sea lying at the mercy of the winds ? What is there with the power to disorder its deep seriousness and consistency ? or think you some unforeseen or sudden chance can do so ? What chance of such a kind can happen to the man who has surveyed in advance all that falls to the lot of man ? For [1] as to the statement that excess should be cut back, natural growth be left, what, I ask, can be natural if it can also be pushed to excess ? For all such growth [2] springs from the roots of deception and it must be torn out and dragged away, not clipped and pruned.

XXVII. But, as I have a notion that your inquiry is not so much directed to the wise man as to your own case (for you think that *he* is free from all disorder, *you* wish to be so), let us note how efficacious is the medicine applied by philosophy to the diseases of souls. For there is assuredly some remedy, and nature has not proved so bitter an enemy of mankind as to discover so many means of providing bodily health without discovering a single one for the soul, to which she has even rendered this better service, that aids for the body are given

[2] The disorders which arise from deception, such as joy, lust, distress, fear and their subdivisions. § 46.

adhibentur extrinsecus, animorum salus inclusa in
ipsis[1] est. Sed quo maior est in eis praestantia et
divinior, eo maiore indigent diligentia. Itaque
bene adhibita ratio cernit quid optimum sit, neg-
59 lecta multis implicatur erroribus. Ad te igitur mihi
iam convertenda omnis oratio est; simulas enim
quaerere te de sapiente, quaeris autem fortasse de
te. Earum igitur perturbationum, quas exposui,
variae sunt curationes. Nam neque omnis aegritudo
una ratione sedatur; alia est enim lugenti, alia
miseranti aut invidenti adhibenda medicina. Est
etiam in omnibus quattuor perturbationibus illa
distinctio, utrum ad universam perturbationem, quae
est aspernatio rationis aut appetitus vehementior,
an ad singulas, ut ad metum, libidinem, reliquas,
melius adhibeatur oratio, et utrum illudne non
videatur aegre ferundum, ex quo suscepta sit aegritudo, an omnium rerum tollenda omnino aegritudo,
ut, si quis aegre ferat se pauperem esse, idne disputes, paupertatem malum non esse an hominem
aegre ferre nihil oportere. Nimirum hoc melius,
ne, si forte de paupertate non persuaseris, sit
aegritudini concedendum: aegritudine autem sublata propriis rationibus, quibus heri usi sumus,
quodam modo etiam paupertatis malum tollitur.
60 XXVIII. Sed omnis eius modi perturbatio animi

<hr>

[1] *in his ipsis* MSS. : *in ipsis* Bake.

<hr>

[1] cf. § 11, *libido, laetitia, metus, aegritudo.*
[2] In attempting consolation, etc.
[3] cf. Bk. III. §§ 77, 78.
[4] Though poverty is not specifically dealt with.

by outward application, the health of souls is comprised within themselves. But the greater and more divine their superiority, the greater their need of assiduous care. And so reason if well employed sees clearly what is best; if left neglected it is entangled in a multitude of deceptions. To your case therefore I must now wholly direct the course of my remarks. For you pretend to be inquiring about the wise man; maybe, however, you are inquiring about yourself. The means then of attending to the disorders I have enumerated are varied. For not every distress is assuaged by one method; for there is one remedy to be applied to the mourner, another to the compassionate or envious. There is too in dealing with all four disorders [1] this difference to be considered, whether our remarks [2] are better addressed to disorder in general, which is contempt of reason or longing of a more violent kind, or to the separate disorders, as for instance, of fear, lust, and the rest; and whether the special cause of the distress which is felt, is to be held undeserving of distress, or whether distress arising from every cause is to be wholly removed; for instance, supposing anyone were distressed at being poor, the question is whether you should argue that poverty is not an evil, or that a human being should not be distressed at anything. Beyond doubt this latter course is better, for fear the sufferer should have to give way to distress, supposing one should fail to convince him about poverty; whereas, once distress is removed by the appropriate reasoning we made use of yesterday,[3] in a certain way [4] the evil of poverty is also removed. XXVIII. But all disturbance of soul of this kind may be cleansed

placatione abluatur illa quidem, cum doceas nec
bonum illud esse, ex quo laetitia aut libido oriatur,
nec malum, ex quo aut metus aut aegritudo.
Verum tamen haec est certa et propria sanatio, si
doceas ipsas perturbationes per se esse vitiosas nec
habere quidquam aut naturale aut necessarium, ut
ipsam aegritudinem leniri videmus, cum obiicimus
maerentibus imbecillitatem animi effeminati cumque
eorum gravitatem constantiamque laudamus, qui
non turbulente humana patiantur; quod quidem
solet eis etiam accidere, qui illa mala esse censent,
ferenda tamen aequo animo arbitrantur.   Putat
aliquis esse voluptatem bonum, alius autem pecuniam, tamen et ille ab intemperantia et hic ab
avaritia avocari potest. Illa autem altera ratio et
oratio, quae simul et opinionem falsam tollit et
aegritudinem detrahit, est ea quidem utilior,[1] sed
61 raro proficit neque est ad vulgus adhibenda. Quaedam autem sunt aegritudines, quas levare illa
medicina nullo modo possit, ut, si quis aegre ferat
nihil in se esse virtutis, nihil animi, nihil officii,
nihil honestatis, propter mala is quidem angatur,
sed alia quaedam sit ad eum admovenda curatio
et talis quidem, quae possit esse omnium etiam de
ceteris rebus discrepantium philosophorum; inter
omnes enim convenire oportet commotiones ani-

---

[1] On the ground that *utilior* does not fit the context
Bentley proposed *subtilior*.

---

[1] The method of showing that that which occasions lust
or delight is not a good, and that which occasions fear or
distress is not an evil. It is seldom effective, for few who
suffer, say, from poverty can be made to see that poverty is
not an evil.

[2] cf. III. § 77.

away by using the method of relief by which one
shows that neither is that a good which occasions
delight or lust, nor that an evil which occasions
fear or distress. Yet on the other hand the sure
and proper means of cure is found in showing that
the disorders are of themselves essentially wrong
and contain nothing either natural or necessary.
For instance, we see that distress is itself mitigated
when we confront mourners with the weakness of
an enervated soul, and when we praise the dignity
and consistency of those who submit to the lot of
mankind without chafing; and this usually happens
with those who think such afflictions evil but nevertheless consider they should be endured with
equanimity. Someone thinks pleasure a good,
another on the other hand thinks money; all the
same the one can be called away from gross indulgence and the other from avarice in the way I
have shown. Our other[1] method and way of speaking however which at one and the same time does
away with erroneous belief and removes distress is
indeed more serviceable, but succeeds in few cases
and is not to be applied to the ordinary ruck of
mankind. There are further certain kinds of distress where the remedy can give no relief, as for
instance, supposing anyone were to be distressed at
having no virtue in himself,[2] no spirit, no sense of
obligation, no rectitude, he would indeed be worried
because of the evil he feels, but a different mode of
treatment would have to be employed in his case
and of such a sort as can win the general approval
of all philosophers even where they disagree upon
all other points; for it ought to be agreed amongst
all of them that agitations of the soul alien to right

397

morum a recta ratione aversas esse vitiosas, ut,
etiam si et mala sint illa, quae metum aegritudi-
nemve, et bona,[1] quae cupiditatem laetitiamve moveant, tamen sit vitiosa ipsa commotio : constantem
enim quendam volumus, sedatum, gravem, humana
omnia spernentem [2] illum esse, quem magnanimum
et fortem virum dicimus.   Talis autem nec maerens
nec timens nec cupiens nec gestiens esse quisquam
potest.   Eorum enim haec sunt, qui eventus humanos superiores quam suos animos esse ducunt.

62   XXIX. Qua re omnium philosophorum, ut ante
dixi, una ratio est medendi, ut nihil quale sit illud,
quod perturbet animum, sed de ipsa sit perturbatione dicendum.

Itaque primum in ipsa cupiditate, cum id solum
agitur, ut ea tollatur, non est quaerendum, bonum
illud necne sit, quod libidinem moveat, sed libido
ipsa tollenda est, ut, sive, quod honestum est, id
sit summum bonum, sive voluptas sive horum utrumque coniunctum sive tria illa genera bonorum,
tamen, etiam si virtutis ipsius vehementior appetitus sit, eadem sit omnibus ad deterrendum adhibenda oratio.   Continet autem omnem sedationem
animi humana in conspectu posita natura, quae quo
facilius expressa cernatur, explicanda est oratione
63 communis condicio lexque vitae.   Itaque non sine

---

[1] *nec mala . . . nec bona* MSS. : *et mala . . . et bona*
Lambinus.
[2] *prementem* MSS. : *spernentem* Anon.

reason are wrong, so that even if both the things which occasion fear or distress are evil and the things which occasion desire or delight are good, nevertheless, the agitation they occasion is in itself wrong : for we wish the man whom we describe as brave and high-souled to be of an equable, settled, dignified character, scorning all human vicissitudes. And such a character is incompatible with either mourning or fear or desire or extravagant delight. For these are the traits of men who think the chances of mortal life of more importance than their souls.

XXIX. That is why, as I have previously said, all philosophers have one single method of cure, namely to refuse to say anything about that which occasions the disorder of the soul, but to attack the feeling of distress itself.

And so in the first place in dealing with the actual feeling of desire, since the only object is to stifle it, we must not inquire whether the stimulating cause of lust is good or not, but the feeling of lust itself must be stifled, in order that, whether the morally right, or pleasure, or a combination of the two, or the recognized three[1] kinds of good be the highest good, nevertheless, even if the unduly violent longing be for virtue itself, the same mode of speaking must be employed by all by way of a deterrent. Moreover human nature, if properly examined, has in itself all means of calming the soul, and in order that a distinct image of it may be discerned more easily, the general conditions and law of life must be clearly explained. And so not without reason, when

---

[1] Of soul, body, fortune, cf. V. § 24.

causa, cum Orestem fabulam doceret Euripides,
primos tris versus revocasse dicitur Socrates:

> *Neque tam terribilis ulla fando oratio est*
> *Nec sors nec ira caelitum invectum malum,*
> *Quod non natura humana patiendo ecferat.*

Est autem utilis ad persuadendum ea, quae acciderint, ferri et posse et oportere enumeratio eorum,
qui tulerunt. Etsi aegritudinis sedatio et hesterna
disputatione explicata est et in Consolationis libro,
quem in medio—non enim sapientes eramus—maerore
et dolore conscripsimus, quodque vetat Chrysippus
ad recentes quasi tumores animi remedium adhibere.
id nos fecimus naturaeque vim attulimus, ut magni
tudini medicinae doloris magnitudo concederet.

64   XXX. Sed aegritudini, de qua satis est disputatum, finitimus est metus, de quo pauca dicenda
sunt.   Est enim metus, ut aegritudo praesentis,
sic ille futuri mali: itaque non nulli aegritudinis
partem quandam metum esse dicebant; alii autem
metum praemolestiam appellabant, quod esset quasi
dux consequentis molestiae. Quibus igitur rationibus instantia feruntur, eisdem contemnuntur sequentia; nam videndum est in utrisque, ne quid
humile, summissum, molle, effeminatum, fractum
abiectumque faciamus. Sed quamquam de ipsius
metus inconstantia, imbecillitate, levitate dicendum
est, tamen multum prodest ea, quae metuuntur,

---

[1] cf. III. § 76. At the time of his daughter's death
Cicero thought he did well to indulge his grief. Chrysippus
thought that comforters should show the afflicted that grief
was not a duty and therefore not to be indulged.

Euripides produced the play of Orestes, did Socrates, we are told, call for the first three lines again :

No speech so terrible in utterance,
No chance, no ill imposed by wrath of heaven,
Which human nature cannot bear and suffer.

Furthermore, in convincing a sufferer that he is able and ought to bear the accidents of fortune, it is helpful to recount the examples of those who have done so. I say this although the method of assuaging distress was set forth in our discussion of yesterday, as well as in my *Consolation,* the book which I composed (for I was no "wise man") in the midst of mourning and grief, and I employed the remedy of which Chrysippus forbids the application to fresh ferments as it were of the soul, and did violence to nature in order that the strength of my grief might yield to the strength of the medicine.[1]

XXX. But fear, about which a few words must be said, is closely related to distress, which has been sufficiently discussed. For as distress is due to present evil, so fear is due to coming evil, and consequently some said that fear was a special branch of distress ; others termed fear apprehensiveness[2] because they held it to be the forerunner of ensuing vexation. Therefore present evils are endured by the same reasoning as that by which ensuing evils are despised ; for we must be careful in both cases that we are guilty of nothing mean, craven, weak, unmanly, humiliating, degraded. But although we ought to speak of the inconsistency, weakness and triviality of fear itself, nevertheless it is a distinct gain to

[2] *praemolestia* is a word that does not occur elsewhere. It was coined to express "the sense of coming *molestia.*"

ipsa contemnere. Itaque sive casu accidit sive consilio, percommode factum est, quod eis de rebus, quae maxime metuuntur, de morte et de dolore, primo et proximo die disputatum est: quae si probata sunt, metu magna ex parte liberati sumus.

65 XXXI. Ac de malorum opinione hactenus. Videamus nunc de bonorum, id est, de laetitia et de cupiditate. Mihi quidem in tota ratione ea, quae pertinet ad animi perturbationem, una res videtur causam continere, omnes eas esse in nostra potestate, omnes iudicio susceptas, omnes voluntarias. Hic igitur error est eripiendus, haec detrahenda opinio atque ut in malis opinatis tolerabilia, sic in bonis sedatiora sunt efficienda ea, quae magna et laetabilia ducuntur. Atque hoc quidem commune malorum et bonorum, ut, si iam difficile sit persuadere nihil earum rerum, quae perturbent animum, aut in bonis aut in malis esse habendum, tamen alia ad alium motum curatio sit adhibenda aliaque ratione malevolus, alia amator, alia rursus 66 anxius, alia timidus corrigendus. Atque erat facile sequentem eam rationem, quae maxime probatur de bonis et malis, negare umquam laetitia adfici posse insipientem, quod nihil umquam haberet boni. Sed loquimur nunc more communi. Sint

---

[1] *i.e.* the Stoic doctrine that only what is honourable is good and only what is disgraceful is evil, cf. II. § 29.

despise the actual things which occasion fear. And so whether by accident or design it fits in most conveniently that the objects of our greatest fear, death and pain, were discussed on the first and following days of our meeting: and if the conclusions then reached are approved we are in great measure relieved of fear.

XXXI. Now so far we have dealt with belief of evil. Let us now deal with belief of good, that is, with delight and desire. For my part I think that the whole train of reasoning which is concerned with disorder of the soul turns upon the one fact that all disorders are within our control, are all acts of judgment, are all voluntary. To think otherwise therefore is a deception to be removed, and a belief to be rejected, and just as where evil is expected the prospect must be met with endurance, so where good is expected the objects held to be momentous and delightful must be regarded in a calmer spirit. Besides there is this feature common to good and evil, that if it should be difficult at the moment to convince the sufferer that none of the things which disorder the soul is to be reckoned among good or evil, nevertheless different modes of treatment are applicable to different emotions, and the malicious must be reformed in one way, the rake in another, the worried again in another and the fearful in another. Now it would be easy for anyone pursuing the best approved line of reasoning[1] upon the nature of good and evil, to deny that the unwise can ever feel delight, because at no time would he be in possession of anything good. But we are at present suiting our language to ordinary thought Grant, if you will, that the

403

sane ista bona, quae putantur, honores, divitiae,
voluptates, cetera: tamen in eis ipsis potiundis
exsultans gestiensque laetitia turpis est, ut, si
ridere concessum sit, vituperetur tamen cachinnatio.
Eodem enim vitio est effusio animi in laetitia quo
in dolore contractio, eademque levitate cupiditas
est in appetendo qua laetitia in fruendo, et, ut
nimis adflicti molestia, sic nimis elati laetitia iure iudi-
cantur leves. Et cum invidere aegritudinis sit, malis
autem alienis voluptatem capere laetitiae, utrumque
immanitate et feritate quadam proponenda casti-
gari solet; atque ut cavere[1] decet, timere non
decet, sic gaudere decet, laetari non decet, quoniam
docendi causa a gaudio laetitiam distinguimus.
67 Illud iam supra diximus, contractionem animi recte
fieri numquam posse, elationem posse: aliter enim
Naevianus ille gaudet Hector:

> *Laetus sum laudari me abs te, pater, a laudato viro,*

aliter ille apud Trabeam:

> *Lena delenita argento nutum observabit meum,*
> *Quid velim, quid studeam: adveniens digito impellam*
> *ianuam,*
> *Fores patebunt: de improviso Chrysis ubi me as-*
> *pexerit,*

[1] *confidere* MSS.: *cavere* Davies.

---

[1] cf. I. § 95. *Levitas* is the opposite of *gravitas*, the quality
which the Romans so highly esteemed, and has no single
English equivalent.
[2] cf. § 13.   [3] cf. § 14 and I. § 90.
[4] For Naevius cf. I. § 3 and App. II.   [5] For Trabea cf. § 35.

things held to be good are good, namely offices, riches, pleasures, and all the rest; nevertheless extravagant and exuberant delight in the acquisition of these selfsame things is disgraceful, just as, supposing one received permission to laugh, it would all the same be inexcusable to guffaw. For it is from one and the same defect that the soul is demonstrative in delight or shrinks up in pain, and eagerness in seeking shows the same weakness[1] as delight in enjoying; and like men unduly depressed by trouble, so men unduly elated by delight are rightly adjudged weak and worthless. And as envy comes under the head of distress, while on the other hand satisfaction at another person's evil comes under that of delight, both are usually corrected by pointing out the degree in which they are inhuman and barbarous. Moreover as it is becoming to be cautious, unbecoming to be afraid, so joy is becoming, delight unbecoming, since for the sake of clearness we make a distinction between joy and delight.[2] We have already earlier made the remark that a shrinking up of soul[3] can never be justifiable, high spirits can. For in Naevius'[4] play Hector rejoices in one spirit:

Praise from you delights me, father, you a man deserving praise;

and Trabea's[5] hero in another:

Caught with coin the procuress will obey my nod and wish,
And my longing; if I go and with my finger touch the doors,
They will open: and when Chrysis sees me unexpected there,

Alacris ob viam mihi veniet complexum exoptans
meum,
Mihi se dedet.

Quam haec pulcra putet ipse iam dicet:

. . . *fortunam ipsam anteibo fortunis meis.*

68 XXXII. Haec laetitia quam turpis sit satis est
diligenter attendentem penitus videre. Et ut
turpes sunt qui efferunt se laetitia tum, cum fruuntur Veneriis voluptatibus, sic flagitiosi, qui eas
inflammato animo concupiscunt. Totus vero iste,
qui vulgo appellatur amor——nec hercule invenio quo
nomine alio possit appellari——, tantae levitatis est,
ut nihil videam quod putem conferendum: quem
Caecilius

deum qui non summum putet,
Aut stultum aut rerum esse imperitum existumat,
Cuius in manu sit quem esse dementem velit,
Quem sapere, quem insanire, quem in morbum iniici,
Quem contra amari, quem expeti, quem arcessier.

69 O praeclaram emendatricem vitae poëticam! quae
amorem, flagitii et levitatis auctorem, in concilio
deorum collocandum putet. De comoedia loquor,
quae, si haec flagitia non probaremus, nulla esset
omnino. Quid ait ex tragoedia princeps ille
Argonautarum?

Tu me amoris magis quam honoris servavisti gratia.

---

[1] Greek has φιλεῖν as well as ἐρᾶν.
[2] cf. III. § 56.   [3] Cf. App. II.

Eagerly she'll come to meet me, yearning for my
    welcome arms,
She will give herself to me.

How fair the prospect his own words now show :

    . . . my fortune Fortune's self shall now outdo.

XXXII. Close attention is sufficient to give anyone complete insight into the degradation of such
delight. And just as those who are transported
with delight at the enjoyment of sexual pleasures
are degraded, so those who covet them with feverish
soul are criminal. In fact the whole passion
ordinarily termed love (and heaven help me if I
can think of any other term to apply to it)[1] is of
such exceeding triviality that I see nothing that I
think comparable with it. Of love Caecilius[2]
expresses the opinion :

    who him of Gods thinks not supreme
A fool is or of life no knowledge hath ;
For Love has power whom he will to craze,
Make wise or senseless, cast disease upon,
But whom he will, make loved, desired and
    sought.

How glorious the reformation of life that poetry
inspires ! since it thinks love, the promoter of shame
and inconstancy, fit for a place in the company
of gods. I speak of comedy which would have no
existence at all did we not approve of such shame.
What does the leader of the Argonauts say in
tragedy ?[3]

You for love's sake more than honour's have
    preserved me safe from harm.

Quid ergo? hic amor Medeae quanta miseriarum excitavit incendia! Atque ea tamen apud alium poëtam patri dicere audet se *coniugem* habuisse

> *Illum, Amor quem dederat, qui plus pollet potiorque*
> *est patre.*

70 XXXIII. Sed poëtas ludere sinamus, quorum fabulis in hoc flagitio versari ipsum videmus Iovem. Ad magistros virtutis, philosophos, veniamus, qui amorem negant stupri esse et in eo litigant cum Epicuro non multum, ut opinio mea fert, mentiente. Quis est enim iste amor amicitiae? Cur neque deformem adolescentem quisquam amat neque formosum senem? Mihi quidem haec in Graecorum gymnasiis nata consuetudo videtur, in quibus isti liberi et concessi sunt amores. Bene ergo Ennius:

> *Flagiti principium est nudare inter civis corpora.*

Qui ut sint, quod fieri posse video, pudici, solliciti tamen et anxii sunt eoque magis, quod se ipsi
71 continent et coërcent. Atque, ut muliebres amores omittam, quibus maiorem licentiam natura concessit, quis aut de Ganymedi raptu dubitat quid poëtae velint aut non intelligit quid apud Euripidem et loquatur et cupiat Laius? quid denique homines doctissimi et summi poëtae de se ipsis et carminibus

---

¹ Pacuvius? in *Medus*?, cf. App. II.
² Epicurus defined love as ὄρεξις ἀφροδισίων.
³ A lost play of Euripides entitled *Chrysippus*, the name of a youth who was son of Pelops.

What then ? What a conflagration of woe this love of Medea's kindled ! And yet in another poet[1] she dares to tell her father that she has won for husband

> Him whom Love had granted, who is stronger, better than a father.

XXXIII. But let us allow the poets to make merry, whose stories let us see Jupiter himself implicated in this shame. Let us have recourse to the teachers of virtue, the philosophers—who say that love has no part in debauchery and on that point are at daggers drawn with Epicurus, who in my belief is not in what he says much of a liar.[2] For what is the so-called love of friendship ? Why is it no one is in love with either an ugly youngster or a beautiful old man ? For my part I think this practice had its origin in the Greek gymnasia where that kind of love-making was free and permitted. Well then did Ennius say :

> Shame's beginning is the stripping of men's bodies openly.

And though such loves be, as I see is possible, within the bounds of modesty, yet they bring anxiety and trouble and all the more because they are a law to themselves and have no other restraint. Again, not to speak of the love of women, to which nature has granted wider tolerance, who has either any doubt of the meaning of the poets in the tale of the rape of Ganymede, or fails to understand the purport of Laius' language and his desire in Euripides' play ?[3] What disclosures lastly do men of the highest culture and poets of supreme merit make about their own life in their poems and

edunt et cantibus? Fortis vir in sua re publica cognitus quae de iuvenum amore scribit Alcaeus! Nam Anacreontis quidem tota poësis est amatoria. Maxime vero omnium flagrasse amore Rheginum Ibycum apparet ex scriptis.

XXXIV. Atque horum omnium libidinosos esse amores videmus. Philosophi sumus exorti et auctore quidem nostro Platone, quem non iniuria Dicaearchus accusat, qui amori auctoritatem tribueremus.

72 Stoici vero et sapientem amaturum esse dicunt et amorem ipsum conatum amicitiae faciendae ex pulcritudinis specie definiunt. Qui si quis est in rerum natura sine sollicitudine, sine desiderio, sine cura, sine suspirio, sit sane; vacat enim omni libidine; haec autem de libidine oratio est. Sin autem est aliquis amor, ut est certe, qui nihil absit aut non multum ab insania, qualis in Leucadia est:

> *Si quidem sit quisquam deus,*
> *Cui ego sim curae.*

73 At id erat deis omnibus curandum, quem ad modum hic frueretur voluptate amatoria!

> *Heu me infelicem!*

Nihil verius. Probe et ille:

> *Sanusne es, qui temere lamentare?*

---

[1] Alcaeus of Lesbos, the lyric poet. Anacreon, lyric poet at the court of Polycrates of Samos.

[2] He refers to Plato's *Symposium* and *Phaedrus*.

[3] There is no apodosis to the "if" clause. This, like the uncompleted sentence at the beginning of § 77, is an instance of the grammatical laxity which Cicero purposely adopted for the style of the *Tusculans*.

songs? What things Alcaeus,[1] a man of bravery
and of note in his country, writes about the love of
youths! Of Anacreon I say nothing, for his work
is all love-poetry. Above all, however, Ibycus of
Rhegium was, it is clear from his writings, a passionate
lover.

XXXIV. In fact we see that love in all the
examples given is lustful. We philosophers have
come forward (and on the authority indeed of our
Plato[2] whom Dicaearchus not unjustly upbraids) to
attribute authority to love. The Stoics actually
both say that the wise will experience love, and
define love itself as the endeavour to form a friendship inspired by the semblance of beauty. And if
in the actual world there is an instance of love free
from disquietude, from longing, from anxiety, from
sighing, then so be it! if you will; for such love
has no element of lust; but our discourse is about
lust. But if[3] on the other hand there is some love,
as assuredly there is, which must be reckoned as
not removed or not far removed from unsoundness
of mind, as for instance in the " Leucadian Girl " :[4]

> Ah! were there but some god,
> Who would have care for me!

But in this case all the gods were to " have care "
how he might enjoy the pleasures of love.

> Ah me unhappy!

Nothing more true. With reason too the other:

> Art thou sane who rashly wailest?

[4] A play of Turpilius, an old Roman comic writer, adapted
from the Greek.

Hic[1] insanus videtur etiam suis. At quas tragoedias efficit!

> Te, Apollo sancte, fer opem, teque, omnipotens
>   Neptune, invoco,
> Vosque adeo, venti!

Mundum totum se ad amorem suum sublevandum conversurum putat; Venerem unam excludit ut iniquam:

> nam quid ego te appellem, Venus?

Eam prae libidine negat curare quidquam: quasi vero ipse non propter libidinem tanta flagitia et faciat et dicat.

74 XXXV. Sic igitur adfecto haec adhibenda curatio est, ut et illud, quod cupiat, ostendatur[2] quam leve, quam contemnendum, quam nihili sit omnino, quam facile vel aliunde vel alio modo perfici vel omnino negligi possit. Abducendus etiam est non numquam ad alia studia, sollicitudines, curas, negotia; loci denique mutatione tamquam aegroti non con-

75 valescentes saepe curandus est: etiam novo quidam amore veterem amorem tamquam clavo clavum eiiciendum putant; maxime autem admonendus est, quantus sit furor amoris; omnibus enim ex animi perturbationibus est profecto nulla vehementior, ut, si iam ipsa illa accusare nolis, stupra dico et corruptelas et adulteria, incesta denique, quorum omnium accusabilis est turpitudo, sed ut haec omittas, perturbatio ipsa mentis in amore foeda per

76 se est. Nam ut illa praeteream, quae sunt furoris,

---

[1] sic MSS.: hic Madvig.

Even his own family think him of unsound mind.
Note what a tragic air of passion he puts on !

> Thee, Apollo holy, help me, Neptune, thee great
>   Lord I call,
> You too, winds of heaven !

The whole universe, he thinks, will conspire to aid
his love ; Venus alone he shuts out as disdainful :

> For why am I to call you, Venus?

He says that goddess because of lust has no care at
all : just as if in fact he were not moved by lust
himself to do and utter such shamelessness.

XXXV. The treatment applicable to a man so
victimized is to make it plain how trivial, con-
temptible and absolutely insignificant is the object
of his desire, how easily it can either be secured from
elsewhere or in another way, or else wholly put out of
mind. Occasionally also he must be diverted to other
interests, disquietudes, cares, occupations ; finally he
is frequently curable by change of scene as is done
with sick people who are slow in making recovery.
Some think, too, that the old love can be driven
out by a new, as one nail can be driven out by
another ; above all, however, he must be warned of
the madness of the passion of love. For of all disturbances of the soul there is assuredly none more
violent, and so even if you be unwilling to accuse
its actual enormities, I mean the intrigues, seductions,
adulteries culminating with incest, the vileness of
all which deserves to be accused—but to say nothing
of these, the disorder of the mind in love is in itself
abominable. For to pass over the excesses which

---

¹ *ostendat* MSS. : *ostendatur* Davies.

haec ipsa per sese quam habent levitatem, quae videntur esse mediocria!

> *Iniuriae,*
> *Suspiciones, inimicitiae, induciae,*
> *Bellum, pax rursum : incerta haec si tu postules*
> *Ratione certa facere, nihilo plus agas,*
> *Quam si des operam ut cum ratione insanias.*

Haec inconstantia mutabilitasque mentis quem non ipsa pravitate deterreat? Est etiam[1] illud, quod in omni perturbatione dicitur, demonstrandum, nullam esse nisi opinabilem, nisi iudicio susceptam, nisi voluntariam. Etenim si naturalis amor esset, et amarent omnes et semper amarent et idem amarent neque alium pudor, alium cogitatio, alium satietas deterreret.

77 XXXVI. Ira vero quae quam diu perturbat animum, dubitationem insaniae non habet, cuius impulsu exsistit etiam inter fratres tale iurgium:

> *A. Quis homo te exsuperavit usquam gentium impudentia?*
> *M. Quis item malitia te?*

Nosti quae sequuntur; alternis enim versibus intorquentur inter fratres gravissimae contumeliae, ut facile appareat Atrei filios esse, eius qui meditatur poenam in fratrem novam:

> *Maior mihi moles, maius miscendumst malum,*
> *Qui illius acerbum cor contundam et comprimam.*

> [1] *enim* MSS. : *etiam* Manutius.

---

[1] Terence, *Eun.* I. 1. 14.   [2] cf. note on § 72.
[3] Agamemnon and Menelaus. Perhaps from Accius' *Atreus,* cf. App. II.

mark its madness, what an intrinsic futility there is
in the effects which count as ordinary!

> Outrages,
> Suspicion, enmity, a patched up truce,
> War, peace again.   Should you by reason sure
> Things unsure claim to do, no more you'll gain
> Than should you try with reason to be mad.[1]

Such inconsistency and capriciousness of mind—
whom would it not scare away by its very vileness?
This characteristic, too, of all disorder must be made
clear, namely, that there is no instance where it is
not due to belief, due to an act of judgment, due
to voluntary choice.   For were love a matter of
nature all men would love, as well as always love
and love the same object, nor should we find one
discouraged by shame, another by reflection, another
by satiety.

XXXVI. Next anger [2] which so long as it disorders the soul undoubtedly implies unsoundness of
mind, and starts a brawl like this even between two
brothers: [3]

> A. What man in all the world in impudence has
>   ever you surpassed?
> M. Who too in malice you?

You know what follows; the bitterest taunts are
hurled from brother to brother in alternate lines,
so that it is easy to see they are sons of the Atreus
who plots an unheard of penalty for his brother: [4]

> More mass of misery must mingled be
> Whereby to break and wring his cruel heart.

[4] Thyestes.

Quo igitur haec erumpit[1] moles? Audi Thyestem:

Ipsus hortatur me frater, ut meos malis miser
Mandarem natos . . . .

Eorum viscera apponit. Quid est enim quo non progrediatur eodem ira quo furor? Itaque iratos proprie dicimus exisse de potestate, id est, de consilio, de ratione, de mente; horum enim potestas in 78 totum animum esse debet. His aut subtrahendi sunt ei, in quos impetum conantur facere, dum se ipsi colligant—quid est autem se ipsum colligere nisi dissipatas animi partes rursum in suum locum cogere?—aut rogandi orandique sunt, ut, si quam habent ulciscendi vim, differant in tempus aliud, dum defervescat ira. Defervescere autem certe significat ardorem animi invita ratione excitatum: ex quo illud laudatur Archytae, qui cum vilico factus esset iratior: *Quo te modo,* inquit, *accepissem, nisi iratus essem!*

79 XXXVII. Ubi sunt ergo isti, qui iracundiam utilem dicunt—potest utilis esse insania?—aut naturalem? An quidquam est secundum naturam, quod fit repugnante ratione? quo modo autem, si naturalis esset ira, aut alius alio magis iracundus esset aut finem haberet prius, quam esset ulta, ulciscendi libido aut quemquam poeniteret quod

---

[1] *erunt* MSS.: *erumpit* Davies.

---

[1] A Pythagorean philosopher of Plato's time.

Which way then is this mass to crash? Hark to Thyestes:

> 'Twas my brother's lips that urged me to consign
>   my sons as food
> To their wretched father's jaws.

He sets their flesh before him. For in what direction will not anger go to the same lengths as madness? And so we say appropriately that angry men have passed beyond control, that is, beyond consideration, beyond reason, beyond intelligence; for these should exercise authority over the entire soul. Either the victims of angry men's attempted onslaught must be withdrawn from their reach until of themselves they gain self-control (but what is to control oneself except to bring together the scattered parts of the soul again into their place?) or, if they have any power of taking revenge, they must be begged and entreated to put it off to another time, until their anger cools down; but cooling down surely implies a fire in the soul kindled against the consent of reason: and hence the approval given to the utterance of Archytas[1] who on becoming angry with his bailiff said, "What a visitation you would have got if I had not been angry!"

XXXVII. Where then are the wiseacres who say that irascibility is useful (can unsoundness of mind be useful?) or natural? or is anything in accordance with nature which is done in opposition to reason? How, moreover, if anger were natural, would either one man be more irascible than another? or how would lust of vengeance come to an end before it had exacted retribution? or how would anyone

fecisset per iram? ut Alexandrum regem videmus,
qui cum interemisset Clitum familiarem suum, vix
a se manus abstinuit: tanta vis fuit poenitendi.
Quibus cognitis quis est qui dubitet quin hic quoque motus animi sit totus opinabilis ac voluntarius?
Quis enim dubitarit quin aegrotationes animi, qualis
est avaritia, gloriae cupiditas, ex eo, quod magni
aestimetur ea res, ex qua animus aegrotat, oriantur?
Unde intelligi debet perturbationem quoque omnem
80 esse in opinione. Et si fidentia, id est firma animi
confisio, scientia quaedam est et opinio gravis non
temere adsentientis, metus quoque est diffidentia
exspectati et impendentis mali; et, si spes est
exspectatio boni, mali exspectationem esse necesse
est metum. Ut igitur metus, sic reliquae perturbationes sunt in malo. Ergo ut constantia scientiae,
sic perturbatio erroris est. Qui autem natura dicuntur iracundi aut misericordes aut invidi aut tale
quid, ei sunt constituti quasi mala valetudine animi,
sanabiles tamen, ut Socrates dicitur. Cum multa
in conventu vitia collegisset in eum Zopyrus, qui
se naturam cuiusque ex forma perspicere profite-
batur, derisus est a ceteris, qui illa in Socrate vitia
non agnoscerent, ab ipso autem Socrate sublevatus,
cum illa sibi insita,[1] sed ratione a se deiecta diceret.
81 Ergo ut optima quisque valetudine adfectus potest

---

[1] *signa* MSS.: *insita* Bentley.

---

[1] cf. III. § 14.
[2] As well as unstable belief.

repent of what he had done in anger? as for instance we see King Alexander did, who could
scarcely keep his hands off himself after he had
killed his friend Clitus: such was the force of
repentance. When this is realized, who is there to
doubt that this movement too of the soul is wholly
a matter of belief and will? For who could doubt
that sicknesses of the soul, such as avarice, or the
thirst for glory, originate in the fact that a high value
is attached to that which occasions the sickness of
the soul? Hence it should be realized that disorder too lies entirely in belief. And if self-confidence,[1] that is, steadfast reliance of soul is a
kind of knowledge and firm belief where assent is
not rashly given, want of self-confidence is also [2]
fear of an expected and threatening evil; and if
hope is expectation of good, fear must be expectation
of evil. Just then as it is with fear, so with the
remaining disorders; their element is evil. Therefore as consistency is the characteristic of knowledge, disorder is the characteristic of deception.
Moreover men who are described as naturally
irascible or compassionate or envious or anything
of the kind, have an unhealthy constitution of soul,
yet all the same are curable, as is said to have been
Socrates' case. Zopyrus, who claimed to discern
every man's nature from his appearance, accused
Socrates in company of a number of vices which
he enumerated, and when he was ridiculed by the
rest who said they failed to recognize such vices in
Socrates, Socrates himself came to his rescue by
saying that he was naturally inclined to the vices
named, but had cast them out of him by the help
of reason. Therefore just as everyone blest with

videri natura ad aliquem morbum proclivior, sic
animus alius ad alia vitia propensior; qui autem
non natura, sed culpa vitiosi esse dicuntur, eorum
vitia constant e falsis opinionibus rerum bonarum et
malarum, ut sit alius ad alios motus perturbationes-
que proclivior. Inveteratio autem ut in corporibus
aegrius depellitur quam perturbatio, citiusque re-
pentinus oculorum tumor sanatur quam diuturna
lippitudo depellitur.

82   XXXVIII. Sed cognita iam causa perturbationum,
quae omnes oriuntur ex iudiciis opinionum et volun-
tatibus, sit iam huius disputationis modus. Scire
autem nos oportet cognitis, quoad possunt ab
homine cognosci, bonorum et malorum finibus nihil
a philosophia posse aut maius aut utilius optari
quam haec, quae a nobis hoc quadriduo disputata
sunt. Morte enim contempta et dolore ad patiendum levato adiunximus sedationem aegritudinis, qua
nullum homini malum maius est. Etsi enim omnis
animi perturbatio gravis est nec multum differt ab
amentia, tamen ceteros, cum sunt in aliqua perturbatione aut metus aut laetitiae aut cupiditatis,
commotos modo et perturbatos dicere solemus, at
eos, qui se aegritudini dediderunt, miseros, adflictos,
83 aerumnosos, calamitosos. Itaque non fortuito fac-

---

[1] cf. § 29.

excellent health can yet appear to have a greater natural proneness to some one disease, so one soul is more disposed to one set of vices, another to others. In the case of those, however, who are said to be vicious, not by nature but by their own fault, their vices are due to erroneous ideas of good and bad,[1] with the result that one is more prone to one set of agitations and disorders than another. But a vice of long standing like a physical ailment is driven out with more distress than a disorder, and a sudden swelling of the eyes is healed more quickly than chronic inflammation is got rid of.

XXXVIII. But now that the cause of disorders is discovered, all of which originate in judgments based upon beliefs and upon consent of the will, let us at last put an end to this discussion. Besides we ought to know, now that the limits of good and evil, so far as they are discoverable by human powers, are discovered, that nothing either more important or more useful can be hoped from philosophy than the subjects which have occupied our four days' discussion. For, after death had been made of little account and pain alleviated so as to be endurable, we added the assuagement of distress, and man has no greater evil to cope with than distress. For although all distress of soul is burdensome and does not greatly differ from loss of mind, we are nevertheless accustomed to say in all the other cases where men are involved in some disorder either of fear or delight or desire, that they are merely agitated and disordered; but where they have surrendered themselves to distress we call them wretched, cast down, victims of trouble and ruin. And so your suggestion does not seem made

tum videtur, sed a te ratione propositum, ut separatim de aegritudine et de ceteris perturbationibus
disputaremus; in ea est enim fons miseriarum et
caput. Sed et aegritudinis et reliquorum animi
morborum una sanatio est, omnes opinabiles esse
et voluntarios ea reque suscipi, quod ita rectum
esse videatur. Hunc errorem quasi radicem malorum omnium stirpitus philosophia se extracturam
84 pollicetur. Demus igitur nos huic excolendos
patiamurque nos sanari; his enim malis insidentibus
non modo beati, sed ne sani quidem esse possumus.
Aut igitur negemus quidquam ratione confici, cum
contra nihil sine ratione recte fieri possit aut, cum
philosophia ex rationum collatione constet, ab ea, si
et boni et beati volumus esse, omnia adiumenta et
auxilia petamus bene beateque vivendi.

accidentally but with good reason, that we should discuss separately the question of distress and all other disorders; for in distress is the fountain-head of wretchedness. But there is one method of healing both distress and all other diseases of the soul, namely to show that all are matters of belief and consent of the will and are submitted to simply because such submission is thought to be right. This deception, as being the root of all evil, philosophy promises to drag out utterly. Let us surrender ourselves therefore to its treatment and suffer ourselves to be cured; for when these evils settle upon us, not merely is it impossible to be happy but we cannot be in a sound state either. Let us then either deny that reason has its perfect work, although on the contrary the fact is that nothing can be done aright without reason, or inasmuch as philosophy consists in the collection of rational arguments, let us, if we wish to be both good and happy, seek to gain from it all aid and support for leading a good and happy life.

M. TULLI CICERONIS TUSCULANARUM DISPUTATIONUM

LIBER V

1 I. Quintus hic dies, Brute, finem faciet Tuscula-
narum disputationum, quo die est a nobis ea de re,
quam tu ex omnibus maxime probas, disputatum :
placere enim tibi admodum sensi et ex eo libro,
quem ad me accuratissime scripsisti, et ex multis
sermonibus tuis virtutem ad beate vivendum se ipsa
esse contentam ; quod etsi difficile est probatu
propter tam varia et tam multa tormenta fortunae,
tale tamen est, ut elaborandum sit quo facilius
probetur ; nihil est enim omnium, quae in philosophia tractantur, quod gravius magnificentiusque
2 dicatur.   Nam cum ea causa impulerit eos, qui
primi se ad philosophiae studium contulerunt, ut
omnibus rebus posthabitis totos se in optimo vitae
statu exquirendo collocarent, profecto spe beate
vivendi tantam in eo studio curam operamque
posuerunt.   Quod si ab iis inventa et perfecta virtus
est et si praesidii ad beate vivendum in virtute satis
est, quis est qui non praeclare et ab illis positam et

---

[1] A book of Marcus Brutus, with the title *De Virtute*,
which has been lost.

[2] αὐτάρκη εἶναι πρὸς εὐδαιμονίαν according to Zeno and
Chrysippus, Diog. Laert. VII. 127.

[3] His political and domestic sorrows, cf. § 121.

M. TULLIUS CICERO'S TUSCULAN DISPUTATIONS

BOOK V

I. This fifth day, Brutus, will bring the Tusculan discussions to an end, and on that day we discussed the subject which of all subjects meets with your warmest approval: for from the book[1] you have written with such sedulous care and dedicated to me, as well as from the numerous conversations I have had with you, I have realized the strength of your conviction that virtue is self-sufficient for a happy life.[2] And though the agony[3] fortune inflicts on me in so many different ways makes proof difficult, the attempt to make it easier is nevertheless one deserving our best energies; for of all the subjects with which philosophy deals there is none that calls for language more dignified and elevated. For since this gave the motive by which those who first devoted themselves to the study of philosophy were stimulated to put aside all other considerations and occupy themselves entirely in the quest for the best condition of life, assuredly it was in the hope of a happy life that they bestowed such a wealth of care and toil on its pursuit. Wherefore if virtue has been made known and the idea of it perfected by their efforts, and if an adequate support for happy life is found in virtue, who can fail to regard both their work in founding the study of philosophy and ours in

a nobis susceptam operam philosophandi arbitretur?
Sin autem virtus subiecta sub varios incertosque
casus famula fortunae est nec tantarum virium est,
ut se ipsa tueatur, vereor ne non tam virtutis fiducia
nitendum nobis ad spem beate vivendi quam vota
3 facienda videantur.   Equidem eos casus, in quibus
me fortuna vehementer exercuit, mecum ipse con-
siderans huic incipio sententiae diffidere interdum et
humani generis imbecillitatem fragilitatemque extimescere.   Vereor enim ne natura, cum corpora
nobis infirma dedisset iisque et morbos insanabiles
et dolores intolerabiles adiunxisset, animos quoque
dederit et corporum doloribus congruentes et se-
4 paratim suis angoribus et molestiis implicatos.   Sed
in hoc me ipse castigo, quod ex aliorum et ex nostra
fortasse mollitia, non ex ipsa virtute, de virtutis
robore existimo.   Illa enim, si modo est ulla virtus—
quam dubitationem avunculus tuus, Brute, sustulit—,
omnia, quae cadere in hominem possunt, subter se
habet eaque despiciens casus contemnit humanos
culpaque omni carens praeter se ipsam nihil censet
ad se pertinere.   Nos autem omnia adversa cum
venientia metu augentes tum maerore praesentia
rerum naturam quam errorem nostrum damnare
malumus.
5   II. Sed et huius culpae et ceterorum vitiorum
peccatorumque nostrorum omnis a philosophia petenda correctio est; cuius in sinum cum a primis

---

[1] Cato Uticensis.

carrying it on as a noble effort? But if on the other hand virtue lies at the mercy of manifold and uncertain accidents and is the handmaid of fortune, and has insufficient strength to maintain herself alone, I fear it seems to follow that in hoping to secure a happy life we should not place our confidence in virtue so much as offer up prayers to heaven. For my part, when I consider with myself the hazards in which fortune has tried me so severely, there are moments when I begin to lose confidence in this opinion of yours and feel exceeding fear of the weakness and frailty of mankind. For I am afraid that nature in giving us, to begin with, feeble bodies, with which she has combined both incurable diseases and unendurable pains, has also given us souls that both share in the suffering of physical pain and, apart from this, have their own entanglement of trouble and vexation. But in such a mood I rebuke myself for forming my judgment of the strength of virtue from the effeminacy of others and perhaps from my own, and not from virtue itself. For virtue, if only any exists—and that doubt your uncle,[1] Brutus, has destroyed—keeps beneath its own level all the issues that can fall to man's lot, and looking down upon them despises the chances of mortal life, and free of all reproach thinks that nothing concerns it besides itself. We on the contrary, magnifying the approach of all adversities by our fears, as well as their presence by our sorrow, prefer to condemn the course of events rather than our own mistakes.

II. But the amendment of this fault, as of all our other failings and offences, must be sought for from philosophy ; to whose bosom I was driven from the

temporibus aetatis nostra voluntas studiumque nos
compulisset, his gravissimis casibus in eundem portum, ex quo eramus egressi, magna iactati tempes-
tate confugimus.   O vitae philosophia dux, o virtutis indagatrix expultrixque vitiorum ! quid non
modo nos, sed omnino vita hominum sine te esse
potuisset ? Tu urbes peperisti, tu dissipatos homines
in societatem vitae convocasti, tu eos inter se primo
domiciliis, deinde coniugiis, tum litterarum et vocum
communione iunxisti, tu inventrix legum, tu magistra
morum et disciplinae fuisti : ad te confugimus, a te
opem petimus, tibi nos, ut antea magna ex parte, sic
nunc penitus totosque tradimus.   Est autem unus
dies bene et ex praeceptis tuis actus peccanti immor-
talitati anteponendus.   Cuius igitur potius opibus
utamur quam tuis, quae et vitae tranquillitatem
6 largita nobis es et terrorem mortis sustulisti ?   Ac
philosophia quidem tantum abest ut proinde ac de
hominum est vita merita laudetur, ut a plerisque
neglecta a multis etiam vituperetur. Vituperare
quisquam vitae parentem et hoc parricidio se inqui-
nare audet et tam impie ingratus esse, ut eam
accuset, quam vereri deberet, etiam si minus percipere potuisset ?   Sed, ut opinor, hic error et haec
indoctorum animis offusa caligo est, quod tam longe
retro respicere non possunt nec eos, a quibus vita
hominum instructa primis est,[1] fuisse philosophos
arbitrantur.

---

[1] *sit* MSS. : *est* Bake.

earliest days of manhood by my own enthusiastic choice, and in my present heavy misfortunes, tossed by the fury of the tempest, I have sought refuge in the same haven from which I had first set sail. O philosophy, thou guide of life, o thou explorer of virtue and expeller of vice! Without thee what could have become not only of me but of the life of man altogether? Thou hast given birth to cities, thou hast called scattered human beings into the bond of social life, thou hast united them first of all in joint habitations, next in wedlock, then in the ties of common literature and speech, thou hast discovered law, thou hast been the teacher of morality and order: to thee I fly for refuge, from thee I look for aid, to thee I entrust myself, as once in ample measure, so now wholly and entirely. Moreover one day well spent and in accordance with thy lessons is to be preferred to an eternity of error. Whose help then are we to use rather than thine? thou that hast freely granted us peacefulness of life and destroyed the dread of death. And yet philosophy is so far from being praised in the way its service to the life of man has deserved, that most men ignore it and many even abuse it. Dare any man abuse the author of his being and stain himself with such atrocity, and be so wickedly ungrateful as to upbraid her whom he ought to have reverenced, even if his powers had not allowed him comprehension? But, as I think, this deception and this mental darkness have overspread the souls of the uninstructed, because they cannot look back far enough into the past and do not consider that the men by whom the means of human life were first provided have been philosophers.

7   III. Quam rem antiquissimam cum videamus,
nomen tamen esse confitemur recens; nam sapientiam quidem ipsam quis negare potest non modo re
esse antiquam, verum etiam nomine ? quae divinarum
humanarumque rerum, tum initiorum causarumque
cuiusque rei cognitione hoc pulcherrimum nomen
apud antiquos adsequebatur.   Itaque et illos septem, qui a Graecis σοφοί, sapientes a nostris et
habebantur et nominabantur, et multis ante saeculis Lycurgum, cuius temporibus Homerus etiam
fuisse ante hanc urbem conditam traditur, et iam
heroicis aetatibus Ulixem et Nestorem accepimus
8 et fuisse et habitos esse sapientes.   Nec vero
Atlans sustinere caelum nec Prometheus adfixus
Caucaso nec stellatus Cepheus cum uxore, genero,
filia traderetur, nisi caelestium divina cognitio
nomen eorum ad errorem fabulae traduxisset.
A quibus ducti deinceps omnes, qui in rerum con-
templatione studia ponebant, sapientes et habebantur et nominabantur, idque eorum nomen usque
ad Pythagorae manavit aetatem, quem, ut scribit
auditor Platonis Ponticus Heraclides, vir doctus in
primis, Phliuntem ferunt venisse cumque [1] Leonte,
principe Phliasiorum, docte et copiose disseruisse

---

[1] *eumque cum* MSS. : *cumque* Davies.

---

[1] "I gave my heart to seek and search out by wisdom
concerning all things that are done under heaven." *Eccl.*
1. 13.

[2] Bias of Priene, Chilon of Lacedaemon, Cleobulus of
Lindus, Pittacus of Mytilene, Periander of Corinth, Solon
of Athens, Thales of Miletus.

[3] Atlas a Titan, brother of Prometheus, was condemned
after the war of the Titans with Zeus to support heaven on
his head and hands in the far West.   For Prometheus cf. II.
§ 23.   Cepheus, King of Ethiopia, was husband of Cassiopea

III. And though we see that philosophy is a fact of
great antiquity, yet its name is, we admit, of recent
origin. For who can deny that wisdom itself at any
rate is not only ancient in fact but in name as well?[1]
And by its discovery of things sacred and human, as
well as of the beginnings and causes of every
phenomenon, it gained its glorious name with the
ancients. And so the famous seven[2] (who were
called σοφοί by the Greeks) were both held and
named wise men by our countrymen, whilst many
generations previously Lycurgus (in whose day
according to tradition Homer also lived before the
foundation of this city) and back in the heroic age
Ulysses and Nestor were, as history relates, wise men
and accounted wise. And surely tradition would
not have told of Atlas upholding the heavens, or
Prometheus nailed to Caucasus, or Cepheus placed
amongst the stars with his wife and son-in-law and
daughter, unless their marvellous discovery of things
heavenly had caused their name to be transferred to
the fairy-tales of myth.[3] And with these began the
succession of all those who devoted themselves to the
contemplation of nature and were both held to be
and named wise men, and this title of theirs
penetrated to the time of Pythagoras[4] who,
according to Heraclides of Pontus, the pupil of Plato
and a learned man of the first rank, came, the
story goes, to Phlius and with a wealth of learning
discussed certain subjects with Leon the ruler of the

and father of Andromeda whom Perseus married. Cicero
regards these tales as allegorical, following Heraclides
Ponticus who said that Atlas was a wise astrologer, προλέγων
χειμῶνας καὶ μεταβολὰς ἄστρων καὶ δύσεις, and hence came the
fable that he carried the world on his shoulders.
[4] cf. I. § 20.

quaedam : cuius ingenium et eloquentiam cum
admiratus esset Leon, quaesivisse ex eo qua maxime
arte confideret; at illum artem quidem se scire
nullam, sed esse philosophum. Admiratum Leontem
novitatem nominis quaesivisse quinam essent philo-
9 sophi et quid inter eos et reliquos interesset ; Pythagoram autem respondisse similem sibi videri vitam
hominum et mercatum eum, qui haberetur maximo
ludorum apparatu totius Graeciae celebritate : nam
ut illic alii corporibus exercitatis gloriam et nobilitatem coronae peterent, alii emendi aut vendendi
quaestu et lucro ducerentur, esset autem quoddam
genus eorum idque vel maxime ingenuum, qui nec
plausum nec lucrum quaererent, sed visendi causa
venirent studioseque perspicerent quid ageretur et quo
modo, item nos quasi in mercatus quandam celebrita-
tem ex urbe aliqua sic in hanc vitam ex alia vita et
natura profectos alios gloriae servire, alios pecuniae ;
raros esse quosdam, qui ceteris omnibus pro nihilo
habitis rerum naturam studiose intuerentur ; hos se
appellare sapientiae studiosos, id est enim philosophos, et ut illic liberalissimum esset spectare nihil
sibi acquirentem, sic in vita longe omnibus studiis
contemplationem rerum cognitionemque praestare.
10   IV. Nec vero Pythagoras nominis solum inventor,
sed rerum etiam ipsarum amplificator fuit: qui cum

---

[1] To begin with the philosopher was a lover of wisdom and
pursued knowledge. Even Aristotle included mathematics
and physics in philosophy. The differentiation of studies
took place at Alexandria.

[2] τὸν βίον ἐοικέναι πανηγύρει, Diog. Laert. VIII. 8; the
festival at Olympia, cf. I. § 111.

[3] Of wild olive.

[4] Pythagorean μετεμψύχωσις.

Phliasians. And Leon after wondering at his talent and eloquence asked him to name the art in which he put most reliance; but Pythagoras said that for his part he had no acquaintance with any art, but was a philosopher.[1] Leon was astonished at the novelty of the term and asked who philosophers were and in what they differed from the rest of the world. Pythagoras, the story continues, replied that the life of man seemed to him to resemble the festival[2] which was celebrated with most magnificent games before a concourse collected from the whole of Greece; for at this festival some men whose bodies had been trained sought to win the glorious distinction of a crown,[3] others were attracted by the prospect of making gain by buying or selling, whilst there was on the other hand a certain class, and that quite the best type of free-born men, who looked neither for applause nor gain, but came for the sake of the spectacle and closely watched what was done and how it was done. So also we, as though we had come from some city to a kind of crowded festival, leaving in like fashion another life and nature of being,[4] entered upon this life, and some were slaves of ambition, some of money; there were a special few who, counting all else as nothing, closely scanned the nature of things; these men gave themselves the name of lovers of wisdom (for that is the meaning of the word philosopher); and just as at the games the men of truest breeding looked on without any self-seeking, so in life the contemplation and discovery of nature far surpassed all other pursuits.

IV. Nor was Pythagoras by any means simply the discoverer of the name, but he extended the actual content of philosophy as well. After his arrival in

post hunc Phliasium sermonem in Italiam venisset, exornavit eam Graeciam, quae magna dicta est, et privatim et publice praestantissimis et institutis et artibus ; cuius de disciplina aliud tempus fuerit fortasse dicendi. Sed ab antiqua philosophia usque ad Socratem, qui Archelaum Anaxagorae discipulum audierat, numeri motusque tractabantur et unde omnia orerentur quove reciderent, studioseque ab iis siderum magnitudines, intervalla, cursus anquirebantur et cuncta caelestia ; Socrates autem primus philosophiam devocavit e caelo et in urbibus collocavit et in domus etiam introduxit et coëgit de vita

11 et moribus rebusque bonis et malis quaerere : cuius multiplex ratio disputandi rerumque varietas et ingenii magnitudo, Platonis memoria et litteris consecrata, plura genera effecit dissentientium philosophorum, e quibus nos id potissimum consecuti sumus, quo Socratem usum arbitrabamur, ut nostram ipsi sententiam tegeremus, errore alios levaremus et in omni disputatione quid esset simillimum veri quaereremus ; quem morem cum Carneades acutissime copiosissimeque tenuisset, fecimus et alias saepe et nuper in Tusculano ut ad eam consuetudinem

---

[1] Archelaus of Miletus, about 450 B.C.
[2] For Anaxagoras cf. I. § 104.
[3] Cicero is thinking of the old Ionian Nature-philosophers beginning with Thales of Miletus and ending with Anaxagoras and Archelaus.

Italy, subsequently to this conversation at Phlius, he enriched the private and public life of the district known as Magna Graecia with the most excellent institutions and arts—of his doctrines we can perhaps speak another time. But from the ancient days down to the time of Socrates, who had listened to Archelaus[1] the pupil of Anaxagoras,[2] philosophy dealt with numbers and movements, with the problem whence all things came, or whither they returned, and zealously inquired into the size of the stars, the spaces that divided them, their courses and all celestial phenomena;[3] Socrates on the other hand was the first to call philosophy down from the heavens and set her in the cities of men and bring her also into their homes and compel her to ask questions about life and morality and things good and evil:[4] and his many-sided method of discussion and the varied nature of its subjects and the greatness of his genius, which has been immortalized in Plato's literary masterpieces, have produced many warring philosophic sects of which I have chosen particularly to follow that one[5] which I think agreeable to the practice of Socrates, in trying to conceal my own private opinion, to relieve others from deception and in every discussion to look for the most probable solution; and as this was the custom observed by Carneades[6] with all the resources of a keen intelligence, I have endeavoured on many other occasions as well as recently in the Tusculan villa to conform to the same fashion in our discussions;

[4] Xen. *Mem.* I. 1. 6. says περὶ τῶν ἀνθρωπείων ἀεὶ διελέγετο. Archelaus had not neglected moral questions (Diog. Laert. II. 16) nor had Pythagoras.
[5] cf. II. § 9.   [6] cf. III. § 54.

disputaremus; et quadridui quidem sermonem superioribus ad te perscriptum libris misimus, quinto
autem die cum eodem in loco consedissemus, sic est
propositum de quo disputaremus.

12 V. A. Non mihi videtur ad beate vivendum satis
posse virtutem. M. At hercule Bruto meo videtur,
cuius ego iudicium, pace tua dixerim, longe antepono
tuo. A. Non dubito, nec id nunc agitur, tu illum
quantum ames, sed hoc, quod mihi dixi videri, quale
sit, de quo a te disputari volo. M. Nempe negas ad
beate vivendum satis posse virtutem? A. Prorsus
nego. M. Quid? ad recte, honeste, laudabiliter,
postremo ad bene vivendum satisne est praesidii in
virtute? A. Certe satis. M. Potes igitur aut, qui
male vivat, non eum miserum dicere aut, quem bene
fateare, eum negare beate vivere? A. Quidni
possim? Nam etiam in tormentis recte, honeste,
laudabiliter et ob eam rem bene vivi potest, dum
modo intelligas quid nunc dicam bene; dico
13 enim constanter, graviter, sapienter, fortiter: haec
etiam in eculeum coniiciuntur, quo vita non aspirat
beata. M. Quid igitur? solane beata vita, quaeso,
relinquitur extra ostium limenque carceris, cum
constantia, gravitas, fortitudo, sapientia reliquaeque
virtutes rapiantur ad tortorem nullumque recusent
nec supplicium nec dolorem? A. Tu, si quid es

and I have in fact written out in the preceding books and sent you the result of four days' conference; on the fifth day, however, after seating ourselves in the same place, the following subject was put forward for discussion.

V. *A.* It does not appear to me that virtue can be sufficient for leading a happy life. *M.* But, I can assure you, my friend Brutus thinks it sufficient and with your permission I put his judgment far above yours. *A.* No doubt you do and yet the question now before us is not the depth of your affection for him, but the view I have stated as it appears to me, and this I wish you to discuss. *M.* Do you really mean that virtue cannot be sufficient for leading a happy life? *A.* I do, absolutely. *M.* Tell me this, does virtue give sufficient aid for living rightly, honourably, praiseworthily, and in a word for leading a good life? *A.* Certainly it does. *M.* Can you then say either that the man who lives an evil life is not wretched, or that the man who, as you admit, leads a good life does not lead a happy one? *A.* Why should I not? for even in torture a man can live rightly, honourably, praiseworthily and for that reason lead a good life, provided only you understand the sense in which I now use the term good; for I mean living consistently, with dignity, wisdom, courage: these qualities too are thrown along with their possessor upon the rack, and for that happy life has no ambition. *M.* What then? is happy life, I ask, left in solitude outside the threshold and gate of the prison-house when consistency, dignity, courage, wisdom and the rest of the virtues are hurried along to the executioner and recoil from no torment or pain? *A.* If you are going to do any

facturus, nova aliqua conquiras oportet: ista me
minime movent, non solum quia pervulgata sunt, sed
multo magis, quia tamquam levia quaedam vina nihil
valent in aqua, sic Stoicorum ista magis gustata
quam potata delectant.   Velut iste chorus virtutum
in eculeum impositus imagines constituit ante oculos
cum amplissima dignitate, ut ad eas cursim perrec-
tura nec eas beata vita a se desertas passura videa-
14 tur: cum autem animum ab ista pictura imaginibusque
virtutum ad rem veritatemque traduxeris, hoc nudum
relinquitur, possitne quis beatus esse quam diu
torqueatur.   Quam ob rem hoc nunc quaeramus;
virtutes autem noli vereri ne expostulent et queran-
tur se a beata vita esse relictas: si enim nulla virtus
prudentia vacat, prudentia ipsa hoc videt, non
omnes bonos esse etiam beatos, multaque de M.
Atilio, Q. Caepione, M'. Aquilio recordatur, beatam-
que vitam, si imaginibus potius uti quam rebus
ipsis placet, conantem ire in eculeum retinet ipsa
prudentia negatque ei cum dolore et cruciatu quidquam esse commune.
15   VI. M. Facile patior te isto modo agere, etsi ini-
quum est praescribere mihi te quem ad modum a
me disputari velis.   Sed quaero utrum aliquid actum
superioribus diebus an nihil arbitremur?   A. Actum
vero et aliquantum quidem.   M. Atqui, si ita est,
profligata iam haec et paene ad exitum adducta
quaestio est.   A. Quo tandem modo?   M. Quia

---

[1] Like the Greeks the Romans usually mixed wine with
water for drinking.
[2] M. Atilius Regulus defeated in Africa in the first Punic
war, 255 B.C., cf. Hor. *Od.* III. 5.   Q. Servilius Caepio
defeated by the Cimbri, 105 B.C.; his imperium was abro-
gated and his property confiscated.   Manius Aquilius cap-
tured by Mithridates, B.C. 88, and cruelly put to death.

good, you must look out for some fresh arguments. Those you have given have no effect on me, not merely because they are hackneyed but much more because, as with certain light wines which lose their flavour in water,[1] there is more delight in a sip than a draught of this Stoic vintage. For instance your troop of virtues, when laid upon the rack, bring before the eyes visions of majestic splendour, making it seem that happy life is on the point of hastening to them speedily and not suffering them to remain deserted by itself. When, however, one has led the soul away from the visions of that picture of the virtues to the truth of reality, there is left this bare question,—can anyone be happy as long as he is tormented? Let us therefore put this question now ; as for the virtues, however, do not be afraid of their remonstrating and complaining that happy life has deserted them, for if there is no virtue without prudence, prudence by itself can see that not all good men are also happy, and recalls many memories of M. Atilius, Q. Caepio or Manius Aquilius,[2] and when happy life (if resolved to resort to visions rather than actual facts) attempts to pass to the rack, prudence in person restrains it and says that it has no partnership with pain and agony.

VI. M. I readily allow you to take such a line, although it is unfair of you to dictate the way in which you wish me to conduct the discussion. But I want to know whether we think any result was arrived at on the days previous to this or not. A. Certainly there was and a result of some moment. M. And yet, if that is so, this question has already been threshed out and brought wellnigh to its conclusion. A. How so, pray ? M.

motus turbulenti iactationesque animorum incitatae
et impetu inconsiderato elatae rationem omnem re-
pellentes vitae beatae nullam partem relinquunt.
Quis enim potest mortem aut dolorem metuens,
quorum alterum saepe adest, alterum semper impendet, esse non miser? Quid? si idem, quod
plerumque fit, paupertatem, ignominiam, infamiam
timet, si debilitatem, caecitatem, si denique, quod
non singulis hominibus, sed potentibus populis saepe
contigit, servitutem, potest ea timens esse quisquam
16 beatus? Quid, qui non modo ea futura timet, verum
etiam fert sustinetque praesentia? adde eodem
exsilia, luctus, orbitates : qui rebus his fractus aegritudine eliditur potest tandem esse non miserrimus?
Quid vero? illum, quem libidinibus inflammatum et
furentem videmus, omnia rabide appetentem cum
inexplebili cupiditate, quoque adfluentius voluptates
undique hauriat, eo gravius ardentiusque sitientem,
nonne recte miserrimum dixeris? Quid? elatus ille
levitate inanique laetitia exsultans et temere gestiens
nonne tanto miserior quanto sibi videtur beatior?
Ergo ut hi miseri, sic contra illi beati, quos nulli
metus terrent, nullae aegritudines exedunt, nullae
libidines incitant, nullae futiles laetitiae exsultantes
languidis liquefaciunt voluptatibus. Ut maris igitur
tranquillitas intelligitur nulla ne minima quidem
aura fluctus commovente, sic animi quietus et placa-

---

[1] The *perturbationes*, cf. Bk. IV.

Because troubled movements and agitations[1] of the soul, roused and excited by ill-considered impulse, in scorn of all reason, leave no portion of happy life behind them. For who can fail to be wretched with the fear of death or pain upon him, one of which is always close at hand and the other always threatening? Further, if the same man (and this happens frequently) is afraid of poverty, disgrace, dishonour, if he is afraid of infirmity, blindness, if lastly he is afraid of slavery (the frequent fate, not of individual men but powerful communities): can anyone be happy with such fears before him? Again, the man who not merely fears such misfortunes in the future, but actually suffers and endures them in the present (add to the list exile, sorrow, childlessness), the man who is broken down by such blows and shipwrecked by distress, can he fail, pray, to be utterly wretched? Further, where we see a man passionately stirred with the madness of lust, desiring all things in a fury of unsatisfied longing, and the more copiously he drains the cup of pleasure wherever offered, the deeper and more consuming his thirst, would you not rightly pronounce him utterly wretched? Again, when a man is frivolously excited, and in a transport of empty delight and reckless extravagance, is he not all the more wretched, the happier his life appears in his own eyes? Therefore as such men are wretched, so on the contrary those are happy whom no fears alarm, no distresses corrode, no lusts inflame, no vain transports of delight dissolve in the melting lassitude of pleasure. Just therefore as the sea is understood to be calm when not even the lightest breath of air ruffles its waves; so a peaceful, still

tus status cernitur, cum perturbatio nulla est qua
17 moveri queat.   Quod si est, qui vim fortunae, qui
omnia humana, quaecumque accidere possunt, tolerabilia ducat, ex quo nec timor eum nec angor attingat, idemque si nihil concupiscat, nulla efferatur
animi inani voluptate, quid est cur is non beatus
sit ? et si haec virtute efficiuntur, quid est cur virtus
ipsa per se non efficiat beatos ?

    VII. A. Atqui alterum dici non potest quin ii, qui
nihil metuant, nihil angantur, nihil concupiscant,
nulla impotenti laetitia efferantur, beati sint, itaque
id tibi concedo, alterum autem iam integrum non
est ; superioribus enim disputationibus effectum est
18 vacare omni animi perturbatione sapientem.   M.
Nimirum igitur confecta res est ; videtur enim ad
exitum venisse quaestio.   A. Propemodum id quidem.   M. Verum tamen mathematicorum iste mos
est, non est philosophorum.   Nam geometrae cum
aliquid docere volunt, si quid ad eam rem pertinet
eorum, quae ante docuerunt, id sumunt pro concesso
et probato, illud modo explicant, de quo ante nihil
scriptum est : philosophi, quamcumque rem habent
in manibus, in eam quae conveniunt, congerunt
omnia, etsi alio loco disputata sunt.   Quod ni ita
esset, cur Stoicus, si esset quaesitum satisne ad beate
vivendum virtus posset, multa diceret ? cui satis
esset respondere se ante docuisse nihil bonum esse

----

    [1] We must not like geometricians take what has pre-
viously been proved for granted, *e.g.* that the angles of a
triangle are together equal to two right angles.   We must
like philosophers assemble all the proofs which belong to
our subject, whether they have been previously discussed
or not.

condition of the soul is discernible when there is no disturbance of strength enough to be able to ruffle it. Therefore if there is a man able to regard the power of fortune, to regard all human vicissitudes that can possibly befall, as so far endurable that neither fear nor worry touch him, and if the same man should covet nothing, feel no transport of empty pleasure in his soul, what reason is there why he should not be happy? And if virtue makes this possible, what reason is there why virtue of its own power alone should not make men happy?

VII. A. Well at any rate there can be no question of the one point—that those who have no fear, no worry, no covetousness, no transport of ungovernable delight are happy, and so I grant you this; moreover the other problem has already had a breach made in it, for the result of our previous discussions was that the wise man is free from all disturbance of soul. M. Surely then the inquiry is finished, for the problem seems to have reached its solution. A. Almost so at any rate. M. And yet you argue here like the mathematicians,[1] not like the philosophers. For geometricians, when they want to demonstrate some proposition, take for granted and proved anything in previous demonstrations which is germane to the subject; they only unravel the difficulty about which nothing has previously been written: philosophers collect together all that is applicable to any inquiry upon which they are engaged, even if it has all been thoroughly discussed elsewhere. Had this not been the case, why should the Stoic wax eloquent when asked whether virtue can be sufficient for leading a happy life? it would be enough for him to reply that he had previously

nisi quod honestum esset, hoc probato consequens
esse beatam vitam virtute esse contentam, et quo
modo hoc sit consequens illi, sic illud huic, ut, si
beata vita virtute contenta sit, nisi honestum quod
19 sit, nihil aliud sit bonum.   Sed tamen non agunt sic ;
nam et de honesto et de summo bono separatim libri
sunt, et cum ex eo efficiatur satis magnam in virtute
ad beate vivendum esse vim, nihilo minus hoc agunt
separatim ; propriis enim et suis argumentis et ad-
monitionibus tractanda quaeque res est, tanta praesertim.   Cave enim putes ullam in[1] philosophia
vocem emissam clariorem ullumve esse philosophiae
promissum uberius aut maius.   Nam quid profitetur ?
o di boni ! perfecturam se qui legibus suis paruisset
ut esset contra fortunam semper armatus, ut omnia
praesidia haberet in se bene beateque vivendi, ut
20 esset semper denique beatus.   Sed videro quid
efficiat : tantisper hoc ipsum magni aestimo, quod
pollicetur.   Nam Xerxes quidem refertus omnibus
praemiis donisque fortunae, non equitatu, non pede-
stribus copiis, non navium multitudine, non infinito
pondere auri contentus, praemium proposuit, qui
invenisset novam voluptatem : qua ipsa non fuisset[2]
contentus : neque enim umquam finem inveniet

---

[1] A few MSS. read *a*.
[2] Bentley's correction for the *fuit* of MSS.

---

[1] *i.e.* in philosophic works.
[2] What else can promise so much ? Can external good or
pleasure ? No, *for* the man like the King of Persia who
looks for happiness from wealth or pleasure will never be
content, but will always crave for more and more, so that
he can never be happy.

explained that there was nothing good save that
which was right, and when this was proved he
would say that it follows that a happy life is bound
up with virtue, and just as this follows from the
premises, so with the converse that, if happy life is
bound up with virtue, there is nothing good save
that which is right. But this nevertheless is not
the way they go to work; for their books deal
separately both with that which is right and with
the highest good, and while from the nature of the
good it is concluded that virtue implies sufficient
power for leading a good life, none the less they
deal separately with the converse; for every subject
must be attacked with its own appropriate proofs
and exhortations, particularly one so momentous.
For do not imagine that there is any utterance in
philosophy [1] delivered more distinctly or any
promise of philosophy more fruitful or important.
For what is the offer made ? that by heaven's grace
she will ensure that the man who has been obedient
to her laws is always armed against the assaults of
fortune, that he has within him all the support
required for leading a good and happy life, that in
fine he is always happy. But I must see another
time how far the claim is made good. Meanwhile
I value highly the simple fact that she does make
such a promise. For [2] in Xerxes we have a case in
point: though loaded with all the privileges and
gifts that fortune bestows, he was not content with
cavalry, with infantry, with a host of ships, with
boundless stores of gold, but offered a reward to
anyone who should discover a new pleasure : and
had it really been found he would not have been
content; for lust will never discover its limit. I

libido. Nos vellem praemio elicere possemus, qui nobis aliquid attulisset, quo hoc firmius crederemus.

21 VIII. A. Vellem id quidem, sed habeo paullum quod requiram. Ego enim adsentior eorum, quae posuisti, alterum alteri consequens esse, ut, quem ad modum, si quod honestum sit, id solum sit bonum, sequatur vitam beatam virtute confici, sic si vita beata in virtute sit, nihil esse nisi virtutem bonum. Sed Brutus tuus auctore Aristo[1] et Antiocho non sentit hoc; putat enim, etiam si sit bonum aliquod praeter virtutem. M. Quid igitur? contra Brutumne me dicturum putas? A. Tu vero, ut videtur; nam

22 praefinire non est meum. M. Quid cuique igitur consentaneum sit, alio loco. Nam ista mihi et cum Antiocho saepe et cum Aristo nuper, cum Athenis imperator apud eum deversarer, dissensio fuit: mihi enim non videbatur quisquam esse beatus posse, cum in malis esset, in malis autem sapientem esse posse, si essent ulla corporis aut fortunae mala. Dicebantur haec, quae scriptitavit[2] etiam Antiochus locis pluribus, virtutem ipsam per se beatam vitam efficere

---

[1] A common reading is *Aristone.* Aristus brother of Antiochus and Aristo pupil of Zeno were often confused. In the *Life of Brutus* Plutarch gives the name *Aristo* to the brother of Antiochus.

[2] The ordinary readings are *scripsit, scripta sit* for which *scriptitavit* has been suggested by Klotz.

---

[1] That virtue is sufficient for a good and happy life.

[2] Aristus was brother of Antiochus. He belonged to the Academic school and was a friend of Cicero. For Antiochus cf. III. § 59. Brutus had a great admiration for both brothers.

[3] The Peripatetics held that there were goods of soul, body and fortune. Aristotle, *Eth.* I. 8 says τὸ εὖ ζῆν καὶ τὸ εὖ πράττειν are requisites for happiness. It casts a shadow

could wish we were able, by offering a reward, to lure someone to provide some means of more assured belief in this truth.[1] VIII. A. I could wish the same, but I have a small point to raise. For while I agree that, of the statements you have made, the one follows from the other, namely that, just as it would follow that a happy life is secured by virtue if that only be good which is right, similarly if happy life lies in virtue, nothing is good except virtue : but your friend Brutus on the authority of Aristus[2] and Antiochus does not accept this; for he thinks happy life lies in virtue even if there should be some good besides virtue.[3] M. What then ? do you think I shall contradict Brutus ? A. Nay, you must do as you please. It is not for me to lay down the law. M. Then let us settle each one's consistency elsewhere. For I had the disagreement you mention both frequently with Antiochus and also recently with Aristus, at the time I stayed with him at Athens whilst I still held my command.[4] For my opinion was that no one could be happy when encompassed with evil ; but the wise man could be encompassed with evil if any evils of body and fortune existed.[5] The arguments used (and Antiochus has also stated them continually in a number of passages in his works), were that virtue alone is of itself able to render life happy and yet

over happiness to be devoid for instance of noble birth, fair offspring or beauty of person.

[4] On Cicero's return from his province of Cilicia, 50 B.C. He had been saluted as *Imperator* by his soldiers on the field of battle at Issus. His *imperium* he would not lay down until he had entered Rome.

[5] The Peripatetics and the Academy called diseases, pain, poverty *evils*: the Stoics called them *inconveniences*, ἀποπροηγμένα.

posse neque tamen beatissimam : deinde ex maiore
parte plerasque res nominari, etiam si quae pars
abesset, ut vires, ut valetudinem, ut divitias, ut
honorem, ut gloriam, quae genere, non numero
cernerentur : item beatam vitam, etiam si ex aliqua
parte clauderet, tamen ex multo maiore parte
23 obtinere nomen suum.   Haec nunc enucleare non
ita necesse est, quamquam non constantissime dici
mihi videntur.   Nam et qui beatus est non intelligo
quid requirat, ut sit beatior—si est enim quod desit,
ne beatus quidem est—et quod ex maiore parte
unam quamque rem appellari spectarique dicunt, est
ubi id isto modo valeat : cum vero tria genera
malorum esse dicant, qui duorum generum malis
omnibus urgueatur, ut omnia adversa sint in fortuna,
omnibus oppressum corpus et confectum doloribus,
huic paullumne ad beatam vitam deesse dicemus,
non modo ad beatissimam ?

24   IX. Hoc illud est, quod Theophrastus sustinere
non potuit ; nam cum statuisset verbera, tormenta,
cruciatus, patriae eversiones, exsilia, orbitates magnam vim habere ad male misereque vivendum, non
est ausus elate et ample loqui, cum humiliter demis-
seque sentiret.   Quam bene non quaeritur, constanter

---

[1] *i.e.* fall short of perfect happiness.
[2] Cicero is giving the Stoic argument.   The *summum
bonum* does not admit of degrees : it cannot increase or
decrease.   If happy life has the *summum bonum*, which is
perfect, it must be perfectly happy.
[3] The Peripatetics, cf. § 76.
[4] As there are three kinds of goods, so there must be three
kinds of evils—their contraries.   If life is happy when goods
preponderate, life must be wretched if evils preponderate,
and therefore if the wise man is very unfortunate and
afflicted he must be miserable,—which to the Stoic is absurd.

not supremely happy; secondly that most things get their name from that which forms, even if a fraction be missing, the greater part of them, such things for instance as strength, as health, as riches, as honour, as glory which are discerned as present in essence if not in every detail; in the same way happy life, even though it should in some part be lame,[1] yet gets its name from what forms by far the greater part of it. It is not at present necessary to give a full explanation of this view, and yet it seems to me that the statement is not wholly consistent; for I do not understand, for one thing, what the man who is happy wants in order to be happier (for if anything is to be missing, he is not so much as happy),[2] and as to the statement that each single thing gets its title and estimation from that which forms the greater part of it, there are cases where this holds in the way described: but as they[3] say there are three kinds of evil—when a man is beset with all the evils of two kinds[4] so that his lot is dogged with every kind of adversity, his body reduced and weakened with all manner of pains—shall we say that such a man "wants but little" to secure a happy life, to say nothing of a supremely happy life?

IX. This is the position Theophrastus[5] proved unable to defend. For after deciding that blows, the rack, torture, ruin of country, exile, childlessness had great influence in rendering life evil and wretched, he did not venture to speak in an exalted and dignified strain, as his thoughts were mean and low: how far he was right is not the question now;

[5] Theophrastus is said to have been given his name, meaning "divine speaker," by Aristotle, cf. I. § 45.

quidem certe. Itaque mihi placere non solet consequentia reprehendere, cum prima concesseris : hic
autem elegantissimus omnium philosophorum et
eruditissimus non magno opere reprehenditur, cum
tria genera dicit bonorum; vexatur autem ab omnibus, primum in eo libro, quem scripsit de vita beata,
in quo multa disputat, quam ob rem is, qui torqueatur, qui crucietur, beatus esse non possit ; in eo
etiam putatur dicere in rotam[1] beatam vitam non
escendere. Non usquam id quidem dicit omnino,
25 sed quae dicit idem valent. Possum igitur, cui
concesserim in malis esse dolores corporis, in malis
naufragia fortunae, huic suscensere dicenti non
omnes bonos esse beatos, cum in omnes bonos ea,
quae ille in malis numerat, cadere possint ? Vexatur
idem Theophrastus et libris et scholis omnium
philosophorum, quod in Callisthene suo laudarit
illam sententiam :

> *Vitam regit fortuna, non sapientia.*

Negant ab ullo philosopho quidquam dictum esse
languidius : recte id quidem, sed nihil intelligo dici

[1] After *rotam* old editions have the words *id est genus
tormenti apud Graecos*, which seem to be an ancient gloss.

[1] The Peripatetics held that there were three kinds of
good, goods of soul, goods of body and goods of fortune or
external goods. Theophrastus, Cicero argues, should not be
blamed for being consistent to his principle and saying that
the man who suffers evils of fortune or body cannot be
happy. It is the principle that there are three kinds of
goods and their opposites, which should be attacked. Admit
the principle and we have no right to be angry with Theophrastus for saying that, as good men can suffer in body and

consistent at any rate he undoubtedly was.[1]   And
so it is not my way to be content with criticizing
conclusions where one has granted the premises :
but this most subtle and learned of all philosophers
is not seriously criticized when he says there are
three kinds of good ; he is, however, bitterly attacked
by everyone, first for the book he wrote about happy
life,[2] in which he discusses at length the reason
why the man who is racked, who is tortured cannot
be happy ; in the course of it too he is thought to
say that happy life cannot mount the scaffold to the
wheel.[3] It is true he does not anywhere say so
completely, but what he does say amounts to the
same thing. Can I therefore, if I have granted him
that bodily pains are counted evils, that shipwreck
of fortune is counted evil, be angry with him when
he says that not all good men are happy, since the
things which he reckons as evil can come upon all
good men ? Theophrastus is again bitterly attacked
both in the books and lectures of all philosophers
for having in his *Callisthenes* [4] approved the maxim :

Fortune, not wisdom, rules the life of men.[5]

They say that nothing more spiritless was ever said
by any philosopher : so far they are right, but I do
not understand that anything could have been said

fortune, like the patriarch Job, they cannot all be happy.
We must argue logically.

[2] περὶ εὐδαιμονίας.

[3] The Greek punishment ἐπὶ τοῦ τροχοῦ στρεβλοῦσθαι.
Breaking on the wheel was a punishment employed in
France and in Germany up to 1827.

[4] cf. III. § 21.

[5] τύχη τὰ θνητῶν πράγματ' οὐκ εὐβουλία, quoted by Plutarch
de Fortuna, p. 97.

potuisse constantius. Si enim tot sunt in corpore
bona, tot extra corpus in casu atque fortuna, nonne
consentaneum est plus fortunam, quae domina rerum
sit et externarum et ad corpus pertinentium, quam
consilium valere?

26   An malumus Epicurum imitari? qui multa praeclare saepe dicit; quam enim sibi constanter con-
venienterque dicat non laborat. Laudat tenuem
victum : philosophi id quidem, sed si Socrates aut
Antisthenes diceret, non is, qui finem bonorum
voluptatem esse dixerit. Negat quemquam iucunde
posse vivere, nisi idem honeste, sapienter iusteque
vivat. Nihil gravius, nihil philosophia dignius, nisi
idem hoc ipsum, honeste, sapienter, iuste ad voluptatem referret. Quid melius quam fortunam exiguam intervenire sapienti? sed hoc isne dicit, qui,
cum dolorem non modo maximum malum, sed solum
malum etiam dixerit, toto corpore opprimi possit
doloribus acerrimis tum, cum maxime contra fortu-
27   nam glorietur? Quod idem melioribus etiam verbis
Metrodorus : *Occupavi te*, inquit, *fortuna, atque cepi
omnesque aditus tuos interclusi, ut ad me aspirare non
posses.* Praeclare, si Aristo Chius aut si Stoicus
Zeno diceret, qui nisi quod turpe esset nihil malum
duceret. Tu vero, Metrodore, qui omne bonum in
visceribus medullisque condideris et definieris summum bonum firma corporis adfectione explorataque

---

¹ Antisthenes, pupil of Socrates and founder of the sect of
the Cynics who had only cloak, wallet and staff.

² οὐκ ἔστιν ἡδέως ζῆν ἄνευ τοῦ φρονίμως καὶ καλῶς καὶ δικαίως
οὐδὲ φρονίμως καὶ καλῶς καὶ δικαίως ἄνευ τοῦ ἡδέως, Diog.
Laert. X. 140.

³ βραχεῖα σοφῷ τύχη παρεμπίπτει, Diog. Laert. X. 144.

⁴ cf. II. § 8.

⁵ cf. II. § 15.

more consistently. For if there is so much of good in the body and so much outside the body in accident and fortune, is it not reasonable for fortune, which is mistress both of things external to the body and things appertaining to it, to have more control than foresight has?

Or do we prefer to follow Epicurus, who often expresses many noble sentiments? For he does not trouble about consistency and coherency in what he says. He praises plain living: that is indeed worthy of a philosopher, but only in the mouth of Socrates or Antisthenes,[1] not of the man who can say that pleasure is the limit of good. He says that no one can live pleasantly unless he also lives honourably, wisely and justly.[2] Nothing could be more dignified, nothing more worthy of philosophy, if he did not go on to make pleasure the standard of this self-same "honourably, wisely, justly." What better than his remark that "fortune has but little weight with the wise"?[3] But is this said by one who, after saying that not only is pain the chief evil but the only evil as well, can bear all over his body the crushing burden of acutest pain at the moment he utters his loudest vaunts against fortune? And the same thing is expressed in even better language by Metrodorus;[4] "I have caught you, fortune," he says, "and have occupied and blocked all your means of access, so that you could not get near me." Nobly said in the mouth of Aristo of Chios[5] or the Stoic Zeno, who would consider nothing evil except what was disgraceful: but you, Metrodorus, seeing you have stored up all good in the flesh and marrow of the body, and have defined the highest good as bound up with a stable condition of body and an

453

eius spe[1] contineri, fortunae aditus interclusisti ?
Quo modo ? Isto enim bono iam exspoliari potes.

28 X. Atqui his capiuntur imperiti, et propter huius
modi sententias istorum hominum est multitudo :
acute autem disputantis illud est non quid quisque
dicat, sed quid cuique dicendum sit videre : velut in
ea ipsa sententia, quam in hac disputatione sus-
cepimus, omnes bonos semper beatos volumus esse.
Quos dicam bonos perspicuum est ; omnibus enim
virtutibus instructos et ornatos tum sapientes, tum
viros bonos dicimus. Videamus qui dicendi sint beati.
Equidem eos existimo, qui sint in bonis, nullo ad-
iuncto malo, neque ulla alia huic verbo, cum beatum
dicimus, subiecta notio est nisi secretis malis omni-
29 bus cumulata bonorum complexio. Hanc adsequi
virtus, si quidquam praeter ipsam boni est, non
potest ; aderit enim malorum, si mala illa ducimus,
turba quaedam, paupertas, ignobilitas, humilitas,
solitudo, amissio suorum, graves dolores corporis,
perdita valetudo, debilitas, caecitas, interitus patriae,
exsilium, servitus denique : in his tot et tantis,—
atque etiam plura possunt accidere,—potest esse
sapiens ; nam haec casus importat, qui in sapientem
potest incurrere. At si ea mala sunt, quis potest
praestare semper sapientem beatum fore, cum vel in
30 omnibus his uno tempore esse possit? Non igitur

---

[1] *explorataque spe* is the reading of the MSS. : *eius* has been
inserted (Wesenberg) and corresponds to Metrodorus' own
words, τὸ περὶ ταύτης πιστὸν ἔλπισμα.

---

[1] cf. *Luke* xii. 20.

assured hope of its continuance, have you blocked
the approaches of fortune? How? Why, of such
a good you can be robbed this night.[1]

X. But all the same, the inexperienced are caught
by these statements, and owing to views of
this kind there is a mass of men who think in this way;
it is, however, the mark of an accurate reasoner to
look, not at what each particular thinker says, but
at what each one ought to say: take, for instance,
the very view which we have maintained in this
discussion—we wish the good man to be happy
always. It is clear whom I mean by good men; for
we say that men equipped with and distinguished
by all the virtues are wise as well as good. Let us
see who are to be described as happy: for my part
I think it is those who are compassed about with
good without any association of evil, and no other
sense underlies the word happy, when we use it,
except the fulness of combined good and complete
separation of evil. Virtue cannot secure this, if
there is any good besides itself; for there will come
as it were a throng of evils, if we regard them as
evils, poverty, obscurity, insignificance, loneliness,
loss of property, severe physical pain, ruined health,
infirmity, blindness, fall of one's country, exile and,
to crown all, slavery: in all these distressing conditions—and more still can happen—the wise man
can be involved; for chance occasions them, and
chance can assail the wise man; but if these are
" evils," who can show that the wise man will be
always happy, seeing that he can be involved in all
of them at one and the same time? Therefore,
since they reckon the things I have enumerated
above to be " evils," I do not readily allow either

facile concedo neque Bruto meo neque communibus
magistris nec veteribus illis, Aristoteli, Speusippo,
Xenocrati, Polemoni, ut cum ea, quae supra enume-
ravi, in malis numerent, idem dicant semper beatum
esse sapientem. Quos si titulus hic delectat insignis
et pulcher, Pythagora, Socrate, Platone dignissimus,
inducant animum illa, quorum splendore capiuntur,
vires, valetudinem, pulcritudinem, divitias, honores,
opes contemnere, eaque, quae his contraria sunt,
pro nihilo ducere, tum poterunt clarissima voce
profiteri se neque fortunae impetu nec multitudinis
opinione nec dolore nec paupertate terreri omniaque
sibi in sese esse posita nec esse quidquam extra
31 suam potestatem quod ducant in bonis. Nunc[1] et
haec loqui, quae sunt magni cuiusdam et alti viri, et
eadem quae vulgus in malis et bonis numerare
concedi nullo modo potest. Qua gloria commotus
Epicurus exoritur, cui etiam, si dis placet, videtur
semper sapiens beatus. Hic dignitate huius sententiae capitur, sed numquam id diceret, si ipse se
audiret; quid est enim quod minus conveniat quam
ut is, qui vel summum vel solum malum dolorem
esse dicat, idem censeat: "Quam hoc suave est!"
tum, cum dolore crucietur, dicturum esse sapientem?
Non igitur singulis vocibus philosophi spectandi sunt,
sed ex perpetuitate atque constantia.

32 XI. A. Adducis me ut tibi adsentiar. Sed tua

---

[1] The MSS. have *nec* or *neque hunc* for which Wesenberg
suggested *nunc*.

---

[1] Antiochus, Aristus and others.   [2] I. § 7.
[3] Nephew of Plato, whom he succeeded as head of the
Academy.
[4] I. § 20.
[5] Succeeded Xenocrates as head of the Academy.

my friend Brutus or those who have taught us both[1] or those thinkers of old, Aristotle,[2] Speusippus,[3] Xenocrates,[4] Polemo,[5] to say also that the wise man is always happy. And if the noble distinction of this title of "wise," most worthy of Pythagoras, Socrates and Plato, so delights them, let them constrain the soul to despise the things which dazzle them, strength, health, beauty, riches, distinctions, wealth, and count as nothing the things that are their opposites: then will they be able in clearest accents to claim that they are terrified neither by the assault of fortune nor the opinion of the mob nor by pain or poverty, and that they regard all things as resting with themselves, nor is there anything beyond their control which they reckon as good. As it is, however, it is in no way possible to allow them both to utter sentiments worthy of a really great and lofty character and reckon as good and evil the same things as the common herd of mankind. Ambitious of such glory[6] Epicurus starts up, and he too, save the mark! thinks the wise man always happy. He is caught by the grandeur of the thought; but he would never say so if he attended to his own words; for what is less consistent than for the man who says that pain is either the highest or the only evil, to suppose also that the wise man at the moment he is tortured by pain will say "How sweet this is!"[7] Philosophers, therefore, must be judged not by isolated utterances but by uninterrupted consistency.

XI. A. You are leading me on to agree with you.

[6] Epicurus aspires to the title of "wise" bestowed on other philosophers, or like them to utter noble sentiments about true happiness.   [7] cf. II. § 17.

quoque vide ne desideretur constantia. M. Quonam
modo? A. Quia legi tuum nuper quartum *de
Finibus* : in eo mihi videbare contra Catonem dis-
serens hoc velle ostendere, quod mihi quidem probatur, inter Zenonem et Peripateticos nihil praeter
verborum novitatem interesse ; quod si ita est quid
est causae quin, si Zenonis rationi consentaneum sit
satis magnam vim in virtute esse ad beate vivendum,
liceat idem Peripateticis dicere? Rem enim opinor
33 spectari oportere, non verba. M. Tu quidem
tabellis obsignatis agis mecum et testificaris quid
dixerim aliquando aut scripserim. Cum aliis isto
modo, qui legibus impositis disputant : nos in diem
vivimus ; quodcumque nostros animos probabilitate
percussit, id dicimus, itaque soli sumus liberi.
Verum tamen, quoniam de constantia paullo ante
diximus, non ego hoc loco id quaerendum puto,
verumne sit quod Zenoni placuerit quodque eius
auditori Aristoni, bonum esse solum quod honestum
esset, sed, si ita esset, tum ut hoc totum, beate
34 vivere, in una virtute poneret.[1] Qua re demus hoc
sane Bruto, ut sit beatus semper sapiens : quam
sibi conveniat ipse viderit. Gloria quidem huius
sententiae quis est illo viro dignior? Nos tamen
teneamus ut sit idem beatissimus.

XII. Et si Zeno Citieus, advena quidam et

---

[1] This is the reading of the MSS., which gives a good
sense. Bentley proposed to read *ni* for *si, num* for *tum ut*
and *poneretur* for *poneret*.

---

[1] Documents were sealed up to prevent any subsequent
tampering with the words ; such documents could be produced in court when an action was tried. Antonius the
orator never published his speeches for fear of having them
quoted against him later.

But take care that your own consistency be not at fault. M. In what way? A. Because I have lately read the fourth book of your *de Finibus*: there it appeared to me that in arguing against Cato you wished to show what for my part I approve, namely, that there is no difference between Zeno and the Peripatetics except novel terminology; and if this is so, what reason is there, if it fits in with Zeno's system for virtue to have great power in securing happy life, why the Peripatetics should not be allowed to say the same? For I think regard should be paid to facts not words. M. You are confronting me with sealed documents, and putting in as evidence what I have sometime said or written.[1] Take that way with other people who are handicapped in argument by rules: I live from day to day; I say anything that strikes my mind as probable;[2] and so I alone am free. All the same, as we spoke a little while back about consistency,[3] I do not consider that the question to be asked at this point is whether the view accepted by Zeno and his pupil Aristo is true, namely, that only what is right is good, but supposing it were true, then how was it that he based the entire possibility of living happily upon virtue alone? Therefore, if you will, let us grant Brutus, that the wise man is always happy: it is his business to consider how far he is consistent. As to the glory of such an opinion, who is more worthy of it than he? Let us nevertheless hold fast our view that the wise man is also supremely happy.

XII. And if Zeno of Citium, a mere foreigner and

---

[2] cf. II. § 9.
[3] §§ 21, 22.

MARCUS TULLIUS CICERO

ignobilis verborum opifex, insinuasse se in antiquam
philosophiam videtur, huius sententiae gravitas a
Platonis auctoritate repetatur, apud quem saepe haec
oratio usurpata est, ut nihil praeter virtutem diceretur
bonum, velut in *Gorgia* Socrates, cum esset ex eo
quaesitum Archelaum, Perdiccae filium qui tum
fortunatissimus haberetur, nonne beatum putaret,
35 "Haud scio" inquit; "numquam enim cum eo collocutus sum." Ain tu? an[1] aliter id scire non potes?
"Nullo modo." Tu igitur ne de Persarum quidem
rege magno potes dicere beatusne sit? "An ego
possim, cum ignorem quam sit doctus, quam vir
bonus?" Quid? tu in eo sitam vitam beatam putas?
"Ita prorsus existimo, bonos beatos, improbos miseros." Miser ergo Archelaus? "Certe, si iniustus."
Videturne omnem hic beatam vitam in una virtute
36 ponere? Quid vero? in Epitaphio quo modo idem?
"Nam cui viro," inquit, "ex se ipso apta sunt omnia,
quae ad beate vivendum ferunt, nec suspensa aliorum
aut bono casu aut contrario pendere ex alterius
eventis et errare coguntur, huic optime vivendi ratio
comparata est. Hic est ille moderatus, hic fortis,
hic sapiens, hic et nascentibus et cadentibus cum
reliquis commodis, tum maxime liberis, parebit et
obediet praecepto illi veteri; neque enim laetabitur
umquam nec maerebit nimis, quod semper in se

---

[1] *Ain tu an* is the common reading. Some editors omit
an as unusual after *Ain tu*?

[1] Plato, *Gorgias* 470 D, E.
[2] King of Macedon at that time.
[3] Plato, *Menexenus*, p. 248.

an obscure coiner of phrases, seems to have wormed
his way into ancient philosophy, let the full weight
of this opinion be obtained afresh from the authority
of Plato, in whose pages we often find the expression
used that nothing should be called good except
virtue. For instance in the *Gorgias*,[1] Socrates,
when he was asked whether he regarded Archelaus,[2]
Perdiccas' son, then held to be the favourite of
fortune, as happy—" I am not quite sure," said he,
" for I have never conversed with him."—" What do
you say? Can you not know this any other way?"
" By no means."—" Do you mean then you cannot say of the great King of Persia either whether
he is happy?" " How can I when I do not know
how he stands in point of education, in point of
goodness?"—" What? do you think happy life
depends on that?" " It is my conviction absolutely
that the good are happy, the wicked wretched."
" Archelaus is therefore wretched?" " Certainly if
he is unrighteous." Don't you think Socrates makes
all happy life rest upon virtue alone? Again!
How does he speak also in the Funeral Oration?[3]
" For the man," he says, " in whom all that con-
tributes to leading a happy life rests upon himself
alone, who is not forced to dangle at the mercy of
other men's good fortune or its reverse, in wavering
dependence upon his neighbour's success, *he* has
secured the means of leading the best life. This is
the man of self-restraint, this the courageous, this
the wise, this the man who, when all other blessings
and, above all, children are both born and die, will
obediently submit to that ancient precept; for
never will he give way to transports of either joy or
grief, because he will always base every hope he

ipso omnem spem reponet sui." [1] Ex hoc igitur
Platonis quasi quodam sancto augustoque fonte
nostra omnis manabit oratio.

37   XIII. Unde igitur ordiri rectius possumus quam
a communi parente natura ? quae, quidquid genuit,
non modo animal, sed etiam quod ita ortum esset e
terra, ut stirpibus suis niteretur, in suo quidque
genere perfectum esse voluit. Itaque et arbores et
vites et ea, quae sunt humiliora neque se tollere a
terra altius possunt, alia semper virent, alia hieme
nudata, verno tempore tepefacta frondescunt : neque
est ullum, quod non ita vigeat interiore quodam
motu et suis in quoque seminibus inclusis, ut aut
flores aut fruges fundat aut bacas omniaque in omnibus, quantum in ipsis est, nulla vi impediente per-
38 fecta sint. Facilius vero etiam in bestiis, quod iis
sensus a natura est datus, vis ipsius naturae perspici
potest. Namque alias bestias nantes aquarum incolas
esse voluit, alias volucres caelo frui libero, serpentes
quasdam, quasdam esse gradientes : earum ipsarum
partim solivagas, partim congregatas, immanes alias,
quasdam autem cicures, non nullas abditas terraque
tectas. Atque earum quaeque suum tenens munus,
cum in disparis animantis vitam transire non possit,
manet in lege naturae. Et ut bestiis aliud alii prae-

---

[1] *Neque enim* to *reponet sui* are printed in some editions as
two lines of poetry, but Cicero is translating Plato's prose,
οὔτε γὰρ χαίρων οὔτε λυπούμενος ἄγαν φανήσεται διὰ τὸ αὑτῷ
πεποιθέναι.

forms upon himself alone." From this doctrine then of Plato, as from a fountain holy and revered, all my discourse will flow.

XIII. What surer starting point can we have than nature our common parent? All that she has given birth to, not merely living creatures but also what springs from the earth and has to support itself on its roots, she has willed to be perfect each after its kind. And so both trees and vines and plants that run along the ground and cannot lift themselves higher from the earth are some of them evergreen, others are stripped bare by winter and in the warmth of the springtime put forth leaves; nor is there any plant which fails, by the energy of a sort of inner movement and the power of the seeds enclosed in each of them, to put out in profusion either flowers or fruit or berries, while all of them are perfect in all things to the limit of their natures, if no outside force prevents. But it is in animals that the force of nature pure and simple can be still more easily discerned, because nature has granted them sensation: for some creatures that have the power of swimming she has willed to have their home in the waters; others, the fowls of heaven, to have the freedom of the open sky; certain of them to be creeping things; certain of them to walk: of these self-same creatures part she has made to wander alone, part to herd together, others to be savage, a certain number on the other hand to be tame, some to be hidden in the shelter of the earth. Moreover each kind holding fast to its own instinct, seeing that it cannot pass into the manner of living of a creature unlike itself, abides by the law of nature. And as with all creatures nature has given to one,

MARCUS TULLIUS CICERO

cipui a natura datum est, quod suum quaeque retinet
nec discedit ab eo, sic homini multo quiddam praestantius, etsi praestantia debent ea dici, quae habent
aliquam comparationem, humanus autem animus
decerptus ex mente divina cum alio nullo nisi cum
ipso deo, si hoc fas est dictu, comparari potest.

39 Hic igitur si est excultus et si eius acies ita curata
est, ut ne caecaretur erroribus, fit perfecta mens, id
est absoluta ratio, quod est idem virtus. Et, si omne
beatum est, cui nihil deest et quod in suo genere
expletum atque cumulatum est, idque virtutis est
proprium, certe omnes virtutis compotes beati sunt.
Et hoc quidem mihi cum Bruto convenit, id est, cum
Aristotele, Xenocrate, Speusippo, Polemone.

40 Sed mihi videntur etiam beatissimi : quid enim
deest ad beate vivendum ei, qui confidit suis bonis ?
aut qui diffidit beatus esse qui potest ? At diffidat
necesse est qui bona dividit tripertito. XIV. Qui
enim poterit aut corporis firmitate aut fortunae
stabilitate confidere ? Atqui nisi stabili et fixo et
permanente bono beatus esse nemo potest. Quid
ergo eius modi istorum est ? ut mihi Laconis illud
dictum in hos cadere videatur, qui glorianti cuidam
mercatori, quod multas naves in omnem oram mari-
timam dimisisset : *Non sane optabilis quidem ista,*

---

[1] According to the Stoics τὰς ψυχὰς συναφεῖς τῷ θεῷ ἅτε
αὐτοῦ μόρια εἶναι καὶ ἀποσπάσματα. Epictet. 1. 14. 6. So in
Plato, *Philebus* 30, Socrates says, "whence comes the soul,
unless the body of the universe, which contains elements
similar to our bodies but fairer, had also a soul?" and Virg.
Aen. VI. 730. *Igneus est ollis vigor et caelestis origo/seminibus.*

[2] *Animi medicina philosophia*, III. § 5.

[3] The Peripatetics admitted that happiness could not
depend upon goods of fortune and body which are uncertain.

[4] cf. § 30.

464

one distinguishing feature, to another another which each of them preserves as its own and does not depart from, so to man she has given something far more pre-eminent—although the term " pre-eminent" ought to be applied to things which admit of some comparison ; but the soul of man, derived as it is from the divine mind,[1] can be compared with nothing else, if it is right to say so, save God alone.   Therefore if this soul has been so trained, if its power of vision has been so cared for [2] that it is not blinded by error, the result is mind made perfect, that is, complete reason, and this means also virtue.   And if everything is happy which has nothing wanting, and whose measure in its own kind is heaped up and running over, and if this is the peculiar mark of virtue, assuredly all virtuous men are happy.[3]   And so far I am in agreement with Brutus, that is to say with Aristotle, Xenocrates, Speusippus, Polemo.[4]

But to me virtuous men seem also supremely happy : for what is wanting to make life happy for the man who feels assured of the good that is his ? Or how can the man who is without assurance be happy ?   But the man who makes a three-fold division of good must necessarily be without assurance.   XIV. For how will he be able to feel assured of either strength of body or security of fortune ?   And yet no one can be happy except when good is secure and certain and lasting.   What is so then in the goods of such thinkers ?   I am led to think that to them applies the saying of the Laconian who, when a certain trader boasted of the number of ships he had despatched to every distant coast, remarked : " The fortune that depends on

inquit, *rudentibus apta fortuna.* An dubium est quin
nihil sit habendum in eo genere, quo vita beata
compleatur;[1] si id possit amitti? Nihil enim
interarescere, nihil exstingui, nihil cadere debet
eorum, in quibus vita beata consistit. Nam qui
timebit ne quid ex his deperdat beatus esse non
41 poterit. Volumus enim eum, qui beatus sit, tutum
esse, inexpugnabilem, saeptum atque munitum, non
ut parvo metu praeditus sit, sed ut nullo. Ut enim
innocens is dicitur, non qui leviter nocet, sed qui
nihil nocet, sic sine metu is habendus est, non qui
pauca[2] metuit, sed qui omnino metu vacat. Quae
est enim alia fortitudo nisi animi adfectio cum in
adeundo periculo et in labore ac dolore patiens tum
42 procul ab omni metu? Atque haec certe non ita se
haberent, nisi omne bonum in una honestate consisteret. Qui autem illam maxime optatam et
expetitam securitatem—securitatem autem nunc
appello vacuitatem aegritudinis, in qua vita beata
posita est—habere quisquam potest, cui aut adsit
aut adesse possit multitudo malorum? Qui autem
poterit esse celsus et erectus et ea, quae homini
accidere possunt, omnia parva ducens, qualem sapientem esse volumus, nisi omnia sibi in se posita
censebit? An Lacedaemonii, Philippo minitante[3]
per litteras se omnia, quae conarentur, prohibiturum,

---

[1] *complectitur* MSS. : *compleatur* Wopkens : *completur* Bentley.

[2] Most MSS. have *parva* which Madvig approves. *Pauca, parum* or *parvo metu est* are conjectures.

[3] The MSS. have *minitanti*, which would be ungrammatical with *quaesiverunt.*

cordage is not quite one to be desired."[1] Or is there any question that nothing that can escape our grasp ought to be reckoned as one in kind with that which makes the fulness of happy life? For nothing of all that goes to make a happy life should shrivel up, nothing be blotted out, nothing fall to the ground. For the man who shall be afraid of the loss of any of such things cannot be happy. For our wish is that the happy man be safe, impregnable, fenced and fortified, and so made inaccessible not only to a little fear, but to any fear at all. For just as the word innocent is applied, not to the man who is guilty of a slight offence, but to the man who is guilty of none; so we must reckon as fearless, not the man who has few fears, but the man who is free from any fear at all. For what is fortitude except a disposition of the soul capable of endurance in facing danger and in toil and pain, as well as keeping all fear at a distance? And these qualities would assuredly not be found unless all good reposed on rectitude and that alone. How, moreover, can anyone, about whom come or can come a throng of evils, enjoy that object of supreme desire and aspiration—security (and security is the term I apply to the absence of distress upon which happy life depends)? How besides can he hold his head erect, in disdain of all the vicissitudes of man's lot, in the spirit we wish the wise man to show, unless he shall think that for him all things depend upon himself? Did the Lacedaemonians in answer to Philip's[2] threat, when he wrote that he would prevent all their efforts, ask

---

[1] οὐ προσέχω εὐδαιμονίᾳ ἐκ σχοινίων ἀπηρτημένῃ. Plutarch, *Apothegm. Lacon.*

[2] Philip of Macedon, father of Alexander the Great.

quaesiverunt num se esset etiam mori prohibiturus :
vir is, quem quaerimus, non multo facilius tali
animo reperietur quam civitas universa ?   Quid ? ad
hanc fortitudinem, de qua loquimur, temperantia
adiuncta, quae sit moderatrix omnium commotionum,
quid potest ad beate vivendum deesse ei, quem
fortitudo ab aegritudine et a metu vindicet, temperantia cum a libidine avocet tum insolenti alacritate gestire non sinat ?   Haec efficere virtutem
ostenderem, nisi superioribus diebus essent explicata.

43   XV. Atque cum perturbationes animi miseriam,
sedationes autem vitam efficiant beatam, duplexque
ratio perturbationis sit, quod aegritudo et metus in
malis opinatis, in bonorum autem errore laetitia
gestiens libidoque versetur, quae omnia [1] cum consilio
et ratione pugnant, his tu tam gravibus concitationi-
bus tamque ipsis inter se dissentientibus atque dis-
tractis quem vacuum, solutum, liberum videris, hunc
dubitabis beatum dicere ?   Atqui sapiens semper ita
adfectus est : semper igitur sapiens beatus est.   Atque etiam omne bonum laetabile est ; quod autem
laetabile, id praedicandum et prae se ferendum ;
quod tale autem, id etiam gloriosum ; si vero gloriosum, certe laudabile ; quod laudabile autem, profecto etiam honestum : quod bonum igitur, id
44 honestum.   At quae isti bona numerant ne ipsi
quidem honesta dicunt : solum igitur bonum quod

---

[1] Bentley's conjecture for the *quom haec . . . pugnent* of
the MSS.

---

[1] An instance of the *Sorites* or chain-argument, a train of
reasoning in a compressed form much used by Chrysippus.
The conclusion predicates the last predicate *right* of the first
subject *good*, cf. III. § 15.

him whether he also intended to "prevent" them
from dying : and shall not the true man of whom we
are in quest be more readily found with such a spirit
than a whole community? Again, when to this
fortitude of which we are speaking there is linked
temperance to have control of all the emotions, what
element of happy life can fail the man whom
fortitude can deliver from distress and fear, while
temperance can both call him away from lust and
forbid him to give way to transports of immoderate
eagerness? That this is virtue's work I should show,
had not the previous day's discussions made it fully
plain.

XV. Further, since disturbances of the soul
produce wretchedness, while tranquillity produces
happy life ; and as the course of disturbance is twofold, because distress and fear rest on evils that are
expected, whilst extravagant joy and lust rest on a
mistaken notion of what is good, and all these things
conflict with deliberation and reason—will you
hesitate to give the name of happy to the man whom
you find undisturbed by, liberated and free from
agitations so oppressive and so mutually discordant
and estranged from one another? And yet this is
always the condition of the wise man : the wise man
therefore is always happy. Furthermore too every
good thing is joyful ; now what is joyful deserves
credit and esteem ; moreover what can be so
described is also glorious ; now if glorious it is
assuredly praiseworthy ; moreover what is praiseworthy is surely also right ; what is good therefore
is right.[1] But what our opponents count as good
things they do not even themselves pronounce right ;
therefore the only good is what is right : and from

honestum; ex quo efficitur honestate una vitam
contineri beatam. Non sunt igitur ea bona dicenda
nec habenda, quibus abundantem licet esse miserri-
45 mum. An dubitas quin praestans valetudine, viribus,
forma, acerrimis integerrimisque sensibus, adde
etiam, si libet, pernicitatem et velocitatem, da
divitias, honores, imperia, opes, gloriam : si fuerit is,
qui haec habet, iniustus, intemperans, timidus,
hebeti ingenio atque nullo, dubitabisne eum miserum
dicere? Qualia igitur ista bona sunt, quae qui
habeat miserrimus esse possit? Videamus ne, ut
acervus ex sui generis granis, sic beata vita ex sui
similibus partibus effici debeat. Quod si ita est, ex
bonis, quae sola honesta sunt, efficiendum est
beatum : ea mixta ex dissimilibus si erunt, honestum
ex iis effici nihil poterit, quo detracto quid poterit
beatum intelligi? Etenim quidquid est quod bonum
sit, id expetendum est; quod autem expetendum,
id certe approbandum; quod vero approbaris, id
gratum acceptumque habendum : ergo etiam dignitas
ei tribuenda est. Quod si ita est, laudabile sit
necesse est : bonum igitur omne laudabile; ex
quo efficitur ut, quod sit honestum, id sit solum
bonum.
46   XVI. Quod ni ita tenebimus, multa erunt quae
nobis bona dicenda sint : omitto divitias, quas cum
quivis quamvis indignus habere possit, in bonis non

---

[1] *e.g.* wheat, barley, oats.
[2] Chain-argument again as in § 43.

this it follows that happy life is bound up with rectitude alone. Those things therefore the abundant
possession of which does not prevent extreme
wretchedness cannot be named or considered good.
Have you any doubt that excellent health, strength,
beauty, senses keen and vigorous in the extreme;
add if you like too suppleness and quickness of
movement; bestow wealth, distinctions, commands,
resources, glory;—if the man who possesses these
things is unjust, intemperate, fearful, with an
intelligence sluggish or even non-existent, will you
hesitate to pronounce him wretched? In what sense
then are those things good in the possession of
which a man can be utterly wretched? Let us be
careful lest it be not true that just as a heap of
anything[1] is made up of grains of its own kind, so
happy life is bound to be made up of parts that are
like itself. And if this is so we must conclude that
happiness is made up of good things which are right
and nothing else; if it is a blend of things which
are unlike, nothing right can be the result: take
that away and what happiness can be understood to
remain? For all that is of the nature of good is
desirable; moreover what is desirable is certainly to
be approved; but what one has approved must be
regarded as welcome and agreeable: therefore also
it must be held worthy of distinction. And if this is
so it must of necessity be praiseworthy. And from
this it follows that what is right is the only good.[2]

XVI. And unless we desire to hold fast this
conclusion there are a number of things we shall
feel bound to pronounce good; I pass over riches
which I do not include in the category of good, as
anyone however unworthy can possess them; for it

numero; quod enim est bonum, id non quivis habere
potest: omitto nobilitatem famamque popularem
stultorum improborumque consensu excitatam: haec,
quae sunt minima, tamen bona dicantur necesse est,
candiduli dentes, venusti oculi, color suavis, et ea,
quae Anticlea laudat Ulixi pedes abluens,

> *Lenitudo orationis, mollitudo corporis,*

ea si bona ducemus, quid erit in philosophi gravitate
quam in vulgi opinione stultorumque turba quod
47 dicatur aut gravius aut grandius?   At enim eadem
Stoici *praecipua* vel *producta* dicunt quae bona isti!
Dicunt illi quidem, sed iis vitam beatam compleri
negant: hi autem sine iis esse nullam putant aut, si
sit beata, beatissimam certe negant. Nos autem
volumus beatissimam, idque nobis Socratica illa
conclusione confirmatur: sic enim princeps ille
philosophiae disserebat, qualis cuiusque animi adfectus esset, talem esse hominem, qualis autem
homo ipse esset, talem eius esse orationem; orationi
autem facta similia, factis vitam; adfectus autem
animi in bono viro laudabilis, et vita igitur laudabilis boni viri et honesta ergo, quoniam laudabilis: ex quibus bonorum beatam vitam esse con-
48 cluditur.   Etenim proh deorum atque hominum

---

[1] Anticlea was the mother of Ulysses. His nurse was
Euryclea. The verse comes from the *Niptra* of Pacuvius,
quoted in II. § 49, cf. App. II.

[2] cf. II. § 29, IV. § 28. To certain things classed as
ἀδιάφορα, *i.e.* neither good nor bad, the Stoics gave the name
προηγμένα, *e.g.* health, strength, etc.

is not anyone you will who can possess what is good :
I pass over good birth and public reputation where
it is called into being by the united voice of fools
and knaves : but take such insignificant things—we
have to *call* them good—as white teeth, fine eyes,
fresh colour and the things that Anticlea[1] praises in
washing the feet of Ulysses,

"Speech of gentle modulation, body that is soft
to touch,"

if we are to reckon such things as good, what shall
we find to describe as more serious and elevated in
the seriousness of the philosopher than in the belief
of the common herd and ruck of fools ? " But stay !
for the Stoics give the name of advantages or pre-
ferences[2] to the same things that the Peripatetics
name good." It is true they do, but they do not
say that happy life is thereby fulfilled ; the
Peripatetics on the contrary think that without
these things no life can be happy, or supposing it be
happy, it certainly cannot be supremely happy.
Now we wish it to be supremely happy and our view
is confirmed by Socrates' well-known conclusion.
For this was the way in which that leader of
philosophy argued, that as was the disposition of
each individual soul so was the man ; and as was
the man in himself so was his speech ; moreover
deeds resembled speech and life resembled deeds.
Further the disposition of the soul in a good man is
praiseworthy, and therefore the life of a good man is
praiseworthy, and for that reason right, seeing that it
is praiseworthy. And from these arguments the
conclusion comes that the life of good men is happy.
And rightly so, for—in the name of gods and men !—

fidem! parumne cognitum est superioribus nostris
disputationibus an delectationis et otii consumendi
causa locuti sumus, sapientem ab omni concitatione
animi, quam perturbationem voco, semper vacare,
semper in animo eius esse placidissimam pacem?
Vir igitur temperatus, constans, sine metu, sine
aegritudine, sine alacritate ulla, sine libidine, nonne
beatus? At semper sapiens talis: semper igitur
beatus. Iam vero qui potest vir bonus non ad id,
quod laudabile sit, omnia referre, quae agit quaeque
sentit? Refert autem omnia ad beate vivendum;
beata igitur vita laudabilis; nec quidquam sine
virtute laudabile: beata igitur vita virtute conficitur.

49   XVII. Atque hoc sic etiam concluditur: nec in
misera vita quidquam est praedicabile aut gloriandum nec in ea, quae nec misera sit nec beata; et
est in aliqua vita praedicabile aliquid et gloriandum
ac prae se ferendum, ut Epaminondas:

   Consiliis nostris laus est attonsa Laconum,

ut Africanus:

   A sole exoriente supra Maeotis paludes
   Nemo est qui factis aequiperare queat.

50 Quod si est,[1] beata vita glorianda et praedicanda et

───────────────────
   [1] *est* is not in the MSS.

───────────────────

   [1] The Stoics said—τέλος εἶναι τὸ εὐδαιμονεῖν, οὗ ἕνεκα πάντα
πράττεται, αὐτὸ δὲ πράττεται μὲν οὐδενὸς δὲ ἕνεκα· τοῦτο δὲ
ὑπάρχειν ἐν τῷ κατ' ἀρετὴν ζῆν.   Stob., *Ecl. Eth.* p. 138.
   [2] ἡμετέραις βουλαῖς Σπάρτη μὲν ἐκείρατο δόξαν, was the first of
the lines engraved on the statue of Epaminondas at Thebes,
Pausanias IX. 15.
   [3] From the epitaph of Ennius over the great Scipio
Africanus, cf. App. II.

has not sufficient been learnt from our previous discussions; or is it for the sake of amusement and passing the time that we have said that the wise man is always free from all agitation of soul to which I give the name of disturbance? that in his soul there reigns the most tranquil calm? The man then who is temperate, steadfast, without fear, without distress, without any eagerness, without lust, is he not happy? But such is the character of the wise man always: therefore the wise man is always happy. Again, how can the good man fail to refer all his acts and feelings to the standard he holds to be praiseworthy? But he refers everything to the standard of living happily;[1] therefore happy life is praiseworthy; and without virtue nothing is praiseworthy; happy life therefore is consummated by virtue.

XVII. And this conclusion is proved again in the following way: neither in a wretched life nor in such a life as is neither wretched nor happy is there anything commendable or worthy of glory; and yet in the lives of some men there is something commendable, illustrious and exemplary, as in the life of Epaminondas:

Shorn by the counsels I gave was the Lacedaemonian glory,[2]

and of Africanus:

West of the dawn where the sun rises over the marsh of Maeotis,
  No one to match my deeds is there on earth to be found.[3]

So then, if happy life is a reality, it is worthy of

475

prae se ferenda est; nihil est enim aliud quod praedicandum et prae se ferendum sit. Quibus positis
intelligis quid sequatur, et quidem, nisi ea vita beata
est, quae est eadem honesta, sit aliud necesse est
melius vita beata. Quod erit enim honestum, certe
fatebuntur esse melius; ita erit beata vita melius
aliquid, quo quid potest dici perversius? Quid?
cum fatentur satis magnam vim esse in vitiis ad
miseram vitam, nonne fatendum est eandem vim in
virtute [1] esse ad beatam vitam? Contrariorum enim
51 contraria sunt consequentia. Quo loco quaero quam
vim habeat libra illa Critolai, qui cum in alteram
lancem animi bona imponat, in alteram corporis et
externa, tantum propendere illam [2] putet, ut terram
et maria deprimat.

XVIII. Quid ergo aut hunc prohibet aut etiam
Xenocratem illum gravissimum philosophorum, ex-
aggerantem tanto opere virtutem, extenuantem
cetera et abiicientem, in virtute non beatam modo
vitam, sed etiam beatissimam ponere? quod quidem
52 nisi fit, virtutum interitus consequetur. Nam in
quem cadit aegritudo, in eundem metum cadere
necesse est; est enim metus futurae aegritudinis
sollicita exspectatio: in quem autem metus, in
eundem formido, timiditas, pavor, ignavia: ergo ut

---

[1] *vim virtutum* in some MSS.
[2] The MSS. have *illam boni lancem*, but *boni* is quite
unsuitable when there are *bona* in each of the scales: *illam*
by itself is clear.

---

[1] cf. IV. § 5. [2] cf. I. § 20.
[3] cf. IV. § 19.

glory and commendable and exemplary; for there
is nothing else to be commendable and exemplary.
And when this is established you realize what is the
conclusion, and in any case, unless the life which is
at the same time right is happy, there must of
necessity be something else better than happy life.
For surely they will admit that what is found to be
right is better: consequently there will be something
better than happy life, and can any statement more
wrong-headed than this be made? Tell me! when
they admit that vice has sufficient power to make
life wretched, must they not admit that virtue has
the same power to make life happy? For from
things that are opposed consequences that are opposites follow logically. And at this point I ask for
the meaning of the famous balance of Critolaus,[1]
who claims that if in one scale he puts the good that
belongs to the soul, and in the other the good that
belongs to the body and good things which come
from outside the man, the first scale sinks so far as
to outweigh the second with land and seas thrown
in as well.

XVIII. What then prevents either this thinker or
the famous Xenocrates [2] as well, that most influential
of philosophers, who exalts virtue so earnestly and
depreciates and rejects everything else, from making
not merely happy life depend upon virtue but
supremely happy life as well? And, in fact, if this is
not done, the annihilation of the virtues will be the
consequence. For the man who is susceptible of
distress must necessarily be also susceptible of fear;
for fear is the anxious anticipation of coming distress;
moreover the man who is susceptible of fear is also
susceptible of fright, timidity, terror, cowardice;[3]

idem vincatur interdum nec putet ad se praeceptum
illud Atrei pertinere:

Proinde ita parent se in vita, ut vinci nesciant.

Hic autem vincetur, ut dixi, nec modo vincetur, sed
etiam serviet: at nos virtutem semper liberam
volumus, semper invictam; quae nisi sunt, sublata
53 virtus est. Atque[1] si in virtute satis est praesidii
ad bene vivendum, satis est etiam ad beate. Satis
est enim certe in virtute, ut fortiter vivamus; si
fortiter, etiam ut magno animo, et quidem ut nulla
re umquam terreamur semperque simus invicti.
Sequitur ut nihil poeniteat, nihil desit, nihil obstet:
ergo omnia profluenter, absolute, prospere, igitur
beate. Satis autem virtus ad fortiter vivendum
54 potest: satis ergo etiam ad beate. Etenim ut
stultitia, etsi adepta est quod concupivit, numquam
se tamen satis consecutam putat, sic sapientia semper
eo contenta est, quod adest, neque eam umquam sui
poenitet.

XIX. Similemne putas C. Laelii unum consulatum
fuisse et eum quidem cum repulsa—si, cum sapiens
et bonus vir, qualis ille fuit, suffragiis praeteritur,
non populus a bono consule potius, quam ille a
populo[2] repulsam fert—sed tamen utrum malles te,

---

[1] The MSS. have *atqui*. But *atque* (Bentley) is needed to
introduce a new proof.
[2] The MSS. have *bono populo*. Thanks to Madvig *bono*
goes out. *Vano* and *malo* have been suggested in its place.

---

[1] The "wise man" of the Stoics never repented, was never
mistaken, never changed his mind. cf. § 81.
[2] C. Laelius Sapiens, the friend of Scipio Africanus Minor,
was defeated by Q. Pompeius for the consulship of 141 B.C.

he must expect then sometimes to be defeated, and cannot think that the well-known maxim of Atreus is made for him :

In life let men learn not to know defeat.

But the man we speak of will, as I have said, be defeated, and not only will he be defeated but be a slave as well : it is our wish on the other hand for virtue to be always free, always undefeated : otherwise virtue is done away with. Again, if virtue gives sufficient aid for leading a good life, it also gives sufficient for a happy one. For surely virtue gives sufficient to make us live bravely ; if bravely, sufficient too to make us high-souled and in fact never appalled by any event and always undefeated. It follows that there is no repentance, no deficiency, no obstacle :[1] there is then always abundance, perfection, prosperity, therefore happiness. But virtue can give sufficient help for living bravely ; sufficient therefore also for living happily. For just as folly, although it has secured its coveted object, yet never thinks it has obtained enough ; so wisdom is always contented with its present lot and is never self-repentant.

XIX. Do you think there has been a resemblance between the one consulship of C. Laelius,[2] and that only granted after the populace had first rejected him (if, when a wise and good man, as he was, is passed over at the election, it is not the populace that is rejected by the good consul rather than he by the populace),[3]—but all the same I ask you whether,

[3] Famous Romans like Aemilius Paullus and Porcius Cato were rejected candidates.

si potestas esset, semel ut Laelium consulem an ut
55 Cinnam quater? Non dubito tu quid responsurus
sis, itaque video cui committam. Non quemvis hoc
idem interrogarem; responderet enim alius fortasse
se non modo quattuor consulatus uni anteponere,
sed unum diem Cinnae multorum et clarorum
virorum totis aetatibus. Laelius, si digito quem
attigisset, poenas dedisset: at Cinna collegae sui,
consulis Cn. Octavii, praecidi caput iussit, P. Crassi,
L. Caesaris, nobilissimorum hominum, quorum virtus
fuerat domi militiaeque cognita, M. Antonii, omnium
eloquentissimi, quos ego audierim, C. Caesaris, in quo
mihi videtur specimen fuisse humanitatis, salis,
suavitatis, leporis. Beatusne igitur qui hos inter-
fecit? Mihi contra non solum eo videtur miser,
quod ea fecit, sed etiam quod ita se gessit, ut ea
facere ei liceret: etsi peccare nemini licet, sed
sermonis errore labimur; id enim licere dicimus,
56 quod cuique conceditur. Utrum tandem beatior
C. Marius tum, cum Cimbricae victoriae gloriam cum
collega Catulo communicavit, paene altero Laelio—
nam hunc illi duco simillimum—, an cum civili bello
victor iratus necessariis Catuli deprecantibus non

---

¹ L. Cornelius Cinna was the leader of the Cinnan revolution of 87 B.C.
² He is again thinking of Julius Caesar who constantly
quoted the lines of Euripides,

εἴπερ γὰρ ἀδικεῖν χρή, τυραννίδος πέρι
κάλλιστον ἀδικεῖν, τἄλλα δ' εὐσεβεῖν χρεών. *Phoen.* 525.

Caesar's first wife was daughter of Cinna.
³ All these perished in Marius' reign of terror in
87 B.C.
⁴ Cinna had the right of might but no moral right to act
as he did in his revolution.

given the choice, you would prefer to be once consul like Laelius or four times like Cinna.[1] I have no doubt what *you* will answer; and so I am sure to whom I confide my question. I should not put this same question to all the world; for another might perhaps answer that not only did he put four consulships before one, but a single day of Cinna's rule before the whole lifetime of many illustrious men.[2] Laelius, if he had laid a finger on anyone, would have given him satisfaction : but Cinna gave orders for the beheading of his colleague, the consul Cn. Octavius, of P. Crassus, of L. Caesar,[3] men of the highest nobility whose great qualities had been proved in peace and war, of M. Antonius the most eloquent of all the speakers I have myself heard, of C. Caesar who represented, I think, the ideal of courtesy, wit, grace and charm. Is then the man who slew them happy? To my mind on the contrary he appears wretched not only because of what he did, but also because he so acted as to make his doing it allowable?[4] and yet it is allowable for no one to do wrong, but a mistaken usage of speech misleads us; for we say that everyone is "allowed" to do what is put into his power.[5] Was C. Marius,[6] pray, happier on the day that he shared the glory of the victory over the Cimbri with his colleague Catulus, almost a second Laelius (for I think he bore a close resemblance to him), or when, in the wrath his victory in the civil war inspired, he replied to the appeal of the friends of Catulus, not once only but

[5] cf. 1 *Cor.* 6. 12. "All things are lawful for me, but I will not be brought under the power of any."

[6] C. Marius who with Q. Lutatius Catulus destroyed the Cimbri in the Raudine Plain, 101 B.C., was six times consul and died in 86 B.C., the year of his seventh consulship.

semel respondit, sed saepe : *" Moriatur "* ? In quo
beatior ille, qui huic nefariae voci paruit, quam is,
qui tam scelerate imperavit. Nam cum accipere
quam facere praestat iniuriam, tum morti iam ipsi
adventanti paullum procedere ob viam, quod fecit
Catulus, quam quod Marius, talis viri interitu sex
suos obruere consulatus et contaminare extremum
tempus aetatis.

57 XX. Duo de quadraginta annos tyrannus Syra-
cusanorum fuit Dionysius, cum quinque et viginti
natus annos dominatum occupavisset. Qua pulcri-
tudine urbem, quibus autem opibus praeditam servitute oppressam tenuit civitatem ! Atqui de hoc
homine a bonis auctoribus sic scriptum accepimus,
summam fuisse eius in victu temperantiam, in rebusque gerundis virum acrem et industrium, eundem
tamen maleficum natura et iniustum : ex quo omnibus
bene veritatem intuentibus videri necesse est miserrimum. Ea enim ipsa, quae concupierat, ne tum
quidem, cum omnia se posse censebat, conseque-
58 batur. Qui cum esset bonis parentibus atque honesto
loco natus, etsi id quidem alius alio modo tradidit,
abundaretque aequalium familiaritatibus et consuetudine propinquorum, haberet etiam more Graeciae
quosdam adolescentes amore coniunctos, credebat
eorum nemini, sed iis, quos ex familiis locupletium
servos delegerat, quibus nomen servitutis ipse de-

---

[1] cf. the Socratic κάκιον εἶναι τὸ ἀδικεῖν τοῦ ἀδικεῖσθαι.

[2] Catulus killed himself. Cicero is thinking too of the
suicide of M. Porcius Cato Uticensis after the battle of
Thapsus, 46 B.C.

[3] Dionysius the elder, tyrant of Syracuse from 405–367 B.C.

[4] *e.g.* that he was son of an ass-driver or a clerk.

repeatedly, " Let him die"? And in this act that
man who obeyed the impious words was happier
than he who gave so criminal a command. For
it is at once better to submit to outrage than
commit it,[1] and to advance a little way to meet the
actual approach of death now close at hand, as
Catulus did,[2] than like Marius by the murder of such
a man to eclipse the fame of his six consulships and
pollute the last period of his life.

XX. For thirty-eight years, after securing despotic
control at the age of twenty-five, Dionysius [3] was
tyrant of Syracuse. How beautiful the city, how
richly provided with resources the State which he
kept under the crushing weight of slavery! And yet
we are told on the authority of trustworthy writers
that while this man was exceedingly temperate in
his way of life and showed untiring energy in the
conduct of affairs, he was yet unscrupulous by nature
and unjust: and this means that in the eyes of all
who have a clear insight into the truth he was
necessarily supremely wretched. For he failed to
secure the very objects of his covetous desires, even
at the moment he thought that he could do all he
wished. Although he came of good parentage and
was born in a respectable position (though as to this
different authorities have given different accounts [4])
and although he had many friendly relations with
contemporaries and enjoyed the intimacy of kins-
folk, and certain youths too were attached to him
in the loverlike fashion recognized in Greece, he
trusted none of them, but committed the care of
his person to slaves whom he had selected from the
households of wealthy men and whom he personally
had relieved of the name that marked their servile

traxerat, et quibusdam convenis et feris barbaris
corporis custodiam committebat; ita propter iniustam
dominatus cupiditatem in carcerem quodam modo
ipse se incluserat. Quin etiam, ne tonsori collum
committeret, tondere filias suas docuit: ita sordido
atque ancillari artificio regiae virgines ut tonstriculae
tondebant barbam et capillum patris; et tamen ab
his ipsis, cum iam essent adultae, ferrum removit
instituitque ut candentibus iuglandium putaminibus
59 barbam sibi et capillum adurerent. Cumque duas
uxores haberet, Aristomachen, civem suam, Doridem
autem Locrensem, sic noctu ad eas ventitabat, ut
omnia specularetur et perscrutaretur ante; et cum
fossam latam cubiculari lecto circumdedisset eiusque fossae transitum ponticulo ligneo coniunxisset,
eum ipse,[1] cum forem cubiculi clauserat, detorquebat.
Idemque cum in communibus suggestis consistere
60 non auderet, contionari ex turri alta solebat. Atque
is cum pila ludere vellet—studiose enim id factitabat
—tunicamque poneret, adolescentulo, quem amabat,
tradidisse gladium dicitur. Hic cum quidam fami-
liaris iocans dixisset: *Huic quidem certe vitam tuam
committis*, adrisissetque adolescens, utrumque iussit
interfici, alterum, quia viam demonstravisset interi-
mendi sui, alterum, quia dictum id risu approba-

---

[1] *ipsum* in MSS.: *ipse* Scheibe.

---

[1] Ammian. Marcell. XVI. 8. 10 says *Aedemque brevem,
ubi cubitare sueverat, alta circumdedit fossa.*

condition, as well as to certain refugees and un-civilized barbarians. In this way he had of his own choice, in order to gratify his unrighteous longing for despotism, almost shut himself up in prison. Nay too he went so far as to have his daughters taught the use of a razor that he might not put his neck at the mercy of a barber; accordingly the young princesses, reduced to the mean employment of drudges, shaved their father's hair and beard like mere barberettes; and all the same, when they were now older, he took the iron utensil out of the hands of these self-same girls and arranged for them to singe his hair and beard with red-hot walnut shells. He had two wives, Aristomache of his own city and Doris of Locris, and visiting them by night, took precautions to have a thorough inspection and examination everywhere before he came. And having surrounded the chamber in which he slept with a wide trench and fitted a gangway over the trench by means of a small wooden bridge, we are told that he drew in this self-same bridge himself as often as he closed the door of the chamber.[1] And as too he did not venture to appear upon the public platform for speakers he used to harangue the people from a lofty tower. Again, when once he wanted to play at ball (for he was devoted to this pastime) and laid aside his undergarment, it is said that he handed his sword to a youngster of whom he was fond. When a certain acquaintance jestingly remarked, "Here at any rate is one to whom you certainly entrust your life," and the young man gave a smile, Dionysius had both executed, the one for having, as he held, pointed out the way to assassinate him, and the other for having greeted

visset; atque eo facto sic doluit, nihil ut tulerit
gravius in vita; quem enim vehementer amarat
occiderat. Sic distrahuntur in contrarias partes im-
potentium cupiditates: cum huic obsecutus sis, illi
est repugnandum.

61 Quamquam hic quidem tyrannus ipse iudicavit
quam esset beatus: XXI. nam cum quidam ex eius
adsentatoribus, Damocles, commemoraret in sermone
copias eius, opes, maiestatem dominatus, rerum
abundantiam, magnificentiam aedium regiarum, ne-
garetque umquam beatiorem quemquam fuisse:
Visne igitur, inquit, *o Damocle, quoniam te haec vita
delectat, ipse eam* [1] *degustare et fortunam experiri
meam?* Cum se ille cupere dixisset, collocari iussit
hominem in aureo lecto strato pulcherrimo textili
stragulo, magnificis operibus picto, abacosque complures ornavit argento auroque caelato; tum ad
mensam eximia forma pueros delectos iussit consistere eosque nutum illius intuentes diligenter
62 ministrare. Aderant unguenta, coronae; incende-
bantur odores; mensae conquisitissimis epulis ex-
struebantur: fortunatus sibi Damocles videbatur.
In hoc medio apparatu fulgentem gladium e lacunari
saeta equina aptum demitti iussit, ut impenderet
illius beati cervicibus. Itaque nec pulcros illos
ministratores aspiciebat nec plenum artis argentum
nec manum porrigebat in mensam; iam ipsae de-

---

[1] *eandem, eadem* in MSS.

the remark with a smile; and the grief he felt for this act occasioned him greater distress than anything else in his life; for he had put to death the being he fondly loved. So true is it that the passions of ungovernable men are in continual conflict: satisfy one and you have to resist another.

And yet this tyrant out of his own mouth passed judgment on the reality of his happiness. XXI. For when one of his flatterers, named Damocles, dilated in conversation upon his troops, his resources, the splendours of his despotism, the magnitude of his treasures, the stateliness of his palaces, and said that no one had ever been happier: "Would you then, Damocles," said he, "as this life of mine seems to you so delightful, like to have a taste of it yourself and make trial of my good fortune?" On his admitting his desire to do so Dionysius had him seated on a couch of gold covered with beautiful woven tapestries embroidered with magnificent designs, and had several sideboards set out with richly chased gold and silver plate. Next a table was brought and chosen boys of rare beauty were ordered to take their places and wait upon him with eyes fixed attentively upon his motions. There were perfumes, garlands; incense was burnt; the tables were loaded with the choicest banquet: Damocles thought himself a lucky man. In the midst of all this display Dionysius had a gleaming sword, attached to a horse-hair, let down from the ceiling in such a way that it hung over the neck of this happy man. And so he had no eye either for those beautiful attendants, or the richly-wrought plate, nor did he reach out his hand to the table; presently the garlands slipped from their place of their own

fluebant coronae; denique exoravit tyrannum, ut
abire liceret, quod iam beatus nollet esse. Satisne
videtur declarasse Dionysius nihil esse ei beatum,
cui semper aliqui terror impendeat? Atque ei ne
integrum quidem erat, ut ad iustitiam remigraret,
civibus libertatem et iura redderet; iis enim se
adolescens improvida aetate irretierat erratis eaque
commiserat, ut salvus esse non posset, si sanus esse
coepisset.

63 XXII. Quanto opere vero amicitias desideraret,
quarum infidelitatem extimescebat, declaravit in
Pythagoriis duobus illis, quorum cum alterum vadem
mortis accepisset, alter, ut vadem suum liberaret,
praesto fuisset ad horam mortis destinatam : *Utinam
ego,* inquit, *tertius vobis amicus ascriberer !* Quam
huic erat miserum carere consuetudine amicorum,
societate victus, sermone omnino familiari, homini
praesertim docto a puero et artibus ingenuis erudito ! Musicorum vero perstudiosum accepimus,
poëtam etiam tragicum—quam bonum, nihil ad rem :
in hoc enim genere nescio quo pacto magis quam
in aliis suum cuique pulcrum est; adhuc neminem
cognovi poëtam (et mihi fuit cum Aquinio amicitia)
qui sibi non optimus videretur ; sic se res habet :
te tua, me delectant mea —, sed, ut ad Dionysium

---

[1] Damon and Phintias. Phintias was condemned to death
for plotting against Dionysius, and Damon became bail for
his friend's appearance at the appointed time.
[2] Aquinius was a bad poet, cf. Catullus XIV. 18.

Caesios, Aquinos,
Suffenum omnia colligam venena.

Aquinius and Aquinus are two forms of the same name.

accord; at length he besought the tyrant to let him go, as by now he was sure he had no wish to be happy. Dionysius seems (does he not?) to have avowed plainly that there was no happiness for the man who was perpetually menaced by some alarm. Moreover it was not even open to him to retrace his steps to the path of justice, to restore to his fellow citizens their freedom and their rights; for with the inconsiderateness of youth he had entangled himself in such errors and been guilty of such acts as made it impossible for him to be safe if he once began to be sane.

XXII. While, however, he had a lively fear of the disloyalty of friends, how deeply he felt the need of them he disclosed in the affair of the two Pythagoreans,[1] one of whom he had accepted as surety for sentence of death, while the other had presented himself at the hour appointed for execution to discharge the surety: "Would," said he, "that I could be enrolled as a third in your friendship!" How wretched it was for him to cut himself off from the intimacy of friendship, from the enjoyment of social life, from any freedom of intercourse at all! particularly in the case of a man who had received instruction from childhood and was trained in the liberal arts. He was in fact we hear an enthusiastic musician, a tragic poet too—how good, matters little; for in this art, more than in others, it somehow happens that everyone finds his own work excellent; so far I have never known the poet (and I have been friends with Aquinius[2]) who did not think himself the best; this is the way with them—"You are charmed with your work, I with mine"—but to come back to Dionysius, he denied himself all the

redeamus, omni cultu et victu humano carebat.
Vivebat cum fugitivis, cum facinerosis, cum barbaris,
neminem, qui aut libertate dignus esset aut vellet
omnino liber esse, sibi amicum arbitrabatur.

64 XXIII. Non ego iam cum huius vita, qua taetrius,
miserius, detestabilius excogitare nihil possum,
Platonis aut Archytae vitam comparabo, doctorum
hominum et plane sapientium : ex eadem urbe
humilem homunculum a pulvere et radio excitabo,
qui multis annis post fuit, Archimedem ; cuius ego
quaestor ignoratum ab Syracusanis, cum esse omnino
negarent, saeptum undique et vestitum vepribus et
dumetis indagavi sepulcrum ; tenebam enim quosdam
senariolos, quos in eius monumento esse inscriptos
acceperam, qui declarabant in summo sepulcro
65 sphaeram esse positam cum cylindro. Ego autem,
cum omnia collustrarem oculis—est enim ad portas
Agragianas [1] magna frequentia sepulcrorum —, animum adverti columellam non multum e dumis
eminentem, in qua inerat sphaerae figura et cylindri.
Atque ego statim Syracusanis—erant autem principes
mecum—dixi me illud ipsum arbitrari esse quod
quaererem. Immissi cum falcibus famuli [2] purgarunt
66 et aperuerunt locum: quo cum patefactus esset aditus,
ad adversam basim accessimus ; apparebat epigramma

---

[1] *Agragianas* in MSS. Suggestions are *Achradinas*,
Agragantinas. The gate led to Agrigentum, Ἀκράγας,
Girgenti.
[2] The MSS. have *multi.* Suggestions made are *famuli,*
tumuli, milites.

---

[1] cf. IV. § 78.
[2] Archimedes was killed when Syracuse was taken by
Marcellus in the year 212 B.C. Cicero had no idea of ranking

spiritual enjoyment of civilized life; he associated with runaways, with criminals, with barbarians: he regarded no man who either felt worthy of freedom or had any wish at all to be free as a friend.

XXIII. With the life of such a man, and I can imagine nothing more horrible, wretched and abominable, I shall not indeed compare the life of Plato or Archytas,[1] men of learning and true sages: I shall call up from the dust and his measuring-rod an obscure, insignificant person belonging to the same city, who lived many years after, Archimedes.[2] When I was quaestor[3] I tracked out his grave, which was unknown to the Syracusans (as they totally denied its existence), and found it enclosed all round and covered with brambles and thickets; for I remembered certain doggerel lines inscribed, as I had heard, upon his tomb, which stated that a sphere along with a cylinder had been set up on the top of his grave. Accordingly, after taking a good look all round (for there are a great quantity of graves at the Agrigentine Gate), I noticed a small column rising a little above the bushes, on which there was the figure of a sphere and a cylinder. And so I at once said to the Syracusans (I had their leading men with me) that I believed it was the very thing of which I was in search. Slaves were sent in with sickles who cleared the ground of obstacles, and when a passage to the place was opened we approached the pedestal fronting us; the epigram was traceable

him with the philosophers. Dust in which they drew their figures was the blackboard of ancient geometricians. Cf. I. § 63. In his life of Marcellus Plutarch says that Archimedes was a kinsman and friend of King Hiero.

[3] Quaestor to Sex. Peducaeus in Lilybaeum, B.C. 75.

exesis posterioribus partibus versiculorum dimidiatis
fere. Ita nobilissima Graeciae civitas, quondam
vero etiam doctissima, sui civis unius acutissimi
monumentum ignorasset, nisi ab homine Arpinate
didicisset.—Sed redeat unde aberravit oratio. Quis
est omnium, qui modo cum Musis, id est cum
humanitate et cum doctrina, habeat aliquod com-
mercium, qui se non hunc mathematicum malit
quam illum tyrannum? Si vitae modum actionem-
que quaerimus, alterius mens rationibus agitandis
exquirendisque alebatur cum oblectatione sollertiae,
qui est unus suavissimus pastus animorum, alterius
in caede et iniuriis cum et diurno et nocturno metu.
Age confer Democritum, Pythagoram, Anaxagoram;
quae regna, quas opes studiis eorum et delecta-
67 tionibus antepones? Etenim quae pars optima est
in homine, in ea situm esse necesse est illud, quod
quaeris, optimum. Quid est autem in homine sagaci
ac bona mente melius? Eius bono fruendum est
igitur, si beati esse volumus; bonum autem mentis
est virtus: ergo hac beatam vitam contineri necesse
est. Hinc omnia, quae pulcra, honesta, praeclara
sunt, ut supra dixi, sed dicendum idem illud paullo
uberius videtur, plena gaudiorum sunt; ex perpetuis
autem plenisque gaudiis cum perspicuum sit vitam

---

[1] Arpinum in Latium was Cicero's native town, cf. § 74.
It was also the native town of Marius.
[2] The best part of a man is his mind, and the good of the
mind is virtue, the "best," of which we are in search.

with about half the lines legible, as the latter portion
was worn away. So you see, one of the most famous
cities of Greece, once indeed a great school of learning as well, would have been ignorant of the tomb
of its one most ingenious citizen, had not a man of
Arpinum[1] pointed it out. But to come back to the
point where I made this digression. Who in all the
world, who enjoys merely some degree of communion
with the Muses, that is to say with liberal education
and refinement, is there who would not choose to be
this mathematician rather than that tyrant? If we
inquire into their manner of life and employment
we see that the mind of the one found its sustenance
in the problems of scientific research and enjoyed
the exercise of its ingenuity—and this is the one
most delightful spiritual food—whilst the mind of
the other dwelt on murder and outrage, and fear
was in its company both by day and night. Come,
compare Democritus, Pythagoras, Anaxagoras with
Dionysius; what thrones, what resources will you
put above the studies in which they found their
delight? For that "best" of which you are in
search must necessarily have its place in what is
the best part in a man.[2] But what is there in man
better than a mind that is sagacious and good? The
good of such a mind then we must enjoy if we wish
to be happy; but the good of the mind is virtue:
therefore happy life is necessarily bound up with
virtue. Consequently all that is lovely, honourable,
of good report,[3] as I have said above,[4] but I must
say it again, it seems, with rather more expansion,
is full of joys; but seeing that it is clear that

---

[3] cf. *Philippians* 4. 8.   [4] § 43.

beatam exsistere, sequitur ut ea exsistat ex honestate.

68　XXIV. Sed, ne verbis solum attingamus ea, quae volumus ostendere, proponenda quaedam quasi moventia sunt, quae nos magis ad cognitionem intelligentiamque convertant. Sumatur enim nobis quidam praestans vir optimis artibus isque animo parumper et cogitatione fingatur. Primum ingenio eximio sit necesse est ; tardis enim mentibus virtus non facile comitatur : deinde ad investigandam veritatem studio incitato ; ex quo triplex ille animi fetus exsistet : unus in cognitione rerum positus et in explicatione naturae ; alter in discriptione expetendarum fugiendarumve rerum et in ratione vivendi ;[1] tertius in iudicando quid cuique rei sit consequens, quid repugnans, in quo inest omnis

69　cum subtilitas disserendi tum veritas iudicandi. Quo tandem igitur gaudio adfici necesse est sapientis animum cum his habitantem pernoctantemque curis ! ut, cum totius mundi motus conversionesque perspexerit sideraque viderit innumerabilia caelo inhaerentia cum eius ipsius motu congruere certis infixa sedibus, septem alia suos quaeque tenere cursus

---

[1] The MSS. differ. Wesenberg suggests *et in ratione vivendi* for the *ne vivendi* which is found in some.

---

[1] *Honestas* or *honestum*, for which Cicero sometimes uses *rectum* and rarely *pulchrum*, answers to τὸ καλόν. Its opposite is *utilitas* or *utile*, expediency. In *De Fin.* II. 14. 45, *honestum* is defined as *quod tale est ut detracta omni utilitate sine ullis praemiis fructibusve per se ipsum possit iure laudari*. By nature man desires self-preservation, possesses reason, investigates truth, has a sense of order and propriety, and these are all elements in *honestum*, *De Off.* I. 4. The word is derived from *honor, honos*, cf. II. § 58.

happy life comes from unceasing fulness of joys, it follows that it comes from rectitude.[1]

XXIV. But that we may not try by the use of argument alone to reach the truth we wish to reveal, we must set before our eyes certain as it were palpable inducements to make us turn more readily to the knowledge and understanding of its meaning. Let us assume a man pre-eminently endowed with the highest qualities and let our imagination play for a moment with the picture. In the first place he must be of outstanding intelligence; for virtue is not easily found to go with sluggish minds; secondly he must have an eager enthusiasm in the quest of truth; and from this springs the famous threefold progeny of the soul:[2] one centred in the knowledge of the universe and the disentanglement of the secrets of nature; the second in distinguishing the things that should be sought out or avoided and in framing a rule of life; the third in judging what is the consequence to every premise, what is incompatible with it, and in this lies all refinement of argument and truth of judgment. With what joy, pray, must then the soul of the wise man be thrilled when in such company he spends his life and passes his nights in their study! When for instance[3] he discovers the movements and revolutions of the whole heaven[4] and sees the countless stars fixed in the sky in unison with the movement of the vault itself as they keep their appointed place, seven others preserving their several courses,

[2] Physica, Ethica, Dialectica, the three parts of Philosophy according to the Stoics. The Epicureans recognized the first two parts only.

[3] Physica.   [4] cf. I. ch. XXVIII.

multum inter se aut altitudine aut humilitate
distantia quorum vagi motus rata tamen et certa
sui cursus spatia definiant—horum nimirum aspectus
impulit illos veteres et admonuit, ut plura quaererent. Inde est indagatio nata initiorum et tamquam seminum, unde essent omnia orta, generata,
concreta, quaeque cuiusque generis vel inanimi vel
animantis vel muti vel loquentis origo, quae vita,
qui interitus quaeque ex alio in aliud vicissitudo
atque mutatio, unde terra et quibus librata ponderibus, quibus cavernis maria sustineantur : qua[1] omnia
delata gravitate medium mundi locum semper ex-
petant, qui est idem infimus in rotundo.

70   XXV. Haec tractanti animo et noctes et dies
cogitanti exsistit illa a deo Delphis praecepta
cognitio, ut ipsa se mens agnoscat coniunctamque
cum divina mente se sentiat, ex quo insatiabili
gaudio completur.[2]   Ipsa enim cogitatio de vi et
natura deorum studium incendit illius aeternitatis
imitandi, neque se in brevitate vitae collocatum[3]
putat, cum rerum causas alias ex aliis aptas et
necessitate nexas videt, quibus ab aeterno tempore
fluentibus in aeternum ratio tamen mensque modera-

[1] *in qua* MSS. : *qua* Davies.
[2] Bentley's correction of *compleatur*.
[3] Other readings are *collocata* and *collocatam*.

---

[1] Thales, Heraclitus, Anaximenes, Anaximander, cf.
§ 10.
[2] *Aeris vi suspensam cum quarto aquarum elemento librari
medio spatio tellurem.* Plin. *Nat. Hist.* II. 4.
[3] The earth had caverns and passages through which the
water passed. Cf. Lucr. V. 268.

though far remote from one another in the height or lowliness of their position, and yet their wandering movements mark the settled and regulated spaces of their course—no wonder the spectacle of all this stimulated those men of old and encouraged them to further search.[1] Hence sprang the investigation into the beginnings and as it were the seeds from which all things got their origin, propagation and growth, to find out what was the beginning of each kind whether inanimate or animate, or mute or speaking, what life is, what death, and what the change and transmutation from one thing into another, what the origin of the earth, what weights preserve its equilibrium,[2] what are the caverns in which the seas are upheld,[3] what force of gravity makes all things tend to the world's centre which is also lowest in what is spherical.[4]

XXV. To the soul occupied night and day in these meditations there comes the knowledge enjoined by the god at Delphi,[5] that the mind should know its own self and feel its union with the divine mind, the source of the fulness of joy unquenchable. For meditation upon the power and nature of the gods of itself kindles the desire of attaining an immortality that resembles theirs, nor does the soul think that it is limited to this short span of life, when it sees that the causes of things are linked one to another in an inevitable chain, and nevertheless their succession from eternity to eternity is governed

---

[4] In the sphere the centre, to which heavy things fall, is lowest. Such in the universe is the earth toward which all things are carried. For nature always guides weights to the lowest point. Cf. I. § 40. In Dante's *Inferno* Satan is placed at the centre, *al qual si traggon d'ogni parte i pesi.*

[5] I. § 52.

71 tur. Haec ille intuens atque suspiciens vel potius
omnes partes orasque circumspiciens quanta rursus
animi tranquillitate humana et citeriora considerat!
Hinc illa cognitio virtutis exsistit, efflorescunt genera
partesque virtutum, invenitur quid sit quod natura
spectet extremum in bonis, quid in malis ultimum,
quo referenda sint officia, quae degendae aetatis
ratio deligenda. Quibus et talibus rebus exquisitis
hoc vel maxime efficitur, quod hac disputatione
agimus, ut virtus ad beate vivendum sit se ipsa
72 contenta. Sequitur tertia, quae per omnes partes
sapientiae manat et funditur, quae rem definit,
genera dispertit, sequentia adiungit, perfecta con-
cludit, vera et falsa diiudicat, disserendi ratio et
scientia; ex qua cum summa utilitas exsistit ad res
ponderandas tum maxime ingenua delectatio et
digna sapientia. Sed haec otii: transeat idem iste
sapiens ad rem publicam tuendam. Quid eo possit
esse praestantius, cum[1] prudentia utilitatem civium
cernat, iustitia nihil in suam domum inde derivet,
reliquis utatur tot tam variisque virtutibus? Adiunge
fructum amicitiarum, in quo doctis positum est cum
consilium omnis vitae consentiens et paene con-
spirans, tum summa iucunditas e cotidiano cultu
atque victu. Quid haec tandem vita desiderat quo

----

[1] After *cum* the MSS. have *contineri*, which was removed
on the conjecture of Lambinus.

----

[1] Ethica.
[2] Dealt with in the *De Finibus bonorum et malorum.*
[3] Dialectica.   [4] Politica.
[5] cf. Arist. *Eth.* IX. 1.

by reason and intelligence. As the wise man gazes upon this spectacle and looks upward or rather looks round upon all the parts and regions of the universe, with what calmness of soul he turns again to reflect upon what is in man and touches him more nearly! Hence comes his knowledge of virtue;[1] the kinds and species of the virtues break into blossom, discovery is made of what nature regards as the end in what is good and the last extremity in what is evil,[2] the object of our duties and the rule for the conduct of life that must be chosen. And by the exploration of these and similar problems the chief conclusion of all attained is the aim of this discussion of ours, that virtue is self-sufficient for leading a happy life. In the third place[3] follows that which spreads freely over all parts of the field of wisdom, which gives the definition of a thing, distinguishes kinds, links up sequences, draws just conclusions, discerns true and false,—the art and science of reasoning; and this, besides its supreme usefulness in weighing judgments, affords particularly a noble delight which is worthy of wisdom. But this is the occupation of leisure : let the wise man we have imagined also pass to the maintenance of the public weal.[4] What course more excellent could he take, since his prudence shows him the true advantage of his fellow citizens, his justice lets him divert nothing of theirs to his own family, and he is strong in the exercise of so many different remaining virtues? Add to this the fruit which springs from friendships[5] in which learned men find the counsel which shares their thoughts and almost breathes the same breath throughout the course of life, as well as the supreme charm of daily social intercourse. What, pray, does

499

sit beatior? Cui refertae tot tantisque gaudiis
Fortuna ipsa cedat necesse est. Quod si gaudere
talibus bonis animi, id est, virtutibus, beatum est
omnesque sapientes iis gaudiis perfruuntur, omnes
eos beatos esse confiteri necesse est.

73 XXVI. A. Etiamne in cruciatu atque tormentis?
M. An tu me in viola putabas aut in rosa dicere?
An Epicuro, qui tantum modo induit personam
philosophi et sibi ipse hoc nomen inscripsit, dicere
licebit, quod quidem, ut habet se res, me tamen
plaudente dicit, nullum sapienti esse tempus, etiam
si uratur, torqueatur, secetur, quin possit exclamare :
"*Quam pro nihilo puto !* ", cum praesertim omne
malum dolore definiat, bonum voluptate, haec nostra
honesta turpia irrideat dicatque nos in vocibus
occupatos inanes sonos fundere neque quidquam ad
nos pertinere nisi quod aut leve aut asperum in
corpore sentiatur : huic ergo, ut dixi, non multum
differenti a iudicio ferarum oblivisci licebit sui et
tum fortunam contemnere, cum sit omne et bonum
eius et malum in potestate fortunae, tum dicere
se beatum in summo cruciatu atque tormentis, cum
constituerit non modo summum malum esse dolorem,
74 sed etiam solum? Nec vero illa sibi remedia comparavit ad tolerandum dolorem, firmitatem animi,
turpitudinis verecundiam, exercitationem consuetu-
dinemque patiendi, praecepta fortitudinis,[1] duritiam
virilem, sed una se dicit recordatione acquiescere

---

[1] The words *praecepta fortitudinis* seem to be a gloss.

such a life require to make it happier? And to a life filled with joys so abundant and intense, fortune itself is bound to yield its place. If then it is happiness to rejoice in such goods of the soul, that is virtues, and all wise men have full experience of such joys, we are bound to admit that they are all happy.

XXVI. A. Even in torture and upon the rack? M. Do you think I meant on beds of violets and roses? Or is Epicurus, who merely puts on the mask of a philosopher and has bestowed the title on himself, to be allowed to say (and say it indeed he does, really and truly, with my pronounced approval, spite of his inconsistency) that there is no time when the wise man, even if burnt, racked, cut in pieces, cannot cry out: "I count it all as nothing," particularly as Epicurus restricts evil to pain and good to pleasure, makes a mock of this "right and base" of ours and says we are busied with words and uttering sounds empty of meaning, and that nothing interests us except the bodily sensation of either rough or smooth? Shall we allow this man, whose judgment differs but little from the instinct of the beasts, to be forgetful of himself and be disdainful of fortune at the moment when all that he holds good and evil is at fortune's disposal; to say that he is happy in the extremity of torture and upon the rack at the moment when he has laid down that not only is pain the worst of evils but is the only one as well? And he has in no way provided for himself those healing aids to the endurance of pain to be found in strength of soul, shame of baseness, the habitual practice of patience, the lessons of fortitude, a manly hardness, but says that he finds peace in the recollection of past

praeteritarum voluptatum, ut, si quis aestuans, cum
vim caloris non facile patiatur, recordari velit sese
aliquando in Arpinati nostro gelidis fluminibus cir-
cumfusum fuisse ; non enim video quo modo sedare
75 possint mala praesentia praeteritae voluptates. Sed
cum is dicat semper beatum esse sapientem, cui
dicere hoc, si sibi constare vellet, non liceret,
quidnam faciendum est iis, qui nihil expetendum,
nihil in bonis ducendum, quod honestate careat,
existimant?

Me quidem auctore etiam Peripatetici veteresque
Academici balbutire aliquando desinant aperteque
et clara voce audeant dicere beatam vitam in
76 Phalaridis taurum descensuram. XXVII. Sint enim
tria genera bonorum, ut iam a laqueis Stoicorum,
quibus usum me pluribus quam soleo intelligo, rece-
damus, sint sane illa genera bonorum, dum corporis
et externa iaceant humi et tantum modo, quia
sumenda sint, appellentur bona, alia¹ autem illa
divina longe lateque se pandant caelumque con-
tingant : ea² qui adeptus sit, cur eum beatum modo
et non beatissimum etiam dixerim ?

Dolorem vero sapiens extimescet ? Is enim huic
maxime sententiae repugnat ; nam contra mortem
nostram atque nostrorum contraque aegritudinem et
reliquas animi perturbationes satis esse videmur

---

¹ *animi* is suggested for *alia*, as the other goods, *corporis et
externa*, are named expressly.
² *ut* comes before *ea* in MSS., but does not fit in gram-
matically.

---

¹ One was the Fibrenus.   ² cf. II. § 17.
³ *Sumenda* are the same as *producta*, cf. § 47, answering to
the προηγμένα of the Stoics.
⁴ *i.e.* goods of the soul.

pleasures and in that alone, just as if a man swelter-
ing in uneasy endurance of violent summer heat
should choose to recollect a dip in the cool freshness
of the streams[1] in my Arpinum; for I do not see
how past pleasures can allay present evils.   But as
this man, who would have no right to say it if he
chose to be self-consistent, says that the wise man is
always happy, what ought to be expected of those
who consider nothing desirable, nothing worth
reckoning as a good where rectitude is not found?

For my part, I should say, let the Peripatetics
also and the Old Academy make an end some time
or other of their stuttering and have the courage
to say openly and loudly that happy life will step
down into the bull of Phalaris.[2]   XXVII. For grant
that there are three kinds of good things (to make
a final escape from the meshes of Stoic subtleties
of which I realize I have made more use than I
generally do), grant if you will the existence of
these kinds of good, provided only that goods of
the body and external goods lie grovelling on the
ground and are merely termed good because they
are to be "preferred,"[3] whilst those other divine
goods[4] extend their influence far and wide and reach
to the heavens: why should I pronounce anyone who
has secured them to be happy only, and not supremely
happy as well?

But will the wise man be terribly afraid of pain?[5]
For pain is the chief obstacle to our view: for against
death, our own and that of our relatives, and against
distress and all other disorders of the soul we have,

---

[5] Pain is the subject of Book II, to which he makes no
reference here and which may accordingly have been written
after this book, but cf. §118.

superiorum dierum disputationibus armati et parati :
dolor esse videtur acerrimus virtutis adversarius, is
ardentes faces intemptat, is fortitudinem, magnitudinem animi, patientiam se debilitaturum minatur.

77 Huic igitur succumbet virtus, huic beata sapientis et
constantis viri vita cedet ? Quam turpe, o di boni !
Pueri Spartiatae non ingemiscunt verberum dolore
laniati ; adolescentium greges Lacedaemone vidimus
ipsi incredibili contentione certantes pugnis, calci-
bus, unguibus, morsu denique, cum exanimarentur
prius quam victos se faterentur. Quae barbaria
India vastior aut agrestior ? in ea tamen gente
primum ei, qui sapientes habentur, nudi aetatem
agunt et Caucasi nives hiemalemque vim perferunt
sine dolore, cumque ad flammam se applicaverunt,

78 sine gemitu aduruntur ; mulieres vero in India, cum
est cuius earum vir mortuus, in certamen iudicium-
que veniunt quam plurimum ille dilexerit—plures
enim singulis solent esse nuptae—quae est victrix,
ea laeta prosequentibus suis una cum viro in rogum
imponitur, illa victa maesta discedit. Numquam
naturam mos vinceret ; est enim ea semper invicta ;
sed nos umbris, deliciis, otio, languore, desidia
animum infecimus, opinionibus maloque more de-

---

¹ cf. II. § 34.

² Cicero is referring to the final stages of the life of the
pious Brahman, when he becomes anchorite and mendicant.
Cf. the reference to Callanus in II. § 52.

³ *i.e.* it is not necessary to suppose that custom has
conquered nature and that Indians do not feel frost and fire:
custom gives them strength to face pain, whereas Roman

I think, been sufficiently armed and provided by the previous days' discussions: pain seems to be the most active antagonist of virtue; it points its fiery darts, it threatens to undermine fortitude, greatness of soul and patience.   Will virtue then have to give way to pain, will the happy life of the wise and steadfast man yield to it?   What degradation, great gods of heaven!   Spartan boys[1] utter no cry when their bodies are mangled with painful blows; I have seen with my own eyes troops of youngsters in Lacedaemon fighting with inconceivable obstinacy, using fists and feet and nails and even teeth to the point of losing their lives rather than admit defeat.   What barbarous country more rude and wild than India?   Yet amongst its people those, to begin with, who are reckoned sages[2] pass their lives unclad and endure without show of pain the snows of the Hindu Kush and the rigour of winter, and when they throw themselves voluntarily into the flames they let themselves be burnt without a moan; whilst the women in India, when the husband of any of them dies, compete with one another to decide whom the husband loved best (for each man usually has more than one wife): and she who is victorious, accompanied by her relatives, goes joyfully to join her husband on the funeral pyre; the conquered rival sadly quits the field.   Never could custom conquer nature;[3] for nature is always unconquered; but as for us we have corrupted our souls with bowered seclusion, luxury, ease, indolence and sloth, we have enervated and weakened them

custom is now enervating and weakening the race.   We may compare the contrast Tacitus draws between the Romans of his day and the Germans in *Germania*, ch. 19.

lenitum mollivimus. Aegyptiorum morem quis
ignorat? quorum imbutae mentes pravis[1] erroribus
quamvis carnificinam prius subierint quam ibim aut
aspidem aut felem aut canem aut crocodilum violent,
quorum etiam si imprudentes quidpiam fecerint,
79 poenam nullam recusent. De hominibus loquor:
quid bestiae? Non frigus, non famem, non monti-
vagos atque silvestres cursus lustrationesque patiuntur? non pro suo partu ita propugnant, ut
vulnera excipiant, nullos impetus, nullos ictus
reformident? Omitto quae perferant quaeque
patiantur ambitiosi honoris causa, laudis studiosi
gloriae gratia, amore incensi cupiditatis. Plena vita
exemplorum est.
80 XXVIII. Sed adhibeat oratio modum et redeat
illuc, unde deflexit. Dabit, inquam, se in tormenta
vita beata, nec iustitiam, temperantiam in primisque
fortitudinem, magnitudinem animi, patientiam pro-
secuta, cum tortoris os viderit, consistet virtutibusque
omnibus sine ullo animi terrore ad cruciatum profectis
resistet extra fores, ut ante dixi, limenque carceris.
Quid enim ea foedius, quid deformius sola relicta,
a[2] comitatu pulcherrimo segregata? quod tamen
fieri nullo pacto potest; nec enim virtutes sine beata
vita cohaerere possunt nec illa sine virtutibus:
81 itaque eam tergiversari non sinent secumque rapient,
ad quemcumque ipsae dolorem cruciatumque du-

---

[1] Suggested by Lambinus for the MSS., *pravitatis.*
[2] *a* not in MSS., added by Lambinus.

---

[1] cf. Hdt. II. 65, τὸ δ' ἄν τις τῶν θηρίων τούτων ἀποκτείνῃ,
ἢν μὲν ἑκών, θάνατος ἢ ζημίη, ἢν δὲ ἀέκων, ἀποτίνει ζημίην τὴν ἂν
οἱ ἱρέες τάξωνται.
[2] cf. § 13.
[3] This is precisely what he has to prove.

by false beliefs and evil habits. Who does not know of the custom of the Egyptians? Their minds are infected with degraded superstitions and they would sooner submit to any torment than injure an ibis or asp or cat or dog or crocodile, and even if they have unwittingly done anything of the kind there is no penalty from which they would recoil.[1] I am speaking of human beings: what of the beasts? Do they not go through cold, through hunger, ranging the mountains and traversing the forests in their wanderings? Do they not fight for their young so fiercely that they sustain wounds and shrink from no assaults, no blows? I pass by all that ambitious men go through submissively to win distinction, men covetous of fame to win glory, men inflamed with love to gratify passion. Life is full of such examples.

XXVIII. But let us check our eloquence and return to the point at which we digressed. Happy life will give itself, I say, to torture, and following in the train of justice, temperance and above all of fortitude, of greatness of soul and patience will not halt at the sight of the face of the executioner, and, when all the virtues, while the soul remains undaunted, pass on to face torment, it will not stay behind outside the doors, as I have said,[2] and threshold of the prison. For what could be more abominable, more hideous than to be left desolate, severed from its glorious companions? And yet this is by no means possible; for neither can the virtues subsist without happy life, nor happy life without the virtues.[3] And so they will not suffer it to make evasions and will hurry it along with them to whatsoever pain and torment they shall

centur. Sapientis est enim proprium nihil quod poenitere possit facere, nihil invitum, splendide, constanter, graviter, honeste omnia, nihil ita exspectare quasi certo futurum, nihil cum acciderit admirari, ut inopinatum ac novum accidisse videatur, omnia ad suum arbitrium referre, suis stare iudiciis; quo quid sit beatius mihi certe in mentem venire non potest.

82 Stoicorum quidem facilis conclusio est, qui cum finem bonorum esse senserint congruere naturae cumque ea convenienter vivere, cum id sit in sapientis[1] situm non officio solum, verum etiam potestate, sequatur necesse est ut, cuius in potestate summum bonum, in eiusdem vita beata sit: ita fit semper vita beata sapientis. Habes quae fortissime de beata vita dici putem et, quo modo nunc est, nisi quid tu melius attuleris, etiam verissime. XXIX. A. Melius equidem adferre nihil possum, sed a te impetrarim libenter, ut, nisi molestum est,[2] quoniam te nulla vincula impediunt ullius certae disciplinae libasque ex omnibus quodcumque te maxime specie veritatis movet, quod paullo ante Peripateticos veteremque Academiam hortari videbare, ut sine retractione libere dicere auderent sapientes esse semper beatissimos, id velim audire, quem ad modum his putes consentaneum esse id

---

[1] Lambinus for *sapiente* of MSS.
[2] For *sit* of MSS. Helm.

---

[1] cf. II. § 9.

themselves be led. For it is characteristic of the wise man to do nothing of which he can repent, nothing against his will, to do everything nobly, consistently, soberly, rightly, not to look forward to anything as if it were bound to come, to be astonished at no occurrence under the impression that its occurrence is unexpected and strange, to bring all things to the standard of his own judgment, to abide by his own decisions. And what can be happier than this I certainly cannot conceive.

For the Stoics indeed the conclusion is easy, since they hold it the sovereign good to live according to nature and in harmony with nature, seeing that not only is this the wise man's settled duty but also it lies in his power, and so for them it follows necessarily that where a man has the chief good in his power, he also has the power of happy life : thus the life of the wise is rendered happy always. Now you know the utterances I think the most courageous about happy life and, at the point we now are—unless you have something better to suggest—the truest as well. XXIX. A. I have no better suggestion to offer for my part, but there is a favour I should like to obtain from you, if it is not troublesome (seeing that you are not hampered by being tied to any definite school of thought, and taste from all of them everything that strikes you most as having the semblance of truth),[1] as a little while back you appeared to be urging the Peripatetics and the Old Academy to have the courage to say freely without reservation that wise men were always supremely happy, this is what I should like to hear, how you think it is con-

MARCUS TULLIUS CICERO

dicere; multa enim a te contra istam sententiam
83 dicta sunt et Stoicorum ratione conclusa. M. Utamur
igitur libertate, qua nobis solis in philosophia licet
uti, quorum oratio nihil ipsa iudicat, sed habetur in
omnes partes, ut ab aliis possit ipsa per sese nullius
auctoritate adiuncta iudicari. Et quoniam videris
hoc velle, ut, quaecumque dissentientium philosophorum sententia sit de finibus, tamen virtus satis
habeat ad vitam beatam praesidii, quod quidem
Carneadem disputare solitum accepimus; sed is, ut
contra Stoicos, quos studiosissime semper refellebat
et contra quorum disciplinam ingenium eius exarse-
rat; nos quidem illud cum pace agemus. Si enim
Stoici fines bonorum recte posiverunt, confecta res
est : necesse est semper beatum esse sapientem.
84 Sed quaeramus unam quamque reliquorum sententiam
si fieri potest, ut hoc praeclarum quasi decretum
beatae vitae possit omnium sententiis et disciplinis
convenire.

XXX. Sunt autem haec de finibus, ut opinor,
retentae defensaeque sententiae. Primum simplices
quattuor : nihil bonum nisi honestum, ut Stoici;
nihil bonum nisi voluptatem, ut Epicurus; nihil

---

[1] That the wise man is happy but not supremely happy,
cf. § 22.

[2] cf. § 11.

[3] Meaning the highest point that can be reached, just
as in II. § 3, *sperandi finis* is the highest that can be hoped
for, and *finis dicendi* the best that can be spoken. *Finis
bonorum* is the chief good, the *summum bonum*, τἀγαθόν.

[4] cf. III. § 54. Carneades agreed that virtue was sufficient

sistent for them to say so; for you have said a
good deal in opposition to the opinion they hold [1]
by adopting the conclusions of the Stoic reasoning.
M. Let me then use the freedom allowed to my
school of philosophic thought alone, which decides
nothing on its own pronouncement but ranges over
the whole field,[2] in order that the question may
be decided by others on its own merits, without
invoking anyone's authority. And since it appears
that what you wish established is that, whatever
the views held by warring sects about the limits [3]
of good and evil, nevertheless virtue is sufficient
security for a happy life, a proposition which
Carneades [4] we are told habitually discussed—but
he did so heatedly, as was his way in opposing the
Stoics whom he was always most eager to refute,
and against whose teaching his temper had fired
up—for my part I shall treat the question calmly.
For if the Stoics have rightly fixed the limits of
the good,[5] the question is settled: it follows of
necessity that the wise man is always happy. But
let us inquire, if possible, into each single opinion
of the remaining schools of thought, that so this
noble dogma, as it were, of happy life, can fit in with
the views and teaching of them all.

XXX. Now these in my opinion are the views
about "limits" still maintained and supported. First
four simple ones: that nothing is good unless it is
morally right, as the Stoics say; no good except
pleasure, as Epicurus; no good except absence of

for happiness but not that the morally right was the only
good, cf. § 33.
[5] As if it was a boundary stone on which was inscribed
"*Finis Posiverunt Vicini*" to mark the limits of a field.

bonum nisi vacuitatem doloris,[1] ut Hieronymus;
nihil bonum nisi naturae primis bonis aut omnibus
aut maximis frui, ut Carneades contra Stoicos dis-
85 serebat.   Haec igitur simplicia, illa mixta.   Tria
genera bonorum, maxima animi, secunda corporis,
externa tertia, ut Peripatetici nec multo veteres
Academici secus; voluptatem cum honestate Dinomachus et Callipho copulavit; indolentiam autem
honestati Peripateticus Diodorus adiunxit.   Hae
sunt sententiae, quae stabilitatis aliquid habeant;
nam Aristonis, Pyrrhonis, Herilli nonnullorumque
aliorum evanuerunt.   Hi quid possint obtinere
videamus omissis Stoicis, quorum satis videor de-
fendisse sententiam.   Et Peripateticorum quidem
explicata causa est: praeter Theophrastum et si
qui illum secuti imbecillius horrent dolorem et
reformidant, reliquis quidem licet facere id, quod
fere faciunt, ut gravitatem dignitatemque virtutis
exaggerent; quam cum ad caelum extulerunt, quod
facere eloquentes homines copiose solent, reliqua
ex collatione facile est conterere atque contemnere:
nec enim licet iis, qui laudem cum dolore petendam
esse dicunt, negare eos esse beatos, qui illam adepti
sint; quamquam enim sint in quibusdam malis,
tamen hoc nomen beati longe et late patet.
86   XXXI. Nam ut quaestuosa mercatura, fructuosa

---

[1] Most MSS. omit *doloris* which is needed.   The phrase
vacuitas doloris occurs frequently in the *De Finibus*.

---

[1] cf. II. § 15.
[2] τὰ πρῶτα κατὰ φύσιν, *e.g.* bodily and mental gifts.
[3] cf. § 21.
[4] Cyrenaic philosophers.
[5] A pupil of Critolaus belonging to the Peripatetic school.

pain, as Hieronymus;[1] no good except enjoyment
of the first goods of nature,[2] either all or the chief
of them, as Carneades argued against the Stoics.
These then are the simple; the next are composite:
three kinds of good,[3] the highest of the soul, second
of the body, third from the outside, as the Peripatetics, and the Old Academy are much the same;
Dinomachus and Callipho[4] have coupled pleasure
with rectitude; the Peripatetic Diodorus[5] has joined,
however, freedom from pain to rectitude. These
are the views which have some solid support; for
those of Aristo, Pyrrho, Herillus[6] and some others
have melted into air. Let us see what these can do
for us, leaving on one side the Stoics whose view I
think I have supported sufficiently already. And
besides them the Peripatetic case is cleared up:
apart from Theophrastus[7] and any who follow him
in a feeble dread and abhorrence of pain, it is
allowable for the rest of them at any rate to do
as they usually do, that is to say, exalt the dignity
and grandeur of virtue. And when they have raised
it to the heavens, in the way habitual to men who
have a fine flow of eloquence, it is easy to trample all
else under foot and despise it in comparison with
virtue; for it is not allowable for men who say that
renown must be sought at the cost of pain to deny
that those who had attained their aim are happy;
for though they are involved in certain evils, yet
this term of happiness has a wide and far-reaching
meaning.

XXXI. For as commerce is termed profitable and

[6] For Aristo and Pyrrho, cf. II. § 15. Herillus of Carthage,
a Stoic and disciple of Zeno.
[7] cf. § 24.

aratio dicitur, non, si altera semper omni damno,
altera omni tempestatis calamitate semper vacat,
sed si multo maiore ex parte exstat in utraque
felicitas, sic vita non solum si undique referta bonis
est, sed si multo maiore et graviore ex parte bona
87 propendent, beata recte dici potest.   Sequetur
igitur horum ratione vel ad supplicium beata vita
virtutem cumque ea descendet in taurum, Aristotele, Xenocrate, Speusippo, Polemone auctoribus,
nec eam minis aut[1] blandimentis corrupta deseret.
Eadem Calliphontis erit Diodorique sententia,
quorum uterque honestatem sic complectitur, ut
omnia, quae sine ea sint, longe retro ponenda
censeat.   Reliqui habere se videntur angustius,
enatant tamen, Epicurus, Hieronymus, et si qui sunt
qui desertum illum Carneadem curent defendere.
Nemo est enim quin verorum[2] bonorum animum
putet esse iudicem eumque condocefaciat, ut ea,
quae bona malave videantur, possit contemnere.
88 Nam quae[3] tibi Epicuri videtur, eadem erit Hie-
ronymi et Carneadis causa et hercule omnium
reliquorum ; quis enim parum est contra mortem
aut dolorem paratus?   Ordiamur ab eo, si placet,
quem mollem, quem voluptarium dicimus.   Quid?
is tibi mortemne videtur an dolorem timere, qui
eum diem, quo moritur, beatum appellat, maximis-
que doloribus adfectus eos ipsos inventorum suorum

---

[1] *minis aut* is Bentley's conjecture for *minimis* of the
MSS.
[2] Bentley's conjecture for *qui eorum* of the MSS.
[3] The reading of most MSS. is *quod.*

---

[1] The Peripatetics and Old Academy, cf. § 22.
[2] *i.e.* of Phalaris, II. § 17.

farming productive, not if the one always escapes all loss, the other always escapes all damage from bad weather, but if in the main there is in each a good margin of prosperity; so life can be termed happy, not only if it is brimful of good things of every sort, but if in the main and on the weightier side there is a marked preponderance of good. Therefore by the reasoning of these philosophers[1] happy life will follow virtue even to torture and in its company pass down into the bull,[2] on the authority of Aristotle, Xenocrates, Speusippus, Polemo,[3] and threats and bribes will not pervert it to abandon virtue. The opinion of Callipho and Diodorus will be the same, both of whom so warmly espouse rectitude that all things that have not got it must, they hold, be ranked a long way behind it. The rest do seem to be in somewhat of a strait, still they manage to swim their way out—Epicurus, Hieronymus, and any who are found to care to support poor deserted Carneades. For there is none of them who does not regard the soul as judge of the true good and join in instructing it to be able to despise such things as have only the semblance of good or evil. For what you hold to be the case of Epicurus, will also be the case of Hieronymus and Carneades and, upon my word, of all the rest of them; for who of them is insufficiently provided against death or pain? Let us begin, if you will, with the man we name effeminate,[4] name a voluptuary. Well, do you think him afraid of death or pain? He calls the day of his death happy and in the sufferings of acute pains he represses those very pains by the living remem-

---

[3] cf. § 30.   [4] Epicurus, cf. II. § 45.

memoria et recordatione confutat, nec haec sic agit,
ut ex tempore quasi effutire videatur? De morte
enim ita sentit, ut dissoluto animante sensum exstinctum putet, quod autem sensu careat, nihil ad
nos id iudicet pertinere; item de dolore certa habet
quae sequatur, cuius magnitudinem brevitate con-
89 solatur, longinquitatem levitate. Qui tandem isti
grandiloqui contra haec duo, quae maxime angunt,
melius se habent quam Epicurus? an ad cetera, quae
mala putantur, non et Epicurus et reliqui philosophi satis parati videntur? Quis non paupertatem
extimescit? neque tamen quisquam philosophorum.

XXXII. Hic vero ipse quam parvo est contentus!
Nemo de tenui victu plura dixit. Etenim quae res
pecuniae cupiditatem adferunt, ut amori, ut ambi-
tioni, ut cotidianis sumptibus copiae suppetant,
cum procul ab his omnibus rebus absit, cur pecuniam
magno opere desideret vel potius cur curet omnino?
90 An Scythes Anacharsis potuit pro nihilo pecuniam
ducere, nostrates philosophi facere non potuerunt?
Illius epistola fertur his verbis: "Anacharsis Han-
noni salutem. Mihi amictui est Scythicum tegimen,
calciamentum solorum callum, cubile terra, pulpa-
mentum fames; lacte, caseo, carne vescor. Qua re
ut ad quietum me licet venias; munera autem ista,
quibus es delectatus, vel civibus tuis vel dis immortalibus dona." Omnes fere philosophi omnium

---

[1] ὁ θάνατος οὐδὲν πρὸς ἡμᾶς· τὸ γὰρ διαλυθὲν ἀναισθητεῖ· τὸ δὲ
ἀναισθητοῦν οὐδὲν πρὸς ἡμᾶς, Diog. Laert. X. 124–126.

[2] οἱ μεγάλοι πόνοι συντόμως ἐξάγουσιν, οἱ δὲ χρόνιοι μέγεθος
οὐκ ἔχουσιν, Plut. De Aud. Poet., p. 36 B, cf. II. § 44.

[3] The Stoics.

[4] The Greek of this letter is extant. It was a forgery of
some sophist and attributed to Anacharsis.

brance of the truths he has discovered, and this he does not do in a spirit that makes it seem the babble of the moment. For in his view of death he holds that with the dissolution of the living creature sensation is extinct and what is without sensation, in his judgment, has no concern with us;[1] also he has definite maxims to obey with regard to pain,[2] the violence of which is relieved by its shortness, its length by its slightness. How, pray, are those pompous[3] friends of yours better off than Epicurus in facing these two causes of the most intense anguish? Or do you think that Epicurus and the rest of the philosophers are not adequately prepared to meet all other things that are considered evil? What man is not sorely afraid of poverty? And yet not a single philosopher is so.

XXXII. Nay, with how little is Epicurus himself contented! No one has said more about plain living. For take the things which make men desire money to provide the means for love, for ambition, for their daily expenditure—as he is far removed from all such things, why should he feel much need of money or rather why should he trouble about it at all? Was it possible for a Scythian like Anacharsis to think nothing of money; has it been impossible for philosophers of a country like ours? There is on record a letter of his in these terms:[4] "Anacharsis to Hanno greeting. My clothing is a Scythian mantle, my shoes the thick skin of the soles of my feet, my bed is the earth, hunger my relish; I live on milk, cheese, flesh. You may come to me therefore as to one at peace; but as for the gifts you delight in, present them to your fellow citizens or to the immortal gods." Almost all philosophers of

disciplinarum, nisi quos a recta ratione natura
vitiosa detorsisset, eodem hoc animo esse potuerunt.

91 Socrates, in pompa cum magna vis auri argentique
ferretur: *Quam multa non desidero!* inquit. Xenocrates, cum legati ab Alexandro quinquaginta ei
talenta attulissent, quae erat pecunia temporibus
illis, Athenis praesertim, maxima, abduxit legatos
ad cenam in Academiam: iis apposuit tantum,
quod satis esset, nullo apparatu. Cum postridie
rogarent eum, cui numerari iuberet: *Quid? vos
hesterna,* inquit, *cenula non intellexistis me pecunia non
egere?* Quos cum tristiores vidisset, triginta minas
accepit, ne aspernari regis liberalitatem videretur.

92 At vero Diogenes liberius, ut Cynicus, Alexandro
roganti, ut diceret, si quid opus esset: *Nunc quidem
paullulum,* inquit, *a sole.* Offecerat videlicet apri-
canti. Et hic quidem disputare solebat quanto
regem Persarum vita fortunaque superaret: sibi
nihil deesse, illi nihil satis umquam fore: se eius
voluptates non desiderare, quibus numquam satiari
ille posset, suas eum consequi nullo modo posse.

93 XXXIII. Vides, credo, ut Epicurus cupiditatum
genera diviserit, non nimis fortasse subtiliter, utiliter
tamen; partim esse naturales et necessarias, partim
naturales et non necessarias, partim neutrum; neces-

---

[1] πόσων ἐγὼ χρείαν οὐκ ἔχω, Diog. Laert. II. 25.
[2] cf. I. § 20.
[3] cf. I. § 104.
[4] μικρὸν ἀπὸ τοῦ ἡλίου μετάστηθι, Plut. *Alexand.* XIV.
[5] τῶν ἐπιθυμιῶν αἱ μέν εἰσι φυσικαὶ καὶ ἀναγκαῖαι, αἱ δὲ φυσικαὶ
καὶ οὐκ ἀναγκαῖαι, αἱ δὲ οὔτε φυσικαὶ οὔτε ἀναγκαῖαι ἀλλὰ παρὰ
κενὴν δόξαν γιγνόμεναι, Diog. Laert. X. 149.

every school, except such as corrupt nature has
turned away from right reason, have been able to
show this same spirit. When a great quantity of
gold and silver was being carried in a procession,
Socrates said, " How much there is I do not need ! "[1]
When ambassadors brought fifty talents to Xenocrates[2] from Alexander, a very large sum for those
days, particularly at Athens, he carried off the
ambassadors to sup with him in the Academy and
put before them just enough to be sufficient, without
any display. On their asking him next day to
whom he required them to count out the money :
" What ? " he said, " Did not yesterday's pot-luck
show you that I have no need of money ? " And
when he saw their faces fall he accepted thirty
minas to avoid appearing scornful of the king's
generosity. But Diogenes,[3] certainly, was more
outspoken, in his quality of Cynic, when Alexander
asked him to name anything he wanted : " Just
now," said he, " stand a bit away from the sun ! "[4]
Alexander apparently had interfered with his bask-
ing in the heat. And in fact Diogenes, to show how
far superior he was to the King of Persia in the conditions of his life, used to argue that while he had no
needs, nothing would ever be enough for the king ;
he did not miss the pleasures with which the king
could never be sated, the king could never enjoy the
pleasures of the philosopher.

XXXIII. You are, I take it, aware that Epicurus
has distinguished different kinds of desires, not
perhaps with over-much exactness, still in a way
that is of service :[5] in part, they are, he says,
natural and necessary, in part natural and not necessary, in part neither one nor the other ; scarcely

sarias satiari posse paene nihilo, divitias enim naturae
esse parabiles; secundum autem genus cupiditatum
nec ad potiendum difficile esse censet nec vero ad
carendum; tertias, quod essent plane inanes neque
necessitatem modo, sed ne naturam quidem attin-
94 gerent, funditus eiiciendas putavit. Hoc loco multa ab
Epicureis disputantur eaeque voluptates singillatim
extenuantur, quarum genera contemnunt,[1] quaerunt
tamen copiam; nam et obscenas voluptates, de quibus
multa ab illis habetur oratio, faciles, communes, in
medio sitas esse dicunt, easque si natura requirat,
non genere aut loco aut ordine, sed forma, aetate,
figura metiendas putant, ab iisque abstinere minime
esse difficile, si aut valetudo aut officium aut fama
postulet, omninoque genus hoc voluptatum optabile
95 esse, si non obsit, prodesse numquam. Totumque
hoc de voluptate sic ille praecipit, ut voluptatem
ipsam per se, quia voluptas sit, semper optandam
expetendamque putet, eademque ratione dolorem
ob id ipsum, quia dolor sit, semper esse fugiendum;
itaque hac usurum compensatione sapientem, ut et
voluptatem fugiat, si ea maiorem dolorem effectura
sit, et dolorem suscipiat maiorem efficientem volup-

---

[1] The MSS. have *non contemnunt*. Madvig says *non*
originated in *con* and should be removed.

---

[1] τὸ μὲν φυσικὸν πᾶν εὐπόριστόν ἐστι, τὸ δὲ κενὸν δυσπόριστον.
[2] The Epicureans despised certain kinds of pleasure such as
obscene pleasures, pleasures of food and the like; they took

anything is required to satisfy the necessary pleasures for the stores of nature are available ;[1] and the second kind of desires is he thinks neither hard to satisfy nor indeed hard to go without ; the third kind he thought should be utterly rejected, because they were completely meaningless, and so far from counting as necessary, had not any relation to nature either. At this point his disciples enter on a long argument, and those pleasures, which belong to kinds they despise, they belittle in detail, yet all the same look out for a plentiful supply of them.[2] For lewd pleasures upon which they dwell at length are, they say, easy to satisfy, general, within reach of all, and should nature demand them, the standard of value should, they think, not be birth, position or rank, but beauty, age, shape, and abstinence is by no means difficult at the call of either health or duty or reputation, and in general this kind of pleasures is desirable, should there be no obstacle, but is never of benefit.[3] The whole teaching of Epicurus about pleasure is that pleasure is, he thinks, always to be wished and sought for in and for itself because it is pleasure, and that on the same principle pain is always to be avoided for the simple reason that it is pain, and so the wise man will employ a system of counterbalancing which enables him both to avoid pleasure, should it be likely to ensure greater pain, and submit to pain where it ensures greater pleasure ; and

them one by one and refined them away, yet all the same preferred to have a plentiful supply of all. Cf. Madvig, *De Finibus*, I. 13. 45.

[3] συνουσία δὲ ὤνησε μὲν οὐδέποτε, ἀγαπητὸν δὲ εἰ μὴ καὶ ἔβλαψεν, Diog. Laert. X. 118.

tatem, omniaque iucunda, quamquam sensu corporis
96 iudicentur, ad animum referri tamen; quocirca
corpus gaudere tam diu, dum praesentem sentiret
voluptatem, animum et praesentem percipere pariter
cum corpore et prospicere venientem nec praete-
ritam praeterfluere sinere: ita perpetuas et con-
textas voluptates in sapiente fore semper, cum
exspectatio speratarum voluptatum cum perceptarum
memoria iungeretur.

97   XXXIV. Atque his similia ad victum etiam trans-
feruntur, extenuaturque magnificentia et sumptus
epularum, quod parvo cultu natura contenta sit.
Etenim quis hoc non videt, desideriis omnia ista
condiri? Darius in fuga cum aquam turbidam et
cadaveribus inquinatam bibisset, negavit umquam
se bibisse iucundius; numquam videlicet sitiens
biberat.   Nec esuriens Ptolemaeus ederat; cui
cum[1] peragranti Aegyptum comitibus non conse-
cutis cibarius in casa panis datus esset, nihil visum
est illo pane iucundius.   Socratem ferunt, cum
usque ad vesperum contentius ambularet quaesi-
tumque esset ex eo qua re id faceret, respondisse
se, quo melius cenaret, opsonare ambulando famem.
98 Quid? victum Lacedaemoniorum in philitiis nonne
videmus?   Ubi cum tyrannus cenavisset Dionysius,

----

[1] *cum* is not in MSS. and is added by Madvig.

----

[1] Pleasure and pain come from bodily sensation, but
Epicurus inconsistently held that the pleasures and pains of
the soul were greater than those of the body, cf. Madvig on
De Fin. I. 17. 55.
[2] Darius Codomanus after his defeat at Arbela by Alexander
the Great, 331 B.C.

all pleasurable things, although judged of by the
bodily senses, are notwithstanding transmitted on
again to the soul;[1] and for this reason while the
body feels delight for the time that it has the sensation of present pleasure, it is the soul which has
both the realization of present pleasure conjointly
with the body and anticipates coming pleasure, and
does not suffer past pleasure to slip away : thus the
wise man will always have an unbroken tissue of
pleasures, as the expectation of pleasures hoped for
is combined with the recollection of pleasures
already realized.

XXXIV. And similar reasoning is also applied to
food, and the costly splendour of banquets is belittled,
because they say nature is contented with little
elaboration. For who does not see that need is the
seasoning for all such things ? When Darius[2] in his
flight drank muddy water polluted by corpses he
said he had never had a more delightful drink ;
obviously he had never before been thirsty when he
drank. And Ptolemy[3] had never been hungry when
he ate : for when he was on a progress through
Egypt and was parted from his escort and given
coarse bread in a cottage, it seemed to him that
nothing was more delightful than this bread.
Socrates, it is said, would walk hard till evening,
and when he was asked in consequence why he did
so, he replied that by walking he was getting
hunger as a relish to make a better dinner.[4] Again !
do we not know of the fare put before the Lacedaemonians at their public meals ? When the tyrant

[3] Perhaps Ptolemy I., King of Egypt, 323–284 B.C.
[4] καὶ πρὸς τοὺς πυνθανομένους Τί τηνικάδε ; ἔλεγεν ὄψον
συνάγειν πρὸς τὸ δεῖπνον, Athenaeus IV. 157.

negavit se iure illo nigro, quod cenae caput erat,
delectatum. Tum is, qui illa coxerat: *Minime
mirum; condimenta enim defuerunt. Quae tandem?*
inquit ille. *Labor in venatu, sudor, cursus ad Euro-
tam,*[1] *fames, sitis. His enim rebus Lacedaemoniorum
epulae condiuntur.* Atque hoc non ex hominum more
solum, set etiam ex bestiis intelligi potest, quae, ut
quidquid obiectum est, quod modo a natura non sit
99 alienum, eo contentae non quaerunt amplius. Civitates quaedam universae, more doctae, parcimonia
delectantur, ut de Lacedaemoniis paullo ante diximus. Persarum a Xenophonte victus exponitur,
quos negat ad panem adhibere quidquam praeter
nasturtium. Quamquam si quaedam etiam suaviora
natura desideret, quam multa ex terra arboribusque
gignuntur cum copia facili tum suavitate praestanti![2] Adde siccitatem, quae consequitur hanc
continentiam in victu, adde integritatem valetudinis.
100 Confer sudantes, ructantes, refertos epulis tamquam
opimos boves, tum intelliges, qui voluptatem maxime
sequantur, eos minime consequi, iucunditatemque
victus esse in desiderio, non in satietate. XXXV.
Timotheum, clarum hominem Athenis et principem
civitatis, ferunt, cum cenavisset apud Platonem
eoque convivio admodum delectatus esset vidissetque eum postridie, dixisse: *Vestrae quidem cenae*

---

[1] Bentley's suggestion for *ab Eurota* of the MSS.
[2] Lambinus' suggestion for *praestantia* of the MSS.

---

[1] Dionysius the elder.
[2] ζωμὸς μέλας, Athenaeus IX. 379.
[3] Xen. *Cyrop.* I. 2. 8.
[4] The four elements were earth, air, fire, and water whose
mixture and cardinal properties dryness, warmth, coldness,
and moistness form the body and its constituent parts. Dry
bodies were healthiest and strongest.

Dionysius [1] dined with them he said that the black broth [2] which was the staple of the meal was not to his taste; whereupon the cook who had made it said: "No wonder; for you did not have the seasoning." "What is that, pray?" said the tyrant. "Toil in hunting, sweat, a run down to the Eurotas, hunger, thirst; for such things are the seasoning of the feasts of Lacedaemonians." And apart from the usage of men the same lesson can be learnt also from animals which, when a thing of any sort is flung to them, are content and look for nothing further, provided it is not repugnant to their instincts. There are certain whole States, like the Lacedaemonians whom I mentioned a little while ago, which by the training of custom have learnt to take delight in frugal living. Xenophon in describing the food of the Persians says that they take nothing but cress with their bread. [3] And yet, if nature should feel the need of something yet more savoury, what a quantity of things are provided by earth and trees in ready abundance and of excellent savour! Add dryness [4] which follows upon restraint in diet, add unimpaired health; contrast with this, sweating, belching men stuffed with food like fatted oxen: then you will understand that those who are hottest in pursuit of pleasure are furthest from catching it, and that the pleasantness of food lies in appetite, not in repletion. XXXV. Timotheus, [5] who bore a great name at Athens and was a leading man in the State, after dining, we are told, with Plato and being much delighted with the entertainment, said, when he saw him next day: "Your

[5] Son of Conon and Athenian General between 378–356 B.C.

*non solum in praesentia, sed etiam postero die iucunda
sunt.* Quid, quod ne mente quidem recte uti possumus multo cibo et potione completi? Est praeclara epistola Platonis ad Dionis propinquos, in qua
scriptum est his fere verbis : " Quo cum venissem,
vita illa beata, quae ferebatur, plena Italicarum
Syracusiarumque mensarum, nullo modo mihi placuit; bis in die saturum fieri nec umquam per-
noctare solum, ceteraque, quae comitantur huic
vitae, in qua sapiens nemo efficietur umquam,
101 moderatus vero multo minus. Quae enim natura
tam mirabiliter temperari potest?" Quo modo
igitur iucunda vita potest esse, a qua absit prudentia,
absit moderatio? Ex quo Sardanapalli, opulentis-
simi Syriae regis, error agnoscitur, qui incidi iussit
in busto :

> *Haec habeo, quae edi quaeque exsaturata libido
> Hausit ; at illa iacent multa et praeclara relicta.*

Quid aliud, inquit Aristoteles, in bovis, non in regis
sepulcro inscriberes? Haec habere se mortuum
dicit, quae ne vivus quidem diutius habebat quam
102 fruebatur. Cur igitur divitiae desiderentur, aut ubi
paupertas beatos esse non sinit? Signis, credo,
tabulis studes :[1] si quis est qui his delectetur, nonne

---

[1] The MSS. have *ludis* which does not fit in. *Studes* and
pictis are suggested.

---

[1] Plato, *Ep.* 7, p. 326 B.
[2] The Greek meals were ἀκράτισμα, light breakfast, ἄριστον,
midday and δεῖπνον, evening meal.
[3] οὐδεὶς . . . οὕτω θαυμαστῇ φύσει κραθήσεται as to combine
temperance and intemperance, according to the letter of
Plato.

dinners are indeed delightful, not only at the time, but on the following day as well." Why so? because we cannot make proper use of our minds when our stomachs are filled with meat and drink. There is a noble letter of Plato [1] to the relatives of Dion which contains a passage written pretty nearly in these words : "On my arrival here I found no pleasure in the celebrated happy life, with all its fulness of Italian and Syracusan feasts; in having two rich meals [2] a day and never passing the night alone, and all the other accompaniments of such a life in which no one will ever be rendered wise, far less indeed temperate. In what nature can the elements be so wonderfully mixed?" [3] What charm then can there be in the life where there is no prudence, no temperance? This shows us the mistake of Sardanapalus, the very wealthy king of Syria, who had carved upon his tomb the lines :

"All I have eaten and wantoned and pleasures of
    love I have tasted,
These I possess but have left all else of my riches
    behind me." [4]

"What else," says Aristotle, "could one inscribe on the grave of an ox, not on that of a king?" He says that in death he possesses the things which even in life he possessed only for the moment of enjoyment. Why then should the need of riches be felt, or in what does poverty refuse to allow of happiness? Statues, I suppose; pictures are your hobby. If there is anyone to find delight in them,

---

[4] κεῖν' ἔχω, ὅσσ' ἔφαγον καὶ ἐφύβρισα καὶ σὺν ἔρωτι
    τέρπν' ἔπαθον, τὰ δὲ πολλὰ καὶ ὄλβια πάντα λέλειπται.
                                        Athenaeus VIII. 336.

melius tenues homines fruuntur quam illi, qui iis
abundant? Est enim earum rerum omnium in
nostra urbe summa in publico copia; quae qui
privatim[1] habent, nec tam multa et raro vident,
cum in sua rura venerunt; quos tamen pungit
aliquid, cum illa unde habeant recordantur. Dies
deficiat, si velim paupertatis causam defendere;
aperta enim res est et cotidie nos ipsa natura
admonet quam paucis, quam parvis rebus egeat,
quam vilibus.

103   XXXVI. Num igitur ignobilitas aut humilitas
aut etiam popularis offensio sapientem beatum esse
prohibebit? Vide ne plus commendatio in vulgus
et haec, quae expetitur, gloria molestiae habeat
quam voluptatis. Leviculus sane noster Demosthenes, qui illo susurro delectari se dicebat aquam
ferentis mulierculae, ut mos in Graecia est, insusur-
rantisque alteri: *Hic est ille Demosthenes.* Quid
hoc levius? At quantus orator! Sed apud alios
loqui videlicet didicerat, non multum ipse secum.

104 Intelligendum est igitur nec gloriam popularem
ipsam per sese expetendam nec ignobilitatem ex-
timescendam. *Veni Athenas,* inquit Democritus,
neque me quisquam ibi agnovit. Constantem hominem
et gravem, qui glorietur a gloria se afuisse! An
tibicines iique, qui fidibus utuntur, suo, non multitudinis arbitrio cantus numerosque moderantur:
vir sapiens multo arte maiore praeditus non quid
verissimum sit, sed quid velit vulgus exquiret? An

---

[1] Lambinus' suggestion for *privati* of the MSS.

---

[1] Roman governors stole them from their provinces as
Verres did from Sicily. Cf. *In Verrem* Bk. IV.

cannot men of narrow means enjoy them better than those who have plenty ? For there is abundant provision of all such things in our city in public places. And those who own them as private property do not see so many, and only on rare occasions when they visit their country seats ; and there all the same they feel a prick of conscience when they remember how they got them.[1] Time would fail me should I wish to maintain the cause of poverty ; for the matter is evident and nature herself teaches us daily how few, how small her needs are, how cheaply satisfied.

XXXVI. Will then obscurity, insignificance, unpopularity prevent the wise man from being happy ? Beware lest the favour of the crowd and the glory we covet be more of a burden than a pleasure. Surely it was petty of my favourite Demosthenes to say he was delighted with the whispered remark of a poor woman carrying water, as is the custom in Greece, and whispering in her fellow's ear—" Here is the great Demosthenes ! " What could be more petty ? " Ah ! but how consummate an orator ! " Yes ! but assuredly he had learnt how to speak before others, not to commune much with himself. It must be understood, therefore, that neither is popular glory to be coveted for its own sake nor is obscurity to be sorely feared. " I came to Athens," said Democritus, " and no one there knew me." What dignified firmness for a man to glory in having no glory ! Are flute-players and harpists to follow their own tastes, not the tastes of the multitude in regulating the rhythm of music, and shall the wise man, gifted as he is with a far higher art, seek out not what is truest, but what is the pleasure of the

quidquam stultius quam, quos singulos sicut operarios barbarosque contemnas, eos aliquid putare esse universos? Ille vero nostras ambitiones levitatesque contemnet honoresque populi etiam ultro delatos repudiabit: nos autem eos nescimus, ante
105 quam poenitere coepit, contemnere. Est apud Heraclitum physicum de principe Ephesiorum Hermodoro: universos ait Ephesios esse morte mulctandos, quod, cum civitate expellerent Hermodorum, ita locuti sint: *Nemo de nobis unus excellat; sin quis exstiterit, alio in loco et apud alios sit.* An hoc non ita fit omni in populo? Nonne omnem exsuperantiam virtutis oderunt? Quid? Aristides— malo enim Graecorum quam nostra proferre—nonne ob eam causam expulsus est patria, quod praeter modum iustus esset? Quantis igitur molestiis vacant qui nihil omnino cum populo contrahunt! Quid est enim dulcius otio litterato? iis dico litteris, quibus infinitatem rerum atque naturae et in hoc ipso mundo caelum, terras, maria cognoscimus.
106 XXXVII. Contempto igitur honore, contempta etiam pecunia quid relinquitur quod extimescendum

---

[1] As Socrates said to Alcibiades, Aelian, *Var. Hist.* II. 1.

[2] Cicero is thinking of his own popularity in the days of his consulship, so soon to be followed by his exile brought about by Clodius, and of the enthusiasm which greeted his return from exile, to be followed only by his impotence in face of the triumvirs.

[3] Heraclitus, the Ionian philosopher, was born at Ephesus and lived about 500 B.C. Cf. § 69.

populace? Can anything be more foolish than to suppose that those, whom individually one despises as illiterate mechanics, are worth anything collectively? [1] The wise man will in fact despise our paltry ambitions and reject the distinctions bestowed by the people even if they come unsought: but we do not know how to despise them before the time for repentance begins.[2] There is a passage in Heraclitus,[3] the natural philosopher, relating to Hermodorus,[4] the leading citizen of Ephesus, where he says that the whole body of the Ephesians ought to be put to death, because, when they drove Hermodorus out of their community, they used this language: "Let no single man among us distinguish himself above the rest; but if any such appear let him live elsewhere and amongst other men." [5] Is this feeling not prevalent with every people? Do not men hate all superiority of virtue? What about Aristides (for I prefer to take Greek instances rather than Roman)—was he not banished from his country because he was too just? What vexations therefore they escape who have no dealings whatever with the people! For what is more delightful than leisure devoted to literature? That literature I mean which gives us the knowledge of the infinite greatness of nature, and, in this actual world of ours, of the sky, the lands, the seas.

XXXVII. Now when distinction is despised, money also despised, what is there left to be

---

[4] The Digest I. 2. 4, speaking of the origin of the Twelve Tables, B.C. 450, says *quarum ferendarum auctorem fuisse decemviris Hermodorum quendam Ephesium exulantem in Italia quidam rettulerunt.*

[5] ἡμέων μηδὲ εἷς ὀνήϊστος ἔστω· εἰ δέ τις τοιοῦτος, ἄλλῃ τε καὶ μετ' ἄλλων. Diog. Laert. IX. 2.

sit? Exsilium, credo, quod in maximis malis ducitur.
Id si propter alienam et offensam populi voluntatem
malum est, quam sit ea contemnenda paullo ante
dictum est; sin abesse patria miserum est, plenae
miserorum provinciae sunt, ex quibus admodum
pauci in patriam revertuntur.—At mulctantur bonis
107 exsules.—Quid tum? parumne multa de toleranda
paupertate dicuntur? Iam vero exsilium, si rerum
naturam, non ignominiam nominis quaerimus,
quantum tandem a perpetua peregrinatione differt?
in qua aetates suas philosophi nobilissimi consump-
serunt, Xenocrates, Crantor, Arcesilas, Lacydes,
Aristoteles, Theophrastus, Zeno, Cleanthes, Chrysippus, Antipater, Carneades, Clitomachus, Philo,
Antiochus, Panaetius, Posidonius, innumerabiles
alii, qui semel egressi numquam domum reverterunt.
At enim sine ignominia. An potest exsilium ignominia adficere[1] sapientem? de sapiente enim haec
omnis oratio est, cui iure id accidere non possit;
108 nam iure exsulantem consolari non oportet. Postremo ad omnes casus facillima ratio est eorum,
qui ad voluptatem ea referunt, quae sequuntur in
vita, ut, quocumque haec loco suppeditetur, ibi
beate queant vivere. Itaque ad omnem rationem
Teucri vox accommodari potest:

> *Patria est, ubicumque est bene.*

Socrates quidem cum rogaretur cuiatem se esse

---

[1] The MSS. have *sine ignominia adficere*. Wesenberg
suggested *An potest exsilium ignominia* before *adficere*.

---

[1] All these philosophers had to leave their native place in
Asia Minor, Africa or the outlying parts of Greece and live
in some centre of learning like Athens or Rome.

dreaded? Exile, I suppose, which is reckoned among the greatest evils. If it is an evil because popularity is impaired and lost, it was explained a little while back how despicable a thing that is ; but if it is wretched to be separated from one's country, our provinces are full of wretched beings, very few of whom return to their country. " But exiles have their property confiscated." What of that ? Is there not sufficient said about the endurance of poverty ? In fact if we now inquire into the real meaning of exile, not the disgrace of the name, how far, pray, does it differ from continual residence abroad ? And in that the noblest philosophers have spent their lives, Xenocrates, Crantor, Arcesilas, Lacydes, Aristotle, Theophrastus, Zeno, Cleanthes, Chrysippus, Antipater, Carneades, Clitomachus, Philo, Antiochus, Panaetius, Posidonius, countless others who, once departed, never returned home.[1] " Yes, but without disgrace." Can exile bring disgrace upon the wise man ? For the wise man is our subject throughout, and such a blot he could not justly incur ; for we are not called upon to comfort the exile whose sentence is just. Finally in facing all mischances the easiest is the method of those who refer the aims they follow in life to the standard of pleasure, and this means that they can live happily wherever this is provided. And so Teucer's saying can be fitted to every condition :

" One's country is wherever one does well." [2]

Socrates, for instance, on being asked to what country

[2] Pacuvius' *Teucer*, cf. App. II and Aristoph. *Plut.* 1151, πατρὶς γάρ ἐστι πᾶσ', ἵν' ἂν πράττῃ τις εὖ.

diceret, "Mundanum" inquit; totius enim mundi
se incolam et civem arbitrabatur. Quid T. Albucius?
nonne animo aequissimo Athenis exsul philosopha-
batur? cui tamen illud ipsum non accidisset, si in
109 re publica quiescens Epicuri legibus paruisset.   Qui
enim beatior Epicurus, quod in patria vivebat quam
quod Athenis Metrodorus? aut Plato Xenocratem
vincebat aut Polemo Arcesilam, quo esset beatior?
Quanti vero ista civitas aestimanda est, ex qua boni
sapientesque pelluntur?   Damaratus quidem, Tarquinii nostri regis pater, tyrannum Cypselum quod
ferre non poterat, fugit Tarquinios Corintho et ibi
suas fortunas constituit ac liberos procreavit.   Num
stulte anteposuit exsilii libertatem domesticae
servituti?
110   XXXVIII. Iam vero motus animi, sollicitudines
aegritudinesque oblivione leniuntur traductis animis
ad voluptatem.   Non sine causa igitur Epicurus
ausus est dicere semper in pluribus bonis esse
sapientem, quia semper sit in voluptatibus; ex quo
effici ʾputat ille, quod quaerimus, ut sapiens semper
111 beatus sit.   Etiamne, si sensibus carebit oculorum,
si aurium?   Etiam; nam ista ipsa contemnit.
Primum enim horribilis ista caecitas quibus tandem
caret voluptatibus? cum quidam etiam disputent
ceteras voluptates in ipsis habitare sensibus, quae

---

[1] οὐκ ᾿Αθηναῖος οὐδ᾽ ῞Ελλην ἀλλὰ κόσμιος, Plut. *De Exil.* 600.
[2] T. Albucius was accused of malversation in Sardinia, 103
B.C., and went into exile at Athens.
[3] λάθε βιώσας.
[4] " For " goes back to the saying of Teucer.
[5] Metrodorus came from Lampsacus, cf. II. § 8.
[6] cf. § 107.
[7] Cypselus tyrant of Corinth 660 B.C.

he claimed to belong, said, " To the world ; " [1] for he regarded himself as a native and citizen of the whole world. What of T. Albucius? [2] Did he not study philosophy at Athens with complete tranquillity in exile? Yet that is the very thing which would not have happened to him if in obedience to the rule of Epicurus [3] he had taken no part in public affairs. For [4] how was Epicurus happier for living in his country than Metrodorus [5] for living at Athens? Or did Plato get the better of Xenocrates [6] or Polemo of Arcesilas in point of happiness? What value indeed can be attached to the sort of community from which the wise and good are driven away? Damaratus for instance, the father of our King Tarquin, left Corinth because he could not endure the tyranny of Cypselus, [7] and fled to Tarquinii, where he set up house and begat children. Surely it was not foolish of him to prefer the freedom of exile to slavery at home?

XXXVIII. Then again, emotions of the soul, anxieties and distresses are alleviated by forgetfulness when the thoughts of the soul are diverted to pleasure. [8] Not without reason therefore Epicurus ventured to say that the wise man always has more of good than evil because he always has pleasures ; and from this he thinks there follows the conclusion we are in quest of, that the wise man is always happy. " Even if he is to be without sense of sight, of hearing?" Even then; for he despises such things in themselves. For to begin with, what pleasures, pray, does the blindness you dread so much have to go without? seeing that some even argue that all the other pleasures reside in the actual sensations, while the perceptions of sight

---

[8] This is the teaching of Epicurus, cf. III. § 33.

autem aspectu percipiantur, ea non versari in
oculorum ulla iucunditate, ut ea, quae gustemus,
olfaciamus, tractemus, audiamus, in ea ipsa, ubi
sentimus, parte versentur; in oculis tale nihil fit:
animus accipit quae videmus.   Animo autem multis
modis variisque delectari licet, etiam si non adhibeatur aspectus; loquor enim de docto homine et
erudito, cui vivere est cogitare; sapientis autem
cogitatio non ferme ad investigandum adhibet oculos
112 advocatos.   Etenim si nox non adimit vitam beatam,
cur dies nocti similis adimat?   Nam illud Antipatri
Cyrenaici est quidem paullo obscenius, sed non
absurda sententia est: cuius caecitatem cum mulierculae lamentarentur: *Quid agitis?* inquit, *an
vobis nulla videtur voluptas esse nocturna?*   Appium
quidem veterem illum, qui caecus annos multos
fuit, et ex magistratibus et ex rebus gestis intelligimus in illo suo casu nec privato nec publico
muneri defuisse.   C. Drusi domum compleri a con-
sultoribus solitam accepimus; cum quorum res esset
sua ipsi non videbant, caecum adhibebant ducem.
Pueris nobis Cn. Aufidius praetorius et in senatu
sententiam dicebat nec amicis deliberantibus deerat
et Graecam scribebat historiam et videbat in litteris.
113 XXXIX. Diodotus Stoicus caecus multos annos
nostrae domui vixit.   Is vero, quod credibile vix
est,[1] cum in philosophia multo etiam magis adsidue

---

[1] *esset* in MSS. : *est* Bake.

---

[1] cf. I. § 46.
[2] Appius ¦Claudius Caecus who made the Appian way,
312 B.C., and brought the Aqua Appia to Rome.
[3] C. Livius Drusus, brother of the more famous M. Livius
Drusus, tribune 91 B.C.

do not go along with any delight felt in the eyes, in the same way as the perceptions of taste, smell, touch, hearing are confined to the actual organ of sensation: nothing of the sort takes place with the eyes:[1] it is the soul which receives the objects we see. Now the soul may have delight in many different ways, even without the use of sight; for I am speaking of an educated and instructed man with whom life is thought; and the thought of the wise man scarcely ever calls in the support of the eyes to aid his researches. For if night does not put a stop to happy life why should a day that resembles night stop it? For the remark of the Cyrenaic Antipater is, it is true, a bit coarse, but its purport is not pointless; when his womenfolk were bemoaning his blindness, "What is the matter?" he said: "is it that you think there is no pleasure in the night?" That famous old worthy, Appius,[2] for example, who was blind for a number of years, was, as we gather both from the posts he filled and the business he transacted, in no way unfitted by his misfortune for his duties whether private or public. C. Drusus,[3] we are told, had his house continually filled by clients unable to see for themselves their way to settle their rights and ready to call in a blind man to guide them. In my childhood Cn. Aufidius the ex-praetor both stated his views in the senate and aided his friends in their consultations, and wrote history in Greek and, in literature, had a seeing eye. XXXIX. The Stoic Diodotus, who was blind, lived for many years at my house. Now whilst—a thing scarcely credible—he occupied himself with philosophical study even far more untiringly than he did previously, and played upon the

quam antea versaretur et cum fidibus Pythagoreorum
more uteretur, cumque ei libri noctes et dies
legerentur, quibus in studiis oculis non egebat, tum
quod sine oculis fieri posse vix videtur, geometriae
munus tuebatur, verbis praecipiens discentibus unde
quo quamque lineam scriberent. Asclepiadem
ferunt, non ignobilem Eretricum philosophum, cum
quidam quaereret quid ei caecitas attulisset, respondisse, puero ut uno esset comitatior; ut enim
vel summa paupertas tolerabilis sit, si liceat quod
quibusdam Graecis cotidie, sic caecitas ferri facile
114 possit, si non desint subsidia valetudinum. Democritus luminibus amissis alba scilicet discernere et atra
non poterat : at vero bona mala, aequa iniqua, honesta
turpia, utilia inutilia, magna parva poterat, et sine
varietate colorum licebat vivere beate, sine notione
rerum non licebat. Atque hic vir impediri etiam
animi aciem aspectu oculorum arbitrabatur, et cum
alii saepe quod ante pedes esset non viderent, ille
in infinitatem omnem peregrinabatur, ut nulla in
extremitate consisteret. Traditum est etiam Homerum caecum fuisse. At eius picturam, non
poësim videmus. Quae regio, quae ora, qui locus
Graeciae, quae species formaque pugnae, quae acies,
quod remigium, qui motus hominum, qui ferarum

---

[1] Pupil of Menedemus whose sect of philosophy took its
name from Eretria in Euboea.

[2] Rich men when they went out in public were attended
by a large retinue of friends : poor philosophers went by
themselves.

[3] *i.e.* be parasites or beggars : *Omnia ̄novit Graeculus
esuriens*, Juv. III. 77. Cicero does not say *parasitari*, to
spare the feelings of genuine Greek philosophers whose
poverty obliged them to seek the hospitality of wealthy
Romans.   [4] cf. I. § 22.

harp in the fashion of the Pythagoreans, and had
books read aloud to him by night and day, in the
study of which he had no need of eyes, he also did
what seems scarcely possible without eyesight, he
went on teaching geometry, giving his pupils verbal
directions from and to what point to draw each line.
It is related that Asclepiades,[1] no obscure follower
of the Eretrian school, on being asked by someone
what blindness had brought him, answered that he
had one more boy in his retinue;[2] for just as the
most utter poverty would be endurable if we could
bring ourselves to do as certain Greeks do daily,[3]
so blindness could readily be borne, should we
be supplied with aids to our infirmities. When
Democritus [4] lost his sight he could not, to be sure,
distinguish black from white: but all the same he
could distinguish good from bad, just from unjust,
honourable from disgraceful, expedient from inexpedient, great from small, and it was permitted
him to live happily without seeing changes of colour;
it was not permissible to do so without true ideas.
And this man believed that the sight of the eyes
was an obstacle to the piercing vision of the soul
and, whilst others often failed to see what lay at
their feet, he ranged freely into the infinite without
finding any boundary that brought him to a halt.
There is the tradition also that Homer was blind:
but it is his painting not his poetry that we see;[5]
what district, what shore, what spot in Greece,
what aspect or form of combat, what marshalling
of battle, what tugging at the oar, what movements
of men, of animals has he not depicted so vividly

[5] The painting is so life-like that we forget the poetry.
Lucian, *Imagin.* c. 8, calls Homer ὁ ἄριστος τῶν γραφέων.

non ita expictus est, ut quae ipse non viderit nos ut videremus effecerit? Quid ergo? aut Homero delectationem animi ac voluptatem aut cuiquam
115 docto defuisse umquam arbitramur, aut, ni ita se res haberet, Anaxagoras aut hic ipse Democritus agros et patrimonia sua reliquissent, huic discendi quaerendique divinae delectationi toto se animo dedissent? Itaque augurem Tiresiam, quem sapientem fingunt poëtae, numquam inducunt deplorantem caecitatem suam. At vero Polyphemum Homerus, cum immanem ferumque finxisset, cum ariete etiam colloquentem facit eiusque laudare fortunas, quod qua vellet ingredi posset et quae vellet attingere. Recte hic quidem; nihilo enim erat ipse Cyclops quam aries ille prudentior.
116 XL. In surditate vero quidnam est mali? Erat surdaster M. Crassus; sed aliud molestius, quod male audiebat, etiam si, ut mihi videbatur, iniuria. Nostri [1] Graece fere nesciunt nec Graeci Latine. Ergo hi in illorum et illi in horum sermone surdi, omnesque item [2] nos in iis linguis, quas non intelligimus, quae sunt innumerabiles, surdi profecto sumus. At vocem citharoedi non audiunt. Ne stridorem quidem serrae tum, cum acuitur, aut grunditum, cum iugulatur, suis, nec, cum quiescere volunt, fremitum murmurantis maris. Et si cantus eos forte delectant, primum cogitare debent, ante

---

[1] *Epicurei nostri* MSS. : *Nostri* Davies or *Operarii nostri.*
[2] *id* MSS. : *item* Manutius : others *idem* or omit.

---

[1] cf. I. § 104.
[2] The blind prophet of ancient Thebes.

that he has made us see, as we read, the things which he himself did not see? What then? Do we think either that Homer failed to feel delight of soul and pleasure, or that any learned man ever did so? Or if this were not true, would Anaxagoras [1] or Democritus himself, whom we have named, have left the fields they inherited, would they have given themselves up entirely to this divine delight of learning and discovery? And so the augur Tiresias, [2] whom the poets represent as wise, is never introduced as bemoaning his blindness. But on the other hand Homer, having represented Polyphemus as a savage monster, depicts him also as conversing with a ram and congratulating it on its good fortune in being able to walk where it would and reach what it would. [3] The poet was right; for the Cyclops himself had no more sense than the ram.

XL. Is there any evil really in deafness? Marcus Crassus was half-deaf; still he suffered another worse annoyance, in hearing himself spoken ill of, even if, as I thought at the time, it was unjustly. Our countrymen do not as a rule know Greek nor the Greeks Latin: therefore we in their tongue and they in ours are deaf, and all of us as well are assuredly deaf in those languages, countless in number, which we do not understand. "But the deaf do not hear the voice of a good singer." No, nor the screech of a saw either, when it is being sharpened, nor the grunting of a pig when its throat is being cut, nor the thunder of the roaring sea when they want to sleep. And if, may be, music has charms for them, they should first reflect that

---

[3] cf. Hom. *Odyss.* IX. 447; but the conversation with the ram is not as Cicero represents.

quam hi sint inventi, multos beate vixisse sapientes,
deinde multo maiorem percipi posse legendis his
117 quam audiendis voluptatem. Tum ut paullo ante
caecos ad aurium traducebamus voluptatem, sic licet
surdos ad oculorum; etenim qui secum loqui poterit,
sermonem alterius non requiret.

Congerantur in unum omnia, ut idem oculis et
auribus captus sit, prematur etiam doloribus acerrimis corporis; qui primum per se ipsi plerumque
conficiunt hominem: sin forte longinquitate pro-
ducti vehementius tamen torquent, quam ut causa
sit cur ferantur, quid est tandem, di boni, quod
laboremus ? Portus enim praesto est, quoniam mors
ibidem est [1] aeternum nihil sentiendi receptaculum.
Theodorus Lysimacho mortem minitanti: *Magnum
vero*, inquit, *effecisti, si cantharidis vim consecutus es.*
118 Paullus Persi deprecanti ne in triumpho duceretur:
In tua id quidem potestate est. Multa primo die, cum
de ipsa morte quaereremus, non pauca etiam postero,
cum ageretur de dolore, sunt dicta de morte, quae
qui recordetur, haud sane periculum est ne non
mortem aut optandam aut certe non timendam
putet. XLI. Mihi quidem in vita servanda videtur
illa lex, quae in Graecorum conviviis obtinetur: *Aut
bibat*, inquit, *aut abeat.* Et recte; aut enim fruatur
aliquis pariter cum aliis voluptate potandi aut, ne

---

[1] *quoniam—est* is suspected of being a gloss by Bentley.

---

[1] Cantharis, Spanish fly or blister-beetle, from which
cantharidin, an irritant poison, is extracted.
[2] ἢ πῖθι ἢ ἄπιθι.

many wise men lived happily before music was invented, secondly that far greater pleasure can be derived from reading than hearing verse. Next, as a little while ago we diverted the blind to the pleasure of hearing, so we may divert the deaf to the pleasure of sight; for the man who can converse with himself will not need the conversation of another.

Let everything be piled up on one single man so that he loses together sight and hearing, suffers too the most acute bodily pains; and these in the first place commonly finish a man of themselves alone: but if, maybe, they are indefinitely prolonged and torture him notwithstanding more violently than he sees reason for enduring, what reason have we, gracious heaven, for continuing to suffer? For there is a haven close at hand, since death is at the same time an eternal refuge where nothing is felt. Theodorus said to Lysimachus when he threatened him with death, "A great achievement indeed of yours if you have got the power of a blister-beetle." [1] When Perses begged not to be led in triumph, Paullus replied, "That is a thing *you* can settle." Much was said about death the first day, when we inquired into the nature of death; a good deal on the next day when pain was being discussed, and he who remembers it surely runs no risk of thinking either that death is not to be wished for or at any rate that it is to be feared. XLI. For my part I think that in life we should observe the rule which is followed at Greek banquets:— "Let him either drink," it runs, "or go!" [2] And rightly; for either he should enjoy the pleasure of tippling along with the others or get away early,

543

sobrius in violentiam vinolentorum incidat, ante dis-
cedat. Sic iniurias fortunae, quas ferre nequeas,
defugiendo relinquas. Haec eadem quae Epicurus,
totidem verbis dicit Hieronymus.

119 Quod si ii philosophi, quorum ea sententia est,
ut virtus per se ipsa nihil valeat, omneque, quod
honestum nos et laudabile esse dicimus, id illi
cassum quiddam et inani vocis sono decoratum esse
dicant, ei tamen[1] semper beatum censent esse
sapientem, quid tandem a Socrate et Platone profectis philosophis faciendum iudicas?[2] Quorum
alii tantam praestantiam in bonis animi esse dicunt,
ut ab his corporis et externa obscurentur, alii autem
haec ne bona quidem ducunt, in animo reponunt
120 omnia. Quorum controversiam solebat tamquam
honorarius arbiter iudicare Carneades; nam cum
quaecumque bona Peripateticis eadem Stoicis commoda viderentur, neque tamen Peripatetici plus
tribuerent divitiis, bonae valetudini, ceteris rebus
generis eiusdem quam Stoici, cum ea re, non verbis
ponderarentur, causam esse discrepandi negabat.
Qua re hunc locum ceterarum disciplinarum philosophi quem ad modum obtinere possint ipsi viderint:
mihi tamen gratum est, quod de sapientium perpetua
bene vivendi facultate dignum quiddam philosophorum voce profitentur.

---

[1] *et tamen* MSS. : *ei tamen* Wesenberg.
[2] *vides* MSS. : *iudicas* and *putas* suggested.

---

[1] Peripatetics and Academy. [2] Stoics.

that a sober man may not be a victim to the violence of those who are heated with wine. Thus by running away one can escape the assaults of fortune which one cannot face. This is the same advice as Epicurus gives and Hieronymus repeats it in as many words.

But if the philosophers who hold the view that virtue in and by itself is quite ineffective—whilst everything that *we* say is honourable and praiseworthy, *they* say is mere emptiness tricked out in a sounding phrase that has no meaning—if nevertheless they think that the wise man is always happy, what, pray, do you conclude that philosophers who go back to Socrates and Plato ought to do? Some [1] of them say that the superiority of goods of the soul is so marked that they eclipse goods of the body or external goods, while others [2] think that such things are not goods at all and make all good rest with the soul. The controversy between them used to be decided by Carneades in his capacity of umpire chosen as a compliment by the disputants; for as all that the Peripatetics regarded as goods were also regarded by the Stoics as advantages, and as the Peripatetics did not in spite of their opinion attach more value to riches, good health and the other things of the same kind than the Stoics did, he said that inasmuch as the determining factor is the thing, not the words, there was no ground for disagreement. Therefore it is for the philosophers of the other schools themselves to consider how they can maintain their position; I nevertheless welcome the fact that in agreeing upon the uninterrupted power of the wise man to lead a good life their avowal is one worthy of the utterance of philosophers.

545

121   Sed quoniam mane est eundum, has quinque
dierum disputationes memoria comprehendamus.
Equidem me etiam conscripturum arbitror—ubi
enim melius uti possumus hoc cuicuimodi est otio?
—ad Brutumque nostrum hos libros alteros quinque
mittemus, a quo non modo impulsi sumus ad philosophiae[1] scriptiones, verum etiam lacessiti.   In quo
quantum ceteris profuturi simus non facile dixerim,
nostris quidem acerbissimis doloribus variisque et
undique circumfusis molestiis alia nulla potuit
inveniri levatio.

[1] *philosophicas, philosophas* MSS. : *philosophiae* in Nonius.

But, as we have to part in the morning, let us fix in our recollections the discussions of the last five days. For my part I think too that I shall write them out (for in what way can I better employ my leisure to whatever cause it is due ?), and I shall send this second set of five books to my friend Brutus[1] by whom I was not only pressed to write on philosophic subjects, but provoked to do so as well. In doing this I cannot readily say how much I shall benefit others; at any rate in my cruel sorrows and the various troubles which beset me from all sides no other consolation could have been found.

[1] The five books, *De Finibus Bonorum et Malorum*, had been dedicated to Brutus.

APPENDIX I

CICERO'S TRANSLATIONS FROM THE GREEK

MARCUS TULLIUS CICERO

I. 41:

Quam quisque novit artem, in hac se exerceat.

I. ch. XXIII. "Quod semper movetur, aeternum est: quod autem motum adfert alicui quodque ipsum agitatur aliunde, quando finem habet motus, vivendi finem habeat necesse est. Solum igitur, quod se ipsum movet, quia numquam deseritur a se, numquam ne moveri quidem desinit: quin etiam ceteris, quae moventur, hic fons, hoc principium est movendi. Principii autem nulla est origo: nam e principio oriuntur omnia, ipsum autem nulla ex re alia nasci potest: nec enim esset id principium, quod gigneretur aliunde. Quod si numquam oritur, ne occidit quidem umquam: nam principium exstinctum nec ipsum ab alio renascetur nec ex se aliud creabit, si quidem necesse est a principio oriri omnia. Ita fit ut motus principium ex eo sit, quod ipsum a se movetur; id autem nec nasci potest nec mori, vel concidat omne caelum omnisque natura consistat necesse est nec vim ullam nanciscatur, qua a primo impulsa moveatur. Cum pateat igitur aeternum id esse, quod se ipsum moveat, quis est qui hanc naturam animis esse tributam neget? Inanimum est enim omne, quod pulsu agitatur externo; quod autem est animal, id motu cietur interiore et suo. Nam haec est propria natura animi atque vis, quae si est una ex omnibus, quae se ipsa moveat, neque nata certe est et aeterna est."

TRANSLATIONS FROM THE GREEK

Arist., *Wasps*. 1431:

ἔρδοι τις ἣν ἕκαστος εἰδείη τέχνην.

Plato, *Phaedrus*, 245 C: ψυχὴ πᾶσα ἀθάνατος. τὸ γὰρ ἀεικίνητον ἀθάνατον· τὸ δ' ἄλλο κινοῦν καὶ ὑπ' ἄλλου κινούμενον, παῦλαν ἔχον κινήσεως, παῦλαν ἔχει ζωῆς. μόνον δὴ τὸ αὐτὸ κινοῦν, ἅτε οὐκ ἀπόλειπον ἑαυτό, οὔ ποτε λήγει κινούμενον, ἀλλὰ καὶ τοῖς ἄλλοις ὅσα κινεῖται τοῦτο πηγὴ καὶ ἀρχὴ κινήσεως. ἀρχὴ δὲ ἀγένητον. ἐξ ἀρχῆς γὰρ ἀνάγκη πᾶν τὸ γιγνόμενον γίγνεσθαι, αὐτὴν δὲ μηδ' ἐξ ἑνός· εἰ γὰρ ἔκ του ἀρχὴ γίγνοιτο, οὐκ ἂν ἐξ ἀρχῆς γίγνοιτο. ἐπειδὴ δὲ ἀγένητόν ἐστι, καὶ ἀδιάφθορον αὐτὸ ἀνάγκη εἶναι. ἀρχῆς γὰρ δὴ ἀπολομένης οὔτε αὐτή ποτε ἔκ του οὔτε ἄλλο ἐξ ἐκείνης γενήσεται, εἴπερ ἐξ ἀρχῆς δεῖ τὰ πάντα γίγνεσθαι. οὕτω δὴ κινήσεως μὲν ἀρχὴ τὸ αὐτὸ αὑτὸ κινοῦν. τοῦτο δὲ οὔτ' ἀπόλλυσθαι οὔτε γίγνεσθαι δυνατόν, ἢ πάντα τε οὐρανὸν πᾶσάν τε γένεσιν συμπεσοῦσαν στῆναι καὶ μήποτε αὖθις ἔχειν ὅθεν κινηθέντα γενήσεται. ἀθανάτου δὲ πεφασμένου τοῦ ὑφ' ἑαυτοῦ κινουμένου, ψυχῆς οὐσίαν τε καὶ λόγον τοῦτον αὐτόν τις λέγων οὐκ αἰσχυνεῖται. πᾶν γὰρ σῶμα, ᾧ μὲν ἔξωθεν τὸ κινεῖσθαι, ἄψυχον, ᾧ δὲ ἔνδοθεν αὐτῷ ἐξ αὑτοῦ, ἔμψυχον, ὡς ταύτης οὔσης φύσεως ψυχῆς. εἰ δ' ἐστὶ τοῦτο οὕτως ἔχον, μὴ ἄλλο τι εἶναι τὸ αὐτὸ ἑαυτὸ κινοῦν ἢ ψυχήν, ἐξ ἀνάγκης ἀγένητόν τε καὶ ἀθάνατον ψυχὴ ἂν εἴη.

551

MARCUS TULLIUS CICERO

I. 97-99: "Magna me" inquit "spes tenet, iudices, bene mihi evenire, quod mittar ad mortem; necesse est enim sit alterum de duobus, ut aut sensus omnino omnes mors auferat aut in alium quendam locum ex his locis morte migretur. Quam ob rem sive sensus exstinguitur morsque ei somno similis est, qui non numquam etiam sine visis somniorum placatissimam quietem adfert, di boni, quid lucri est emori! aut quam multi dies reperiri possunt, qui tali nocti anteponantur, cui si similis futura est perpetuitas omnis consequentis temporis, quis me beatior? Sin vera sunt quae dicuntur, migrationem esse mortem in eas oras, quas qui e vita excesserunt incolunt, id multo iam beatius est. Tene, cum ab iis, qui se iudicum numero haberi volunt, evaseris, ad eos venire, qui vere iudices appellentur, Minoem, Rhadamanthum, Aeacum, Triptolemum, convenireque eos, qui iuste et cum fide vixerint: haec peregrinatio mediocris vobis videri potest? Ut vero

552

TRANSLATIONS FROM THE GREEK

Plato, *Apol.* **40** C : ἐννοήσωμεν δὲ καὶ τῇδε, ὡς
πολλὴ ἐλπίς ἐστιν ἀγαθὸν αὐτὸ εἶναι. δυοῖν γὰρ
θάτερόν ἐστι τὸ τεθνάναι· ἢ γὰρ οἷον μηδὲν εἶναι
μηδ' αἴσθησιν μηδεμίαν μηδενὸς ἔχειν τὸν τεθνεῶτα,
ἢ κατὰ τὰ λεγόμενα μεταβολή τις τυγχάνει οὖσα
καὶ μετοίκησις τῇ ψυχῇ τοῦ τόπου τοῦ ἐνθένδε
εἰς ἄλλον τόπον. καὶ εἴτε δὴ μηδεμία αἴσθησίς
ἐστιν, ἀλλ' οἷον ὕπνος, ἐπειδάν τις καθεύδων
μηδ' ὄναρ μηδὲν ὁρᾷ, θαυμάσιον κέρδος ἂν εἴη ὁ
θάνατος. ἐγὼ γὰρ ἂν οἶμαι, εἴ τινα ἐκλεξάμενον
δέοι ταύτην τὴν νύκτα, ἐν ᾗ οὕτω κατέδαρθεν,
ὥστε μηδ' ὄναρ ἰδεῖν, καὶ τὰς ἄλλας νύκτας τε
καὶ ἡμέρας τὰς τοῦ βίου τοῦ ἑαυτοῦ ἀντιπαρα-
θέντα ταύτῃ τῇ νυκτὶ δέοι σκεψάμενον εἰπεῖν,
πόσας ἄμεινον καὶ ἥδιον ἡμέρας καὶ νύκτας
ταύτης τῆς νυκτὸς βεβίωκεν ἐν τῷ ἑαυτοῦ βίῳ,
οἶμαι ἂν μὴ ὅτι ἰδιώτην τινά, ἀλλὰ τὸν μέγαν
βασιλέα εὐαριθμήτους ἂν εὑρεῖν αὐτὸν ταύτας
πρὸς τὰς ἄλλας ἡμέρας καὶ νύκτας. εἰ οὖν
τοιοῦτον ὁ θάνατός ἐστι, κέρδος ἔγωγε λέγω· καὶ
γὰρ οὐδὲν πλείων ὁ πᾶς χρόνος φαίνεται οὕτω
δὴ εἶναι ἢ μία νύξ. εἰ δ' αὖ οἷον ἀποδημῆσαί
ἐστιν ὁ θάνατος ἐνθένδε εἰς ἄλλον τόπον, καὶ
ἀληθῆ ἐστὶ τὰ λεγόμενα, ὡς ἄρα ἐκεῖ εἰσὶν
ἅπαντες οἱ τεθνεῶτες, τί μεῖζον ἀγαθὸν τούτου
εἴη ἄν, ὦ ἄνδρες δικασταί ; εἰ γάρ τις ἀφικόμενος
εἰς "Αιδου, ἀπαλλαγεὶς τούτων τῶν φασκόντων
δικαστῶν εἶναι, εὑρήσει τοὺς ὡς ἀληθῶς δικαστάς,
οἵπερ καὶ λέγονται ἐκεῖ δικάζειν, Μίνως τε καὶ
'Ραδάμανθυς καὶ Αἰακὸς καὶ Τριπτόλεμος, καὶ
ἄλλοι, ὅσοι τῶν ἡμιθέων δίκαιοι ἐγένοντο ἐν τῷ
ἑαυτῶν βίῳ, ἆρα φαύλη ἂν εἴη ἡ ἀποδημία ; ἢ αὖ

colloqui cum Orpheo, Musaeo, Homero, Hesiodo liceat, quanti tandem aestimatis? Equidem saepe emori, si fieri posset, vellem, ut ea, quae dico, mihi liceret invenire. Quanta delectatione autem adficerer, cum Palamedem, cum Aiacem, cum alios iudicio iniquo circumventos convenirem! Temptarem etiam summi regis, qui maximas copias duxit ad Troiam, et Ulixi Sisyphique prudentiam, nec ob eam rem, cum haec exquirerem, sicut hic faciebam, capite damnarer. Ne vos quidem, iudices ii, qui me absolvistis, mortem timueritis. Nec enim cuiquam bono mali quidquam evenire potest nec vivo nec mortuo, nec umquam eius res a dis immortalibus negligentur, nec mihi ipsi hoc accidit fortuito. Nec vero ego iis, a quibus accusatus aut a quibus condemnatus sum, habeo quod suscenseam, nisi quod mihi nocere se crediderunt." Et haec quidem hoc

554

Ὀρφεῖ ξυγγενέσθαι καὶ Μουσαίῳ καὶ Ἡσιόδῳ
καὶ Ὁμήρῳ ἐπὶ πόσῳ ἄν τις δέξαιτ᾽ ἂν ὑμῶν;
ἐγὼ μὲν γὰρ πολλάκις ἐθέλω τεθνάναι, εἰ ταῦτ᾽
ἐστὶν ἀληθῆ· ἐπεὶ ἔμοιγε καὶ αὐτῷ θαυμαστὴ
ἂν εἴη ἡ διατριβὴ αὐτόθι, ὁπότε ἐντύχοιμι Παλα-
μήδει καὶ Αἴαντι τῷ Τελαμῶνος καὶ εἴ τις ἄλλος
τῶν παλαιῶν διὰ κρίσιν ἄδικον τέθνηκεν· ἀντιπα-
ραβάλλοντι τὰ ἐμαυτοῦ πάθη πρὸς τὰ ἐκείνων,
ὡς ἐγὼ οἶμαι, οὐκ ἂν ἀηδὲς εἴη. καὶ δὴ τὸ
μέγιστον, τοὺς ἐκεῖ ἐξετάζοντα καὶ ἐρευνῶντα
ὥσπερ τοὺς ἐνταῦθα διάγειν, τίς αὐτῶν σοφός
ἐστι καὶ τίς οἴεται μέν, ἔστι δ᾽ οὔ. ἐπὶ πόσῳ
δ᾽ ἄν τις, ὦ ἄνδρες δικασταί, δέξαιτο ἐξετάσαι
τὸν ἐπὶ Τροίαν ἀγαγόντα τὴν πολλὴν στρατιάν,
ἢ Ὀδυσσέα, ἢ Σίσυφον, ἢ ἄλλους μυρίους ἄν τις
εἴποι καὶ ἄνδρας καὶ γυναῖκας; οἷς ἐκεῖ διαλέγεσ-
θαι καὶ ξυνεῖναι καὶ ἐξετάζειν ἀμήχανον ἂν εἴη
εὐδαιμονίας πάντως. οὐ δήπου τούτου γε ἕνεκα
οἱ ἐκεῖ ἀποκτείνουσι· τά τε γὰρ ἄλλα εὐδαιμονέσ-
τεροί εἰσιν οἱ ἐκεῖ τῶν ἐνθάδε, καὶ ἤδη τὸν λοιπὸν
χρόνον ἀθάνατοί εἰσιν, εἴπερ γε τὰ λεγόμενα
ἀληθῆ ἐστίν. ἀλλὰ καὶ ὑμᾶς χρή, ὦ ἄνδρες
δικασταί, εὐέλπιδας εἶναι πρὸς τὸν θάνατον, καὶ
ἕν τι τοῦτο διανοεῖσθαι ἀληθές, ὅτι οὐκ ἔστιν
ἀνδρὶ ἀγαθῷ κακὸν οὐδὲν οὔτε ζῶντι οὔτε τελευ-
τήσαντι, οὐδὲ ἀμελεῖται ὑπὸ θεῶν τὰ τούτου
πράγματα· οὐδὲ τὰ ἐμὰ νῦν ἀπὸ τοῦ αὐτομάτου
γέγονεν, ἀλλά μοι δῆλόν ἐστι τοῦτο, ὅτι ἤδη
τεθνάναι καὶ ἀπηλλάχθαι πραγμάτων βέλτιον
ἦν μοι. διὰ τοῦτο καὶ ἐμὲ οὐδαμοῦ ἀπέτρεψε τὸ
σημεῖον, καὶ ἔγωγε τοῖς καταψηφισαμένοις μου
καὶ τοῖς κατηγόροις οὐ πάνυ χαλεπαίνω. καίτοι

modo ; nihil autem melius extremo : " Sed tempu
est " inquit " iam hinc abire me, ut moriar, vos, u
vitam agatis.   Utrum autem sit melius di immortale
sciunt : hominem quidem scire arbitror neminem."

I. 101 :

> Dic, hospes, Spartae, nos te hic vidisse iacentes
> Dum sanctis patriae legibus obsequimur.

I. 115 :

> Nam nos decebat coetus celebrantes domum
> Lugere, ubi esset aliquis in lucem editus,
> Humanae vitae varia reputantes mala ;
> At, qui labores morte finisset graves,
> Hunc omni amicos laude et laetitia exsequi.

I. 115 :

> Ignaris homines in vita mentibus errant ;
> Euthynous potitur fatorum numine leto.
> Sic fuit utilius finiri ipsique tibique.

I. 117 :

> Mors mea ne careat lacrimis : linquamus amicis
> Maerorem, ut celebrent funera cum gemitu.

οὐ ταυτῃ τῇ διανοιᾳ κατεψηφίζοντό μου καὶ
κατηγόρουν, ἀλλ᾽ οἰόμενοι βλάπτειν· τοῦτο αὐτοῖς
ἄξιον μέμφεσθαι. ἀλλὰ γὰρ ἤδη ὥρα ἀπιέναι,
ἐμοὶ μὲν ἀποθανουμένῳ, ὑμῖν δὲ βιωσομένοις.
ὁπότεροι δὲ ἡμῶν ἔρχονται ἐπὶ ἄμεινον πρᾶγμα,
ἄδηλον παντὶ πλὴν ἢ τῷ θεῷ.

Simonides, *Bergk III.* 451 :

ὦ ξεῖν᾽, ἀγγέλλειν Λακεδαιμονίοις, ὅτι τῇδε
κείμεθα τοῖς κείνων ῥήμασι πειθόμενοι.

Euripides, *Frag.* 452 (Dindorf) :

ἐχρῆν γὰρ ἡμᾶς σύλλογον ποιουμένους
τὸν φύντα θρηνεῖν, εἰς ὅσ᾽ ἔρχεται κακά·
τὸν δ᾽ αὖ θανόντα καὶ πόνων πεπαυμένον
χαίροντας εὐφημοῦντας ἐκπέμπειν δόμων.

In Plutarch *Cons. ad Apoll.*, p. 109 :

ἦ που, νήπιε 'Ηλύσι', ἠλίθιαι φρένες ἀνδρῶν·
Εὐθύνοος κεῖται μοιριδίῳ θανάτῳ.
οὐκ ἦν γὰρ ζώειν καλὸν αὐτῷ οὔτε γονεῦσιν.

Solon quoted in Plutarch's *Lives*, Comparison of
Solon and Publicola :

μηδέ μοι ἄκλαυστος θάνατος μόλοι, ἀλλὰ
φίλοισι
ποιήσαιμι θανὼν ἄλγεα καὶ στοναχάς.

557

MARCUS TULLIUS CICERO

II. 20–21 :

O multa dictu gravia, perpessu aspera,

Quae corpore exanclata atque animo pertuli !

Nec mihi Iunonis terror implacabilis

Nec tantum invexit tristis Eurystheus mali,

Quantum una vaecors Oenei partu edita.

Haec me irretivit veste furiali inscium,

Quae lateri inhaerens morsu lacerat viscera

Urguensque graviter pulmonum haurit spiritus :

Iam decolorem sanguinem omnem exsorbuit.

Sic corpus clade horribili absumptum extabuit :

Ipse illigatus peste interemor textili.

Hos non hostilis dextra, non Terra edita

Moles Gigantum, non biformato impetu

Centaurus ictus corpori inflixit meo,

Non Graia vis, non barbara ulla immanitas,

Non saeva terris gens relegata ultimis,

Quas peragrans undique omnem ecferitatem expuli :

Sed feminae vir, feminea interemor manu.

O nate, vere hoc nomen usurpa patri,

Neve occidentem matris superet caritas.

Huc adripe ad me manibus abstractam piis.

Iam cernam mene an illam potiorem putes.

558

TRANSLATIONS FROM THE GREEK

Sophocles, *Trach*. 1046 ff.:

ὦ πολλὰ δὴ καὶ θερμὰ κοὐ λόγῳ κακὰ
καὶ χερσὶ καὶ νώτοισι μοχθήσας ἐγώ·
κοὔπω τοιοῦτον οὔτ' ἄκοιτις ἡ Διὸς
προὔθηκεν οὔθ' ὁ στυγνὸς Εὐρυσθεὺς ἐμοί,
οἷον τόδ' ἡ δολῶπις Οἰνέως κόρη
καθῆψεν ὤμοις τοῖς ἐμοῖς Ἐρινύων
ὑφαντὸν ἀμφίβληστρον, ᾧ διόλλυμαι.
πλευραῖσι γὰρ προσμαχθὲν ἐκ μὲν ἐσχάτας
βέβρωκε σάρκας, πλεύμονός τ' ἀρτηρίας
ῥοφεῖ ξυνοικοῦν· ἐκ δὲ χλωρὸν αἷμά μου
πέπωκεν ἤδη, καὶ διέφθαρμαι δέμας
τὸ πᾶν, ἀφράστῳ τῇδε χειρωθεὶς πέδῃ.
κοὐ ταῦτα λόγχῃ πεδιάς, οὔθ' ὁ γηγενὴς
στρατὸς Γιγάντων οὔτε θήρειος βία,
οὔθ' Ἑλλὰς οὔτ' ἄγλωσσος οὔθ' ὅσην ἐγὼ
γαῖαν καθαίρων ἱκόμην, ἔδρασέ πω·
γυνὴ δέ, θῆλυς φῦσα κοὐκ ἀνδρὸς φύσιν,
μόνη με δὴ καθεῖλε φασγάνου δίχα.
ὦ παῖ, γενοῦ μοι παῖς ἐτήτυμος γεγώς,
καὶ μὴ τὸ μητρὸς ὄνομα πρεσβεύσῃς πλέον.
δός μοι χεροῖν σαῖν αὐτὸς ἐξ οἴκου λαβὼν
ἐς χεῖρα τὴν τεκοῦσαν, ὡς εἰδῶ σάφα
εἰ τοὐμὸν ἀλγεῖς μᾶλλον ἢ κείνης ὁρῶν
λωβητὸν εἶδος ἐν δίκῃ κακούμενον.
ἴθ', ὦ τέκνον, τόλμησον· οἴκτιρόν τέ με
πολλοῖσιν οἰκτρόν, ὅστις ὥστε παρθένος
βέβρυχα κλαίων· καὶ τόδ' οὐδ' ἂν εἷς ποτὲ
τόνδ' ἄνδρα φαίη πρόσθ' ἰδεῖν δεδρακότα,
ἀλλ' ἀστένακτος αἰὲν εἱπόμην κακοῖς.
νῦν δ' ἐκ τοιούτου θῆλυς ηὕρημαι τάλας.

559

MARCUS TULLIUS CICERO

Perge, aude, nate, illacrima patris pestibus,
Miserere ! Gentes nostras flebunt miserias.
Heu ! virginalem me ore ploratum edere,
Quem vidit nemo ulli ingemescentem malo !
Ecfeminata virtus adflicta occidit.
Accede, nate, adsiste, miserandum aspice
Eviscerati corpus laceratum patris !
Videte, cuncti, tuque, caelestum sator,
Iace, obsecro, in me vim coruscam fulminis,
Nunc, nunc dolorum anxiferi torquent vertices,
Nunc serpit ardor.   O ante victrices manus,
O pectora, o terga, o lacertorum tori !
Vestrone pressu quondam Nemeaeus leo
Frendens efflavit graviter extremum halitum ?
Haec dextra Lernam, taetra mactata excetra,
Pacavit, haec bicorporem adflixit manum,
Erymanthiam haec vastificam abiecit beluam,
Haec e Tartarea tenebrica abstractum plaga
Tricipitem eduxit Hydra generatum Canem :
Haec interemit tortu multiplicabili
Draconem auriferam obtutu adservantem arborem :
Multa alia victrix nostra lustravit manus,
Nec quisquam e nostris spolia cepit laudibus.

καὶ νῦν προσελθὼν στῆθι πλήσιον πατρός,
σκέψαι δ' ὁποίας ταῦτα συμφορᾶς ὕπο
πέπονθα· δείξω γὰρ τάδ' ἐκ καλυμμάτων.
ἰδού, θεᾶσθε πάντες ἄθλιον δέμας,
ὁρᾶτε τὸν δύστηνον, ὡς οἰκτρῶς ἔχω.
αἰαῖ, ὦ τάλας, αἰαῖ,
ἔθαλψεν ἄτης σπασμὸς ἀρτίως ὅδ' αὖ,
διῆξε πλευρῶν, οὐδ' ἀγύμναστόν μ' ἐᾶν
ἔοικεν ἡ τάλαινα διαβόρος νόσος.
ὦναξ Ἀΐδη, δέξαι μ',
ὦ Διὸς ἀκτίς, παῖσον.
ἔνσεισον, ὦναξ, ἐγκατάσκηψον βέλος,
πάτερ κεραυνοῦ. δαίνυται γὰρ αὖ πάλιν
ἤνθηκεν, ἐξώρμηκεν. ὦ χέρες χέρες,
ὦ νῶτα καὶ στέρν', ὦ φίλοι βραχίονες,
ὑμεῖς δὲ κεῖνοι δὴ καθέσταθ', οἵ ποτε
Νεμέας ἔνοικον, βουκόλων ἀλάστορα
λέοντ', ἄπλατον θρέμμα κἀπροσήγορον,
βίᾳ κατειργάσασθε, Λερναίαν θ' ὕδραν,
διφυᾶ τ' ἄμικτον ἱπποβάμονα στρατὸν
θηρῶν, ὑβριστήν, ἄνομον, ὑπέροχον βίαν,
Ἐρυμάνθιόν τε θῆρα, τόν θ' ὑπὸ χθονὸς
Ἅιδου τρίκρανον σκύλακ', ἀπρόσμαχον τέρας,
δεινῆς Ἐχίδνης θρέμμα, τόν τε χρυσέων
δράκοντα μήλων φύλακ' ἐπ' ἐσχάτοις τόποις.
ἄλλων τε μόχθων μυρίων ἐγευσάμην,
κοὐδεὶς τροπαῖ' ἔστησε τῶν ἐμῶν χερῶν.

III. 18 :

> Corque meum penitus turgescit tristibus iris,
> Cum decore atque omni me orbatum laude
>   recordor.

III. 29 :

> Nam qui haec audita a docto meminissem viro,
> Futuras mecum commentabar miserias ;
> Aut mortem acerbam, aut exsili maestam fugam,
> Aut semper aliquam molem meditabar mali,
> Ut, si qua invecta diritas casu foret,
> Ne me imparatum cura laceraret repens.

III. 59 :

> Mortalis nemo est, quem non attingat dolor
> Morbusque ; multis sunt humandi liberi,
> Rursum creandi, morsque est finita omnibus,
> Quae generi humano angorem nequiquam adferunt.
> Reddenda terrae est terra, tum vita omnibus
> Metenda, ut fruges : sic iubet Necessitas.

III. 63 :

> Qui miser in campis maerens errabat Aleïs,
> Ipse suum cor edens, hominum vestigia vitans.

III. 65 :

> Namque nimis multos atque omni luce cadentis
> Cernimus, ut nemo possit maerore vacare.
> Quo magis est aequum tumulis mandare peremptos
> Firmo animo et luctum lacrimis finire diurnis.

Iliad 9. 646:

ἀλλά μοι οἰδάνεται κραδίη χόλῳ, ὅππoτ᾽
ἐκείνων
μνήσομαι, ὥς μ᾽ ἀσύφηλον ἐν Ἀργείοισιν
ἔρεξεν.

Eurip., *Frag.* 392 (Dindorf):

ἐγὼ δὲ τοῦτο παρὰ σοφοῦ τινος μαθὼν
εἰς φροντίδας νοῦν συμφοράς τ᾽ ἐβαλλόμην,
φυγάς τ᾽ ἐμαυτῷ προστιθεὶς πάτρας ἐμῆς
θανάτους τ᾽ ἀώρους καὶ κακῶν ἄλλας ὁδούς,
ἵν᾽ εἴ τι πάσχοιμ᾽ ὧν ἐδόξαζον φρενί,
μή μοι νεωρὲς προσπεσὸν μᾶλλον δάκοι.

Eurip., *Frag.* 757 (Dindorf):

ἔφυ μὲν οὐδεὶς ὅστις οὐ πονεῖ βροτῶν,
θάπτει τε τέκνα χἄτερα κτᾶται νέα,
αὐτός τε θνήσκει· καὶ τάδ᾽ ἄχθονται βροτοὶ
εἰς γῆν φέροντες γῆν. ἀναγκαίως δ᾽ ἔχει
βίον θερίζειν ὥστε κάρπιμον στάχυν.

Iliad 4. 201:

ἤτοι ὁ καπ πεδίον τὸ Ἀλήϊον οἶος ἀλᾶτο,
ὃν θυμὸν κατέδων, πάτον ἀνθρώπων ἀλεείνων.

Iliad 19. 226:

λίην γὰρ πολλοὶ καὶ ἐπήτριμοι ἤματα πάντα
πίπτουσιν· πότε κέν τις ἀναπνεύσειε πόνοιο;
ἀλλὰ χρὴ τὸν μὲν καταθάπτειν, ὅς κε θάνῃσιν,
νηλέα θυμὸν ἔχοντας, ἐπ᾽ ἤματι δακρύσαντας.

III. 67 :

> Si mihi nunc tristis primum illuxisset dies,
> Nec tam aerumnoso navigassem salo ;
> Esset dolendi causa, ut iniecto eculei
> Freno repente tactu exagitantur novo ;
> Sed iam subactus miseriis obtorpui.

III. 71 :

> Nec vero tanta praeditus sapientia
> Quisquam est, qui aliorum aerumnam dictis ad
> levans
> Non idem, cum fortuna mutata impetum
> Convertat, clade subita frangatur sua,
> Ut illa ad alios dicta et praecepta excidant.

III. 76 :

> Oc. Atqui, Prometheu, te hoc tenere existimo,
> Mederi posse orationem iracundiae.
> Pr. Si quidem qui tempestivam medicinam ad
> movens
> Non adgravescens vulnus inlidat manu.

IV. 63 :

> Neque tam terribilis ulla fando oratio est,
> Nec sors, nec ira coelitum invectum malum,
> Quod non natura humana patiendo ecferat.

V. 25 :

> Vitam regit fortuna, non sapientia.

V. 27 : Occupavi te, fortuna, atque cepi omnesque aditus tuos interclusi, ut ad me adspirare non posses.

TRANSLATIONS FROM THE GREEK

Eurip., *Frag.* 818 (Dindorf):

εἰ μὲν τόδ' ἦμαρ πρῶτον ἦν κακουμένῳ
καὶ μὴ μακρὰν δὴ διὰ πόνων ἐναυστόλουν,
εἰκὸς σφαδάζειν ἦν ἂν ὡς νεόζυγα
πῶλον χαλινὸν ἀρτίως δεδεγμένον·
νῦν δ' ἀμβλύς εἰμι καὶ κατηρτυκὼς κακῶν.

Sophocles, *Frag.* 964 (Dindorf):

τοὺς δ' αὖ μεγίστους καὶ σοφωτάτους φρενὶ
τοιούσδ' ἴδοις ἄν, οἷός ἐστι νῦν ὅδε,
καλῶς κακῶς πράσσοντι συμπαραινέσαι·
ὅταν δὲ δαίμων ἀνδρὸς εὐτυχοῦς τὸ πρὶν
μάστιγ' ἐρείσῃ τοῦ βίου παλίντροπον,
τὰ πολλὰ φροῦδα καὶ καλῶς εἰρημένα.

Aesch., *Prom. Vinct.* 377:

'Ωκ. οὔκουν, Προμηθεῦ, τοῦτο γιγνώσκεις ὅτι
ὀργῆς ζεούσης εἰσὶν ἰατροὶ λόγοι ;
Πρ. ἐάν τις ἐν καιρῷ γε μαλθάσσῃ κέαρ
καὶ μὴ σφυδῶντα θυμὸν ἰσχναίνῃ βίᾳ.

Eurip., *Orestes* 1:

οὐκ ἔστιν οὐδὲν δεινὸν ὧδ' εἰπεῖν ἔπος,
οὐδὲ πάθος, οὐδὲ συμφορὰ θεήλατος,
ἧς οὐκ ἂν ἄροιτ' ἄχθος ἀνθρώπου φύσις.

Attributed to Chaeremon:

τύχη τὰ θνητῶν πράγματ', οὐκ εὐβουλία.

Metrodorus: προκατείλημμαί σε, ὦ τύχη, καὶ
πᾶσαν τὴν σὴν ἀφῄρημαι παρείσδυσιν.

V. 35 : Cum esset ex eo quaesitum, Archelaum, Perdiccae filium, qui tum fortunatissimus haberetur, nonne beatum putaret : Haud scio, inquit ; nunquam enim cum eo collocutus sum.—Ain tu ? an aliter id scire non potes ?—Nullo modo.—Tu igitur ne de Persarum quidem rege magno potes dicere, beatusne sit ?—An ego possim, cum ignorem quam sit doctus, quam vir bonus ?—Quid ? Tu in eo sitam vitam beatam putas ?—Ita prorsus existimo, bonos beatos, improbos miseros.—Miser ergo Archelaus ?—Certe, si iniustus.

V. 36. Nam cui viro ex se ipso apta sunt omnia, quae ad beate vivendum ferunt, nec suspensa aliorum aut bono casu aut contrario pendere ex alterius eventis et errare coguntur, huic optime vivendi ratio comparata est. Hic est ille moderatus, hic fortis, hic et nascentibus et cadentibus cum reliquis commodis, tum maxime liberis, parebit et oboediet praecepto illi veteri ; neque enim laetabitur unquam nec maerebit nimis, quod semper in se ipso omnem spem reponet sui.

TRANSLATIONS FROM THE GREEK

Plato, *Gorgias* 470 D : Πωλ. Ἀρχέλαον δήπου τοῦτον τὸν Περδίκκου ὁρᾷς ἄρχοντα Μακεδονίας ; Σω. Εἰ δὲ μή, ἀλλ' ἀκούω γε. Πωλ. Εὐδαίμων οὖν σοι δοκεῖ εἶναι ἢ ἄθλιος ; Σω. Οὐκ οἶδα, ὦ Πῶλε· οὐ γάρ πω συγγέγονα τῷ ἀνδρί. Πωλ. Τί δαί ; συγγενόμενος ἂν γνοίης, ἄλλως δὲ αὐτόθεν οὐ γιγνώσκεις, ὅτι εὐδαιμονεῖ ; Σω. Μὰ Δί' οὐ δῆτα. Πωλ. Δῆλον δή, ὦ Σώκρατες, ὅτι οὐδὲ τὸν μέγαν βασιλέα γιγνώσκειν φήσεις εὐδαίμονα ὄντα. Σω. Καὶ ἀληθῆ γε ἐρῶ· οὐ γὰρ οἶδα παιδείας ὅπως ἔχει καὶ δικαιοσύνης. Πωλ. Τί δέ ; ἐν τούτῳ ἡ πᾶσα εὐδαιμονία ἐστίν ; Σω. Ὡς γε ἐγὼ λέγω, ὦ Πῶλε· τὸν μὲν γὰρ καλὸν κἀγαθὸν ἄνδρα καὶ γυναῖκα εὐδαίμονα εἶναί φημι, τὸν δὲ ἄδικον καὶ πονηρὸν ἄθλιον. Πωλ. Ἄθλιος ἄρα οὗτός ἐστιν ὁ Ἀρχέλαος κατὰ τὸν σὸν λόγον ; Σω. Εἴπερ γε, ὦ φίλε, ἄδικος.

Plato, *Menexenus* 247 E : ὅτῳ γὰρ ἀνδρὶ εἰς ἑαυτὸν ἀνήρτηται πάντα τὰ πρὸς εὐδαιμονίαν φέροντα ἢ ἐγγὺς τούτου, καὶ μὴ ἐν ἄλλοις ἀνθρώποις αἰωρεῖται, ἐξ ὧν ἢ εὖ ἢ κακῶς πραξάντων πλανᾶσθαι ἠνάγκασται καὶ τἀκείνου, τούτῳ ἄριστα παρεσκεύασται ζῆν, οὗτός ἐστιν ὁ σώφρων καὶ οὗτος ὁ ἀνδρεῖος καὶ φρόνιμος· οὗτος γιγνομένων χρημάτων καὶ παίδων καὶ διαφθειρομένων μάλιστα πείσεται τῇ παροιμίᾳ· οὔτε γὰρ χαίρων οὔτε λυπούμενος ἄγαν φανήσεται διὰ τὸ αὑτῷ πεποιθέναι.

567

V. 49:

Consiliis nostris laus est attonsa Laconum.

V. 101:

Haec habeo, quae edi quaeque exsaturata libido
Hausit; at illa iacent multa et praeclara relicta.

APPENDIX II

REFERENCES TO EARLY LATIN AUTHORS

(Many of the passages quoted from Ennius,
Caecilius, etc., will be found in the first three
volumes of *Remains of Old Latin*, published in the
Loeb Classical Library. References to these passages are given below.)

Page of *Tusculan Disputations*.	Source of quotation.	Ref. to *Remains of Old Latin*.
22, note 2	Ennius, *Annals*	I. p. 120.
32, note 1	Ennius, *Annals*	I. p. 12.
34, note 1	Ennius, *Annals*	I. p. 38.
35, note 6	Ennius, *Annals*	I. p. 22.
38, note 1	Caecilius, *Synephebi*	I. p. 538.
40, note 1	Ennius, *Epigrams*	I. p. 402.
42, note 2	Unknown author	II. p. 602.
44, note 4		
54, note 2	Ennius, *Medea*	I. p. 312.
55, note 3	Ennius, *Scipio* or *An-nals* ?	I. p. 204.
59, note 3	Ennius, *Andromacha*	I. p. 254.
100, note 2	Ennius, *Andromacha*	I. p. 250–53.

TRANSLATIONS FROM THE GREEK

Paus. IX. 15. 6 :

ἡμετέραις βουλαῖς Σπάρτη μὲν ἐκείρατο
    δόξαν.

Quoted in Athenaeus VIII. 336 :

κεῖν' ἔχω ὅσσ' ἔφαγον καὶ ἐφύβρισα σὺν
    ἔρωτι
τέρπν' ἔπαθον· τὰ δὲ πολλὰ καὶ ὄλβια πάντα
    λέλειπται.

Page of *Tusculan Disputations*.	Source of quotation.	Ref. to *Remains of Old Latin*.
124	(1) Ennius, *Andromacha*	I. p. 248.
	(2) Accius (unassigned fragment of a play)	II. p. 566.
126–8	(1) Pacuvius, *Iliona*	II. pp. 238–41.
	(2) Ennius, *Thyestes*	I. p. 354–57.
140, note 2	Ennius, *Epigrams*	I. p. 402.
146, note 1	Ennius (unassigned fragment of a play)	I. p. 368.
158, note 2	Accius, *Atreus*	II. p. 392.
166, note 1	Accius, *Philoctetes*	II. p. 512–16.
181, note 5	Accius, *Philoctetes*	II. p. 510.
188, note 2	Ennius, *Hectoris Lytra*	I. p. 278.
192, note 3	Lucilius, *Satires IV*	III. p. 56.
202, note 1 ⎱ 204 ⎰	Pacuvius, *Niptra*	II. p. 270–73.
237, note 1	Laws of the XII. Tables (Table V.)	III. p. 451.
248, note 4	Accius, *Melanippus*	II. p. 470.
256, note 2	Ennius, *Thyestes*	I. p. 352.
258, note 1	Pacuvius, *Medus*	II. p. 260.
260, note 2	Ennius, *Telamo*	I. p. 336.
277, note 5	Ennius, *Thyestes*	I. p. 354.
278, note 1	Ennius, *Andromacha*	I. p. 250–53.
292, note 1	Caecilius (unassigned fragment of play)	I. p. 552.
300, note 4	Ennius, *Medea*	I. p. 314.

APPENDIX II

Page of *Tusculan Disputations*.	Source of quotation.	Ref. to *Remains of Old Latin*.
330, note 2	Laws of the XII. Tables (Table VIII.)	III. p. 474.
347, note 3	Ennius, *Alcmeo*	I. p. 230.
379, note 4	Lucilius, *Satires IV*.	III. p. 58.
388, note 1	Accius, *Atreus*	II. p. 390.
404, note 4	Naevius, *Hector Proficiscens*	II. p. 118.
406, note 2	Caecilius (unassigned fragment of play)	I. p. 548.
406, note 3	Ennius, *Medea*	I. p. 322.
408, note 1	Pacuvius, *Medus*	II. p. 262.
414, note 3	Accius, *Atreus*	II. p. 382–91.
472, note 1	Pacuvius, *Niptra*	II. p. 266.
474, note 3	Ennius, *Epigrams*	I. p. 398–401.
533, note 2	Pacuvius, *Teucer*	II. p. 302.

INDEX

(References are to pages, and for italicized and Greek words chiefly to notes.)

571

INDEX

INDEX

Clitomachus of Carthage, 288
Clitus, 419
Cocytus, 13
Codrus, 140
confidens, confidere, 240
consensus, 36
Consolatio, 77, 89, 400
constantiae, 342
contentio, intentio, 208
contractio, 192, 342
copula, 14
Corinth, 27, 259, 289
Corinthian vases, 180; aes Corinthium, 360
Crantor of Soli, Academic, 139, 239, 308
Crassus, (1) L. Licinius, 12; (2) P. Licinius, 95; (3) M. Cr. Agelastus, 264; (4) Publius, 481; (5) M. Licinius, triumvir, 14, 541
Cratippus of Mytilene, xii
Cresphontes, 139
Critias, 115
Crito, friend of Socrates, 122
Critolaus of Phaselis, 332, 477
crows, 91
Cumae, 259
Curius, Manius Curius Dentatus, defeated Pyrrhus 275 B.C., 133
Cypselus, 534
Cyrenaeus, 122
Cyrenaics, xiii, 261, 265, 287, 315, 512

D

Damaratus, 534
Damocles, 486
Damon, 488
Danai, 384
Darius Codomanus, 522
Decii, 106, 212
declamatio, 10, 172
Deianira, 166
Delphi, 137, 497
Democritus of Abdera, 29, 50, 97, 375, 389, 493, 528, 538
Demosthenes, the orator, 13, 299, 375, 389, 528
desiderium, 348
Deucalion, survivor with Pyrrha his wife of flood which destroyed all other mortals, 27
Diagoras of Rhodes, 132
dialectica, xv, 498

διαμαστίγωσις, 182
Dicaearchus of Messana, 26, 31, 49, 60, 90, 410
Dii Consentes, 35
Dinomachus, 512
Diodorus of Tyre, 513
Diodotus, Stoic, xi, 536
Diogenes of Babylon, Stoic, 333
Diogenes of Sinope, Cynic, 122, 292, 518
Dion, 527
Dionysius (1) of Heraclea, the "turn-coat," 214, 247; (2) Stoic of Cicero's day, 173; (3) the elder, tyrant of Syracuse, 483, 525; (4) the younger, 258
Dolabella, xxiii
dolere, maerere, 36
dolor, labor, 182
Drusus, C. Livius, 536

E

earth, 47, 80, 496
Egyptians, 129, 507
elections, 216
elements, four, 26, 47, 51, 524; fifth, 28, 47, 77
Elysius of Terina, 139
Empedocles of Agrigentum, xii, 22
ἐνδελέχεια, 28
Endymion, 110
Ennius, Q., 4, 22, 32, 34, 41, 59, 100, 127, 141, 146, 188, 228, 260, 278, 301, 347, 384, 408, 474
ἔννοιαι, 68
Epaminondas, Theban statesman and general, 6, 39, 133, 140, 213, 474
Ephesus, 531
Epicharmus, 18
Epicurei, 90, 266, 284, 520
Epicurus, xix, 96, 153, 160, 163, 175, 259, 265, 271, 274, 277, 281, 285, 319, 408, 453, 457, 501, 511, 515, 518, 535, 544
Epigoni, 215
Epitaphium, or Menexenus, of Plato, 460
Erasmus, xxviii
Erechtheus, 139
Eretricus, also Eretriacus, 539
Erymanthia belua, 168, 382
Ethics, xv, 498
Etrusci, 106
Euclid of Megara, xiii

573

INDEX

INDEX

575

INDEX

INDEX

INDEX

V

Venus, 412
Venusia in Apulia, 106
virtues, all connected, 180; overlap, 246; cardinal virtues, 179, 271
vitiositas, vitium, 356, 358, 362
Vulcan, 183

X

Xanthippe, 264
Xenocrates of Chalcedon, 24, 456, 465, 477, 515, 518, 535

Z

Xenophon, pupil of Socrates, 217, 525
Xerxes, King of Persia, 444

Zeno, (1) of Citium in Cyprus, xv, 25, 161, 177, 215, 315, 339, 379, 453, 459; (2) of Elea, xii, 207; (3) of Sidon, Epicurean, 272
Zodiac, 80
Zopyrus, physiognomist, 418